AN ANNOTATED SECONDARY BIBLIOGRAPHY SERIES ON ENGLISH LITERATURE IN TRANSITION

1880–1920

W. EUGENE DAVIS

GENERAL EDITOR

JOSEPH CONRAD

THOMAS HARDY

E. M. FORSTER

JOHN GALSWORTHY

GEORGE GISSING

D. H. LAWRENCE

WALTER PATER

G. B. SHAW

CONTRIBUTORS

Jean-Claude Amalric   *Université Paul Valéry,*
Montpellier, France
Werner Bies   *Universitat Trier, Germany*
Mario Curreli   *Universita di Pisa*
Richard Farr Dietrich   *University of South Florida, Tampa*
Robert Langenfeld   *University of North Carolina,*
Greensboro
Masahiko Masumoto   *Nagoya University*
Alice C. Patterson   *Greenville, South Carolina*
Lisë B. Pedersen   *McNeese State University, Louisiana*
Asela Rodriguez de Laguna   *Rutgers University*
Charles Sanders   *University of Illinois, Urbana-Champaign*
Kristina A. Valaitis   *Champaign, Illinois*
David Welsh   *London, England*

ASSOCIATE CONTRIBUTORS

Peter Bell   *San Diego, California*
Lidia W. Haberman   *Arizona State University*
Betty Richardson   *Southern Illinois University,*
Edwardsville
Karl-Heinz Schoeps   *University of Illinois*
Eugene Steele   *University of Jos, Nigeria*

G. B. Shaw

AN ANNOTATED BIBLIOGRAPHY OF WRITINGS ABOUT HIM

VOLUME II: 1931–1956

COMPILED AND EDITED BY

ELSIE B. ADAMS
with
DONALD C. HABERMAN

NORTHERN ILLINOIS UNIVERSITY PRESS

DEKALB, ILLINOIS 1987

ELSIE B. ADAMS is professor of English and Comparative Literature at San Diego State University. Her areas of special interest are drama, Victorian and Edwardian literature, and women's studies. She holds a Ph.D. from the University of Oklahoma and is the author of *Bernard Shaw and the Aesthetes* as well as numerous critical works on Shaw and other transitional British authors, including George Gissing, Rudyard Kipling, D. H. Lawrence, and Israel Zangwill.

DONALD C. HABERMAN is professor of English at Arizona State University, Tempe, where his areas of special interest are drama and modern British literature. The recipient of a Yale Ph.D., he has also taught at Lafayette College and the University of Montana. He is the author of *The Plays of Thornton Wilder, A Critical Study* and has also written articles on Ford Madox Ford, Marcel Proust, Stéphane Mallarmé, James Joyce, Plautus, and Evelyn Waugh.

Library of Congress Cataloging-in-Publication Data

Wearing, J. P.
  G. B. Shaw: an annotated bibliography of writings about him.
  (Annotated secondary bibliography series on English literature in transition, 1880–1920)
  Vol. 2 compiled and edited by Elsie B. Adams with Donald C. Haberman.
  Vol. 3 compiled and edited by Donald C. Haberman.
  Includes bibliography and indexes.
  Contents: v. 1. 1871–1930—v. 2. 1931–1956—v. 3. 1957–1978.
  1. Shaw, Bernard, —1856–1950—Bibliography.
I. Adams, Elsie Bonita, 1932–   . II. Haberman, Donald C., 1933–   . III Title. IV. Series.
Z8814.5.W4 1986 016.822'912 86-8649 [PR5366]
ISBN 0-87580-121-8

Preface

G. B. SHAW: AN ANNOTATED BIBLIOGRAPHY OF WRITINGS ABOUT HIM
is a part of the Annotated Secondary Bibliography Series,
conceived and nourished by the late Helmut E. Gerber, who
defined the purposes of the series thusly:

1. To provide for scholars-in-the-making and established
scholars a comprehensive record of everything that has
been said, in any language, about a given author: (a) to
eliminate duplication of scholarship on selected authors;
(b) to eliminate long hours of fruitless research; (c) to
make available some scholarship that is not readily
accessible (work in obscure journals, foreign languages
unfamiliar to most scholars, etc.).
2. To provide a ready reference to materials for studies
of the history of taste in a limited period for scholars
concerned not with individual authors but with cultural
history.
3. To provide, by means of five indexes, a reference work
that will simplify studies in an author's reputation
(generally or in a particular nation), a periodical's
critical position, a particular critic's criteria for
judging literary works, etc.

Shortly after undertaking the SHAW bibliography, the
editors of the projected three volumes realized that the
goal of abstracting "everything that has been said, in any
language" about Shaw was unrealistic, given the tremendous
number of reviews, news items, and critical assessments of
Shaw around the world. We decided that we would attempt
instead to be representatively inclusive—that is, we would
try to provide an extensive sampling of items to reflect
the variety and scope of Shaw's fame. We of course have

tried to include all important criticism of Shaw and all other reasonably important items about him, including reviews of important performances of his plays in major theaters. Items of little or no interest to a literary critic have been included to reflect Shaw's wide-ranging interests and opinions on practically any and all subjects. It is our hope that no significant work on Shaw has been omitted.

We have made no attempt to include reviews of secondary works about Shaw, unless the reviewer is especially noteworthy or the review widely circulated in reprints. We include bibliographical information about dissertations listed in standard sources, but we do not abstract them. When several reviews or notices of a particular Shaw production exist, we frequently list only one as representative. In those instances in which an item that promised to be important has been located but not seen, we include the item, indicate "Not seen" in brackets, and list the reference source whenever possible. We do not include M.A. theses on Shaw.

The present volume, covering the "middle years" of Shaw criticism and commentary, is the second of a three-volume set. The volume is arranged chronologically by year (1931 through 1956); within each year the items are arranged alphabetically by author. The listing of each item is under the date of its first publication. The abstracts reflect the point of view of the author of the item; any editorial comment appears in brackets. At the end of the volume are five indexes: these have been organized according to authors, secondary titles, primary titles, periodicals and newspapers, and foreign language items appearing in the bibliography.

In this volume, Elsie B. Adams is responsible for the items from 1931 to 1950. The co-editor, Donald C. Haberman, who is also the editor of Volume III of G. B. SHAW: AN ANNOTATED BIBLIOGRAPHY..., is responsible for the items covering 1951 through 1956.

Elsie B. Adams and Donald C. Haberman

PREFACE

ACKNOWLEDGEMENTS

This bibliography is the result of the labor of many people. One of the high points in the making of SHAW II has been my introduction to scholars who were willing to take time from busy schedules and projects of their own to contribute their expertise and talents. Those who have made major contributions to the volume are listed on a separate page under Contributors and Associate Contributors. Without them, the volume could not have been done.

Others to whom I owe a debt for generous contributions to foreign language items are Daniel Brink, Arizona State University (Dutch); Thomas Cox, San Diego State University (French and Italian); W. Eugene Davis, Purdue University (German); John Ellis, Arizona State University (Norwegian); and Lee Fetzer, San Diego State University (Slavic). Norma Jenckes, Bryant College, Smithfield, Rhode Island, contributed a number of abstracts of English items, as did Joseph S. Tedesco, St. Bonaventure University, St. Bonaventure, New York (who also assisted with the abstracting of Italian items).

A number of past and present students have provided me with valuable assistance in library checking, reading and notetaking, typing, filing, and abstracting. For their careful and conscientious work, always performed cheerfully and efficiently, I thank Geoffrey R. Adams, Vivian Camberg, Lisa M. Gomer, Donald Risty, Yvonne Turpening, and Carole Zinck (all from San Diego State University) as well as Lea Jacobs (from the University of California at San Diego).

I am grateful to the Interlibrary Loan Department of Love Library at San Diego State University, where the librarians have always proved eminently resourceful in locating and obtaining books for me. In Spring 1982 the Interlibrary Loan Department of California State University at Fullerton also provided me with efficient, cooperative service. During the early years of my research for this project, San Diego State University gave me special encouragement and support in the form of two Grants-in-aid of Research (from the Graduate Division). As the project neared completion, the College of Arts and Letters provided me with substantial grants for typing the manuscript into camera-ready copy and for assistance in proofreading and preparation of the indexes.

The list of people to whom I owe special debts of gratitude are Mrs. Mary Pedersen, who is the best typist I have ever known; Mary Ellen Cummings, who assisted me during the last few nervous weeks of the project; W. Eugene Davis, who provided valuable editorial guidance; and my co-editors of SHAW, J. P. Wearing (Volume I) and Donald C. Haberman (Volumes II and III). To the late Helmut E. Gerber, who originated the idea of the Series and of the Shaw bibliography, I am eternally grateful: he served as mentor and as model for me in many ways. Finally, I offer grateful acknowledgment to my husband, Frank Marini, who provides an emotional center in my otherwise chaotic life.

Elsie B. Adams

- --

To the Contributors and Associate Contributors credited on a separate page I offer special acknowledgement and praise for their industry, their professional judgment and knowledge, and their skill and care. Among many others who have aided in crucial ways are Rodica Jackson, Tempe, Arizona; Gwen Stowe, Arizona State University, Tempe; LaVeda Musser, Arizona State University; Jane E. Conrow, Interlibrary Loan Services, Arizona State University; and Stella Wachsler, Baltimore, Maryland.

Donald C. Haberman

Contents

A Selective Checklist

OF THE WORKS OF G. B. SHAW.

COLLECTIONS

The Complete Plays of Bernard Shaw (Lond: Constable, 1931-
  1951)
Prefaces by Bernard Shaw (Lond: Constable, 1934)
Selected Novels of G. Bernard Shaw (NY: Caxton House, 1946)
The Selected Prose of Bernard Shaw, ed by Diarmiud Russell
  (NY: Dodd, Mead, 1952)

LETTERS

Ellen Terry and Bernard Shaw: A Correspondence, ed by
  Christopher St. John (NY: Fountain P; Lond: Constable,
  1931)
Florence Farr, Bernard Shaw and W. B. Yeats, ed by Clifford
  Bax (Dublin: Cuala P, 1941)
Bernard Shaw and Mrs. Patrick Campbell: Their
  Correspondence, ed by Alan Dent (NY: Knopf; Lond: Victor
  Gollancz, 1952)
Advice to a Young Critic and Other Letters, ed by E. J.
  West (NY: Crown Publishers, 1955)

PLAYS

Too True to Be Good, Village Wooing & On the Rocks: Three
  Plays (1934)
The Simpleton of the Unexpected Isles, The Six of Calais &
  The Millionairess: Three Plays (1936)
Cymbeline Refinished (1937)
Geneva (1939)
In Good King Charles's Golden Days (1939)
Pygmalion (Screen Version) (1941)

Major Barbara: A Screen Version (1946)
Geneva, Cymbeline Refinished & Good King Charles (1947)
Buoyant Billions (1950)
Buoyant Billions, Farfetched Fables & Shakes versus Shav
   (1951)
Why She Would Not (1956)

FICTION

The Adventures of the Black Girl in Her Search for God
   (1932)
Short Stories, Scraps and Shavings (1934)

OTHER WORKS

What I Really Wrote About the War (1932)
The Political Madhouse in America and Nearer Home (American
   title: The Future of Political Science in America) (1933)
William Morris as I Knew Him (1936)
London Music in 1888-89 by Corno di Bassetto (1937)
Everybody's Political What's What (1944)
The Crime of Imprisonment (new edition of Imprisonment,
   1925) (1946)
Sixteen Self Sketches (1949)

PREMIERES OF PLAYS

Too True to Be Good (Boston, 1932; NY, 1932)
On the Rocks (Warsaw, 1933; Lond, 1933)
Village Wooing (Dallas, 1934)
The Six of Calais (Lond, 1934)
The Simpleton of the Unexpected Isles (NY, 1935)
The Millionairess (Vienna, 1936; Bexhill, 1936)
Cymbeline Refinished (Lond, 1937)
Geneva (Malvern, 1938; Lond, 1938)
In Good King Charles's Golden Days (Malvern, 1939; Lond,
   1940)
Buoyant Billions (Zurich, 1948; Malvern, 1949; Lond, 1949)
Shakes versus Shav (Malvern, 1949)
Farfetched Fables (private performance) (Lond, 1950)

SELECTIVE CHECKLIST

FILMS

How He Lied to Her Husband (British, 1931)
Arms and the Man (British, 1932)
Pygmalion (German, 1935)
Pygmalion (Dutch, 1937)
Pygmalion (British, 1938)
Major Barbara (British, 1941)
Caesar and Cleopatra (British, 1945)
Androcles and the Lion (American, 1953)

Abbreviations of Secondary Works

Altick and Matthews	Guide to Doctoral Dissertations in Victorian Literature 1886-1958
American N&Q	American Notes and Queries
BDDTG	Blatter des Deutchen Theatres in Gottigen
BNYPL	Bulletin of the New York Public Library
CRITICAL HERITAGE	T. F. Evans (ed), SHAW: THE CRITICAL HERITAGE (Lond, Henley & Boston: Routledge & Kegan Paul, 1976)
CShav	California Shavian
DA	Dissertation Abstracts
DAI	Dissertation Abstracts International
DAID	Dissertations on Anglo-Irish Drama
DRAMA	Drama, The Quarterly Theatre Review
DramS	Drama Survey
ETJ	Educational Theatre Journal
G.B.S. 90	S[tephen] Winsten (ed), G.B.S. 90 (Lond & NY: Hutchinson, 1946)
ILN	Illustrated London News
ISh	Independent Shavian
List	Listener
McNamee	Dissertations in English and American Literature
McNamee, Supp I	Dissertations in English and American Literature, Supp I
MD	Modern Drama
NStat	New Statesman
NS&Nation	New Statesman and Nation
NYHT	New York Herald Tribune

NYHTBR	New York Herald Tribune Book Review
NYT	New York Times
NYTBR	New York Times Book Review
NYTMag	New York Times Magazine
NYer	New Yorker
N&Q	Notes and Queries
P&P	Plays and Players
PMLA	Publications of the Modern Language Association of America
QQ	Queen's Quarterly
Reg	Regional
SAT REV	Saturday Review of Literature (Lond)
SRL	Saturday Review of Literature (NY)
ShawB	Shaw Bulletin
ShawR	Shaw Review
ShawSB	Shaw Society Bulletin
TAM	Theatre Arts Monthly
TH	Theater Heute
TLS	Times Literary Supplement

Introduction

During the years from 1931 to 1956 (Bernard Shaw's centenary year) Shaw was at the apogee of his fame. Any news about him made headlines; he was reminisced about, railed at, and revered. His face appeared on the covers of magazines: SATURDAY REVIEW OF LITERATURE (New York) ran his picture on its cover on 6 July 1935; he appeared on the cover of THEATRE WORLD (London) in March 1939. He made the cover of LIFE in February 1944, and the SATURDAY REVIEW OF LITERATURE ran a special birthday issue devoted completely to him in the same year.

Shaw's ninetieth year, 1946, produced hundreds of tributes to him: NEWSWEEK carried his picture on the July 29 cover, accompanied by the condescending caption, "George Bernard Shaw: Naughty at Ninety." THEATRE ARTS MONTHLY also featured him on its cover and included within "Ave to a Nonagenarian," in which the anonymous writer declared that Shaw defied analysis. Stephen Winsten edited a festschrift for Shaw, G.B.S. 90, which was filled with essays, letters, and poetry from Shaw's friends and contemporaries. Eric Bentley published "Bernard Shaw's Politics (A Birthday Tribute)" in KENYON REVIEW, placing Shaw in the Victorian socialist tradition; in "Shaw at Ninety," in ATLANTIC MONTHLY, Bentley maintained that Shaw had had no real influence because he had never been taken seriously. Other birthday tributes included "An Illustrated Guide to George Bernard Shaw," in NATION; a cover feature in the ILLUSTRATED LONDON NEWS; a special exhibition in London of first editions and opening night programs (sponsored by the National Book League); and a dinner at the Waldorf-Astoria in New York on July 25 at which friends and business acquaintances reminisced about Shaw.

It is obvious from the numerous accolades to Shaw from 1931 to 1956 that the world had apparently agreed to honor the prophet and ignore or denigrate his prophecy, a fate Shaw anticipated and feared. Perhaps the 29 July 1946 issue of LIFE best illustrates the phenomenon that occurred: the magazine carried a pictorial essay on Shaw at home, along with an article eloquently entitled, "G.B.S.: All honor to his genius; but his message is irrelevant to our problems today." According to LIFE, the world needed a less pragmatic morality than Shaw's, less biology in its politics, and no socialism at all. As early as the Epistle Dedicatory to Man and Superman (1903), Shaw had complained of a tendency to admit books to the canon "by a compact which confesses their greatness in consideration of abrogating their meaning; so that the reverend rector can agree with the prophet Micah as to his inspired style without being committed to any complicity in Micah's furiously Radical opinions." Similarly, Shaw found himself and his radicalism defeated "by a simple policy of non-resistance. In vain do I redouble the violence of the language in which I proclaim my heterodoxies....instead of exclaiming 'Send this inconceivable Satanist to the stake,' the respectable newspapers pith me by announcing 'another book by this brilliant and thoughtful writer.' And the ordinary citizen, knowing that an author who is well spoken of by a respectable newspaper must be all right, reads me, as he reads Micah, with undisturbed edification from his own point of view." As Shaw aged, this compact to denigrate genius became more obvious. While Shaw remained intellectually vigorous and politically radical, the world, as reflected in the press, treated him as a Grand Old Man—interesting and cranky but essentially harmless. And thus, as Shaw had feared, he was "defrauded of [his] just martyrdom" and canonized instead. At Shaw's death in 1950 there was a world-wide outpouring of obituaries, the overall effect of which was to pay tribute to genius without acknowledging its power.

The hundreds of news items, theater reviews, book reviews, and critical assessments of Shaw as social critic, philosopher, and artist that appear from 1931 to 1956 are for the most part unoriginal and at times obtuse. With a few notable exceptions, the prevailing criticism of Shaw—whether of his work in print or plays in production—echoes familiar cliches about his art. According to this criticism, Shaw sacrifices character to problem and theory and uses his characters as mouthpieces for his own views, so that the characters have no life of their own but are always Shaw. He deals with the head and not with the heart, and thus loses an emotional dimension in his drama. He is too voluble, too repetitious, and too much the clown. He allows laughter, paradox, and brilliant wit to obscure serious themes. He is not an original thinker, and his ideas are rapidly going out of date because he does not treat eternal verities but social problems.

While this essentially wrong-headed criticism was being produced, Shaw continued speaking and writing vigorously; the Shaw message did not mellow with old age. One sees in the plays and the philosophical, biographical, and political essays and speeches of Shaw's late years unrelenting attacks on capitalism, political ineptitude, dilettantism in art, sexual inequality, religious hypocrisy, ineffective educational systems, parent-child relationships, and other socio-politico-educational-aesthetic concerns. In the 1930's Shaw became a world traveller, visiting Russia, South Africa, China, Japan, India, the United States, New Zealand, and Mexico in a series of world cruises. Wherever he went, he produced headlines and created controversy. He offended England and the United States on his return from a trip to Russia in 1931 by insisting that Russian communism was superior to Anglo capitalism; his "dear old boobs" radio address to the United States produced a furor. An even greater furor resulted from his 1933 address in New York to the Academy of Political Science on American economic and political problems (published in England as The Political Madhouse in America and Nearer Home). The speech prompted a London newspaper to observe that the United States was suffering from "three plagues: the bank closing, the earthquake, the visitation of Mr. Shaw" (quoted in NEWS-WEEK, I [1 April 1933], 16). After his 1932 trip to South Africa, Shaw wrote his controversial The Adventures of the Black Girl in Her Search for God. Though some critics found it brilliant— one called it worthy of Voltaire (Cabell, 1933), most complained that it was vulgar, tedious, unoriginal, and lacking in satiric focus.

Similar criticism greeted the steady stream of new plays from Shaw's prolific pen. Too True to Be Good, first produced in Boston and New York in 1932, was attacked as

having no subject and no dramatic interest. George Jean
Nathan called it a "substitute for playwrighting" and found
it "dull, dull, dull" (THE INTIMATE NOTEBOOKS, 1932,
pp. 265-68). Other critics were in shock over the pervading
sense of disillusionment and despair: "Heartbreak
Universe," said one (Woollcott, 1932). On the Rocks, which
premiered in the Theatr Polski in Warsaw (1933), found an
essentially unimpressed English audience when it opened in
London in December: it was "simply three hours of talk"
(Fleming, 1933). When On the Rocks was published, Shaw's
Preface—with its argument in favor of political killing—
attracted predictably unfavorable reviews. By the time The
Simpleton of the Unexpected Isles was produced (1935),
critics were talking of Shaw's declining powers and hinting
at possible senility. The London TIMES reviewer found
Simpleton "stale and shop-worn," with too much talk and too
little structure. The Malvern reviewer said that it was
simply not a play. Surprisingly, Geneva (first produced
London, 1938) was better received, though the familiar
complaints about Shaw's sermonizing and loquaciousness
persisted and its New York production in 1940 prompted
negative reviews. During the war years, In Good King
Charles's Golden Days (first produced Malvern Festival,
1939) came as a welcome relief to the somber present;
critics liked the purple passages, the dialog, and the
likeable characters, but criticized the lack of action and
plot. For the most part, the criticism of Shaw's late plays
did not treat them as experimental products of an active
imagination but as tired reworkings of earlier Shavian
ideas. Nevertheless, one sees during this period the
beginning of a tendency to lionize Shaw as a man who
single-handedly fought against the assumptions of his time
—a man whose artistry might outlive his views. By his
ninetieth birthday, Shaw was on his way to literary
sainthood, in spite of bad reviews of his late work.

If his tours and plays attracted world-wide notice, the
films of his plays brought Shaw even greater fame.
Especially praised was the Gabriel Pascal film of
Pygmalion, which premiered in 1938 and which critics found
excellent in every way. (Apparently Shaw agreed; according
to NEWSWEEK [5 Dec 1938], Shaw told Bennett Cerf that it
was the best movie he had ever seen.) Pascal's subsequent
film of Major Barbara (1941) received mixed reviews: some
found its dialog brilliant and the theme powerful; others

found it dated and verbose. Critics found the British production of <u>Caesar and Cleopatra</u>, starring Claude Rains and Vivien Leigh, technically interesting but with an obscure theme and a plot that drags. The film elicited a hysterical attack in BERNARD SHAW AMONG THE INNOCENTS (1945).: E. W. and M. M. Robson maintained that the film demonstrates Shaw's inhumanity, abnormality, and perversion and might lead to World War III.

Numerous revivals of Shaw plays also kept Shaw in the public eye. The most popular plays in revival were <u>Candida</u> and <u>Saint Joan</u>. Katharine Cornell gave New York audiences a critically acclaimed performance of Candida in 1937, and again in 1942 in a benefit for the American Theater Wing War Service. In the latter performance, hailed the "Best Work of the Year" by Brooks Atkinson in the NEW YORK TIMES, Burgess Meredith played a mettlesome, boyish Marchbanks, with Raymond Massey as Morell. Cornell revived <u>Candida</u> once again in 1946 in New York in what was called "one of her better interpretations" (Nathan, 1946). Marlon Brando played Marchbanks, and the NEW YORK TIMES complained of the "monotonously intoning poet." Other notable Candida interpretations were offered by Ann Harding (London, 1937) and by Congresswoman Clare Boothe Luce (Stamford, Conn., 1945). The Luce Candida attracted much publicity but received essentially unfavorable reviews.

Katharine Cornell's portrayal of Saint Joan (Guthrie McClintic production, New York, 1936) received excellent critical commentary on both the play and the production. In the same year, Wendy Hiller played Joan at the Malvern Festival, which also included productions of <u>Pygmalion</u> and <u>On the Rocks</u> in honor of Shaw's eightieth birthday. In 1938 Elizabeth Bergner played Joan at Malvern with "childlike pathos"; critics contrasted her performance unfavorably with that of Cornell. Another important interpretation of Joan was that of Siobbhan McKenna in 1955 (London).

With the exception of the war years, each year brought numerous Shaw revivals. It would be interesting to time travel back to see some of them: for example, the Mercury Theater (New York, 1938) production of <u>Heartbreak House</u>, in which Orson Welles played Shotover. Writing for PARTISAN REVIEW, Mary McCarthy found fault with both the play and the production, claiming that the best of Shaw was only equal to the worst of Chekhov and maintaining that the production missed all levels of Shaw's attack on the "moral

bankruptcy" of the English upper middle class. In the same
year, the Federal Theater Project players produced in
Harlem an all black production of Androcles and the Lion,
in which the cast translated the theme to the persecution
of blacks. The Katharine Cornell revival of The Doctor's
Dilemma in 1941 brought forth mixed reviews, though mostly
praise for the acting of Cornell and Raymond Massey. 1944
was a big year for Shaw revivals in London: the Old Vic
produced Arms and the Man, with Laurence Olivier as
Saranoff and Ralph Richardson as Bluntschli; the Lyric
Theater in Hammersmith presented Candida, Pygmalion, and
Too True to Be Good; while the Arts Theater revived The
Philanderer and Fanny's First Play. Other remarkable Shaw
revivals included the Theater Incorporated production of
Pygmalion (New York, 1945); the Maurice Evans production of
Man and Superman (New York, 1947); the Dublin Gate Theater
production of John Bull's Other Island (New York, 1947);
the National Theater production of Caesar and Cleopatra
(New York, 1949); the First Drama Quartet production of Don
Juan in Hell (Carnegie Hall, New York, 1951); the New York
City Center Theater production of Misalliance (1953); and
many others, all attesting to the popularity of Shaw with
producers and actors. Significantly, in 1949 the Bedford
Theater in Camden Town replaced Shakespeare with Shaw
plays; and Laurence Olivier and Vivien Leigh performed
Caesar and Cleopatra and Antony and Cleopatra on alternate
nights in the Ziegfield Theater (New York, 1951).

In addition to the publicity and criticism drawn forth by
premieres of his new plays, revivals of his old ones, and
his pre-eminence as a world "character," Shaw attracted
considerable attention through his collections of prose
published between 1931 and 1956. When in 1937 he published
his early music criticism for the London STAR in London
Music in 1888-89 by Corno di Bassetto, critics declared it
some of the best music criticism ever written—refreshing,
original, and entertaining. His political opinions in
Everybody's Political What's What (1944) received a less
friendly evaluation: critics were upset with Shaw's
skepticism concerning democracy and his insistence on
equality of income; Eric Bentley thought the book
demonstrated that Shaw was out of touch with contemporary
reality. The book was, however, undeniably interesting,
though provocative. Shaw had clearly not lost his edge:
Edmund Wilson stated that Shaw was still the best mind

around. Collections of letters published during the period under review show a different side of Shaw: the private man, as distinct from the public figure. Ellen Terry and Bernard Shaw: A Correspondence (1931) brought praise for the revelation through his letters of the human side of Shaw, along with interest in the drama history brought to life therein. (The son of Ellen Terry, Gordon Craig, did, however, in his biography of his mother, attempt to correct for what he saw as Shaw's detraction from Terry's fame [ELLEN TERRY AND HER SECRET LIFE, 1931].) Florence Farr, Bernard Shaw and W. B. Yeats (1941) gave critics another glimpse of the private Shaw and his interactions with the actress and the aesthete. So too Bernard Shaw and Mrs. Patrick Campbell: Their Correspondence (1952) presented Shaw the infatuated philanderer as well as the committed dramatic artist. The biographical details revealed in the letters were enhanced in 1949 with the publication of Shaw's Sixteen Self Sketches, a book frequently reviewed along with Stephen Winsten's DAYS WITH BERNARD SHAW (1949). The Self Sketches, in which critics found not much new on Shaw, served to cap the long career of the enigmatic Shaw, who had spent his life explaining himself.

Critics found Winsten's DAYS WITH BERNARD SHAW not very helpful in explaining Shaw. But I have already observed that the commentary on Shaw from 1931 to 1956 is not, in general, particularly helpful; much of it is mediocre to bad. There are, of course, exceptions. Several reviewers of Shaw during these years were to make an impact on the world of letters: Edmund Wilson was writing for the NEW REPUBLIC in the 1930's; Joseph Wood Krutch was regularly reviewing books, art, music, films, and drama for the NATION; John Mason Brown was "Seeing Things" (sometimes not too astutely) for the SATURDAY REVIEW OF LITERATURE; Wolcott Gibbs was writing a theater column for the NEW YORKER; and Bennett Cerf was writing on Shaw and sundry in "Trade Winds" in the SATURDAY REVIEW. It was the period when Archibald Henderson brought out the standard biography of Shaw: GEORGE BERNARD SHAW: MAN OF THE CENTURY (1956), an expanded version of BERNARD SHAW, PLAYBOY AND PROPHET (1932) and of GEORGE BERNARD SHAW: HIS LIFE AND WORKS (1911, reprinted 1918). Eric Bentley placed Shaw among the hero-worshippers—Carlyle, Wagner, and Nietzsche—in A CENTURY OF HERO-WORSHIP (1944); in THE PLAYWRIGHT AS THINKER (1946), Bentley analyzed Shaw's dramatic theory and practice, finding Shaw close to William James's pragmatic pluralism and arguing that Shaw had created a new form and standard for comedy. In BERNARD SHAW: A RECONSIDERATION (the Makers of Modern Literature Series, 1947), Bentley explained, as other critics had failed to do, Shaw's central paradox: impulse and passion, which Shaw considers the essence of humanity, evolve into thought and pure ideas, and Shaw thus becomes at once both rationalist and irrationalist. In the analysis of Shaw's politics, dramatic method, and world view, Bentley's BERNARD SHAW is possibly the best single introduction to Shaw.

In 1942 Hesketh Pearson brought out his anecdotal biography, G.B.S., A FULL LENGTH PORTRAIT, to which he added G.B.S., A POSTSCRIPT in 1950. There were as well a number of major critical studies produced during the period. Martin Ellehauge's book on THE POSITION OF BERNARD SHAW IN EUROPEAN DRAMA AND PHILOSOPHY (1931) traces continental influences—including naturalism and vitalism—on Shaw's art and thought. Jacques Barzun's "Bernard Shaw in Twilight" (KENYON REVIEW, 1943) assesses Shaw's prose style, dramatic technique, and complex philosophy of life; Barzun ranks Shaw's prose next to Swift's, and finds his plays good theater, combining late nineteenth-century formulae and classical technique. E. J. West's "G.B.S., Music, and Shakespearean Blank Verse" (ELIZABETHAN STUDIES AND OTHER ESSAYS, 1945) discusses Shaw's contribution to Shakespearean performance and criticism: the insistence on not cutting Shakespeare in performance and on paying attention to Shakespeare's "word music." William Irvine's monumental THE UNIVERSE OF G.B.S. (1949) takes a biographical-historical approach to Shaw's political views and artistic efforts, including his music criticism and his novels. Irvine finds two basic themes in Shaw: the individual as robber of society, and the individual martyred by society. C. E. M. Joad's SHAW (1949) views Shaw as essentially a rationalist, more interested in ideas than in drama; Joad's commentary echoes conventional opinions of Shaw's dramatic art, and his analysis of Shaw's style is taken without acknowledgement, and at times verbatim, from Dixon Scott's essay on Shaw in MEN OF LETTERS (1916). Edmund Fuller's GEORGE BERNARD SHAW: CRITIC OF WESTERN MORALE (1950) focusses on Shaw's eclectic thought, explaining that Shaw adopted "Both/And" instead of "Either/Or" as his method. The major works on Shaw vary in value and significance: some, like Bentley's BERNARD SHAW, are landmark studies; some, like Joad's or Fuller's, add little new.

As a final commentary on the Shaw criticism produced from 1931 to 1956, I will note that reading this material in the books and periodicals published during the period sharply calls into question the relative significance of all such criticism. What I have characterized as mostly trivial—often erroneous—Shaw criticism occurs on the world stage of the 1930's, 40's, and early 50's. The pages of the London and the New York TIMES, of news magazines and of popular and scholarly journals remind us of the grim world situation that is making the news: not the theater and book news, but the news that counts. There is a world-wide economic depression, the collapse of European diplomacy, the rise of Nazi Germany, World War II, the emergence of the atomic age and the Cold War. Against this background, theater reviews and literary criticism pale. Shaw continued writing plays and polemics alerting us to the dangers as he saw them. His critics concentrated on his failures in logic or in dramatic technique, and his admirers exclaimed about his wit and wisdom. In all this, we writers of literary criticism (and makers of bibliographies) should be able to find a lesson for today: in view of daily reminders of the war in Central America, an explosive Middle Eastern situation, South African apartheid, wasted natural resources, domestic political corruption, ineffective economic policies, and the threat of atomic annihilation, we might do well to take our scholarly plowshares and beat them into swords of protest.

Elsie B. Adams
June 1987

For Geoffrey and Lea,
in memory of a marvelous summer
of good fellowship
divided between beach and bibliography

G. B. Shaw

AN ANNOTATED BIBLIOGRAPHY

OF WRITINGS ABOUT HIM

VOLUME II

The Bibliography

1931
---

1 Abascal, Luis. "El dilema del doctor: comedia en 5 actos de G. Bernard Shaw, por la companía de Alexander Moissi, en el San Martín" (The Doctor's Dilemma: G. Bernard Shaw's Comedy in 5 Acts, by the Company of Alexander Moissi, in the San Martin) CRITERIO (Argentina), IV, No 165 (30 April 1931), 176-77.
The Doctor's Dilemma is a caustic play, ridiculing the medical profession but with good taste. The dialog is full of substance and thought, but it is deplorable that, through the amoral artist Dubedat, Shaw aims to establish the foundation of a new ethics. The play is good theater, but Shaw should not be taken seriously. [In Spanish.]

2 Abascal, Luis. "El teatro: La temporada de Berta Singerman" (The Season of Berta Singerman), CRITERIO (Argentina), IV, No 187 (1 Oct 1931), 23-24.
[A review of Berta Singerman's production of Arms and the Man at the San Martín.] [In Spanish.]

3 Archer, Charles. WILLIAM ARCHER: HIS LIFE, WORK AND FRIENDSHIPS (New Haven: Yale UP, 1931), pp. 13, 14, 119, 121, 131, 135, 139, 144, 146, 147, 156, 170, 172, 174n, 177, 196, 199, 208, 217n, 219-20, 236, 237n, 241-43, 245, 252, 255-57, 261, 263-64, 266, 272, 274, 284, 295-96, 303-6, 321, 330, 337, 340, 363, 375-78, 383n, 384n, 390-92, 400, 407, 411.

1

[Included are a number of Shaw letters with varying degrees
of commentary. The letters are broken into chronological
groupings, with accompanying titles.]

4 Atkinson, J. Brooks. "The Play: Shaw and the
Guild," NYT, 31 March 1931, p. 25.
Getting Married (Guild Theater, NY) is too long: the first
half is humorous and thoughtful, but the second half is
tedious. The characters are interesting, but the play has
only "the illusion of drama," being instead a conversation
with touches of horseplay.

5 B., J. "The Play: Irish Act Shaw Playlet," NYT, 11
April 1931, p. 17.
O'Flaherty, V. C. (Barbison Theater, NY) is a diverting
"piece of conversation" which was understandably suppressed
in England until after armistice.

6 Bakshy, Alexander. "Films: Shaw's First Movie,"
NATION, CXXXII (4 Feb 1931), 135-36.
The film of How He Lied to Her Husband, produced under
Shaw's personal direction, does not take account of the
difference between stage and screen. The action takes place
in one room; the plot is too much like "a stunt"; the
characters and dialog lack Shaw's characteristic
brilliance.

7 Becker, May Lamberton. "The Reader's Guide," SRL,
VII (10 Jan 1931), 525-26.
[Answers a query from J. R. M. (Princeton, N.J.), who wants
a bibliography of current works on Shaw. Lists significant
works since Henderson's 1911 biography.]

8 BERNARD SHAW: ANEKDOTEN UND AUSSPRÜCHE (Bernard
Shaw: Anecdotes and Sayings), ed by Ludwig Möllhausen
(Wien: Phaidon, 1931).
[A selection of about fifty anecdotes and sayings without
any critical import. Includes ten drawings by Tibor
Gergely. A prefatory letter to Shaw, pp. 5-12, calls the
selection the mythological part of Shaw's biography.] [In
German.]

9 Bidou, Henri. [On The Apple Cart], JOURNAL DES
DÉBATS, 11 May 1931, p. 3.

2

In The Apple Cart, a desperate passion for the common good discourages bitterness. There are some amusing episodes and not a word which is not action. [In French.]

10 Brinser, Ayers. THE RESPECTABILITY OF MR. BERNARD SHAW (Cambridge, Mass: Harvard UP, 1931).
Shaw's truth-telling is restricted to the area of social conditions, and his mainspring is the idea of himself the dramatist, not his characters. In Alfred Doolittle, Andrew Undershaft, Julius Caesar, and Mrs. Clandon "the prophetic white beard of Shaw is always discernible." Saint Joan has vigor but that arises from "a certain unexpected flippancy . . . in violent contrast to the preconceived notions of her"; the Epilog "restores the usual atmosphere of Hyde Park on Sunday afternoon." In Shaw's plays "intellectual super-snobs" are contemptuous of "morons." Shaw has simply turned the tears of eighteenth-century comedy into bitter ridicule. His is not classic comedy. He ignores inherent human weakness by exaggerating poverty as the real cause of sin. Doolittle is an example that affluence leads merely to hypocrisy, not moral stamina. Broadbent, Lickcheese, the Emperor in Androcles and the Lion, and Mrs. Warren therefore form "a superlative rogues' gallery of moral cowardice," without conscience or sense of responsibility; and Shaw praises them for their emancipation. Shaw makes a straw man out of a half-truth, and hypocritically pretends that he is dealing with reality. Shaw is not a dramatist, but a preacher-showman, with one central worn-out idea, as The Apple Cart makes all too evident.

11 Brisson, Pierre. [On The Apple Cart], LE TEMPS, 20 April 1931, p. 2.
Never was Shaw less dramatic than in The Apple Cart. The Preface is a massive, confused pamphlet. Shaw's volcanic ideology only expresses his need to fight romance. The play is not in Shaw's grand style, but is nevertheless an entertainment of a rare quality. [In French.]

12 Brown, Ivor. "THE APPLE CART: A Political Extravaganza, by Bernard Shaw...THE THEATRE OF MY HEART, by Geoffrey Whitworth," FORTNIGHTLY REVIEW, ns CXXIX (Feb 1931), 280-81.
The Apple Cart is not a major Shaw work, nor is the Preface, which summarizes doubts about democracy from a

stale point of view. England needs a National Theater to produce such works.

13 Brown, Ivor. "The Play: Two Players," WEEK-END REVIEW, III (28 March 1931), 474.
Widowers' Houses is "one of the Little Plays of St. Bernard" with a great comic character, Lickcheese. In this role, as in others in the past, Cedric Hardwicke (Birmingham Repertory Company production) seemed magnificently real.

14 Brown, John Mason. "Paper Love and Mr. Shaw," SRL, VIII (3 Oct 1931), 161-62.
The letters in Ellen Terry and Bernard Shaw: A Correspondence, edited by Christopher St. John, use the language of love, but record at first-hand the story of the emergence of the modern English theater. Through the letters, Shaw attacked Henry Irving "from within the ranks of his own camp." Shaw has not only proved himself a great drama critic but also a dramatist who dared break with the past. His letters combine "passion and precision."

15 Bullock, J. M. "The Shavian Theatre," TIMES (Lond), 24 May 1931, p. 6.
The Complete Plays of Bernard Shaw (Constable) remind one that Shaw has written over a million words in plays—words which carry the actors and the Shavian message to appreciative audiences. It is "a wonderful achievement."

16 Carb, David. "Seen on the Stage: Getting Married," VOGUE, LXXVII (15 June 1931), 100, 102.
The directors of the Theater Guild (NY) appear to have set out to remove the "halo of greatness" from Shaw. Getting Married is not a good play, indeed, not a play at all, but merely a tedious disquisition on a hackneyed subject.

17 Carbon, Emile. [De notre correspondant particulier: The Apple Cart] (From Our Special Correspondent: The Apple Cart) COMOEDIA, 12 March 1931.
The Apple Cart is a most astounding political fantasy. A perfect rendering of the play given by the Pitoeff Company left the audience enthusiastic. [In French.]

4

18 Caro, J. "The Apple Cart von Bernard Shaw" (<u>The Apple Cart</u> by Bernard Shaw), DIE NEUEREN SPRACHEN, XXXIX (1931), 189-92.
[A summary of Shaw's Preface and quotations from his paradoxical remarks about democracy.] Trebitsch, the German Shaw translator, has aptly translated the title as <u>Der Kaiser von Amerika</u> (The Emperor of America). [In German.]

19 Chatfield-Taylor, Otis. "The Latest Plays," OUTLOOK (NY), CLVII (15 April 1931), 538.
<u>Getting Married</u> (Theater Guild production) is dated, platitudinous, and boring. Shaw attempts to introduce movement in his essentially static play with the character of Mrs. George. But Helen Westley is an "unfortunate" choice for the role.

20 Chesterton, G[ilbert] K[eith]. "George Bernard Shaw," FORTNIGHTLY REVIEW, ns CXXX (Aug 1931), 150-59.
Despite much nonsense he has knowingly written, Shaw, a man of honor, has never shirked responsibility. Because he grew up in narrow circumstances, he was disinherited from the full culture of the past, and so could judge Shakespeare superficial in comparison to Ibsen. An Irish Calvinist who had lost his Calvinism as Ibsen had lost his Scandinavian Lutheranism, Shaw became his own admirer, feeling the need to debunk what "thousands of millions of people" believed as true because "all culture and experience" equals "cant and prejudice." Shaw's original moral philosophy was then one of "opportunism." However, Shaw's later works contradict this earlier opportunism in their championing the idealistic Life Force. Still, Shaw, like H. G. Wells, became nervous and did not go far enough: his very fertility prevented him from seeing the necessity to lay foundations for a religion much needed by the world today.

21 Closset, F. G. BERNARD SHAW, SON OEUVRE (LES CÉLÉBRITÉS ETRANGÈRES) (G. Bernard Shaw, His Work [Foreign Celebrities]) (Paris: Nouvelle Revue Critique, 1931).
[An essentially non-critical, brief survey of Shaw's work to date.) [In French.]

22 "Court Theatre: Fanny's First Play," TIMES (Lond), 5 March 1931, p. 12.
Fanny's First Play (Court Theater, Lond) is not profound, but it has the grace of a "brilliant occasion piece." Mrs. Knox is saved from tiresomeness by one redeeming speech; and comic reversals unify the play.

23 "Court Theatre: 'Mrs. Warren's Profession,'" TIMES (Lond), 31 March 1931, p. 12.
Mrs. Warren's Profession (Court Theater, Lond) is a rarity in Shaw in its expression of free and open emotion, especially in Mrs. Warren and Vivie. Some of the other characters have lost their brilliance with time.

24 Craig, Edward Gordon. ELLEN TERRY AND HER SECRET LIFE (Lond: Sampson Low, Marston, 1931) [not seen in this form]; rptd NY: Dutton, 1932, pp. vii-viii, 2, 14, 38, 97, 117-19, 131, 151, 160, 183.
This biography of Craig's mother was made necessary because Shaw, vain and jealous, detracted from Ellen Terry's fame by permitting publication of their correspondence and adding insult in his "apologetic" Preface.

25 de Pawlowski, G. "La Charrette de Pommes au Théâtre des Arts" (The Apple Cart at the Théâtre des Arts), LE JOURNAL, 16 April 1931.
The Apple Cart is not a play to be performed and is therefore unacceptable for a Latin mind. The first act is too long: only an English audience can sit through it. The second act is a charming interlude. The defense of individualism is fascinating, but Shaw's views on politics are old-fashioned. [In French.]

26 Dickinson, Thomas H. "Bernard Shaw and Woodrow Wilson," VIRGINIA QUARTERLY REVIEW, VII (Jan 1931), 11-17.
Shaw and Woodrow Wilson were similar intellectually—in their Puritanism, freedom from illusions, weariness at conventional thought, and dissatisfaction with the social conditions that created World War I. Both rose from amateur reformers to recognized statesmen through "radical and forthright thought and speech." In fact, Wilson may have been influenced by Shaw's comments on the War in Common Sense about the War and Peace Conference Hints; their

substance as well as their "comic and corrective method" would have appealed to Wilson. After America entered the War, Shaw's pronouncements declined, because "the War was now under the supreme direction of a man he could trust."

27   Dinamov, S. BERNARD SHOU (Bernard Shaw), (Moscow: GIKhA, 1931).
Shaw's first lines were directed against the tenets of religion and the hypocrisy of society. He entered English literature as a rebel and iconoclast; his art was that of the agitator, though he was not a mere journalist. Nor was he a mere jester. He believed that great art should be closely associated with militant contemporary questions. His growth was marked by increasing popularity among the bourgeoisie, and he became an educator, though this aspect of Shaw's work was concealed by his paradoxes. The bourgeoisie did not fear him, because his heroes merely talk and do not act. He never depicts the class which genuinely fights for a proletarian revolution or for communism. His humanism is bourgeois. He seeks to pacify those who might take up the class struggle, and seeks forgiveness for the sins of capitalism.

In Man and Superman, the most characteristic of Shaw's plays before 1914, the hero calls himself a socialist and is bold in verbal attacks on bourgeois society and bourgeois ideology in general. But Shaw himself was a socialist-opportunist who saw Marxism as unscientific and preached socialism without destroying capitalism.

World War I taught Shaw a great deal and made his attitude to the Soviet Union sympathetic after the 1917 October Revolution. However, his attitude toward the Soviet Union was contradictory. He was unable to join capitalism, but failed to unite his protests with the only revolutionary class, the proletariat. His revolt was isolated and helpless. He believed a new mankind could evolve slowly, without a class struggle. But reality shattered these petit-bourgeois illusions.

Now, having freed himself of the ruins of the past and having gained proper understanding of the Soviet Union, hopefully Shaw will see all his earlier mistakes and enter upon the same path as Romain Rolland. [In Russian.]

7

28 Dubech, Lucien, Jacques de Montbrial, Claire Éliane Engel, and Madeleine Horn-Monval (eds.). HISTOIRE GÉNÉRALE ILLUSTRÉ DU THÉÂTRE (An Illustrated General History of the Theater) 5 vols. (Paris: Librairie de France, 1931-1934), V, 326, 328, 329.

The best known English author on the continent, Shaw has won the admiration of his compatriots by satirizing his time and attacking serious questions of religion, society, and morality. He uses history as a mine for arguments and presents historical figures—Caesar, Napoleon, the Christian martyrs, Joan—as human beings, showing that the past was no more beautiful than the present, which he presents as ugly. But he remains an optimist, is even almost sentimental (though he denies it). His plays are generally poorly constructed; he writes interminably and his characters become Shaw and harangue the public. Yet his influence has been enormous. [In French.]

29 d'Uhalde, Jean. "Création au Gymnase: 'La Charrette de Pommes,' la dernière oeuvre de M. Bernard Shaw" (Creation in the Gymnasium: The Apple Cart, the Last Work of M. Bernard Shaw), MASSALIA (Marseille), 7 and 14 March 1931.

The Apple Cart is a curious, bitter, sarcastic play. In its first performance in France (Marseille, 9 March 1931), the play disappointed the audience by its remoteness from the French public. [In French.]

30 Dukes, Ashley. "Letters of an Artist and a Genius," YALE REVIEW, XXI (Dec 1931), 393-95.

Shaw "writes as he talks"—with an intellectual conviction that the world needs his correction. In Ellen Terry and Bernard Shaw: A Correspondence, he writes love letters in a Shavian vein, inspired by devotion to Terry's art and jealous of her wasting her talent on Henry Irving's theater. He wanted her to be a New Woman acting in Ibsenite drama, a truly romantic aspiration since it presupposes a unified theater and audience devoted to "the New Movement." Shaw has "always stood alone," even today when his importance to English theater is recognized. "And this essential loneliness lends an especial sympathy to his marvellous letter-writing."

31 Ellehauge, Martin. THE POSITION OF BERNARD SHAW
IN EUROPEAN DRAMA AND PHILOSOPHY (Copenhagen: Levin &
Munksgaard, 1931); rptd NY: Haskell House, 1966.

Shaw inherited the Continental tradition of the problem
play. From the problem play emerges modern realistic drama
in which "colliding ideas or principles" result in
intellectual conflict. Action is artificial and is reduced
to a minimum; events are arbitrarily arranged to illustrate
theory. Characters are molded to suit the intellectual
motif. Shavian characters rarely have "much independent
value." Dramatic dialog is sacrificed to argumentation and
philosophy. Shaw inherited three intellectual traditions.
Following Mill and Marx, he is part of a "regenerative
movement" that pits rational ethics against conventional
morality; this revolt had been incorporated in many
continental plays before Shaw began writing. He also
inherited theories of naturalism developed earlier on the
continent; his notion of the experimental nature of the
evolutionary process belongs to the naturalistic tradition.
Finally, he inherited vitalism. Shaw's originality lay in
giving a "novel turn" to these ideas, in phrasing old
theories in a peculiarly "lucid and concrete way," in
deducing different and further-reaching inferences than
earlier thinkers and writers, and in "expounding old
theories in the lights of newer theories." He differs from
Continental playwrights in his "jesting and jocular mode of
expression, due perhaps to the conservative mind of the
English audience, which requires very careful handling if
it is not to be shocked." But Shaw's attempt to synthesize
these various creeds is a failure. It is difficult to
discern "harmonious and original" Shavian theories because
of Shavian inconsistencies, and he is too intellectual to
produce true art.

32 "The Embattled 'Boobs' Retort to Shaw," LITERARY
DIGEST, CXI (24 Oct 1931), 7.

Shaw loves to exasperate Americans, referring to them as
"dear old boobs" in a recent radio address, when he praised
the Russian economy and criticized that of England the
United States. The fact is that Shaw loves communism from a
safe distance. [Quotes from American periodicals in
response to Shaw's broadcast.]

33 "A Famous Dramatist Portrayed by a Famous Painter: 'G.B.S.,'" ILN, CLXXVIII (11 April 1931), 597.
[Photograph of portrait by Sir John Lavery, R.A.; brief biographical sketch, with announcement of Saint Joan revival at His Majesty's Theater and praise for Shaw's recent work.]

34 Farjeon, Herbert. "The London Talkies," GRAPHIC (Lond), CXXXI (24 Jan 1931), 128.
Perhaps one day Shaw's plays will be filmed in more than an acceptable fashion, but the "strictly respectful version" of How He Lied to Her Husband reveals simply an "antiquated playlet." Unfortunately, the whole text is spoken without any editing of the film.

35 Fergusson, Francis. "A Month of the Theatre: The Shuberts and the Guild," BOOKMAN (NY), LXXIII (June 1931), 408-411, espec 411.
Getting Married (Guild Theater, NY) is a Shavian argument with points of view in place of characters and "two endings, one when the plot...has been resolved...and the other, five or ten minutes later, when Shaw has finished his train of thought." [Attack on Shaw's "shiny half-truths" and the Guild's historical attraction to them.]

36 "Film Notes: Mr. Shaw's Talkie," WEEK-END REVIEW, 17 Jan 1931, p. 76.
Cecil Lewis has produced How He Lied to Her Husband in a mechanical fashion. He has been too faithful to the text, presenting forty minutes of epigrams without any attempt at cinematic idiom.

37 Firkins, O. W. "New Plays: From Boards to Cover," YALE REVIEW, XX (June 1931), 815-18.
The Apple Cart is "the highest-hearted" of Shaw's comedies. King Magnus is perhaps an abstraction but is nevertheless engaging. But the exaggeration of the play reduces its credibility.

38 Forrest, Mark. "The Film: Herr Lubitsch Again," SAT REV, CII (24 Jan 1931), 120.
Cecil Lewis and British International Pictures have produced How He Lied to Her Husband; unfortunately, it is

nothing but a record of the play supported by animated
photography. If more of Shaw's plays are produced along the
same lines, audiences will soon tire of his works.

39 Fyfe, Hamilton. "The Journalist as Playwright,"
SPECTATOR, CXLVII (8 Aug 1931), 191.
Shaw's plays are not first-class drama but first-class
journalism. They entertain, stir the intellect, "sometimes
even a little . . . the imagination." But one is thankful,
nevertheless, for their brilliance, ruthlessness,
diversion, and acuteness. Shaw's criticism is destructive
when it is effective; when it attempts to be constructive,
it is incomprehensible (as in The Devil's Disciple) or
"sentimentally crude" (as in The Shewing-Up of Blanco
Posnet). His sense of theater is as strong as Ibsen's, but
Shaw cares more about problems and theories than he does
about human beings. Saint Joan, his play closest to drama
in the usual sense, has no characters as real as
Shakespeare's Falstaff, Lady Macbeth or Richard II.

40 "A G. B. S. Omnibus," WEEK-END REVIEW, III (30
May 1931), 822.
The Complete Plays of Bernard Shaw (Constable) is a
remarkable one-volume bargain. The complete prefaces, in
"the best pamphleteering prose style since Swift," should
follow.

41 Gerhardi, William. MEMOIRS OF A POLYGLOT (NY:
Knopf, 1931; Lond: Duckworth, 1931) [not seen in this
form]; rptd Lond: Macdonald, 1973, pp. v, 54-55, 66,
106, 143, 146, 148, 204, 213, 224, 229, 236, 240-49,
268, 280-81, 311.
[Passing references to and anecdotes about Shaw, including
an account of a meeting of Gerhardi with Shaw and Charlotte
Shaw at the H. G. Wells'.] Shaw writes only "in one
dimension, by intellect alone," and lacks poetic quality.
His range of experience is narrow, and his style is "cold,
rigid, colourless, strait-laced."

42 "Getting Married," DRAMA (NY), XXI (May 1931),
10.
The Theater Guild revival of Getting Married proves that
Shaw's plays are at first moving but ultimately out of
date. Soon they "will be dead issues in our theatre."

11

43 "Getting Married," NEW CATHOLIC WORLD, CXXXIII (May 1931), 207.
The Theater Guild production of Getting Married provides "two hours of verbiage, some of it clever and some of it dull." The thesis is that marriage as it is practiced is a necessary evil.

44 Hall, Mordaunt. "The Screen: Mr. Shaw's First Film," NYT, 17 Jan 1931, p. 23.
How He Lied to Her Husband (Elstree Studios) lacks cinematic action but, in that it reflects Shaw's "agile wit," it "makes for a jolly half an hour."

45 Harris, Frank. BERNARD SHAW: AN UNAUTHORIZED BIOGRAPHY BASED ON FIRST HAND INFORMATION, WITH A POSTSCRIPT BY MR. SHAW (Garden City, NY: Garden City Publishing Co.; Lond: Victor Gollancz; NY: Book League of America; NY: Simon and Schuster, 1931); rptd Hamburg: Albatross (Albatross Modern Continental Library, vol. 36), 1932; as VITA E MIRACOLI DI BERNARD SHAW, trans by Antonio Agresti (Milan: Mondadori, 1934); also Paris: Gallimard (Les contemporains vus de pres, 2nd series, no. 5), trans by Madeleine Vernon and H. D. Davray; and Buenos Aires: Editorial Losada, 1943, trans by Ricardo Baeza and Fernando Baeza Martos.
[A controversial biography of Shaw which includes many first-hand impressions by a man not noted for an impartial and truthful-to-fact approach to affairs. The books include a chapter on "Shaw's Sex Credo" and a Postscript by Shaw, who edited the biography by "supplying or correcting the facts" but leaving in "the criticisms, jibes, explosions of passing ill humour, and condemnations" (Shaw's words).]

46 Harris, Frank. "Correspondence: Material on G.B.S.," NATION, CXXXII (7 Jan 1931), 16-17.
[Letter from Harris to the public stating that he has contracted to write the biography of Shaw and inviting Shaw information.]

47 Hazlitt, Henry. "Books, Music, Drama: With a Preface," NATION, CXXXII (22 April 1931), 453-60, espec 453-54.

12

The Apple Cart is one of Shaw's "feeblest plays." Some scenes could have been omitted. The Preface offers "not a solution but a self-contradictory day dream."

48 Hergesíc, I. "O 75-godišnjici roÞenja Shawa" (On Shaw's Seventy-Fifth Birthday), OBZOR (Zagreb), LXXII: 173 (1931), 2. (Not seen but listed in BIBLIOGRAFSKA RASPRAVA, Zagreb, 1956, 9064.) [In Croatian.]

49 Heynen, W. "Inland and Ausland: Zeitschriftenschau: Dreimal Shaw" (At Home and Abroad: Survey of the Journals: Three Times Shaw), PREUSSISCHE JAHRBUCH, CCXVI (1931), 313-22.
[Extended excerpts from and commentary on two publications on Shaw: the most recent issue of NEUE RUNDSCHAU (reprinting Shaw's Preface to Immaturity) and Ellen Terry and Bernard Shaw: A Correspondence. Nothing new.] [In German.]

50 "His Majesty's Theatre: 'Saint Joan,'" TIMES (Lond), 7 April 1931, p. 8.
[Praise for Sybil Thorndike's "human, amusing, and touching" portrayal of Saint Joan, in His Majesty's Theater, Lond, revival.]

51 Irzykowski, Karol. "G. B. Shaw: Lekarz na rozdrożu" (G. B. Shaw: The Doctor's Dilemma), ROBOTNIK (Warsaw), No 92 (1931), p. 2; rptd in RECENZJE TEATRALNE: WYBÓR (Theatrical Reviews: A Selection) (Warsaw: Państwowy Instytut Wydawniczy, 1965), pp. 328-31.
Shaw makes the stage a Dionysian altar and a pulpit. In The Doctor's Dilemma the doctors represent English cant, while Shaw takes the side of his painter, though the latter is full of faults. The Poles have a great deal more sympathy than the English for such scoundrels (at least they had in 1906, when Shaw wrote the play). But Shaw spoiled the play slightly by caricaturing the doctors, and his satire on the medical profession is already out of date. [In Polish.]

52 "Kingsway Theatre: 'Man and Superman,'" TIMES (Lond), 19 May 1931, p. 14.

Shaw's plays typically quarrel aggressively; the philosophically-based argument in Man and Superman (Kingsway Theater, Lond) is too long and too oratorical. But the play is saved by Tanner's and Ann's vivacity, well acted in the Macdona Players' performances.

53 "Kingsway Theatre: 'Pygmalion,'" TIMES (Lond), 5 May 1931, p. 12.

The characterization of Pygmalion (Kingsway Theater, Lond) is weak and the social theme slight; thus it is a forgettable, though enjoyable, play. The plot is a series of dextrous "sparring matches," well-played in this production, though Esmé Percy's Higgins is not impetuous and brusque enough.

54 Lengnick, Paul. EHE UND FAMILIE BEI BERNARD SHAW (Marriage and Family in Bernard Shaw's Works). Published dissertation, University of Königsberg, 1931.

According to Shaw, marriage as an institution is a contrivance of the Life Force. Man is the pursued, Woman the pursuer. Shaw prefers companionable and affectionate partnerships to love matches. He fights against the financial dependence of women on men and favors marriage as a private contract and the extension of divorce. He attacks the British marriage law and forced family affection. [Attacks Shaw's opinions and defends the family as a necessary and welcome human institution.] [In German.]

55 Leonard, Baird. "Theatre," LIFE, XCVII (17 April 1931), 20.

The Theater Guild production of Getting Married is lively and colorful. Some of the characters hypothesize Shaw's views on life itself, and the subject matter makes the play interesting and entertaining.

56 Lunacharskiĭ, A[natoli] V[asil'evich]. "Bernard Shou" (Bernard Shaw), PROLETARSKII AVANGARD (Moscow), No 8 (1931); rptd in O THEATRE I DRAMATURGII: IZBRANNOE STAT'I (On Theater and Dramaturgy), Vol. 2 (Moscow: Iskusstvo, 1958), 481-84.

Shaw's fellow countryman and predecessor was Jonathan Swift, but the kind of laughter each inspired differed: Swift's humor, like Russia's Shchedrin's, had its dark side, while that of Shaw is lighter. When Shaw was in Russia, he said that he was an old revolutionary; his revolutionary work is concentrated in his plays and prefaces. Shaw is 75 today, at a time when the capitalism he so hates is in its final phase. Shaw believed it natural for an intelligent, educated individual to be a socialist: anyone who is not is a strange creature. But it is one thing to be a socialist by conviction, another to bring it about. Destruction of the capitalist world is not socialism. As Shaw said in the talking film made in Leningrad, Lenin's way promises salvation and transition to higher forms. [In Russian.]

57 Lunacharskiĭ, A[natoli] V[asil'evich]. "Bernard Shou—nash gost" (Bernard Shaw—Our Guest), IZVESTIIA (Moscow), 21 July 1931, p. 2. [Not seen. Source: K. Muratova. LUNACHARSKII O LITERATURE (Leningrad, 1964), 1419.]

58 Lunacharskiĭ, A[natoli] V[asil'evich]. "Rech' na vechere posviashchennom 75-letiiu B Shou" (Speech at the Evening Celebrating B. Shaw's 75th Birthday), LITERATURNAIA GAZETA (Moscow), 30 July 1931, p. 3.
On 26 July 1931, in the Colonnade Hall of the Trade Union House, Moscow, Shaw was honored on his seventy-fifth birthday; members of the government, diplomatic corps, representatives of literature and art, and the press were present. Comrade A. Khapotov greeted Shaw's ability to unmask all the horrors of the bourgeois system, adding, "Shaw has now come to the Soviet Union to see with his own eyes the enthusiasm and success of the working class which is bringing a new socialist system into being." Comrade A. V. Lunacharskii then praised Shaw's ability to combine laughter and exposure of "the dark nature of capitalist reality." Shaw is reaching old age at a time when the capitalist system which he so hated is also at its last stages. Shaw believes it natural for an educated and intelligent man to be a socialist. [In Russian.]

59 Marcu, Valeriu. "Bernard Shaw und andere Russlandpilger" (Bernard Shaw and Other Pilgrims to Russia), DIE LITERARISCHE WELT, VII (21 Aug 1931), 3.

His visit to Russia has moved Shaw to enthusiasm. Obviously he did not realize that his hosts were concealing their enmity under an appearance of friendliness. [In German.]

60 Marriott, J[ames] W[illiam]. THE THEATRE (Lond: Harrap, 1931; new ed rvd Lond: Harrap, 1946), pp. 43, 63, 74, 112-15, 137, 157, 201, Index, espec 112-15.
Shaw is "the arch-heretic of the day," as his iconoclastic plays show. Unlike most propagandist dramatists, Shaw writes excellent plays, saved by his wit, his sense of humor, his ability to create novel scenes (a dentist's office, a motor-car being repaired, etc.), and his ability to present multiple points of view. Some of his plays touch "deep springs of emotion." His prefaces are brilliant. He towers over the repertory movement. [Extremely adulatory appraisal.]

61 Martin, Edward S. "Wanted: Needles That Point North," HARPERS MAGAZINE, CLXIII (Nov 1931), 765-66.
Shaw has talent but lacks direction. He lives profitably under capitalism, but praises socialism; and he is "indiscriminate" in his praise of Russia. His success is due to his ability to ridicule those more stupid than his readers.

62 Miller, Anna Irene. THE INDEPENDENT THEATRE IN EUROPE 1887 TO THE PRESENT (NY: R. Long & R. R. Smith, 1931; NY: Benjamin Blom, 1966), pp. 1, 5, 8, 11, 45, 83, 90, 132, 134, 157, 164-65, 166, 170, 172-75, 177, 180, 181, 182, 185, 199, 212, 230, 251, 261, 284, 380, 382, Index.
[Account of the production of Widowers' Houses by J. T. Grein's Independent Theater, and passing references to Shaw's place in the independent theater in Europe.

63 Morgan, Charles. "Mr. Shaw in London, Too: Amid a Host of Revivals, There Is Brought Back His 'Widowers Houses,'" NYT, 12 April 1931, Section 9, p. 2.
Widowers' Houses "is a dismal, stiff little pamphlet" with a love story and theatrical temper tantrums dragged into it. Cedric Hardwicke's Lickcheese (Stage Society production, Lond) steps "out of the Pickwick Papers"; what vitality the play has is Dickensian.

64 Morton, Frederick. "Theatre Arts Bookshelf: The Terry-Shaw Letters," TAM, XV (Dec 1931), 1046-47, 1049.

The correspondence of Ellen Terry and Shaw was a book "born great." Shaw's introduction to it may well be, "next to Candida, the finest thing Shaw has written." The letters bring to life London dramatic history from 1892 to 1920.

65 "Mr. Shaw and Russia," NATION, CXXXIII (5 Aug 1931), 122.

Shaw was once "the bad boy of the articulate world" but became "the best intellect of his time." Russia is now "the bad boy of nations"—but in fifty years? [Written during Shaw's visit to Russia.]

66 Nathan, George Jean. "Books: Androcles and the Lioness," NATION, CXXXIII (14 Oct 1931), 398-400; rptd as "Vegetarian Amour," in THE INTIMATE NOTEBOOKS OF GEORGE JEAN NATHAN (NY: Knopf, 1932), pp. 294-99.

Ellen Terry and Bernard Shaw: A Correspondence is not so much a love story as drama criticism on Shaw's part. Ellen Terry's letters present a "curiously disturbing picture" of her as a wily female.

67 Nathan, George Jean. TESTAMENT OF A CRITIC (NY & Lond: Knopf; Lond: Allen & Unwin, 1931), pp. 56, 59, 77, 140, 145, 163-68 ("Shaw"), 169-78 ("Ditto and Sex"), 224-25, 240; "Ditto and Sex" rptd as "Mr. Shaw and the Ogre," in GEORGE BERNARD SHAW: A CRITICAL SURVEY, ed by Louis Kronenberger (Cleveland & NY: World, 1953), pp. 114-19.

Shaw was "until lately a genius of comedy." Even his "talkiest" plays, e.g., Misalliance and Getting Married, employ diverting characters and stage tricks to keep audience interest. But his talents have collapsed. The Apple Cart is repetitious and banal—except for a few moments merely a ghost of former Shavian wit. The situations are borrowed from old farce, and the jokes are equally stale. Shaw is averse to, perhaps fearful of, sex. He created "a virginal Cleopatra"; a slapstick Great Catherine; a Pygmalion who rejects Galatea; a philosophical Don Juan, etc. Again and again in his writing occur romantic animadversions to sex. [Numerous examples.]

68 Norwood, Gilbert. "Stage and Screen: Two Shaw Plays," CANADIAN FORUM, XI (March 1931), 236, 238-39.
Shaw is not a constructive nor even a consistent thinker. The last act of Major Barbara (Hart House Theater, Toronto) is a "fiasco" in which the idea of the play breaks down. And The Apple Cart has no ideas at all; it is essentially a one-act play lengthened by Shaw's crude intrusions to a "bungling exordium." Only Lysistrata's tirade against Breakages, Ltd. has the vigor of "the old Shaw"; but she and the other characters are failures. After Saint Joan, Shaw has become popular with audiences who cannot understand him.

69 "The Old Vic: 'Arms and the Man,'" TIMES (Lond), 17 Feb 1931, p. 12.
Arms and the Man (Old Vic, Lond) has the "joyous succulence" of a chocolate cream. Bluntschli combines dominance and insolence, and the other characters have equally challenging parts in this witty, impudent, and paradoxical play.

70 Ould, Hermon. "Mr. Shaw's 'Apple Cart': The Political Extravaganza Published," BOOKMAN (Lond), LXXIX (Jan 1931), 275.
The Apple Cart is a hodgepodge of wisdom and buffoonery, bad style and eloquence, sense and nonsense. Shaw's portrait of the King's Ministers "recalls the Mad Hatter's Tea-party, and leaves the reader as bewildered as Alice" in this shapeless play. It lacks the unity and political coherence of Heartbreak House.

71 Pierre, Emile. "La politique au théâtre" (Politics in the Theater), LE SOLEIL, 10 March 1931.
The Apple Cart is a powerful, humorous satire of British politics. [Draws a parallel between the play and LE ROI by de Flers and Caillavet.] [In French.]

72 "Plays and Pictures: An Early Shaw Play," NS&Nation, I (14 March 1931), 108-9.
Fanny's First Play is a perfect example of a "potboiler" that is so stimulating it may outlast more important Shavian dramas. The Court Theater production demonstrates that the play is not out of date.

73 "Plays and Pictures: <u>Man and Superman</u> in Modern Dress," NS&Nation, I (23 May 1931), 463-64.
All in all, <u>Man and Superman</u> "wears amazingly well." Certainly it must have been written with "one eye on posterity." Esmé Percy (Kingsway Theater, Lond) plays Jack Tanner with "conviction" and "vitality."

74 Rose, Enid. GORDON CRAIG AND THE THEATRE (Lond: S. Low, 1931; NY: Frederick A. Stokes, 1932), pp. 30, 32-34, 39, 41, 60, 96, 119, 122, 128, 130-31, 150, 161, 178, 204-6, 208-9, 219-20.
Shaw, a rationalist, was of course opposed to Craig, the defender of artistic inspiration and intuition. Shaw's admiration for the Elizabethan Stage Society was misplaced, and <u>The Admirable Bashville</u> shows his historical and aesthetic ignorance of the Elizabethan stage. The letters of Ellen Terry and Shaw are from an artist (Terry) to a "bargain driver" (Shaw). [Rancorous passing attacks on Shaw for failing to champion Craig.]

75 Rothenstein, William. MEN AND MEMORIES, 2 vols. (NY: Coward-McCann, 1931-1932), I, 138, 179-80, 208-11, 213, 229-30, 250, 276, 282, 283-84, 287, 298, Index; II, 44, 68, 72, 75-76, 87, 100, 108-9, 157, 162, 183-84, 202, 264, 265, 315, 317, 379, Index.
[An admiring first-hand portrait of Shaw in the 90's: he "did not wait until he was famous to behave like a great man." Also reminiscences of various later encounters with Shaw, including Shaw's sitting for Rodin, Joseph Conrad's hostility to Shaw, etc.]

76 Rummel, Walter. "George Bernard Shaw Talks on Modern Music," ETUDE, XLIX (Dec 1931), 841-42.
Shaw believes that concert artists should explain more to their audiences. He likes to provoke argument, and has refreshing vitality. [Anecdotal, based on pianist Rummel's visits with Shaw.]

77 Sawyer, Newell W. THE COMEDY OF MANNERS FROM SHERIDAN TO MAUGHAM (Phila: University of Pennsylvania P, 1931) [not seen in this form]; rptd NY: A. S. Barnes (Perpetua Book), 1961, pp. 47, 83, 86n, 115, 145, 152, 158, 197, 198, 199, 200-2, 213, 214, 231, 239, Index, espec 200-202.

Shaw's announced purpose of using the stage as a forum for discussion is antithetical to the purpose of comedy. For example, Getting Married is a prolix symposium on marriage as an institution, with character development sacrificed to the presentation of Shaw's opinions; yet the ideas of the play could have been developed in a comedy of manners. So too You Never Can Tell, How He Lied to Her Husband, and Pygmalion demonstrate Shaw's capacity—thwarted by his doctrinaire nature—for social comedy. [Passim references to Shaw's theory and place in modern comic drama.]

78 Schöpflin, Aladár. "Okos ember az a Bernard Shaw?" (Is That Bernard Shaw a Clever Man?), NYUGAT (1931), II, 254-55.
To a skeptical reader who has never seen or read Shaw's plays but has read newspaper interviews: "Read one or two of Shaw's plays and then you will see that Shaw isn't as simple-minded after all as he presents himself. But it seems as if he's being frugal with his wit. He sticks the good jokes into his plays and the bad ones into the newspapers." [In Hungarian.]

79 Schöpflin, Aladár. "Szinház: BemutatÓk" (Theater: Openings), NYUGAT I, No 10 (16 May 1931), 703-7, espec. 703-4.
Notwithstanding Shaw's extensive prefaces to his works, there is often controversy over their real meaning. This is particularly so because of Shaw's critical perspective—his ability to illuminate the negative aspects of issues—and his tendency to express views diverging from the ordinary. In The Apple Cart, Shaw uses dialog, argument, and dialectic, not action or even conflicting mores, to advance his points. The one actor who does not appear—Shaw himself —shines throughout the play with his sparkling dialog, witty jibes, original ideas, and lack of respect for truisms. [In Hungarian.]

80 "Shaw Twits America on Reds' 'Prosperity,'" NYT, 12 Oct 1931, p. 30.
After a ten-day visit to Russia, Shaw is as convinced as Dr. Pangloss that he saw the best of all possible worlds. Shaw told American radio listeners that the Russian government was simply following ideas he set forth years

ago. And he called Americans "dear old boobs" for not seeing the merits of communism.

81 "Shavian Biographies," TLS, XXX (3 Dec 1931), 976.
Immaturity has well-delineated characters but is "as gloomy as Gissing." The one touch of the better Shaw is the household of the Irish MP, which as wit and vitality. Frank Harris' BERNARD SHAW is wrong in seeing Shaw as a cold Englishman: he is instead passionate about socialism and fastidious and imaginative in his dealings with women.

82 "Shou, Bernard" (Bernard Shaw), MALAĬA SOVETSKAĬA ENTŜIKLOPEDIĬA, Vol. 10 (Moscow: "Sovetskaĭa entŝiklopediĭa," 1931), columns 93-94.
In his plays, Shaw mocks the most characteristic features of the English bourgeoisie: hypocrisy, religious bigotry, respectability, etc. He attacks the worst forms of social injustice (prostitution, the inequality of women, the oppression of Ireland, etc.) However, Shaw does not answer the questions that arise from his generally good-natured criticism of bourgeois civilization. He wrongly gained the reputation of a socialist during the Second International, though he was a liberal. [In Russian.]

83 Sinclair, Upton. "Shaw Might Be Safe Here," OPEN FORUM, VIII (12 Dec 1931), 1.
[A reply to a letter by Shaw (LOS ANGELES EXAMINER, 3 Dec 1931, p. 6) about an incident in Glendale, California, in which a socialist party leader was forcibly restrained by the Glendale American Legion from speaking to a college audience. Sinclair assures Shaw that, thanks to the American Civil Liberties Union, free speech has been restored to Los Angeles and "the Socialists won a complete victory in Glendale."]

84 Skinner, R[ichard] Dana. OUR CHANGING THEATRE (NY: Dial P; Toronto: Longmans, Green, 1931), pp. 31, 124, 136, 204, 243-48, 257, 259, 305, Index, espec 243-48.
Shaw combines wit and satire, a Puritan conscience, Victorian sentimentality, and adolescent intellectual rebellion. But he lacks a universal sense, except in certain passages of Saint Joan. Most of his plays are

therefore dated, since they treat fads rather than human instincts and emotions, as for example The Doctor's Dilemma and Getting Married. Shaw's mind is "poorly balanced," dealing with only the surface of things. Arms and the Man and Pygmalion lack the bitterness of his other comedies; the former is Shaw at his best. But Fanny's First Play and Major Barbara only knock down straw men, and Androcles and the Lion violates Shaw's own most deeply held religious feelings in ridiculing Christians.

85 Skinner, Richard Dana. "The Play: Getting Married—and Shaw," COMMONWEAL, XIII (15 April 1931), 666.

Getting Married (Theater Guild production) is not about marriage but about British divorce laws. It is dull, rambling, impoverished of ideas. Shaw's plays are concerned only with the here and now and (except in some parts of Saint Joan) never touch universals. His mind is "poorly balanced"; he worries more about "the abuse of a principle" than about the principle itself. He is not creative, poetic, or even a good reporter, and has only "pseudo-humor."

86 Sorani, Aldo. "Shaw e Gordon Craig" (Shaw and Gordon Craig), IL MARZOCCO (Florence), 1 Feb 1931, pp. 3-4.

[On the use of stage directions.] [In Italian.]

87 Speth, William. "Le Théâtre: La charrette de pommes" (The Theater: The Apple Cart), LA REVUE MONDIALE, CCIII (1 May 1931), 93-95.

The Apple Cart is boring, except for a charming interlude between the King and his favorite. The ideas are not fresh. [In French.]

88 St. John, Christopher [pseud Christabel Marshall]. "Introductory Note," ELLEN TERRY AND BERNARD SHAW: A CORRESPONDENCE, ed by Christopher St. John (NY: G. P. Putnam's, 1931), pp. vii-xxviii.

St. John came to know Terry through her daughter, Ellen Craig, and through her memoirs. The omissions in Ellen Terry and Bernard Shaw: A Correspondence do not distort the character of Terry, who "would do credit to many a saint."

89 "Stage Society: Widowers' Houses," TIMES (Lond), 24 March 1931, p. 14.
Widowers' Houses (Prince of Wales Theater, Lond) is "neither dead nor fully alive." Its "Shavian puppets," now familiar characters in Shaw, have endurance, and are well presented in this Stage Society production.

90 Strachey, John. "Admitted Impediment," SPECTATOR, CXLVII (19 Sept 1931), 357.
The best reading in Ellen Terry and Bernard Shaw: A Correspondence is Shaw's Preface. The letters help, however, to show why his genius took the course it did, being transformed into "one of the most particular of great British writers" rather than into "one of the most complete."

91 "Terry-Shaw Letters," TLS, XXX (10 Sept 1931), 679.
The letters in Ellen Terry and Bernard Shaw: A Correspondence show Shaw's battle against the romantic theatrical tradition. However, when Shaw recognized that Ellen Terry's aim in theater was to make people happy, he became less intense, more friendly.

92 Tobin, A. I., and Elmer Gertz. FRANK HARRIS: A STUDY IN BLACK AND WHITE (Chicago: Madelaine Mendelsohn, 1931), pp. 1, 11, 13, 25, 33, 91, 99, 118, 131, 133, 134, 144, 150, 157, 162, 168, 174, 179, 188, 191, 195, 200, 203, 208, 212, 214, 225-27, 232, 238, 240, 245, 268, 273, 275, 301, 311, 313, 316, 319, 329, 331-34, 338, 349, 350.
[Many references dealing with Shaw and his relationship with Harris as well as other authors, critics, censors, and publishers. Also many excerpts from Shaw's letters, prefaces, and articles.]

93 Trebitsch, Siegfried. "How I Discovered Bernard Shaw," BOOKMAN (Lond), LXXX (April 1931), 1-3.
[Account of Trebitsch's introduction to Shaw through William Archer, who in 1900 gave Trebitsch copies of Shaw's published plays and then arranged a meeting with Shaw personally. Brief account of that meeting, and of Trebitsch's successful attempts to get theater managers to produce Shaw's plays in Vienna.]

94 Vallese, Tarquinio. IL TEATRO DI G. B. SHAW (The Theater of G. B. Shaw), (Milano, Genova, Roma, & Napoli: Società Anonima Editrice Dante Alighieri, 1931).

In the history of English drama, Shaw is a major figure who is behind Shakespeare and Marlowe but ahead of Jonson and Sheridan. Shaw's work should be evaluated not in the light of his personality but in terms of the characters and the worlds he creates in his plays. The major weakness in his dramatic works is his creation of characters who preach and advocate different philosophical and social positions to the point of becoming marionettes, thereby distorting a play's structure. Examples of such characters are in The Devil's Disciple, Man and Superman, Caesar and Cleopatra, Major Barbara and Getting Married. On the other hand, the characters in Candida (the strongest of Shaw's dramas), The Doctor's Dilemma, Act I of Pygmalion, Androcles and the Lion, Heartbreak House and Saint Joan have autonomy and are not troubled with Shaw's intrusions. In these plays Shaw exercises consummate skill in blending tragic and comic aspects of drama. [In Italian.]

95 Van Doren, Mark. "Drama: The Changing Shaw," NATION, CXXXII (15 April 1931), 430-31.

Shaw does not change; the public does. His reputation has gone through three periods: the view of him as "an irresponsible clown"; the discovery of the serious socialist and Nietzschean; and the present skepticism toward Shaw's message. Getting Married (Theater Guild, NY) has intriguing ideas and characters, and that is more important to comedy than truth.

96 Van Doren, Mark. "The Letters of George Bernard Shaw and Ellen Terry," THEATRE GUILD MAGAZINE (NY), IX (Oct 1931), 20-23.

The unusual love affair between Shaw and Ellen Terry may be one of the most touching in literary history. The letters the two exchanged reveal Shaw's warmth and wit; she appears sympathetic but not sentimental. In fact, in a real sense, this is one of Shaw's most accomplished works, full of wisdom, passion, nonsense and love.

97 Wakefield, Gilbert. "The Theatre," SAT REV, CLI
   (14 March 1931), 376.
Although almost twenty years have elapsed since Fanny's
First Play first appeared, Fanny's language, philosophy,
and behavior are not in the least "old fogyish." The Court
Theater revival is excellent.

98 Wakefield, Gilbert. "The Theatre: Fin de siècle,"
   SAT REV, CLI (11 April 1931), 529.
If Oscar Wilde "was Aestheticism in extremis," "Shaw was
intellectualism in excelsis," practicing what he preached
about the propagandistic value of art. Both Widowers'
Houses (Stage Society production, Lond) and Mrs. Warren's
Profession (Court Theater, Lond) are crude plays, and—
being attacks on contemporary issues—will date.

99 Walbrook, H. M. "The Shavian Epic," ENGLISH
   REVIEW, LIII (Sept 1931), 446-55.
Shaw has always attacked majority opinion, but is
nevertheless immensely popular. His Common Sense About the
War opposed both radical and majority opinion. The Apple
Cart satirized Labour government. His drama is innovative
in that it denies love and passion, flesh and blood, and
romance in favor of caustic wit and intellect. It is hard
to say whether or not it will endure. His characters lack
amiability; he eschews style but at times has an
"admirable" one; and he is above all impishly provocative.

100 Walpole, Hugh. "The Book of the Month," ENGLISH
   REVIEW, LIII (Oct 1931), 586-90.
Ellen Terry and Bernard Shaw: A Correspondence is not a
collection of love letters. The letters contain no
insidious revelations or indiscretions, but reveal two
important and interesting personalities. Moreover, they
present the development of Shaw's plans for his own future
achievement.

101 "Week by Week: G. B. S. on the U.S.S.R.,"
   COMMONWEAL, XIV (9 Sept 1931), 433.
Shaw's account of Soviet Russia in the NEW YORK TIMES lacks
wit and style, and is "a little like a map of the island
valley of Avalon."

102 Welby, T. Earle. "The Shaw-Terry Correspondence," WEEK-END REVIEW, IV (5 Sept 1931), 282-83.
Ellen Terry and Bernard Shaw: A Correspondence reflects the theater of an earlier time, when actors were a separate people. The letters show the friendship of an actress without principles and of a man with a highly developed moral sense.

103 West, Rebecca. "Blessed Are the Pure in Heart," OUTLOOK AND INDEPENDENT, CLVII (28 Jan 1931), 132-33, 156.
[Reflections on Thomas Hardy, Shaw, and Einstein, partly based on a Zionist dinner at which both Shaw and Einstein spoke.]

104 W[ilson], E[dmund]. "A Half-Baked Shaw Production," NEW REPUBLIC, LXVI (15 April 1931), 236.
In Getting Married (Theater Guild, NY) the actors do not understand the intellectual subject of their art, and they fail to put any poetry into the rational arguments. Shaw's plays are like Beethoven symphonies where Shaw "manipulates ideas as the composer does musical themes."

105 Wyatt, Euphemia Van Rensselaer. "The Drama: Plays of Some Importance: Getting Married," CATHOLIC WORLD, CXXXIII (May 1931), 206-11, espec 207.
Getting Married (Guild Theater, NY) is too wordy and at times dull. The "comedy is static," and the female cast disappointing.

106 Young, Stark. "Ellen Terry and Bernard Shaw," NEW REPUBLIC, LXVIII (4 Nov 1931), 327-29.
The letters in Ellen Terry and Bernard Shaw: A Correspondence are rich in revealing the theory and history of the period. Shaw used Terry to further his battle against the old school of theater as typified by the productions of Henry Irving.

107 Zucker, Irving. "LE 'COURT THEATRE' (1904-1914) ET L'EVOLUTION DU THÉÂTRE ANGLAIS CONTEMPORAIN" (The Court Theater, 1904-1914, and The Evolution of the Contemporary English Theater) (Paris: Les Presses

26

Modernes,   1931),   pp.   24-31,   68-101,   133-45   et
passim.)
The new spirit of English drama emerging in the 1890's was
embodied by Shaw, among others, in his first plays, his
defense of Ibsen, and his critical essays and reviews. From
The Philanderer to The Doctor's Dilemma, the themes and
techniques of Shaw's plays demonstrate the development of
the new comedy of ideas, admirably produced and performed
by Harley Granville-Barker, who, like Shaw, believed in the
social function of dramatic art. Shaw's influence on the
realistic problem plays in his use of prefaces, of stage
directions, and of various comic devices cannot be
overestimated. [In French.]

1932

---

108 "The age of youth," VANITY FAIR, XXXIX (Dec
1932), 38-39.
"Youth is all a matter of heart and not of years."
[Photographs of a number of old (over 70), vigorous people,
including Shaw at 76.]

109 Anderson, John. "Drama," ARTS WEEKLY (NY), I (16
April 1932), 122-23; rptd in AMERICAN THEATRE AS SEEN
BY ITS CRITICS, 1752-1934, ed by Montrose J. Moses
and John Mason Brown (NY: Norton; Toronto: McLeod,
1934), pp. 283-86.
Too True To Be Good is about Shaw's emotional disillusionment in his old age. The play is "garrulous, tiresome,
brilliant, idiotic" and at times inept. It is heart-
breaking to see Shaw, who has devoted his life to reason,
renouncing his convictions.

110 Anderson Imbert, Enrique. "Filosofía de Bernard
Shaw" (The Philosophy of Bernard Shaw), LA VANGUARDIA
(1932) [not seen in this form]; rptd in LA FLECHA EN
EL AIRE (The Arrow in the Air) (Buenos Aires: La
Vanguardia, 1937), pp. 68-72; enlarged edition Buenos
Aires: Ediciones Gure, 1972.

The Adventures of the Black Girl in Her Search for God sketches the development of the metaphysics Shaw began in Man and Superman.

111 Armstrong, Martin. "Who Wrote Shaw?" WEEK-END REVIEW, VI (20 Aug 1932), 203-4.

Since the case of Bacon and Shakespeare, it has become clear that if a dramatist becomes famous he did not write his own plays. Shaw enjoys a substantial reputation; therefore it is unlikely he wrote his own plays. Critics should explore the contemporary possibilities and find out who really wrote Shaw. "It is not too much to say that W. R. Inge is written all over the plays of G. B. Shaw."

112 Aronstein, Philipp. "George Bernard Shaw als Persönlichkeit" (George Bernard Shaw as a Personality), DIE NEUEREN SPRACHEN, XL (Nov 1932), 458-73.

Shaw is a revolutionary idealist, a socialist, a man of strength and restless energy and full of fads, a Fabian and an Irishman, a fierce fighter against romanticism, an extreme individualist, a self-mad man, a born rebel, a severe critic of traditions, cant and sham, and an aggressive iconoclast. [In German.]

113 Atkinson, J. Brooks. "Acting at the Guild," NYT, 10 April 1932, VIII, p. 1.

The Theater Guild (NY) production of Too True To Be Good is good; but the play is tedious.

114 Atkinson, J. Brooks. "G. B. S., Lecturer: In 'Too True to Be Good' He Discusses the Collapse of the World—'Stage Sermons' On Many Topics," NYT, 6 March 1932, VIII, p. 1.

If Too True To Be Good were by an unknown author, it would not reach the stage (Colonia Theater, Boston). It is disorganized, reflecting a surrender to Shaw's "weakness for chatter." But Colonel Tallboys and Private Meek enliven the action, which is, unfortunately, mostly "a collection of sermons."

115 Atkinson, J. Brooks. "The Play: Over the Coffee Cups With George Bernard Shaw in a Play Entitled 'Too Good to Be Good,'" NYT, 5 April 1932, p. 27.

<u>Too True To Be Good</u> owes to its actors (Guild Theater, NY) its vigor and eloquence; the script is infirm, having no theme, but the performance is versatile and animated. The final speech is magnificent, though much of the play is discursive and dull.

116 Atkinson, J. Brooks. "Shaw's New Play Tedious With Talk: 'Too True to Be Good' Given Its World Premier by Theatre Guild in Boston," NYT, 1 March 1932, p. 19.
<u>Too True To Be Good</u> (Theater Guild, Colonial Theater, Boston) has no subject or dramatic point. It hs the familiar Shavian puppets--cynical, ironic, and iconoclastic. The dialog rambles to a conclusion which expresses the futility of talk.

117 B., S. "Shaw on War and Diplomacy," CURRENT HISTORY, XXXVI (May 1932), vii, x.
Shaw's power as a battling pamphleteer is not waning, as is evident in <u>What I Really Wrote about the War</u>. He has a penetrating mind and an ability to present facts clearly. His <u>Common Sense About the War</u> offended wartime Britain, but history has proved him right. Unfortunately, the issues of war and peace with which he dealt are still alive.

118 Barling, E. M. BACK TO G. B. S.: SHAW TERCENTARY CELEBRATION, MALVERN, A.D. 2156 (Lond: Panton House, 1932; rptd, with illustrations by Paul Shelving, Malvern Festival Book, 1936).
[Play, broadcast Tuesday, 15 Nov 1932. On 26 July 2156, at the Memorial Talkiechrome, Malvern, science has made dramatic performances possible with "no actors present in the flesh." Attending a performance of <u>Widowers' Houses</u>, Skepticus the critic holds forth that Shaw was really a minor dramatist whose plays were written by H. G. Wells. The shades of Shakespeare and Shaw appear to bemoan the fact that they remain misunderstood.]

119 "Books in Brief: What I Realy Wrote About the War," CHRISTIAN CENTURY, XLIX (1 June 1932), 710-11.
In <u>What I Really Wrote About the War</u> Shaw shows uncanny prescience. But his analysis of how nationalism and socialism are compatible causes puzzlement.

120 Brisson, Pierre. [On Too True To Be Good], LE
TEMPS, 26 Dec 1932, p. 2.
Too True To Be Good is insipid; the fantasy is labored. The
soldier is the only Shavian character, with true humor. [In
French.]

121 Brown, Ivor. "Goings On: The Play," WEEK-END
REVIEW, V (7 May 1932), 581.
Shaw, once the terror of the popular press, is now the
"Whiteheaded Boy of Press and Public." Though Heartbreak
House was facetiously called "Jawbreak House" during its
1921 run, the author's altered status as well as the
performance of the present company (Queen's Theater, Lond)
make the play one of his best. It has, moreover, the
Ibsenite quality of surprise.

122 Brown, Ivor. "Goings On: The Play," WEEK-END
REVIEW, VI (3 Dec 1932), 668.
Getting Married (Little Theater, Lond) is now "dressed
Edwardian." This is necessary, for sexual life has been so
exposed to uninhibited discussion that what stimulated
playgoers in 1908 has now become commonplace. Shaw,
however, is never tedious, though one assumes in Shaw that
the butler will be sage and the general foolish.

123 Brown, Ivor. "Goings On: The Sermon," WEEK-END
REVIEW, VI (13 Aug 1932), 183-84.
Too True To Be Good simply offers a series of sermons. The
indictments excoriate an age without direction, without
creed, and without solution to its spiritual problems. Shaw
is, however, "not satirising our negativity without
positive counsel," though it would appear so when the
sermons are taken in isolation from the entire Shaw canon.
Unfortunately, the sermons are mixed with the lowest form
of Shakespearean clowning, giving the "groundlings a
laugh."

124 Carb, David. "Seen On The Stage," VOGUE, LXXVIV
(1 June 1932), 45, 76.
Too True To Be Good seems to have little or no plan. It
says practically everything Shaw has said previously, and
in the same fashion. Despite several delightful interludes
of low comedy, the play is enveloped in a depressing
atmosphere. Shaw exudes not senility, but "maundering age."

The Theater Guild, however, has done a splendid job of casting.

125 Castro, Cristobal de. "Bernard Shaw o el guiño" (Bernard Shaw or the Ironic Wink), VIDAS FERTILES (Fertile Lives) (Madrid: no publisher, 1932), pp. 249-55.

For over forty years of writing, Shaw has shown that he thrives on argument and polemics. His theater is profoundly anti-bourgeois, though eminently social; it is a parade of political, social, religious, health and economic problems. Throughout his works one finds that his mission is to stir up the sleepy, inactive bourgeoisie. [In Spanish.]

126 Chesterton, G[ilbert] K[eith]. "Bernard Shaw and America," SIDELIGHTS ON NEW LONDON AND NEWER YORK, AND OTHER ESSAYS (NY: Dodd, 1932), pp. 112-18; rptd Freeport, NY: Books for Libraries P [Essay Index Reprint Series], 1968.

Shaw's ideas are shared by much of America; his total abstinence has become American prohibition, and many Americans share his prejudice against tea and tobacco. But, because American education narrows the mind, America turns his fads into fanaticism.

127 Chesterton, G[ilbert] K[eith]. "Bernard Shaw and Breakages," SIDELIGHTS ON NEW LONDON AND NEWER YORK, AND OTHER ESSAYS (NY: Dodd, 1932), pp. 240-46; rptd Freeport, NY: Books for Libraries P [Essay Index Reprint Series], 1968.

The Apple Cart is Shaw's best play. In it, Shaw shows a thorough knowledge of the world. The Prime Minister's rages are the manipulative devices characteristic of the modern politician. Breakages, Ltd., reveals a change in capitalism. Individual enterprise is no longer valued; instead, giant trusts destroy independence, individuality, liberty, efficiency, and practical progress.

128 Chesterton, G[ilbert] K[eith]. "On Mr. Shaw's Puritanism," ALL IS GRIST, A BOOK OF ESSAYS (NY: Dodd, 1932), pp. 175-81; rptd Freeport, NY: Books for Libraries P [Essay Index Reprint Series], 1967.

Shaw has not understood some matters "even sufficiently to disagree" [with Chesterton]. One of Shaw's limitations is his refusal to include Napoleon on his list of great men; Shaw feels the typical Puritan compulsion to hate military glory. What Shaw does not realize is that the modern world, including socialism, was made possible by Napoleonic France, which "established everywhere the modern theories of civic right and equal opportunity."

129 Chesterton, G[ilbert] K[eith]. "Shakespeare and Shaw," SIDELIGHTS ON NEW LONDON AND NEWER YORK, AND OTHER ESSAYS (NY: Dodd, 1932), pp. 234-39; rptd Freeport, NY: Books for Libraries P [Essay Index Reprint Series], 1968.

Shakespeare is more frivolous than Shaw; Shaw, not Shakespeare, is the "earnest sage and seer." Shakespeare came at the end of an era, inheriting the best of an old culture. Shaw inherited a fragmented culture, since a "sort of barbaric interruption" had cut off northern Europe from classicism and humanism. Thus Shakespeare "passes by in the woods with the elusive laughter of a faun" while Shaw has the "gravity of the god, or at least of the prophet or oracle of the god."

130 Chesterton, G[ilbert] K[eith]. "The Spirit of the Age in Literature," SIDELIGHTS ON NEW LONDON AND NEWER YORK, AND OTHER ESSAYS (NY: Dodd, 1932), pp. 205-21; rptd Freeport, NY: Books for Libraries P [Essay Index Reprint Series], 1968.

Shaw, the greatest and last of the "old visionaries of social construction," is an influence on Rebecca West.

131 "Chronicle and Comment," BOOKMAN (NY), LXXV (Nov 1932), 682-98, espec 686.

[Photograph of Shaw with J. B. Priestley at the third Malvern Shaw festival.]

132 "Chronicle and Comment: The Playboy Philosopher," BOOKMAN (NY), LXXV (Sept 1932), 449-64, espec 464.

In reply to the question of suicide versus persevering in "the battle of life" (posed to fifty famous people), Shaw countered with questions of his own: "How the devil do I know? Has the question itself any meaning?"

133 "Chronicle and Comment: Who Wrote Shaw's Plays?"
BOOKMAN (NY), LXXV (Sept 1932), 449-64, espec 451-52.
In a recent WEEK-END REVIEW, Martin Armstrong tried to
prove that Dean W. R. Inge is the author of Shaw's work,
thus possibly creating a controversial issue for a doctoral
candidate of 2232 A.D.

134 Clark, Emily. "Actress and Critic," VIRGINIA
QUARTERLY REVIEW, VIII (April 1932), 282-85.
In Ellen Terry and Bernard Shaw: A Correspondence, Shaw's
letters tell less about him than Terry's letters tell about
her, "the most appealing figure of any stage then or now."
The letters also document the birth of the modern English
theater, "with Mr. Shaw in the role of mother, writhing,
far more than Miss Terry, in labour pains." The paper
romance diminished when business (the production of Captain
Brassbound's Conversion, written for Terry) and marriage
intervened between them. Yet the feeling of friendship
endured.

135 Cooke, Alistair. "The English Scene:
Sophistication and Mr. Coward," TAM, XVI (Nov 1932),
874-80, espec 877-78.
Too True To Be Good has less force for Americans than for
the English, since its dialectic is aimed at Shaw's
"unsubstantiated theory of new world materialism." The play
is an "admission of defeat"; even the Shavian creed cannot
cope with a disintegrating world. It is Shaw's Inferno.

136 Cordell, Richard A. HENRY ARTHUR JONES AND THE
MODERN DRAMA (NY: Long & Smith, 1932) [not seen in
this form]; rptd Port Washington, NY: Kennikat P,
1968, pp. 2, 24-25, 44, 52, 54, 55, 72, 73, 74, 84,
93, 95, 103, 116-17, 120, 122-23, 125, 132, 142-43,
148, 154, 159, 167, 185, 186, 189, 195, 202, 204,
206, 211, 213, 214, 222, 224, 245, 246, 247, 249,
Index.
Shaw and Henry Arthur Jones were precursors of the
realistic drama emerging at the turn of the century. Shaw
defended Jones' THE RENASCENCE OF THE ENGLISH DRAMA (1895),
a collection of Jones' essays and addresses. Shaw also
praised Jones' technical skill in drama but lamented Jones'
antiquated ideas; Shaw's usual criticism of Jones was "that
Henry Arthur Jones is Jones and not Bernard Shaw." Unlike

33

Jones, Shaw can defy the laws of dramaturgy because of his iconoclasm and his stage sense. Finally, Jones was enraged at Shaw for his World War I stance and his espousal of socialism and communism.

137 Croce, Benedetto. "George Bernard Shaw," CONVERSAZIONI CRITICHE (Critical Conversations) (Bari: Laterza, 1932), III, 397-98.

In <u>Saint Joan</u> Shaw cultivates his interest in history and gives a clear judgment of the crisis of the Church and of the medieval order of society. His imagination helps him, through dialog, to present his conception of history in a concise and clear way; even though the things he says are not always original, he says them with a new sense of truth. [In Italian.]

138 Crouch, A. P. MR. G. B. SHAW. A SKETCH... (Bath: Harold Cleaver, 1932); rptd Folcroft, Pa.: Folcroft Library Editions, 1975.

Shaw's first act of rebellion occurred when he was fifteen and learned that he must begin work as a clerk, not as an employer. When his letter about Moody and Sankey scandalized his relatives, his career was decided; he would achieve fame, or notoriety, by shocking. His Fabian speech-making turned him into the "finest word-juggler in the British Empire." He took up arms against authority in any form and devoted himself to an "elaborate system of self-advertisement" to which his "anti-Shakespeare stunt" proved a valuable addition. His flair for self-advertisement, had he not become a playwright, would have led him to make a fortune as a vendor of patent medicines. Taking every opportunity to attack the Seven Deadly Virtues, he never portrayed a sympathetic woman and seemed most pleased to be the first playwright to use "a certain vulgar oath" on the stage. Shaw's plans for a socialist state are "almost too farcical for comment."

139 Dana, H. W. L. "Shaw in Moscow," AMERICAN MERCURY, XXV (March 1932), 343-52; rptd in OPINIONS AND ATTITUDES IN THE TWENTIETH CENTURY, ed by S. S. Morgan and W. H. Thomas (NY: Nelson, 1934), pp. 520-33.

Before his trip to the Soviet Union, the world wondered how Shaw would react to the Russians. He returned determined to say only good of Russia, since he knew that the press would emphasize any negative thing he said. He shows "good sales resistance" against both communist propaganda and capitalist counter-propaganda. [First-hand detailed account of Shaw's trip to the Soviet Union.]

140 "Doctors' Delusions," TLS (Lond), XXXI (25 Aug 1932), 592.
Doctors' Delusions: Crude Criminology and Sham Education has inaccuracies and "perversions of fact." Shaw's knowledge of medicine was reasonably sound in the 1880's but lacks much today.

141 F., D. C. "TOO TRUE TO BE COOD," THEATRE WORLD (Lond), XVIII (Oct 1932), 172.
Too True To Be Good is difficult to describe. It breaks many accepted canons of the theater; yet the speeches are delicately modulated.

142 Falser, Margarete. "Gedanken über das Verhaltnis von Mann und Frau bei Bernard Shaw" (Thoughts about the Relationship between Men and Women in Bernard Shaw). Unpublished dissertation, University of Innsbruck, 1932. [Listed in Altick and Matthews, Item 1720.] [In German.]

143 Fergusson, Francis. "A Month of the Theatre: recalling the high lights," BOOKMAN (NY), LXXV (June-July 1932), 288-91, espec 290.
Too True To Be Good catches Shaw "in his present rather disillusioned mood." It is a turning point, "the swan-song of the Shavian brisk, self-satisfied social satire."

144 Fergusson, Francis. "A Month of the Theatre: remarks on recent shows," BOOKMAN (NY), LXXV (April 1932), 75-77.
Shaw is out of date, and knows it. But Too True To Be Good (Theater Guild production) "has a new depth"; Shaw seems to be skeptical of himself, "seems to be folding up his box of tricks." His characters are always Shaw, with different masks on.

145 Fleming, Peter. "The Theatre," SPECTATOR, CXLVIII (30 April 1932), 625.

Shaw's Preface to Heartbreak House makes extravagant claims for the work, but the first two acts are the usual Shavian "comedy of bad manners." Only in the final act is there a sense of the decadence of Europe before 1914. Heartbreak (Queen's Theater, Lond) cannot be seen as allegory, satire, or sermon; it has enough wit, however, to make it a successful comedy.

146 Fyfe, W[illiam] H[amilton]. "George Bernard Shaw," QQ, XXXIX (Feb 1932), 29-45.

Like Socrates, Shaw is "an indefatigable gadfly." The moral of his plays is "Know Yourself." Shaw believes that virtue is knowledge. Trust in reason and distrust in the heart unite Shaw and Socrates in a puritanical suspicion of art and in a preoccupation with social reform. Shaw is, thus, not an artist but a reformer; except for Saint Joan—which "escapes from its author and lives a triumphant life of its own"—Shaw's plays are not likely to be enjoyed forever because they lack "the independent vitality which characterizes all great art, and express the views rather than the personality of their author." The interest of Shaw's plays centers not in the fate and character of the dramatis personae but in social problems "which will lose their interest." Shaw is, finally, a great and enjoyable critic, if not a great dramatist.

147 Garland, Hamlin. MY FRIENDLY CONTEMPORARIES: A LITERARY LOG (NY: Macmillan, 1932; Lond: Macmillan, 1933), pp. 428-32, 507-21.

[Personal reminiscences of meetings with Shaw in Adelphi Terrace and at Ayot St. Lawrence in 1922 and 1923; describes Shaw's appearance, speech, manner, and recounts his conversation.] "He laughs while exposing absurd and stupid laws. That is his way of reforming society."

148 "Getting Married at the Little," ILN, CLXXXI (3 Dec 1932), 912.

Getting Married is "an amazing tour de force." The lack of action is atoned for by the vivid dialog, though the third act is a bit boring. It appears that the text has been revised, for Shaw would never have omitted such a topical subject as "Votes for Women."

149 Grein, J. T. "The World of the Theatre," ILN, CLXXX (16 April 1932), 568.
Oscar Straus' THE CHOCOLATE SOLDIER is the most "tuneful and brillant" operetta since those of Johann Strauss. The plot, adapted from Shaw, is plausible enough, and the music mixes melody, the romantic, and the martial in its own orchestration.

150 Hardwicke, Cedric. LET'S PRETEND: RECOLLECTIONS AND REFLECTIONS OF A LUCKY ACTOR (Lond: Grayson, 1932; rptd NY: Benjamin Blom, 1972), pp. 47, 118, 126, 132, 152, 177, 180, 199, 201, 205, 209, 211, 218, 225, 230, 233, 237, 240.
Shaw's reputation made many actors anxious, but the "dreadful dragon" was actually "one of the most sympathetic and genial of men, the most helpful of producers," and "no mean actor himself." [Many anecdotes and background to various productions of Shaw's plays.]

151 Harvey, Sir Paul (ed.) "Shaw, George Bernard (1856-   )," THE OXFORD COMPANION TO ENGLISH LITERATURE (Oxford: Clarendon Press, 1932), p. 713.
[Brief résumé of Shaw's works to date.]

152 Henderson, Archibald. "Bernard Shaw: Big Noise or Flash-in-the-pan?" WESTMINSTER MAGAZINE, XVII (Winter 1932), 15-18.
Shaw is a combination of personae, recognized even by those hostile to him as a writer of extraordinary power. Whereas Shaw is indebted to others for his socialism, his style is his own. He is always "fiercely partisan," portraying not character but "ethical propaganda." He founded the school of "debate drama" and wrote "the greatest drama written in English since Shakespeare" in Saint Joan.

153 Henderson, Archibald. BERNARD SHAW, PLAYBOY AND PROPHET (NY & Lond: Appleton, 1932).
[An expanded version of Henderson's GEORGE BERNARD SHAW: HIS LIFE AND WORKS (Lond: Hurst & Blackett; Cincinnati: Stewart & Kidd, 1911); rptd NY: Boni & Liveright, 1918. The 1932 biography was later expanded in GEORGE BERNARD SHAW: MAN OF THE CENTURY (NY: Appleton-Century-Crofts, 1956); rptd NY: Da Capo P, 1972. The standard biography of Shaw by his authorized biographer. Anecdotal and badly organized

(hence hard to use), but nevertheless essential to the study of Shaw because of its wealth of information about him.]

154 Hill, Ralph. "George Bernard Shaw as Musical Critic," BOOKMAN (Lond), LXXXII (Aug 1932), 237-38.
Shaw in <u>Music in London: 1890-1894</u> is the ideal musical critic, combining scholarly knowledge with literary ability, objectivity and subjectivity. His abhorrence of pedantry causes him to exaggerate when he attacks composing by rules. And he misunderstands Brahms.

155 Hutchins, John. "End of a Season: Broadway in Review," TAM, XVI (June 1932), 437-48, espec 437-39.
<u>Too True To Be Good</u> is too discursive; it covers "old Shavian territory." It suffers from an incredibly tenuous framework of narrative and heavy phrasing. The despairing end, however, gains majesty with the "heightened passion and momentum" of the rhythms of speech.

156 Ireland, Baron. "Literary Note," BOOKMAN (NY), LXXV (Aug 1932), 373.
[A short, humorous verse on the subject of Shaw's love notes to Ellen Terry.]

157 Ishida, Kenji. BERNARD SHAW SHINZUI (The Quintessence of Bernard Shaw) (Kyoto & Tokyo: Kobundo, 1932).
A thorough and detailed exposition of almost all of Shaw's works up to 1930. After completing the manuscript, however, Ishida became critical of Shaw's thought. In the final chapter he attempts its reassessment, which in some points reverses his own views expressed in the preceding pages.] Shaw advocates that we should set ourselves free from all morals and ideals, and that we should act only on the promptings of the Life Force. But his theory is inconsistent. As a matter of fact, he lays stress on human values, and aspires to a morallyd esirable world. It will, however, not be realized by equality of income. Furthermore, there is no hope at the moment of its realization by creating the Superman. Shaw's Superman is like a person described by Confucius: a man who does everything just as he pleases, but nver oversteps the bounds of moderation. In the Preface to <u>Androcles and the</u>

38

Lion Shaw regards Jesus Christ as social thinker, and says that his teachings would be realized by laws alone. Shaw's thought, particularly his most recent, lacks credibility. The most lively and attractive portion of it is his holding up the humanistic and moralistic ideal that has clearly been influenced by Christianity. [In Japanese.]

158 Jevtic, B. "Bernard So" (Bernard Shaw), PREGLED (Belgrade), VII (1932), 146-47. [Not seen but listed in BIBLIOGRAFSKA RASPRAVA, Zagreb, 1956, 10502.] [In Serbian.]

159 Joad, C. E. M. "A Lively Correspondence," FORTNIGHTLY REVIEW, CXXXVII (Jan 1932), 119-20.
The letters in Ellen Terry and Bernard Shaw: A Correspondence are about "everything and nothing," with particular emphasis on plays and players. Whereas the letters are delightful, the most interesting part of the book is Shaw's Preface, which is as significant as the prefaces to Saint Joan and The Apple Cart.

160 Kingsmill, Hugh. "Oscar Wilde by the Styx," BOOKMAN (NY), LXXV (May 1932), 131-34.
[An imaginary conversation in which Oscar Wilde, in the underworld, discusses with the author various writers, including Shaw. "Shaw is reasonable and repulsive, and bids men realize themselves through parsnips, and the dwellers in his Utopia cast no shadows because they have no bodies."]

161 Kingsmill, Hugh. "Some Modern Light-Bringers as they might have been extinguished by Thomas Carlyle," BOOKMAN (NY), LXXV (Dec 1932), 766-68, espec 766.
[Parody on what Carlyle might have written about Wells, Shaw, Lawrence, Proust, Joyce, and Strachey. Shaw is compared to a shrill spinster who wants to put the world's parlor to rights, and, as a cure-all to the world's problems, would present every person with a weekly check.]

162 Krutch, Joseph Wood. "Drama: Alas, Poor Yorick," NATION, CXXXIV (20 April 1932), 277-78.
In general, Too True To Be Good (Guild Theater, NY) is a bad play, but it is impressive because in it Shaw "stripped

himself bare." In this play Shaw speaks in his own person, declaring himself and humankind a failure.

163 Lalou, René. "Le Théâtre," LES NOUVELLES LITTÉRAIRES, 31 Dec 1932, p. 8.
Too True To Be Good is unrestrained words, words, words— few of them funny. Considering Shaw's crackers and bangers which fail to explode, Anatole France seems to be a bold revolutionary. [In French.]

164 "Lecturing Mr. Shaw," LITERARY DIGEST, CXIV (12 Nov 1932), 15.
In Too True To Be Good Shaw is "in the doldrums," despairing of humanity.

165 "Little Theatre: 'Getting Married,'" TIMES (Lond), 26 Nov 1932, p. 8.
Getting Married (Little Theater, Lond) is little more than "an inconclusive discussion"; yet its argument mvoes swiftly and gracefully in this "well-mounted and well-acted revival."

166 Loewenstein, F[ritz] E[rwin]. "Mr. Bernard Shaw Regrets..," AMERICAN MERCURY, LXIII (Aug 1946), 174-76.
Shaw copes with the many letters he receives with color-coded postcards containing witty, sometimes curt, pre-printed messages.

167 Loveman, Amy. "Books of the Spring," SRL, VIII (16 April 1932), 667.
What I Really Wrote About the War is too much a self-advertisement, in which Shaw maintains that he wrote "the whole truth" about the war during the war years.

168 Lunn, Hugh Kingsmill. FRANK HARRIS: A BIOGRAPHY (Lond: Jonathan Cape, 1932), pp. 89, 99, 113, 146, 166, 188, 203, 218, 249-53.
Harris was displeased that Shaw would not write a preface to his collected works. Shaw did praise Harris for his "range of sympathy and understanding," although he refused to voertly repay Harris for making him a drama critic on the SATURDAY REVIEW.

169 M., H. G. "TOO TRUE TO BE GOOD," THEATRE WORLD (Lond), XVIII (Sept 1932), 118, 121.
Too True To Be Good is a kaleidoscope of ideas; but it contains one central idea: the need for dogma, for certainty. The sense of futility permeating modern thought is echoed by several characters. The darkness, however, is streaked by moments of lurid wit.

170 MacCarthy, Desmond. "Miscellany: Mr. Shaw's Play," NS&Nation, IV (13 Aug 1932), 178-79; rptd as "Too True to be Good," in MacCarthy, SHAW'S PLAYS IN REVIEW (NY: Thames & Hudson, 1951; rptd Folcroft, Pa.: Folcroft P, 1969), pp. 188-92.
Shaw has never shown much concern for structure, but in Too True To Be Good he shows even "more complete indifference to form." However, this conforms to his erroneous belief that art is less valuable than philosophy. Thus Too True has dozens of subjects, but "no focus to group them around." The play is simply a "series of snapshots."

171 Maine, Basil. "Shaw, Wells, Binyon—and Music," MUSICAL QUARTERLY, XVIII (July 1932), 375-82, espec 375-77.
In calling Roger Fry's concept of art "Confectionery," Shaw startles at first, but he means to attack the notion of art as "mechanical process." But Fry does not extol technique over vision as primary in an artist.

172 "The Malvern Festival: Mr. Shaw's New Play, 'Too True to be Good,'" TIMES (Lond), 8 Aug 1932, p. 8.
Too True To Be Good (Malvern Festival production) has style but no form or dramatic interest. Yet Shaw's "badness, like his goodness, is unique." The play is a patchwork of ideas, touching on a great theme wasted "as ballast for a leaky farce."

173 Marble, Annie Russell. "George Bernard Shaw: Dramatist, Satirist, and Prophet," THE NOBEL PRIZE WINNERS IN LITERATURE, 1901-1931 (NY and Lond: Appleton-Century, 1932), pp. 277-95.
While many critics are skeptical of Shaw's idealism, there is ample evidence that he possessed the qualities described in the Nobel Prize citation: "idealism and humanity ...lively satire associated with peculiar poetic beauty."

In actuality, Shaw is more of a satirist than an idealist, and anti-romantic before the word became a characteristic description of modern literature. Shaw defies conventional orthodoxy in his plays by portraying conflicts between individual wills and social systems in forms varying from satire verging on invective to extreme statement and braggadoccio. [Anecdotal resume of his life from birth to Widowers' Houses followed by description and thematic commentary on plays up to The Apple Cart.]

174 Morgan, Charles. "London, With Examples: Three New Productions Epitomize That Metropolis's Current Stage," NYT, 16 Oct 1932, IX, p. 3.
Caesar and Cleopatra (Old Vic, Lond) has "solid character-drawing and swift narrative," and is infinitely better than Too True To Be Good, "with its quips and puppets."

175 [Morgan, Charles.] "The Malvern Festival: Mr. Shaw's New Play, 'Too True to be Good,'" TIMES (Lond), 8 Aug 1932, p. 8; rptd CRITICAL HERITAGE, pp. 327-28, Item 104.
Too True To Be Good is like an "undigested notebook"—formless, yet unique in its combined wisdom and childishness. It is filled with stale dramatic effects, and its message is lost amidst buffoonery. [C. B. Purdom, "Shaw Needs no Defense," EVERYMAN, 18 Aug 1932, answers Morgan, defending Shaw's style in a play which "makes its own rules."]

176 Morgan, Charles. "Malvern Upholds an American Verdict," NYT, 28 Aug 1932, IX, p. 1.
Idolization of Shaw makes him tedious, as in Too True To Be Good, with its pasteboard characters, sermons, and feeble slapstick.

177 Nathan, George Jean. THE INTIMATE NOTEBOOKS OF GEORGE JEAN NATHAN (NY: Knopf, 1932), pp. 51-52, 166, 175, 265-70, 294-99.
Shaw was once a good critic and a witty, humorous playwright. Now he ought to "shut up." He has of late made a fool of himself in his public appearances, and he has become a "lamentable bore." Too True To Be Good is a "substitute for playwrighting"; "It is dull, dull, dull" and belongs in the trash basket. Shaw seems to be trying to

placate his critics by dealing with sex and sentiment in
the play.

178 "New Books and Reprints: Political," TLS, XXXI
(1 Sept 1932), 608-12, espec 610.
Essays in Fabian Socialism is of great value to a historian
of ideas. "Socialism and Superior Brains" is the most
characteristic, while "The Transition to Social Democracy"
is a model of academic work.

179 "New Theatre: 'Too True to be Good,'" TIMES
(Lond), 14 Sept 1932, p. 8.
Audiences will laugh at any Shavian joke and listen to any
Shavian sermon; therefore, Shaw should not throw sops to
his audience, as he does in Too True To Be Good (New
Theater, Lond). The first act is a bit dull; the third act,
a wild "mixture of strength and weakness." The theme of the
world's struggle to overcome spiritual despair emerges in
pieces.

180 Nieuwenhuis, W. "Bernard Shaw," DIETSCHE WARANDE
EN BELFORT, XXXII (1932), 73-77.
Shaw strove intellectually to be both an absolute protester
and an absolute individualist. His successful dramatic
characters were created in spite of Shaw's intellectual
strivings because of his powerful dramatic instincts. [In
Dutch.]

181 "Noble Kinsmen," TLS, XXXI (12 May 1932), 346.
Pen Portraits and Reviews is "a miniature masterpiece of
biography." Some of the essays use human beings to
illustrate ideas which can either be put forward or fought
against. Unlike G. K. Chesterton [whose SIDELIGHTS is also
reviewed here], Shaw surveys humanity with "ironical
exasperation," advocating a change in human nature rather
than a realistic and traditionalist acceptance of it.

182 "The Old Vic: 'Caesar and Cleopatra,'" TIMES
(Lond), 20 Sept 1932, p. 8.
Caesar and Cleopatra is Shaw's "swiftest and plainest
narrative." Britannus is "out of the Shavian slot-
machine," but Caesar is witty and wise, and Cleopatra sly
and alive. [General praise for the acting.]

183 [On <u>Too True To Be Good</u>], LES NOUVELLES
LITTÉRAIRES, 5 Nov 1932, p. 2.
<u>Too True To Be Good</u> was a hit in Birmingham but not in
London. The pessimism in the last act is terrifying. [In
French.]

184 Osma, J. M. de. "Variaciones sobre el tema de
Don Juan" (Variations on the Don Juan Theme),
HISPANIA, XV (1932), 55-62.
Shaw's <u>Man and Superman</u> is a caricature of the traditional
libertine. John Tanner is not a superman or a "macho man"
but a "slave of the spirit," a poor devil who fell into the
nets of a woman in love. [In Spanish.]

185 "The Play of the Moment: 'Too True To Be Good,'"
THEATRE WORLD (Lond), XVIII (Oct 1932), 175-86.
<u>Too True To Be Good</u> does not resemble a play, for it is
mostly discourses in well-modulated and balanced prose. [A
plot synopsis, with photographs and stage description of
the New Theater, London, production.]

186 "A Playgoer's Afterthoughts," THE STAGE (NY), IX
(May 1932), 5-7.
The Theater Guild (NY) production of <u>Too True To Be Good</u>
lends "beguiling pomp and circumstance" to Shaw's
"collection of stage sermons." He can write a better play
if he wants to.

187 "The Playhouse: 'Too True To Be Good,' At the
New," ILN, CLXXI (24 Sept 1932), 474.
<u>Too True To Be Good</u> is a second-rate drama full of
provocative dialog.

188 "Plays and Pictures: <u>Heartbreak House</u>,"
NS&Nation, III (30 April 1932), 557.
<u>Heartbreak House</u> (Queen's Theater, Lond) is well worth a
visit. Cedric Hardwicke understands and loves the part of
Shotover, and the other players are excellent as well.

189 "Queen's Theatre: 'Heartbreak House,'" TIMES
(Lond), 26 April 1932, p. 14.
The first act of <u>Heartbreak House</u> (Queen's Theater, Lond)
is beautifully unified in both form and substance, but the

second and third acts are uneven, "buffeted to and fro by every gust of dialogue." The acting is also uneven.

190 Redman, Ben Ray. "Old Wine in New Bottles,"
NYHTBR, 22 May 1932, p. 12.
In Shaw's What I Really Wrote About the War, inconsistencies are prevalent, but many of his ideas on the war
are "accepted by even semi-thoughtful people as truthful
commonplaces." He really has the right to say I told you
so.

191 Rhys, Ernest. "Miscellany: Shaw versus
Shakespeare," NS&Nation, III (30 April 1932), 555-56.
[A conversational account of a journey to Stratford for the
Shakespeare Festival, where Rhys stops at Shakespeare's
Head Press for a drink and meets the Bard himself.
Shakespeare mistakes Rhys for Shaw, and a dialog on their
plays ensues.]

192 Richards, Grant. MEMORIES OF A MISSPENT YOUTH,
1872-1896 (Lond: Heinemann, 1932; NY & Lond: Harper,
1933), pp. 24, 106, 123, 164, 232-36, 241, 285-89,
321-23, Index.
[Reminiscences concerning James Welch as Lickcheese in
Widowers' Houses and Richards' early encounters with Shaw;
includes letters from Shaw to Richards and Grant Allen.]

193 Roberts, R. Ellis. "Shaw after Shaw," NS&Nation,
IV (10 Dec 1932), 764, 766.
The Adventures of the Black Girl in Her Search for God is
witty, balancing "in the polyptych of Shaw's work" The
Shewing-Up of Blanco Posnet. The latter has God tracking
down the soul; the former shows the soul in search of God.
Shaw's theology is shaky. He prefers the 19th-century
humanitarian image of Jesus to the Psalms and the "advanced
doctrine of Jonah." The ending of Adventures is
anticlimactic: "Shaw, in the search for God, meets Bernard
Shaw." But the parable is in Shaw's "clear, definite prose
—the best plain prose since Defoe's." [Also includes a
review of Henderson's BERNARD SHAW: MAN OF THE CENTURY, a
"cumbrous necessity to all students of Shaw."]

194 "Shaftesbury Theatre: 'The Chocolate Soldier,'"
TIMES (Lond), 1 April 1932, p. 10.

Arms and the Man has more fun and excitement than this
unauthorized parody (THE CHOCOLATE SOLDIER), which
nevertheless is a good comic opera.

195 "Shaw the Prophet," TLS, XXXI (8 Dec 1932), 939.
The Adventures of the Black Girl in her Search for God
shows nothing new of Shaw's theories, but it does expose
"current religious errors." Whereas the ex-clergyman in Too
True To Be Good goes on preaching and preaching, the black
girl gives up and raises a houseful of children. [Also
reviews Archibald Henderson's BERNARD SHAW, PLAYBOY AND
PROPHET.]

196 "Shaw's 'Shofar-Blast,'" LITERARY DIGEST, CXIV
     (22 Oct 1932), 20.
THE AMERICAN HEBREW AND JEWISH TRIBUNE (NY) asked Shaw to
sound a "Shofar-blast" to all nations to celebrate the
Jewish New Year. Shaw wrote that both races and nations are
anachronisms, that "The future belongs to the citizens of
the world." This of course brought forth irate replies from
various Jewish sources. The NYT observed taht Shaw can be
depended on to offend propriety.

197 "Shaw's Valedictory?" LITERARY DIGEST, CXIII (30
     April 1932), 14-15.
The finale of Too True To Be Good (Guild Theater
production) "is in the nature of a valedictory." [Summary
of critical comments on the play.]

198 Sinclair, Upton. AMERICAN OUTPOST: A BOOK OF
     REMINISCENCES (NY: Farrar & Rinehart; pub as CANDID
     REMINISCENCES, Lond: T. Werner Laurie, 1932), pp.
     204, 254-55.
[Brief account of a luncheon meeting between "Thyrsis"
(Sinclair) and Shaw.]

199 Skinner, Richard Dana. "The Play: Too True To Be
     Good," COMMONWEAL, XV (20 April 1932), 691.
Too True To Be Good has some wit and some scenes of
brilliant extravaganza, but it rehashes old Shaw and
deliberately avoids dramatic form. Its interest is in
Shaw's retreat from Moscow, determinism, and certainty. The
last act reflects his bewilderment at trying to adjust to a

world in which 19th-century atheism, socialism, and pragmatism have collapsed. The last speech is very moving.

200 St. John, Christopher [pseud Christabel Marshall], and Edith Craig, eds. ELLEN TERRY'S MEMOIRS (NY: G. P. Putnam's, 1932), v-viii, ix-x, 27, 115, 116, 191, 251, 252, 256-84, 287-301, 315, 324, 329, 348, 357, 362.
[Many brief references to Shaw by Terry, as well as editorial notes on those references.]

201 Strong, L. A. G. "Fiction," SPECTATOR, CXLIX (9 Dec 1932), 844.
Shaw's concept of what children are taught about God is outdated. In The Adventures of the Black Girl in her Search for God he "falls into the error of judging a belief by its silliest adherents." The allegory is vigorous and economical, but it finally loses momentum. Shaw's purpose is sincere; "His exposition, however, is bound to be offensive to many readers." The John Farleigh illustrations "combine humour with beauty."

202 Takenaka, Toshikazu. "Shaw to Galsworthy" (Shaw and Galsworthy), CORONA AUSTRALIS (Hiroshima), No 6 (June 1932), pp. 1-3.
Shaw and Galsworthy are both now Grand Old Men of British drama. Their characteristics are, however, contrary to each other. Shaw's plays are didactic, dogmatic and satiric. But Galsworthy's motto is impartial delineation. He depicts things with sympathy and love. His plays appeal to emotion; Shaw's to intellect. Yet both have succeeded as practicing dramatists. Shaw poses as a propgandist, and Galsworthy looks upon himself as an artist. It may, however, be correct to say that Shaw is an artist in spite of himself, and that Galsworthy is a propagandist in spite of himself. [In Japanese.]

203 Tetauer, Frank, "The Utopias of Butler and Shaw," from "Philosophical and Ethical Attitudes of G. B. Shaw and its Relation to the Philosophy of Samuel Butler," CHARISTERIA GUILELMO MATHESIO QUINQUAGENARIO A DISCIPULIS ET CIRCULI LINGUISTICI PRAGENSIS SODALIBUS OBLATA (Prague: "Prazský linguistický krouzek," 1932), pp. 139-40.

Shaw's philosophical and ethical attitude in many respects is a direct continuation of Samuel Butler's philosophy. The strongest link between them is the belief in Creative Evolution. [In English.]

204 Tilby, A. Wyatt. "Love by Post," SAT REV, CLII (19 Sept 1932), 360.
Ellen Terry and Bernard Shaw: A Correspondence reveals two distinct but attractive personalities. Shaw is the determined iconoclast who always has something to say on almost any topic. Terry, a conservative, really has very little to say, but she says it even better than Shaw.

205 "'Too True to be Good': Mr. Shaw's Play Produced at Boston," TIMES (Lond), 2 March 1932, p. 10.
The original idea of Too True To Be Good (Colonial Theater, Boston)—"an attack on doctors and meat-eating"—has been obscured by other ideas, many of which have been familiar for years. [Résumé of the plot.]

206 Verschoyle, Derek. "Theatre," SPECTATOR, CXLIX (24 Sept 1932), 367.
Too True To Be Good follows a Shavian formula: farcical action, attacks on medicine, ridicule of the army, and a last-act sermon giving Shaw's philosophy.

207 Wakefield, Gilbert. "Theatre," SAT REV, CLIII (7 May 1932), 470-71.
Perhaps Mr. Shaw considers Heartbreak House his best play, but much of it is repetitious Shavian doctrine, and thus dramatically it is among his worst plays. Unfortunately, it is a symposium on "things in general"; often one group of characters is replaced by another which discusses a subject wholly unrelated to the dramatic issue at hand. Moreover, the usual dialectic continuity is absent. Originally, the play was intended to criticize cultural Europe before World War I, but too much of it is topical, with nothing to relate to 1914.

208 Wakefield, Gilbert. "Theatre," SAT REV, CLIV (24 September 1932), 322.
Shaw is unquestionably the most remarkable living English playwright. Unfortunately, Too True To Be Good is "empty and fatiguing." The play is a shapeless conglomeration of

political diatribes, sermons, and clowning. Shaw predicts more devastating wars in the future, admonishes us that the truths of science and philosophy lack any credibility; yet he fails to explain what is to be done.

209 "The Week," NEW REPUBLIC, LXXII (12 Oct 1932), 216-19, espec 218.
Shaw recently wrote to THE AMERICAN HEBREW AND JEWISH TRIBUNE (NY) that he looked forward to Jewish assimilation (and thus the disappearance of Jewry). That is in fact happening in America. Shaw's manner rather than his matter offended, and Shaw no doubt is delighted at the stir he caused.

210 Welby, T. Earle. "Frank Harris: Bernard Shaw: An Antithesis," FORTNIGHTLY REVIEW, ns CXXI (Jan 1932), 94-100.
[A hostile sketch of Frank Harris, with Shaw as the touchstone of quality.] Unlike Harris, Shaw developed an art responsive to his public, and his life was well conducted. Shaw is a great pamphleteer and critic, and justly esteemed today. Unfortunately, other artists (e.g., Ellen Terry, Harris) are being accorded recognition to the extent that they were entangled with Shaw.

211 "What Shall We Do to Be Saved?" THEATRE GUILD MAGAZINE (NY), IX (April 1932), 14-17.
Too True To Be Good has no semblance of plot or logic, but it possesses various moods: the amusing, the fantastic, the bawdy, the romantic or the evangelical. Indeed, the play is like a morality play, for the characters incarnate virtues or vices. Shaw is not simply addressing spiritual problems, but the survival of the modern Western world.

212 Wilson, Edmund. "Bernard Shaw and the War," NEW REPUBLIC, LXX (13 April 1932), 241-42.
In What I Really Wrote About the War Shaw defends himself too glibly. His view of the war was essentially Marxist. He spoke intelligently and coolly at a time when most writers were carried away by panic, but finally he did not denounce the war.

213 Wilson, Edmund. "Post-War Shaw and Pre-War Bennett," NEW REPUBLIC, LXXI (8 June 1932), 92-94.

Shaw has lived through the war to see Fabianism sell out; probably his defense of the Bolshevik Revolution and Stalin is the only alternative he sees to his outdated convictions. He has made great efforts to keep in accord with the changing times. [The development of his opinions is traced by means of Annajanska, the Bolshevik Empress; Back to Methuselah; The Intelligent Woman's Guide to Socialism and Capitalism; The Apple Cart; and Too True To Be Good.]

214 Wilson, P. W. "Mr. Shaw and the World War," NYTBR, 27 March 1932, pp. 1, 16.
Shaw's What I Really Wrote About the War attempts to administer a moral shock to the accepted interpretation of the war. As usual, Shaw's notions are replete with inconsistencies and clever irresponsibility, yet they are needed. Shaw is not a prophet but a Mephistophelian wit where "the classical coincides with the cheap."

215 Wingfield-Stratford, Esmé. THE VICTORIAN SUNSET (NY: William Morrow, 1932), pp. 136, 211, 254, 332, 333, 335-39, Index.
Shaw created the "genuine new drama" (i.e., realistic, truth-telling drama) of the nineties. He surpasses his contemporaries not in character drawing or structural unity or wit but in scope: he illuminates the whole of contemporary life without pandering to popular tastes.

216 Woolf, S[amuel] J[ohnson]. "George Bernard Shaw," DRAWN FROM LIFE (NY & Lond: Whittlesey House, 1932), pp. 19-29.
[Account of Woolf's visit to Adelphi Terrace to draw Shaw, in which Shaw discoursed for two hours or more on Strindberg, Rodin, economics, religion, and modern art.]

217 Woollcott, Alexander. "Shouts and Murmurs: World Premiere," NYer, VIII (12 March 1932), 32.
Too True To Be Good (Theater Guild production, Boston) has the aura of a valedictory. It is unashamedly and admittedly "talky." "It might have been called 'Heartbreak Universe'" —being "a wilderness...of lost dogmas." The final speech is among the finest in modern theater.

218 Wyatt, Euphemia Van Rensselaer. "The Drama: <u>Too True To Be Good</u>," CATHOLIC WORLD, CXXXV (May 1932), 206-12, espec 206-7.
<u>Too True To Be Good</u> (Theater Guild production) is a "philosophical treatise" animated by farce. The curtain speech is "tragic and compelling." Shaw, weary and tired, is seeking a secure faith and a guide to it.

219 Yamamoto, Shuji. EIBEI GENDAIGEKI NO DOKO (Tendency of the Contemporary English and American Drama) (Tokyo & Osaka: Sogensha, 1932), pp. 140-44, 283-308.
Apart from King Magnus, almost all characters in <u>The Apple Cart</u> are blind ritualists of democracy. Therefore they cannot understand anything that Magnus stands for: "great abstractions," "conscience and virtue," "the eternal against the expedient," "the evolutionary appetite against the day's gluttony" and so forth. They are not aware, either, that Breakages, Ltd. pulls the wires behind the scene.

The antagonism between Henry Irving and Shaw was aroused by their opposing views of the stage. Irving was the champion and leader of the theater, while Shaw, the pioneer of drama, applied to the British theater the standards of philosophical seriousness and psychological depth set by Goethe, Ibsen, and Wagner. [In Japanese.]

220 Young, Stark. "Little Flowers," NEW REPUBLIC, LXX (20 April 1932), 271-73.
<u>Too True To Be Good</u> (Theater Guild production) rehashes Shaw's cheap didactic tricks. However, there is a slight dramatic touch in the last scene.

1933

---

221 Abe, Isoo. "Bernard Shaw no Seitokan" (Bernard Shaw's View of Politics), KAIZO (Tokyo), XV, No 4 (April 1933), 287-89.
[Shaw visited the headquarters of the Japanese Federation of Labor on 6 March 1933 and met some thirty union

leaders.] Shaw is certainly one of the foremost writers of the day, but not a statesman. His observations are those of a writer. They are synthetic, not analytical; intuitive, not experimental. [In Japanese.]

222 Arns, Karl. LITERATURE UND LEBEN IM HEUTIGEN ENGLAND (Literature and Life in Contemporary England) (Leipzig: Emil Rohmkopf, 1933), pp. 23, 54-55, 67, 69, 74, 76, 77-78, 82, 84, 88, 107, 111, 112, 116.
Shaw did not deserve the Nobel Prize. Back to Methuselah is a feeble and artificial play; Too True To Be Good is a mixture of satire and farce. The mocking attitude of C. E. M. Joad's autobiography, UNDER THE FIFTH RIB (1932), recalls Shaw's prefaces. [In German.]

223 Arvin, Newton. "Erin Go Blah," NEW REPUBLIC, LXXIV (22 March 1933), 163.
As philosophy or theology, The Adventures of the Black Girl in Her Search for God fails to go deep enough to say anything profound. As art, it is vulgar and tedious. The black girl only discovers what "most educated people have known for many decades."

224 Baba, Tsunego. "Shaw Inshoki" (Impressions of Shaw), KAIZO (Tokyo), XV, No 4 (April 1933), 304-6; rptd as "Bernard Shaw" in KUNI TO JINBUTSU (Country and Character) (Tokyo: Takayama Shoin, 1941), pp. 217-22.
Shaw is not so much a philosopher as an artist, and not so much a practicing social theorist as an amiable man. [Based on two personal meetings with Shaw in Tokyo, March 1933.] [In Japanese.]

225 Bergholz, Harry. DIE NEUGESTALTUNG DES MODERNEN ENGLISCHEN THEATERS 1870-1930 (The New Form of the Modern English Theater), (Berlin: Karl Bergholz Verlag, 1933), pp. 38, 42, 47ff., 54, 80, 86, 98, 101, 105, 108, 116, 118, 120, 124, 128, 137, 141, 143ff., 148, 160, 162ff., 166, 170ff., 176, 180ff., 187ff., 203ff., 209ff., 213, 218, 223, 230, 236, 242, 245ff., 251ff., 258, 265, 268, 273.
[Brief references to Shaw's plays and performances.]

226   Bernard, J. J. "Témoignages: Bernard Shaw et
Paris" (Testimonies: Bernard Shaw and Paris),
MASQUES, April 1933, pp. 65 ff.
Shaw's dramatic works are not as much appreciated in France
as they might be because of the lack of understanding
between Shaw and the average Frenchman. [In French.]

227   "'Bishop' Bernard Shaw's Search for God,"
LITERARY DIGEST, CXV (11 Feb 1933), 18.
The Adventures of the Black Girl in Her Search for God is
"half fairy-tale and half polemics." [Quotes other
reviewers, espec Robert Lynd, Lond NEWS CHRONICLE, and John
A. Hutton, THE BRITISH WEEKLY.]

228   Bishop, G[eorge] W[alter]. BARRY JACKSON AND THE
LONDON THEATRE (Lond: Barker, 1933; rptd NY & Lond:
Benjamin Blom, 1969), pp. vii, xii, 3, 7-11, 19, 23-
36, 43-46, 47, 54, 57, 58, 71, 83, 85-86, 102, 109-
22, 123, 127-31, 133, 136-38, 141-46, 149, Index.
[Accounts of Barry Jackson's productions of Shaw plays,
including their critical reception: Back to Methuselah
(Court Theater, 1924; Court Theater, 1928); Caesar and
Cleopatra (Kingsway Theater, 1925); The Apple Cart (Malvern
Festival, 1929; Queen's Theater, 1932); Too True To Be Good
(New Theater, 1932). Shaw is credited with having
contributed significantly to the success of the Malvern
festival and Jackson's venture in the Queen's Theater by
giving Jackson first refusal of The Apple Cart.]

229   "Books in Brief," FORUM, LXXXIX (April 1933), v-
vii.
Shaw's "observations about the deficiencies of the Bible"
in The Adventures of the Black Girl in Her Search for God
are hardly original. His old wit appears in places, but the
parable lacks brilliance.

230   Brande, Dorothea. "The Bishop of Everywhere's
Bull," AMERICAN REVIEW, I (April 1933), 110-15.
The Adventures of the Black Girl in Her Search for God "is
very nearly Shaw at his worst." Shaw has expressed many of
the ideas before, especially in Androcles and the Lion.
Shaw urges a rational, down to earth view of the Bible.

231 Brown, Ivor. "Goings On: The Play," WEEK-END REVIEW, VIII (2 Dec 1933), 576-77.

In On The Rocks (Winter Garden, Lond) Shaw mopes over the spectacle of free will abused, failing in the process to suggest new modes of creative activity. Why does he insist on doom-saying as well as lamenting the corruption and ineptitudes of democracy? The governments of Russia and Germany would not tolerate his lampoons. The play is, nevertheless, "a bargain in all-around mental battery."

232 Burdett, Osbert. "A Critical Stroll Through Bernard Shaw," LONDON MERCURY, XXVIII (June 1933), 136-42.

Shaw's success results more from his being a journalist than from being an artist. His journalism is praiseworthy; however, "a brilliant surface is not beauty." The novels and plays are "less interesting for their narrative or drama" than for "the social or abstract analysis introduced." [Evaluates the novels and many of Shaw's plays, finding best those that have most narrative.] Shaw's prose in his prefaces and essays has the "effectiveness of a steam-engine" and lacks idiom; it contains information, humor, and combativeness—the mainsprings of journalism, not literature. The bulk of Shaw's information is compressed in The Intelligent Woman's Guide to Socialism and Capitalism. Common Sense about the War finds "unpopular reasons for popular causes." In this and other work Shaw displays a frigid quality. However, as a critic of the more absurd pretentions of scientists, Shaw has been "a pillar of sanity." Pen-Portraits and Reviews is a worthy collection.

233 Cabell, Branch. "Shaw, Voltaire, a Black Girl and God," NYHTBR, 26 Feb 1933, pp. 1-2.

The Adventures of the Black Girl in Her Search for God is Shaw's best story; it might have been written by Voltaire. It is well-constructed and profound. The end smacks of the confessional, as the girl concludes that truth cannot be found by smashing things with her knobkerry.

234 "Chronicle and Comment: A Prize for Mr. Shaw," BOOKMAN (NY), LXXVI (Jan 1933), 47-64, espec 59-61.

[Anecdote from Archibald Henderson's BERNARD SHAW: PLAYBOY AND PROPHET concerning the prize Shaw won and returned in

1908 to COLLIER'S WEEKLY for his short story "Aerial Football: The New Game." The original BOOKMAN report of the incident is also reprinted.]

235 "Chronicle and Comment: Bee-keeping and Literature," BOOKMAN (NY), LXXVI (Feb 1933), 148-65, espec 149-50.
Shaw has been threatened with expulsion from a bee-keeping society because of his blasphemy in The Adventures of the Black Girl in Her Search for God, though what bee-keeping has to do with authorship or religion is not clear.

236 Cunliffe, J[ohn] W[illiam]. ENGLISH LITERATURE IN THE TWENTIETH CENTURY (NY: Macmillan, 1933; rptd Freeport, NY: Books for Libraries P, 1967), pp. 34, 45-85, 89, 93, 95, 145, 223, 271, espec 45-85, Index.
The leading European dramatist of his time, Shaw rescued drama from "the slough into which it had fallen." He exercised a profound influence on English drama, raising its intellectual tone and enlarging the "range and variety of subject and treatment." He sugar-coated his pills of instruction, and embodied his religious views in dramatic form. [A good sketch of his life and works.]

237 Cunliffe, J[ohn] W[illiam]. PICTURED STORY OF ENGLISH LITERATURE FROM ITS BEGINNINGS TO THE PRESENT DAY (NY & Lond: Appleton-Century, 1933), pp. 172, 301, 386-94, Index.
[Cursory biographical-historical account of Shaw's dramatic career.]

238 "Dilly Tante Observes: The Gloomy Dean," WILSON BULLETIN FOR LIBRARIANS, VIII (Sept 1933), 50-52.
[Mention of Shaw's verse response to Archibald Henderson's request for proper pronunciation of Dean W. R. Inge's name (in Henderson's biography) and of Shaw's vitality in New York speech of last year.]

239 The Drifter. "In the Driftway," NATION, CXXXVI (3 May 1933), 503.
Shaw's speech to the United States during his visit, broadcast and printed in its entirety, created a stir. 399 people called the radio station to complain; one called in commendation.

240 Dunton-Green, L. "G. B. Shaw, critique musical" (G. B. Shaw, Music Critic), REVUE MUSICALE, May 1933, pp. 334-39.

Music in London, 1890-1894 is a first-class document on the taste and the musical events of an era. Shaw's style is full of hyperbole, sarcasm and far-fetched comparisons, but he has an unerring gift for distinguishing what is truly musical from what is not. To conductors and singers, Shaw gives sound, positive advice. The book is highly readable and instructive, as Shaw shows himself to have been the greatest musical critic England produced at that time. [In French.]

241 Ensor, R. C. K. "Shaw in the Pulpit," SPECTATOR, CLI (15 Sept 1933), 350.

Shaw's The Political Madhouse in America and Nearer Home excoriates Americans and the World Economic Conference. It also predicts a day of judgment for the English. Shaw is in the pulpit, combining a Voltairian wit with a growing sense of political indirection.

242 Ervine, St. John. THE THEATRE IN MY TIME (Lond: Rich & Crown, 1933; NY: Mussey, 1934); rptd Lond: Rich; Toronto: Ryerson P, 1946, pp. 84, 87-89, 94, 105, 106, 119-20, 124, 128, 142, 143, 144, 146, 150-54, 160, 169, 247, Index.

[Passim references to Shaw as the author reminisces about the state of the theater from the end of the century to 1933; includes an account of attending a Forbes-Robertson production of The Devil's Disciple and of the Irving-Shaw feud.]

243 Fleming, Peter. "Stage and Screen," SPECTATOR, CLI (1 Dec 1933), 801.

On the Rocks (Winter Garden, Lond) is simply three hours of talk. Once again Shaw has substituted a conversation piece for the legitimate business of the stage. The play reflects not defeat but disorientation.

244 Fukuhara, Rintaro. EIBUNGAKU NI ARAWARETARU FUSHI TO HUMOR (Satire and Humor in English Literature) (Tokyo: Iwanami Shoten [Iwanamikoza Sekaibungaku], 1933), pp. 26-28; rptd in EIBUNGAKU

KENKYUHO (Methods for the Study of English Literature) (Tokyo: Shingetsusha, 1949), pp. 254-60. Shaw is the most important satirical writer in twentieth-century literature before World War I. He stands in the direct tradition of nineteenth-century satirical literature, particularly that of Samuel Butler. [In Japanese.]

245 G., W. E. [Winfred Ernest Garrison]. "Shaw's Flight from God," CHRISTIAN CENTURY, L (29 March 1933), 425.
The Adventures of the Black Girl in Her Search for God is irreverent but has a serious purpose: to attack Church dogmatism, intolerance, and hypocrisy. The book is also clever. Whereas Shaw's black girl searches for God, Shaw himself seeks to escape God.

246 Godfrey, Philip. BACK-STAGE: A SURVEY OF THE CONTEMPORARY ENGLISH THEATRE FROM BEHIND THE SCENES (Lond, Bombay, & Sydney: Harrap, 1933), pp. 105-6, 107-8, 146-47, 159, 163.
[References to Shaw as theater critic and in relation to actors, the dramatic censorship, and the art theater movement.] Shaw invented "slam-criticism" and used it effectively in the SATURDAY REVIEW. His use of the theater as a pulpit or platform is inappropriate, and his detailed stage instructions "often muddle the actor or interfere with his imagination."

247 Graham, D. Cunningham. "Mr. Shaw's Swan Song," COMMONWEAL, XVIII (19 May 1933), 76.
Shaw's speech to New Yorkers (reported in "Mr. Shaw's Swan Song," COMMONWEAL, XVII, 26 April 1933, 701-2) caused rancor between Great Britain and the United States and made Shaw appear foolish. Ramsey Macdonald, not Shaw, represents the British attitude.

248 Gregor, Joseph. WELTGESCHICHTE DES THEATERS (A World History of Theater) (Zürich: Phaidon, 1933), pp. 683-85.
Shaw is the representative of the typical British drama, i.e., the ironic drama. [In German.]

249 Grein, J. T. "The World of the Theatre," ILN, CLXXXIII (9 Dec 1933), 932.
Although there is little action in <u>On the Rocks</u> (Winter Garden, Lond), except perhaps intellectual movement, the play provokes and agitates discussion on contemporary problems. The drama admittedly lacks a closely developed narrative; nevertheless, it compels our interest by thematically dwelling on democracy and dictatorship, as well as employing effective stagecraft.

250 Hallowell, Charlotte Rudyard. "Shaw the Black Girl," SRL, IX (4 March 1933), 461, 463.
<u>The Adventures of the Black Girl in Her Search for God</u>, divided into an essay and a narrative, is cumbersome. If the narrative had been stronger artistically, the essay might not have been necessary. All the characters are Shaw —a typical failing of his. The satire misses its mark; the puns are terrible; the argument is almost orthodox in that it preaches that Christ's theories were ruined by his apostles.

251 Hamilton, Cosmo. PEOPLE WORTH TALKING ABOUT (Lond: McBride, 1933; rptd Freeport, NY: Books for Libraries P, 1970), pp. 3-10.
[A brief standard history of Shaw's life and rise to fame. He is called a "Swift without bitterness" who believed "life is a probation" and human beings are the instrument of God in service to others.]

252 Hamilton, Mary Agnes. SIDNEY AND BEATRICE WEBB (Boston & NY: Houghton Mifflin; Lond: Sampson Low, Marston, 1933), pp. 13-37, 76-77, 106, 139, 140, 143, 155, 160, 266, 267, Index.
Shaw wrote most of the early Fabian history and drew "the most vivid picture" of Sidney Webb, "his closest friend and associate." Shaw and Webb, along with Graham Wallas and Sydney Olivier, made an "amazing quartette" in the early Fabian days. [References and anecdotes pertaining to Shaw's relationship to the Webbs.]

253 Hazlitt, Henry. "Books, Art, Drama: Bernard's Progress," NATION, CXXXVI (8 March 1933), 264-70, 272, espec 264.

The Adventures of the Black Girl in Her Search for God has "not a single idea . . . that could not have been found in Shaw himself thirty years ago."

254 Hearnshaw, F. J. C. EDWARDIAN ENGLAND: A.D. 1901-1910 (Lond: Ernest Benn, 1933), pp. 26, 200, 201, 243, Index.
With Man and Superman and John Bull's Other Island Shaw began to be recognized as the greatest English playwright since Sheridan. "More of a satirist and less of a preacher than Galsworthy," Shaw brought to the drama a "concern with the practical actuality of things," "unconventional but masterly stagecraft," and "vivid dramatic language."

255 Henderson, Archibald. "Bernard Shaw as a World Power," CAROLINA PLAY-BOOK, VI (1933), 46-49.
[Speech on the occasion of a "Festival in honor of Bernard Shaw" (Chapel Hill, North Carolina), in which Henderson recounts how he came to be Shaw's biographer and plays on the victrola an address by Shaw, "Spoken English and Broken English."]

256 Henríquez Ureña, Pedro. "Bernard Shaw: Vida y obra" (Bernard Shaw: His Life and Work) CURSOS Y CONFERENCIAS (Argentina), III, No 6 (July 1933), 593-636; Part II, "Shaw y la economía política" (Shaw and Political Economy), III, No 8 (Jan-July 1934), 785-95; Part III, "Filosofía y estética" (Philosophy and Esthetics), III, No 11 (Jan-July 1934), 1155-64; Part II rptd as "Bernard Shaw y la economía política" (Bernard Shaw and Political Economy), in LA NACIÓN (Argentina), 12 May 1934; entire work rptd in REPERTORIO AMERICANO (Costa Rica): Part I, XXXI, No 17 (16 April 1936), 257-59; Part II, XXXI, No 19 (7 May 1936), 296-99; Part III, XXXI, No 21 (21 May 1936), 325-27.
[Compilation of an entire course taught by Henríquez Ureña at the Colegio Libre de Estudios Superiores in Buenos Aires. It covered Shaw's life and works, his ideas in political economy, and his philosophy and esthetics as revealed from Widowers' Houses to On the Rocks. Until 1933 the most complete study of Shaw in Spanish.]

257 Hidaka, Tadaichi. EIKOKUGEKI TAIKAN (A Survey of British Drama) (Tokyo: Eigo Eibungakukoza Kankokai [Eigo Eibungakukoza 8], 1933), pp. 40-46.
Shaw is a writer of the play of ideas, and he commits himself to the theater in order to propagate his ideas. Unlike John Galsworthy, he is more of a social reformer than an artist. [Briefly surveys Shaw's major works, focusing on their philosophic sides.] [In Japanese.]

258 Horwill, Herbert W. "News and Views of Literary London," NYTBR, 24 Sept 1933, p. 6.
Shaw makes it clear to the British in his recently published The Political Madhouse in America and Nearer Home, an updated version of The Future of Political Science in America, that the futilities ascribed to Americans are not peculiar to them alone. A pure American is in fact a harmless and well-meaning child compared to the English, French, Germans, and Japanese.

259 Hutchison, Percy. "Shaw Writes a Parable on Mankind's Quest for God," NYTBR, 26 Feb 1933, p. 3.
Shaw's The Adventures of the Black Girl in Her Search for God is a "compact and biting satire calculated to provoke as much furious discussion as any dramatic work from his nimble pen." In it, Shaw directs his satire at both the fundamentalist and the scientist.

260 Irwin, Alan. "Pen Picturing a Personality," CANADIAN MAGAZINE, LXXIX (June 1933), 14, 24.
In three interviews from Havana to NY on the Empress of Britain liner, Shaw not once spoke "one of the famous barbed quips at the expense of his fellow men." Shaw said reporters had misquoted him for years. He talked of everything with brilliance, but he is not the man that legend has him—he is "genial and very kindly."

261 Ishida, Kenji. SHAW (Tokyo: Iwanami Shoten [Iwanamikoza Sekaibungaku], 1933); rvd in EIGUNGAKU: KANMEI TO KOSATSU (English Literature: Impressions and Observations) (Tokyo: Takashimaya Shuppanbu, 1949), pp. 179-212.
Shaw clings to life in his work too much, and overlooks the Being that rises above the world. This characteristic of his can be consistently seen in all aspects of his life,

thought, and art. In ignoring such Being, which sheds light
on dark, mundane life, a great sage is, after all, taken
for a great fool. [In Japanese.]

262 Kimura, Ki. "Toyo niokeru Bernard Shaw—Tokuhain
no Zuikonikki--" (Bernard Shaw in the Orient—a
Special Correspondent's Journal), KAIZO (Tokyo), XV,
No 4 (April 1933), 331-58.
[A detailed report of Shaw's tour in China and Japan from
17 Feb through 9 March 1933.] [In Japanese.]

263 Kreft, Bratko. "Bernard Shaw: 'Sveta' Ivana"
(Bernard Shaw: "Saint" Joan), GLEDALIŠKI LIST
(Ljubljana) (1933); rptd in his DRAMATURSKI FRAGMENTI
(Ljubljana: Knižnica mestnogo gledališča, 1965), pp.
69-75.
Saint Joan (National Theater, Ljubljana, 1933) depicts Joan
in her social, realistic and national background. In
France, divided by English imperialism, Joan becomes the
only individual in whom are centralized all the
opportunities for the leader needed by the collective in
the class struggle between feudalism and the bourgeoisie.
[In Slovene.]

264 Langner, Lawrence. "Proposals: A Morning with G.
B. S.," THE STAGE (NY), X (June 1933), 16.
During breakfast on the **Empress of Britain** on his visit to
New York, Shaw recounted his recent trip to Russia as well
as the Far East, offering several anecdotes. Afterward, he
was interviewed by New York reporters, who consistently
asked inane and simplistic questions.

265 Lengnick, Paul. "Ehe und Familie bei Bernard
Shaw" (Marriage and the Family in Bernard Shaw).
Unpublished dissertation, University of Königsberg,
1933. [Listed in McNamee, and in Altick and Matthews,
Item 1735.] [In German.]

266 Liddon, Hugh. "Bernard Shaw and the National
Theatre: What to do with L-125,000," SAT REV, CLVI
(29 July 1933), 130-31.
The Shakespeare Memorial National Theatre Committee, of
which Shaw is a member, is reluctant to allocate the funds
to build a small theater where Shakespeare and the classics

can be staged. Indeed, two theaters probably will be needed, one the size of the Globe (for popular plays) and one the size of Blackfriars (for intimate plays). Shaw's "flatulent megalomania" interferes with such plans.

267 Lu Hsün. "Shaw to Shaw o minikita hitobito o miru" (Looking at Shaw and at Those Who Came to Look at Him), KAIZO (Tokyo), XV (April 1933), 276-78; rptd as "Lusin Looks at Bernard Shaw," SHAW BULLETIN, I, No 10 (Nov 1956), 11-13; and in LU HSUN BUNSHU (Collected Works of Lu Hsun), (Tokyo: Chikuma Shobo, 1978), V, 99-103.

[An impression of Shaw based on a meeting with him on his visit to Shanghai, 16 Feb 1933. Quotes Shaw; comments on the newspapers' distortions of his speech.] [In Japanese.]

268 Lunacharskiĭ, Anatoli. "Bernard Shaw eshche raz govorit pravdu" (Bernard Shaw Speaks the Truth Again), VECHERNAIA MOSKVA (1933), No 2 [not seen in this form]; rptd in O TEATR I DRAMATURGII. IZBRANNYE STAT'I 2 (On Theater and Dramaturgy 2) (Moscow: Iskusstvo, 1958), pp. 485-95.

Bourgeois critics do not take Shaw seriously, but he is capable of serious, tragic creativity, e.g., in Too True To Be Good. The play is more than mere witty dialog. If one has revolutionary tendencies, one can be moved by Shaw's lack of faith, nihilism, and the hopeless impasse presented by this play. Shaw has extraordinary virtuosity and theatrical skill combined with ruthless revolutionary criticism of post-war collapse. The complaints that Shaw's message is superfluous or that he does not say the essential are not important. In his filmed speech on Lenin, Shaw said bourgeois Europe is hopeless; and if he does not close his eyes in despair, this is only because he believes in the success of communism. He says the same about Europe in his latest play, but remains silent about the "new world," and his attitude toward it. [In Russian.]

269 Lunacharskiĭ, A[natoli]. "Predislovie" (Foreword), Bernard Shaw: CHERNOKOZHNAIA DEVUSHKA V POISKAKH BOGA (The Adventures of the Black Girl in Her Search for God) (Moscow: Gos. Izd-stvo "Khudozhestvennaia literatura," 1933) [not seen in this form]; rptd in A. Lunacharskiĭ, STATI O

LITERATURE (Moscow: Gos. Izd-stvo "Khudozhestvennaĩa
    literature," 1957), pp. 685-93.
Shaw's biting criticism of the bourgeois social order and
his bold replies to the bourgeois press following his visit
to the Soviet Union in 1931 cannot be overestimated. But in
addition to ideas of amazing sharpness, Shaw also falls
into empty paradoxes, and it is difficult to accept
everything he says without reservation. His recent Too True
To Be Good has irrelevant and feeble criticism of atheism.
The play contains no references to the Soviet Union or to
the Communist Party. But since Shaw is a faithful ally, he
must be accepted as he is. The Adventures of the Black Girl
in Her Search for God is truly Voltairian in content and
form, with robust humor, unexpected and amusing. [In
Russian.]

270 M., F. "Der Clown Europas" (Europe's Clown), DER
    GRAL (Munich), XXVIII (1933-34), 377.
In On the Rocks, a mockery of parliamentary democracy, Shaw
presents himself as an ethical clown. [In German.]

271 MacKay, L. A. "Liberal Surveys of Dictatorship,"
    CANADIAN FORUM, XIV (Dec 1933), 108-9.
In The Political Madhouse in America and Nearer Home, which
stresses American economic problems and lack of a political
system, Shaw, as usual, points out the obvious. However,
his is a necessary task, for the rationally obvious is
usually last to be grasped.

272 Marley, Harold P. "Bernard Shaw—Missionary,"
    UNITY, CXI (29 May 1933), 205-6.
Shaw is an iconoclastic missionary, preaching the need for
political reorganization and for a revitalized religious
sense, proclaiming—as in his visit to the United States—
that the socialist kingdom is at hand.

273 Martin, Kingsley. "On the Rocks," NS&Nation, VI
    (2 Dec 1933), 694-95; rptd in CRITICAL HERITAGE, pp.
    337-40, Item 110.
In On the Rocks (Winter Garden, Lond), Shaw condemns
democracy in an amusing but "easy" attack. The play lacks
the intellectual quality of the best of Shaw. Although this
has been called a fascist play, it "warns rather than
advocates."

274 Matthews, W. R. THE ADVENTURES OF GABRIEL IN HIS
SEARCH FOR MR. SHAW: A MODEST COMPANION FOR MR.
SHAW'S BLACK GIRL, illustrated by Ruth Wood (Lond:
Hamish Hamilton, 1933).
[A satire in which St. Peter commissions Gabriel to seek
"the real Shaw" in "the Shavian wilderness." Gabriel finds
Shaw beating a large drum, making love, deflating
respectable people, and preaching--but all these are
illusory. He finally finds the real Shaw: a miniature man
in a miniature house. Shaw explains that his major
interests are drama, philosophy, and "rage...against the
unreason and injustice of human society." In reply to why
he is so small, he says, "There is the fellow who will beat
that terrible drum, the one who is always philandering, the
one who runs the waxwork show (puncturing images of
respectable people), and, worst of all, the bore who is
never happy without his pulpit. They have taken the
subsistence which I ought to have had. They have prevented
me from growing."]

275 Maurois, André. ÉDOUARD VII ET SON TEMPS (Edward
VII and His Time) (Paris: Les Éditions de France,
1933 [not seen in this form]; rptd Paris: Éditions B.
Grasset, 1937; Paris: Flammarion, 1949; trans by
Hamish Miles as THE EDWARDIAN ERA, NY: Appleton-
Century, 1933, and as KING EDWARD AND HIS TIMES,
Lond: Cassell, 1933), pp. 278, 284, 290, 291, 292,
298.
[In this portrait of an age and of a sovereign, a short
section of chap. VII is devoted to "The Theater"; it speaks
of the impact of Ibsen; the great dramatists of the day,
including Shaw; and the struggle against censorship.] The
Fabian Society united intellectuals who preferred ideas to
action. Shaw was one of the representative Edwardian
writers, setting up "cynical realism against English
sentimentalism"; like Voltaire, he was iconoclastic and
brilliant. [In French.]

276 McCarthy, Lillah. MYSELF AND MY FRIENDS (NY:
Dutton, 1933), pp. 1-8, 33-34, 55-61, 62-70, 108-9,
114-15, 124-25, 126, 134-37, 139, 144-45, 149, 157,
162, 164-74, 188, 190, 192, 201-211, 279, 288-89,
Index; excerpt from p. 65 rptd in CRITICAL HERITAGE,
p. 335, Item 108.

[Reminiscences of Shaw from McCarthy's first experience of him, as drama critic of the SATURDAY REVIEW reviewing her Lady Macbeth, to the end of their "happy association," when Shaw refused her desire to play Ellie in Heartbreak House and to play Saint Joan. Includes information on Shaw's manner with actors of his plays—his comments on their lines, gestures, and costumes—from one who played Raina in Arms and the Man, Ann in Man and Superman, Nora in John Bull's Other Island, Margaret Knox in Fanny's First Play, Lavinia in Androcles and the Lion, Jennifer Dubedat in The Doctor's Dilemma, and Annajanska. Her characterization of Shaw: an Irishman who saw problems rather than poetry in Ireland; a "vivid personality," sane and free of "humbug and sentimentality"; an essentially "tidy" man. Her characterization of Ann Whitefield: an "earthy," not a "stagey," woman who "set the world of women free." Also includes an impression of Rodin, working on his bust of Shaw; Shaw's account of his infatuation with Mrs. Patrick Campbell; and McCarthy's estimate of Shaw's characters (filled with laughter, but never cruel or derisive).]

277 Moore, Mina. "Bernard Shaw et la France" (Bernard Shaw and France). Published dissertation, University of Strasbourg, 1933; pub under same title (Paris: Champion, 1933).
[Analyzes Shaw's relationship to France, including the history of France in Shaw's work, especially in his portraits of Joan of Arc and Napoleon; Shaw's critical reception in France; and his use of the French language and culture in his plays.] Contrary to Augustin Hamon, Shaw is not an English Molière. Lamarck, of course, was of paramount importance to Shaw's thought. The judgment of French critics of Shaw varies; the paradoxes of the humorist and the advanced ideas of the socialist are far from being accepted and admired by everybody. At times, the Hamon translation of Shaw fails to render Shaw's brilliant prose and dialog accurately. [In French.]

278 Morgan, Charles. "The Messrs. Shaw and Priestley," NYT, 17 Dec 1933, IX, p. 4.
On the Rocks follows the latest English vogue for admiring dictatorships. It has less clowning than usual, and avoids the discursive tedium of Too True To Be Good.

GEORGE BERNARD SHAW

279 Morgan, Charles. "New Shaw Play Greeted in London: 'On the Rocks' Presents Political Pamphlet in Criticism of Democracy," NYT, 26 Nov 1933, II, p. 2.

On the Rocks (Winter Garden, Lond) seems to renounce Fabian socialism for dictatorship in a play that has more of "street-corner oratory" than of passion. It is "a political pamphlet," "almost innocent of Shavian excursions into romantic farce."

280 "Mr. Shaw's Swan Song," COMMONWEAL, XVII (26 April 1933), 701-2; response by D. Cunningham Graham, "Mr. Shaw's Swan Song," COMMONWEAL, XVIII (19 May 1933), 76.

Shaw's speech to New Yorkers was foolish and disgusting, "a cluttered and rambling dissertation" on Shavian ideas. His call for either a superman or a collective sense to restore intelligence to humanity, influenced by Nietzsche and Ibsen, fails to understand the world's need for "the Word" and the "Rock."

281 "'Mrs. G. B. S.': The Power Behind the Dome," LITERARY DIGEST, CXV (22 April 1933), 31-33.

Mrs. Shaw is said to be self-effacing; yet she is "an active force" in Shaw's career. [Mostly quotations from Hayden Church's article in NYTMag on the facts of the meeting, marriage, and relationship between Shaw and Charlotte Payne-Townshend.]

282 Myoga, Yukiya. "G. B. Shaw no Seito Seijikan" (G. B. Shaw's View of Democracy), EIBUNGAKU KENKYU (Tokyo), XIII, No 1 (Feb 1933), 66-73.

Shaw's ideal political system is a socialism under the control of several supermen; it requires work of all citizens and has for its motto "equality of income." [In Japanese.]

283 "New Books: Shorter Notices," CATHOLIC WORLD, CXXXVII (April 1933), 113-27, espec 124-25.

The Adventures of the Black Girl in Her Search for God is a "fitting anti-climax" to Shaw's career. It rambles, distorts, lacks style. Shaw seems moving toward madness, having become "not the thinking world's inspired clown but its tragic warning."

284 "New Shaw Play Given in Warsaw: 'On the Rocks' Sounds Sombre Note of Warning in Anxious Fatherly Pleading," NYT, 25 Nov 1933, p. 10.
Instead of criticism, On the Rocks (premiere production, Teatr Polski, Warsaw) reflects fatherly anxiety on Shaw's part. It contains warnings and pleadings instead of satire.

285 "News-Week Headliners: SHAW: Greeted in New York with Criticism and Applause," NEWS-WEEK, I (22 April 1933), 18.
Shaw had a bad press in New York. His speech to the Academy of Political Science (Metropolitan Opera House) was applauded as he spoke of the "anarchy" of Americans living under a constantly changing constitution, the need to nationalize American banks, Russian communism, etc. The papers called the speech "dull" and "rambling."

286 "News-Week Headliners: SHAW: His Visit Classed With Plagues by London Paper," NEWS-WEEK, I (1 April 1933), 16.
[Report of Shaw's visit to America; quotations of his various quips to reporters.]

287 "New York Welcomes Shaw," PUBLISHERS' WEEKLY, CXXIII (22 April 1933), 1340-41.
Shaw was welcomed in his visit to New York, and delighted the audience at the Opera House.

288 Nogami, Toyoichiro. "Tetsugakushateki, Yogenshateki, Kaigyakusha--Bernard Shaw no Hyogenhonshitsu--" (A Philosophic and Prophetic Humorist--The Nature of Bernard Shaw's Artistic Presentation), KAIZO (Tokyo), XV, No 4 (April 1933), 359-71.
Shaw regards himself as a philosopher reflecting the inner will of the world, i.e., the Life Force. The originality of his Life Force theory is that, while creating it out of Lamarck, Schopenhauer, Nietzsche, and Bergson, he expresses it very plainly, and adds a religious flavor to it. His means to fulfill that will is to write Life Force comedies. Recent Shaw studies tend to see Shaw either as a prophet or a playboy; however, it is his dramatic works that will be remembered. They are worth being studied seriously as unique, artistic presentations. [In Japanese.]

289 Noguchi, Yonejiro. "Hito no tameni umareta Shaw" (Shaw, Who Was Born for Other People), KAIZO (Tokyo), XV, No 4 (April 1933), 281-86.
Shaw offers a concrete example of the tragedy of being a prominent man of the time. [A personal impression based on a recent meeting with Shaw in Tokyo after almost twenty years.] [In Japanese.]

290 Okey, Thomas. A BASKETFUL OF MEMORIES: AN AUTOBIOGRAPHICAL SKETCH (Lond & Toronto: J. M. Dent, 1933), pp. 46, 59-60, 118-26.
[Memoirs by the organizer of the Italian tours of 1891 and 1894 taken by Shaw with the Art Workers Guild. Contains anecdotes about the trips as well as Shaw's letter to William Morris from Venice (23 Sept 1891).]

291 Parsons, Louella O. "Bernard Shaw at San Simeon," LOS ANGELES EXAMINER, 26 March 1933 [not seen in this form]; rptd in CALIFORNIA SHAVIAN, I (Sept-Oct 1960) [2 pp].
At 77 Shaw entertained the other guests at the William Randolph Hearst ranch with his witty opinions on every subject.

292 Perthel, Johannes. "Bernard Shaws letztes Bekenntnis" (Bernard Shaw's Last Confession), DIE CHRISTENGEMEINSCHAFT (Stuttgart), X (April 1933), 29-30.
In Too True To Be Good, Shaw has, ironically, turned preacher in an age of nihilism. [In German.]

293 "Plays and Pictures: St. Joan at Croydon," NS&Nation, I (25 Nov 1933), 663.
Saint Joan is well-suited for a small stage, as in the Croydon Repertory Theater. Both Joan and the Dauphin are well acted in this production.

294 Redman, H. Vere. "Shaw in and on Japan," CONTEMPORARY JAPAN (Tokyo), II, No 1 (June 1933), 111-22.
[A succinct report of what Shaw saw and said during his short visit to Japan in 1933.]

295 [Review of <u>On the Rocks</u>]. MORNING POST (Lond),
27 Nov 1933, p. 12 [not seen in this form]; rptd
CRITICAL HERITAGE, p. 336, Item 109.
<u>On the Rocks</u> (Winter Garden, Lond) is witty and highly
interesting.

296 Sansom, George Bailey. "Shawshi no No Hyo
sonota" (Mr. Shaw's Criticism of No and Others),
KAIZO (Tokyo), XV, No 4 (April 1933), 316-17.
Shaw saw Noh plays (on 8 March 1933 in Tokyo), and said he
was interested in the following three points: its splendid
dramatic form; its singular music; and its three-
dimensional representation on the stage. [In Japanese.]

297 Schallert, Edwin. "Mr. Shaw Shakes Up
Hollywood," MOVIE CLASSIC (Chicago), IV (June 1933),
26, 62.
[Anecdotal accounts of Shaw's tour through Hollywood, where
he mingled with many movie lions.]

298 Schöpflin, Aladár. "Színházi bemutatók"
(Theatrical Openings), NYUGAT II (1933), 614-17.
Shaw creates a great figure in Caesar, anachronistic and
more real than the heroes of pathetic historical dramas.
Caesar is like the English empire builder, who hates
killing but can carry it out dispassionately and
purposefully. He prefers to work with conviction, rather
than with force; he always wins and he combines
utilitarianism with irony. For him the woman is a political
tool. In no way does Caesar speak Cicero's language. His
movement and speech are informal and droll; he lacks
history's pathos. His dignity derives from the power
radiating from his person. [In Hungarian.]

299 "Shaw as America's Thersites," LITERARY DIGEST,
CXV (1 April 1933), 13.
[Account of Shaw's remarks when visited by Helen Keller.
Also quoted are other of his comments on Americans.]

300 "SHAW: Greeted in New York With Criticism and
Applause," NEWS-WEEK, I (22 April 1933), 18.
Shaw received a hostile press on his visit to New York last
week. His speech to the Metropolitan Opera House was
bewildering, but at times applauded.

301 "SHAW: His Visit Classed With Plagues by London Paper," NEWS-WEEK, I (1 April 1933), 16.
On his first visit to America, Shaw treated journalists to various Shaw witticisms (here recorded in part). The London MORNING POST observed that the United States is being cursed with "three plagues: the bank closing, the earthquake, the visitation of Mr. Shaw."

302 "The Shaw Show," LITERARY DIGEST, CXV (22 April 1933), 6.
In his address to the Metropolitan Opera House Shaw disappointed his listeners perhaps because "he had something serious to say, and was not merely acting the clown." [Quotations from the EVENING POST (NY), NYT, and WORLD TELEGRAM (NY).]

303 Sherard, Robert Harborough. OSCAR WILDE, "DRUNKARD AND SWINDLER"; A REPLY TO GEORGE BERNARD SHAW, DR. G. J. RENIER, FRANK HARRIS, ETC., WITH AN INTERVIEW WITH G. B. SHAW BY HUGH KINGSMILL [pseud of Hugh Kingsmill Lunn] (Calvi [Corsica], France: Vindex Publishing Co., 1933); rptd as BERNARD SHAW, FRANK HARRIS & OSCAR WILDE, WITH A PREFACE BY LORD ALFRED DOUGLAS (NY: Greystone P; Lond: T. Werner Laurie, 1937).
Shaw's endorsement of Frank Harris' OSCAR WILDE: HIS LIFE AND CONFESSIONS (1916) lent a degree of respectability to an irresponsible book. Harris was a plagiarist and liar, exploiting a friend's memory for financial gain; and Shaw was blind to obvious contradictions and improbabilities in Harris' book. Shaw erroneously characterized Wilde's last years as those of a "drunkard and swindler." ["Pharaoh Hardens His Heart: An Interview with Bernard Shaw," by Hugh Kingsmill, tells of an unsuccessful attempt in 1932 to get Shaw to retract his endorsement of Harris. Shaw admired Harris' power of portraiture, finding Harris' biography "more interesting than the real Wilde."]

304 Sinclair, Upton. "In Defense of Bernard Shaw," REAL AMERICA, I (July 1933), 59, 81-82.
Contrary to the opinion of some who met Shaw on his recent United States visit, Shaw "is the kindest man in the world." Shaw intends to deflate American smugness, not to give offense.

305 Startŝev, A. "Shou" (Shaw), BOLSHAÎA SOVETSKAÎA ENTŜIKLOPEDIÎA, LXII (Moscow: OGIZ, 1933), 614-15.
The foundations of Shaw's outlook and artistic method were laid during the industrial crisis of 1879-1880, which was accompanied by a sharp rise in the workers' movement and crash of the ideas of Free Trade, supported by the successes of socialist propaganda among the petit-bourgeois intelligentsia. Shaw's acquaintance with Marx' DAS KAPITAL led him to become an opponent of the capitalist system. In Widowers' Houses and Mrs. Warren's Profession, Shaw came forward as a merciless realist-sociologist, though the limitations of his social viewpoint are evident in them. The liberal, reformist ideas of Fabianism influenced Shaw's further development and literary work: he aimed to enlighten the bourgeoisie on socialism; he introduced timid attempts at humanism, overcoming contradictions by his intellectual and moral superiority. Except for Man and Superman, which attempted a synthetic solution to his searchings, his work, up to World War I, is full of doubts and inconsistencies. During World War I, he condemned the decomposition and parasitism of the ruling classes, and he became disillusioned with bourgeois democracy after the war. The world crisis of capitalism made Shaw change his position; since his 1931 visit, he has contrasted the socialist structure of the Soviet Union with the decomposition of the bourgeois world. Too True To Be Good demonstrates the serious processes taking place in his work, though the play cannot be termed epoch-making. But for all his weaknesses, Shaw is a writer of superior social penetration and great intellectual honesty, though isolated and misunderstood. [In Russian.]

306 "St. Bernard," NATION, CXXXVI (26 April 1933), 461.
Shaw's speech to the Academy of Political Science at the Metropolitan Opera House (NY) had him "impersonating himself." Shaw, who refused to come to the United States for many years, is no more real to people once they have seen him.

307 Streeter, B. H. "The Misadventures of the Little Black Shaw in His Search for God," CHRISTIAN CENTURY, L (5 April 1933), 454-56.

In The Adventures of the Black Girl in Her Search for God Shaw's religio-historical facts are incorrect and his theological ideas are half a century old. Shaw has the stages of humanity's religious development out of order, uses the least historical gospel for his historical reconstruction of Jesus, and presents only self-evident religious concepts.

308 Tezuka, T. "George Bernard Shaw," THE RISING GENERATION (Japan), 13 April 1933 [not seen in this form]; rptd in INDEPENDENT SHAVIAN, IV (Fall 1965), 12. [Poem.]

309 Thonssen, Lester. "George Bernard Shaw at New York, April 11," QUARTERLY JOURNAL OF SPEECH, XIX (Nov 1933), 596-99.
Shaw's April 11 speech on "The Future of Political Science in America" (Metropolitan Opera House, NY) was well delivered but presumptuous and confused in content. It lacked direction and was merely "a rich collection of conclusions."

310 Tissi, Silvio. AL MICROSCOPIO PSICANALITICO: PIRANDELLO, IBSEN, SHAKESPEARE, TOLSTOI, SHAW, BOURGET, GIDE, DOSTOJEWSKIJ ALLA LUCE DELLA PSICANALISI (Under the Psychoanalytic Microscope: Pirandello, Ibsen, Shakespeare, Tolstoy, Shaw, Bourget, Gide, Dostoevski in the Light of Psychoanalysis) (Milan: Hoepli, 1933), pp. 63-83; rptd 1946.
Shaw's complex ideas are difficult to examine from a psychoanalytical point of view: his sarcastic views of the evils of humankind are more important than his romantic, amusing follies. Shaw is a playwright of extreme clarity: he has no hesitations, though hesitations are to be found in his characters, who are driven and mastered by blind chance. The drama of his characters springs from their unconscious. [In Italian.]

311 "Trade Winds Turn Table (By Quercus Associates)," SRL, IX (27 May 1933), 624.
[A table which "scores" a number of books, including The Adventures of the Black Girl in Her Search for God, which

ranks low on "Author's Score" and higher on "Publisher's Score."]

312 Tsurumi, Yusuke. "Bernard Shaw Kaikenki" (An Interview with Bernard Shaw), KAIZO (Tokyo), XV, No 3 (March 1933), 52-63; rptd in OBEITAIRIKU YUKI (Travelling Notes in Europe and America) (Tokyo: Kodansha, 1933), pp. 721-46; rptd in TSURUMI YUSUKE JINBUTSURON SENSHU (Selected Character Sketches by Yusuke Tsurumi) (Tokyo: Diamondsha, 1968), pp. 190-212.
[Tsurumi called on Shaw at Whitehall Court, Lond, on 16 Oct 1932. Topics discussed include war, world situations, literature, and literary style.] [In Japanese.]

313 Ubugata, Kaname (ed). SHOOKATARU (On Shaw) (Tokyo: Fudo Shobo, 1933).
[Includes articles by A. Lunacharsky, S. Dinamov, K. Wittfogel, M. Gold, J. Cunliffe, F. Harris, and J. Bab; Shaw's speech on 26 July 1931 in Moscow; two short reviews of The Adventures of the Black Girl in Her Search for God and Too True To Be Good; a short biography and bibliography; and excerpts from Ellen Terry and Bernard Shaw: A Correspondence.] [In Japanese.]

314 Vöhringer, Otto. "Die Verzweiflung eines Rationalisten. Bernard Shaw in seinen letzten Werken" (The Desperation of a Rationalist. Bernard Shaw in His Latest Works), HOCHLAND (Kempten and Munich), XXX, No 2 (April 1933-Sept 1933), 433-42.
The Adventures of the Black Girl in Her Search for God gives a new variation of Shaw as a theologian. Too True To Be Good is the product of a desperate preacher who has lost all belief in rationalism and enlightenment. [In German.]

315 Wilder, Amos N. "Mr. Shaw's Fable," YALE REVIEW, XXII (June 1933), 858-60.
In The Adventures of the Black Girl in Her Search for God, Shaw makes palatable many elementary ideas and brilliantly demonstrates the art of teaching. Yet this teaching is filled with misconceptions and errors about Christianity.

316 Wilson, Edmund. "Shaw in the Metropolitan," NEW REPUBLIC, LXXIV (26 April 1933), 298-99; rptd as

"Bernard Shaw at the Metropolitan," in TRAVELS IN TWO DEMOCRACIES (NY: Harcourt, Brace, 1936), pp. 49-55; and THE AMERICAN EARTHQUAKE (Garden City, NY: Doubleday, 1958), pp. 490-95.
[Written on the occasion of Shaw's speech before the Metropolitan Opera House, NY.] Shaw cannot decide who he is speaking to, the bourgeois or the radicals. He is paradoxical, but still a poet.

317 Wingfield-Stratford, Esmé. THE VICTORIAN AFTERMATH: 1901-1914 (Lond: George Routledge, 1933; NY: Morrow, 1934), pp. 150-58, 161, 162, 164-67, 170, 185, 186, 198, 336, Index, espec 164-67.
In an age of "journalization of thought," artists had to have a mountebank's talent to be heard; Shaw was a master of public acrobatics, shocking and entertaining his audience and thereby avoiding serious criticism of his ideas.

318 "Winter Garden Theatre: Mr. Shaw's New Play, 'On the Rocks,'" TIMES (Lond), 27 Nov 1933, p. 12.
On the Rocks (Winter Garden, Lond) preaches a message with "fewer sops of buffoonery" than usual with Shaw. [A very enigmatic, overwritten review.]

319 Wolter, Karl Kurt. "Bernard Shaw, Junger Wein gärt" (Bernard Shaw, Immaturity), JUGEND (Munich), XXXVIII (1933), 387.
The style of Immaturity is pedantic. The most important part of the book is its Preface. [In German.]

320 Woollcott, Alexander. "Shouts and Murmurs: The Nostrils of G. B. S.," NYer, IX (18 Feb 1933), 30; rptd in Woollcott, WHILE ROME BURNS (NY: Viking, 1934), pp. 315-18, and in THE PORTABLE WOOLLCOTT, ed by John Hennessey (NY: Viking, 1946), pp. 351-54.
The Adventures of the Black Girl in Her Search for God treats Pavlovian science more contemptuously than any other deities encountered by the black girl. The thing that motivates all Shaw's messages is his hatred of "the odor of burning flesh"; understanding this explains his aversion to Noah's God, his anger at Saint Joan's martyrdom, and his vegetarianism.

321   Yoshida, Chosho. G. BERNARD SHAW SANTO SANPOSURU (Steps of Mr. G. Bernard Shaw in Japan) (Osaka: pvtly ptd by Chosho Yoshida, 1933).
[Records Shaw's movements when he visited Japan in 1933.] [In Japanese.]

322   Young, Stark. "Loin du Bal: A Letter to Mr. Shaw," NEW REPUBLIC, LXXIV (22 Feb 1933), 45-47.
Shaw is an egotist, an exhibitionist, a second-rate thinker and certain to say "silly things" in America. [A polemic that approaches incoherence, written on the occasion of Shaw's visit to America.]

1934

---

323   Anderson Imbert, Enrique. "Con una comedia de Bernard Shaw debutó la compañía inglesa" (The English Company Debuts with a Comedy of Bernard Shaw), LA VANGUARDIA (Argentina), 30 July 1934.
[Review of performance of Arms and the Man by the English Players in Argentina, at the Odeón Theater.] [In Spanish.]

324   Anderson Imbert, Enrique. "Teatro: Odeón, Exitoso estreno de 'You Never Can Tell,' de G. B. Shaw" (Theater: Odeón, Successful Opening Night of You Never Can Tell, by G. B. Shaw), LA VANGUARDIA (Argentina), 3 Aug 1934.
The English Players' performance of You Never Can Tell was a great success in Buenos Aires. But the Spanish translation of the title, "Lucha de sexos" (Battle of the Sexes), did not express all the other conflicts in the play. A better choice would be "¿Quién sabe?" (Who Knows?). [In Spanish.]

325   Angly, Edward. "Bernard Shaw, to be Taken Lying Down," NYHTBR, 20 May 1934, p. 5.
Shaw's Short Stories, Scraps and Shavings is delightful reading for those late nights under the bed-lamp. The best of these shavings is "The Domesticity of Franklyn Barnabas."

75

326 Bland, J. O. P. "Concerning Bernard Shaw: The Alien Enemy Within Our Gates," SAT REV, CLVII (6 Jan 1934), 19-20.
Being Irish, Shaw is an alien to England and should be asked to live elsewhere unless he stops his offensive attacks on British foreign policy, as in Common Sense about the War and his recent pronouncements on the "Japanese Menace."

327 Boza, Masvidal Aurelio. "La dramática de Shaw y Pirandello" (The Dramatic Art of Shaw and Pirandello), ESTUDIOS DE LITERATURA ITALIANA (Havana) (1934), pp. 7-36; also in UNIVERSIDAD DE LA HAVANA, I (Jan-May 1934), 61-81; rptd in LA REVISTA AMERICANA (Buenos Aires), XIII, No 154 (Feb 1937), 99-118.
Both Shaw and Pirandello are pessimistic destroyers, thinkers, researchers of the human soul and of society, apostles of logical reasoning, innovators, humorists, and great masters of the theater. Shaw's work is directed to the betterment of society, while Pirandello is more imaginative and sensitive, able to understand the nature of passion. [In Spanish.]

328 Cehan, B. BERNARD SHAW. SCHITĂ BIOGRAFICĂ (Bucaresti: Colectia "Excelsior," Editura "Rampa," n.d. [1934]).
[Contains a biographical account of Shaw's early years; a chap on the Fabian Society; a character sketch—"Critic, novelist, vegetarian, and teetotaler"; and a chap on "Shakespeare Dethroned." Includes analyses of the philosopher and feminist, the English theater under Shaw, and Shaw's attitude toward immortality. A separate chap on the Malvern production of The Apple Cart.] [In Romanian.]

329 Compton, C. H. WHO READS WHAT? (NY: Wilson, 1934; rptd Freeport, NY: Books for Libraries P, 1962), pp. 70-90.
[A long letter is addressed to Shaw, describing 431 readers of his works from the St. Louis Public Library and why they read him.]

330 Cookman, A. V. "G. B. S. Considers the Burghers of Calais," NYT, 12 Aug 1934, IX, p. 1.

In The Six of Calais (Regents Park Open Air Theater, Lond) Shaw draws on both Froissart and Rodin to produce a comic history "which is nine-tenths buffoonery and only one-tenth comic invention." Androcles and the Lion (on the same bill) is much wittier.

331 Cunliffe, John W. "George Bernard Shaw," LEADERS OF THE VICTORIAN REVOLUTION (NY and Lond: Appleton-Century, 1934), pp. 315-32.

Shaw's genius was a Victorian phenomenon, and Shaw a representative champion of the late Victorians. His life falls into distinct periods: youth in Ireland (to 1879); novel writing (1879-83); journalism and pamphleteering (1884-98); playwrighting (beginning in the preceding period). [Outline of Shaw's career to date.]

332 Davies, Hugh Sykes. REALISM IN THE DRAMA (NY: Macmillan; Cambridge: University P, 1934), pp. 112-15.

Ibsen is more realistic than Shaw, for Ibsen deals with problems in a personal, human way, whereas Shaw writes more abstractly—as a "dramatic sociologist and politician." Shaw deals with opinions, not feelings, thus lacking a poetic and universal dimension.

333 Davison, Max. "Shaw on Stalin," NS&Nation, VIII (24 Nov 1934), 751.

Shaw the satirist is more amusing than Shaw the Stalin apologist.

334 Dobrée, Bonamy. "Killing No Murder," SPECTATOR, CLII (16 March 1934), 415.

In spite of the fact that Too True To Be Good has a first act that "is an insult to any audience" and that On the Rocks has out-of-date characters, the plays have the best prose for the stage since Congreve, with "brilliant destructive criticism." The prefaces are however, evidence of a confused mind in Shaw's pronouncements on political killing.

335 Dobrée, Bonamy. "The Shavian Situation," SPECTATOR, CLIII (13 July 1934), 46; rptd in CRITICAL HERITAGE, pp. 342-45, Item 113.

Shaw is a man of the eighteenth century in his idealization of women and his emphasis on social virtue. His Collected Prefaces, more direct than comedic, prove him England's "greatest pamphleteer since Swift," a master of style and controversial matter.

336 Dukes, Ashley. "The Scene in Europe: Shaw-Shakespeare-Sherwood-Bergner," TAM, XVIII (Feb 1934), 78-105, espec 98-100.
Seeing On the Rocks is a grim experience. Shaw's discussion drama leads nowhere; it has brought neither new forms of drama nor new directors, actors, or other authors to public attention.

337 Eaton, Walter Prichard. "New Plays by Bernard Shaw," NYHTBR, 4 March 1934, p. 8.
After Saint Joan, Shaw's plays "ran pretty thin," and Too True To Be Good, Village Wooing, and On the Rocks are no exception. The Preface to On the Rocks, however, is timely, forecasting what can happen to democracy in an age of dictators. Here, at least, is a "flare-up of the oldtime Shaw."

338 "Embassy School of Acting: 'Saint Joan,'" TIMES (Lond), 19 July 1934, p. 12.
[Praise for Eileen Thorndike's direction of Saint Joan and for Sara Luce's portrayal of Joan in the Embassy School of Acting, Lond, production.]

339 Galsworthy, John. LETTERS FROM JOHN GALSWORTHY, 1900-1932, ed by Edward Garnett (NY: Scribner's; Lond: Cape; Toronto: Nelson, 1934), pp. 96, 107, 121, 131, 144, 145, 154, 155, 162, 203, Index.
Shaw "is not a dramatist," and Shaw the man is preferable to the author and speaker. [References to enlisting Shaw to oppose the censoring of Garnett's THE BREAKING POINT; also a reaction to the 1906 performance of Major Barbara.] Major Barbara has "too much Shawdom, and Nietscheism of course in the third Act, which is bad." Cusins is "an admirable Shawesque puppet," but Bill Walker lives and breathes.

340 Garland, Hamlin. AFTERNOON NEIGHBORS (NY: Macmillan, 1934), pp. 193-96.

[A conversation with Shaw is recounted in which Shaw talks about a lecture tour, Scotland, Joan of Arc, and the "vulgarity of the stage."]

341 Gilder, Rosamond. "Prepare for Plays," TAM, XVIII (May 1934), 382-88, espec 387.
Modern playwrights are spared the Elizabethan necessity of composing dedicatory epistles for the printed versions of their plays. It is amusing to imagine Shaw, "supreme insulter and Preface writer," penning such an epistle. His vitriolic tone is exemplified in the Preface to his latest collection of plays, Three Plays (Too True To Be Good, Village Wooing, On the Rocks).

342 Gregory, Russell. "Should a Producer Act?" SAT REV, CLVII (28 July 1934), 901.
[Brief review of Saint Joan, Embassy Theater, Lond, praising William Devlin's work and Sara Luce's acting.]

343 Gregory, Russell. "Theatre Notes: Little Theatre," SAT REV, CLVII (30 June 1934), 774.
Village Wooing (Little Theater, Lond) is not worthy of public presentation. It is "quite incredibly stupid," with a plot "not worth describing" and dialog that "would disgrace a child of twelve."

344 Gregory, Russell. "Theatre Notes: 'St. Joan,'" SAT REV, CLVIII (8 Dec 1934), 507.
[Brief, unfavorable review of the acting of Joan by Mary Newcombe in the Old Vic production, Lond.]

345 Heuser, Hilde. "Die Eigenart des Sozialismus George Bernard Shaws" (The Peculiar Feature of George Bernard Shaw's Socialism). Published dissertation, University of Frankfurt, 1934; pub under same title (Frankfurt/Main: Blazek und Bergmann, 1934).
[A survey of Shaw's socialism. Gives biographical reasons for it (his Irish heritage, Puritanism, fight for justice, sympathy with the poor, esthetic dislike of poverty).] Shaw postulates the equal distribution of income and the nationalization of production. He attacks the unequal distribution of work, the leisure of the rich, the exploitation of workers, all private enterprise and high prices caused by entrepreneurs' high profits. He does not,

however, want to abolish private property in general. He
wants equal working time for all and disfavors the party
system. He is an enemy of class warfare and criticizes the
"dramatic" illusions of socialism (simplifying antagonisms
such as the capitalist devil and the socialist angel) and
the scientific illusions of socialism (the law of rent, the
law of value). [In German.]

346 Jack, Peter Monro. "Mr. Shaw Is Too Shavian to
Be True," NYTBR, 1 April 1934, pp. 5, 22.
With On the Rocks, Shaw has written as many plays as
Shakespeare; and, as the Bard unlocked his heart in the
Sonnets, Shaw "unburdened his mind in the Prefaces." While
his later plays—On the Rocks, Village Wooing, Too True To
Be Good—lack the old variety, the prefaces are vigorous as
ever. Indeed, often the characters talk themselves into a
predicament that the author "talks himself out of in the
preface."

347 Jack, Peter Monro. "Mr. Shaw's Basket of Shavian
Scraps and Shavings," NYTBR, 27 May 1934, pp. 2, 17.
Shaw's Short Stories, Scraps and Shavings is a "miscellany
of unconsidered trifles" which is not even enlivened with
new prefaces. A piece on Shakespeare's Lady Macbeth and on
OTHELLO will disgust many. Still, it seems impossible for
Shaw to make himself unreadable.

348 Joad, C. E. M. "Shaw Stories," NS&Nation, ns VII
(9 June 1934), 887-88.
Short Stories, Scraps and Shavings contain embryos of later
Shaw ideas. Some of the early works are mere padding, but
"A Glimpse of the Domesticity of Franklyn Barnabas" is a
witty parody of G. K. Chesterton, and The Adventures of the
Black Girl in Her Search for God is a persuasive
presentation of Shaw's Creative Evolution philosophy.

349 Ketchum, Roland and Adolph Gillis. [Introduction
to Caesar and Cleopatra], THREE MASTERS OF ENGLISH
DRAMA (NY: Dodd, Mead, 1934), pp. 3-31.
Shaw is a many-sided enigma: a man of heart "behind the
Mephistophelian mask." His novels contain the germ of his
later works. He uses laughter to accomplish his primary
purpose, i.e., social reform. In Caesar and Cleopatra,
Caesar's greatness lies not in romantic heroism but in his

virtue and his humanity. In this play as elsewhere, Shaw appeals to "the highest consciousness of the thinking man." [An introduction to a student's edition of Caesar and Cleopatra.]

350 Krzhyzhanovskiĭ, S. "Dramaticheskie Premy Bernarda Shou" (Dramatic Methods of Bernard Shaw), LITERATURNYĬ KRITIK (Moscow), IV (1934), 81-97.
At least thirty of Shaw's plays have complex architectonic features in structure, sub-texts, and dramatic counter-forces, e.g. the little-known The Doctor's Dilemma, of which the title and Preface reveal the play's special theses. Shaw's wit can be analyzed in the terminology of formal logic (content and volume). All Shaw's dramatic methods arise from specific social roots which are firmly in the bourgeois world. Soviet playwrights should be acquainted with them, but should use them with great caution. [In Russian.]

351 L., D. L. "Mr. Bernard Shaw's Prefaces," SAT REV, CLVIII (27 Oct 1934), 310.
Prefaces to plays are superfluous, yet Shaw's have been collected in a monumental volume (Constable). Shaw "does not care whether he writes nonsense or not so long as he entertains." The prefaces are entertaining.

352 Lehmann, Wilhelm. "G. Bernard Shaws Verhältnis zu Romantik und Idealismus" (G. Bernard Shaw's Relationship to Romanticism and Idealism). Published dissertation, University of Bonn, 1934. [Listed in McNamee, and in Altick and Matthews, Item 1734.]
Shaw may be called both a romantic and anti-romantic, an idealist and an anti-idealist. The ambiguity of his works results from his satiric tendencies toward both realism and idealism. His female characters are often anti-romantic, while many of his male characters are romantic. [Too many simplifications.] [In German.]

353 "London Enjoys Two Diverting Comedies," NYT, 20 June 1934, p. 24.
Village Wooing (Little Theater, Lond) proceeds gaily and at random to "the theme of man and superman." It (and Galsworthy's THE LITTLE MAN) and "diverting trifles."

354 M., B. W. "'On the Rocks,'" THEATRE WORLD (Lond), XXI (Jan 1934), 13.
Shaw makes his audiences "work for their pleasure." His characters present clashing ideas with equal force, and not even Shaw knows what the fight is about. On the Rocks (Winter Garden, Lond) is such a play, and it offers no solution to the problems of modern statesmanship. It is, however, a "masterly"—"provocative and amusing"—statement of the situation.

355 "The Malvern Festival: 'You Never Can Tell,'" TIMES (Lond), 28 July 1934, p. 10.
You Never Can Tell (Malvern Festival production) unites through wit and light satire a number of still topical social problems.

356 Marriott, J. W. MODERN DRAMA (Lond, Edinburgh, Paris, Toronto, NY: Thomas Nelson & Sons, 1934), pp. 18, 36, 54, 80, 87, 94, 96, 100, 106-18, 255.
[One chapter presents a brief history of Shaw's background, novels, political writings, and plays. He is singled out as a "master of dramatic dialogue" who did "as much as any man to revolutionize stage dialogue" and who dramatizes propaganda most effectively.]

357 Marsh, D'Arcy. "Potpourri," CANADIAN FORUM, XIV (Aug 1934), 448.
Short Stories, Scraps and Shavings is a "minor Shavian cavalcade." The Adventures of the Black Girl in Her Search for God strikes a death blow at religious dogma. John Farleigh's chaste engravings suit the intellectualism of Shaw's writings.

358 Marsh, D'Arcy. "The Shavian Hegira," CANADIAN FORUM, XIV (July 1934), 385.
With the writing of Candida Shaw passed through the passion of Marchbanks to the detachment of Shaw. The play is an "emotion, re-collected in tranquility," and possesses alone among Shaw's works a "structural purity" and humanity.

359 Martin, Burns. "Shaw on Shakespeare," DALHOUSIE REVIEW, 13 (1934), 478-88.
Shaw smacked of the charlatan and the jester when he used Shakespeare as the flogging horse to advance Ibsen. In

prefaces to the later plays, however, there is less exaggeration and conceit; especially in those to <u>Back to Methuselah</u> and <u>Saint Joan</u>, "we see into the heart of Shaw." He has managed at least to win for the twentieth century a healthier attitude toward Shakespeare than prevailed in the nineteenth.

360 "Mr. Shaw's Conversion," TLS (Lond), XXXIII (15 Feb 1934), 105.

Shaw's plays must be judged by their content, not their art. <u>Too True To Be Good</u>, which argues for socialism from the viewpoint of the very rich, is rambling and dull. <u>On the Rocks</u> holds glaring inconsistencies about the proper degree of government power, reflecting Shaw's romantic attempt to reconcile the Soviet dictatorship with humanitarianism and freedom of speech. <u>Village Wooing</u> is fun to read.

361 Nogami, Toyoichiro. "B. Shaw no Kingyo" (Recent Works of B. Shaw) EIBUNGAKU KENKYU (Tokyo), XIV, No 3 (July 1934), 432-34; incorporated as chap 16 in his enlgd ed of BERNARD SHAW (Tokyo: Tokyodo, 1949 [first pub in 1935]).

Shaw's recent three plays (<u>Too True To Be Good</u>, <u>Village Wooing</u>, and <u>On the Rocks</u>) indicate that his political concern grows with the years, and that his belief in the Life Force becomes deeper. [In Japanese.]

362 [<u>On the Rocks</u> review]. IRISH TIMES, 10 July 1934 [not seen in this form]; rptd in CRITICAL HERITAGE, p. 340, Item 111.

<u>On the Rocks</u> (Abbey Theater, Dublin) alternates brilliance and dullness; "one feels that the real Shaw was writing it only part time."

363 "The Open Air Theatre: 'The Six of Calais,'" TIMES (Lond), 18 July 1934, p. 12.

Shaw corrects Froissart's view of women in his portrait of the manipulative Queen Philippa in <u>The Six of Calais</u>, which is "very good fun," in spite of the somewhat "thin and forced" humor.

364 Pellizzi, Camillo. "Shaw polemico ed umorista" (Shaw as Polemicist and Humorist), IL TEATRO INGLESE

(The English Theater) (Milan: Treves, 1934), 101-27; trans by Roward Williams as ENGLISH DRAMA: THE LAST GREAT PHASE (Lond: Macmillan, 1935), pp. 76-97.
Paradoxically in Shaw the man and in Shaw the playwright is found an authentic nineteenth-century bourgeois and an anti-bourgeois, in whose works polemics prevail over dramatic balance. His humor glosses over his contradictions and precludes cynicism. [In Italian.]

365 Petrescu, Camil. TEZE SI ANTITEZE (Thesis and Antithesis) (Bucaresti: Editura Cultura Nationala, 1934). [Two chaps on Shaw, "D-ra Maria Ventura şi B. Shaw," pp. 343-54; and "Pirandello şi Bernard Shaw," pp. 358-73.] [In Romanian.]

366 "Plays and Pictures: The People's National Theatre," NS&Nation, VII (30 June 1934), 995.
The Little Theater's production of <u>Village Wooing</u> shows that Shaw's conception of the "female boa-constrictor remains unchanged."

367 "Plays and Pictures: <u>Saint Joan</u> at the Old Vic," NS&Nation, VIII (8 Dec 1934), 829.
<u>Saint Joan</u> (Old Vic, Lond) is static. The historical background, France, England, or the battle "never become real."

368 Quiz, Quintus. "This Shavian World," CHRISTIAN CENTURY, LI (21 March 1934), 385.
Shaw is indebted to the United States: his first publication responded to American evangelists; Henry George influenced his socialism; his biographer is from North Carolina. Shaw has made a success out of violating all laws of dramatic construction. [Letter to the Editor.]

369 Rattray, R[obert] F[leming]. BERNARD SHAW: A CHRONICLE AND AN INTRODUCTION (Lond: Duckworth, 1934); rptd as BERNARD SHAW: A CHRONICLE, with photos by Thérèse Bonney (Luton: Leagrave P; NY: Roy, 1951; NY: Haskell House, 1974).
[A pastiche of biographical information, historical background, quotations from Shaw, and critical comments arranged year by year in chronological order. Not a useful approach to Shaw's biography, his ideas, or his art. For

example, the entry for 1934 quotes Shaw and others writing on sundry ideas and events; gives a brief history of the composition and production of The Simpleton of the Unexpected Isles, with a quotation from the play; mentions the writing and production of The Six of Calais; and ends with a quotation of Shaw's refusal to address the Boy Scouts of Derby. The entry is typical: no attempt is made to present materials coherently.]

370 Richards, Grant. AUTHOR HUNTING BY AN OLD LITERARY SPORTS MAN (NY: Coward-McCann, Inc., 1934; rptd Lond: Unicorn Press, 1960), pp. 9n, 12-14, 16, 19, 31, 47, 51, 79, 80-83, 105, 117-34, 135-64, 222-24, 238, Index.
[On Richards' publication of Plays Pleasant and Unpleasant and The Perfect Wagnerite; includes numerous letters from Shaw revealing his interest in printing, publishing, and bookselling, and his business acumen.] Influenced by William Morris, Shaw insisted that his printed pages be pictorial in themselves.

371 Rodway, Phillis Philip and Lois Rodway Slingsby. PHILIP RODWAY AND A TALE OF TWO THEATRES (Birmingham: Cornish Brothers Ltd., 1934), pp. 120, 152, 222, 325, 338, 387-88, 389, 597.
[A number of productions of Shaw's plays are briefly reviewed.]

372 Sarma, D. S. "Short Stories, Scraps and Shavings," ARYAN PATH, V (Dec 1934), 775-76.
In Short Stories, Scraps and Shavings, "The Miraculous Revenge" is least artistic; "The Domesticity of Franklyn Barnabas" has brilliant dialog; "A Sunday on the Surrey Hills" has vivid description. The Adventures of the Black Girl in Her Search for God traces "the evolution of the idea of God." Again Shaw attacks "Crosstianity." Though Shaw's "irreverent raillery" may be repellent, one has to face such hostile criticism of one's faith with courage.

373 Scheiner, Eitelfritz. G. B. SHAW NATIONALSOZIALIST? (G. B. Shaw—National Socialist?) (Berlin: Elsner, 1934).
Shaw's way of writing is strange to the German people because he is not German. As long as there are good German

authors who are not as well known in Germany as Shaw, the Nazi movement has no motivation to promote his works. Shaw's economic ideas may be termed national socialist to some extent; his philosophy, however, forms a sharp contrast to the main ideas of national socialism. [Written from a Nazi point of view; includes a summary of The Intelligent Woman's Guide to Socialism and Capitalism.] [In German.]

374 Scott, Temple. "The New Ecclesiastes," SRL, X (24 Feb 1934), 501, 503.
Too True To Be Good says that, though money will not buy happiness, it is needed to find what will; the play depicts the struggles of the rich "to find happiness under the present social system." The Preface to On the Rocks is a rational, not emotional, approach to the problem of state extermination of undesirables.

375 Scott, Temple. "Shavian By-Products," SRL, X (9 June 1934), 742.
[A listing of the contents of Short Stories, Scraps and Shavings, with a synopsis of The Adventures of the Black Girl in Her Search for God.]

376 Sears, William P., Jr. "Social Order Attacked by Bernard Shaw in New Play," LITERARY DIGEST, XVIII (18 Aug 1934), 24.
On the Rocks (Abbey Theater, Dublin) brings to a climax Shaw's theories of the earlier plays. With the old fire, he blasts the present social structure. The play has little action, but is nevertheless compelling, more brilliant and provocative, critics say, than The Apple Cart.

377 "Shavian Shavings," TLS, XXXIII (17 May 1934), 357.
Short Stories, Scraps and Shavings is a "mixed bag" of entertaining though not particularly profound pieces. "A Glimpse of the Domesticity of Franklyn Barnabas," the best in the book, says more of value about the institution of marriage than does Getting Married.

378 "Shaw on the Oxford Accent," LITERARY DIGEST, CXVII (3 March 1934), 23.

[Shaw's answer when asked by the London TIMES to define the Oxford accent.]

379 "SHAW PREMIERE: 'Village Wooing' First Takes Place in Dallas, Texas," NEWS-WEEK, III (28 April 1934), 39.
Village Wooing, an "amusing trifle," premiered in the Little Theater at Dallas, Texas.

380 "Shaw's New Play Produced in Texas: Dallas Audience Is Amused by 'Village Wooing,' Staged as a World Premiere," NYT, 18 April 1934, p. 22.
Village Wooing (Little Theater, Dallas, Texas) seems to have theatrical amusement as its only purpose, though the dialog "inevitably reflects Shaw's opinionated philosophical background."

381 "Shaw's New Play Proves Dublin Hit: Irish Crowd the Abbey Theatre to See a Political Satire, 'On the Rocks,'" NYT, 11 July 1934, p. 20.
On the Rocks lacks action but not "mental stimulation." The audience at the premiere performance (Abbey Theater, Dublin) revelled in the provocative, witty satire.

382 Spender, J. A. "Shaw and Wells," NS&Nation, VIII (15 Dec 1934), 899.
Shaw's attitude toward "the teachability of his Russian friends" is astonishing. The Russians have persecuted and killed their fellows in order to gain what Shaw calls "bitter [learning] experience."

383 Swinnerton, Frank. THE GEORGIAN SCENE: A LITERARY PANORAMA (NY: Farrar & Rinehart, 1934; rptd NY: Farrar, Straus, 1949, as THE GEORGIAN LITERARY SCENE 1910-1935: A PANORAMA), pp. 4, 5, 10, 11, 43-65, 67, 76, 82-84, 87, 103, 112, 114, 183, 200, 211, 212, 269, 299, 369, Index, espec 43-65.
Both Shaw and H. G. Wells shaped the modern irreverent attitude toward morals and civilization. After Shaw came to England, he discovered socialism, Lamarckian or Butlerian evolutionism, and feminism. He brings to drama the debater's ability to present both sides of an issue. People objected not to the themes of his plays but to their irreverent tone. With Arms and the Man, the best of Shaw's

farcical comedy, Shaw abandoned realism for comic exposure of lies and pretense. Candida and The Devil's Disciple are morality plays illustrating the power of natural virtue. Man and Superman, with its interlude, postscript, and Preface, is the epitome of Shaw's versatility and genius. Back to Methuselah is somewhat dull, but The Apple Cart is lively and stimulating. Saint Joan is overvalued by critics who do not understand that Shaw has always valued simplicity and unpretentiousness.

384 "The Theatre: Comediettina in Dallas," TIME, XXIII (30 April 1934), 26.
"For no particular reason at all," Dallas, Texas (Little Theater) offered the world premiere of Village Wooing. The play consists of "agreeable small talk" and no particular message. [Quotations of praise from Dallas critics.]

385 Ulrich, Walter. "Drama und Schule im England der Gegenwart" (Drama and School in Contemporary England), DIE NEUEREN SPRACHEN, XLII (1934), 291-97.
Shaw's Heartbreak House is very popular with amateur actors. [In German.]

386 Van Amerongen, J. B. "Some Notes on Bernard Shaw as a Dramatist," NEOPHILOLOGUS, XIX (1934), 46-52.
With few exceptions, Shaw's characters have no life of their own but are mouthpieces for Shaw. His drama is of the head, not the heart, as in the anti-climactic epilog to Saint Joan. Yet Shaw's intelligence and wit—and his knowledge of theatrical devices—make his drama effective on the stage. Shaw is a master at contrast, producing the unexpected, and leading up to big scenes (e.g., the trial in Saint Joan). Occasionally he plays to the groundlings. At times he succeeds in "arousing genuine emotion," as in the characters of Lady Cicely, Candida, and Blanco Posnet; at these times he is a "true dramatist."

387 Wells, H. G. EXPERIMENT IN AUTOBIOGRAPHY: DISCOVERIES AND CONCLUSIONS OF A VERY ORDINARY BRAIN (SINCE 1866) (NY: Macmillan, 1934), pp. 13, 193, 198, 202, 216, 396, 438-39, 445, 454-57, 529, 530, 564-65, Index; excerpt from pp. 454-57 rptd in CRITICAL HERITAGE, p. 341, Item 112.

[References to Shaw's early socialist days, his relationship with Frank Harris, his meeting with Joseph Conrad, and Wells' disagreements with the Fabian Society.] Shaw "was as distinctly...on the aesthetic side of life as Henry James." Unlike Wells, Shaw "philanders" with Fact; he is like Rousseau in his respect for Nature.

388 "Wells Repertory Players: 'Village Wooing,'" TIMES (Lond), 2 May 1934, p. 12.
Village Wooing plays better than it reads, as the Wells Repertory Players production (Tunbridge Wells) demonstrates. The incredible incidents and emotionless characters come to life in this amusing, fanciful farce.

389 Weltzien, Erich. "'St. Joan' als national politischer Bildunsstoff" (Saint Joan as National-Political Educational Material), NEUEREN SPRACHEN, XLII (1934), 143-54.
[A lengthy, heavy-footed, interpretation in which "current circumstances" in 1934 Germany dictate the reading of the play.] Saint Joan is an inspired leader ("ein genialer Führer"); her great goal, rescuing of her Fatherland. [In German.]

390 Wilson, Edmund. "Bernard Shaw's Latest Phase," NEW REPUBLIC, LXXIX (18 July 1934), 269-70.
Short Stories, Scraps and Shavings presents the old revolutionary hero in a "satire on radical intransigence." On the other hand, On the Rocks depicts a liberal Prime Minister whose politics of gradualism fail. Both he and the King of The Apple Cart are too refined to lead a revolution—the only way to effect social change. The Prime Minister's predicament is well presented, but Shaw's theater cannot accommodate the rebellion of the people.

391 "Winter Garden: 'Androcles and the Lion,'" TIMES (Lond), 21 Sept 1934, p. 10.
Androcles and the Lion has "warmer humour, a less barbed humanitarianism, and a kindlier brevity" than other Shaw works. [Praise for the play and the production, Winter Garden Theater, Lond.]

392 Wood, Herbert G. "G. B. S. on the Rocks," CONTEMPORARY REVIEW, CLVI (July 1934), 58-65.

In On the Rocks Shaw defends the paradox that humankind does not have the right to live but does have the right to speak freely. He advocates efficient dictators who can exterminate a distinct criminal class, although he hopes they will leave the individual "right to grouse." He has surrendered "to the reactionary currents of the present age." His Creative Evolution has landed him on the rocks.

393 Woolf, Leonard. "Too True To Be Good," NS&Nation, VIII (8 Sept 1934), 298.
Shaw's collected prefaces hold a "mixture of pain and pleasure." In the 1890's, Shaw jarred Victorian complacency with wit, vigor, art, and humanity. In these barbarous times, the "conscience" in Shaw's plays and prefaces is reassuring.

394 "The World and the Theatre," TAM, XVIII (Jan 1934), 3-6, espec 6.
On the Rocks (Winter Garden, Lond) uses the dramatic scene for a political platform, as do The Apple Cart and Too True To Be Good.

1935

---

395 Anderson Imbert, Enrique. "Fue vivamente celebrada 'Pygmalion' de B. Shaw en su versión original" (The Original Version of Pygmalion by B. Shaw Was Enthusiastically Praised), LA VANGUARDIA (Argentina), 7 July 1935.
The English Players' production of Pygmalion was enthusiastically received by the public. [In Spanish.]

396 Atkinson, Brooks. "Helen Hayes Opens in Shaw Revival: Appears With Francis Compton in 'Caesar and Cleopatra' at Suffern Theatre," NYT, 22 Aug 1935, p. 21.
Caesar and Cleopatra seems "wise and reasonable" with clear character portraits and a concrete story; but the Suffern County Theater (NY) production has rough edges. Helen Hayes' Cleopatra, however, is witty and passionate.

397 Atkinson, Brooks. "The Play: Bernard Shaw's 'The Simpleton of the Unexpected Isles' Has World Premiere at Guild Theatre," NYT, 19 Feb 1935, p. 27.
The Simpleton of the Unexpected Isles is "labored, loquacious and soporific"; the actors (Guild Theater, NY) do what they can with an infirm script and a play with no structure.

398 Atkinson, Brooks. "When G. B. S. Was Shaw," NYT, 24 Feb 1935, VIII, p. 1.
There was a time when Shaw was startling and vital, making Shavians idolaters of youth, but Shaw has given up being the superman. The Simpleton of the Unexpected Isles (Guild Theater, NY) relies on Emerson and the Orient for its values and "is only a frisky ruin on the stage."

399 "Books," STAGE (NY), XII (July 1935), 62-63.
Nine Plays (Dodd, Mead) contains Shaw plays which will live, but it should have included Great Catherine, a grand piece of tomfoolery, as well.

400 Brentano, Lowell. "Between Covers—I," FORUM, XCIII (Jan 1935), 5-10, espec 7-9.
Shaw is both a propagandist and a writer. In 1923, when Brentano first met Shaw, Shaw turned down an offer for the screen rights for all his plays. Gene Tunney refused to act in Cashel Byron's Profession; both Tunney and Shaw are careful and fair-minded in business matters. Shaw differs from George Moore in that Shaw was social and Moore aesthetic.

401 Brentano, Lowell. "Between Covers—III," FORUM, XCIII (March 1935), 162-67, espec 163-66.
The biggest and most difficult publishing contract Brentano ever negotiated was the collected edition of Shaw. A careful but scrupulously fair business man, Shaw battled "clause by clause" over the contract. [Reminiscence about attending the London opening of The Apple Cart, where Ramsay MacDonald saw little humor in the play.]

402 Bridie, James [pseud of Henry Mavor Osborne]. "George Bernard Shaw," MEN OF TURMOIL: BIOGRAPHIES OF LEADING AUTHORITIES OF THE DOMINATING PERSONALITIES OF OUR DAY (NY: Minto, Balch, 1935; pub as GREAT

91

CONTEMPORARIES: ESSAYS BY VARIOUS HANDS, Lond: Cassell, 1935), pp. 130-40.

After Hardy's death in 1928, Shaw became England's revered Sage—in spite of his irreverent attacks on English institutions. His middle-class Irish Presbyterian background gave him the advantages of an inquiring mind, articulate expression, social confidence, and dissatisfaction with the status quo. The ménage a trois in which he grew up shaped his personality. His novels were "appallingly incompetent love stories." Widowers' Houses had a familiar structure but its subject, Shaw's treatment of it, and his characters upset audiences. Contrary to the "half-witted" criticism that says that Shaw's characters are mere puppets, Shaw creates characters that show "variety, invention, and life." He characteristically examines all points of view. He uses techniques of classical dramatic form in delivering his essentially religious message. Contrary to what he says, his politics have little in common with modern communism.

403 Brown, Ivor. "Angels Over Malvern," NS&Nation, X (3 Aug 1935), 163-64.

The Simpleton of the Unexpected Isles is not a play, but a collection of Shavian notions illustrated by a cast of characters which includes a "semi-imbecile" curate, an Angel, and a priest and priestess of "Pacific Paganism." It is not very good Shaw, but it has "a few nice passages."

404 Brown, Ivor. "Miscellany: Shaw's First Manager," NS&Nation, X (6 July 1935), 12-13.

[Account of the memorial service for J. T. Grein.] Grein opened the doors for Shaw, and for that reason alone he deserves the accolades and honors of his adopted country, England.

405 Brown, Ivor. "The World of the Theatre: Useful People," ILN, CLXXXVII (17 Aug 1935), 294.

The Simpleton of the Unexpected Isles (Malvern Festival production) needs an economic specialist to judge it. The curate in it "is as innocent as Mr. Chesterton's Father Brown," and Shaw's attack on idlers fails to take account of modern machine-age productivity. Contrary to Shaw, the world needs "a cult of dignified and civilised idling." The

old Puritan work ethic no longer applies; Shaw needs to
redefine "social usefulness."

406 Brown, John Mason. "Time and Mr. Shaw," NEW YORK
EVENING POST (23 Feb 1935) [not seen in this form];
rptd in Brown, TWO ON THE AISLE (NY: Norton, 1938),
pp. 100-102.
Shaw has aged but has not lost his amazing energy. However,
The Simpleton of the Unexpected Isles is disturbing
evidence of declining powers.

407 "Cambridge Theatre: 'Man and Superman,'" TIMES
(Lond), 13 Aug 1935, p. 10.
The parts in Man and Superman (Cambridge Theater, Lond) are
oratorical, and can be played only "in the sense in which
music is played." The characters are not recognizable human
beings. [Praise for the acting in this production.]

408 "Cambridge Theatre: 'The Apple Cart,'" TIMES
(Lond), 26 Sept 1935, p. 10.
The Apple Cart has excellent set-pieces but is difficult to
perform, as demonstrated by the plodding production at the
Cambridge Theater (Lond).

409 Colum, Mary M. "Life and Literature: Short
Stories and Plays," FORUM, XCIV (Dec 1935), 354-59,
espec 357-58.
Shaw, like Oscar Wilde, shook the complacent London theater
of the 1890's. He has been influential on modern drama
(e.g., on O'Neill), though a great deal in Shaw is dead.
Exceptions are Arms and the Man, the character of Morell,
the first act of Caesar and Cleopatra, and the insightful
long discussions in Man and Superman. Shaw knew more about
ideas than about people. His prefaces equal the plays in
artistry.

410 Davis, Elmer. "Shaw and the Inner Light," SRL,
XII (6 July 1935), 3-4, 16-17; rptd in BY ELMER
DAVIS, ed by Robert Lloyd Davis (Indianapolis: Bobbs-
Merrill, 1964).
Nine Plays (Dodd, Mead) remind one of Shaw's value as a
prophet: his search for truth, his break with society's
traditions, his faith in individual conscience and human
evolution. He dreams of a society which would respect the

genius of its Saint Joans and Lavinias, but understands in his later years that this is unlikely. He is "Mr. Valiant-for-Truth, the individualist Protestant prophet, and saint."

411 Disher, M. Willson. "Jubilee Years in the Theatre," THEATRE WORLD (Lond), XXIII (May 1935), 201-6.
[A history of the modern stage, with Shaw mentioned here and there.] Pygmalion united the theater of actors and the theater of authors.

412 Eaton, Walter Prichard. "Shaw's Plays Icing for the Preface-Cake," NYHTBR, 30 June 1935, p. 5.
In Shaw's Nine Plays, the "prefaces are the cake; the plays are the icing." There is a side of Shaw that considers his drama trivial, as only a vehicle to convey social propaganda. Yet the "life blood of the English comedy of manners" in his work still makes it all good entertainment. Indeed, his "dramatic humor may survive the vitality of his ideas."

413 Ell. "Bernard Shaw. Die Insel der Überraschungen" (Bernard Shaw. The Simpleton of the Unexpected Isles), LEBENDIGE DICHTUNG, I, No 8 (June 1935), 198.
The Simpleton of the Unexpected Isles is a mixture of wit, satire and meaningful thought, and is full of fantasy and symbols. [In German.]

414 "Embassy Theatre: 'Arms and the Man,'" TIMES (Lond), 16 July 1935, p. 14.
Shaw's attack in Arms and the Man (Embassy Theater, Lond) on romantic notions about war has "sometimes the effect of a slightly stale newspaper." The strength of the play is its romantic manner and amusing story. The performance is competent if not dazzling.

415 Ervine, St. John. "Shaw: Socialist and Aristocrat," CURRENT HISTORY, XLII (July 1935), 387-92.
[Biographical sketch honoring the seventy-ninth birthday of Shaw.]

416 Fitzhugh, Harriet Lloyd and Percy K. Fitzhugh. "George Bernard Shaw," CONCISE BIOGRAPHICAL DICTIONARY OF FAMOUS MEN AND WOMEN (NY: Grosset, 1935; rptd 1950, ed by Harriet Lloyd Fitzhugh, Percy K. Fitzhugh, and William Morris), pp. 622-23.

As a critic of art, music, drama, society, and social conventions, Shaw has been "original and outspoken, often caustic, biased and extravagant, but always a brilliant writer and an independent thinker." He is regarded as a "sort of witty mountebank" by many; others see him as "a philosophic socialist interested in ideas rather than in dramatic action."

417 Fort, Alice Buchanan and Herbert S. Kates. "George Bernard Shaw," MINUTE HISTORY OF THE DRAMA (NY: Grosset & Dunlap, 1935), pp. 106-9.

[Brief and inadequate biographical sketch, followed by plot summaries of Arms and the Man, Candida, and Man and Superman.]

418 Hart-Davis, Rupert. "Stage and Screen: The Theatre," SPECTATOR, CLV (6 Sept 1935), 353.

In Pygmalion (Cambridge Theater, Lond), "To see five acts doing the work of three is as tiresome as driving a pre-war motor-car"; the production "proceeds at a snail's pace." The Shavian sallies "simply fly about loose in the air."

419 Irzykowski, Karol. "G. B. Shaw: Matołek z wysp nieoczekiwanych" (G. B. Shaw: The Simpleton of the Unexpected Isles), PION (Warsaw), No 14 (1935), p. 7; rptd in his RECENZJE TEATRALNE: WYBÓR (Theatrical Reviews: A Selection) (Warsaw: Panstwowy Instytut Wydawniczy, 1965), pp. 421-23.

The first-night audience was disappointed by The Simpleton of the Unexpected Isles; it expected wit and did not appreciate humor, which pervades the play from its beginning. English utilitarianism is evident in the play. The production and direction of the play at the Teatr Polski (Warsaw, 15 March 1935) was so good that it concealed the faults of construction. [In Polish.]

420 Isaacs, Edith J. R. "Merry Feast of Play-Going: Broadway in Review," TAM, XIX (April 1935), 244-58, espec 244, 247.

<u>The Simpleton of the Unexpected Isles</u> is amusing but lacks a sense of theater. Shaw satirizes a "badly managed world," attacking social classes and the professions. But his solution is ridiculous. The last ten minutes spoil the whole play (NY Theater Guild production).

421 J., L. "'Too True to be Good'--'Candida,'" THEATRE WORLD (Lond), XL (Dec 1944), 6.
The Lyric Theatre (Hammersmith) has opened with a Shaw season. In <u>Too True To Be Good</u> Shaw's criticisms "hit the target very neatly," though the situations are fantastic and the characters allegorical. The play's philosophy is "pungent and witty." The production of <u>Candida</u> shows the play's "swift movement, easy development and contrast of characters." (<u>Village Wooing</u> and <u>The Dark Lady of the Sonnets</u> have been added as well.)

422 Jack, Peter Monro. "Mr. Shaw as He Appears in His First Omnibus Volume," NYTBR, 23 June 1935, pp. 4, 13.
<u>Nine Plays</u>, which contains probably the best of Shaw's works, presents in the long prefaces the playwright as instructor to actors, critics, and audience alike. From page to page there is "vitality and vigilance of writing" from a man intoxicated with his own invention.

423 Krutch, Joseph Wood. "Drama: Shaw for Shaw's Sake," NATION, CXL (6 March 1935), 286-87.
Most critics consider Shaw senile, but he is only "to the point where he feels justified in doing exactly as he likes." <u>The Simpleton of the Unexpected Isles</u>, <u>The Apple Cart</u>, and <u>Too True To Be Good</u> show that Shaw is convinced that humanity is doomed—so Shaw can abandon the useful and practical and indulge in horseplay and random commentary. For example, <u>Simpleton</u> is entertaining vaudeville.

424 Krutch, Joseph Wood. "The Shavian Dilemma," NATION, CXLI (11 Sept 1935), 291-93; rptd in GEORGE BERNARD SHAW: A CRITICAL SURVEY, ed by Louis Kronenberger (Cleveland & NY: World, 1953), pp. 120-25.
Ibsen furnished the inspiration and Shaw generated a revolution in nineteenth-century drama; they popularized "modern" ideas taken for granted in twentieth-century

thought. Unlike Shakespeare, Ibsen and Shaw were fighting their audience, which had to change its "moral and intellectual equipment" in order to appreciate the plays. Thus the plays are of necessity awkward, with much boring exposition and argument.

425 Longstreth, T. Morris. "Fanny's First Play," SRL, XII (14 Sept 1935), 9.
[Letter to the Editor recounting Shaw's opinion that, left to itself, Fanny's First Play would run in London forever.]

426 M., B. W. "'St. Joan,'" THEATRE WORLD (Lond), XXII (Jan 1935), 13.
Mary Newcombe played Saint Joan (Old Vic production) in "the 'traditional' (i.e., the [Sybil] Thorndike) manner"; she was best in the trial scene, and played the part with suppressed intensity.

427 M., H. G. "'The Simpleton of the Unexpected Isles,'" THEATRE WORLD (Lond), XXIV (Sept 1935), 110.
The Simpleton of the Unexpected Isles (Malvern Festival production) demonstrates Shaw's verbal artistry, but "at no point does it convincingly reflect real life." The play is puzzling, with "mystic make-believe" and an Angel of Judgment as deus ex machina. It is a decline from Shaw's previous work.

428 "The Malvern Festival: 'Fanny's First Play,'" TIMES (Lond), 1 Aug 1935, p. 12.
The subject matter of Fanny's First Play is outdated, but the Shavian wit saves the play (Malvern Festival production).

429 "The Malvern Festival: 'Misalliance,'" TIMES (Lond), 3 Aug 1935, p. 8.
Shaw seems to have been "clearing his mind" when he wrote Misalliance. The play is inconclusive, lively, and good-humored, as demonstrated by the Malvern Festival production.

430 "The Malvern Festival: Mr. Shaw's New Play," TIMES (Lond), 30 July 1935, p. 12.
The Simpleton of the Unexpected Isles (Malvern Festival production) lacks purpose and shape; it is "a slow moving

political harlequinade with a poetic finale." Through no fault of the actors, the production was dull.

431 Mason, A. E. W. SIR GEORGE ALEXANDER AND THE ST. JAMES' THEATRE (Lond: Macmillan, 1935), pp. 6, 46, 92, 93, 183, 185, 203-4, 208-9, 218, Index.
[Passim references to Shaw; account of George Alexander's request to Shaw for a play resulting in Pygmalion, though it was finally not produced at the St. James' Theater; nor were any of Shaw's plays during Alexander's management (1891-1913).]

432 Maurois, André. "Bernard Shaw, le prophete sceptique" (Bernard Shaw, The Skeptical Prophet), REVUE HEBDOMADAIRE, 16 March 1935, pp. 308-25; and 23 March 1935, pp. 443-55; rptd in MAGICIENS ET LOGICIENS (Magicians and Logicians) (Paris: Grasset, 1935), pp. 101-38; and in PROPHETS AND POETS, trans by Hamish Miles (NY & Lond: Harper, 1935), pp. 95-138; rptd in POINTS OF VIEW: FROM KIPLING TO GRAHAM GREENE (NY: Ungar, 1968), pp. 95-138.
[A lecture delivered at the "Société des Conférences" on Shaw's life, the main themes of Shaw's theater, Shaw's morals, and the main features of his art.] Shaw's hero is an antisentimental realist; he can face facts and tear away the mask of hypocrisy. Woman, especially when she is driven by the Life Force, is realistic and merciless to serve the purpose of the species; she is the pursuer of man, who is always defeated because he has too much imagination. The artist is also a realist; he is unscrupulous like woman because his work alone is important. The men of action, kings or statesmen, are also realists for the same reason, and they discard fictitious morals and pompous ideals to achieve their purpose. The metaphysical development of that morality is the Utopia of the Superman, though the ultimate stage, the disincarnate thoughts of Back to Methuselah, is not very engaging. Shaw's art rests on his dialog, his comic strength, his paradoxes, the masterliness of his brilliant intellectual tirades. His prefaces are also masterpieces. Shaw is better compared with Voltaire than with Molière; there is in him a secret emotion that refuses vulgar sentimentality. [In French.]

433 Millett, Fred and Gerald Eades Bentley. THE ART OF THE DRAMA (NY: Appleton-Century, 1935), pp. 82, 112-15, 197, 236, Index.

Modern comedy, under the influence of Shaw and Ibsen, often concentrates on ideas. Shaw also has satiric Jonsonian comedy (e.g., in The Doctor's Dilemma and Major Barbara) and Molière's "comedy of character" (in Candida).

434 Morgan, Charles. "Shaw at Home—Schwartz Abroad," NYT, 25 Aug 1935, X, p. 1.

The Simpleton of the Unexpected Isles (Malvern Festival production) shows that Shaw no longer feels impelled to either tell a story or find a form for his drama; "he has ceased to coordinate his messages," having become "an oracle over-pleased by the sound of his own voice." [Also reviews YOSHE KALB, with Maurice Schwartz.]

435 Morgan, Walter. WHY I LIKE BERNARD SHAW (Lond: Westminster City Publishing Company, n.d. [1935]; rptd Folcroft, Pa.: Folcroft Library Editions, 1976).

Though his critics complain that Shaw is conceited personally, unreliable as a thinker, and undramatic as a playwright, Shaw is the "greatest playwright since Shakespeare," and the greatest writer of English comedy. Contrary to his critics, Shaw's characters are not mere mouthpieces for ideas, and his plays have "imperishable qualities" that will allow them to endure when their manners and morals are outdated. He must be taken seriously as a realistic pioneer thinker, "the greatest living iconoclast." He nevertheless has a "genuinely religious spirit": he is an ascetic with faith in a "social [and socialist] religion." [Character sketch emphasizes Shaw's good nature, as illustrated in Henry Arthur Jones' quarrel with Shaw after publication of Common Sense about the War; Shaw's enlightened attitude toward women; and his humanitarianism.]

436 "Mr. Shaw Says It All Over Again: A Torpid Restatement of All His Familiar Prides and Prejudices," LITERARY DIGEST, CXIX (2 March 1935), 23.

[A plot summary of The Simpleton of the Unexpected Isles.]

437 Nathan, George Jean. "The Theatre," VANITY FAIR, XLIV (May 1935), 37-38; revised and rptd as "Shaw," in Nathan, THE THEATRE OF THE MOMENT: A JOURNALISTIC COMMENTARY (NY & Lond: Knopf; Toronto: Ryerson P, 1936), pp. 309-10.
Shaw should have stopped writing ten years ago and avoided the accusation of senility. The Simpleton of the Unexpected Isles is dull and repetitive of old Shaw ideas. Once spry and vital, Shaw has become "an increasingly addled and rather futile old man."

438 "New Plays in Manhattan: The Simpleton of the Unexpected Isles," TIME, XXV (4 March 1935), 38-39.
Shaw has not improved since Widowers' Houses "as a dramatic structuralist." The Simpleton of the Unexpected Isles (Theater Guild production) is "woefully stale and shopworn," tiresome and nonsensical.

439 Nogami, Toyoichiro. SHAW (Tokyo: Kenkyusha [Kenkyusha Hyodensosho 72], 1935; rptd in 1980); enlgd as BERNARD SHAW (Tokyo: Tokyodo, 1949).
[A concise critical appreciation of Shaw's life and works up to 1931.] [In Japanese.]

440 "The Old Vic: 'Major Barbara,'" TIMES (Lond), 5 March 1935, p. 14.
Shaw's characters should wear masks since they represent "types, systems, walking morals" rather than men and women. Undershaft, as representative of the philosophy of power, is the focus of the Old Vic production of Major Barbara. The play is still very much alive.

441 "Plays and Pictures: Major Barbara at the Old Vic," NS&Nation, IX (16 March 1935), 381.
Major Barbara (Old Vic production) is a "vigorous but outmoded play." But the skillful production cannot dissolve the contradictions in the final act.

442 "Plays and Pictures: Shaw at the Cambridge," NS&Nation, X (17 Aug 1935), 222-23.
Man and Superman (Cambridge Theater, Lond) demonstrates that ordinary play technique has "unjustly been neglected" since the play was first written. With such an approach,

even an apathetic audience can become engrossed, and Superman is "still dazzling and fascinating

443 "'Q' Theatre: 'Caesar and Cleopatra,'" TIMES (Lond), 12 March 1935, p. 14.
Caesar and Cleopatra ("Q" Theater, Lond) is a serious presentation of historical figures in crisis; the play moves smoothly from incident to incident, with Britannus supplying mischievous jolts on occasion.

444 "'Q' Theatre: 'Candida,'" TIMES (Lond), 14 May 1935, p. 14.
The modern dress production of Candida ("Q" Theater, Lond) shows that Candida is never dated, but that Marchbanks and Morell belong to the nineties. Yet the play is "beautifully constructed," moving to an "intellectually intricate and emotionally simple" climax.

445 "The Q Theatre: ' Major Barbara,'" TIMES (Lond), 5 Nov 1935, p. 14.
The "all or nothing" argument of Major Barbara ("Q" Theater, Lond) is not clear in the play, which seems to be a series of unconnected brilliant scenes.

446 "'Q' Theatre: 'Misalliance,'" TIMES (Lond), 5 March 1935, p. 14.
Misalliance ("Q" Theater, Lond) is loosely constructed and a hodge-podge of Shavian afterthoughts, but nevertheless sparkling with wit.

447 "'Q' Theatre: 'Mrs. Warren's Profession,'" TIMES (Lond), 23 July 1935, p. 12.
In Mrs. Warren's Profession ("Q" Theater, Lond), the characters of Mrs. Warren and Vivie overshadow the play's thesis. The skillful dialog proceeds by indirection to develop "the essential theme of tragedy." The minor characters, unfortunately, lack reality.

448 "The 'Q' Theatre: 'Widowers' Houses,'" TIMES (Lond), 19 Nov 1935, p. 12.
Widowers' Houses ("Q" Theater, Lond) is designed to cause an uproar. In the midst of light comedy appears a shocking revelation, made more relevant by the modern costuming of the production.

449 Rubenstein, R. "Cleopatra in Moscow," NS&Nation, IX (19 Jan 1935), 74-75.
The Kamerny Theater, founded in 1914 by Tairov, is celebrating its birthday with a composite production of Shakespeare's Antony and Cleopatra, Shaw's Caesar and Cleopatra, and "a dash" of Pushkin's Egyptian Nights. Shaw's Cleopatra will be the basis of the Queen's character, for her features are clearer than those of Shakespeare's heroine. Indeed, Shaw's play will, in a sense, be used as a dramatic overture to Shakespeare's play. Prokofiev has written the music, and Cleopatra will be played by the great Soviet actress, Alice Koonon.

450 S., C. "Theatre Notes: 'Pygmalion,'" SAT REV, CLX (14 Sept 1935), 191.
Pygmalion (Cambridge Theater, Lond) is a dead, dull play, and "should be played in costume if it is played at all."

451 Sears, William P., Jr. "A New Play by Shaw," LITERARY DIGEST, CXIX (2 Feb 1935), 24.
The Simpleton of the Unexpected Isles will have its world premiere in a NY Theater Guild production. The Six of Calais, "a twentieth century commentary on the heroic burghers of Calais," was performed in the Regents Park Theater (Lond) last July, with Shaw present for a curtain call.

452 "Seventh Malvern Festival: 'The Simpleton of the Unexpected Isles,'" PLAY PICTORIAL, LXVII, No 400 (1935), 23-27.
The Simpleton of the Unexpected Isles is Shaw's attempt at soul-purging through humor, poetry, and fantasy. [A resume of the plot and photographs of the Malvern production.]

453 Smith, Hugh. "Dublin on That End," NYT, 27 Oct 1935, IX, p. 2.
Village Wooing "is less a play than a highly diverting and audacious duologue." [Favorable review of Abbey Theater, Dublin, performance of this and Candida.]

454 "STAGE: Hedgerow Honors Shaw's Birthday With 6 Shavian Plays," NEWS-WEEK, VI (3 Aug 1935), 20.
The Hedgerow Players, of Maylan Rose Valley, Pa., celebrated Shaw's seventy-ninth birthday by presenting six

Shaw plays: <u>Saint Joan</u>, <u>Heartbreak House</u>, <u>Candida</u>, <u>Arms and the Man</u>, <u>Androcles and the Lion</u>, <u>The Doctor's Dilemma</u>.

455 Vernon, Grenville. "The Play: Shaw at the Guild," COMMONWEAL, XXI (8 March 1935), 542.

<u>The Simpleton of the Unexpected Isles</u> (Theater Guild production) offers no new Shaw ideas and lacks his former style. His powers have declined with old age.

456 Williams, Harcourt. FOUR YEARS AT THE OLD VIC, 1929-1933 (Lond: Putnam, 1935), pp. xi-xiii, 12, 45-62, 68, 75, 104-7, 176-79, 180-82, 185-87, 188-89, 211, Index; espec 45-62.

[Letter from Shaw regarding responsibilities of a producer when writing about actors; passing comments on productions of <u>The Dark Lady of the Sonnets</u>, <u>Androcles and the Lion</u>, <u>Arms and the Man</u>, and <u>Caesar and Cleopatra</u>.]

457 Withington, Robert. "The Sage of Dubdon: A Critical Note on G. B. Shaw," SEWANEE REVIEW, XLIII (April-June 1935), 224-29.

Shaw is more like Ben Jonson than like Shakespeare. Both Jonson and Shaw write satirical comedies, use character types, despise their public, and let their personalities intrude in their work. For Shaw, the idea behind the play is most important; for Jonson, the dialog is. Both are "conscious" dramatists. Shaw stays too near the surface of life, and on an economic rather than a moral level.

458 Wood, Frederick T. "Individualism in Religious Thought in the Plays of Ibsen and Bernard Shaw," CALCUTTA REVIEW (June 1935), pp. 243-55.

<u>Saint Joan</u> is the greatest modern play on the question of religious authority versus private judgment. The trial scene focusses the issue, in which individualism finally triumphs. Shaw has in this and in <u>The Devil's Disciple</u>, <u>The Shewing-Up of Blanco Posnet</u>, and <u>Major Barbara</u> "stated the case for the immanence of the Divine Spirit more clearly than any other"; in play after play he affirms the innate goodness—the divine spark—in humanity.

459 "The World and the Theatre: British National Theatre," TAM, XIX (Aug 1935), 573-76.

Nine Plays (Dodd, Mead) marks the end of an era of change in the British theater. But Shaw has not changed much since his youth.

460 Wyatt, Euphemia Van Rensselaer. "The Drama: The Simpleton of the Unexpected Isles," CATHOLIC WORLD, CXLI (April 1935), 86-92, espec 87-88.
The Simpleton of the Unexpected Isles (Theater Guild production) is a children's religious tract, with the Simpleton representing the Established Church. The one truly dramatic moment comes with the clergyman's speech on the disappearance of love. Shaw may yet be converted.

461 Young, Stark. "Mr. Fresnay, Mr. Shaw," NEW REPUBLIC, LXXXII (6 March 1935), 105.
The Simpleton of the Unexpected Isles (Theater Guild production, NY) is less boring than The Apple Cart. Shaw preaches too much.

1936

462 "Among the New Books: The New Shavian Trio," CHRISTIAN SCIENCE MONITOR, 3 June 1936, pp. 12-15, espec 13.
The Six of Calais is not impressive. The Simpleton of the Unexpected Isles has a worthy theme, but this "shambling farce" cheats it of wit, theatrical sense, and style. The Millionairess is entertaining.

463 Anderson, John. "It's a Small World: Theatre," PICTORIAL REVIEW, XXXVII (June 1936), 4, 55-56.
Saint Joan is a majestic and wise play—Shaw's best. It reflects faith and truth, with Joan not the author dominating the play. Katharine Cornell's Joan (Martin Beck Theater, NY) captures the spirit of Shaw's work.

464 Anderson, John. [Saint Joan review], NY JOURNAL, 10 March 1936 [not seen in this form]; rptd in Katharine Cornell, I WANTED TO BE AN ACTRESS (NY: Random House; Toronto: Macmillan, 1939), pp. 317-21.

Saint Joan (Martin Beck Theater, NY) is a great play in
need of a better epilog. It is eloquent, wise, and
dramatically powerful; the issues are sharply drawn. The
trial scene impressively combines melodrama and history.

465 Arthur, Sir George. FROM PHELPS TO GIELGUD:
REMINISCENCES OF THE STAGE THROUGH SIXTY-FIVE YEARS
(Lond: Chapman and Hall, 1936; rptd Freeport, NY:
Books for Libraries P, 1967), pp. 104, 130, 131, 147,
148, 150, 152, 163, 207, 226-31, Index.
[Brief references to Shaw's contributions to the New
Drama.] Shaw persuaded his readers that dramatic criticism
could be readable and that the drama of ideas need not be
dull.

466 Atkinson, Brooks. "Joan of G. B. S.: Katharine
Cornell's Revival of a Major Chronicle Drama," NYT,
15 March 1936, X, p. 1.
Shaw's "heartless egotism" has earned him deep resentment
from his public, but Saint Joan, with its human passion,
pity, and affirmation of the power of faith, almost redeems
him. The play contains Shaw's finest speeches, and the
McClintic production (Martin Beck Theater, NY) does justice
to them.

467 Atkinson, Brooks. "The Play: Katharine Cornell
and Her Associates Revive Bernard Shaw's 'Saint
Joan,'" NYT, 10 March 1936, p. 27; rptd in ON STAGE:
SELECTED THEATER REVIEWS FROM THE NEW YORK TIMES
1920-1970, ed by Bernard Beckerman and Howard Siegman
(NY: Arno P, 1973), pp. 174-75.
Saint Joan ranks with the best modern drama, though it has
some merely competent scenes, and the epilog is tedious.
But the trial scene is a masterpiece, and Cornell's Joan
has "flesh, blood and spirit" (Martin Beck Theater, NY).

468 Bab, Julius. "Mein Verhältnis zu Bernard Shaw"
(My Relationship to Bernard Shaw), SHAW KOMPENDIUM:
VERZEICHNIS UND ANALYSE SEINER WERKE: VERZEICHNIS
SEINER WERKE IN ENGLAND UND DEUTSCHLAND (Shaw
Compendium: List and Analysis of His Works: List of
the Performances of His Works in England and Germany)
(Paris: Henri Didier, 1936), ed by X[avier] Heydet,
pp. 147-49.

[Not about a personal relationship; rather, Bab traces the genesis of his 1910 book, republished much revised in 1926, on Shaw and the grounds for the deep, lasting impression Shaw's works made on him.] [In German.]

469 "Bernard Shaw en México" (Bernard Shaw in Mexico), REVISTA DE REVISTAS (Mexico), XXVI, No 1349 (22 March 1936).
[Three photographs, with comments on Shaw's declarations to the news media when he visited Mexico.] [In Spanish.]

470 "Books: Shaw's Friends," TIME, XXVIII (14 Dec 1936), 91-93.
William Morris as I Knew Him reveals more about Shaw than about Morris, since it "takes for granted a great deal of information about Morris."

471 Borges, Jorge Luis. "Las últimas comedias de Shaw: Demasiado cierto para ser bueno. El Bobalicón de las islas inesperadas" (The Last Comedies of Shaw: Too True To Be Good and The Simpleton of the Unexpected Isles), SUR (Argentina), No 24 (Sept 1936), 127-30.
Too True To Be Good and The Simpleton of the Unexpected Isles are inferior to Shaw's first dramatic works, but nonetheless better than the works of other playwrights of the time. The world of these comedies is unreal and opaque. They lack the humor and ironic spark, for example, of Caesar and Cleopatra. [In Spanish.]

472 Brown, Ivor. "New Plays: G.B.S. and U.S.A.," MANCHESTER GUARDIAN, 24 March 1936, p. 5.
Even a trifle like Fanny's First Play is better than Shaw's recent efforts—The Millionairess, a "helter-skelter" piece with characters who are mere mouthpieces for Shaw, The Simpleton of the Unexpected Isles, and The Six of Calais.

473 Brown, Ivor. "The World of the Theatre: The Meek and the Mighty," ILN, CLXXXVIII (28 March 1936), 562.
The Millionairess is "a helter-skelter kind of comedy," with social satire on "the politics and ethics of Bossing." The heroine is "a Natural Boss," and would be well played

by Edith Evans. But the theater usually loves the bossed ("the little fellows") more than the bosses.

474 Brown, Ivor. "The World of the Theatre: Young Men and Old," ILN, CLXXXVIII (18 Jan 1936), 100.

1935 was not "a Shavian vintage year." The Simpleton of the Unexpected Isles (Malvern Festival) was like a parody of Shaw, with "all the annoying tricks and the familiar japes without the old driving power and dramatic pertinence"; the revival of Fanny's First Play had more "savour." The Millionairess, produced in Vienna, is apparently witty and thoughtful, and should allow Shaw to scale "the Malvern summits."

475 Brown, John Mason. "Katharine Cornell Presents Bernard Shaw's 'Saint Joan,'" NY POST, 10 March 1936 [not seen in this form]; rptd in TAM, XX (June 1936), 463-64; rptd as "Miss Cornell's Saint Joan," in Brown, TWO ON THE AISLE (NY: Norton, 1938), pp. 102-6, and as "The Prophet and the Maid: Cornell's Joan," in Brown, DRAMATIS PERSONAE: A RETROSPECTIVE SHOW (NY: Viking, 1963), pp. 141-44.

In Saint Joan, Shaw achieves eloquence as a poet and discipline as a playwright. "It is the most stirring expression the modern theatre has produced of the hungry rationalities of the spirit which transcend the limited rationalities of the mind."

476 Canby, Henry Seidel. "Merlin Speaking," SRL, XIV (13 June 1936), 10.

Shaw remains vital in Three New Plays. The Six of Calais is "a grand piece of character action"; The Simpleton of the Unexpected Isles, though rather dull, presents the Fabian belief that only the useful deserve to stay alive; The Millionairess rambles, but has an important Preface and theme (the wedding of the superman and socialism).

477 Cecchi, Emilio. "George Bernard Shaw," ENCICLOPEDIA ITALIANA (Rome: Treccani, 1936), XXXI, 602-3.

In his handling of dialog Shaw stands comparison with classic authors. His targets are the conventional ideas of the English middle class with its stereotypes and prejudices. To his criticism he added a constructive element with his theory of the Life Force, whose supreme depository is woman. His poignant remarks make up for his occasional shortcomings. In his aggressive realism he sometimes is unfair, but one should acknowledge his courage and sense of justice, particularly in connection with the Italian-English clash over Ethiopia in December 1935. [A concise, perceptive analysis.] [In Italian.]

478 Chesterton, G. K. THE AUTOBIOGRAPHY OF G. K. CHESTERTON (NY: Sheed & Ward, 1936), pp. 115, 143, 151, 153, 158, 178, 179, 197, 201, 225, 228, 229-36, 256, 259, 266, 277, 306, 312, 347, 351.
Shaw is "at his best when he is antagonistic" and when he is wrong; in fact, "everything about him is wrong except himself." Oddly enough, he is an imperialist on the Boer War question. A small war to force backward people to open their resources is acceptable to Shaw, but a war of great powers to determine the religious and moral destiny of humanity is unacceptable. Arguments with Shaw, however, are not limited to the nature of war. It is easy to dispute with him "about sex, about sin, about sacraments, about personal points of honour, about all the most sacred or delicate essentials of existence." Yet through it all Shaw demonstrates "fair-mindedness and intellectual geniality."

479 Cookman, A. V. "Of 'The Boy David' and 'The Millionairess,'" NYT, 13 Dec 1936, Section 11, p. 5.
The Millionairess (Forsyth Players, Bexhill) lacks characterization and replaces drama with elocution; yet it moves "swiftly and brightly" and is better than other recent Shaw plays. Epifania is an Ann Whitefield with millions.

480 "Drama and Music: Saint Joan Stirs Broadway, Too," LITERARY DIGEST, CXXI (21 March 1936), 19.
The stature of Saint Joan has grown through the years, evidence of a great play. [Rave reviews of Chicago Grand Opera House production, with Katharine Cornell. Also quotations of John Mason Brown, NY POST, and Brooks Atkinson, NYT.]

481 Eaton, Walter Prichard. "The Wit of Bernard Shaw Still Crackles," NYHTBR, 17 May 1936, p. 7.

It is now fashionable to deride Shaw and think of him as "a doddering old gentleman." But The Simpleton of the Unexpected Isles, The Six of Calais, and The Millionairess as well as the accompanying prefaces just issued revitalize the traditional comedy of manners. The Millionairess in particular is a Jonsonian comedy that raises fundamental questions about human nature. It is a well constructed play, and the "dialogue spits and crackles." The younger generation may find it difficult to keep pace with this doddering old man.

482 "The Encirclement of Mr. Bernard Shaw: Social Doctrines in a Dilemma," TLS (Lond), XXXV (28 March 1936), 267; rptd in CRITICAL HERITAGE, pp. 346-50, Item 114.
The Simpleton of the Unexpected Isles is in an obscure style and lacks "constructive originality." The Millionairess illustrates Shaw's current impasse; Epifania is dangerous to the state but cannot be controlled by communism and democracy. Shaw attempts "to apply economic remedies to spiritual evils"—such as humanity's desire for riches and fear of death; he also refuses to recognize the difference between Jesus' and Lenin's communism.

483 Erdmann, Lothar. "George Bernard Shaw," DIE HILFE, XLII, No 15 (1 Aug 1936), 353-56.
[A brief portrait of Shaw on the occasion of his eightieth birthday.] Shaw is a passionate fighter and disturber of the peace, a playwright, artist, philosopher, and socialist—all in one person. [In German.]

484 Farrell, James T. "G. B. S. Interviews the Pope: An Imaginary Conversation," NATION, CXLIII (3 Oct 1936), 287-88.
[A playlet in which Shaw visits Pope Pius XI to complain about Catholics and the Legion of Decency, a group which was trying to censor the film of Saint Joan. Shaw argues that Saint Joan is a pro-Catholic play; the Pope responds with euphemisms, bits of Latin, and admonitions to pray for guidance.]

485 "G. B. S. and the Catholic Censorship," NEW REPUBLIC, LXXXVIII (23 Sept 1936), 173.

Shaw's letter to the NYT protesting the attempted censorship by Catholic Action of the film of Saint Joan deals a damaging blow to Catholic motion-picture censorship.

486 Gedye, G. E. R. "Vienna Premiere for Shaw's Play: 'The Millionairess,' Written 18 Years Ago, Is Given For the First Time," NYT, 5 Jan 1936, p. 39.
The Millionairess is a witty satire divested of Shaw's Fabian propaganda. The Vienna audience at the premiere performance (Akademie Theater) responded favorably to the implausibilities of the fantastic play.

487 Green, Alice A. [pseud of Michael Orme]. J. T. GREIN: THE STORY OF A PIONEER, 1862-1935 (Lond: John Murray, 1936), pp. 1-5, 78, 97, 117-18, 126, 130, 138, 142, 148-49, 153, 192, 206-7, 234, 264, 286-87, 297, 310-11, 328, 329, 340.
In 1918 J. T. Grein was a principal figure in the debut of the Amsterdam Municipal Theater, which opened with Shaw's Candida. Edvard Verkade was the director, and his production "surpassed all expectations." Shaw once noted that Grein dropped two "bombshells" on the British theater, one being Ibsen. The other—Shaw—made people "stare and laugh."

488 Green, E. Mawby. "Echoes from Broadway," THEATRE WORLD (Lond), XXV (May 1936), 233.
The Katharine Cornell version of Saint Joan (Martin Beck Theater, NY) is magnificent. But Shaw preaches too much in the play, which at times becomes boring. A good production should curb Shaw's "garrulous propensity."

489 Gwynn, Stephen. IRISH LITERATURE AND DRAMA IN THE ENGLISH LANGUAGE: A SHORT HISTORY (Lond, Edinburgh, Paris, Melbourne, Toronto, NY: Thomas Nelson and Sons, 1936), pp. 146-48, 180-81, 207, 217, 226, 233.
Shaw's audiences at first "resented the idea of being asked to think," for they were accustomed to amusement only. His preoccupation was not with Irish problems but with the "vastly larger field of Great Britain." Yet his mind was "unEnglish" with a "special note of hostility that is Irish." The Irish were delighted when he "made war on the

most cherished convictions of English respectability."
Shaw's main service to literature in Ireland was the
impetus he gave to a "theatre of ideas not merely box
returns."

490   Hartmann, Alfons. DER MODERNE ENGLISCHE EINAKTER
(The Modern English One-act Play) (Leipzig: Robert
Noske, 1936), pp. 2, 4, 7, 9, 24, 52, 61-67, 88, 122,
172, 173, 178.
Not all playlets by Shaw can be defined as one-act plays,
for Shaw does not conform to the dramatic rules of the
genre. Some plays, such as Getting Married and Misalliance,
are too long. Some, such as Annajanska, the Bolshevik
Empress or Press Cuttings, are sketches rather than plays.
[In German.]

491   "Headliner: G. B. S.: Teetotaler, Vegetarian,
Fabian, and Britain's Best Wit," NEWS-WEEK, VIII (25
July 1936), 23.
Shaw's "greatest creation is probably himself, a living
caricature called G.B.S." [Biographical sketch on the
occasion of Shaw's eightieth birthday.]

492   Henderson, Ray. [Account of Guthrie McClintic's
meeting with Shaw], NY TRIBUNE, 1 March 1936 [not
seen in this form]; rptd in Katharine Cornell, I
WANTED TO BE AN ACTRESS (NY: Random House; Toronto:
Macmillan, 1939), pp. 324-28.
[Account of a meeting between producer Guthrie McClintic
and Shaw at Whitehall Court (1935) concerning the planned
Cornell-McClintic production of Saint Joan.]

493   Hevesi, Sándor. "A huszadik század Shakespeare-
je" (Shakespeare in the Twentieth Century), BUDAPESTI
SZEMLE, No 706 (1936), pp. 287-309.
Dramatic interpretations of Shakespeare have changed
considerably from the nineteenth to the twentieth century;
undoubtedly the modern interpretations stand closer to the
original than those of intervening centuries. Although
consciously "anti-Shakespeare" in his own dramatic style,
Shaw as a theater critic played a great role in bringing
true Shakespearean text back to the stage. In the 1890s,
Shaw was the most vehement critic of the theatrical
deforming of Shakespeare through the shifting of scenes and

characters to fit a rigid act- (not scene-) oriented structure. [In Hungarian.]

494 Hevesi, Sándor. "Shaw, a megfordított Shakespeare" (Shaw, the Reverse of Shakespeare), SZÍNHÁZI ÉLET, No 7 (1936), pp. 8-11.
Whereas Shakespeare's HENRY VI presents Joan as a lecherous witch and loudly praises the English, Shaw glorifies Joan and mercilessly exposes the English. Shaw presents the inquisition with jarring objectivity and with an unparalleled stroke closes the play (which is unassailably faithful to history). The end provides a new perspective in drama: past dramatists wrote about the lives and deaths of heroes; Shaw brings the immortality of a heroine to the stage and thus creates a real "happy ending." [In Hungarian.]

495 Heydet, X[avier]. SHAW KOMPENDIUM: VERZEICHNIS UND ANALYSE SEINER WERKE; SHAW-BIBLIOGRAPHIE: VERZEICHNIS DER LITERATUR ÜBER SHAW; VERZEICHNIS DER AUFFÜHRUNGEN SEINER WERKE IN ENGLAND UND DEUTSCHLAND (Shaw Compendium: List and Analysis of His Works; Shaw Bibliography: List of the Literature about Shaw; List of the Performances of his Works in England and Germany) (Paris: Henri Didier, 1936).
[Includes a chronology of Shaw's life; a list of his works, with dates of composition and appearance in England and Germany; and a list of books about Shaw. Shaw's works and selected books about him are summarized through excerpts from reviews and books about Shaw. A section on "Deutsche Ubersetzer und Biograph" (German Translators and Biographers) includes brief articles by Siegfried Trebitsch, "Der Deutsche Aufsteig Bernard Shaws" (Bernard Shaw's German Ascent), q.v., and by Julius Bab, "Mein Verhältnis zu Bernard Shaw" (My Relationship to Bernard Shaw, q.v.). Bibliography includes lists of articles about Shaw and by Shaw appearing in German newspapers and magazines.] [In German.]

496 "Huésped ilustre: George Bernard Shaw" (Illustrious Guest: George Bernard Shaw), REVISTA DE REVISTAS (Mexico), XXVI, No 1347 (8 March 1936), 1.
Shaw's visit to Mexico is momentous; perhaps it will contribute to a better understanding between English-

speaking countries and Mexico. Shaw's keen observations should provide a new vision of Mexico. [In Spanish.]

497 Irzykowski, Karol. "G. B. Shaw: Milionerka" (G. B. Shaw: The Millionairess), PION (Warsaw), No 23 (1936), pp. 7-8; rptd in Irzykowski, RECENZJE TEATRALNE: WYBÓR (Theatrical Reviews: A Selection) (Warsaw: Pánstwowy Instytut Wydawniczy, 1965), pp. 467-70.
Shaw is a socialist, but like a genuine Englishman admires the self-made man, and states that eighty per cent of cases of poverty are due to ignorance. But he is a socialist who regards socialism as a problem of organization, not of altruism. This is why he admires Stalin. [In Polish.]

498 Irzykowski, Karol. "G. B. Shaw: Profesja pani Warren" (G. B. Shaw: Mrs. Warren's Profession), PION (Warsaw), No 26 (1936), p. 7; rptd Irzykowski, RECENZJE TEATRALNE: WYBÓR (Theatrical Reviews: A Selection) (Warsaw: Pánstwowy Instytut Wydawniczy, 1965), pp. 471-73.
Sociologically, the fate of Mrs. Warren is most interesting. The scene between Mrs. Warren and her daughter is dialectic in the manner of later Shaw; there is also the clash of two temperaments, generations, and cultures. But Shaw's criticism of capitalism forty years ago is now well-known, and the audience accepts it with approval. As at a familiar opera, the audience knows what is going to happen, but is not bored (Teatr Malicki production, Warsaw, June 1936). [In Polish.]

499 Isaacs, Edith J. R. "Saints and Law-Makers: Broadway in Review," TAM, XX (May 1936), 333-43; rptd as "Saint Joan," in THEATRE ARTS ANTHOLOGY, ed by Rosamond Gilder, Hermine Rich Isaacs, Robert M. MacGregor, and Edward Reed (NY: Theatre Arts Books; Robert M. MacGregor, 1950), pp. 639-41; and as "Argumentative Martyrs," in Stanley Weintraub (ed), SAINT JOAN: FIFTY YEARS AFTER (Baton Rouge: Louisiana State UP, 1973), pp. 102-5.
Saint Joan is a major imaginative achievement, though too long and too verbose. Shaw rescues from legend both her judges and Joan, who, according to Shaw, "sees clearly

because she is never blinded by fear or prejudice."
Katharine Cornell acts Joan as Shaw envisioned her.

500 Knowlton, Thomas Anson. ECONOMIC THEORY OF
GEORGE BERNARD SHAW (Orono, Me.: University P
[University of Maine Studies, 2nd Series, No 39;
MAINE BULLETIN, XXXIX, Nov 1936, No 4], 1936).
Shaw's importance is not as an economist but as an
influence on his generation's thought. He forces his
readers to consider new values, using economics as he uses
biology—to create a world. He makes few contributions to
theoretic socialism: he is at times unreasoning, or filled
with bourgeois bias, or unwilling to sacrifice for his
ideals. He is, furthermore, "a _carrier_ of socialism,"
advocating it but personally immune to it. [Surveys Shaw's
early years; his conversion to socialism; his relationship
to the Fabian Society; his opinions on production and
consumption, capital and interest, rent, money and banking;
his "war record" (concerning World War I); and his portrait
of the socialist state. Frequent reference to his _Essays in
Fabian Socialism_ and _The Intelligent Woman's Guide to
Socialism and Capitalism_; little reference to the plays or
novels.]

501 Krutch, Joseph Wood. "Drama: Shaw's Classic,"
NATION, CXLII (25 March 1936), 392.
Saint Joan (Martin Beck Theater, NY) is a classic of the
modern theater, timely and powerful, and getting better
with time. Dominated by Shavian mysticism, the play "offers
no intellectual solution for the problem it discusses," but
tips the balance toward Joan by virtue of her passionate
conviction.

502 Lawson, John Howard. THEORY AND TECHNIQUE OF
PLAYWRITING (NY: Putnam; Toronto: T. Allen, 1936; new
edition, THE THEORY AND TECHNIQUE OF PLAYWRITING AND
SCREENWRITING, NY: Putnam; Toronto: T. Allen, 1949
[not seen in these editions]; rptd NY: Hill and Wang
[Dramabook], 1960), pp. xxxii, 57, 71, 78, 86, 107-
13, 115, 127, 129, 135, 151, 194, 208, 214, espec
107-13.
Shaw is unable to solve his mental contradictions. He tends
to look for an easy solution to social problems, creates
essentially static drama, and blurs ideas through talk. His

female characters—e.g., Candida, Ann Whitefield, Joan—are vital. But his plays reflect a progressive technical disintegration.

503 M., A. "Notas" (Notes), UNIVERSIDAD (Mexico), I, No 2 (March 1936), 47.
In Shaw's visit to Mexico, he laughed a lot, and made Mexicans laugh even more. [In Spanish.]

504 "Malvern Festival Honors G. B. Shaw: Dramatist's 80th Birthday Eve Marked by Performance of 'St. Joan,'" NYT, 26 July 1936, II, p. 1.
[Praise for Wendy Hiller's performance of Joan (Malvern Festival) on occasion of Shaw's eightieth birthday.]

505 "Malvern Festival: 'On the Rocks,'" TIMES (Lond), 28 July 1936, p. 12.
The form of On the Rocks defies analysis; its politics remain alive and interesting; its conclusion is vague.

506 "Malvern Festival: 'Pygmalion,'" TIMES (Lond), 31 July 1936, p. 12.
Eliza and Higgins, in Pygmalion, are fantastic, delightful characters set in "a series of sparring matches." [Praise for the Malvern Festival performance.]

507 "Malvern Festival: 'Saint Joan,'" TIMES (Lond), 27 July 1936, p. 10.
Saint Joan suffers from a lack of poetry in the trial scene, and fails to give a sense of the cruel punishment for heresy in the Middle Ages. [Praise for Wendy Hiller's stubborn and humble Joan.]

508 Mantle, Burns. [Saint Joan review], NY NEWS, 10 March 1936 [not seen in this form]; rptd in Katharine Cornell, I WANTED TO BE AN ACTRESS (NY: Random House; Toronto: Macmillan, 1939), pp. 321-23.
The McClintic production of Saint Joan (Martin Beck Theater, NY) is inspired, though Shaw's argument gets a bit "sluggish" and the epilog changes the tragic mood.

509 "Mr. Shaw's New Play: 'The Millionairess,'" TIMES (Lond), 18 Nov 1936, p. 12.

Epifania in <u>The Millionairess</u> (Forsyth Players, Bexhill) is an "exuberant addition to the Shavian theatre"--an irresistible oppressor in this entertaining cartoon of a play.

510 Navarro, Mary Anderson de. A FEW MORE MEMORIES (Lond: Hutchinson, 1936), pp. 180, 216-19.
[Personal recollections of Shaw at a Shakespeare birthday lunch in Stratford-on-Avon and at Malvern, by the actress Mary Anderson (de Navarro).]

511 Nicoll, Allardyce. FILM AND THEATRE (NY: Crowell; Lond: Harrap; Toronto: Oxford, 1936), pp. 34, 61, 164-65, Index.
[Mentions Shaw's readable prefaces and stage directions in urging screen plays be made intelligible to non-technical readers. Gives an account of a film version of <u>Arms and the Man</u> which followed faithfully Shaw's stage version, with the result that the wit and vitality of Shaw's plays disappeared on screen; asserts that the stage can present characters as types, but the screen requires character individualization.]

512 Norwood, Gilbert. "A Voice From the Past," CANADIAN FORUM, XVI (July 1936), 24-25.
The "greatest wit since Anatole France" and "finest playwright since Ibsen" says nothing new in <u>The Simpleton of the Unexpected Isles</u>, <u>The Six of Calais</u>, and <u>The Millionairess</u>. These plays contain only "thin echoes" of Shaw. <u>Simpleton</u> is the worst of the three.

513 "Novels and Plays: Chicago Under Depression; Dream versus Fact; G. B. S. Again," LITERARY DIGEST, CXXI (30 May 1936), 25.
<u>Three Plays by Bernard Shaw</u> show that Shaw has not lost "his pithy Shavian wit." The Preface to <u>The Six of Calais</u> is a model of invective, and <u>The Simpleton of the Unexpected Isles</u> is a profound attack on the worship of delusions. [Critical opinions quoted from the NYT, NY SUN, HARTFORD (Conn.) TIMES, NYHTBR, and NYTBR.]

514 Poore, C. G. "Bernard Shaw in His Role As Grand Disquisitor," NYTBR, 17 May 1936, p. 2.

Shaw's plays have not become better in recent times; in fact, some playwrights who learned from him are surpassing their master. Still, he remains the "Grand Disquisitor of the modern stage." The prefaces to his recent plays are seditious, stirring people to look at the world as it is. He does repeat himself, though, as in the Preface to The Six of Calais.

515 Saxe, Joseph. BERNARD SHAW'S PHONETICS: A COMPARATIVE STUDY OF COCKNEY SOUND-CHANGES (Copenhagen: Levin & Munksgaard; Lond: George Allen & Unwin, 1936).
[A comparison of the Cockney dialect of the middle and of the end of the nineteenth century, using PUNCH, THE LOND CHARIVARI from the 1850's and 1860's as the source of mid-century Cockney and using Shaw's examples of Cockney speech in his plays as the source of late-nineteenth century Cockney. Deals in passing with Shaw's advocacy of phonetic spelling, Shavian eccentricities in spelling, typographical anomalies in Shaw, and Shaw's interest in Cockney vowels. Concludes that little phonetic difference exists in Cockney speech between the two periods.]

516 Schnell, Jonathan. "Books: A Causerie," FORUM, XCVI (July 1936), iv-vii, espec iv.
Shaw is waning, and his faults are being exaggerated. In The Simpleton of the Unexpected Isles, he is a puppet master manipulating figures who nevertheless "talk divertingly enough." Shaw "still deserves a crowd...and strong handclaps."

517 Schöpflin, Aladár. "Szent Johanna a Belvárosiban" (Saint Joan in the Downtown [Theater]), NYUGAT (1936), I, 241-244.
In Saint Joan, Shaw's theme of natural human rationality confronting the convolutions and falsehoods of society is carried through more clearly and unequivocally than in his other plays. Saint Joan is one of the few plays of our time that can lay claim to being of lasting and timeless worth. [In Hungarian.]

518 Scott-James, R. A. "Stimulus for Drama," CHRISTIAN SCIENCE MONITOR MAGAZINE, 16 Feb 1936, p. 9.

Shaw for twenty-five years has been a member of the committee to establish a National Theater which has not yet materialized. [An argument for the establishment of a National Theater in England.]

519 Sedgwick, Ruth Woodbury. "Saint Joan," STAGE (NY), XII (April 1936), 30-33.
The Katharine Cornell version of Saint Joan is intellectually stimulating and emotionally intense. Shaw's play has "power and beauty"; it is "an epic of the soul." [A résumé of Joan in literature and on stage.]

520 Sen Gupta, S[ubodh] C[handra]. THE ART OF BERNARD SHAW (Lond, NY, Bombay, Calcutta, Madras: Oxford UP, 1936; 2nd rvd ed Calcutta: A. Mukherjee, 1936; rptd Folcroft, Pa.: Folcroft P, 1969).
Shaw defies convention, romance, and sentimentalism and places credence in instinct and intuition; he sees world problems as having either biological or economic solutions. Such theoretical ideas form the basis of Shaw's drama. He is able to combine both art and morality in sui generis plays that combine "deadly earnestness" with "light-hearted triviality." This combination of the serious and comic leads to comic plays which do not adequately represent the author's philosophy (explained in prefaces). For example, The Doctor's Dilemma, Getting Married, Misalliance, Fanny's First Play, The Apple Cart, On the Rocks, Heartbreak House, and Too True To Be Good fall short of excellence because Shaw approaches problems indirectly and because he insists on discussing "serious questions in romping farces." In most of his plays, he fails to understand deep, serious human emotions (exceptions: Pygmalion and John Bull's Other Island). At his best, however, Shaw gives life and concreteness to abstract social forces (as in Androcles and the Lion, Major Barbara, Widowers' Houses, Mrs. Warren's Profession, O'Flaherty, V. C., Candida, Captain Brassbound's Conversion, Saint Joan) or draws a picture of a superman-hero in which the conflict is not external but between will and passion. Shaw's "metabiological drama" is spoiled by his regarding sexual attraction as a mere instrument of creative will. As a novelist, Shaw lacks the ability to invent and manage complex plots; and as a critic, Shaw applies a personal standard that leads to a misunderstanding of Shakespeare and a distortion of Ibsen.

118

521 "The Shape of Things: Mr. Shaw Is Always at His Happiest When," NATION, CXLIII (26 Sept 1936), 349-51.
Shaw is in an argument with a Catholic action group which is purportedly trying to censor the movie version of Saint Joan.

522 "SHAW: Alarmed at Censorship, He Writes Letter to the Times," NEWS-WEEK, VIII (19 Sept 1936), 44.
In a three-column letter to the NYT, Shaw attacked a Catholic action organization for threatening to censor Saint Joan. Shaw's invective was merely free publicity for Saint Joan.

523 "Shaw Bounces His Wit Into Miami," LITERARY DIGEST, CXXI (15 Feb 1936), 29.
[Account of Shaw's visit to Miami—mostly quotations of his remarks.]

524 "Shaw on Catholic Censorship," CHRISTIAN CENTURY, LIII (23 Sept 1936), 1244.
In a letter to the NYT, Shaw shows what Catholic standards are. Saint Joan is a great, truly religious play. Yet in order to have Catholic approval of its filming in Hollywood, "the play must be destroyed." The trial scene must be rewritten, and words such as "paradise," "halo," "damned," "God," etc., must be deleted.

525 "Shaw's Latest Play Given in England: One Critic's View Is Playwright Had Eye on Films When He Wrote 'Millionairess,'" NYT, 18 Nov 1936, p. 30.
The Millionairess is like an entertaining cartoon, with its central character "an extraordinary, exuberant addition to the Shavian theatre" (British premiere performance, Forsyth Players, Bexhill).

526 Smodlaka, Luka. "Bernard Šo: povodom njegove 80-godišnjice" (Bernard Shaw: On the Occasion of his 80th Birthday), JAVNOST (Belgrade), II, No 31 (1936), 683-85.
Shaw's work has two aspects: one critical of contemporary life and conventionality, the other with visions of great possibilities in the future. In his first period, Shaw was a dialectical writer; in the second, a poet and thinker.

Shaw represents the drama of ideas and dramatized thought, and is the most versatile of English writers. [In Serbian.]

527 Sobra, Adrien. "Les Femmes dans le théâtre de G. Bernard Shaw," (Women in the Theater of G. Bernard Shaw), REVUE DE L'ENSEIGNEMENT DES LANGUAGES VIVANTES, No 2 (Feb 1936), pp. 49-57; No 3 (March 1936), pp. 109-115; No 4 (April 1936), pp. 164-74; No 5 (May 1936), pp. 198-211.

Shaw's women are mere puppets, voicing their author's ideas. They are the victims of the Life Force, mother-women bent on perpetuating the species. Sometimes the puppet revolts and becomes a real, living woman. Sometimes the Galatea is an intelligent creature who, in a paradoxical situation, transforms Pygmalion. Shaw's women therefore are often stronger than men, and the forerunners of a new civilization. Some minor characters embody the different types Shaw discovered in the universe: the Instinct-Woman, the Brain-Woman, and the Statue-Woman. The first is of little interest; the third only reveals the character of man. Only the second, who abounds in Shaw's plays, is worth studying. [In French.]

528 St. John, Christopher [pseud of Christabel Marshall]. "Socrates or Polonius?" NS&Nation, XI (4 April 1936), 531.

The Simpleton of the Unexpected Isles will not play well; it is Shaw's "most puzzling play," and is unintelligible. The Angel is Shaw's own voice; his conception of the Last Judgment does not take into account "where the eternal impinges on the temporal." In The Millionairess, the Preface explains the theme. Epifania dominates "through vulgar abuse, and physical violence." The Six of Calais is "a childish extravaganza about which the less said the better." Shaw should have curbed his pen in writing these plays.

529 "STAGE: 'Saint Joan'--Artistic, But Not a Financial, Triumph," NEWS-WEEK, VII (21 March 1936), 22.

Saint Joan (Martin Beck Theater, NY) is an artistic success but a financial failure because of large production costs. [Photographs of Cornell as Joan.]

530 Stresau, Hermann. "George Bernard Shaw," NEUE RUNDSCHAU, XLVII (1936), 818-25.
Shaw is a passionate moralist with a preference for paradox. He has a Puritan fear of the ambiguous and the abysmal. An ascetic view of life urged him to become a teacher rather than a poet. [In German.]

531 Swinnerton, Frank. SWINNERTON: AN AUTOBIOGRAPHY (NY: Doubleday, Doran & Co, 1936), pp. 57, 58-62, 63, 64, 184-85, 219-20.
When the intellects of the day congregated at Essex Hall or Memorial Hall, heated discussions sometimes became inhumane. Shaw often restored everyone to good humor with his mixture of "chaff," "seriousness," and "flattery." Indeed, he could capture the wise as well as the malcontent. Moreover, his incisive mind made him the best debater in London.

532 "Theatre Arts Bookshelf: More Shaw," TAM, XX (Sept 1936), 748-50.
The plays in Three Plays (Dodd, Mead) say something of value, though it is hidden in "prolixity or excess preachment." And the prefaces are always lively and interesting.

533 "The Theatre: Shaw's Saint," TIME, XXVII (23 March 1936), 55.
Katharine Cornell's revival (Grand Opera House, Chicago) of Saint Joan shows Shaw in "one glorious swoop of spiritual free-wheeling."

534 Timmler, Markus. "Die Anschauungen Bernard Shaws über die Aufgabe des Theaters auf Grund seiner Theorie und Praxis" (Bernard Shaw's Opinions on the Function of the Theater on the Strength of his Theory and his Practice). Published dissertation, University of Königsberg, 1936; pub under same title (Breslau: Priebatsch, 1936).
Shaw chose the theater as a vehicle for his convictions because of its great influence on public life, on morals and on the individual life. His theater is a social organ; his plays are didactic, being neither comedies nor tragedies. His plays of ideas offer little humor, but much satire and irony. As a philosopher-artist Shaw considers

language to be a way of communication and does not favor an ornamental style. Enlightenment, education, and amusement are the main functions of Shaw's theater. [In German.]

535 Titterton, W[illiam] R[ichard]. G. K. CHESTERTON: A PORTRAIT (Lond: A. Ouseley, 1936; rptd Lond: D. Organ, 1947), pp. 19, 42, 44, 56, 62-74, 75, 79, 93, 94, 182-83, 184-87, 227.
[An account of the Shaw-Chesterton debate (1927) from the point of view of a Chesterton partisan.] Shaw is intelligent, intelligible, sincere—a worthy antagonist for Chesterton. The debate destroyed socialism.

536 Trebitsch, S[iegfried]. "Der deutsche Aufstieg Bernard Shaws" (Bernard Shaw's German Ascent), SHAW KOMPENDIUM: VERZEICHNIS UND ANALYSE SEINER WERKE: VERZEICHNIS SEINER WERKE IN ENGLAND UND DEUTSCHLAND (Shaw Compendium: List and Analysis of His Works: List of the Performances of his Works in England and Germany) (Paris: Henri Didier, 1936), ed by X[avier] Heydet, pp. 139-47.
[Trebitsch surveys his own work, as translator and promoter, to gain a hearing for Shaw's work in Germany.] [In German.]

537 Van Doren, Mark. "The Rest of William Morris," NATION, CXLIII (15 Aug 1936), 192-93.
It is difficult to say whether or not a generation that never knew William Morris will value his life and work as highly as Shaw does. [Review of three volumes on Morris, one containing William Morris As I Knew Him.]

538 Vernon, Grenville. "The Play and Screen: Saint Joan," COMMONWEAL, XXIII (27 March 1936), 609.
The only two Shavian figures who are not merely replicas or abstracts of Shaw himself are Candida and Joan. In the presence of Joan (played by Katharine Cornell, Martin Beck Theater, NY) Shaw is humble. His ideas have not changed over fifty years.

539 Whitman, Willson. "A Pair of Protestants," STAGE (NY), XIII (June 1936), 66-67.
Saint Joan explains not only the Maid but Shaw as playwright. Shaw identifies with the rebelliousness and

independence of spirit of Joan. Like her, Shaw wants to do God's work. Both establish themselves as heaven's messengers, fight impersonally for their goals, and are personally abstemious. Significantly, Saint Joan does not end with martyrdom; the epilog revives Joan. So too Shaw has survived the Great War, when most dramatists have not. His late plays are challenging, on a higher level than the early ones; "when religion again becomes popular, Mr. Shaw will be canonized."

540 Wilson, Edmund. "The Octogenarian Shaw," NEW REPUBLIC, LXXXVII (24 June 1936), 209-10.
In Three New Plays Shaw is showing his age; his ideas are finally becoming outdated. His susceptibility to romantic individualism leads him to look for strong men to lead society rather than for a revolutionary leader. His ideas lead to fascism as easily as to communism. In The Simpleton of the Unexpected Isles he sets up a theocratic rather than a Marxist tribunal; and in the Preface to The Millionairess he glorifies Mussolini and even praises Hitler.

541 Woolf, S. J. "Outwitting the Wittiest," READER'S DIGEST, XXVIII (April 1936), 24.
[Account of getting Shaw to pose for a sketch.]

542 Wyatt, Euphemia Van Rensselaer. "The Drama: St. Joan," CATHOLIC WORLD, CXLIII (April 1936), 85-90, espec 85-86.
Saint Joan (Martin Beck Theater, NY) is "not only the epic of a saint but the tragedy of this world's reactions to sanctity." Shaw found in Joan a subject "greater than he had imagined." Contrary to Shaw, Joan was orthodox, and her trial was unfair.

543 Young, Stark. "The McClintics' Shaw," NEW REPUBLIC, LXXXVI (25 March 1936), 198.
The Guthrie McClintic direction of Saint Joan (Martin Beck Theater, NY) cuts down on Shavian fooling and makes the characters seem more real. Saint Joan, however, is not a great play; it is flawed by garrulousness, confusion in detail, the author's personal assertions, and "a stupid and obvious epilogue." But the clash of individual conscience versus traditional authority lifts the play "to the plane of greatness" in the trial scene.

544 Zeller, Hermann. "Die Frauengestalten in Bernard Shaws Dramatischen Werken" (The Women in Bernard Shaw's Plays). Unpublished dissertation, University of Tübingen, 1936. [Listed in McNamee, and in Altick and Matthews, Item 1764.] [In German.]

1937

---

545 Agate, James. "The Dramatic World: Wuthering Depths," TIMES (Lond), 21 Nov 1937, p. 6; rptd Agate, THE AMAZING THEATRE (Lond, Toronto, Bombay, Sydney: Harrap, 1939), pp. 49-54, espec 51-53.
Shaw's emendation of Shakespeare in Cymbeline Refinished (Embassy Theater, Lond) is like Gershwin to Mozart, or calico to brocade. The audience is unprepared for Imogen the emancipated woman.

546 Anderson Imbert, Enrique. "De Ibsen a Shaw" (From Ibsen to Shaw), LA FLECHA EN EL AIRE (The Arrow in the Air) (Buenos Aires, La Vanguardia, 1937), pp. 8-15; rptd enlarged edition Buenos Aires: Ediciones Guré, 1972.
Ibsen and Shaw are linked in the history of modern theater by mutual preoccupations. The main difference is the abundance of philosophy in Shaw, and the absence of it in Ibsen. [In Spanish.]

547 Anderson Imbert, Enrique. "'Santa Juana,' de Shaw, en una interpretación magnífica de M. Xirga" (Shaw's Saint Joan, in a Magnificent Interpretation by M. Xirga), LA VANGUARDIA (Argentina), 22 May 1937. [Favorable review of Saint Joan, as interpreted by the Spanish actress Margarita Xirga.] [In Spanish.]

548 Atkinson, Brooks. "The Play: Katharine Cornell Appearing in a Revival of Shaw's 'Candida,'" NYT, 11 March 1937, p. 20.
Katharine Cornell's Candida (Empire Theater, NY) has "pity and wisdom" in Shaw's "most perfect stage piece."

549 Atkinson, Brooks. "Shaw's 'Candida': Katharine Cornell's Revival Restores Interest in a Fine Play," NYT, 21 March 1937, XI, p. 1.
Candida has humanity, sincerity and charm; its theme is the need for love. With Katharine Cornell (Empire Theater, NY) in the lead, it offers "one of the most winning portraits of a woman in the English drama."

550 Barzun, Jacques. RACE: A STUDY IN MODERN SUPERSTITION (NY: Harcourt, Brace, 1937), pp. 12, 282-93, 302.
To place Shaw in a category of race, typically white and Irish, is misleading. The "race-national classification" does not work with him, for he could not be a socialist if he were truly an Irishman. Indeed, to call him either "a bourgeois mind or a revolutionary mind without further qualification is patently absurd."

551 Becker, May Lamberton. "Read this one First," SCHOLASTIC, XXXI (2 Oct 1937), 24-E.
Shaw is "as much an institution as a man." Though much of his writing is dated, his spirit looks toward the future.

552 Brown, Ivor. "The World of the Theatre: A Season of Performance," ILN, CXC (27 Feb 1937), 356.
Unlike much of Shaw's work, Candida (Globe Theater, Lond) "touches humanity keenly." The political parson is not assaulted but treated sympathetically. Ann Harding plays a serene and strong Candida.

553 Bruton, Percy. "Shavian Adventures," ADVENTURES AMONG IMMORTALS: PERCY BRUTON—IMPRESARIO, AS TOLD TO LOWELL THOMAS (NY: Dodd; Toronto: McClelland, 1937; Lónd: Hutchinson, 1938), pp. 183-201.
Shaw is "a first-rate practical man of the theatre." [Anecdotes by a manager of stars about Shaw's business sense, his way with actors and other celebrities, and his dealings with productions of his plays.]

554 C., N. "Mr. Shaw on Music," MANCHESTER GUARDIAN, 8 Oct 1937, p. 8.
London Music reflects in magnificent prose a professional knowledge of music and an ability to see through the second-rate.

555 Churchill, Winston S. "George Bernard Shaw," GREAT CONTEMPORARIES (Lond: Butterworth; NY: Putnam's, 1937), pp. 35-44; rev. ed. Lond: Butterworth, 1938; rptd Lond: Reader's Union, Butterworth, 1939; Lond: The Reprint Society, 1941; Lond: Fontana Books, 1959; Freeport, NY: Books for Libraries P, 1971; Chicago: University of Chicago P, 1973; rptd in A RHETORIC READER, ed by Erwin Hester (Englewood Cliffs, NJ: Prentice-Hall, 1967), pp. 175-77.

Shaw invented the Life Force to replace religion, made God a socialist, and fashioned heaven in his own political image. The main innovation of his plays was to depend on the interplay of ideas for dramatic effect; he broke the well-made play "by not 'making' it at all." Shaw was an original and profound thinker, but often inconsistent; and his keen wit was often mixed with "bombinating nonsense." He was frequently unmindful of the effects of his remarks on the convictions of others and sometimes misused his genius and fame, e.g., in his praise of Russia after his trip there. Despite all this, he is still "the greatest living master of letters in the English-speaking world."

556 "Corno di Basetto," TLS, XXXVI (2 Oct 1937), 709.

London Music in 1888-89 has a good autobiographical Preface and refreshing criticism. However, Shaw was too enamored of Wagner, and thus slighted Brahms and Weber.

557 Cunningham, James P. "The Play and Screen: Candida," COMMONWEAL, XXV (26 March 1937), 612.

Katharine Cornell's revival of Candida (Empire, NY), "Shaw's best play," is among her finest efforts. In Saint Joan and Candida Shaw created real characters (except for Marchbanks, "a hang-over from the poets of the YELLOW BOOK"). But otherwise Shaw's ideas and characters are dead.

558 Delpech, Jeanine. "A propos de 'Candida': des influences subies par Bernard Shaw" (Concerning Candida: Some Influences on Bernard Shaw), LES NOUVELLES LITTÉRAIRES, 10 July 1937.

Candida, performed in English at the Théâtre des Champs-Elysées, provides one of the greatest figures of Shaw's theater. Yet Shaw is little known in France in spite of his

126

struggle to defend values that are now recognized (e.g., Wagner and Ibsen). He has a caustic wit but at the same time a great sense of discretion. He was influenced by Shelley, Dickens, Butler, and Ibsen, who forced audiences to face unpleasant facts. [In French.]

559 Dickinson, Thomas H. THE THEATER IN A CHANGING EUROPE (NY: Holt, 1937; Lond: Putnam; Toronto: McClelland, 1938), pp. 87, 155, 184, 214, 241, 261, 283, 289, 303, 309, 340, 346, 353, 420, 428, 430, Index.
[Passing brief references in articles by various authors to Shaw's similarity to or difference from various modern European dramatists, and to productions of his plays in various European theaters. Neither comprehensive nor very helpful.]

560 Downes, Olin. "A Promising Young Critic Called Bernard Shaw," NYTBR, 31 Oct 1937, pp. 4, 24.
London Music in 1888-89 is not a profound critical exploration in the art of music, but it is full of the "sparkle of [Shaw's] thought and his overflowing abundance of ideas." He has a good ear and a solid knowledge of music. In Shaw's introduction, he makes many hasty, ill-advised remarks about Brahms as well as Wagner. Still, the musical criticism is entertaining and original.

561 Drew, Elizabeth. DISCOVERING DRAMA (NY: Norton; Lond: Cape; Toronto: McLeod, 1937), pp. 26, 36, 91, 92, 110, 120, 137, 147, 148-50, 152-55, 164, 169, 170, 180, 197, 199, 208, Index.
The two great writers of English satiric comedy, Ben Jonson and Shaw, write very different satire: "Jonson is passionate, violent and abusive; Shaw is suave, rational and witty." Yet both see life as it is. Shaw attacks romantic illusions, using intellect and reason to challenge convention. In his plays, his ideas—not his characters— are alive; his characters, who symbolize his ideas, constitute a full-scale comment on modern life. Shaw's gospel may never be fulfilled, but his comedy will live because of its style and intellectual verve. [Passim references to Shaw's works and opinions as illustrations of the dramatist as craftsperson, as artist, etc.]

562 Ehrmann, Ruth. "George Bernard Shaw und der Viktorianische Sozialismus" (George Bernard Shaw and Victorian Socialism). Unpublished dissertation, University of Basel, 1937. [Listed in Altick and Matthews, Item 1718.] [In German.]

563 F., D. C. "'Candida,'" THEATRE WORLD (Lond), XXVII (March 1937), 110.
Candida is "strangely archaic and unmoving"; its problem is dated, and "the period is not sufficiently remote to give the play the value of a museum piece." The Globe (Lond) revival is well-acted.

564 Fotez, Marko. "Shaw opet na nasoj pozornici. Pred današnjiu izvedbu drame Candida" (Shaw Again on our Stage: Before Today's Production of Candida), NOVOSTI (Zagreb), XXI, No 130 (1937), 9. [Not seen but listed in FILOLOGIJA (Zagreb), III (1962), 263.] [In Croatian.]

565 Funke, Otto. DIE SCHWEIZ UND DIE ENGLISCHE LITERATUR (Switzerland and English Literature) (Bern: A. Francke, 1937), pp. 12, 56.
Bluntschli in Arms and the Man is the embodiment of the Swiss national character. He bears abundant evidence of the resemblance of the Swiss race to the English race. [In German.]

566 Hackett, J. P. GEORGE VERSUS BERNARD (NY: Sheed & Ward, 1937; rptd Folcroft, Pa.: Folcroft Library Editions, 1974).
Shaw is steadfast of purpose and honest in thought and expression. After his early novels, art became his religion, with creative artists the prophets. He used the mask of clown as "a special license to go anywhere and say anything." Though he purported to reject reason as the motivating force for humanity, he accepted it in terms of "conscience" or "self-control." "He hugs his contradictions and magically turns them into an international reputation for anti-climax." His dramatic technique is to offer a series of pictures, each with high emotional content; he begins with his conclusion and then illustrates it with lively applications and instances. [Includes analysis of

the novels; The Quintessence of Ibsenism, "the keel of his dramatic career"; and the major plays.]

567 Henderson, Archibald. "Bernard Shaw at Eighty," YALE UNIVERSITY LIBRARY GAZETTE, XII (Oct 1937), 18-30.
[Lecture delivered 15 Feb 1937 at Yale University on the occasion of the exhibit of the Archibald Henderson Collection of Shaviana, given to Yale.] Shaw has common sense, though he has written much nonsense. He gives "unusual and bizarre reasons for taking the right course of action." [Adulatory comments on Shaw's integrity, his greatness of soul.] He is not modest and self-deprecatory; he challenges majority opinion. He is "a passionate worshipper with an authentic martyr complex." He sacrifices himself to his work; is an ascetic; is—contrary to critics—"a natural dramatist." He wrote "five weird novels, full of a horrible humor and a shocking lack of good taste." But he is "a first-class playwright" and "a master of rehearsal." His plays contain "most of the leading ideas of the day"; their structure is innovative—organic rather than "constructed," discussions resulting from the clash of ideas. He is a poet, as revealed in Dubedat, Caesar, and Saint Joan. he was a captivating speaker, music critic, drama critic. He is in politics, as once in philosophy, a pragmatist; in matters of sex, a literary romancer.

568 HENDERSON MEMORIAL COLLECTION OF SHAW, YALE UNIVERSITY LIBRARY GAZETTE, XII (Oct 1937).
[Issue focusses on the Henderson Memorial Collection of Shaw, given to Yale; contains William Lyon Phelps, "Introduction to Archibald Henderson," p. 17; Archibald Henderson, "Bernard Shaw at Eighty," pp. 18-30, q.v.; "The Henderson Memorial Collection of Shaw," pp. 31-37, an account of the lecture, collection, and exhibit; various photographs of art works of Shaw in the exhibit; and reprints of some Shaw letters and inscriptions.]

569 Heydet, Xavier. "Richard Wagner et Bernard Shaw" (Richard Wagner and Bernard Shaw), REVUE DE L'ENSEIGNEMENT DES LANGUES VIVANTES, June 1937, pp. 245-58.

Shaw and Wagner are kindred spirits, with the same interest in revolution and social justice, the same conception of art and its function. Wagner's influence on Shaw corresponds to Wagner's ideas in the 1848-1854 years but does not extend beyond that period. In The Perfect Wagnerite, Shaw gives his personal, Fabian interpretation of Wagner's ideas and of Siegfried, the anarchist, immoralist hero. [In French.]

570 Honma, Hisao. "Shaw to Nihon" (Shaw and Japan), WAGA KANSHO NO SEKAI (The World of My Appreciation) (Tokyo: Toen Shobo, 1937), pp. 44-47.
Shaw first attracted wide attention in Japan with The Quintessence of Ibsenism around 1909 when the naturalistic literary movement was flourishing. His iconoclasm was received with keen interest. Shaw also exerted a considerable influence over the Japanese feminist movement in the 1910's. [In Japanese.]

571 Irzykowski, Karol. "G. B. Shaw: Szczygli zaulek" (G. B. Shaw: Widowers' Houses), PION (Warsaw), No 7 (1937), p. 5; rptd in Irzykowski, RECENZJE TEATRALNE: WYBÓR (Theatrical Reviews: A Selection) (Warsaw: Państwowy Instytut Wydawniczy, 1965), pp. 552-54.
In Widowers' Houses Shaw is primarily a dramatist, losing no opportunity for powerful scenes, though the play is really a lecture on socialism. Unfortunately, his opponents are weakly characterized: Trench has no notion of economic or social matters. The play is reminiscent of Ibsen and some Polish plays and novels of the 1890's. [In Polish.]

572 Isaacs, Edith J. R. "The Pleasure in Good Acting: Broadway in Review," TAM, XXI (May 1937), 339-49, espec 344-48.
Candida "seems today better, more surely written, kinder, more human than ever." Katharine Cornell's Candida (Empire Theater, NY) makes the play "fresh and relevant to our day."

573 Krutch, Joseph Wood. "Drama: What Every Woman Knows," NATION, CXLIV (27 March 1937), 361-62.
Candida (Katharine Cornell revival, Empire Theater, NY) is intellectually iconoclastic but comes to a Victorian conclusion: that understanding outweighs romantic passion,

and that the best husband is the one who needs his wife
most. In fact, Candida is the same as James M. Barrie's
WHAT EVERY WOMAN KNOWS, with Shavian fireworks added.
Shaw's characters are lively, and have a theatrical
concreteness that makes them more than puppets.

574   Lockridge, Richard. [Candida review], NY SUN, 11
March 1937 [not seen in this form]; rptd in Katharine
Cornell, I WANTED TO BE AN ACTRESS (NY: Random House;
Toronto: Macmillan, 1939), pp. 338-40.
Candida (Katharine Cornell revival, Empire Theater, NY) is
an "untarnished" play—stimulating and moving. Marchbanks
is perhaps too intense, so that one is relieved when
Candida chooses the parson.

575   Lorenz, Rolf. "Bernard Shaws Auseinandersetzung
mit der Tragik des Daseins" (Bernard Shaw's Quarrel
with the Tragedy of Existence). Unpublished
dissertation, University of Marburg, 1937. [Listed in
McNamee, and in Altick and Matthews, Item 1736.] [In
German.]

576   McCague, Wilma Gallagher. "The Influence of
Shaw's Experience as a Director of Plays on his Stage
Directions." Unpublished dissertation, Ohio State
University, 1937. [Listed in Frederic M. Litto,
AMERICAN DISSERTATIONS ON THE DRAMA AND THE THEATRE
(Kent: Kent UP, 1969), p. 62.]

577   MacCarthy, Desmond. "Miscellany: 'Candida,
Candida, Candida,'" NS&Nation, XIII (20 Feb 1937),
284-85.
Candida (Globe Theater, Lond) is still capable of riveting
an audience, but the ideas are no longer startling. And
casting a lovely movie star, Ann Harding, as the "clever,
hardworking, unfathomably sensible wife of an East End
clergyman" is a blunder.

578   McKay, Claude. "Adventuring in Search of George
Bernard Shaw," A LONG WAY FROM HOME (NY: Lee Furman,
1937), pp. 59-65.
Shaw has a wise and penetrating intellect, and is capable
of poetic utterance (e.g., in Candida). He also has "animal

cunning and cleverness." [Personal account of meeting with Shaw.]

579 Mackworth, Margaret Haig (Thomas) (2nd Viscountess Rhondda). "The Apple Cart," NOTES ON THE WAY (NY: Macmillan, 1937; rptd Freeport, NY: Books for Libraries P, 1968), pp. 186-93.
The Apple Cart reflects Shaw's consistently pro-socialist and anti-democratic stance. Shaw has a genius for diagnosing problems but his judgment is impaired when he proposes solutions. For example, the villain of The Apple Cart is human heartlessness, but Shaw puts up private enterprise as the whipping boy.

580 Mackworth, Margaret Haig (Thomas) (2nd Viscountess Rhondda). "Shaw on Sex," NOTES ON THE WAY (NY: Macmillan, 1937; rptd Freeport, NY: Books for Libraries P, 1968), pp. 71-75.
Shaw's views on sex are unpopular, but they are a truthful reflection of most normal people's views.

581 Mackworth, Margaret Haig (Thomas) (2nd Viscountess Rhondda). "That Gadfly," NOTES ON THE WAY (NY: Macmillan, 1937; rptd Freeport, NY: Books for Libraries P, 1968), pp. 194-98.
Old age is usually treated chivalrously by the press. But Shaw, in his eighties, is attacked for senility by his exasperated critics. Shaw has spent his life advocating unpalatable ideas—and continues with wit and acumen to do so.

582 Mackworth, Margaret Haig (Thomas) (2nd Viscountess Rhondda). "Too True to Be Good," NOTES ON THE WAY (NY: Macmillan, 1937; rptd Freeport, NY: Books for Libraries P, 1968), pp. 198-205.
The reputation of Too True To Be Good will grow with the years. It combines excellent melodrama, unforgettable character portraits, and a magnificent final speech. The Burglar-Clergyman offers "a masterly analysis of the world chaos and depression of today"; and Mops is a clever reflection of an entire tendency in modern women toward independence and sisterhood.

583 "Malvern Festival: 'The Millionairess,'" TIMES (Lond), 27 July 1937, p. 12.
The Millionairess combines "farce and fisticuffs" with an unobtrusive political moral (mostly confined to the Preface). Some of the "Shavian tricks" in the play have worn thin.

584 María y Campos, Armando. "'Santa Juana,' de Shaw" (Shaw's Saint Joan), PRESENCIAS DE TEATRO (CRÓNICAS 1934-1936) (Theater Appearances [Chronicles 1934-1936]) (Mexico: Ediciones Populares, 1937), pp. 285-94.
Saint Joan is not a chronicle, as Shaw called it, but rather an essay on the "case" around Joan of Arc. She represents the two forces that destroyed the horizon of the Middle Ages and made possible the modern world: the free examination of the spiritual order and nationalism. Both concepts share the same ground: the acknowledgement of God over the ecclesiastical hierarchy and of the king over the feudal society. It is necessary, then, that both orders suppress Joan, a patriot and a protestant. [In Spanish.]

585 Morgan, Charles. "Of Miss Ann Harding as Candida," NYT, 28 Feb 1937, XI, p. 1.
Candida is an exception to Shaw's cold-blooded characters; she is, at least as portrayed by Ann Harding (Globe Theater, Lond), "his only character is whom kindness, charity and wisdom shine through the wit."

586 "Music: Basset Horn," TIME, XXX (11 Oct 1937), 48-49.
London Music in 1888-89 reminds readers that Shaw succeeded as a music critic by "being flip" and ignoring music's technical aspect, though he had a thorough background in music.

587 N[ogami], T[oyoichiro]. "G.B.S. no Kingyo 3 Pen" (Recent Three Plays of G.B.S.), EIBUNGAKU KENKYU (Tokyo), XVII, No 2 (April 1937), 284-90; incorporated as chap 17 in his enlgd ed of BERNARD SHAW (Tokyo: Tokyodo, 1949 [first pub in 1935]).
The theme of The Simpleton of the Unexpected Isles, presupposing a group marriage as a eugenic experiment, can be traced back to Shaw's earlier works, such as Getting

Married, Misalliance, and Back to Methuselah. But Simpleton
is more fantastic and more allegorical, though its
expression is more realistic than romantic. The
Millionairess proposes that not all are equal before the
law. And there exists always a boss like Epifania. It is
only democracy or communism that can put a boss like her to
good use for everybody. [In Japanese.]

588 Norwood, Gilbert. "G. B. S. Respectful,"
CANADIAN FORUM, XVII (May 1937), 64.
William Morris As I Knew Him is both a contribution to the
history of socialism and a vivid portrait of early Shaw
associates. The prose is creditable and the memoir is
engaging, reflecting Shaw's respect for Morris.

589 "Plays and Pictures: Heartbreak House,
Westminster," NS&Nation, XIII (20 March 1937), 480.
Heartbreak House (Westminster Theater, Lond) has "wildly
improbable" characters who are merely a burlesque, although
they do not really burlesque anything. But Shaw's
argumentative reasoning and wit are felicitous.

590 "Plays and Pictures: Pygmalion, The Old Vic,"
NS&Nation, XIV (2 Oct 1937), 488.
Pygmalion was "rapturously received" at the Old Vic by an
audience that still thinks middle-class morality is a "good
joke."

591 Praz, Mario. "George Bernard Shaw," STORIA DELLA
LETTERATURA INGLESE (History of English Literature)
(Florence: Sansoni, 1937), pp. 367-70.
Shaw was in a position to consider England with all the
irreverence of an Irishman. It is not in his positive
aspect of social reformer, but in his apparently frivolous
denunciation of property, religion, and science that Shaw
made his subversive point of view palatable to his British
audience. [Brief bio-bibliographical sketch.] [In Italian.]

592 "'Pyg' Show Stands on Own Feet," STAGE (NY), XIV
(Aug 1937), 76.
[A review of the NY opening of Pygmalion in 1914, as though
it were written by Sime Silverman, for the "Fond Memories
Number" of STAGE.] Pygmalion has funny situations and

lines, though the "sanguinary word" that shocked London makes less impact on American audiences.

593 "REVIVAL: Katharine Cornell Fails Bernard Shaw in Candida, or Vice Versa," NEWS-WEEK, IX (20 March 1937), 22.
Candida is "high-powered hokum," and Katharine Cornell (Empire Theater, NY) is "a Candida of sexless serenity."

594 Savchenko, S. "Tvorchiĭ shliakh Bernarda Shou" (Bernard Shaw's Creative Progress), LITERATURNA KRITIKA, XII: 1 (1937), 74-75. [Not seen but listed in Bunich Remizov, RADIANSKA LITERATUROZNAVSTVO, XII: 1, 1968, 60.] [In Ukrainian.]

595 Schlöser, Anselm. DIE ENGLISCHE LITERATUR IN DEUTSCHLAND VON 1895 BIS 1934 (English Literature in Germany from 1895 to 1934) (Jena: Verlag der Frommannschen Buchhandlung Walter Biedermann, 1937), pp. 44-45, 51, 55, 60, 61, 92-101, 126-27, 138, 144, 290-94, 431, 489-90.
Shaw is one of the most popular authors in Germany. The Germans have played Shaw more constantly and widely than the British or Americans have. [Discusses the quality of Siegfried Trebitsch's translations. A survey of the most important first nights in Germany and a complete list of all German translations of Shaw's works.] [In German.]

596 Schöpflin, Aladar. "Színház: Bemutatók" (Theater: Openings), NYUGAT, II (1937), 462-66, espec 464-65.
Through its characters Major Barbara provides Shaw numerous mouthpieces for his views on modern society. He turns the machine guns of his wit on some of the pillars of society: religious hypocrisy, uncritical sentimentality, and capitalistic cynicism. Though Shaw himself is the only figure revealed as a whole person, the characters have enough human traits to be accepted as people. Shaw as dramatic poet manages to rise above Shaw as preacher. [In Hungarian.]

597 Sedgwick, Ruth Woodbury. "From G106-107," STAGE (NY), XIV (April 1937), 78, 80, espec 78.

"Candida seems not only undated but practically advance news." The Katharine Cornell revival (Empire Theater, NY) makes Candida "a unique monument to the greatness and wisdom of a woman's heart."

598 "Shaw on Music," SRL, XVII (13 Nov 1937), 14.
The criticism in London Music is good for an amateur. The forty pages of autobiographical particulars are a must for Shavians.

599 Shawe, Christopher. "Corno di Bassetto," SPECTATOR, CLIX (12 Nov 1937), 860, 862.
Shaw "never missed anything": he used his eyes; knew music; has "astonishingly sure" taste. London Music in 1888-89 is good, though not as good as Music in London, 1890-94, "the most entertaining books on music in existence."

600 "Stage and Screen: Katharine Cornell: Superb Candida," LITERARY DIGEST, CXXIII (20 March 1937), 28.
Katharine Cornell (NY Empire Theater production) plays Candida "for what she is; completely the woman; amused and not at all mystified by the vagaries of her men." Cornell, the supporting cast, and Shaw are "superb."

601 Stillman, Clara Gruening. "One Great Talker Talks About Another," NYHTBR, XIII (7 Feb 1937), 3.
Shaw's William Morris As I Knew Him is "done with affection, respect and engaging sprightliness, with the figure of Shaw as complement and foil." Shaw sees Morris as a man of noble and creative vision who wrote some of the best socialist books. Shaw's account is incisive and of course witty.

602 Tarantino, Vincent D. "Shaw the Orthodox," SAN FRANCISCO QUARTERLY, III (May 1937), 1-12.
Shaw's philosophy, derived from Ibsen, is "rather unhealthy" in that it fails to distinguish between seeming virtue and real virtue. Thus Shaw satirizes both hypocrisy and genuine goodness. Androcles and the Lion disparages Christianity and Christ; Man and Superman ridicules marriage. On the other hand, Arms and the Man, Candida, and The Devil's Disciple attack, respectively, orthodox heroism, smugness, and religiosity. Shaw lucidly portrays

stupid and wicked characters, but his noble characters are confusing. Finally, Shaw is an excellent dramatist who preaches merely to amuse himself.

603 "The Theatre: Shaw's 'Cymbeline,'" TIME, XXX (29 Nov 1937), 33.
Shaw's contempt for Shakespeare's Cymbeline led him to rewrite the play. [Statement of changes Shaw made, and quotation from Shaw's version of it.]

604 "Westminster Theatre: 'Heartbreak House,'" TIMES (Lond), 10 March 1937, p. 12.
Unlike Tolstoy and Chekhov—both artists at root—Shaw is basically a preacher using drama for moral purposes. Yet the first half of Heartbreak House is a pastiche of Chekhov, and Captain Shotover an impressive "Tolstoyan doll."

605 W[ilson], E[dmund]. "Books in Brief," NEW REPUBLIC, LXXXIX (6 Jan 1937), 309.
In William Morris As I Knew Him, Shaw admires Morris as a poet with a vision of a socialist state which is much more beautiful than pragmatic Fabian economics. It is a good memoir. Shaw is "nowadays better on the past than on the present."

606 Wilson, N. Scarlyn. EUROPEAN DRAMA (Lond: Ivor Nicholson and Watson; Toronto: S. J. R. Saunders, 1937; rptd Folcroft Library Editions, 1978), pp. 238-44.
Shaw is largely responsible for the modern revival of drama in England. He compensates for bad construction in drama with his wit and incisive social criticism. He has "a disquieting knack of being right"; insists on questioning convention; and attacks "sham idealism and sentimentality." Though a few plays—e.g., Fanny's First Play, You Never Can Tell, How He Lied to Her Husband, and Candida—are "pure comedy," most of them are profound, witty, sometimes beautiful explorations of ideas.

607 Wyatt, Euphemia Van Rensselaer. "The Drama: Candida," CATHOLIC WORLD, CXLV (May 1937), 211-15, espec 211-13.

Shaw writes some tedious plays, but Candida, Saint Joan, and the last speech in Too True To Be Good have "immortal lines." And Candida has timeless wisdom. In the current production (Empire Theater, NY) Candida is more medieval than Victorian. The triangle is really a conflict between action and spirit, and Candida embodies both domestic and ethereal realms. Shaw understood celibacy; Marchbanks must (like Saint Joan) remain alone.

608 Young, Stark. "Candida, Candida, Candida!" NEW REPUBLIC, XC (21 April 1937), 322; revised and rptd in IMMORTAL SHADOWS: A BOOK OF DRAMATIC CRITICISM (NY: Scribner's, 1948; rptd NY: Hill & Wang, 1959).
Candida (Empire Theater, NY) is an interesting melange of thoughts and theories; it is "healthy and strictly theatre," though the last scene is tiresome taken out of the context of the rest of the play.

1938

---

609 Agate, James. "The Malvern Festival (I)," TIMES (Lond), 7 Aug 1938; rptd in Agate, THE AMAZING THEATRE (Lond, Toronto, Bombay, Sydney: Harrap, 1939), pp. 148-53, espec 148-50.
The third act of Geneva (Malvern Festival production) redeems the first two, but the play needs drastic cutting. Begonia Brown is another Shavian "lifeless doll."

610 Agate, James. "The Malvern Festival (II)," TIMES (Lond), 14 Aug 1938; rptd in Agate, THE AMAZING THEATRE (Lond, Toronto, Bombay, Sydney: Harrap, 1939), pp. 154-59, espec 157-59.
Saint Joan, "one of the greatest glories in English Theatre," could well become grand opera. But Elizabeth Bergner's Joan portrayed a childish, waif-like Joan.

611 Anderson Imbert, Enrique. "Shaw, el austero" (Shaw the Austere), REPERTORIO AMERICANO (Costa Rica), XXXV, No 7 (19 Feb 1938), 109.
[Brief reference to Cunninghame Graham and Shaw.] [In Spanish.]

612 Atkinson, Brooks. "Hero of Heartbreak House," NYT, 8 May 1938, X, p. 1.
The Preface to Heartbreak House heroically told "ugly truths" to an uncomprehending world. The play (Mercury Theater, NY) is less precise and cogent. Unlike Chekhov, Shaw is a "master pamphleteer," not a realist poet; he substitutes burlesque and wit for compassion.

613 Atkinson, Brooks. "The Play: George Bernard Shaw's 'On the Rocks' Acted by a Federal Theatre Company," NYT, 16 June 1938, p. 20.
On the Rocks is too voluble and lacks structure, but it has a high level of intelligence. The Federal Theater production (Daly's Theater, NY) "is practically a flawless performance."

614 Atkinson, Brooks. "The Play: Laurette Taylor Offers 'Candida' as Postscript to the Summer Theatre Season in Westchester," NYT, 31 Aug 1938, p. 13.
[Review of Candida, Tuttle & Skinner Westchester Playhouse, NY—"no great shakes as a revival."]

615 Atkinson, Brooks. "The Play: Mercury Theatre Restores George Bernard Shaw's 'Heartbreak House' to the Stage," NYT, 30 April 1938, p. 18.
Heartbreak House is too garrulous and too long, but it contains wisdom and fun. Orson Welles plays Shotover as Shaw (Mercury Theater, NY).

616 Atkinson, Brooks. "The Play: New Bernard Shaw Play, 'The Millionairess,' Has Its American Premiere is Westport, Conn.," NYT, 16 Aug 1938, p. 22.
The Millionairess (Westport County Playhouse, Westport, Conn.) has wit and impudence, but lacks point. The story, of "a rich virago," is commonplace and at times silly.

617 Atkinson, Brooks. "The Play: Shaw's 'Androcles and the Lion' Acted by the Harlem Unit of the Federal Theatre," NYT, 17 Dec 1938, p. 10.
The Federal Theater Project players (Lafayette Theater, Harlem, NY) uses a black cast to translate Androcles and the Lion into a play about the persecution of the black race. [Praise for the acting, espec of Ferrovius.]

618 Batho, Edith, Bonamy Dobrée, and Guy Chapman. THE VICTORIANS AND AFTER, 1830-1914 (Lond: Cresset P, 1938), Vol. IV of INTRODUCTIONS TO ENGLISH LITERATURE, ed by Bonamy Dobrée, pp. 18, 23, 29, 31, 73, 117, 118, 124, 125-26, 129, 147, 151, 177, 261, 269, 270-71, 275, 334, Index.

Shaw is "the most typical advanced product of the Edwardian era": an agnostic-mystic, a Fabian socialist, and anti-esthetic. He writes rationalist comedy in an admirable prose tinged with vitalism and mysticism. His prefaces "are the finest pamphleteering since Swift."

619 Brown, Ivor. "The World of the Theatre: The Critic Criticised," ILN, CXCIII (3 Dec 1938), 1036.

Shaw's drama criticism lives because it deals with ideas; his Quintessence of Ibsenism is enduring and easily readable. So too his drama Geneva (Saville Theater, Lond) deals with ideas. Priestley incorrectly asserts that critics should focus on method rather than ideas.

620 Brown, Ivor. "The World of the Theatre: The Drama in a Changing World," ILN, CXCIII (13 Aug 1938), 274.

Geneva (Malvern Festival production) treats the stage as a pulpit and the actors as Shaw's mouthpieces. It lacks stage realism, is too discursive, and is only "intermittently amusing."

621 Caudwell, Christopher [pseud of Christopher St. John Sprigg]. "George Bernard Shaw, A Study of the Bourgeois Superman," STUDIES IN A DYING CULTURE (Lond: The Bodley Head, 1938; rptd Lond: John Lane, 1947), pp. xi, xvii, 1-19.

Shaw's Utopia is described in Back to Methuselah. The weakness of his "characteristically bourgeois" socialism lies in his stress on pure contemplation. His is a familiar intellectual error. By retreating into the imagination, humankind creates categories and magic spells in an attempt to "subjugate reality contemplatively." The real artist and the scientist do not make this mistake; rather, they seek reality outside themselves. Thus, Shaw rejects science, for he, by a typically neurotic device, must reject "this tough, distressing, gritty environment." Shaw's inability to face the reality of the emotions, the instincts, and the unconscious robs his work of both political and artistic value. His characters are inhuman. Their conflicts are merely rational ones. Shaw, like Wells, wants a world of "intellectual Samurai" who guide "poor muddled workers"; in this view Shaw is fascist. He writes comedies to sugar-coat his argument for childish minds, thus becoming the "world's buffoon," for "the sugar he put on his pill prevented the pill from acting."

622 "Cinema: Old Show, New Trick," TIME, XXXII (5 Dec 1938), 26, 28.
Gabriel Pascal's movie version of Pygmalion is praiseworthy. Shaw usually refuses to sell cinema rights to his plays, but Pascal managed to persuade him to film Pygmalion. [Brief description of plot, Pascal's background, and Shaw's part in the movie's production.]

623 Connolly, Cyril. ENEMIES OF PROMISE, AND OTHER ESSAYS: AN AUTOBIOGRAPHY OF IDEAS (Lond: G. Routledge, 1938; rev ed NY: Macmillan, 1948; rptd Garden City, NY: Anchor, 1960), pp. 6, 19-20, 96, 208.
Shaw is no artist. He helped invent "the idiom of our time"—i.e., "the way people talk."

624 Cookman, A. V. "Mr. Priestley Ventures: In 'Music at Night' He Tries a New and Promising Experiment—And 'Geneva,'" NYT, 21 Aug 1938, IX, p. 2.
Geneva (Malvern Festival) gives no new Shaw message, and the farcical elements and improbable ending come close "to a long-winded parody of Mr. Shaw's own conventions."

625 Dent, Alan. "Stage and Screen: The Theatre," SPECTATOR, CLXI (5 Aug 1938), 232; rptd in CRITICAL HERITAGE, pp. 357-58, Item 116.
Geneva (Malvern Festival production) is nothing to laugh about. It expresses despair at the world's plight, in spite of its farcical effects and Shavian quips.

626 Dukes, Ashley. "The Scene in Europe," TAM, XXII (March 1938), 181-86.
Shaw has neither school nor followers; he is isolated by his intelligence and his habit of correcting wrong-

headedness. He represents his philosophy in a rarefied, unconvincing world, peopled by inhuman, unpoetic, and dispassionate characters. Therefore the common man cannot —indeed, no one can—understand Shaw.

627 Ferguson, Otis. "The Federal Theatre's Shaw," NEW REPUBLIC, XCV (6 July 1938), 251.
On the Rocks (Federal Theater production, Daly's Theater, NY) has too much lecturing; it is rather a bore though there is some sort of charm in it.

628 Ferguson, Otis. "The Good with the Bad," NEW REPUBLIC, XCVII (28 Dec 1938), 231-32, espec 231.
The film version of Pygmalion is popular, but it "has none of that sense of spring you get when comedy seems to leave the humdrum of its manufacture naturally and with its own crazy grace."

629 Galway, Peter. "The Movies: Pygmalion, at the Leicester Square Theatre," NS&Nation, XVI (8 Oct 1938), 529.
The film version of Pygmalion faithfully follows the original. The direction and acting are first-rate.

630 "G. B. Shaw's 'Pygmalion' Is the Best Motion Picture G. B. Shaw Has Ever Seen," NEWSWEEK, XII (5 Dec 1938), 24-25.
The film of Pygmalion, which leavens "acid wit with warmth and poignance," is better than the play. Shaw told Bennett Cerf that it is the best movie he has ever seen.

631 "'Geneva,' at the Saville," ILN, CXCIII (10 Dec 1938), 1132.
Geneva "is as witty as anything [Shaw] has written." The first half is slow, but the second is "exhilarating entertainment."

632 Griffin, Gerald. THE WILD GEESE: PEN PORTRAITS OF FAMOUS IRISH EXILES (Lond: Jarrolds, 1938), pp. 11, 13-21, 22, 43, 63, 130, 216.
[A portrait of Shaw which dwells on his iconoclastic views. An interview with Shaw is woven into the text.]

633 Haggin, B[ernard] H. "Shaw as Critic," NATION, CXLVI (1 Jan 1938), 748-49; rptd in Haggin, MUSIC IN THE NATION (NY: William Sloan, 1949), pp. 337-39.

In London Music in 1888-1889 Shaw is a model for music critics. He brings all his knowledge, taste, and wit to bear on an evaluation of a work or performance; yet he avoids using the material as an occasion to display his own competence. He has a sound approach and technique, is relevant and appealing, and is better than many modern music critics.

634 Halász, Gyula. "Shaw és a nyelvmuvelés" (Shaw and the Effort to Maintain Correct Language Usage), NYUGAT, I, No 5 (May 1938), 405-406.

On reading that the 82-year-old Shaw has written a new will earmarking his five million pound fortune to efforts to maintain correct English language usage, one sees that maintaining the correctness and purity of the language is a problem for many peoples. Those engaged in such efforts must weigh a variety of factors in dealing with something as dynamic and socially based as language. [In Hungarian.]

635 Hamilton, T. J. "Shaw Gets Spotlight Again: His Latest Play, 'Geneva,' Wins Some Praise But Not the Pardon of His Former Allies," NYT, 7 Aug 1938, IV, p. 5.

Geneva is not so much a play as a judgment on human political failure. The play was better received (Malvern Festival production) than other recent Shaw efforts. Shaw has recently come under attack for alleged fascist leanings.

636 Hevesi, Sándor. "Bernard Shaw mint színházi kritikus" (Bernard Shaw as a Theater Critic), ÚJ IDŐK, No 34 (1938), 270.

Shaw's theater reviews were clearly ahead of their time. Some of Shaw's interesting and still timely observations demonstrate his modernity and show his ability to overcome any possible bias. [In Hungarian.]

637 Hoellerling, Franz. "Films," NATION, CXLVII (24 Dec 1938), 701-2.

The movie of Pygmalion follows the play too closely, and thus fails to show Eliza's falling in love with Higgins;

the character and the picture thus lose depth by ignoring the irrational dimension.

638 "Kako nastaje drama: Bernard So o svom stvaranju" (How a Play Is Made: Bernard Shaw On His Work), SCENA (Belgrade), IV (1938/39), 2, 4. [Not seen: listed in BIBLIOGRAFSKA RASPRAVA (Zagreb, 1956), 19292.] [In Serbian.]

639 Keunen, J. "Ellen Terry en Bernard Shaw" (Ellen Terry and Bernard Shaw), DIETSCHE WARANDE EN BELFORT (1938), pp. 745-59.
[A history of the Terry-Shaw relationship from Shaw's initial lukewarm impression of the actress in the 1870's and 1880's to the appearance of their published correspondence in 1931.] [In Dutch.]

640 Keunen, J. "G. B. Shaw's eerste opvoeding" (G. B. Shaw's Early Upbringing), DIETSCHE WARANDE EN BELFORT (1938), pp. 592-602.
Shaw's early years were a formative influence on Shaw's thought. The father's influence is found in Shaw's self-satire and in his dislike of pretension. His mother served as the model for Shaw's many strong, wise, emancipated female characters. His early poverty contributed to Shaw's thinking on social issues and drew him to Fabianism. His difficulties in school are reflected in the scholastic failure of the hero of Cashel Byron's Profession. [In Dutch.]

641 Keunen, J. "Rond G. B. Shaw's Quintessence of Ibsenism" (On G. B. Shaw's Quintessence of Ibsenism), DIETSCHE WARANDE EN BELFORT (1938), pp. 377-85.
The difficulty of getting Ibsen produced in England caused Shaw to publish The Quintessence of Ibsenism in 1891, in support of the movement to get HEDDA GABLER on the stage. Although chapters were added in 1913 with a primarily literary focus, the original work was actually more an explication of Shaw's own moral views, which Ibsen's plays just happened to support. [In Dutch.]

642 Krutch, Joseph Wood. "Drama: Better than Shakespeare?" NATION, CXLVI (14 May 1938), 566-67.

Heartbreak House (Mercury Theater, NY) is not like a Chekhov play: it lacks a synthesis of moods and relies on farce and caricature. The best scene is Ellie's attempt to justify her impending marriage to Boss Mangan to Captain Shotover, a scene that points up forcefully and wittily Shaw's unresolved conflict between rational materialism and mysticism.

643 Lombard, Paul. "Le théâtre et l'argent" (The Theater and Money), L'HOMME LIBRE, 24 Sept 1938.
For more than one reason, Widowers' Houses is a very interesting play. This kind of theater had great influence on the evolution of ideas at the time of its composition. [In French.]

644 Loraine, Winifred. ROBERT LORAINE: SOLDIER, ACTOR, AIRMAN (Lond: Collins, 1938); also as HEAD WIND: THE STORY OF ROBERT LORAINE (NY: William Morrow, n.d.), pp. 35, 75-86, 89-96, 177, 178, 199-201, 203-6, 216, 237, 242-47, 260-62, 267-73, 276, 286, 289, 295-96, 299, 310, 329, 337, 361, 364, 370, Index.
[Account of Loraine's immensely successful 1905-6 performance of Jack Tanner in Man and Superman (Charles Frohman production, Hudson Theater, NY) and of other Loraine performances (e.g., of Don Juan, Bluntschli, St. John Hotchkiss). Records Loraine's personal friendship with the Shaws; includes excerpts from Loraine's diary, letters from Shaw, and the interpolations in the text by Shaw.]

645 Lorentowicz, Jan. TEATR POLSKI W WARSZAWIE 1913-1938 (The Polish Theater in Warsaw, 1913-1938) (Warsaw: Biblioteka polska, 1938).
[Productions of Shaw's plays in Polish translation at the Teatr Polski (Polish Theater), Warsaw: Pygmalion, 10 March 1914 (31 performances), revived 9 March 1916 (17), 17 April 1920 (41), new production 30 March 1938 (53), 13 March 1937 (46); Great Catherine and How He Lied to Her Husband, 30 August 1916 (16); Fanny's First Play, 29 March 1919 (26); Major Barbara, 30 November 1919 (26); Arms and the Man, 5 August 1921 (20); You Never Can Tell, 10 August 1923; Saint Joan, 3 December 1924 (32); Man and Superman, 24 February 1928 (38); The Apple Cart, 14 June 1929 (39), revived 31 December 1929 (11); The Doctor's Dilemma, 5 March 1931

(25); Too True To Be Good, 4 June 1932 (37); On the Rocks, 15 December 1933 (30); The Simpleton of the Unexpected Isles, 15 March 1935 (27); The Millionairess, 28 May 1936 (37).] [In Polish.]

646 Lux, George L. "His Excellency, Luigi Pirandello: Random Comparisons with Other Writers," SOUTH ATLANTIC QUARTERLY, XXXVII (Jan 1938), 67-72, espec 67-68.

Shaw and Pirandello both have technical facility, attack sentimentalism and convention, and aim at idea rather than story. But Shaw, unlike Pirandello, is concerned with social problems, portrays "certainty and hope," and creates powerful women. Shaw sees the world with normal sight, Pirandello with abnormal. "To Shaw the stage is a pulpit; to Pirandello, a clinic."

647 MacCarthy, Desmond. "A Play of the Moment," NS&Nation, XVI (3 Dec 1938), 914-15; rptd as "Geneva: A Play of the Moment," in MacCarthy, SHAW'S PLAYS IN REVIEW (NY: Thames & Hudson, 1951; rptd Folcroft, Pa.: Folcroft P, 1969), pp. 193-97.

Geneva has some "good jokes" in it, but they are repeated too often. Moreover, some of the characters are boring, particularly Begonia Brown. Shaw, who once believed all men should put justice and mercy into an unjust and merciless world, has changed; old age has "blunted his human sympathies." Furthermore, watching the "most merciless of all revolutions" in Russia has led him to "inhuman lenience" in tolerating totalitarian states.

648 McCarthy, Mary. "Theater Chronicle: New Sets for the Old House," PARTISAN REVIEW, V (June 1938), 41-44; rptd as "Shaw and Chekhov," in McCarthy, SIGHTS AND SPECTACLES 1937-1956 (NY: Farrar, Straus and Cudahy, 1956), pp. 39-45, and MARY MCCARTHY'S THEATRE CHRONICLES 1937-1962 (NY: Farrar, Straus and Company, 1963), pp. 39-45.

Heartbreak House is layered with meanings: it portrays the directionless English upper middle class, their "moral and political bankruptcy," and "the protean character of human nature." The characters constantly change shape, as does the play's schema, which ends on a note of uncertainty. The apocalyptic air raid releases Shaw from the necessity of ending his story. The Orson Welles' production (Mercury Theater, NY) misses all significant levels of meanings. Heartbreak House compares well with Chekhov's THE SEA GULL —that is to say, the best of Shaw equals the worst of Chekhov. Both Shaw and Chekhov show the futility of a cultured, leisured class; emphasize contradictory human nature; and reveal character through "confession." But the two playwrights are, finally, more dissimilar than similar.

649 "Malvern Festival: 'Saint Joan,'" TIMES (Lond), 8 Aug 1938, p. 8.
Elizabeth Bergner's acting of Joan was magnetic in the opening scene of Saint Joan (Malvern Festival production), but in the rest of the play she relied too heavily on childlike pathos. Likewise many of the other characters gave unsuitable performances.

650 Maugham, W. Somerset. THE SUMMING UP (NY: Literary Guild of America; Garden City, NY: Doubleday; Lond: Heinemann; Toronto: Ryerson; NY: Star Books, 1938; rptd NY: Garden City Publishing Co.; Lond: Heinemann; Toronto: Ryerson, 1940), pp. 132-33, 136-40, 145.
Shaw's emergence as a thinker in modern drama coincided with youthful rebellion against Victorian convention. Shaw had "high spirits, rollicking humour, wit and fertility of comic invention"; but his ideas were quickly antiquated. His influence on the modern English stage "has been devastating" because lesser talents wrote plays of ideas in imitation of his success. Shaw is an inimitable dramatist who capitalized on the English malaise concerning romantic love, presenting it as "a tiresome, secondary business."

651 "Mercury Theatre: 'The Man of Destiny,'" TIMES (Lond), 8 Oct 1938, p. 10.
Shaw's method in The Man of Destiny is inconclusive argument; both Shaw's play and Valentin Kataev's SQUARING THE CIRCLE (on the same bill) seem written "as a relaxation for revolutionaries."

652 "Movie of the Week: Bernard Shaw's Pygmalion, Introducing Wendy Hiller," LIFE, V (12 Dec 1938), 30-32.

Shaw, considered "the world's greatest dramatist since Ibsen," is iconoclastic and controversial. Though his recent works are somewhat senile, he is nevertheless an acknowledged seer. Gabriel Pascal's Pygmalion introduces Shaw's comic genius to the films. [Photograph of Shaw, p. 30, and scenes from the movie, pp. 31-32.]

653 "Mr. Shaw's New Play: 'Geneva' at Malvern," TIMES (Lond), 2 Aug 1938, p. 8.
Shaw's recent philosophy has reached an impasse as he attempts to find economic solutions to spiritual problems. The satire in Geneva thus relies on "bluster and defiance of the dictators" as discussion arises out of farce.

654 Murray, Gilbert. "Mr. Shaw's 'Geneva,'" SPECTATOR, CLXI (26 Aug 1938), 330-31.
Geneva is "disrespectful," fantastic in facts, unsympathetic, one long Shavian conversation. But Shaw touches on an important truth at the play's end when the Judge brands one and all scoundrels but is unable to inflict a sentence.

655 "Music Teacher-seer at Eighty-Two," ETUDE, LVI (Sept 1938), 570.
Shaw never "lost his intimate contact with the musical art." He exemplified in his own life his epigram that one should live "so that when you die God is in your debt." [Photograph of Shaw.]

656 N., L. "G. B. S. at 55," NYT, 27 Jan 1938, p. 16.
[Favorable review of Pygmalion, "the Shavian version of 'All That Glitters,'" Federal Theater Project production, Maxine Elliott's Theater, NY.]

657 "New York! Première of George Bernard Shaw's PYGMALION," STAGE (NY), XVI (Dec 1938), 20-21.
The film of Pygmalion, making its Western hemisphere première at the Astor Theater, has a "brilliant and vigorous plot" written by Shaw.

658 Newman, Robert George. "The Charm of Bernard Shaw," READING AND COLLECTING, II (Feb-March 1938), 47-48.

In spite of his didacticism and certain technical defects
in his plays, Shaw remains popular with the very public he
ridicules. This is because of his fresh, vital point of
view and his ability to present his message through wit,
paradox, and brilliant comedy.

659 Nugent, Frank S. "The Screen in Review: G. B. S.
Makes Debut as Screen Writer in 'Pygmalion' at
Astor," NYT, 8 Dec 1938, p. 34.
Pygmalion should be taken lightly and played accordingly,
as it is in the film version. [High praise for Wendy
Hiller's Eliza.] Some scenes are too static, and the ending
needs improvement.

660 Orme, Michael. "The World of the Kinema: Past
and Present," ILN, CXCIII (15 Oct 1938), 682.
The film version of Pygmalion is a brilliant adaptation of
a witty, lively play. It is well-directed, well-acted,
excellent in every component.

661 Petrović, S. "Velike figure moderne engleske
književnosti: Đorđa Bernard Šo—lakrdijăs i apostol"
(Great Figures of Modern English Literature: George
Bernard Shaw—Clown and Apostle), PRAVDA (Belgrade),
XXXIV, No 13 (1938), 130. [Not seen but listed in
BIBLIOGRAFSKA RASPRAVA (Zagreb) (1956), 16896.] [In
Serbian.]

662 "Plays and Pictures: Man and Superman, at Old
Vic," NS&Nation, XVII (26 Nov 1938), 873.
The use of modern dress in Man and Superman (Old Vic
production) is not a good idea. What was once shocking is
now commonplace in the play, whose main fault lies in the
"absence of tenderness." The characters talk about sex, but
nobody seems capable of warmth, except perhaps Ramsden.

663 "Plays and Pictures: The Man of Destiny and
Squaring the Circle, at the Mercury," NS&Nation, XVI
(15 Oct 1938), 569.
Shaw wrote The Man of Destiny to display the virtuosity of
Henry Irving and Ellen Terry, and to affront the popular
notion that Napoleon was a genius. The first production on
the London stage in thirty-one years (Mercury Theater) is
excellent entertainment.

664 "Plays and Pictures: <u>You Never Can Tell</u>, at the Westminster," NS&Nation, XV (14 May 1938), 834.
<u>You Never Can Tell</u> (Westminster Theater) "wears well." Mrs. Clandon and Gloria still represent "sexual fakes and bores" perfectly.

665 "Q Theatre: 'John Bull's Other Island,'" TIMES (Lond), 13 Dec 1938, p. 14.
The appeal of <u>John Bull's Other Island</u> is journalistic, and current Irish politics are "stranger than the wilder Shavian paradoxes." Furthermore, some of the characters seem drawn from literature rather than from life.

666 Routley, Clare. "A Criticism of George Bernard Shaw." Unpublished dissertation, University of Ottawa, 1938. [Listed in Altick and Matthews, Item 1748.]

667 "Saville Theatre: 'Geneva,'" TIMES (Lond), 23 Nov 1938, p. 12.
<u>Geneva</u> is an overlong farce leading to a brilliant "fantasia on the theme of international justice." The last act is witty and shrewd, with most of the good lines going to Bombardone. Curiously, the play seems dated.

668 Schöpflin, Aladár. "Szinházi bemutatók" (Theatrical Openings), NYUGAT, II (1938), 368-72.
To present a genius in a stage production in a believable manner is difficult. Yet Shaw in <u>The Doctor's Dilemma</u> is able to portray convincingly a genius in the form of a young, dying rascal, who otherwise remains a scoundrel but in intellect rises above all. In conjunction with this, Shaw ridicules the societal and medical "bluffing" of doctors, carrying on successfully the satire of social facades common to his other works. [In Hungarian.]

669 "Shaw on the Screen," SRL, XIX (24 Dec 1938), 8.
In the movie version of <u>Pygmalion</u>, Shaw has changed the emphasis from class structure, phonetics, and the New Woman to the struggle between two personalities. He wisely changed the ending and rewrote a few lines.

670 Short, Ernest and Arthur Compton-Rickett. RING UP THE CURTAIN: BEING A PAGEANT OF ENGLISH

ENTERTAINMENT COVERING HALF A CENTURY (Lond: Herbert Jenkins, 1938), pp. 172-73, 222, 268.
THE CHOCOLATE SOLDIER was adapted from Arms and the Man without Shaw's permission. When he was finally sent the libretto and music, with a check, he returned the check but eventually gave his permission for the adaptation of his plot.

671 Soskin, William. "Corno Di Bassetto (Later Known as G.B.S.)," NYHTBR, 2 Jan 1938, p. 6.
Shaw's London Music in 1888-89 shows the perfect Wagnerite doing battle with Tory opponents who were "attuned to melodic perfume." The most telling sections of the book deal with the human characteristics involved in music. It is clear that Shaw knew music well.

672 SZÍNHÁZ (Theater) (Budapest: Singer és Wolfner Irodalmi Intézet, 1938), pp. 5-7, 18, 53-55, 70, 86, 132, espec 53-55.
Many English critics do not consider Shaw a genuine dramatist. Works such as Candida and Mrs. Warren's Profession are moving and reach a high literary level, but other works, especially his later ones, take on the form of intellectual dialogs written for the stage. The technique of concentrating less on plot and more on the development of his own ideas or of his characters is not new with Shaw, having also been used by Aristophanes, Molière, Shakespeare and others. [Passing references to Shaw's drama theory and technique and his relationship to other European dramatists.] [In Hungarian.]

673 "Theatre: New Play in Manhattan," TIME, XXXI (27 June 1938)', 33.
On the Rocks, produced by the Federal Theater (NY), is filled with "sparkling, perfectionist common sense," but it has no physical action.

674 "Theatre: Old Play in Manhattan," TIME, XXXII (26 Dec 1938), 25.
The Federal Theater (NY) revival presents Androcles and the Lion, with an all-black cast, "as a Negro problem play." Shaw's play is good, but this production is not.

675 Vernon, Grenville. "The Stage and Screen: Heartbreak House," COMMONWEAL, XXVIII (13 May 1938), 77.

Heartbreak House (Mercury Theater, NY) is a baffling and an annoying play, with heights and depths. There is some tedium, wordiness, and repetition; yet there is genius in the character of Shotover. "Much of Shaw is...an attitude, as artificial as other attitudes."

676 Vernon, Grenville. "The Stage and Screen: On the Rocks," COMMONWEAL, XXVIII (1 July 1938), 273.

On the Rocks (Daly's Theater, NY) is not a play: it has no story, no dramatic interest, no arrangement of parts, no characterization. Yet it is amusing, thought-provoking, and "well phrased." Its meaning is obscure.

677 "Westminster Theatre: 'You Never Can Tell,'" TIMES (Lond), 4 May 1938, p. 12.

Shaw can tell a great story with brilliant light-heartedness, and does so in You Never Can Tell. The characters are taking on the "glamour of immortality," and the period-dress production (Westminster Theater, Lond) does justice to them.

678 Whitfield, George. AN INTRODUCTION TO DRAMA (Lond: Oxford, 1938; 2nd ed Lond: Oxford UP, 1963), pp. 164-65.

Shaw's work defies categorization: he strips facts of their familiar covering so that they can be intellectually scrutinized. [Introd to a rptd excerpt from Saint Joan.]

679 Wilhelmsen, Leif J. "Fortalens Betydning I Bernard Shaws Produksjon" (The Significance of the Preface in Bernard Shaw's Production), EDDA, XXXVIII (1938), 449-56.

Like Dryden, Synge, and Dumas, Shaw has raised prefaces to a genre equal to his drama. Often autobiographical, they contribute much to an understanding of Shaw and his work. In them, he often accounts for a play's genesis and says something about its reception. Censorship in large part prompted his writing prefaces, because they did not come under the censor, as plays did. Thus he could use them to develop ideas with a freedom not permitted in the drama. They also attracted him because the form itself is more convenient for discussing ideas per se than the drama is. In them, he sets forth his Puritanism and socialism, and reveals, often unconsciously, the influences on him of other European writers. He writes prefaces as a thinker rather than as a poet. It is perhaps as an essayist that Shaw will be best remembered. [In Norwegian.]

680 Wilson, Edmund. "Bernard Shaw at Eighty," ATLANTIC MONTHLY, CLXI (Feb 1938), 198-215; rptd in Wilson, THE TRIPLE THINKERS (NY: Harcourt, 1938; revised and enlarged ed NY: Oxford UP, 1948, pp. 165-96; also rptd in Louis Kronenberger (ed), GEORGE BERNARD SHAW: A CRITICAL SURVEY (Cleveland and NY: World, 1953), pp. 126-52; excerpted in CRITICAL HERITAGE, pp. 394-95, Item 115.
Shaw is a better artist than thinker. His social snobbery, his romanticism (in spite of his satire on it), and his striving to realize himself in art deflected his socialism. Instead of a crusader, he became a social success. Common Sense about the War attacks capitalism but finally supports the war; The Intelligent Woman's Guide to Socialism and Capitalism is not realistically grounded in post-war England; and his defense of Mussolini and Hitler does not take into account Nazi persecutions of Shaw's own political camp. Shaw's mind fluctuates to produce various points of view, a characteristic that weakens his public utterances but strengthens his art, where economic insight joins literary genius. His drama has "a logic and grace, a formal precision" like eighteenth-century music. The major pattern in his best plays is the conflict between the saint and the world. Heartbreak House, with its failure to resolve problems, was a new direction for Shaw. All his plays, even the latest ones, where old age is beginning to show, are the "chronicle of a soul in relation to society." [Comments on The Apple Cart, Major Barbara, Androcles and the Lion, Tragedy of an Elderly Gentleman, Saint Joan, Too True To Be Good, On the Rocks, The Simpleton of the Unexpected Isles, The Millionairess.]

681 Wright, Basil. "Stage and Screen: The Cinema," SPECTATOR, CLXI (14 Oct 1938), 603.
The movie version of Pygmalion translated Shaw's uncinematic "static and stagey" work into the "fluid terms of the screen."

682 Wyatt, Euphemia Van Rensselaer. "The Drama: Heartbreak House," CATHOLIC WORLD, CXLVII (June 1938), 344-48.
Heartbreak House (Mercury Theater, NY) is "a brilliant symposium"—with slapstick—on disillusionment, with full diagnosis and suggested cure. It needs cutting.

683 Wyatt, Euphemia Van Rensselaer. "Theater: The Devils' Disciple," CATHOLIC WORLD, CLXX (March 1950), 468-69.
Probably Burgoyne inspired The Devil's Disciple. A different character dominates each act. Dick lives and is willing to die for Christian standards, and all the characters are not who they think they are (New York City Theater Company Production, Royale Theater). "I wonder if Mr. Shaw knows the end of the story?"

684 Young, Stark. "Heartbreak House," NEW REPUBLIC, XCV (8 June 1938), 130-31; revised and rptd in Young, IMMORTAL SHADOWS: A BOOK OF DRAMATIC CRITICISM (NY: Scribner's, 1948; rptd NY: Hill & Wang, 1959), pp. 188-92; rptd in ESSAYS IN THE MODERN DRAMA, ed by Morris Freedman (Boston: Heath, 1964).
Shaw compares Heartbreak House (Mercury Theater, NY) to Chekhovian drama, but Shaw lacks Chekhov's ability to portray character. Shaw sees people only in the light of their opinions; thus his characters do not seem real or distinct from each other.

1939

---

685 Agate, James. "A Flood at Kew," TIMES (Lond), 19 Feb 1939; rptd in Agate, THE AMAZING THEATRE (Lond, Toronto, Bombay, Sydney: Harrap, 1939), pp. 226-30.
The Doctor's Dilemma (Westminster Theater, Lond) is a masterpiece of "sheer theatricality." The central thesis and the satire on doctors will wear well over time, as will Dubedat's death scene.

686 Agate, James. "A Great Shaw Play: In Good King

Charles's Golden Days," TIMES (Lond), 13 Aug 1939, p.
17; rptd in CRITICAL HERITAGE, pp. 360-62, Item 118.
In Good King Charles's Golden Days (Malvern Theater
production) is long and lacks action; yet it is filled with
the essence of Shaw and several purple passages that assure
its immortality.

687 Agate, James. "Shavian Phonetics," TIMES (Lond),
18 June 1939; rptd in Agate, THE AMAZING THEATRE
(Lond, Toronto, Bombay, Sydney: Harrap, 1939), pp.
259-63.
Shaw's representations of Cockney speech in Pygmalion
(Haymarket Theater, Lond) are inaccurate, and the play is
hopelessly dated, since ladies are now extinct. Stage
speech should be "well-bred speech."

688 Anderson Imbert, Enrique. "Bernard Shaw:
Geneva," SUR (Argentina), No 60 (Sept 1939), 57-59.
Geneva is a play which follows a series of anti-democratic
comedies by Shaw. It is not one of Shaw's best, and in 1939
its theme appears to be old and outmoded. [In Spanish.]

689 Backlund, Alice Moss. "Forerunner of Eliza
Doolittle," SRL, XX (9 Sept 1939), 9, 21.
The Pygmalion story resembles chap 87 of Tobias Smollett's
PEREGRINE PICKLE. Shaw's version is done with more genius.

690 Bernigau, Karl Franz. "Der Weg" (The Way [of
English Instruction]), HANDBUCH DES ENGLISCHEN
UNTERRICHTS (Handbook to English Instruction), ed by
Gustav Gräfer (Leipzig & Berlin: Teubner, 1939), pp.
13-144.
[References to the use of Shaw's plays—Major Barbara and
John Bull's Other Island—in English instruction.] [In
German.]

691 Block, Anita. THE CHANGING WORLD IN PLAYS AND
THEATRE (Boston: Little, Brown, 1939), pp. 7, 10, 16,
29, 45-57, 76, 83, 101, 194, 279, 406, 429.
Shaw carried forward into new realms Ibsenite drama, with
its avowed purpose to serve life. His many political
writings were never tempered; his socialism was the guiding
philosophy of a lifetime. Both his admiration for socialism
and for Ibsen center on moral passion, which is embodied in
plays like Mrs. Warren's Profession and Major Barbara.

692 "Books in Brief: Three Plays: Too True to Be Good, Village Wooing, and On the Rocks," CHRISTIAN CENTURY, LI (18 April 1939), 530-31.
Village Wooing is "a slight Shavian whimsey"; On the Rocks is pungent political satire. As usual, Shaw's prefaces are as interesting as the plays.

693 Breĭtburg, S. "Bernard Shou v spore s Tolstym o Shekspire" (Bernard Shaw's Quarrel with Tolstoy over Shakespeare), LITERATURNOE NASLEDSTVO (Moscow), 37/38 (1939), 617-32.
Shaw and Tolstoy reached similar conclusions about Shakespeare, but from different artistic positions. Shaw had not yet risen above a closed social group, and remained a long time on the edge of a narrow, petit-bourgeois ideology. Both writers shared a critical attitude toward capitalism. But the deism of Tolstoy did not find an echo in Shaw. Both were critical of Shakespeare's world-view and hated the thoughts, aims and feelings of his characters. Both viewed Shakespeare's use of language negatively, but neither denied his artistic power. Shaw's attitude to Tolstoy in this respect was that Tolstoy, as a foreigner, could not be enchanted by the music of Shakespeare's words. Shaw agreed only with the last chapters of Tolstoy's "Essay on Shakespeare and the Drama" (1908), which deal with the "emptiness" of Shakespeare's philosophy, its superficiality, and its lack of originality. Shaw also noticed Tolstoy's mistaken and inaccurate readings of Shakespeare's text. The go-between, Chertkov, who translated for both, believed Shaw's vehemence was due to professional envy. But the exchange did not terminate their friendship. Three of Shaw's letters to Chertkov (1905) are in the Chertkov archives. [In Russian.]

694 Brooks, Benjamin Gilbert. "Mr. Shaw's 'Geneva,'" NINETEENTH CENTURY AND AFTER, CXXVI (Oct 1939), 449-57.
Though its style is admirable, Geneva belongs to the historic past. It has lost meaning for the average reader.

695 Brown, Ivor. "The World of the Theatre: History on the Stage," ILN, CXCV (26 Aug 1939), 350.

In In Good King Charles's Golden Days Shaw rescues Charles II from his romantic reputation as a playboy and gives him intellect and political acumen. The play, "almost entirely a conversation-piece," has no plot.

696 Brown, Ivor. "The World of the Theatre: Salute to Methuselah," ILN, CXCIV (17 June 1939), 1104.

Age has not slowed Shaw down. He "is the dramatist of the year," with Geneva having "outlived international crises and changes of address" and numerous Shaw revivals in London having achieved popularity. Shaw's detractors have not replaced him either in thought or art. "He prefers good prose to bad poetry and common-sense methods of stating a concrete case to fantastic methods of suggesting abstractions." Thus the English playgoer prefers Shaw's realism and individualized characters—like Doolittle—to Expressionist abstraction.

697 Calverton, V. F. "Cultural Barometer," CURRENT HISTORY, XLIX (Feb 1939), 47-48.

Shaw's recent plays have been dull, but the critics have withheld attack out of "kindly tolerance." However, with the film version of Pygmalion, Shaw is making a come-back, as with the "incredible" Federal theater (Daly's Theater, NY) production of On the Rocks. The latter is not always dramatic because of Shaw's interest in theater as a vehicle for ideas.

Shaw is the world's most lucid, logical, penetrating, and intelligent dramatist; his only modern competitor is Voltaire. Though Shaw lacks "organization genius" and emotional or erotic sense, he excels in social vision, using Marxism as "a tool, not a religion."

698 Castelli, Alberto. "Santa Giovanna" (Saint Joan) SCRITTORI INGLESI CONTEMPORANEI (Contemporary English Writers) (Milan: Principato, 1939), 108-38.

The artistic value of Saint Joan is strictly linked to the theory of the Immanent Will; in applying this theory, Shaw fully succeeds in achieving his artistic aim, that is, the creation of a Protestant martyr. [In Italian.]

699 Clemens, Cyril C. CHESTERTON AS SEEN BY HIS CONTEMPORARIES (Webster Groves, Mo.: International Mark Twain Society, 1939; rptd NY: Haskell House, 1969), pp. 15, 27, 44, 46, 55-56, 75-76, 85, 95, 96, 141-42, 146, Index.
[Superficial references to Shaw by S. Lewis May, Coulson Kernahan, Holbrook Jackson, William Platt, Hugo C. Riviere, Thomas Caldecot Chubb, Rafael Sabatini, and W. B. Yeats. Shaw's recollections of G. K. Chesterton, pp. 75-76.]

700 Condon, Frank. "Shaw Man," COLLIER'S, CIII (29 April 1939), 48-50, 54.
Gabriel Pascal's Pygmalion (premiere at Four Star Theater, Los Angeles) achieves a miracle with an old play; people are lining up to see the movie. Pascal and Shaw work well together: they added a ballroom scene (a "lollipop diversion") and plan to do more movies of Shaw plays.

701 Cornell, Katharine. I WANTED TO BE AN ACTRESS (NY: Random House; Toronto: Macmillan, 1939), pp. 74-75, 126, 128, 133-34, 136, 146, 150, 161, 163-64, 167, 169-70, 218-19, 284-85, 316-28, 338-40, 343.
[Records Cornell's acting in Candida (Actors Theater, NY, 1924; on tour 1933-34; Empire Theater, NY, 1937) and Saint Joan (Martin Beck Theater, NY, 1936); includes a letter from Shaw to Cornell, her account of a visit to Shaw, and reprints of selected reviews.]

702 Darlington, W. A. "Shaw at Malvern," NYT, 3 Sept 1939, IX, p. 2.
In In Good King Charles's Golden Days (Malvern Festival production) "nothing happens whatever." Shaw dispenses with the craft of play construction to give a three-act lecture, some of it entertaining and some of it exhausting.

703 Dent, Alan. "Stage and Screen: The Theatre," SPECTATOR, CLXIII (18 Aug 1939), 252.
In Good King Charles's Golden Days is an "irruption of mind." Technically, it is "indefensible"; historically, "inadmissible." But the audience cannot bring itself to leave it.

704 Disher, M. Willson. "Man with a Load of _____?" THEATRE WORLD (Lond), XXXI (March 1939), 104, 129.

The flavor of Shaw is not in his imitators but only in Shaw himself. He single-handedly fought against his time. Yet his genius also lies in the creation (like Dickens) of memorable fictions. As time passes, his views may give way to the artistry of his plays. For example, the "'Women's Rights' propaganda" of <u>Candida</u> will become "an excellent jest." His current plays—<u>The Apple Cart</u>, <u>The Simpleton of the Unexpected Isles</u>, and <u>Geneva</u>—"prove that the Shaw of the nineties is the Shaw of 1939," with the same purpose though with a different method.

705 Dukes, Ashley. "The English Scene," TAM, XXIII (Feb 1939), 99-105, espec 100, 102.

<u>Geneva</u> is not really topical; it is rather an emotionless "argument proceeding somewhere through the space or void of human experience." <u>Man and Superman</u> is witty and ingenious, having become more comedy and less manifesto than when it was first performed.

706 "An 83-Year Old G.B.S. Adventures in a New Genre: 'In Good King Charles's Golden Days,'" ILN, CXCV (26 Aug 1939), 351.

[Photographs of the Malvern Festival production of <u>In Good King Charles's Golden Days</u>.]

707 Ellis-Fermor, Una. THE IRISH DRAMATIC MOVEMENT (Lond: Methuen, 1939; 2nd ed 1954; rptd 1964; also in University Paperbacks, 1967; 1971), pp. 6, 13, 20, 21, 22, 25, 28, 31, 46, 48, 49, 51-54, 57, 107, 133, 136, 197, 223, Index.

[Passing references to Shaw and the English theater of the 1890's and the early history of the Irish dramatic movement. Account of the Abbey Theater production of <u>The Shewing-Up of Blanco Posnet</u> (1909) in defiance of English and attempted Irish censorship.]

708 Eyrignoux, Louis. "La dette de Shaw envers Samuel Butler, deux documents" (Shaw's Debt to Samuel Butler—Two Documents), ETUDES ANGLAISES, IV (Oct-Dec 1939), 361-64.

[A letter from Shaw (6 Jan 1937) to a French student who was working on an M.A. thesis on Butler's influence on Shaw; and an account of an interview granted to Eyrignoux (12 Aug 1937) in which Shaw answers questions on his debt to Butler, on the emerging race of superior beings, and on his rationalism and mysticism.] [In French.]

709 Furukaki, Tetsuro. "Bernard Shawou to Kataru" (An Interview with Bernard Shaw), LONDON NO YUUTSU (Melancholy in London) (Tokyo: Sanseido, 1939), pp. 356-64; rptd as "Bernard Shawou" (Old Mr. Bernard Shaw), in LONDON NO YUUTSU (Melancholy in London) (Tokyo: Meikyokudo, 1950), pp. 139-48; rvd as "Bernard Shaw" in KOKORONIKUKI HITOBITO (People I Admire) (Tokyo: Asahi Shinbunsha, 1966), pp. 85-90.
An interview with Shaw in the spring of 1935 in which Shaw told the author, among other things, that the British parliamentary system was completely out of fashion; that the friendly relationship of China and Japan would solidify the foundation of peace and prosperity in the Far East; and that African nations would soon achieve their independence.] [In Japanese.]

710 Galinsky, Hans. "Englische und angloirische Dichtung" (English and Anglo-Irish Literature), DIE GEGENWARTSDICHTUNG DER EUROPÄISCHEN VÖLKER, ed by Kurt Wais (Berlin: Junker und Dünnhaupt, 1939), pp. 77-160.
[Brief introduction to Shaw's plays, emphasis on his attack on capitalism, his iconoclasm.] In Shaw's writings the preacher is more important than the poet. [In German.]

711 "'Geneva': A Play of the Moment by Bernard Shaw," THEATRE WORLD (Lond), XXXI (March 1939), 106, 113-20.
Geneva is a "brilliant journalistic summary of the current European situation." It is lively and funny. Bombardone and Battler are "wittily and accurately observed," and their viewpoints are presented fairly. [Photographs of the St. James' Theater (Lond) production.]

712 "Geneva in Warsaw: August '39," TAM, XXIII (Nov 1939), 779-80.
Geneva, at the Polski Theater in Warsaw, "is alive from start to finish." It is "fantastic, ironical and satiric," and sensible—"almost a part of reality."

713 Glendinning, Alex. "Commentary," NINETEENTH CENTURY AND AFTER, CXXV (Jan 1939), 87-92, espec 88-90.
Geneva (Saville Theater, Lond) has little conflict or pointed satire. It is lighthearted, but irrelevant to the issues it raises.

714 [Godfrey, Eleanor]. "Propaganda Drama," CANADIAN FORUM, XIX (Dec 1939), 288-89.
The first half of Geneva has a "fine, jeering survey of the international situation," but the second half fades into side issues and ambiguity. The effect is of "plenty of powder and no ammunition." Shaw enjoys confronting audiences with the unexpected and thus causing "intelligences [to] disintegrate."

715 "Haymarket Theatre: 'Pygmalion,'" TIMES (Lond), 14 June 1939, p. 12.
Pygmalion has shape, is larger than life, and is magnificently playable. The Haymarket Theater (Lond) production is vigorous and fresh, but Eliza has an unsanctioned final line that refutes the Shavian ending.

716 Hicks, Granville. FIGURES OF TRANSITION: A STUDY OF BRITISH LITERATURE AT THE END OF THE NINETEENTH CENTURY (NY: Macmillan, 1939), pp. 72, 83, 85, 100, 101, 103, 104, 106, 107, 108, 154, 157, 171, 176, 215, 228, 238, 244, 252.
After the 1887 rout of the radicals from Trafalgar Square, Shaw, William Morris, and Henry Hyndman began preparing a manifesto to encourage cooperation among socialist groups in London. While Shaw was on the friendliest terms with Morris, he did not share his thorough hostility to nineteenth-century institutions. Indeed, Shaw wanted socialism, but "not at the sacrifice of whatever capitalism had accomplished in the way of order and comfort." He was interested not in a romantic notion of destruction, but in conservation, and thus he became a Fabian. Moreover, the Fabians offered intellectuals of Shaw's own class, as he once noted.

717 Kuhn, Ferdinand, Jr. "Shaw's New Play Has Its Premiere: Charles II No 'Merry Monarch' in Portrait of Him Given at Malvern Festival," NYT, 13 Aug 1939, p. 28.

In Good King Charles's Golden Days (Malvern Festival production) is a dull history lesson which "ends nowhere and proves nothing in particular" except that Shaw can still write vigorously at times and that he admires King Charles.

718 Lo Duca, Giuseppe Maria. "Colloquio con Shaw" (Conversation with Shaw), CINEMA, LXX (1939), 326-27.

Shaw's deep-rooted mistrust of an art based on images rather than words was modified by Gabriel Pascal's film version of Pygmalion. Leslie Howard succeeded, according to Shaw, in satisfactorily representing his ideal of the professor. [An interview in Italian.]

719 Lorentz, Pare. "Pygmalion," MCCALLS (Feb 1939); rptd in MOVIES 1927 TO 1941: LORENTZ ON FILM (NY: Hopkinson & Blake, 1975), pp. 161-62.

In Pygmalion Shaw makes an auspicious debut in films. It is not merely a re-created stage play, though it retains Shaw's dialog and occasional laughs from the old play. The acting and sound score are excellent.

720 M., F. "'Geneva,'" THEATRE WORLD (Lond), XXXI (Jan 1939), 12-13.

Geneva (Saville Theater, Lond) is audacious and witty. The first two acts are simply "a somewhat long-winded lead-up" to the last-act trial. The latter is one of Shaw's "most brilliant tours de force," with the dictators richly comic; their points of view are presented fairly.

721 MacCarthy, Desmond. "Pygmalion," NS&Nation, XVIII (1 July 1939), 12-13.

While some of the language in Pygmalion is considered tame and dated today, the theme is as fresh as ever. The movie version, however, seems to portray merely a "wish fulfillment love story of a poor girl who became a lady and married the man who made her one." The dialog is, unfortunately, "swamped by impressions conveyed pictorially."

722 MacLiammóir, Michael. "Problem Plays," THE IRISH THEATRE: LECTURES DELIVERED DURING THE ABBEY THEATRE

FESTIVAL HELD IN 1939 (Lond: Macmillan, 1939; rptd NY: Haskell House, 1971), pp. 199-227, espec 211-13. Shaw tried to explode the myth of Irish charm in John Bull's Other Island but succeeded in creating "undeniably charming" characters, e.g., Larry Doyle, Nora, Father Keegan, and Aunt Judy—all familiar Irish types. The play is an amusing and nostalgia-producing picture of Irish provincial life, as out of date now in Ireland as Ibsen's Doll's House must be in Norway.

723 "Malvern Festival: Mr. Shaw's New Play, 'In Good King Charles' Golden Days,'" TIMES (Lond), 14 Aug 1939, p. 8.
Shaw's version of King Charles (Malvern Festival production) is of a "subtle politician, a man of taste and the best of husbands." The play proceeds on a variety of political, scientific, and artistic levels—some surface and some profound. The dialog is excellent, moving to a final act of quiet beauty.

724 Marsh, Sir Edward. "A Number of People," HARPERS MAGAZINE, CLXXIX (June 1939), 60-61.
[Marsh discusses his acquaintances among eminent Edwardians, including Shaw; a combination of reminiscence, anecdote, quotations.]

725 "Motion Pictures: Stage Awards the Palm," STAGE (NY), XVI (June 1939), 26-27.
[A "palm" to Shaw for his screen-play of Pygmalion, the best script "since the sound track was invented." Other film celebrities receive "palms" as well.]

726 Perry, Henry Ten Eyck. MASTERS OF DRAMATIC COMEDY AND THEIR SOCIAL THEMES (Cambridge, Mass.: Harvard UP; Lond: Oxford, 1939; rptd Port Washington, NY: Kennikat P, 1968), pp. xiv, xix, 338, 366-408, Index.
Like Aristophanes, Shaw felicitously combines sarcasm with idealism. In fact, Shaw belongs with the greatest satirists, men of letters, and writers of comedy. Shaw is "an apostle of ideas," and his dramatic genius lies in his social criticism rather than in the creation of action and characters of universal significance. [A thorough resume of

Shaw's work to 1939, with <u>Man and Superman</u>, <u>Heartbreak House</u>, and <u>Saint Joan</u> held up as his best.]

727 "Playhouse Theatre: 'The Shewing-Up of Blanco Posnet,'" TIMES (Lond), 15 Feb 1939, p. 10.
<u>The Shewing-Up of Blanco Posnet</u> is a sentimental drama—unusual in the Shaw canon. Esmé Percy (People's National Theater production, Playhouse Theater, Lond) plays Blanco as a fantastic character, so that there are "occasional splashes of vivid colour" in the place of Shaw's idea.

728 "The Playhouses: 'Pygmalion,' at the Haymarket," ILN, CXCIV (24 June 1939), 1186.
<u>Pygmalion</u> is still amusing, but not very well acted at the Haymarket Theater (Lond).

729 "Plays and Pictures: <u>Candida</u>, at the Actors' Theatre," NS&Nation, XVII (14 Jan 1939), 49.
<u>Candida</u> presents the "arts of the orator" and offers a warmth of feeling rarely seen in Shaw. The actors of the Actors' Theater production were surprisingly good; Candida was played with appropriate "sincerity and niceness" but with "too little glamour."

730 "Plays and Pictures: <u>Candida</u>, at the Westminster," NS&Nation, XVII (29 April 1939), 647-48.
<u>Candida</u> (Westminster Theater, Lond) is Shaw's only play that comes from the heart. Love is not an "obstruction," nor is woman "a puppet of the life force." Burgess is one of Shaw's best comic parts. But the play is dated.

731 "Plays and Pictures: <u>The Doctor's Dilemma</u>, at the Westminster," NS&Nation, XVII (25 Feb 1939), 281.
Ideas germinate in <u>The Doctor's Dilemma</u> to make it a "rotund comedy." The London Mask Theater production (Westminster Theater, Lond) has "ease and exuberance."

732 "Plays and Pictures: <u>In Good King Charles's Golden Days</u>, at Malvern Festival," NS&Nation, XVIII (26 Aug 1939), 309.
<u>In Good King Charles's Golden Days</u> is a "hypothetical study depending on the 'clash' of well-chosen but ill-assorted personalities." The problem of governing Englishmen is

never solved, except to teach them "citizenship and the necessity of being governed." The first scene is the most dynamic.

733 "Plays and Pictures: Major Barbara at the Westminster," NS&Nation, XVIII (30 Dec 1939), 955.
In Major Barbara (London Mask Theater revival, Westminster Theater) the "incidentals rather than the essential argument and point" are dated. In fact, the argument for "Scientific Socialism" in the mouth of an arms magnate would made a relevant movie today.

734 "Plays and Pictures: Misalliance, at Torch Theatre, Knightsbridge," NS&Nation, XVII (24 June 1939), 976.
Misalliance, "the most Wildean" of Shaw's plays, is particularly suited to a small theater. The Torch Theater production, Knightsbridge, is the best performance of the play to appear on the stage.

735 Price, Clair. "82 Years 50 Plays 1 Shaw: G. B. S. Talks of Old Age and New Work," NYTMag, 26 March 1939, pp. 3, 19.
In In Good King Charles's Golden Days Shaw plans to write history as it might have happened. The play may or may not be produced for the screen, but it will be presented at the Malvern Festival. Shaw, who believes that politicians do not live long enough to become statesmen, has no recipe for longevity.

736 Rivoallan, Anatole. LITTÉRATURE IRLANDAISE CONTEMPORAINE (Contemporary Irish Literature) (Paris: Hachette, 1939), pp. 4, 152, 172, 190.
Shaw struggled in England against English prejudices. John Bull's Other Island shows the triumph of Broadbent. [In French.]

737 "Shaw and the Freudians," NEWSWEEK, XIII (13 Feb 1939), 29-30.
Metro-Goldwyn-Mayer, prior to the release of the film of Pygmalion, hired two Freudian psychologists to analyze the movie, a "Symbol Simon approach to the screen."

738 Shaw, Charles Macmahon. BERNARD'S BRETHREN. (Lond: Constable; NY: Holt; Toronto: Macmillan, 1939).

Lecturers, biographers and critics (notably Frank Harris), and Shaw himself have necessitated the present biographical account by their portraying the Shaw clan incorrectly as one of "futile gentility, . . . woebegone miserable creatures, slightly out of elbow, yet polishing their toppers before appearing before the world." [Shaw read the manuscript and made comments and interpolations, preserved in the published book on separate pages printed in red.]

739 "Sidelights of the Week: Octogenarian," NYT, 20 Aug 1939, IV, p. 2.

Eighty-three-year-old Shaw's latest play, <u>In Good King Charles's Golden Days</u>, substitutes brilliant stage discussion for action.

740 Sinclair, Upton. "An Open Letter to George Bernard Shaw about Lady Astor," LIBERTY (NY), XVI (22 April 1939), 11-12; rptd in Sinclair, TELLING THE WORLD (Lond: T. Werner Laurie, 1939), pp. 69-75.

Contrary to Shaw's claim in a letter to LIBERTY, he has not been a "Marxist Communist" for years. Furthermore, his defense of Lady Nancy Astor ignores her Tory opposition to labor representatives, the NY slum property from which she derives part of her fortune, and the part the Cliveden set had in appeasement of the Axis powers.

741 "Streatham Hill Theatre: 'Saint Joan,'" TIMES (Lond), 12 Oct 1939, p. 6.

Constance Cummings does well with the childlike Joan (<u>Saint Joan</u>, Old Vic production), but she cannot portray the sharp-tongued, realist Joan; "her gallantry has more the flourish of a Peter Pan out to discomfort the pirates." But the production as a whole is admirable.

742 "Theatre: Bernard Shaw and a Biographer: Re-Drawing the Caroline Age," TLS, XXXVIII (18 Nov 1939), 672.

<u>In Good King Charles's Golden Days</u> is very mellow Shaw, with likeable characters, and heart. But Shaw fails to see the value of gallantry and heroes because of his worship of

reason. Maurice Colbourne in THE REAL BERNARD SHAW describes "the unmellow Shaw."

743 "Theatre: A Fancied Page of History," TLS, XXXVIII (17 June 1939), 353.
In Geneva Shaw idealistically concludes that humanity must improve if politics are to become humane. The third act trial of the dictators is both amusing and strong. But, in the first act, the death of the English bishop is a feeble joke, the American journalist is "a lay figure," and Begonia Brown lacks reality.

744 "The Theatre: New Play in Toronto," TIME, XXXIV (13 Nov 1939), 59-60.
Geneva (revised and with its world premiere in Toronto), is "Anti-fascist in a typically Shavian way." The dictators are not villains, but fools, as is everybody in the play. Shaw "bumbles on far too long, says far too little"; his ideas are old, and his jokes forced.

745 Vodnik, France. "B. Shaw: Hudičev učenec," (B. Shaw: The Devil's Disciple), SLOVENEC (Ljubljana), XXIX (Sept 1939), 223; rptd in Vodnik, KRITIČNA DRAMATURGIJA (Ljubljana: Slovenska matica, 1968), pp. 112-16.
In The Devil's Disciple (National Theater, Ljubljana, 1939) Shaw uses the weapons of laughter, satire and cynicism. His hero, the "devil's disciple," depicts a new ethical ideal and altruism, which Shaw opposes to faulty morality. Apart from some ideological propositions, the work is closer to farce than comedy. [In Slovene.]

746 Wall, Vincent C., Jr. "Shaw the Statesman," SUMMARIES OF DOCTORAL DISSERTATIONS, University of Wisconsin, III (1939), 311-13. Unpublished dissertation, University of Wisconsin, 1938. [Listed in McNamee, and in Altick and Matthews, Item 1762.]

747 Watts, Stephen. "Promoter of Pygmalion," LIVING AGE (NY), CCCLVI (May 1939), 345-47; rptd from the SUNDAY EXPRESS (Lond).
The film of Pygmalion is a tremendous financial success to all: producer, director, actors, set designer, cameraman, and Shaw. Gabriel Pascal sees Shaw not as a cynic but as a

man with a "great heart"; he plans to bring Shaw's message to the masses by making other films of Shaw plays.

748 "Westminster Theatre: 'Candida,'" TIMES (Lond), 25 April 1939, p. 12.
The Westminster Theater (Lond) presentation of Candida is refreshingly straightforward, but slow-moving and lacking in eloquence.

749 "Westminster Theatre: 'The Doctor's Dilemma,'" TIMES (Lond), 18 Feb 1939, p. 10.
Dubedat in The Doctor's Dilemma (Lond Mask Theater production) is a cross between a rare flower and a poisonous weed. In the play Shaw proves a careful story-teller. [Praise for the acting.]

750 "Westminster Theatre: 'Major Barbara,'" TIMES (Lond), 21 Dec 1939, p. 6.
Major Barbara (Westminster Theater, Lond) is indeed, as Shaw says, "a discussion in three acts," more like a public meeting than a play, with characters that embody ideas. The Undershaft creed remains controversial and topical.

751 "Whitehall Theatre: 'The Doctor's Dilemma,'" TIMES (Lond), 29 March 1939, p. 14.
The Lond Mask Theater production (Whitehall Theater, Lond) of The Doctor's Dilemma loads the dice toward condemning Dubedat, thus obscuring the dilemma.

752 Winter, Ella. "An Interview with George Bernard Shaw," LOS ANGELES EXAMINER, 23 Nov, 30 Nov, and 7 Dec 1939; rptd in CALIFORNIA SHAVIAN, V (July-Aug 1964), 18-24.
[An interview with Shaw at the Malvern Festival, in which were discussed parallels between Mussolini and King Magnus, American industry, Wilsonian liberalism, democracy, and the original of Shotover.]

753 "Winter Garden Theatre: 'Saint Joan,'" TIMES (Lond), 21 Feb 1939, p. 12.
The English School Theater's production of Saint Joan (Winter Garden Theater, Lond) has tedious spots (e.g., the Inquisitor's defense of heresy hunting) in the midst of excellent acting. Mary Morris' Joan is simple and direct.

754 Wyatt, Euphemia Van Rensselaer. "The Drama: Androcles and the Lion," CATHOLIC WORLD, CXLVIII (Feb 1939), 601.
The all black production (Lafayette Theater, NY) of Androcles and the Lion is sincere, tender, human. Androcles is Shaw's most endearing character.

1940

---

755 Atkinson, Brooks. "The Play: English Comedy Brings Bernard Shaw's 'Geneva' to N. Y. After Tour Across Canada," NYT, 31 Jan 1940, p. 15; rptd in CRITICS' THEATRE REVIEWS (NY), I (1940), 403, and in CRITICAL HERITAGE, p. 359, Item 117.
Geneva (Henry Miller Theater, NY) is dull. The court scene is static and the dialog "diffuse and scrappy."

756 Brown, Ivor. "The World of the Theatre: Matters of Place and Time," ILN, CXCVI (1 June 1940), 758.
Shaw's "Restoration silks and periwigs" and debate on beauty in In Good King Charles's Golden Days (New Theater, Lond) is a welcome relief to the sombre present. He clears Charles of the charge of being "the light-headed leader of a light-principled court," making him a man of science and the first English constitutional monarch. The play discusses "everything from mathematics to the nature of the Universe, but much of it is about the art of governing." It is a "wartime consolation of the thinking classes."

757 Brüser, Ernst. "Bernard Shaw als Kritiker des Kapitalismus—und wir" (Bernard Shaw as a Critic of Capitalism—and We), DIE NEUEREN SPRACHEN, XLVIII (1940), pp. 101-7.
[A discussion of Shaw's article "Socialism" (for the ENCYCLOPEDIA BRITANNICA) from a National Socialist point of view.] [In German.]

758 Carter, John. "The Theatre," SPECTATOR, CLXV (2 Aug 1940), 119.
In The Devil's Disciple the ideas may be well-worn and the

wit familiar, but the political background is relevant to the present.

759 Clemens, Cyril. "Bernard Shaw as a Letter Writer," DALHOUSIE REVIEW, XIX (1940), 403-8.
[Shaw's comments to Clemens in person and in letters on Mark Twain, A. E. Housman, and G. K. Chesterton; his inscriptions in Clemens' copies of Cashel Byron's Profession and The Irrational Knot.]

760 D'Amico, Silvio. "L'irreverente Bernard Shaw" (The Irreverent Bernard Shaw), NUOVA ANTOLOGIA (Rome), No 411 (16 Sept 1940), 169-89.
In his comedies, Shaw amuses himself standing people and things upside-down and off-center, as in Russian anarchist comedies, with the coming and going of puppets, each with its own speech, made without any apparent logical justification. Examples are You Never Can Tell and The Philanderer, of which the former is a KING LEAR of the twentieth century, while Man and Superman is a broader variation on ideas in The Philanderer. Shaw does not hesitate to use satire even when handling the most august themes, as in the farcical and grotesque tone of Androcles and the Lion. He even sent The Shewing-Up of Blanco Posnet to Tolstoy, which irritated the latter. In The Doctor's Dilemma, Shaw caricatures English physicians, and brings an incredible situation to a surprising conclusion. He also uses caricature and satire in the political comedies. In Saint Joan, one of Shaw's typical plays, he makes an inglorious page of English history the subject of a polemic, and lets himself be seduced by poetry. After Saint Joan, Shaw becomes increasingly prolix and, as with all playwrights with a thesis, the ideology fades. What saves his plays is art. [In Italian.]

761 "'The Devil's Disciple,'" THEATRE WORLD (Lond), XXXIII (Nov 1940), 105-10.
The Devil's Disciple was "an unprecedented success at the Piccadilly Theatre"; with Robert Donat in the leading role, it is not touring the provinces. The play has much drama and Shavian wit. [Photographs of the production.]

762 Dietrich, Gerhard. "Shavian Phonetics," BEIBLATT ZUR ANGLIA, LI (1940), 284-86.

The phonetic transcription of Cockney speech in Shaw's works is not reliable. [In German.]

763 Dirnbach, Ernst. "Djavolov učenik" (The Devil's Disciple), HRVATSKI LIST (Osijek), XXI, No 291 (1940), 247. [Not seen but listed in FILOLOGIJA (Zagreb), 3 (1962), 265.] [In Croatian.]

764 "Embassy Theatre: 'Misalliance,'" TIMES (Lond), 23 Jan 1940, p. 4.
Misalliance is a shapeless, though delightful, discussion of many subjects. The Embassy Theater (Lond) production seems "both misguided and underrehearsed."

765 Flanagan, Hallie. ARENA (NY: Duell, Sloan and Pearce; Toronto: Collins, 1940), pp. 138, 163, 192-93, 245, 254, 262, 263, 282, 284, 296, 318, 319, 322, 343, 352, Index.
[Passim references to Shaw plays produced by the WPA Federal Theater Project; Shaw released all his plays for a $50 weekly rental and advocated other serious playwrights do the same.]

766 Fraser, Grace Lovat. "Scenes from the Shows," STUDIO, CXX (July 1940), 14-16.
The scenery and costumes for In Good King Charles's Golden Days lack pictorial unity.

767 Fricker, Robert. DAS HISTORISCHE DRAMA IN ENGLAND VON DER ROMANTIK BIS ZUR GEGENWART (The Historical Drama in England from the Romantic Age to the Present) (Bern: Francke [Schweizer Anglistische Arbeiten, 8] 1940), pp. 232-46.
Shaw's character drawing is revolutionary. His historical characters—Napoleon, Caesar and Cleopatra, Saint Joan, and Shakespeare—are aggressive attacks on the nineteenth-century tradition of the Romantic hero and the Victorian gentleman. [In German.]

768 Gassner, John. MASTERS OF THE DRAMA (NY: Random House, 1940; rptd 3rd revised and enlarged ed NY: Dover, 1954), pp. 286, 350, 363, 364, 383, 398, 428, 445, 507, 556, 571, 575, 580-81, 582, 585, 586, 587, 590, 591-616, 619, 628, 681.

Shaw is a lineal descendant of the Victorian writers in his love for polemics and social reform, in his belief in evolution, and in his skepticism of the middle class. His penchant for music is evident in the fugue-like variations in Getting Married, the overture conversation between the King's secretaries in The Apple Cart, and the "varied use of the coda" in the final scenes of The Doctor's Dilemma and Saint Joan. In his public life he castigates competitive society; in his private life he is most generous. His critical opinions on his contemporaries are accepted as "nearly perfect." The subject matter of his drama is broad. Candida shows he is never "an iconoclast for the mere pleasure of being one." The Devil's Disciple explores the "obscured question of sainthood and deviltry." Heroism is the subject of Caesar and Cleopatra. After Man and Superman, almost anything he wrote seems anticlimactic. Although Shaw had several worthy companion playwrights, after reading and seeing Shaw, "one has little patience to listen to anyone else."

769 Gilder, Rosamond. "Manhattan Music: Broadway in Review," TAM, XXIV (April 1940), 230-38, espec 238.
Geneva, like all Shaw's plays, is in a category of its own. Disillusionment is at the core of the play. The first act is slow moving, but then follows "pithy discourse, sharp caricature and malicious wit" (Henry Miller Theater, NY).

770 Hobson, Harold. "George Bernard Shaw," ENGLISH WITS, ed by Leonard Russell (Lond: Hutchinson, 1940), pp. 281-306; excerpted in CRITICAL HERITAGE, pp. 365-66.
What one remembers from Shaw's plays are the ideas, not the characters, who have Shaw's brain but no heart. Shaw also cannot invent character-revealing incident. Yet the flamboyant character of G. B. S., his (somewhat overrated) reputation as thinker, his rhetorical eloquence, and—above all—his wit have made him a theatrical success. His wit is characterized by his ability to disturb complacency and by his good nature. It is a curious combination of "shock-tactics" and good humor.

771 Hübner, Walter. DIE KUNSTPROSA IM ENGLISCHEN UNTERRICHT (Imaginative Prose in English Instruction) (Leipzig: Quelle & Meyer, 1940), pp. 11, 13-14.

[A brief analysis of an excerpt from Shaw's <u>The Intelligent Woman's Guide to Socialism and Capitalism</u>.] [In German.]

772 "'In Good King Charles's Golden Days,'" THEATRE WORLD (Lond), XXXIII (June 1940), 127.
The conversations in <u>In Good King Charles's Golden Days</u> are stimulating and entertaining. The play portrays Charles as a shrewd statesman. The final scene between Charles and Queen Catherine is best, being "an affectionate and moving episode."

773 "'In Good King Charles's Golden Days,'at the New," ILN, CXCVI (18 May 1940), 676.
<u>In Good King Charles's Golden Days</u> is a thought-provoking and amusing play, portraying Charles as introspective rather than merry. The final scene between Charles and his wife is realistic; Shaw "is at his best in showing that affection and passion are things apart."

774 Kenter, Heinz Dietrich. "Ein Blick auf G. B. Shaw im Jahre 1940" (A View of G. B. Shaw in the Year 1940), MÜCHNER NEUESTE NACHRICHTEN, No 334 (29 Nov 1940), p. 3.
The power of wit, the passion of thought, the strife for a new philosophy of life, and the belief in an ethos of work are characteristic of Shaw's works. All his so-called plays are discussions rather than dramatic literature. [In German.]

775 Keun, Odette. "G. B. Shaw and the Amazon," LILLIPUT: A POCKET MAGAZINE FOR EVERYONE (Lond), VI (Jan-June 1940), 335-39.
Shaw worships "power, force and despotism" and endorses "brutality, barbarism, oppression." He has a perverse spirit and an insane ego. [A reply to an article by Shaw, in which he allegedly asserted that women are bloodthirsty, and that England and France are no better than Nazi Germany. Shaw's reply to the attack, "Think, Odette, Think," appears on p. 340.]

776 Lockridge, Richard. "Bernard Shaw Talks of Europe's Troubles in 'Geneva,' at Henry Miller's," NY SUN (31 Jan 1940) [not seen in this form]; rptd in CRITICS' THEATRE REVIEWS (NY), I (1940), 403.

Shaw's ideas are muddled in <u>Geneva</u> (Henry Miller Theater, NY). The play rambles; the lengthy debates are inconclusive; and the wit is dim.

> **777** MacCarthy, Desmond. "Good 'Old' Shaw," NS&Nation, XX (3 Aug 1940), 109-10; rptd as "The Devil's Disciple," in MacCarthy, SHAW'S PLAYS IN REVIEW (NY: Thames & Hudson, 1951; rptd Folcroft, Pa.: Folcroft P, 1969), pp. 198-202.

<u>The Devil's Disciple</u> (Piccadilly Theater, Lond) is basically melodrama, but it asserts a "deeper emotion and a moral contrary to the ethics of melodrama." The hero reverses the expectations raised by his romantic role. Indeed, "heroism itself is finally exhibited to a disadvantage."

> **778** Madariaga, Salvador de. "G B S: Domestic Mephistopheles," LISTENER, XXIII (29 Feb 1940), 411; excerpted in CRITICAL HERITAGE, pp. 363-65, Item 119.

Shaw liberated England from the dead past through his negative and destructive criticism. He has become predictable in that he is always the reverse of the average Englishman, an opposition that produces sparks but no consistent philosophy.

> **779** Mantle, Burns. "G. B. Shaw Meets the Dictators In a Town Hall 'Geneva,'" NY DAILY NEWS (31 Jan 1940) [not seen in this form]; rptd in CRITICS' THEATRE REVIEWS (NY), I (1940), 405.

<u>Geneva</u> (Henry Miller Theater, NY) is a kind of "Town Hall of the World" meeting rather than a play. It is witty, though perhaps not as intellectually weighty as former Shaw. The dictators and the British are smartly satirized.

> **780** Marcus, Hans. "Sozialpolitisches bei G. B. Shaw" (G. B. Shaw's Social-Political Views) NEUEREN SPRACHEN, XLVI (1940), 495-508.

[After surveying Shaw's social-political theories in his speeches, novels, plays and miscellaneous prose, Marcus concludes that Shaw's theories are incoherent.] While Shaw may have worked sincerely for the removal of social injustice in his speeches and essays, in the plays he was content merely to point it out, wittily criticize it, or make it ridiculous. [In German.]

781 Marx, Milton. ENJOYMENT OF DRAMA (NY: Crofts, 1940; 2nd ed. NY: Appleton-Century-Crofts, 1961), pp. 15, 32, 34, 39, 49, 94, 116-17, 149, Index.
[Passing references to Shaw in a general discussion of the nature of drama; e.g., Joan's recantation is used to illustrate the turning point of a play. Brief account of Shaw as "The greatest name in modern comedy."] Shaw was a constructive critic of modern life, dealing with ideas more than characters or situations, presenting provocative argument as witty entertainment.

782 Nathan, George Jean. "Theatre Week: Mind and Matter," NEWSWEEK, XV (12 Feb 1940), 38-40.
Shaw's mind and alertness are on the decline, as evidenced in Geneva, his most static play. It is exaggerated propaganda, ineffective and dull.

783 "New Theatre: 'In Good King Charles's Golden Days,'" TIMES (Lond), 10 May 1940, p. 4.
Shaw's King Charles views the Restoration as an intelligent twentieth-century Fabian Irishman would. He is lively, witty, and shrewd. The play (New Theater, Lond) is a conversation, with touches of caricature and horseplay.

784 "Plays and Pictures: In Good King Charles's Golden Days," NS&Nation, XIX (18 May 1940), 643.
In Good King Charles's Golden Days is not funny, "not even provoking." There are interminable scenes and dialog. Indeed, there is no drama, "not one moment of suspense." Style is all that is left, and while Shaw has little to say, he says it elegantly.

785 Price, Clair. "G.B.S. is Still At It," NYTMag, 11 Feb 1940, pp. 3, 16.
Shaw is still fighting against formidable odds to convene a conference to end the war, having recently endorsed Ribbentrop's Russian pact but not endorsed Stalin's invasion of Finland. Of course, he has taken up many challenges before, from Oxford accents to a new London theater. Though he does not have the physical stamina he once possessed, he still has intellectual verve.

786 Protopopescu, Dragoş. "George Bernard Shaw," REVISTA FUNDAŢIILOR REGALE (Bucharest), VII, No 9 (1940), 558-88.
Shaw abandoned horizontal drama for vertical (like medieval moralities) to depict conflicts between equals (Caesar and Cleopatra, Undershaft and Barbara). His plays have dynamic not static morality, and are dramas of the human condition and ultimate vital truth. He learned a new vision of death and longevity from the German biologist Weismann, as witness the Creative Evolution in <u>Back to Methuselah</u>. [In Romanian.]

787 Vernon, Grenville. "The Stage and Screen: Geneva," COMMONWEAL, XXXI (16 Feb 1940), 367.
<u>Geneva</u> (Henry Miller Theater, NY) is not a play but "an interesting, at times an exhilarating, discussion."

788 Waldorf, Wilella. "Shaw's 'Geneva' Presented at Henry Miller's Theatre," NY POST (31 Jan 1940) [not seen in this form]; rptd in CRITICS' THEATRE REVIEWS (NY), I (1940), 404.
"'Geneva' finds Shaw still inclined to talk his audience to death," but the trial scene is lively. Shaw remains provocative and amusing (Henry Miller Theater, NY).

789 Wanderscheck, Hermann. "Shaw und Churchill" (Shaw and Churchill), DER GOLDENE BORN (Leipzig), V (1940), 67-68.
Shaw is a critic of "Churchill's war against Germany"; Shaw knows that Britain is an exploitative country. [An aggressive product of the Nazi period.] [In German.]

790 Watts, Richard, Jr. "Mr. Shaw Nods," NYHT, (31 Jan 1940) [not seen in this form]; rptd in CRITICS' THEATRE REVIEWS (NY), I (1940), 404.
<u>Geneva</u> (Henry Miller Theater, NY) is tedious, with only moments of the former Shavian fire. There is little action and too much talk in this "static debate about the state of the world."

791 Whipple, Sidney B. "Shaw's Geneva a Study of International Turmoil," NY WORLD-TELEGRAM (31 Jan 1940) [not seen in this form]; rptd in CRITICS' THEATRE REVIEWS (NY), I (1940), 405.

Geneva (Henry Miller Theater, NY), "a treatise on international politics," seems to be the culmination of Shaw's warnings in Heartbreak House that political incompetence and military solutions to problems will lead again to war. Shaw casts obvious truths in dramatic and entertaining language; but the subject may be too big—too horrible—to be contained in a play.

792 Wyatt, Euphemia Van Rensselaer. "The Drama: Moral Disarmament," CATHOLIC WORLD, CL (March 1940), 728-29.

In Geneva, Shaw has put his play into the Preface. Shaw's direct prose makes even political platitudes worth hearing. The Spanish Señora is puzzling, and the Deaconess needs "a more triumphant role."

793 Yamamoto, Jitsuhiko. "Bernard Shaw," KAIZO (Tokyo), XXII, No 12 (Dec 1940), 284-95; rptd in SEKAI BUNKAJIN JUNREI (Pilgrimage to Men of Culture) (Tokyo: Kaizosha, 1948), pp. 108-128.

[Yamamoto called on Shaw at Whitehall Court, Lond, on 19 April 1940. He records Shaw's views on various subjects from the world situation to his impression of Japan.] [In Japanese.]

1941

---

794 Anderson Imbert, Enrique. [Review of In Good King Charles's Golden Days], SUR (Argentina), No 77 (Feb 1941), 72-74.

In Good King Charles's Golden Days is the first historical play of Shaw's which does not follow the past through the spiritual forms of the present. It is a weak play. [In Spanish.]

795 Anderson, John. "'Doctor's Dilemma' Revived by Cornell," NY JOURNAL AND AMERICAN (12 March 1941) [not seen in this form]; rptd in CRITICS' THEATRE REVIEWS (NY), II (17 March 1941), 366.

The Doctor's Dilemma needs cutting, and it has structural flaws, e.g., an abrupt ending, but its dialog is witty and vigorous. Bramwell Fletcher as Dubedat (Shubert Theater, NY) lacks the conviction of Shaw's artist; but the play is "chiefly about doctors, not the Dubedats," and the actors playing the doctors are excellent, as is Katharine Cornell as Jennifer.

796 Anstey, Edgar. "The Cinema," SPECTATOR (Lond), CLXVI (11 April 1941), 395.
Major Barbara, unlike Pygmalion, "never quite carried its point" on screen. Major Barbara is a "philosophical variety-show."

797 Atkinson, Brooks. "Bernard Shaw Speaking," NYT, 1 June 1941, IX, p. 1.
In his prolog to the movie version of Major Barbara, Shaw's wit is caustic; his voice is warm. His film appearance is a "deeply moving episode."

798 Atkinson, Brooks. "No One Is Fooled By the Stars," NYT, 30 March 1941, IX, p. 1.
[High praise for Katharine Cornell's acting, most recently in The Doctor's Dilemma (Shubert Theater, NY).] Shaw is "frightfully talkative" and frequently boring.

799 Atkinson, Brooks. "The Play: Cornell and Massey Appear in a Revival of Bernard Shaw's 'The Doctor's Dilemma,'" NYT, 12 March 1941, p. 18; rptd in CRITICS' THEATRE REVIEWS (NY), II (17 March 1941), 364.
The Doctor's Dilemma is "skittish and garrulous," but is partially redeemed by Katharine Cornell's portrayal (Shubert Theater, NY) of the "romantic, sincere and womanly" Jennifer Dubedat. But Shaw refuses to do anything with the characters except to talk about them.

800 Barzun, Jacques. DARWIN, MARX, WAGNER: CRITIQUE OF A HERITAGE (Boston: Little, Brown, 1941; rev 2nd ed Garden City, NY: Doubleday Anchor, 1958), pp. 20, 106, 111, 158n, 197-98, 214, 264, 287-88, 307, 310, 323, Index.
Shaw promoted Wagner the musician but combatted the Wagnerian cult by linking the Ring to socialism. [Passing references to and quotations from Shaw.]

801 Bax, Clifford. "Prefatory Note," FLORENCE FARR, BERNARD SHAW, W. B. YEATS: LETTERS (Dublin: Cuala P, 1941; rptd NY: Dodd, Mead, 1942, and Lond: Home & Van Thal, 1946), pp. v-viii.
Florence Farr visited Bax in 1912 and sent him a locked black box containing the letters from Yeats and Shaw when she left England. Bax opened the box after Farr's death in 1917. Shaw's letters are admirable, and will be valued by posterity.

802 Bookwright. "Reprints, New Editions," NYHTBR, XVIII (14 Sept 1941), 21.
Pygmalion and Major Barbara, two of the Six Plays by Bernard Shaw (Dodd, Mead), are highly successful movies; hopefully, Heartbreak House, though "talky," will be made into a movie.

803 Bower, Anthony. "Films," NATION, CLII (10 May 1941), 565.
The film of Major Barbara is "too argumentative, too subtle, too verbose," and the discussion of religion seems dated. Barbara thus emerges as a "charming crank." But the dialog is brilliant and the cast superb.

804 Branch, Lesley. "Warring Britain's New Movie, 'Major Barbara,'" VOGUE, XCVII (1 April 1941), 72-73, 105-6, 111.
Major Barbara was filmed between air raids at Denham Studios near London. The director, Gabriel Pascal, believes that Shaw is a "great universal writer," equal to Shakespeare and Goethe. Indeed, Shaw is Pascal's "creed," and "all is harmony between them."

805 Brown, John Mason. "Cornell and Massey in 'The Doctor's Dilemma,'" NY POST (12 March 1941) [not seen in this form]; rptd in CRITICS' THEATRE REVIEWS (NY), II (17 March 1941), 367.
The Katharine Cornell production (Shubert Theater, NY) of The Doctor's Dilemma compares favorably with the 1927 Theater Guild production with Alfred Lunt and Lynn Fontanne —except in Dubedat's death scene. There Bramwell Fletcher conveys self pity, whereas Lunt conveyed "simple ecstasy" in uttering the artist's creed. The play is not a tragedy, as Shaw says, but one of Shaw's most amusing comedies.

806 Chaning-Pearce, M[elville]. "Beyond the Tragic Climax," THE TERRIBLE CRYSTAL: STUDIES IN KIERKEGAARD AND MODERN CHRISTIANITY (NY: Oxford, 1941), pp. 194-201.

Shaw surpasses his powers in the visionary glory of Saint Joan, "the most salient example of tragic art in modern English." The play presents Joan in conflict between time and eternity, leading respectively to martyrdom and sainthood—a conflict focussed in the majestic sixth scene. Shaw's Joan illustrates the Christian themes of sacrifice and resurrection.

807 Chesterton, Mrs. Cecil [Ada Elizabeth]. THE CHESTERTONS (Lond: Chapman & Hall, 1941), pp. 7, 13, 14, 58, 127, 135, 147-48, 188, 201, 278, Index.

[Anecdotes and Shavian quips pertaining to Shaw's relations with G. K. and Cecil Edward Chesterton.]

808 "CINEMA: The Chocolate Soldier," TIME, XXXVIII (17 Nov 1941), 92-93.

The movie of THE CHOCOLATE SOLDIER combines the plot of Ferenc Molnar's THE GUARDSMAN and the music of Oscar Straus's operetta into a "sapless hybrid." "The music doesn't fit the plot, and vice versa."

809 "CINEMA: The New Pictures," TIME, XXXVII (2 June 1941), 80, 82-83.

The film of Major Barbara has "brilliant, provocative, richly comic" dialog. Gabriel Pascal had to contend with Shaw's irascible nature, but the two produce great movies. The eight-minute prolog with Shaw as actor is "unsurpassed by the performances which follow."

810 Crowther, Bosley. "The Screen in Review: George Bernard Shaw's 'Major Barbara,' at the Astor, Seen as a Triumph," NYT, 15 May 1941, p. 27.

Major Barbara is a triumphant proof of British wit and wry satire, even in the face of adversity. The powerful theme has not lost its relevancy. The film version is perhaps even more coherent and better drama than the play.

811 "The Doctor's Dilemma: Katharine Cornell revives Shaw," LIFE, X (5 May 1941), 82-84, 86.

[A pictorial essay of Cornell production of <u>The Doctor's Dilemma</u>. Plot synopsis given through pictures.]

812 Dunkel, Wilbur Dwight. SIR ARTHUR PINERO (Chicago: University of Chicago P, 1941; Lond: Cambridge UP, 1943), pp. 2, 4, 6, 8, 18, 23, 38, 47, 58, 60, 74, 81, 88, 90, 103, 106, 125, Index.
Unlike most of his contemporaries, Shaw disliked Pinero's early drama; his adverse criticism, however, should be discounted as the rancor of a frustrated unpublished author. <u>Mrs. Warren's Profession</u> has more merit than the average playgoer perceived; and <u>Widowers' Houses</u> develops "an important social thesis." Shaw is unique among English playwrights because of his ideas, which he expounded in long prefaces and essays.

813 Esdaile, Ernest. SHOW ME SHAW: MR. BERNARD SHAW'S CONVERSION TO THE FILMS (Lond: Mitre P, 1941; rptd Folcroft, Pa.: Folcroft Library Editions, 1973).
Shaw stands as "the cosmic Comedian" of English drama, having triumphed over misunderstanding, even abuse. He wrote plays as he made speeches, out of an inner compulsion to give utterance to his message. The plays all have a combative tone. The prefaces reveal "heart and sentiment" as well as intellect. [A superficial sketch of Shaw's life, ending with brief reference to Shaw's response to Esdaile's 1938 lecture at the Metro-Goldwyn-Mayer studios on "The Art of Speaking on the Pictures."]

814 Ferguson, Otis. "Not So Good," NEW REPUBLIC, CIV (9 June 1941), 793-94.
The film of <u>Major Barbara</u> is a bore. Shaw's theater is all ideas, and all talk. The theme of religious hypocrisy is true but trite, and the plot lacks life and power.

815 Freedley, George and John A. Reeves. A HISTORY OF THE THEATRE (NY: Crown, 1941), pp. 204, 330, 364, 373, 405, 433, 437, 439, 481, 482, 490, 493, 531, 569, 570-74, Index; espec 570-74.
Shaw takes precedence among modern British dramatists. [Résumé of his work.] <u>Saint Joan</u> is his best play. All his plays have "magnificent writing, actable parts, provocative thinking, and a good deal of garrulousness." [Passing

references to Shaw apropos of other modern dramatists and his place in world drama.]

816 Fuller, Edmund. A PAGEANT OF THE THEATRE (NY: Crowell, 1941), pp. 164, 211, 216, 218, 220, 226-30, 251, Index, espec 226-30.
Shaw and Ibsen are the two giants of the modern European theater. Shaw's plays are a rich variety of genres and themes, and his prefaces are "brilliant controversial documents." His wit and satire "make him something of a modern Aristophanes." [The Devil's Disciple and Heartbreak House are offered as examples.]

817 Gassner, John. PRODUCING THE PLAY, with THE NEW SCENE TECHNICIAN'S HANDBOOK, by Philip Barber (NY: Dryden P, 1941; rev ed NY: Holt, Rinehart and Winston, 1953), pp. 19, 30, 49, 51, 60, 124, 159-60, 165, 171, 337, 348, 418, 448, 454, 532, 651, Index.
[Brief references to some of Shaw's plays, naming them as examples of certain types of comedy, giving examples of stage business in Shaw's plays, and mentioning the use of music in Man and Superman.]

818 Gibbs, Wolcott. "The Theatre: Shaw's Sawbones," NYer, XVII (22 March 1941), 36, 38.
In The Doctor's Dilemma Shaw is amusing but "powerfully given to talking nonsense."

819 Gilder, Rosamond. "Glamour and Purpose: Broadway in Review," TAM, XXV (May 1941), 327-35, espec 327-29.
In The Doctor's Dilemma (Shubert Theater, NY) Shaw uses the stage as a platform to expose medical stupidity. Shaw wittily attacks six types of doctors through "the pixie malice" of the artist's mind of Dubedat. The play is a "stately intellectual minuet." Dubedat's death is no more death than Shaw's play is life.

820 Green, E. Mawby. "Echoes from Broadway: G.B.S. on Stage and Screen," THEATRE WORLD (Lond), XXXV (July 1941), 17-18.
The Katharine Cornell version of The Doctor's Dilemma (Shubert Theater, NY) compliments "this old Shaw chestnut," though it needs cutting. Gabriel Pascal's film version of

Pygmalion and Major Barbara "are really no more than embellished stage productions, trimmed of most of the unnecessary talk." Pascal intends to film other Shaw plays. Perhaps he should consider doing Cornell in The Doctor's Dilemma.

821 Joad, C[yril] E[dwin] M[itchinson]. "Shaw, On This Birthday, Brings Back to Mind the Qualities Which Have Made Him Britain's Outstanding Man of Letters," NYTMag, 20 July 1941, pp. 5, 26, 27.
The hero-worship of Shaw is based on his reputation as a revolutionary propagandist and pamphleteer turning against the conventions of Victorian England and the "solid foundation of the plays themselves." Though his preeminence has declined with the later plays, his place in English letters is assured.

822 Kronenberger, Louis. "Shaw's Satire Is Like His Beard—Neat But Long," NY NEWSPAPER "PM" (12 March 1941) [not seen in this form]; rptd in CRITICS' THEATRE REVIEWS (NY), II (17 March 1941), 366.
The Doctor's Dilemma has "some first-rate dialog, and a couple of first-rate scenes,...a first-rate ending," and "a first-rate character," Dubedat. But it is somewhat static; its form intermingles ideas rather than advances a plot; and the satire on the medical profession is worn. [Praise for Guthrie McClintic's direction (Shubert Theater, NY) and the acting.]

823 Krutch, Joseph Wood. "Drama: A Pretty Problem," NATION, CLII (22 March 1941), 331.
The Doctor's Dilemma (Katharine Cornell production, Shubert Theater, NY) provides "irresponsible wit and satiric farce-comedy." The characters have nothing of human nature about them; e.g., Dubedat's dying statement is rhetorically effective but not moving. And the dilemma lacks credibility. Yet the play still seems "shrewder and funnier than ninety-nine out of a hundred plays."

824 Kutzsch, Gerhard. DER FALL "CANDIDA": EINE KRITISCHE STUDIE ÜBER GEORGE BERNARD SHAW (The Case of Candida: A Critical Study of George Bernard Shaw) (Leipzig: Koehler & Ameling, 1941).

[Chapters: "Bernard Shaw and The Early 1900s in London," "Bernard Shaw's Candida," "The Verdict on Candida," "Actors and Public."] "Candida is neither an artistic revelation of lofty beauty nor a creation full of the spirit which embraces still and deep thoughts about the eternal-human. It is rather an occasional piece—written for Ellen Terry [sic] in order, with her help, to win reputation and to achieve fame for Shaw."

825 Lockridge, Richard. "Miss Cornell Revives 'The Doctor's Dilemma' at the Shubert Theater," NY SUN (12 March 1941) [not seen in this form]; rptd in CRITICS' THEATRE REVIEWS (NY), II (17 March 1941), 345.
The Doctor's Dilemma (Shubert Theater, NY) sparkles with light-hearted satire in which prestigious medical practitioners are dissected in the midst of "delightful dissertations on art and morals." The play's only flaws are abrupt changes of mood and too-obvious wit at times.

826 "Love and Mr. Shaw," HARPER'S BAZAAR, LXXV (15 March 1941), 54-55.
Jennifer Dubedat's love for her genius husband lends nobility to the somewhat tedious talk in The Doctor's Dilemma. Major Barbara as a thinking and loving heroine has become today's Everywoman. [Praise for Katharine Cornell's Jennifer and for Wendy Hiller's Barbara.]

827 Mackail, Denis. THE STORY OF J. M. B. (Lond: Peter Davis, 1941), pp. 169, 178, 348, 387, 397, 401, 410, 413, 415, 418, 421, 422, 432, 435, 443, 444, 449, 468, 469, 486, 575, 608, 681, 683.
There were similarities between James M. Barrie and Shaw, although they perhaps never fully appreciated each other. They were much the same age. Both came to London with "nothing but their brains." Both had been "struggling and then successful journalists." Both were infatuated with the stage.

828 Mantle, Burns. "'The Doctor's Dilemma' Is a Handsome Revival by Cornell," NY DAILY NEWS (12 March 1941) [not seen in this form]; rptd in CRITICS' THEATRE REVIEWS (NY), II (17 March 1941), 367.
The satire on doctors is still incisive and amusing in The Doctor's Dilemma (Shubert Theater, NY); and the Dubedats

are of a universal type—loyal wife to waster husband. [Compares the Alfred Lunt and Lynn Fontanne Theater Guild production (1927) with the current one, which better preserves the satiric tone by means of a more cynical Dubedat.]

829 Miró, Cesár. "Teatro-Cine-Radio: Pigmalión," (Theater-Cinema-Radio: Pygmalion), CULTURA PERUANA (Peru), I, No 4 (Sept 1941).
The performance of Pygmalion, a play of profound psychological and sociological implications, by the Asociación de Artistas Aficionados, was well received by the public. [In Spanish.]

830 Monner-Sans, José María. "Shaw, Pirandello, Lenormand," MÁSCARA (Argentina), I, No 9 (May 1941), 5; rptd MÁSCARA, X, No 112 (Jan-March 1951), 3.
Shaw deals with ethical problems, but as a satirist writes comedies and farces. Pirandello treats ontological problems; as a humorist he writes grotesque dramas. Shaw's is a theater of synthesis, Pirandello's of disruption, while Lenormand's worries at the problem of the being in oneself, and of ethics and behavior. [In Spanish.]

831 "MOVIES: Second Shaw in Celluloid: 'Major Barbara' in New Clothes Comes to American Screen," NEWSWEEK, XVII (19 May 1941), 74.
The excellent film of Major Barbara makes delightful "the frequent long speeches full of the G. B. S. wit and wisdom."

832 O'Hara, John. "Entertainment Week: George Rx," NEWSWEEK, XVII (24 March 1941), 70.
Shaw's satire of the medical profession in The Doctor's Dilemma (Shubert Theater, NY) is correct, though Shaw is too ready to criticize everything. [Adverse criticism of Katharine Cornell as Jennifer.]

833 Sampson, George. THE CONCISE CAMBRIDGE HISTORY OF ENGLISH LITERATURE (Lond: Cambridge UP, 1941; 1961), pp. 607, 759, 858, 944, 977, 993, 1020, 1021, 1027, 1028, 1029.

[Passing references to Arms and the Man, The Quintessence of Ibsenism, Widowers' Houses, Mrs. Warren's Profession, and The Philanderer.]

834 Smith, Winifred. "Bernard Shaw and His Critics (1892-1938)," POET LORE, XLVII (Spring 1941), 76-83.
From the 1890's Shaw has been idolized by friends and pilloried by political enemies and romanticists who do not recognize in him a fellow idealist. [Review of criticism of Shaw's ideas, technique, patriotism, place in modern drama, and attitude toward the Soviet Union.] He is just now beginning to be appreciated.

835 Sörensen, Edith D. "George Bernard Shaws Puritanismus" (The Puritanism of George Bernard Shaw). Unpublished dissertation, University of Hamburg, 1941. [Listed in McNamee, and in Altick and Matthews, Item 1756.] [In German.]

836 "The Talk of the Town: Shaw's Royalties," NYer, XVII (3 May 1941), 9-13, espec 12-13.
[Discussion of Shaw's profitable royalty arrangement and control over sets, scenery, cuts in dialog, and advertising —as exemplified in the Cornell production of The Doctor's Dilemma.]

837 "The Theatre: Revival in Manhattan," TIME, XXXVII (24 March 1941), 43.
The Doctor's Dilemma (Shubert Theater, NY) is "pretty artificial," though it contains "tangy Shavian broadsides" which are still relevant in spite of occasionally dated vocabulary.

838 Thompson, Dorothy. "Major Barbara," LADIES HOME JOURNAL, LVIII (Aug 1941), 6, 105.
The film of Major Barbara demonstrates that "humanitarianism is not enough." All Shaw's plays, like Shakespeare's, contain great women. Shaw is a feminist, and looks to women to achieve a good society. Major Barbara, for example, reconciles and gives purpose to "the man of Power and the man of Intellect."

839 Vernon, Grenville. "The Stage and Screen: The Doctor's Dilemma," COMMONWEAL, XXXIII (28 March 1941), 547-75.
Though the basic idea of The Doctor's Dilemma (Shubert Theater, NY) is dated, the dialog and humor are vivid. The play combines Shaw the "sage,...poet,...harlequin and...bad boy."

840 Watts, Richard, Jr. "Doctors at Bay," NYHT (1? March 1941) [not seen in this form]; rptd in CRITICS' THEATRE REVIEWS (NY), II (17 March 1941), 365.
"Shaw's celebrated sneer" at doctors remains witty and vital in The Doctor's Dilemma (Shubert Theater, NY), and Dubedat "has one of the great speeches of the modern theater." Though the play's structure is unsteady, the acting saves it from any dullness.

841 Wells, H. G. [Letter to Shaw, 16 April 1941], in G. B. S. 90, p. 55; rptd in CRITICAL HERITAGE, pp. 366-67, Item 121.
Major Barbara (Pascal film version) is delightful, though Undershaft needs "a more subtle face."

842 Whipple, Sidney B. "The Doctor's Dilemma Magnificently Played," NY WORLD-TELEGRAM (12 March 1941) [not seen in this form]; rptd in CRITICS' THEATRE REVIEWS (NY), II (17 March 1941), 364.
The satire on the medical profession in The Doctor's Dilemma has lost its bite, but the play remains an "exquisitely written" comedy. Katharine Cornell (Shubert Theater, NY) masterfully suggests Jennifer Dubedat's reserve of power, in spite of the fact that Shaw's character is only a sketch. The doctors caricatured in the play are equally well-acted.

843 Whitebait, William. "The Movies: Major Barbara at the Odeon," NS&Nation, XXI (12 April 1941), 387.
The movie version of Major Barbara is different from Shaw's play. The play's argument has been cut, and Undershaft is altered into a magnetic businessman, instead of an amoral figure. Rex Harrison's Greek professor takes on more significance than called for in the drama.

844 "Wigs on the Green," TIME, XXXVIII (24 Nov 1941), 32.
CAVALCADE submitted questions to Shaw and he answered them. [Two of those answers—both dealing with the war—are included.]

845 Wyatt, Euphemia Van Rensselaer. "The Drama: The Doctor's Dilemma," CATHOLIC WORLD, CLIII (May 1941), 215-19, espec 216-17.
Shaw's treatment of women in drama is chivalric, as in the case of Jennifer Dubedat, whose love balances scientific coldness in The Doctor's Dilemma (Shubert Theater, NY). The dialog of the play is sharp and witty.

846 Young, Stark. "Doctor in Spite of Himself," NEW REPUBLIC, CIV (24 March 1941), 404-5.
In The Doctor's Dilemma (Shubert Theater, NY) Shaw's thesis that artists have only one point of integrity, their art, is platitudinous; and it is wrong because it implies a separate moral standard for artists. The play does have, however, a degree of poetry.

1942

847 Alvaro, Corrado. "Le case del vedovo di G. B. Shaw" (Shaw's Widowers' Houses), IL POPOLO DI ROMA (Rome), 27 Feb 1942; rptd in Alvaro, CRONACHE E SCRITTI TEATRALI (Theater News and Other Writings on Theater) ed by A. Barbina (Rome: "Abete," 1976), pp. 207-9.
Like all vital plays, Widowers' Houses does not seek a moral, a conclusion, or a remedy. Shaw goes straight to the origins of all bourgeois fortunes: house property, which is the fundamental necessity, dream, and incubus of humankind. [In Italian.]

848 Anderson, John. "Katharine Cornell in 'Candida' Matinees," NY JOURNAL-AMERICAN (28 April 1942) [not seen in this form]; rptd in CRITICS' THEATRE REVIEWS (NY), III (4 May 1942), 301.

Candida is a modern classic, and Katharine Cornell understands both the bewitching and "kerosene and onion aspect" of the title role. Burgess Meredith plays Marchbanks as tough-minded rather than dreamy and thus improves on Shaw's "stencil idea of a poet." Raymond Massey's Morell is vigorous and distinguished. All in all, the production, under Guthrie McClintic's direction (American Theater Wing War Service, Inc., Shubert Theater, NY), is superb.

>   **849** Atkinson, Brooks. "Best Work of the Year," NYT, 3 May 1942, VIII, p. 1; rptd as "Katharine Cornell in Candida," in Atkinson, BROADWAY SCRAPBOOK (NY: Theatre Arts, 1947), pp. 208-12.

Burgess Meredith's Marchbanks has "poise and strength of spirit," and Raymond Massey's Morell has stature. Katharine Cornell's Candida is beautiful, warm, proud, and understanding. In fact, the McClintic production of Candida (Shubert Theater, NY) "is a richer comedy than Shaw imagined."

>   **850** Atkinson, Brooks. "The Play in Review: Katharine Cornell, Massey And Meredith Appear in Revival of Shaw's 'Candida,' For the Army-Navy Relief," NYT, 28 April 1942, p. 24; rptd in CRITICS' THEATRE REVIEWS, III (4 May 1942), 303; and in ON STAGE: SELECTED THEATER REVIEWS FROM THE NEW YORK TIMES 1920-1970, ed by Bernard Beckerman and Howard Siegman (NY: Arno P, 1973), p. 241.

Candida is "an association of several rare people": a sensitive poet struggling with a real problem, a superior man who can learn humility, a "luminous, tender and entrancingly wise" woman. Even the minor characters are humanized in the Katharine Cornell production (Shubert Theater, NY).

>   **851** Auden, W. H. "The Fabian Figaro," COMMONWEAL, XXXVII (23 Oct 1942), 12-13; rptd in Louis Kronenberger (ed), GEORGE BERNARD SHAW: A CRITICAL SURVEY (Cleveland and NY: World, 1953), pp. 153-57.

Shaw is an artist, not a propagandist. His plays are a joy not because they are serious ("He cannot, thank God, be serious for very long") but because of their excess of energy. Shaw's virtuous characters (e.g., Candida, Joan)

189

are insufferable; he cannot portray convincing artists
(e.g., Marchbanks, Dubedat); his political heroes are best.
[Review of Hesketh Pearson's G .B. S., A FULL LENGTH
PORTRAIT (1942); includes biographical comments.]

852 Brown, John Mason. "G. B. S.: Satan, Saint, and
Superman," SRL, XXV (24 Oct 1942), 6-7, 46-47; rptd
in Brown, SEEING THINGS (NY & Lond: McGraw-Hill,
1946), pp. 69-83; and in Brown, DRAMATIS PERSONAE: A
RETROSPECTIVE SHOW (NY: Viking, 1963), pp. 103-112.
Shaw the man is more interesting than anything he ever
wrote. A writer of flowing letters, he is a cold lover; he
was a brave man during World War II, though something of a
fascist. He "reoriented and liberated the English-speaking
stage," with disagreement, exaggeration, and paradox his
stocks in trade. His prefaces and letters will endure, but
his plays suffer from outdated ideas, a failure to
understand "the average values of average living," and
characters who are all G. B. S. He is, however, a better
playwright than Ibsen. [Review of Hesketh Pearson's G .B.
S., A Full Length Portrait (1942).]

853 Brown, John Mason. "A Magnificent Revival of Mr.
Shaw's Candida," NY WORLD-TELEGRAM, 28 April 1942
[not seen in this form]; rptd in CRITICS' THEATRE
REVIEWS, III (4 May 1942), 302.
Candida contains deeply human laughter and wisdom, wedding
wit and compassion. Katharine Cornell's Candida (Shubert
Theater, NY) is both sage and simple; Raymond Massey's
Morell is admirable; and Burgess Meredith's Marchbanks is
brilliant—neither a whiner nor a Bunthorne.

854 Burnham, David. "The Stage & Screen,"
COMMONWEAL, XXXVI (29 May 1942), 135-36.
Candida catches Shaw "off-guard, beguiling in place of
reviling," his satire reaching "the heart rather than the
brain." Katharine Cornell (Shubert Theater, NY) is a great
Candida; all the other parts are over-written and must be
underplayed.

855 Clemens, Cyril. "Mr. Shaw and Biographers," SRL,
XXV (24 Jan 1942), 11.

[In a letter to the editor, Clemens claims to have a letter from Shaw denouncing biographers as "the plagues of my life."]

856 Dent, Alan. PRELUDES & STUDIES (Lond & Toronto: Macmillan, 1942; rptd NY & Lond: Kennikat P, 1970), pp. 121, 160.
Shaw liked ALL'S WELL THAT ENDS WELL and its "unromantic wrangling" so much that Man and Superman might be called its modern variant.

857 Dunkel, Wilbur Dwight. "George Bernard Shaw," SEWANEE REVIEW, L (April-June 1942), 255-62.
Shaw's reputation as a public-minded author may not surpass his contribution as a playwright. The journalist and dramatist in him are not so disparate as he would have his public believe. But his laughter at human foibles obscures his meaning for the people whom he most needs to convince in order to bring about his reforms. Ridicule is his chief characteristic as a dramatist but also his weakness.

858 Dunstan, W. B. "The Doctor's Dilemma," NS&Nation, XXIII (14 March 1942), 194.
[A letter to the editor recalls several anecdotes about Shaw and Sir Almroth Wright, a doctor. Written in response to a critique on The Doctor's Dilemma.]

859 Esdaile, Ernest. BERNARD SHAW'S POSTSCRIPT TO FAME (Lond: Quality P, 1942; rptd Folcroft, Pa.: Folcroft Library Editions, 1972).
Shaw's "postscript to fame" are the films, which give new life to his plays. The prefaces, with their miraculous "profundity of knowledge," are "the most unique things about his Plays." [Adulatory biographical sketch of Shaw, "the arch foe of everything dirty, mean, and cruel."]

860 "Florence Farr and Her Friends: Mr. Shaw on the Art of Acting," TLS, XLI (7 March 1942), 118.
The letters from Shaw in Florence Farr, Bernard Shaw and W. B. Yeats offer some first rate advice on acting. Shaw urges Farr to improve her technique and look to her professional improvement, while Yeats is delighted by her and writes poetry for her to recite. Yeats found Caesar and Cleopatra moving but "vulgar."

861 Greene, Graham. BRITISH DRAMATISTS (Lond: William Collins, 1942), pp. 41, 42.
Shaw is fond of adopting ideas for the sake of their paradoxes, but he will discard them as soon as they fail to startle an audience. Often Shaw gives people a sense of intellectual activity when they have not exercised their brains but merely strained their eyes at the "startling convolutions of a tumbler."

862 "Haymarket Theatre: 'The Doctor's Dilemma,'" TIMES (Lond), 5 March 1942, p. 6.
The Doctor's Dilemma is resilient in its sparkling dialectics, but the Haymarket Theater production (Lond) lacks the buoyancy and fun of earlier revivals.

863 Illes, Bela. "Books and Writers: Meetings with Bernard Shaw," SOVIET LITERATURE (1942), pp. 87-89.
[Recounts conversations with Shaw in Moscow during his 1931 visit to the Soviet Union; quotes Shaw on writers and publishers, birthday celebrations, and Stalin.]

864 Isaacs, Edith J. R. "The Playwright as Critic: G. B. S.," TAM, XXVI (Dec 1942), 755-62.
Shaw understood costume, stage scenery, acting--the business of the theater; his drama criticism is trenchant and illuminating. He fought the theater's stagnation, using Henry Irving as chief target. But he was kind to rival playwrights. he demanded "fine shades of quality in acting," expecting clear and accurate speech and musical qualities from actors. He recognized the beauty, the music, of acted Shakespeare.

865 K., F. "Drama Note," NATION, CLV (25 JULY 1942), 79.
THE CHOCOLATE SOLDIER (Carnegie Hall revival) is "a pleasantly nostalgic" experience, with a score that seems fresh, action a bit slow, and adequate stage design and casting.

866 Kronenberger, Louis. "'Candida' Tops Season's Plays," NY NEWSPAPER 'PM' (28 April 1942) [not seen in this form]; rptd in CRITICS' THEATRE REVIEWS, III (4 May 1942), 303.

The Katharine Cornell production of <u>Candida</u> (Shubert Theater, NY) is witty, alive, and moving. Marchbanks is usually insufferable—but Burgess Meredith plays him as mettlesome, boyish, and with a sense of humor. And Cornell's Candida is simple and human. Shaw is more himself when he forgets the plot and simply lets Burgess, Prossy, et al. make fools of each other, and themselves.

867 Kunitz, Stanley J. and Howard Haycraft (eds). "Shaw, George Bernard," TWENTIETH CENTURY AUTHORS (NY: H. H. Wilson, 1942), pp. 1268-70.
[Biographical sketch, with emphasis on Shaw's inconsistent public stance as humorist, crank, and mystic hiding "the innermost Shaw, the timid, tender, modest, idealistic Shaw."]

868 Lockridge, Richard. "Shaw's 'Candida' Is Brilliantly Revived at the Shubert Theater," NY SUN (28 April 1942) [not seen in this form]; rptd in CRITICS' THEATRE REVIEWS, III (4 May 1942), 302.
Candida is the best part Shaw has written for a woman, and Katharine Cornell (Shubert Theater, NY) portrays perfectly Shaw's tranquil, wise woman. Raymond Massey and Burgess Meredith avoid the staginess and shrillness usually attributed to Morell and Marchbanks. The production is, in short, an ideal one.

869 Loewenstein, F[ritz] E[rwin]. "A Collection of Shaviana," TLS, XLI (22 Aug 1942), 420.
It is difficult to locate copies of all Shaw's work since 1875. The Fabian tracts, early novels, syllabi of lectures, notes for theater programs, notes for exhibition catalogs, prefaces to others' books present a challenge to the collector of Shaviana. [Lists bibliographies of Shaw's work. Allan Wade, "Shaviana," TLS, XLI (5 Sept 1942), 444, adds a few items to the list of program notes.]

870 Mantle, Burns. "'Candida' Revival Wins Cheers For Cornell and Her Co-Stars," NY DAILY NEWS, 28 April 1942 [not seen in this form]; rptd in CRITICS' THEATRE REVIEWS, III (4 May 1942), 303.
The Katharine Cornell-Raymond Massey-Burgess Meredith revival of <u>Candida</u> (Shubert Theater, NY) gives to the central figures more humanity than even Shaw intended. The

characters achieve "a spiritual stature unsuspected by their father confessor."

871 Monner Sans, José María. "George Bernard Shaw, Satírico" (George Bernard Shaw, Satirist), PANORAMA DEL NUEVO TEATRO (An Overview of the New Theater) (Buenos Aires) 1942, pp. 93-114.
Shaw's iconoclasm is the key to understanding his dramatic works. His satire is subtly veiled by his sense of humor, which utilizes puns, irony, descriptions in the stage directions, paradoxes, and the diminishing of historical events and personalities. Shaw is a hidden and satirical moralist. [Works alluded to are Mrs. Warren's Profession, Pygmalion, Arms and the Man, Androcles and the Lion, Candida, and You Never Can Tell.] [In Spanish.]

872 "News and Notes: Aryanization," TLS, XLI (21 Feb 1942), 1.
The Germans, in their search for artistic talent, have taken to staging Shaw and Shakespeare. They can justify productions of Shaw as an Irishman stifled under British tyranny.

873 Orwell, George [pseud of Eric Blair]. "The Rediscovery of Europe," LIST, 19 March 1942; rptd in TALKING TO INDIA, 1943 [not seen in these forms]; and in THE COLLECTED ESSAYS, JOURNALISM AND LETTERS OF GEORGE ORWELL, ed by Sonia Orwell and Ian Angus. Vol. II: My Country Right or Left, 1940-1943 (NY: Harcourt, Brace & World, 1968), pp. 197-207.
[Passing references to Shaw, including the observation that "The basis of all Bernard Shaw's attacks on Shakespeare is really the charge—quite true, of course—that Shakespeare wasn't an enlightened member of the Fabian Society."]

874 Pearson, Hesketh. G.B.S., A FULL LENGTH PORTRAIT (NY & Lond: Harper, 1942; rptd Garden City, NY: Garden City Publishing Co., 1946); pub as BERNARD SHAW: HIS LIFE AND PERSONALITY (Lond & Toronto: Collins, 1942; rptd 1944, 1950; rptd Lond: Reprint Society, 1948; NY: Atheneum, 1963). This and G. B. S., A POSTSCRIPT (NY: Harper; Lond: Collins, 1950) rptd as G.B.S., A FULL LENGTH PORTRAIT, AND A POSTSCRIPT (NY: Harper, 1952); rptd as BERNARD SHAW:

A BIOGRAPHY, Introd by Richard Ingrams (Lond:
Macdonald & Jane's, 1975).
Shaw was "a mystic in spiritual matters and an
institutionalist in temporal matters." His greatness lay in
his humor and eccentric personality, not in his beliefs and
preaching, though he was "in the forefront of a revolution
in morals." He was "a classical dramatist" who returned to
"primitive dramaturgy"; yet his characters are seldom
lifelike, except in his best plays—<u>Caesar and Cleopatra</u>,
<u>Androcles and the Lion</u>, and <u>Saint Joan</u>. Shaw was unique in
his ability to portray the religious temperament, and his
best characters express religious emotion. His criticism is
readable, irreverent, original, and courageous—especially
attractive in its personal digressions, "irresponsible
gaiety of spirit," and self-portraiture. His novels lack
his characteristic exuberance and humor. His prefaces,
which cost him more labor than the plays, are invaluable to
the biographer because of their expression of personal
views. [A biography of Shaw for which the author consulted
Shaw on doubtful points, having him check the facts in the
book. Contains much anecdotal material and little
criticism. Detailed information on Shaw's relationship with
William Morris, William Archer, Ellen Terry, the Webbs, H.
G. Wells, Charlotte Payne-Townshend, Frank Harris, and many
others.]

875 Pilger, Else. "George Bernard Shaw in
Deutschland." Unpublished dissertation, University of
Münster, 1942. [Listed in McNamee, and in Altick and
Matthews, Item 1746.] [In German.]

876 "Plays and Pictures: <u>The Doctor's Dilemma</u>, at
the Haymarket," NS&Nation, XXIII (14 March 1942),
175.
In <u>The Doctor's Dilemma</u> (Haymarket Theater, Lond), the real
dilemma lies in the "patient's preference for being
bamboozled, his demand not for science, but for faith and
necromancy."

877 Reynolds, Horace. "Farr to Yeats to Shaw,"
CHRISTIAN SCIENCE MONITOR MAGAZINE, 2 May 1942, p.
12.
<u>Florence Farr, Bernard Shaw, W. B. Yeats: Letters</u> shows
Shaw to be a creditable drama critic and an honorable man.

In his letters, he exhibits both an aesthetic attitude and common sense. Yeats found him a bit vulgar.

878 Robinson, Lennox. CURTAIN UP: AN AUTOBIOGRAPHY (Lond: Michael Joseph, 1942), pp. 24, 25, 26, 37, 122, et passim.
[Robinson became Shaw's "secretary" at the age of 23; he had no duties but attended rehearsals (e.g., of Misalliance at Frohman's repertory theater). Memoirs. No criticism.]

879 Roetel, Erich ("Maroko"). "Obrácenje kapetana Brassbounda" (Captain Brassbound's Conversion), OSJEČKA POZORNICA (Osijek), II, No 18 (1942/43), 1-4. [Not seen but listed in FILOLOGIJA (Zagreb), 3 (1962), 264.] [In Croatian.]

880 S., F. "'The Doctor's Dilemma,'" THEATRE WORLD (Lond), XXXVII (April 1942), 5-6.
The Haymarket Theater (Lond) revival of The Doctor's Dilemma shows that Shaw can still produce laughter "in an age that has almost forgotten how to laugh or cry." The doctor's dilemma, as well as Mrs. Dubedat's loyalty, is "age-old." But "only Shaw could give us such a death-bed scene." The production does well with "the long passages of inaction in which the play abounds, notwithstanding the brilliant dialog."

881 Short, Ernest. THEATRICAL CAVALCADE (Lond: Eyre & Spottiswoode, 1942), pp. 11, 37, 42, 51, 55-72, 142, 214, 215, Index, espec 55-72.
Shaw's genius was to present politics and philosophy in dramatic—and amusing—form. He is at his best when he is being "unpleasant." Both rationalist and idealist, he preaches his message in play after play. He is an actors' dramatist because of the profusion of amusing, interesting and significant characters. [Includes a survey of Shaw's major plays to date.]

882 Smith, Winifred. "Mystics in the Modern Theatre," SEWANEE REVIEW, L (Jan 1942), 34-48, espec 44-45.
Shaw's post-World War I plays show "a tragic sense of life" anticipated in Act III of Man and Superman. Back to Methuselah, with its return to the Life Force religion,

196

attempts to restore hope after the despair of <u>Heartbreak House</u> and <u>Saint Joan</u>, but it fails. It is too long, mixes fantasy and satire, and has tedious debates.

883 Stefanescu, Mircea. "Cronica dramatica: Teatrul Munca si Lumina: <u>Sa nu pui minan foc</u>: Comedie in patru acte de Bernard Shaw" (Dramatic Chronicle: Theater of Labor: <u>You Never Can Tell</u>: Comedy in Four Acts by Bernard Shaw), CURENTAL (Bucharest), 6 Dec 1942.

Shaw's subject in <u>You Never Can Tell</u> provides for a discussion on various social aspects, and sets two abstract ideas in conflict—a principled London society, and free love. [In Romanian.]

884 Strauss, E[rich]. BERNARD SHAW: ART AND SOCIALISM (Lond: Victor Gollancz, 1942; rptd Folcroft, Pa.: Folcroft P, 1969).

[Examines in detail how Shaw's socialism affected his art.] Shaw's socialism permeates his dramatic work; it gives his art dramatic tension between life and art, between action and thought. Admittedly, the plays are not dramatized treatises and the problems of socialism rarely overtly surface in them; yet they abound in social criticism. Shaw's personal change from a man of action to a man of ideas is reflected in his early change from plays of disillusionment (e.g., <u>Widowers' Houses</u>, <u>Mrs. Warren's Profession</u>, <u>Plays Pleasant</u>, <u>Man and Superman</u>) to plays of conversion (<u>Captain Brassbound's Conversion</u>, <u>The Devil's Disciple</u>). Shaw uses love-interest symbolically: the possessive, romantic, emotional woman (e.g., Blanche Sartorius, Henrietta Trefusis, Julia Craven, Mrs. Warren, Ann Whitefield, the Millionairess) represents "the world as it is," particularly capitalist society, in contrast with the self-possessed realistic, intellectual woman. The Superman philosophy is an attempt to escape "the forces of reality." Some of the plays reflect a disillusionment with socialism in depicting the defeat of those espousing Shavian values, and in portraying hateful working-class characters and sympathetic capitalists. Ironically, Shaw was able to create excellent representatives of the powers he attacks and failed to create suitable representatives of his own views. But Shaw did not abandon his dreams; he merely transferred his social to religious concerns in the plays.

885 "Theater: Cornell's 'Candida,'" NEWSWEEK, XIX (25 May 1942), 60, 62.
Five benefit performances of Candida, the proceeds going to the Army Emergency Fund and the Navy Relief Society, constituted the "biggest hit of the season."

886 "The Theatre: Shaw-Inspiring Spectacle," TIME, XXXIX (11 May 1942), 40.
Candida was revived with a cast that played benefit performances for the Army and Navy Relief Funds. It was warm and witty, with Katharine Cornell in the lead and Burgess Meredith as "a winning...rather than a whining" Marchbanks. Shaw waived his royalties.

887 Thompson, Alan Reynolds. THE ANATOMY OF DRAMA (Berkeley: University of California P, 1942; Lond: Cambridge UP, 1943; 2nd ed University of California P, 1946), pp. 44, 102, 162, 233-35, 296, 357, Index.
Shaw's comedies, some of them masterpieces, successfully subordinate plot to intellectual action used to develop a central theme. His plays are unique in that they combine both preaching and clowning, employing a formula that destroys conventional sentiment. Shaw has also proved that intellectual discussion is effective in drama as well, e.g., in the last act of Saint Joan, which functions like a Greek chorus.

888 Villaurrutia, Xavier. "Crítica cinematográfica: Seda, sangre y sol: El soldado de chocolate" (Movie Criticism: Silk, Blood, and Sun: THE CHOCOLATE SOLDIER, ASÍ (Mexico), No 79 (16 May 1942), 60, 63.
Shaw's Arms and the Man is one of the most theatrical and best of Shaw's plays. [Review of THE CHOCOLATE SOLDIER.] [In Spanish.]

889 Waldorf, Wilella. "'Candida' Brilliantly Played By a Star Cast at the Shubert," NY POST (28 April 1942) [not seen in this form]; rptd in CRITICS' THEATRE REVIEWS, III (4 May 1942), 301.
"'Candida' is a well-nigh deathless play,...second only to 'Saint Joan.'" And the Katharine Cornell production

(Shubert Theater, NY) received—and deserved—a standing ovation.

890 Watts, Richard, Jr. "Something Memorable," NYHT, 28 April 1942 [not seen in this form]; rptd in CRITICS' THEATRE REVIEWS, III (4 May 1942), 302.
Candida stands with Saint Joan and Heartbreak House as one of Shaw's best plays, and the cast of the Katharine Cornell production (Shubert Theater, NY) is a tribute to Candida's greatness. Burgess Meredith lends "masculine intensity" and dignity to Marchbanks; Cornell brings "a luminous, lyric quality" to Candida; and Raymond Massey's Morell is not priggish, but warm and human.

891 Woollcott, Alexander. "G. B. S. forever: Or, Required Reading for Meatless Days," GOOD HOUSEKEEPING, CXV (Dec 1942), 21, 199; rptd as "Required Reading for Meatless Days," in Woollcott, LONG, LONG AGO (NY: Viking; Toronto: Macmillan, 1943), pp. 29-33; and in THE PORTABLE WOOLLCOTT, ed by John Hennessey (NY: Viking 1946), pp. 486-90.
[Reminiscence of tea with Shaw at Ayot St. Lawrence in Nov 1941, emphasizing Shaw's "inextinguishable vitality."]

892 "The World and the Theatre," TAM, XXVI (July 1942), 421-22.
Candida (Shubert Theater, NY) is a brilliant and popular revival; it continued for 35 performances.

893 Wright, Basil. "The Theatre," SPECTATOR, CLXVIII (13 March 1942), 254.
In The Doctor's Dilemma (Haymarket Theater, Lond), Shaw succeeded with the character of Dubedat. Schutzmacher, however, has impact (in a way Shaw never intended or foresaw) largely because of World War II events.

894 Wyatt, Euphemia Van Rensselaer. "The Drama: Candida," CATHOLIC WORLD, CLV (June 1942), 337-41, espec 338-40.
Candida (Shubert Theater, NY) is "a classic"—witty, founded on a knowledge of humanity. Candida, who is both "domestic paragon" and "lady of romance," "may have seemed an anomaly to the generation of 1897 but was well known in the fourteenth century."

1943

895 "Arts Theatre: 'Androcles and the Lion,'" TIMES
  (Lond), 3 Feb 1943, p. 6.
Androcles and the Lion (Arts Theater, Lond) is a
"masterpiece of anti-climax"—a "brilliant absurdity" that
brings extravagance to serious themes on faith and
martyrdom.

896 "Arts Theatre: 'Misalliance,'" TIMES (Lond), 11
  Aug 1943, p. 6.
Misalliance is an inconclusive, good-humored conversation
piece on a variety of subjects. The modern dress production
(Arts Theater, Lond) does not hurt the slightly dated
arguments, since the play has little surface plausibility.

897 Barton, Robert. "Letters to the Editor: The
  Generous G.B.S.," SRL, XXVI (13 Nov 1943), 11.
[Instances of Shaw's generous actions; asserts that Shaw
allowed Frank Harris' "malevolent" biography to be
published because Harris' widow was destitute.]

898 Barzun, Jacques. "Bernard Shaw in Twilight,"
  KENYON REVIEW, V (Summer 1943), 321-45; rptd in Louis
  Kronenberger (ed), GEORGE BERNARD SHAW: A CRITICAL
  SURVEY (Cleveland & NY: World, 1953), pp. 158-77.
Shaw is "a one-man Ministry of All the Talents," self-
aware, weighty, imperturbable. His prose ranks next to
Swift's; his plays are good theater, combining late
nineteenth-century formulas and classical techniques. His
characters are articulate and self-conscious, discuss "high
matters," and sometimes function as a chorus. Because Shaw
does not echo conventional sentiments, he is called
heartless. He has a complex, not politically doctrinaire,
view of life and an amazing awareness of history. He
combines rebellion against nineteenth-century materialism,
realism, and determinism with a "robust strain of
aestheticism" inherited from Shelley, Beethoven, Turner,
and Blake. The Christian idea is basic to Shaw.

899 Bonney, Thérèse. "The George Bernard Shaws,"
VOGUE, CII (15 Oct 1943), 60-61.
[Memories of meeting Shaw at Lord and Lady Astor's. Shaw
was attentive to his wife; a conversationalist, not a
polemicist; and a wit and philosopher even at the breakfast
table.]

900 "Cambridge Theatre: 'Heartbreak House,'" TIMES
(Lond), 19 March 1943, p. 6.
Unlike other Shaw plays, Heartbreak House (Cambridge
Theater, Lond) has organic unity—at least until the second
act, when the characters become mere Shavian mouthpieces.
The actors, however, keep the audience pleasantly shocked
or amused by the intermittently brilliant discussion.

901 Church, Richard. "George Bernard Shaw," BRITISH
AUTHORS: A TWENTIETH CENTURY GALLERY (Lond, NY &
Toronto: Longmans, 1943), pp. 25-28.
[A short biography and adulatory assessment.] Shaw is
guided by an "ultra-mental illumination," is "the apostle
of clear-minded thinking."

902 Clemens, Cyril. "Bernard Shaw and Frank Harris,"
SRL, XXVI (23 Oct 1943), 14.
[Cites two instances of Shaw's generosity.]

903 Cohen, A. D. "The Religion of G. B. S.,"
ADELPHI, XX (Oct-Dec 1943), 12-16.
Shaw's "God is the Life Force and Lamarck is its prophet."
Back to Methuselah, which is amusing but not very
convincing, and The Adventures of the Black Girl in Her
Search for God, constitute the canon of his religion. Both
Shaw and Julian Huxley turn God out and enthrone man; yet
Shaw scorns the ordinary man. Shaw is a prophet without a
faith.

904 "'Heartbreak House' at the Phoenix," THEATRE
WORLD (Lond), XXXVIII (May 1943), 22-23.
The H. M. Tennent, Ltd., production of Heartbreak House
(Phoenix Theater, Lond) shows the play to be "amazingly
modern in mood." The old Captain's words of wisdom are
still to the point. [Photographs of the production.]

905 Hone, Joseph Maunsell. W. B. YEATS, 1865-1939 (NY, Lond & Toronto: Macmillan, 1943; rptd NY: Macmillan, 1947), pp. 68, 113-14, 144, 163n, 247, 248, 251-52, 269, 310, 336, 352, 393, 415, 430, 440, 454, 457, 473, Index.

[Passim references to Shaw as his life touched Yeats': e.g., their meeting at Kelmscott House; Yeats' opposition to the censorship of The Shewing-Up of Blanco Posnet and The Adventures of the Black Girl in Her Search for God; their support of an Academy of Irish Letters; Yeats' dislike of The Apple Cart, which he found "theatrical in the worst sense of the word" and superficial.]

906 Hoops, J. "Bernard Shaw, The Four Pleasant Plays," ENGLISCHE STUDIEN, LXXV (June 1943), 377-78.

Shaw's irony and satire are admirable in The Four Pleasant Plays (Leipzig: Tauchnitz, 1940). [Brief summaries of the plays.] [In German.]

907 Joad, C[yril] E[dwin] M[itchinson]. "An Imaginary Dialogue," NS&Nation, ns XXVI (3 July 1943), 6; rptd in Joad, SHAW (Victor Gollancz, 1949), pp. 135-44.

[Joad asks Shaw if the world is any better as a result of Shaw's teachings. Shaw quotes from his works, pointing to his influence on contemporary Labour politics and education.]

908 Kemp, Thomas C. BIRMINGHAM REPERTORY THEATRE: THE PLAYHOUSE AND THE MAN (Birmingham: Cornish Brothers, 1943; 2nd ed rev, 1948), pp. 28, 30, 31, 32, 33, 37, 40, 41, 49, 56, 68, 70, 78.

[Brief references to Shaw's involvement in the Malvern Festival.]

909 MacCarthy, Desmond. "Heartbreak," NS&Nation, XXV (3 April 1943), 222-23; rptd as "Chekhov and Shaw," in MacCarthy, SHAW'S PLAYS IN REVIEW (NY: Thames & Hudson, 1951; rptd Folcroft, Pa.: Folcroft P, 1969), pp. 149-54.

Heartbreak House (Cambridge Theater, Lond) lacks the love and pain that lead to real heartbreak; in fact, Shaw's drama characteristically contains only "jocular despair."

Yet the play has a fine character in Shotover, and atmosphere.

910 "Mrs. Shaw's Profession," TIME, XLII (27 Sept 1943), 38; abridged in SCHOLASTIC, XLIV (20 March 1944), 20.
[Brief account of Charlotte Payne-Townshend's first meeting with Shaw, the circumstances of their marriage, their differences, her influence. Written a week after her death.]

911 "Plays and Pictures: Misalliance, at Arts Theatre," NS&Nation, XXVI (14 Aug 1943), 104.
Misalliance (Arts Theater, Lond) "goes all out for talk." There is a point in Shaw's plays when it is evident that "he is getting nowhere" and "spirits droop." Still, Misalliance wears well.

912 "Plays and Pictures: Plays at the Arts Theatre," NS&Nation, XXV (2 April 1943), 224-25.
Don Juan in Hell (Arts Theater, Lond) is "Irish and eloquent." The play is speech-making rather than conversation, but it is "brilliant and interminable."

913 Redfern, James. "The Theatre," SPECTATOR, CLXX (26 March 1943), 291.
Heartbreak House (Cambridge Theater, Lond) gives a true and comprehensive picture of pre-World War I English society. The characters are individualized; the play is superbly written.

914 Redfern, James. "The Theatre: 'The Magistrate' and 'Misalliance,'" SPECTATOR, CLXXI (20 Aug 1943), 171.
Misalliance (Arts Theater, Lond) is a great achievement, comparable in achievement to the work of writers of comedy from Farquhar through Wilde.

915 Sewell, W. Stuart. "George Bernard Shaw," FAMOUS PERSONALITIES (NY: Garden City Publishing Co.) [Self-Education Quiz Book No 2, New Home Library], 1943), pp. 349-50; rptd in BRIEF BIOGRAPHIES OF FAMOUS MEN AND WOMEN (NY: Permabooks, 1949), pp. 216-17.
[Résumé of standard biographical facts.]

916 Thúrzó, Gábor. "Színház: Warrenné Mestersége" (Theater: Mrs. Warren's Profession), MAGYAR CSILLAG, III, No 19 (1 Oct 1943), 437-40.
Mrs. Warren's Profession stands at the peak of Shaw's work. Structurally it is excellent. Dialectics are kept to the background, while in the foreground are an interesting plot, especially stubborn figures, and extraordinarily well-presented characters. Shaw presents in this play people first and principles later. The fine polemic is an added bonus. The two main characters are stirring and human. [In Hungarian.]

1944

917 "Arts Theatre: 'Fanny's First Play,'" TIMES (Lond), 15 Sept 1944, p. 6.
Fanny's First Play (Arts Theater, Lond) no longer shocks conventional morality, and it has not enough wit to survive—until the last act, when the Shavian discussion brings the play to life.

918 "Arts Theatre: 'The Philanderer,'" TIMES (Lond), 8 April 1944, p. 2.
The Philanderer (Arts Theater, Lond) reflects a strain between author and material; the dialog resembles "the report of a Fabian Society meeting." The "new woman," no longer new, here lacks personality and vitality, as do the other characters. Yet modern plays do not have as many good lines or as much intellectual life.

919 Astrana Marín, Luis. "Dos comedias de Bernard Shaw" (Two Comedies by Bernard Shaw), CERVANTINAS Y OTROS ENSAYOS ("Cervantinas" and Other Essays) (Madrid: Afrodisio Aguado, 1944), pp. 375-83.
[Favorable review of The Devil's Disciple and Caesar and Cleopatra.] [In Spanish.]

920 Barzun, Jacques. "Books and the Arts: Who's Who in Shaw's 'What's What,'" NATION, CLIX (28 Oct 1944), 521-22.

Popular misconceptions concerning Shaw's ideas are caused
by unfair critical abuse and inaccurate labelling. In
Everybody's Political What's What Shaw gives "not simply
another plausible prediction in an age teeming with
prophets, but a possible meaning of that impossible
necessary notion, the superman."

921 Barzun, Jacques. "The Shavian System Simplified:
Half a Century of Criticism and of Constitution
Making," NYHTBR, 5 Nov 1944, p. 6.
Everybody's Political What's What presents half a century
of Shaw's thought in a "simplified, and up-to-date form."
Shaw's politics take into account human demand to be
governed (leading to dictatorships); yet he prefers a
democracy of economic as well as political rights for all
citizens. But the democratic ideal will require a new kind
of human: the superman.

922 Benét, William Rose. "The Phoenix Nest," SRL,
XXVII (18 Nov 1944), 30-31.
Shaw might have been a good philosopher if he had dispensed
with his silliness and eccentricity (as he did in his essay
in the first volume of Fabian Essays).

923 Bentley, Eric Russell. "Bernard Shaw, Caesar,
and Stalin," A CENTURY OF HERO-WORSHIP, A STUDY OF
THE IDEA OF HEROISM IN CARLYLE AND NIETZSCHE, WITH
NOTES ON OTHER HERO-WORSHIPPERS OF MODERN TIMES
(Phila & NY: Lippincott, 1944), pp. 183-201; rptd as
THE CULT OF THE SUPERMAN: A STUDY... (Lond: Hale,
1947), Pt iii, ch 2, pp. 164-82 ("Richard Wagner and
Bernard Shaw"); rptd Gloucester, Mass.: P. Smith,
1969; 2nd ed, A CENTURY OF HERO-WORSHIP; A STUDY OF
THE IDEA OF HEROISM IN CARLYLE AND NIETZSCHE, WITH
NOTES ON WAGNER, SPENGLER, STEFAN GEORGE, AND D. H.
LAWRENCE (Boston: Beacon, 1957), omits the chapter on
Shaw.
Shaw's hero-worship, like that of Carlyle, Wagner, and
Nietzsche, arose out of a sense of contemporary political
failure. Though he leans toward Heroic Vitalism, he is
really "an Aristocratic Radical" who, like Ruskin, was
contemptuous of the people. The Shaw hero is a prosaic man
of action: Caesar is shrewd and steady in purpose; Joan is
"a capable housewife enlarged to heroic proportions." In

Major Barbara, Undershaft is a devil's advocate, while Cusins unites Barbara's social purpose and Undershaft's social analysis in a play which synthesizes "a businessman's ethics and a salvationist's religion." Finally, Shaw rejects the separate, sublime, individual hero; his "ideal of manhood is not the blond beast but the disembodied mind."

924 Bentley, Eric Russell. "Bernard Shaw's Fabian Platonism," SRL, XXVII (28 Oct 1944), 9-10.

Everybody's Political What's What advocates only a marginally democratic political system, in which the competence of those to be elected to office is determined by examination. The style of the book insures that Shaw's audience will not take him seriously. Because he has gradually lost contact with contemporary reality, knows no country outside England, and has not really studied fascism or Sovietism, Shaw has had little influence in the twentieth century.

925 Bentley, Eric Russell. "The Theory and Practice of Shavian Drama," ACCENT, V (Autumn 1944), 5-18; rptd in ACCENT ANTHOLOGY, ed by Kerker Quinn and Charles Shattuck (NY: Harcourt, Brace, 1946), pp. 447-66; and in Bentley, THE PLAYWRIGHT AS THINKER (NY: Reynal & Hitchcock, 1946), pp. 136-57, 168-72.

Shaw says little about dramatic theory. He found in Ibsen that morality was not a given, but to be discussed and worked out. He defends discussion drama and attacks all other, especially the romantic well-made play. He insists on the morality of art, equating (and attacking) both commercialized art and art for art's sake. He is a polemical artist, primarily employing antithesis. Captain Brassbound's Conversion illustrates Shaw's technique of inversion and of irony contrasting romance and realism. Shaw's pre-war (1892-1912) and post-war (1913-1939) periods show that his talent is for dramaturgy as well as dialog. His philosophy is close to William James' pragmatic pluralism.

926 Berger, Meyer. "Mrs. Shaw's Will Starts 'Big Wind' Among Irish Here, But Eire is Calm," NYT, 17 and 18 Feb 1944; rptd in ISh, II (1972-73), 2-4.

[An account of the indignant reaction of the American Irish to Mrs. Shaw's will leaving $400,000 to the improvement of Irish education and manners.]

927 "Books: From Shaw—Without Love," TIME, XLIV (30 Oct 1944), 99-100, 102.

The philosophy expressed in Everybody's Political What's What is belied by Shaw's own life, which "quarrels at so many points with his arguments."

928 "Brains and Ballot-Boxes," TLS, XLIII (16 Sept 1944), 451.

Shaw should treat the democratic dream more seriously; his belief in political intelligence tests to choose those fit to govern fails to recognize that, after all, democracy rests on the critical judgment of the voter. Either there is democracy or tyranny.

929 Bridges-Adams, W[illiam]. THE BRITISH THEATRE (Lond, NY, & Toronto: Longmans Green [British Life and Thought, No 14], 1944; 3rd ed Lond: Longmans, 1947), pp. 32-33, 34, 35, 38, 46, 51.

[References to Shaw's importance as a critic as well as a writer; a brief history of six centuries of British theater.]

930 Brown, John Mason. "Back to Methuselah: A Visit to an Elderly Gentleman in a World of Arms and the Man," SRL, XXVII (22 July 1944), 6-9; rptd Brown, MANY A WATCHFUL NIGHT (NY: Whittlesey House [McGraw-Hill], 1944), pp. 81-90; and in Brown, DRAMATIS PERSONAE: A RETROSPECTIVE SHOW (NY: Viking, 1963), pp. 112-20.

Shaw's intellectual courage corresponds to the physical courage of men fighting in World War II. [Account of an interview with Shaw.]

931 Canby, Henry Seidel. "G. B. S. in the Last War," SRL, XXVII (22 July 1944), 12.

In an interview on 5 July 1938, Shaw revealed himself to be "a keen political and economic thinker," a brilliant conversationalist offering "destructive criticism." [Quotes Shaw on English and Irish political figures, a Federation of Nations, and Irish home rule.]

932 Carnegie, Dale. DALE CARNEGIE'S BIOGRAPHICAL ROUNDUP: HIGHLIGHTS IN THE LIVES OF FORTY FAMOUS PEOPLE (NY: Breemberg, 1944), pp. 1-6.
Shaw's life was "full of sharp and striking contrasts." He attended school only five years but became one of the most distinguished writers of the age. He wrote for years before he could make a living at writing. Though he stood before large audiences and audaciously denounced many cherished traditions, he once "suffered from shyness and timidity and an inferiority complex."

933 Cerf, Bennett. "Oh, Shaw!" SRL, XXVII (22 July 1944), 24-25.
[Anecdotal account of Cerf's first meeting with Shaw (in Spring 1936), Shaw's financial acumen, his witty exchanges with various celebrities, his attitude toward art and life. In Cerf's "Trade Winds," SRL, XXVII (7 Oct 1944), 22-23, appears a letter to Cerf from Lawrence Langner, who says that Cerf misquoted Shaw's exchange with Helen Keller in "Oh, Shaw!"]

934 Clapp, Charles E., Jr. "American Peanuts for G. B. S.," NYTMag, 6 Feb 1944, p. 18.
A visit with Shaw is almost always an event. [Quotes Shaw on the British-American language barrier and on his receiving some American peanuts.]

935 Clemens, Cyril. "G.B.S.," SRL, XXVII (12 Aug 1944), 15.
[In a letter to the editor, Clemens presents excerpts of a letter by Shaw on Mark Twain.]

936 Cortina, Augusto. "El Donjuanismo y Doña Juana de Tirso a Bernard Shaw en dos jornadas y en éxodo" (Donjuanism and Doña Juana from Tirso to Bernard Shaw in Two Acts and an Epilog), INSTITUTO POPULAR DE CONFERENCIAS, ANALES DE BUENOS AIRES, XXIX (1944), 69-82.
Shaw's Don Juan has diminished his sexual cravings in favor of philosophical speculations. Instead of Ovid, he reads Schopenhauer and Nietzsche; and he looks like Hamlet instead of the traditional Trickster. Jack Tanner is a comic-tragic figure, a man chased by a woman. [In Spanish.]

937 Darlington, W. A. "Letter from London: Laurence Olivier and Ralph Richardson Win Laurels in Old Vic Repertory," NYT, 1 Oct 1944, II, p. 1.
[Praise of Richardson's Bluntschli and Olivier's Saranoff in Arms and the Man (Old Vic production, New Theater, Lond).] The audience, after two World Wars, has finally learned Shaw's lesson in Arms and the Man.

938 Elliot, Walter. "Books of the Day: The Sage of Eyot [sic] St. Lawrence," SPECTATOR, CLXXIII (22 Sept 1944), 268.
Only Britain and India tacitly appoint sages, and Shaw is the most successful sage ever produced. But Shaw's Everybody's Political What's What is not his most successful piece of visionary work. It is really concerned with the autobiographical details of an intelligent man, for the political observations are merely blurred "recollections of what someone else once told him."

939 "G. B. S.—A Bibliography," SRL, XXVII (22 July 1944), 28, 30, 32.
[An "up-to-date bibliography of Shaviana," including a list of Shaw's collected works and a list of the first published editions of his works (omitting his "countless writings appearing in newspapers and periodicals").]

940 "G.B.S. at 88," NYTMag, 6 Aug 1944, p. 21.
Shaw observed his birthday by sawing wood, saying "to hell with all birthday wishes; I am not celebrating." He also told reporters that a lasting peace would be impossible, and that Hitler would end up in the Viceregal Lodge in Dublin.

941 Hackett, Francis. "Books of the Times," NYT, 26 Oct 1944, p. 21; rptd as "St. Bernard at 88," in ON JUDGING BOOKS: IN GENERAL AND IN PARTICULAR (NY: John Day, 1947), pp. 201-4.
In Everybody's Political What's What Shaw repeats himself, but has not lost his edge in attacking others' sins. The book shows his "lively and audacious detachment," his shrewd politics, his "sense of honor and devotion," and the "natural toughness and bounce of his mind." Shaw is unique. He controls "the crank and zealot in himself," lives by and defends humane convictions.

942 Handlin, Oscar. "Everybody's Political What's What" ATLANTIC MONTHLY, CLXXIV (Dec 1944), 137, 141.
Everybody's Political What's What is an intelligent but not a wise book. Shaw cloaks his political ideas with the dramatist's devices of wit, paradox, overstatement. "The attractiveness of the paradox sometimes obscures the necessity for resolving the contradiction."

943 "Ignorant Old Gentleman," NEWSWEEK, XXIV (30 Oct 1944), 106-9.
Everybody's Political What's What contains Shaw's "ready answers" to economic, political, scientific, educational, and religious problems. Shaw seems at times more genial than in the past.

944 Johnson, Wendell. "Shaw's Political Pshaw," CHICAGO SUN BOOK WEEK, 12 Nov 1944, p. 28.
Shaw is unable to reason coherently and systematically, as is proved in Everybody's Political What's What. The only parts of the book that are accurate deal with banking and with social class stratification, and these parts are highly derivative.

945 Langner, Lawrence. "The Sinner-Saint as Host: Diary of a Visit to G. B. S. at Stresa," SRL, XXVII (22 July 1944), 10-12; rptd as "A Visit to G. B. S.," in Langner, THE PASSIONATE PLAYGOER: A PERSONAL SCRAPBOOK, ed by George Oppenheimer (NY: Viking, 1958).
[Anecdotal account of the Langners' stay with the Shaws in Italy.]

946 "Leaders of Britain," LIFE, XVI (7 Feb 1944), 87-95, espec 87.
[Account of the trouble Shaw gave Yousuf Karsh when he took Shaw's picture for a series called "Leaders of Britain."]

947 "Life's Cover," LIFE, XVI (7 Feb 1944), 20.
Shaw (on cover of magazine) at 87 "has given a lifetime to cracking the British superiority complex."

948 Loewenstein, F[ritz] E[rwin]. "Letters to the Editor: A Shaw Adaptation," TLS, XLIII (16 Sept 1944), 451.

A chance remark written by Shaw to Ellen Terry makes it possible to identify a Shaw play in four acts entitled The Gadfly, a dramatic opera version of Mrs. E. L. Voynich's novel, THE GADFLY.

949 "Lyric Theatre, Hammersmith: 'Candida,'" TIMES (Lond), 15 Nov 1944, p. 6.

In Candida Shaw presents a masterful unmasking of the liberal hypocrite Morell, but the satire could have been accomplished in two acts. The third act is like an amusing, unessential appendix.

950 "Lyric Theatre, Hammersmith: 'Pygmalion,'" TIMES (Lond), 13 Dec 1944, p. 8.

At first Eliza, played by Ellen Pollock (Pygmalion, Lyric Theater, Hammersmith), seems a bit exaggerated, but finally she is a triumphant comment on convention and sentiment.

951 "Lyric Theatre, Hammersmith: 'Too True to be Good,'" TIMES (Lond), 1 Nov 1944, p. 6.

Too True To Be Good consists "of one excellent sermon and the notes for many more," but lacks a clear theme and narrative line, with Shavian jokes and Fabian politics as distractions.

952 MacCarthy, Desmond. "'Fanny's First Play,'" NS&Nation, XXVIII (30 Sept 1944), 219-20; rptd in MacCarthy, SHAW'S PLAYS IN REVIEW (NY: Thames & Hudson, 1951; rptd Folcroft, Pa.: Folcroft P, 1969), pp. 203-5.

Fanny's First Play, contrary to Shaw, is not a pot-boiler but one of "his religious farces" on the theme of rebellion against unthinking, unquestioning morality. The Arts Theater (Lond) production fails to portray Mrs. Knox as the pivotal character, and it omits the "amusing and pointful" prolog and epilog.

953 MacCarthy, Desmond. "What Is Sauce For the Goose...," NS&Nation, XXVII (15 April 1944), 255.

The Philanderer (Arts Theater, Lond) is "moderately good." It is a difficult play to produce, for there is "no limit to the verve required from the actors." Today's audience has little difficulty with what was once shocking in the play.

954 Meissner, Paul. ENGLISCHE LITERATURGESCHICHTE. III: ROMANTIK UND VIKTORIANISMUS (English Literary History. III: Romanticism and Victorianism) (Berlin: Walter de Gruyter, 1944), pp. 60, 134, 146.
[References to Shaw as a member of the Fabian Society; his comedies as a continuation of Wilde's plays; Byron's DON JUAN as a forerunner of Shaw's comedies.] [In German.]

955 Meissner, Paul. ENGLISCHE LITERATURGESCHICHTE. IV: DAS 20. JAHRHUNDERT (English Literary History. IV: The Twentieth Century) (Berlin: Walter de Gruyter, 1944), pp. 42-46, 51, 59, 68, 129.
[An introduction to Shaw's works, with emphasis on the allegorical tendencies of Shaw's plays, on his Fabian outlook, and on his idea of the Life Force.] In Shaw the reformer exceeds the artist. [In German.]

956 Merriam, Charles E. "G.B.S. Takes His Fling at Politics," NYTBR, 29 Oct 1944, p. 3.
Everybody's Political What's What is a scroll of systematic politics that covers economics, religion, art, class structures, and familial relations. Marxian-Fabian economics are modified, and the "Russian way" is not enthusiastically treated, nor ignored. Socialism, moreover, comes under a new, less sympathetic scrutiny. The book is at times true, false, or dubious, but always interesting.

957 Morgan, Charles. THE HOUSE OF MACMILLAN (1843-1943) (NY: Macmillan, 1944), pp. 119-20, 125, 126-33, 134, 200, 201, 230, Index.
[Contains the Macmillan readers' letters evaluating Immaturity, The Irrational Knot, Cashel Byron's Profession, and An Unsocial Socialist; Shaw's letter of 11 Sept 1943 commenting on the Mfacmillan letters (which he had read in galleys of the book), characterizing himself at 23, and discussing his relationship to the great publishers of the day; brief mention of Shaw's part in a "Book War" (1905-7) between the TIMES (Lond), publishers, and booksellers over observance of a Net Book Agreement.]

958 "Mr. Shaw's Utopia: Equal Income in a new order; Examination for Statesmanship," TLS, XLIII (16 Sept 1944), 450, 452.

Everybody's Political What's What is a convincing argument
for the need for socialism but is weak on how to achieve
it. One wonders how close Russian socialism is to Shaw's
early ideal, since it is far from William Morris' vision.
Shaw exaggerates too much, and trusts too much in equality
of income as a panacea for social ills. He places his faith
in an aristocratic elite, inhuman evolution—"a Promised
Land and a regenerate people."

959 Murry, J. Middleton. "Everybody's Political
What's What, by Bernard Shaw," FORTNIGHTLY, ns CLVI
(Dec 1944), 402, 404.
Everybody's Political What's What is "without faults." It
is educational, lively, Shaw's "final effort to clear our
minds of cant." His analysis of democracy is pertinent; in
fact, his book should be required reading for politicians
and journalists. But there is no evidence that humanity can
respond to Shaw's call for a changed morality.

960 Nathan, George Jean. "George Bernard Shaw,"
AMERICAN MERCURY, LVIII (Feb 1944), 233-38; rev and
rptd as "An Evening with George Bernard Shaw. July
13, 1945," in THE THEATRE BOOK OF THE YEAR, 1945-
1946 (NY: Knopf, 1946), pp. 45-51; and as "George
Bernard Shaw—Hail and Farewell!" in THE WORLD OF
GEORGE JEAN NATHAN, ed by Charles Angoff (NY: Knopf,
1952), pp. 411-17.
[A chronological sketch of Shaw's plays to date, with
emphasis on Shaw's contributions to English theater.] Shaw
introduced sociology and economics to drama with Widowers'
Houses; outraged morality with Mrs. Warren's Profession;
proved that intellectual drama could be amusing; created
remarkable heroines, while avoiding sex; and wrote
beautiful prose. Saint Joan secured his place as the
greatest English dramatist of his time. In the late plays
his powers declined; yet these plays are still better than
their contemporaries. Shaw is actually a romanticist,
covering his romanticism with irony and humor.

961 "New Theatre: 'Arms and the Man,'" TIMES (Lond),
6 Sept 1944, p. 6.
The "impish and inapt mockery" of bellicose virtues in Arms
and the Man probably provided the audience (New Theater,
Lond) with a kind of "joyous release." The well-acted

comedy had a kind of "two-edged topicality" in the jokes about Balkan honor.

962 Olesha, Iu. "Pigmalion" (Pygmalion), TURKMENSKAIA ISKRA (Ashkhabad), 20 May 1944; rptd in P'ESY: STAT'I O TEATRE (Plays: Articles about the Theater) (Moscow: "Iskusstvo," 1968), 358-61.
Shaw's plays, including Pygmalion (Pushkin Theater, Ashkhabad), lack the complex intrigues and theatrical virtuosity characteristic of other European playwrights. Shaw's strength is dialog, and his plays always have social depths expressed in exchanges of remarks and aphorisms, so that his plays are difficult to produce. [In Russian.]

963 Papier, Sara. "Tipos femeninos en las obras de Ibsen y Bernard Shaw" (Feminine Types in the Works of Ibsen and Bernard Shaw), SABER VIVIR (Argentina), IV, No 41 (Jan 1944), 44-45.
Ibsen's feminine characters (from HEDDA GABLER, GHOSTS, LADY FROM THE SEA, A DOLL'S HOUSE) are continued in Shaw's females in Getting Married, Misalliance, Candida, Mrs. Warren's Profession, and Fanny's First Play. They wish ardently to realize themselves. [In Spanish.]

964 "Plays and Pictures: Arms and the Man, at the New Theatre," NS&Nation, XXVIII (16 Sept 1944), 184.
The two wars of this century reinforce the theme of Arms and the Man: war is not romantic. The dialog is still fresh and sharp, and the "situations evolve with a most professional sureness."

965 Redfern, James. "The Theatre," SPECTATOR, CLXXIII (29 Sept 1944), 287.
Shaw's wit and invention are "dateless" in Fanny's First Play (Arts Theater production). The dated epilog has been wisely cut.

966 Redfern, James. "The Theatre," SPECTATOR, CLXXIII (10 Nov 1944), 431.
Too True To Be Good (Lyric Theater, Lond) has form, brilliance of dialog, wit, invention, "and moments of profound good sense."

967 Redfern, James. "The Theatre: 'Arms and the Man,'" SPECTATOR, CLXXIII (15 Sept 1944), 242.
The New Theater production of Arms and the Man is one of "outstanding brilliance," flawed only by a lack of realism in the initial scene and exaggeration of the comic in the last.

968 Redfern, James. "The Theatre: 'The Philanderer,'" SPECTATOR, CLXXII (21 April 1944), 359.
The Philanderer (Arts Theater, Lond) may be a minor work, but it is also an ambitious one, for it is an analytical study of the emergence of feminism and the New Woman at the turn of the twentieth century. The play remains witty, penetrating, and comprehensive.

969 S., H. [Harrison Smith]. "On an Elderly Gentleman," SRL, XXVII (22 July 1944), 20.
Shaw is many-faceted and a profound and serious thinker. [Uncritical praise, in the "GBS Birthday Issue."]

970 Shuster, George N. "Books of the Week: Everybody's Political What's What" COMMONWEAL, XLI (1 Dec 1944), 177-82.
Everybody's Political What's What sums up Shaw—an "Anglo-Irish Plato whose Socrates is Beatrice Webb." The book is a sort of handbook for statesmen; though flawed, it is "trim, spare, disciplined."

971 Smalley, Donald. "Mephistopheles at the Conventicle: G. B. S. Amid the Browningites," SRL, XXVII (22 July 1944), 13-15.
[History of Shaw's career in the London Browning Society. Presents his opinion of the work of other members and his opinion of Browning.]

972 Stern, James. "GBS in Extremis," NEW REPUBLIC, CXI (20 Nov 1944), 666-67.
Everybody's Political What's What is repetitious and badly organized. The premises of the book carried out to their logical extremes mean fascism.

973 Thomas, J. D. "The 'Unsocial Socialist' Pitchforking His Way to the Millenium," SRL, XXVII (22 July 1944), 17-18.
Shaw's five novels attack society and "the ideals of the English gentleman," with the family and romantic love his primary satiric targets. In An Unsocial Socialist Shaw brings his attack into a framework, socialism. And his optimistic opinion that socialism would succeed leads to the theory of creative evolution developed in his plays.

974 Tintner, Anny. "Shaw und Platon" (Shaw and Plato). Unpublished dissertation, University of Vienna, 1944. [Listed in Altick and Matthews, Item 1760.] [In German.]

975 Ward, Maisie. GILBERT KEITH CHESTERTON (Lond: Sheed & Ward, 1944), pp. 111, 135-36, 139, 182, 191-208, 237, 281, 311, 313, 315, 376, 428, 429, 451, 465.
While Shaw and Chesterton argued constantly, they represented something in common, a stern rejection of the self-satisfied smugness of the middle and upper classes in England. When Shaw declared his atheism or described all property as theft, he roused "real moral indignation" in many people. Indeed, they "hated his questions before they began to hate his answers." But Shaw did not merely offer questions; through his characters he gave inspired answers, bringing philosophy back to the drama.

976 "What They Said About Shaw: Some of the Early Reviews of His Books and Plays," SRL, XXVII (22 July 1944), 16-17.
[Brief excerpts from selected reviews (1905 to 1925) of The Irrational Knot, John Bull's Other Island, Major Barbara, Heartbreak House, Back to Methuselah, and Saint Joan.]

977 Whitebait, William. "The Movies: Pygmalion, at the Leicester Square," NS&Nation, XXVII (29 April 1944), 288.
The film of Pygmalion is lively, but no screen dialog captures the genius of Shaw's touch. Shaw's ideas and the battle of the sexes "strike afresh almost brutally."

978 Willis, Katherine Tappert. "Shaw, George Bernard: Everybody's Political What's What," LIBRARY JOURNAL, LXIX (1 Oct 1944), 812.
Everybody's Political What's What is "Shavian essays but in a mellower mood."

979 Wilson, Edmund. "Books: Bernard Shaw on the Training of a Statesman," NYer, XX (28 Oct 1944), 68, 70, 73; rptd in CLASSICS AND COMMERCIALS: A LITERARY CHRONICLE OF THE FORTIES (NY: Farrar, Strauss & Giroux, 1950), pp. 238-43.
Everybody's Political What's What is a handbook for statesmen in the tradition of Castiglione's COURTIER or Machiavelli's THE PRINCE. The book combines anecdotes, examples from history, and some brilliant passages, e.g., Shaw's analysis of World War II and the explanation of fascism as state capitalism. The contradiction between his approval of Stalin's tactics and his objection to compulsory vaccination is evidence of an aging mind—but his is still the best mind around.

980 Woolf, Leonard. "G. B. S.: Everybody's Political What's What," NS&Nation, XXVIII (16 Sept 1944), 188.
Everybody's Political What's What contains Shaw's most important or persistent doctrines. Because Shaw talks nonsense to the world to get its attention, the world does not listen to him when he speaks common sense. Though Shaw is still alive intellectually, he is confusing sense and nonsense on crucial issues, e.g., the franchise, doctors, democracy, Nazism, etc.

981 Woollcott, Alexander. THE LETTERS OF ALEXANDER WOOLLCOTT, ed by Beatrice Kaufman and Joseph Hennessey (NY: Viking; Toronto: Macmillan, 1944; rptd Lond: Cassel; Garden City, NY: Garden City Publishing Co., 1945), pp. 103, 109, 121, 362.
[References to Ellen Terry giving away Shaw's personally inscribed first edition of Plays Pleasant and Unpleasant; to the great number of Dickens allusions in Shaw; to Shaw's irritating Charlotte Shaw with a long luncheon talk about Mrs. Patrick Campbell.]

1945

982 Anderson Imbert, Enrique. "Bernard Shaw:
Everybody's Political What's What," SUR (Argentina),
XIV, No 133 (Nov 1945), 71-73.
Everybody's Political What's What is the "Summa" of Shaw's
thought, the last will of an old citizen who represents the
most exemplary conscience of the liberal epoch. [In
Spanish.]

983 Anstey, Edgar. "The Cinema," SPECTATOR, CLXXV
(21 Dec 1945), 591.
The film of Caesar and Cleopatra achieves little because
the play is thin, static, with a "wordiness of the head
rather than the heart."

984 "Arts Theatre: 'The Simpleton of the Unexpected
Isles,'" TIMES (Lond), 8 March 1945, p. 6.
The Simpleton of the Unexpected Isles lacks a clear
narrative and moves slowly to an unsatisfactory conclusion.
Farce and satirical attacks on English stupidity obscure
the allegory.

985 Brooks, Donald. ROMANCE OF THE ENGLISH THEATRE
(Lond: Rockliff, 1945; rev ed Lond: Rockliff, 1952;
rptd NY: Macmillan, 1953), pp. 163, 165, 170, 172-73,
176, 178-79, 188, 191, 195, 199.
Many of Shaw's early plays, such as Widowers' Houses and
Mrs. Warren's Profession, "won him favor in Liberal
circles." His plays were "provocative criticisms of customs
and characters in modern society," and he succeeded in a
hostile intellectual climate. Between the Great Wars, Shaw
reflected deeply on the nature of war with Heartbreak
House. He was easily master of the stage after World War I.

986 Brown, John Mason. "Theatre Arts Bookshelf: Shaw
on Politics," TAM, XXIX (Jan 1945), 62-64.
Everybody's Political What's What may be second-rate Shaw
but "it is first-rate anyone else." An "old man's book," it
is discursive and repetitious, but provocative and amusing.
It needs more research and more editing; yet it is a

milestone in exposition, wit, progressive ideas, and style. Shaw "is too brilliant not to make sheer brilliance monotonous in his pages."

987 "Caesar and Cleopatra," VOGUE, CV (15 Jan 1945), 64-65.
The film of Caesar and Cleopatra is "a miracle of illusion." [Photographs of Claude Rains and Vivien Leigh on the set in London.]

988 "'Candida': A glittering audience turns out for Congresswoman Clare Luce's performance in famous Shaw play," LIFE, XIX (20 Aug 1945), 65-66.
[Pictorial essay on Clare Boothe Luce as Candida (Stamford, Conn., production).]

989 Castelli, Alberto. LETTURA DI GEORGE BERNARD SHAW (On Reading George Bernard Shaw) (Milan: Società Editrice Vita e Pensiero, 1945).
[Part I: General survey (in 32 chapters) of all aspects and themes of Shaw's life and works, with detailed plot summaries and long quotations (in translation) from plays. Part II: Biographical sketch of the historical Joan of Arc followed by summaries of single scenes of play.] [In Italian.]

990 Chapman, John. "Lawrence Stars in Revival of Shaw Play," DAILY NEWS (NY) (27 Dec 1945) [not seen in this form]; rptd in THEATRE CRITICS' REVIEWS (NY), VI (1945), 60.
The wit and satire of Pygmalion remain current; the Theater Incorporated production (Barrymore Theater, NY) is well-directed (by Sir Cedric Hardwicke) and well-acted (by Gertrude Lawrence and Raymond Massey).

991 Church, Hayden. "It's the Same Shaw—And He's Still Writing," NYTMag, 21 Oct 1945, pp. 13, 55.
After a lapse of six years, Shaw is writing another play, a topical comedy like The Apple Cart; he hopes it will be ready for the Malvern Festival next year. He talked about his writing practices, his correspondence, and his craft in general.

992 "Cinema: Good Enough for Americans?" TIME, XLVI (31 Dec 1945), 88-90.
The film of Caesar and Cleopatra is "a Technicolor camel, exotic but unromantic." It is technically perfect but the plot drags and Shaw's theme is not clear. The British expect something better for five million dollars, but the film may be good enough for American crowds.

993 Clurman, Harold. THE FERVENT YEARS: THE STORY OF THE GROUP THEATRE AND THE THIRTIES (NY: Alfred A. Knopf, 1945), pp. 9-10, 21, 26, 99, 215.
[A few passing references to Shaw, Caesar and Cleopatra and Shaw's criticism.]

994 Clyman, Rhea G. "Stalin Outwits Shaw," AMERICAN MERCURY, LX (Feb 1945), 220.
[Account of witty exchange between Shaw and Stalin on the last day of Shaw's 1937 visit to Russia.]

995 Cuatrecasas, J. F. "Libros: Everybody's Political What's What" (Books: Everybody's Political What's What), REVISTA DE LAS INDIAS (Colombia), XXII, No 73 (Jan 1945), 146-47.
Everybody's Political What's What is a summary of Shaw's sociological theories, modified by external, universal conflicts. The ideas expressed in the prologs and epilogs of his works and pamphlets are now integrated into a body of thought with didactic aims and goals. Through the uses of irony and paradox, Shaw aims to achieve the political education of leaders and citizens. However, some conclusions tend to confuse rather than to illuminate. [In Spanish.]

996 "'Dark Lady of the Sonnets'—'Village Wooing'— 'Pygmalion,'" THEATRE WORLD (Lond), XLI (Jan 1945), 6.
In Village Wooing "Shaw is at his cheekiest and wittiest"; The Dark Lady of the Sonnets is "a satisfying curtain raiser," and "Pygmalion needs no introduction." [Photograph of Ellen Pollock as Eliza; all are at Lyric Theater (Hammersmith).]

997 Döring, Anneliese. "Untersuchungen zu Bernard Shaws 'The Perfect Wagnerite'" (Investigations in

Bernard Shaw's <u>The Perfect Wagnerite</u>). Unpublished dissertation, University of Giessen, 1945. [Listed in Altick and Matthews, Item 1715.] [In German.]

998 Dukes, Ashley. "Repertory at Last! The English Scene," TAM, XXIX (Jan 1945), 22-31, espec 26, 29.
<u>Arms and the Man</u> (produced by the Old Vic) has "razor-edge" satire, though its "triviality...proves to be its charm." [Photograph, p. 26.]

999 Ellis-Fermor, Una. THE FRONTIERS OF DRAMA (Lond: Methuen & Co, 1945), 20, 39, 124.
The theme of <u>Saint Joan</u> is the "outward career of the character it has formed." In <u>Man and Superman</u>, Shaw uses an old dramatic device, the transfer of action to a world which is "virtually a fairyland." However, the scene in hell may contain significant truth.

1000 Erichsen, Svend. "Bernard Shaw: Strejflys over hans personlighed og produktion" (Bernard Shaw: A Brief View of His Personality and Works), TEATER-STREJFLYS (Theater-Glimpses) (Copenhagen: Gyldendalske Boghandel—Nordisk Forlag, 1945), pp. 123-30.
The best of Shaw's writing is in his plays and their prefaces. The prefaces are charming and combative; the plays expose society's biggest lies, very bluntly in Shaw's first plays and more subtly in his later ones. The plays reveal his ability to combine a sense of reality and its demands with a vision which sees past the moment to the centuries ahead, as in <u>Man and Superman</u> and <u>Back to Methuselah</u>. His most recent play (<u>Geneva</u>) shows that his breadth and intellectual vitality remain undiminished. Whether Shaw should be classed among the greatest dramatists is, however, doubtful. His plays are always dazzling, witty and full of ideas, but their psychology is not deep and they often lack poetry and dramatic vigor. [In Danish.]

1001 F., L. B. "Miss Lawrence Returns," NYT, 27 Dec 1945, p. 16; rptd in THEATRE CRITICS' REVIEWS, VI (31 Dec 1945), 58.
Though <u>Pygmalion</u> is not Shaw's best, and though some of its lines have "lost their luster," the Theater Incorporated

production (Barrymore Theater, NY) proves that the play stands the test of time. At times Gertrude Lawrence is not quite believable; yet she can "wring the fun" from Shaw's lines. Raymond Massey is also fine, though a bit exaggerated at times.

1002 Funke, Otto. EPOCHEN DER NEUEREN ENGLISCHEN LITERATUR (Epochs of Modern English Literature) (Bern: A. Francke, 1945), pp. 188, 221, 232-34.
[A brief introduction to Shaw's life and work.] [In German.]

1003 Gibbs, Wolcott. "The Theatre: Excursion," NYer, XXI (18 Aug 1945), 45.
Candida is "almost unbearably tedious and quaint." The Clare Boothe Luce performance (Stamford, Conn.) does nothing to bring life to it.

1004 Guernsey, Otis L., Jr. "Christmas Champagne," NYHT (27 Dec 1945); rptd in THEATRE CRITICS' REVIEWS, VI (31 Dec 1945), 58.
Pygmalion (Barrymore Theater, NY), is immensely entertaining, and the Theater Incorporated production is "immaculate."

1005 Haggin, B. H. "Books and the Arts: Music," NATION, CLX (10 March 1945), 285-86.
London Music in 1888-1889 is "some of the most perceptive and readable writing that has ever been done about music."

1006 Hamilton, Robert. "The Philosophy of Bernard Shaw: A Study of 'Back to Methuselah,'" LONDON QUARTERLY AND HOLBORN REVIEW, CLXX (July 1945), 333-41.
Shaw is not a convincing writer or thinker; yet Back to Methuselah has great imaginative power. Shaw sometimes argues for the sake of argument, degenerating "into uncontrolled and exuberant dialectic"; furthermore, he is "torn between materialism and Theism," between belief in "either blind matter or an omniscient Creator." Back to Methuselah, however, reaches out to God, to a perfectible universe, and to human brotherhood. The cycle, though marred by topical references and humor at the expense of the Elderly Gentleman, has "an epic dignity."

222

1007 Leslie, Louis A. "Personal Shorthand Systems,"
AMERICAN N&Q, IV (Jan 1945), 156.
Shaw extensively used shorthand. He originally learned
Sweet's system, but had to change to Pitman's (which he
called the "pitfall system") because he could not find a
secretary who knew Sweet's.

1008 Lynd, Helen Merrell. ENGLAND IN THE 1880's:
TOWARD A SOCIAL BASIS FOR FREEDOM (Lond & NY: Oxford
UP, 1945; rptd Lond: Frank Cass; NY: A. M. Kelley
[Reprints of Economic Classics], 1968), pp. 104, 179-
80, 383-84, 385, 387, 389, 391, 395, 396, 400-401,
403n, 406, 422, 425, 430, Index.
[References to Shaw's place in the socialist movement of
the 1880's, including his relationship with the Social
Democratic Federation and his Fabian activities.] "Shaw's
socialism became indistinguishable from bourgeois
liberalism."

1009 MacCarthy, Desmond. "Desperate Remedies,"
NS&Nation, XXXIX (24 March 1945), 187-88; rptd as
"The Simpleton of the Unexpected Isles: Desperate
Remedies," in MacCarthy, SHAW'S PLAYS IN REVIEW (NY:
Thames & Hudson, 1951; rptd Folcroft, Pa.: Folcroft
P, 1969), pp. 206-11.
The Simpleton of the Unexpected Isles (Arts Theater, Lond)
is bright and imaginative, but has little intrinsic value.
Inferior to the plays of Shaw's prime, Simpleton repeats
Heartbreak House on an inferior dramatic level in its four
representatives of Love, Pride, Heroism, and Empire and its
apocalyptic ending. Shaw moved from reformer to eugenics in
his search for a solution to social problems; the Day of
Judgment as a remedy can only be seen as comedy.

1010 Nathan, George Jean. "Pygmalion. December 26,
1945," THE THEATRE BOOK OF THE YEAR, 1945-1946 (NY:
Knopf, 1946), pp. 242-45.
Contrary to Maxwell Anderson's charge that Shaw is a
philosopher but no dramatist, Shaw wrote several excellent
dramas. Even Pygmalion, "one of Shaw's lesser efforts," has
wit, character, and farcical situations superior to
Anderson's plays. The Theater Incorporated production
(Barrymore Theater, NY) is, however, not very good.

GEORGE BERNARD SHAW

1011 Nichols, Lewis. "Clare Boothe Luce as Candida
Draws Celebrities to Stamford: Her Interpretation of
Shaw's Heroine Is Letter-Perfect but Lacks Warmth—
Shaw Is a Sell-Out, Nevertheless," NYT, 7 Aug 1945,
p. 25.
Congresswoman Luce deserves "credit for trying" in her
portrayal of Candida (Strand Theater, Stamford, Conn.) but
her Candida lacks gentleness and humanity.

1012 Panesso, Robledo Antonio. "Everybody's
Political What's What," REVISTA DE LAS INDIAS
(Colombia), XXV, No 81 (Sept 1945), 481-88.
For many Shaw is nothing but an acrobat of words; yet his
social ideas are the natural outcome of his common sense,
applied indiscriminately to the economy as well as to
representative democracy, industrial problems, and
international relations. Besides covering political
thought, Shaw discusses a wide range of other subjects in a
nervous but direct style. [In Spanish.]

1013 "Plays and Pictures: Getting Married, at the
Arts Theatre," NS&Nation, XXX (15 Sept 1945), 176.
Getting Married (Arts Theater, Lond) has farcical speeches
answering truly comic lines. Yet it remains witty, and
contains much about marriage that is "wise and true."

1014 "Plays and Pictures: Mrs. Warren's Profession,
at the Torch," NS&Nation, XXX (13 Oct 1945), 244.
Mrs. Warren's Profession must have seemed "staggering" in
1894; its main idea is valid even today. Both the innocent
and successful are proved to be products of an evil social
system (Torch Theater, Lond).

1015 "Plays and Pictures: The Simpleton of the
Unexpected Isles, Arts Theatre Club," NS&Nation, XXIX
(17 March 1945), 172.
The pattern of The Simpleton of the Unexpected Isles (Arts
Theater, Lond) is familiar to Shaw's audiences: light
entertainment and political jesting lead to "very serious
social sermonising." The Day of Judgment is not the end of
the world, but the end of people who cannot adjust to the
world's needs.

1016 Redfern, James. "The Theatre," SPECTATOR, CLXXV (14 Sept 1945), 243.
Getting Married (Arts Theater, Lond) is loquacious, and the characters are no more than types; yet the effect is that of amusement and brilliance.

1017 Robson, E[manuel] W. and M. M. BERNARD SHAW AMONG THE INNOCENTS. Lond: Sydneyan Society, 1945.
Shaw's Caesar and Cleopatra shows his inhumanity, abnormality, inaction, sadism, and perversion. The play is "unfeeling, anti-Christian and uncharitable"; films like it could lead to another war like World War II. Both Shaw and Hitler advocated intuitive action. Shaw slings mud at the British royal family, at Britons, at Nelson. He believes only in subjective reality, and many of his characters look like Shaw. [Pamphlet ends with an attack on the Irish State and DeValera, linking Shaw, DeValera, and Hitler because DeValera paid his respects at the German embassy when Hitler's death was announced, and Shaw defended DeValera's action. "Innocents" in the title refers to admirers of Shaw.]

1018 Sainz de Robles, Federico. "George Bernard Shaw," EL CARRO DE LAS MANZANAS (The Apple Cart) (Madrid: Aguilar, 1945), pp. 11-16.
[Biographical and introductory material to the Spanish translation of The Apple Cart.] [In Spanish.]

1019 Samuel, Herbert. MEMOIRS (Lond: Cresset P, 1945), pp. 13, 17, 29, 30, 57, 59-62; rptd as GROOVES OF CHANGE: A BOOK OF MEMOIRS (Indianapolis & NY: Bobbs-Merrill, 1946), pp. 27, 31, 46, 47, 77, 80-83.
[Reminiscences of early contacts with Shaw at Oxford when leading Fabians came to speak, and at the Webbs. Also letters from Shaw about confrontation with death, about the licensing of plays, and about a parliamentary commission reviewing the licensing laws.]

1020 Schirmer, Walter. KURZE GESCHICHTE DER ENGLISCHEN LITERATUR VON DEN ANFÄNGEN BIS ZUR GEGENWART (Short History of English Literature from the Beginning to the Present) (Halle/Saale: Max Niemeyer, 1945), pp. 216, 231, 254, 258, 262, 264, 265-66, 267.

[Brief introduction to Shaw's works.] [In German.]

1021 "Shaw, (George) Bernard," CURRENT BIOGRAPHY, V (1944), ed by Anna Rothe and Helen Demarest (NY: H. W. Wilson, 1945), pp. 613-16.
[Biographical sketch and résumé of Shaw's career to date.]

1022 Slochower, Harry. NO VOICE IS WHOLLY LOST...: WRITERS AND THINKERS IN WAR AND PEACE (NY: Creative Age, 1945), pp. 2, 9, 81, 279-80, Index.
Shaw is filled with contradictions; he vacillates between "Fabian sociality" and the cult of personality. He is concerned with the results rather than the causes of social ills. The influence of Nietzsche led to his Supermen heroes such as Undershaft and Saint Joan. He favors Lamarck over Darwin, Jevons over Marx. He defended Mussolini, Hitler, and the Soviet Union.

1023 "Theater: The Audience Was Polite," NEWSWEEK, XXVI (20 Aug 1945), 89.
Though Stamford, Conn., was hostile to Clare Boothe Luce at the polls, on the opening night of her performance of Candida (Stamford summer theater) the audience was polite and did not distribute anti-Luce pamphlets prepared for the occasion. [Includes a list of others who have played Candida.]

1024 Titterton, W. R. SO THIS IS SHAW (Lond: Douglas Organ, 1945).
[A character portrait by a fellow Fabian.] Shaw is conceited, but not vain. He uses his art to convince, combining seriousness with humor. Instead of holding the mirror up to nature, he takes snap-shots of people caught in undignified poses. He is not an original thinker, but instead follows trends, e.g., Ibsenism, Wagnerism, Nietzscheism. He is an aristocrat, and a deeply religious man--a Protestant revolutionary [which to Titterton signifies a reactionary]. Furthermore, he is "completely virtuous," "a lonely man upon the heights."

1025 "Transition: Birthday," NEWSWEEK, XXVI (6 Aug 1945), 64.
[A note of Shaw's eighty-ninth birthday.]

1026 "Transition: Nonsense," NEWSWEEK, XXVI (24 Dec 1945), 72.
[An account of Shaw's tongue-in-cheek proposal of marriage to Lady Astor.]

1027 Ward, Alfred Charles (ed). SPECIMENS OF ENGLISH DRAMATIC CRITICISM, XVII-XX CENTURIES (Lond & NY: Oxford, 1945); rptd Westport, Conn.: Greenwood P, 1970, pp. 13-17, 18, 189n, 190-97, 208-217, 237n, 238, 242-43, 244, 246, 247, 284, 290, 319, Index.
While Shaw disliked theaters, his dramatic criticism is "undoubtedly the most satisfying as well as the most brilliant in the English language." A man of integrity, he produced honest work that at the same time was erudite, informative, provocative, and delightful. His criticism of Irving's staging of KING ARTHUR (<u>Our Theatres in the Nineties</u>) is a masterpiece. [Includes William Archer's review, "Arms and the Man," WORLD (25 April 1894), abstracted under year of first publication, and Shaw's review, "Forbes Robertson's Hamlet," SAT REV (2 Oct 1895). Passim references to Shaw in other reviews.]

1028 West, E. J. "G. B. S., Music, and Shakespearean Blank Verse," ELIZABETHAN STUDIES AND OTHER ESSAYS: IN HONOR OF GEORGE F. REYNOLDS (Boulder, Colorado: University of Colorado Studies, [Series B. Studies in the Humanities], Oct 1945), pp. 344-56.
Shaw made a positive contribution to Shakespeare criticism. He had a genuine knowledge of and appreciation for Shakespeare, and admired him as a professional man of the theater. He objected to cutting Shakespeare, and insisted on sensitive attention to the "word music" of Shakespeare's plays. Furthermore, Shaw "was one of the last critics with a real ability to understand and analyze the art of acting."

1029 Whitebait, William. "The Movies: <u>Caesar and Cleopatra</u>, at the Marble Arch Odeon," NS&Nation, XXX (15 Dec 1945), 404-5.
The film version of <u>Caesar and Cleopatra</u> is simply a transliteration of the original. Gabriel Pascal, the director, creates a picture that "transmits very deficiently." Claude Rains as Caesar and Vivien Leigh as Cleopatra do, however, understand the royal relationship.

1030 Wilson, Walter. "Letters to the Editors: G. B. Shaw's Vinegar Method," NATION, CLX (3 March 1945), 258-60.
The United States should use vinegar rather than honey to control the recently defeated fascists. Shaw successfully used this method against Victorianism and wrote a prescription for it in <u>What I Really Wrote About the War</u>.

1031 "Yes, Mr. Shaw, but—Presenting a synthetic colloquy over six questions put to George Bernard Shaw, Britain's pungent dramatist, by Dorothy Royal...then submitted with his answers to James Truslow Adams, America's Number 1 historian...with this result:" ROTARIAN, LXVI (April 1945), 8-10.
[An exchange on the subjects of war, capitalism, a United States of Europe, state control of individual productivity, and self-government for Japan and Germany.]

1946

1032 "About Two Authors," SENIOR SCHOLASTIC, XLIX (11 Nov 1946), 18.
[Brief sketch of early life and career of H. G. Wells and Shaw.]

1033 "Acierta G. B. Shaw" (G. B. Shaw Guesses Right Again), QUE (Argentina), I, No 2 (15 Aug 1946), 7-8.
Shaw correctly recognizes that the most pressing and frequent fault of the leaders of the Western World is their anachronism; neither institutions nor humanity advance at the same rate as history. [In Spanish.]

1034 Agandekián, A. "Letopis sovetskogo teatra perioda Velikoĭ Otechestvennoĭ voĭny" (Chronicle of the Soviet Theater in the Period of the Great Patriotic War), TEATRAL'NYI ALMANAKH (Moscow) I (1946), 340.
On 30 April 1944, the company of the Bolshoi Dramatic Theater performed <u>Pygmalion</u> at Ivanov (155 miles Northeast of Moscow) on their return from war-time evacuation in the East. [In Russian.]

1035 Agee, James. "Films," NATION, CLXIII (17 Aug 1946), 193-95.
The film of Caesar and Cleopatra is perhaps too gaudy, but Shaw's dialog and message are excellent and his analysis of Caesar's genius profound. [Agee again reviews Caesar in "Films," NATION, CLXIII (31 Aug 1946), 249-51.]

1036 "Arts Theatre: 'The Apple Cart,'" TIMES (Lond), 8 Aug 1946, p. 6.
The Apple Cart combines "intellectual restlessness," wit, profundity, and "humourless buffoonery." It seems to satirize democracy and eulogize monarchy. Does it apply to England in 1946?

1037 "Arts Theatre: 'Don Juan in Hell,'" TIMES (Lond), 4 July 1946, p. 6.
Except for the cheap jokes about heaven and hell, the dialog in hell from Man and Superman is brilliant entertainment, consisting of every subject that came into Shaw's head in an hour and a half.

1038 Atkinson, Brooks. "The Play in Review," NYT, 20 Dec 1946, p. 29.
Androcles and the Lion (American Repertory Theater production, International Theater, NY) "lampoons the world and idolizes the Christians." Like Saint Joan, it is a respectful, understanding portrayal of religious faith. It is inventive, with excellent characterization and brilliant logic. [Atkinson again reviews Androcles, calling it "the wittiest play in New York at the moment," in "Bernard Shaw: 'Androcles and the Lion' Revived by the American Repertory Theatre," NYT, 29 Dec 1946, II, p. 1.]

1039 "Ave to a Nonagenarian," TAM, XXX (Aug 1946), 435-37.
Shaw's writings are "gay, fiery, trenchant, contradictory, wise." Shaw himself defies analysis.

1040 Banwell, Marjory [Mrs. H. G. Mecredy]. "Bernard Shaw and His Birthdays," DALHOUSIE REVIEW, XXVI (April 1946), 27-29.
Shaw's parents, his upbringing, his kindness to struggling writers like W. H. Davies, and his sympathy with the inarticulate masses explain the real Shaw, not the

recklessly censorious one. As an Irishman, he loves to shock people. Does he pose? He advises young people to challenge parents, but he should have been a father to daughters who would have laughed at him irreverently.

1041 Barnes, Sir Kenneth. "G. B. S. and the R. A. D. A.," G. B. S. 90, pp. 174-80.
[Account of Shaw's work as a member of the Royal Academy of Dramatic Art Council (1911-1942).] Shaw saw a link between education and theater. He regarded acting as a fine art; he worked with students at rehearsal, explaining dialog, demonstrating characters in action, and emphasizing good speech.

1042 Barr, Donald. "Mr. Shaw as a Novelist," NYTBR, 15 Dec 1946, p. 10.
The Irrational Knot, Cashel Byron's Profession, and An Unsocial Socialist can be read as early works that foreshadow the characters in Shaw's plays, or as the daydreams of a young man. Stylistically, the novels begin resembling the "intellectual extravagance" of Disraeli and end up, mostly in dialog, resembling the plays. Here as elsewhere Shaw's "imperfections as a thinker are his merits as a dramatist."

1043 [Beerbohm, Max]. "A Letter from Sir Max Beerbohm," G. B. S. 90, p. 56.
[A letter to Stephen Winsten expressing admiration for Shaw's genius, disagreement with Shaw's views, and faith in Shaw's enduring fame.]

1044 Bentley, Eric [Russell]. "Bernard Shaw's Politics (A Birthday Tribute)," KENYON REVIEW, VIII (Summer 1946), 347-71.
Shaw's political philosophy is misunderstood, partly because of Marxist attacks on Fabianism. The Fabian society was a group of intellectuals rather than a political party, and Shaw was "a critic and a prophet" rather than "a philosopher and a scientist." Shaw's opposition to fascism and nineteenth-century liberalism is closer to Rousseau than to Machiavelli. Shaw is a Victorian socialist in the tradition of Ruskin and Carlyle. "We have had many vaster and many more logical thinkers but none whose thinking is

more closely knit. Shaw's views are all firmly based on a Baconian faith in human control."

1045 Bentley, Eric [Russell]. THE PLAYWRIGHT AS THINKER: A STUDY OF DRAMA IN MODERN TIMES (NY: Reynal & Hitchcock, 1946), pp. 136-57, 162-72, 335-41, 348-51; NY: World, 1946; rptd NY: Harcourt, 1948?; NY: Meridian, 1955, 1957, 1965; Cleveland and NY: World, 1965
[Comments on Shaw's dramatic theory and technique and on Captain Brassbound's Conversion originally appeared in Bentley, "The Theory and Practice of Shavian Drama" (1944) (q.v.).] Shaw created a new form and standard for comedy. Candida is not a vindication of bourgeois marriage (à la Augier) nor a protest against it (à la Dumas fils), but a dialectical justification of both. ["Notes" include Shaw's letter to James Huneker on Candida and F. Scott Fitzgerald's letter on Candida as a reworking of Eugene O'Neill's STRANGE INTERLUDE.]

1046 Bentley, Eric [Russell]. "Shaw at Ninety," ATLANTIC MONTHLY, CLXXVIII (July 1946), 109-15.
Shaw has never been taken seriously, so that his primary aim--to "save civilization"--has failed. He prevented himself from having any real influence. He was an Outsider (in society, politics, sports, the church) as well as Insider (in music, painting, literature, science). His drama expresses his many-faceted nature; it does not champion particular doctrines.

1047 Berger, Oscar. "An Illustrated Guide to George Bernard Shaw," NATION, CLXIII (27 July 1946), 98-99.
[A birthday tribute to Shaw of eight illustrations, with captions, showing the high points of Shaw's life: birth, arrival in London, first novel, socialist activities, marriage, fame, visit to Russia, and G. B. S. at 90.]

1048 Bernal, J. D. "Shaw the Scientist," G. B. S. 90, pp. 93-105.
Shaw fought current science (Darwin, Pasteur, vivisection, vaccination) and supported "scientific lost causes" (e.g., Lamarckian evolution). His interest in physical science is reflected in The Irrational Knot, with its physical scientist hero, and in In Good King Charles's Golden Days.

The Preface to <u>Back to Methuselah</u> is lucid but wrongheaded. The Preface to <u>The Doctor's Dilemma</u> shows a keen social awareness in its analysis of the medical profession and of poverty as the cause of poor health. The Preface to <u>The Simpleton of the Unexpected Isles</u> seems to turn against science. In general, Shaw failed to distinguish between inner and exterior forces, between conscious and unconscious matter; his faith in the community of living things became "a religion by which to live a most effective and fruitful life." In spite of his aberrant scientific beliefs, he was a profound analyst of society.

1049 "Bernard Shaw et la France" (Bernard Shaw and France), ADAM INTERNATIONAL REVIEW, XIV (Aug 1946), 17-18.
[An account of Shaw's commissioning Augustin Hamon to translate his works into French and the enthusiastic reception of Hamon's translation of <u>Candida</u> when it was performed in Brussels in 1907.] [In French.]

1050 Bernt, H. H. A. "Shaw, George Bernard: <u>The Crime of Imprisonment</u>," LIBRARY JOURNAL, LXXI (15 April 1946), 586.
<u>The Crime of Imprisonment</u> is a brilliant, though somewhat dated, book.

1051 "Books: Nonage Novels," TIME, XLVIII (7 Oct 1946), 110, 112, 114.
<u>The Irrational Knot</u>, <u>Cashel Byron's Profession</u>, and <u>An Unsocial Socialist</u> (all in Caxton House <u>Selected Novels of G. Bernard Shaw</u>) are poor novels. They show little promise of Shaw's later achievements, but they "give a good idea of the audacious, irreverent young Shavian mind."

1052 Bookwright. "Reprints, New Editions," NYHTBR, 6 Octo 1946, p. 35.
Shaw's novels are conventional, with stilted plot and dialog. <u>An Unsocial Socialist</u>, the best, is an imperfect anticipation of <u>Man and Superman</u>.

1053 Bridie, James. "Shaw as Dramatist (including a Surrealist Life of G. B. S.)," G. B. S. 90, pp. 77-91.

Shaw uses the theater as an escape from ordinary life. Like Molière, Shaw brings wit and philosophical ideas to the theater; both attack injustices and experiment in theatrical forms. But Shaw lacks the "easy confident grace" of Molière in handling material. For example, in making Getting Married, Shaw tries a daring experiment, but he loses his nerve and fills the play with "Gilbertian grotesques" and "a welter of small plots." And The Doctor's Dilemma reflects Shaw's ignorance of medicine and employs overly obvious satire. Yet Shaw has an impressive range of subject matter and the courage to explore anything except erotic emotion.

1054 "Briefly Noted," NYer, XXII (27 April 1946), 86, 89-92, espec 90.
The Crime of Imprisonment denounces the prison system and the society which tolerates it. The book is not out of date.

1055 Brophy, Liam. "Veritable Saint or Privileged Lunatic? The Enigma of George Bernard Shaw," CATHOLIC WORLD, CLXIII (July 1946), 319-23.
Shaw's pose as a playboy and enfant terrible belies his message. He lacks the humility to be great. Both Shaw and Wilde were masters of the language, witty and paradoxical, talented (though not geniuses). They lacked heart. [Résumé of Shaw's youth and early success, with quotations from Shaw and others on his fame.] Shaw's perversity can be attributed to his break with his childhood religion without replacing it with Roman Catholicism.

1056 Broughton, Philip S. "The Crime of Imprisonment," AMERICAN JOURNAL OF PUBLIC HEALTH AND THE NATION'S HEALTH, XXXVI (July 1946), 808.
In The Crime of Imprisonment, Shaw combines an attack on the penal system with general social criticism.

1057 Brown, John Mason. "Seeing Things: Eliza Off the Ice," SRL, XXIX (12 Jan 1946), 24-26; rptd in Brown, SEEING THINGS (NY & Lond: McGraw-Hill, 1946), pp. 160-66.
Pygmalion is a second-rate Shaw play, but Shaw's second-rate is good. The dialog (Barrymore Theater, NY) shows evidence of a superior mind, a "literary athlete."

1058 Brown, John Mason. "Seeing Things: Marchbanks vs. Shaw," SRL, XXIX (4 May 1946), 28-30.
Shaw ruins the tension of Candida (Cort Theater, NY) by making Marchbanks a sniveling idiot. Thus Candida does not have a choice between two attractive men, and the actor who plays Marchbanks (Marlon Brando in this production) has an impossible role.

1059 Brown, John Mason. "Seeing Things: The Unbeautiful and the Damned," SRL, XXIX (28 Dec 1946), 26-29, espec 28-29; rptd in Brown, SEEING MORE THINGS (NY and Toronto: McGraw-Hill, 1948), pp. 85-91, espec 90-91.
Shaw's hell in Man and Superman, created in his own witty and wise image, seems "innocent and healthy" compared to Sartre's in NO EXIT.

1060 Bruton, J. G. "George Bernard Shaw," REVISTA DE AMERICA (Columbia), VII, No 20 (Aug 1946), 157-60.
Irony is a unique trait of the Irish people, and Bernard Shaw, in this regard, is as Irish as Sheridan, Goldsmith, and Oscar Wilde, dramatists who in their comedies criticize and mock society, but with elegance. This irony is enriched by the dislike the Irish have for England, and by the ability to speak sharply. Therefore, those writers are distinguished for their brilliant dialog. [Biographical information on Shaw, and reference to the merits of works such as John Bull's Other Island, You Never Can Tell, The Devil's Disciple, Man and Superman, Saint Joan, Everybody's Political What's What. [In Spanish.]

1061 "Caesar and Cleopatra: Vivien Leigh and Claude Rains ornament Shaw's comedy," LIFE, XXI (29 July 1946), 44-46.
[Picture essay on the movie version of Caesar and Cleopatra, one of Shaw's best comedies; brief plot synopsis.]

1062 Canton, Wilberto L. "Teatro" (Theater), LETRAS DE MÉXICO (Mexico), V, No 120 (1 Feb 1946), 217.
The performance in Mexico of Candida received a favorable public reaction. [In Spanish.]

1063 Cerf, Bennett. "Trade Winds: Lawrence Langner,"
SRL, XXIX (7 Dec 1946), 8-10.
Shaw asked Lawrence Langner to depict him not as a "lovable human being" but as detestable in order to discourage "begging letters." Shaw is playing with the idea of writing a musical comedy.

1064 Church, Hayden. "A 'Confession' By G. B. S.,"
NYTMag, 10 March 1946, p. 29.
Shaw confessed that his mother created "spirit paintings" and conversed with the dead. He also confessed that he partakes in seances.

1065 Church, Hayden. "En Route to 'Maturity': G. B.
S. Talks with His Favorite Interviewer," SRL, XXIX
(27 July 1946), 7-8, 10.
[Interview with Shaw, who discusses Back to Methuselah, the political necessity for men to live longer, his diet, the role of the preface-play combination and the novel.]

1066 Crowther, Bosley. "The Screen in Review: Shaw's
'Caesar and Cleopatra' as Film Opens at the
AstorRains and Leigh Co-Star," NYT, 6 Sept 1946, p.
18.
Caesar and Cleopatra is conversational and intellectual, and the discussion becomes tedious at times. The play lacks structure and theatrical effect; yet Gabriel Pascal (film version) has produced pictorial splendor, and the actors capture the charm of Shaw's characters.

1067 Cuatrecasas, J. F. "'Guía política de nuestro
tiempo' por Bernard Shaw" (Everybody's Political
What's What, by Bernard Shaw), DAVAR (Argentina), No
8 (Sept-Oct 1946), 88-90.
[Favorable review of Everybody's Political What's What.]
[In Spanish.]

1068 D., F. J. "'Saint Joan,'" THEATRE WORLD (Lond),
XLII (April 1946), 9.
In the King's Theater (Hammersmith) production of Saint Joan, Ann Casson plays Joan with "youthful simplicity, mature confidence, and unquenchable faith."

1069 Davies, A. Emil. "G. B. S. and Local Government," G. B. S. 90, pp. 152-57.
From the early Fabian tracts to Everybody's Political What's What, Shaw advocated freeing municipal services from the profit motive. As vestryman for St. Pancras (1987-1903) and in his writings, he urged administrative reforms: the municipalization of milk, gas, hospitals, etc., and the right of women to serve on the Council and on committees. Most of his municipal work is still topical.

1070 Davis, Elmer. "Notes on the Failure of a Mission," SRL, XXIX (31 Aug 1946), 6-8.
Shaw and H. G. Wells lived in the hope that collectivization and science would bring an earthly paradise. Wells was more practical than Shaw, with a horror of a collectivized society under the rule of a strong individual and less faith in human improvement. Both Wells and Shaw taught humanity to think clearly and work out its own salvation.

1071 Deans, Marjorie. MEETING AT THE SPHINX: GABRIEL PASCAL'S PRODUCTION OF BERNARD SHAW'S CAESAR AND CLEOPATRA. Lond: Macdonald & Co., n.d. [1946].
England's claim to literary fame rests on Shakespeare and Shaw, who both wrote for the common people. It was inevitable that Shaw would write for the screen, and fortunate that he and Gabriel Pascal, who understands and reveres Shaw, became a team. [Excerpts from correspondence between Pascal and Shaw about the details of production of Caesar and Cleopatra.] Caesar and Cleopatra reads like a film script; it has an "intrinsic cinematic quality." And Shaw, in rewriting for the screen, thinks "in terms of music and light." [An account of the filming of Caesar and Cleopatra, including a Foreword by Shaw, Pascal's "Credo," the script for an unshot scene, and discussion of the actors, production difficulties, the music, costumes, decor and sets. Photographs from the movie.]

1072 Dent, Edward J. "Corno di Bassetto," G. B. S. 90, pp. 122-30.
England is a better country musically as a result of Shaw's music criticism. He writes conscientiously in all his reviews, but his passion is opera. He sees Wagner, like Mozart, as the consummation of an era rather than as a

beginning. He makes scathing criticisms of Mahler and vituperative attacks on Italian opera. His criticism is truculent, yet humorous and graceful, free of rancor. His faults are discursiveness and occasional triviality. Music is for Shaw a religion, "a spiritual force in its own right."

1073 Dobb, Maurice. "Bernard Shaw and Economics," G. B. S. 90, pp. 131-39; rptd in Dobb, ON ECONOMIC THEORY AND SOCIALISM (NY: International, 1955), pp. 205-14.

Shaw's influence on economic thought owes more to his lucid, deft style than to a systematic economic doctrine. His economic ideas are eclectic, conceived "in a Ricardo-Georgian rather than a Marxian setting," though the inspiration of Marx is clear in Shaw's denunciation of capitalism and his championship of the dictatorship of the proletariat. The prefaces to Widowers' Houses and Mrs. Warren's Profession expose social abuses in the economic system; Fabian Essays espouses gradual change. The Intelligent Woman's Guide to Socialism and Capitalism exhibits the essential rationalism that characterizes Shaw's social philosophy and defines his socialism. His economic writings never have an apologetic tone: they are cast in "the invigorating language of confidence in ultimate success and of undaunted iconoclasm."

1074 Dunsany, Lord. "A Permanent Quality," G. B. S. 90, p. 92.

Shaw's work shows no sign of deterioration with time.

1075 "Education: Gungs and Boms," TIME, XLVII (7 Jan 1946), 40.

Shaw explained in a letter to the London TIMES what was wrong with the atom bomb: it was misspelled; it is more economical to spell "bomb" as "bom." According to Shaw, non-phonetic English spelling is wasteful and the British government should do something about it. One might as well spell "gun" as "gung."

1076 "Education: Pshaw on Pspelling," NEWSWEEK, XXVII (7 Jan 1946), 76-77.

Shaw's proposal for a phonetic English alphabet would not work, according to American philologist Charles E. Funk.

1077 "G. B. S.: All honor to his genius; but his message is irrelevant to our problems today," LIFE, XXI (12 Aug 1946), 26.

The celebrations of Shaw's ninetieth birthday ignored Shaw's message, which does not serve today's moral, political, and philosophical needs. The world needs a less pragmatic morality and less biology in its politics. It also does not need Shaw's socialism.

1078 "G.B.S.—859 Years to Go," NEWSWEEK, XXVIII (29 July 1946), 72-74.

[Biographical sketch, photographs, reference to several of Shaw's works, quotations from Shaw.]

1079 "G. B. S. is 90: He has survived Queen Victoria, two wars and the atom bomb, with unflagging faith in Bernard Shaw," LIFE, XXI (29 July 1946), 41-43.

[Pictorial essay on Shaw at home, with various facts of his life presented, including his daily routine.]

1080 "G. B. S. Writing New Play," CHRISTIAN SCIENCE MONITOR MAGAZINE, 10 Aug 1946, p. 14.

Shaw is writing a new play, which he says is like The Apple Cart. He also chops wood, prunes fruit trees, and always dresses for dinner. He has no idea which of his works have brought him the most money.

1081 "Gallery of Gallant Ladies," INDEPENDENT WOMAN, XXV (April 1946), 100-102.

Shaw's Saint Joan, introduced by Katharine Cornell some years ago [1936], is "a searching comment upon political and social bigotry, stupidity and opportunism." Joan keeps faith with her own inner vision and goes to her death. Cornell also portrayed Candida as "a 'womanly woman' who is also a personan individual who is ready to take risks and to fight for her rights as an individual." [Review of various heroines played by Cornell; emphasis on individualism of the women portrayed.]

1082 Gassner, John. "The Theatre Arts," FORUM (Philadelphia), CV (Feb 1946), 561-65, espec 562.

"Shaw wrote Pygmalion out of his head, not his heart"; but the play has intellectual passion. Gertrude Lawrence's

Eliza (Theater Incorporated, Barrymore Theater, NY) "almost comes up to Shaw's writing." The play is not Shaw's best, but is nevertheless brilliant. And "what other dramatist would have dared to conclude the play without having Pygmalion marry his Galatea?"

1083 Gassner, John. "The Theatre Arts," FORUM (Philadelphia), CVI (Sept 1946), 271-75.
At ninety, Shaw is honored by the world; but this is because of his role as gadfly. [Resume of the tributes to him, e.g., G.B.S. 90, the Penguin editions of some of his plays, the Dodd, Mead reissuance of his work.] He writes better prose than Shakespeare, writes well for the screen in adapting his own plays. "The screen version of Major Barbara is the most readable, as well as most intelligent screen play yet published." The Preface to Barbara "is a masterpiece of English prose." Shaw has a genius for seeing the significant in life, and serves as an example of how to write modern social comedy.

1084 Gibbs, Wolcott. "The Theatre: Fourth Down," NYer, XXII (28 Dec 1946), 36, 38.
Androcles and the Lion (American Repertory Company, International Theater, NY) is a "combination of low, almost abysmal comedy and a neat sardonic and sometimes rather moving discussion of comparative religion."

1085 Gibbs, Wolcott. "The Theatre: When You and I Were Young," NYer, XXI (5 Jan 1946), 38, 40-41.
Pygmalion (Theater Incorporated production, Barrymore Theater, NY) is dated and overpoweringly British in humor. The plot is ingenious but "not very filling emotionally." Though typical of that "absurd and whiskery personality" (Shaw), the play is "tame and disappointing."

1086 Gielgud, Val. "Bernard Shaw and the Radio," G. B. S. 90, pp. 171-73; rptd in CRITICAL HERITAGE, pp. 369-71.
Shaw's plays would make excellent radio productions if Shaw would allow editing and cutting. But he will not. He has a magnificent voice and a simple, convincing approach to the microphone. [Includes an account of Shaw's reactions to radio productions of Captain Brassbound's Conversion, Saint Joan, and The Millionairess.]

1087 Gilder, Rosamond. "Sprightly Entertainment: Broadway in Review," TAM, XXX (March 1946), 133-41. espec 134, 136-37.
Gaiety characterizes the Theater Incorporated revival of Pygmalion (Barrymore Theater, NY): the scene in Mrs. Higgins' drawing room is "among the funniest in modern theatre."

1088 Gill, W. W. "G. B. S.," TLS, XLV (10 Aug 1946), 379.
After all the attention at Shaw's ninetieth birthday, his one hundredth birthday will be an anti-climax. Contrary to an assertion in "Shaw and the Ancients" (TLS, XLV, 27 July 1946, 349-50), numbers may indeed have something to do with the goodness of humanity.

1089 [Gillis, James M.]. "American G.B.S.?" CATHOLIC WORLD, CLXIII (Sept 1946), 486-89.
H. L. Mencken is "a rather dim carbon copy of G.B.S." Both writers flout elementary decencies.

1090 [Gillis, James M.]. "What Shaw Really Taught," CATHOLIC WORLD, CLXIII (Sept 1946), 481-86.
Shaw's ready-made formula is "to ridicule what the human race reverences, and to extol what the human race abominates." Yet his critics idolize him, a form of "devil-worship."

1091 Gonzalez Lanuza, Eduardo. "Bernard Shaw: Guía política de nuestro tiempo" (Bernard Shaw: Everybody's Political What's What), SUR (Argentina), XV, No 143 (Sept 1946), 61-65.
In Everybody's Political What's What, Shaw declares himself a convinced adherent of the death penalty for incorrigible criminals. This is a genial book which reflects the manias and obsessions of the dramatist. [In Spanish.]

1092 Gray, James. "Four Rich Uncles: Arnold Bennett, John Galsworthy, H. G. Wells, George Bernard Shaw," ON SECOND THOUGHT (Minneapolis: University of Minnesota P, 1946), pp. 13, 28, 36-58, 95, Index, espec 36-58; translated into German as HALBGOTTER AUF DER LITERARISCHEN BUHNE (Demigods on the Literary Stage) (München, 1950).

Rebecca West regarded Arnold Bennett, John Galsworthy, H. G. Wells, and Bernard Shaw as the uncles of the generation that came to maturity after World War I. Their fame placed them beyond censure, despite the "marital irregularities of the first three uncles and the verbal audacities of the fourth." Of the four, Shaw is the most picturesque. He never mastered the art of the well-made play; instead, each of his plays is "a tract in dramatic form." But he is unique in his gift for "setting off the firecrackers of ideas under the throne of stuffiness." Although Shaw is prone to human error, as is shown in his revolt against medical science and his espousal of other fads such as vegetarianism, in the end "it is possible to go on living in a world that produces Adolf Hitler only because it produces an occasional Bernard Shaw as well."

1093 Green, E. Mawby. "Echoes from Broadway," THEATRE WORLD (Lond), XLII (Feb 1946), 27-30, espec 29.
The Theater Incorporated production of Pygmalion (Barrymore Theater, NY) is disappointing, after the "utter perfection" of the motion picture version. Gertrude Lawrence is too restrained as Eliza, and Raymond Massey makes Higgins "unpleasantly boorish."

1094 Gregory, Isabella Augusta. LADY GREGORY'S JOURNALS, 1916-1930, ed by Lennox Robinson (Lond: Putnam, 1946; NY: Macmillan, 1947), pp. 9, 55-59, 62-63, 65-67, 72, 80, 84, 85, 88, 91, 103, 110-11, 112-13, 115, 124, 125, 154, 180, 190-91, 198, 199-200, 201-16, 232, 245, 253, 266, 289, 292-93, 295-96, 329, Index.
During a number of visits, Shaw reminisced about his mother's interest in gardens and the supernatural, discussed T. E. Lawrence and William Morris, read a story he was preparing for the Belgian Children's Milk Fund and the first part of Heartbreak House, and described Back to Methuselah; he commented on his early novels, on his preparation for Saint Joan, and on a production of Henry James' Guy Domville. [Account of Shaw's various dealings with the Abbey Theater. Includes Shaw's poem to Lady Gregory's grandchildren.]

1095 Haley, Sir William. "The Stripling and the Sage," G. B. S. 90, pp. 167-70.

Shaw's criticism and encouragement helped the infant art of broadcasting to mature. His plays depend on brilliant dialog and are hence excellent for broadcasting. Shaw chaired the Spoken English Committee of the BBC and occasionally appeared at the microphone. His reading of O'Flaherty, V. C. (24 Oct 1924) was a great success.

1096 Halperín Doughi, Tulio. "Bernard Shaw: Guía política de nuestro tiempo" (Bernard Shaw: Everybody's Political What's What), CURSOS Y CONFERENCIAS (Argentina), XV, Nos 169-70 (April-May 1946), 349-51.
Everybody's Political What's What is a well-organized guide, written by one who instead of being merely an expositor of ideas, is an arguer, a person who enjoys discussion. [In Spanish.]

1097 Hartung, Philip T. "Happy Birthday GBS," COMMONWEAL, XLIV (16 Aug 1946), 433-34.
The film of Caesar and Cleopatra is amusing satire, "full of wisecracks." However, it lacks cinematic technique, and the script is too verbose.

1098 Horzyca, Wilam. "G. K. C. i G. B. S.," PROGRAM TEATRU ZIEMI POMORSKIEJ (Toruń), No 7 (1945/6); rptd in Horzyca, O DRAMACIE (About Drama) (Warsaw: Wydawnictwa artystyczne i filmowe, 1969), pp. 206-13.
Although Chesterton and Shaw differed greatly, their aim was the same: the creation of a new orthodoxy. Shaw chose socialism, Chesterton Catholicism. Both Shaw and Chesterton were able to turn everything into a joke in order to dazzle people with the truth. In Chesterton's MAGIC, the characters are "bigots of rationalism," whereas in The Dark Lady of the Sonnets, God is a deus absconditus, though real. But Shaw is too great a realist not to perceive the "shadow of eternity," the presence of which rarely appears as clearly as in the final dialog of the Dark Lady. He is a great joker, but a still greater poet. [In Polish.]

1099 Horzyca, Wilam. "Komedia o Królestwie Bozym" (A Comedy on the Kingdom of Heaven), PROGRAM TEATRU ZIEMI POMORSKIEJ (Toruń), No 7 (1945/6); rptd in

Horzyca, O DRAMACIE (About Drama) (Warsaw:
Wydawnictwa artystyczne i filmowe, 1969), pp. 219-25.
Few can see that under Shaw's clowning and irony beats the
heart of an apostle endowed with "holy impatience." Major
Barbara is his most contemporary play, in which Shaw
attempts to realize "the Kingdom of God" on earth. [In
Polish.]

1100 Housman, Laurence. "G. B. S. and the
Victorians," G. B. S. 90, pp. 47-49.
Shaw devastated Victorian hypocrisy with his wit more than
with his wisdom. With his kind heart and occasionally cruel
tongue, he combines the benevolent wisdom of Socrates and
the sharp wit of Voltaire, as for example in The Adventures
of the Black Girl in Her Search for God.

1101 Hsiung, S. I. "Through Eastern Eyes," G. B. S.
90, pp. 194-99.
[Personal impressions of Shaw.] Shaw is a greater
philosopher than a dramatist. Saint Joan talks endlessly
and talks "exactly like Shaw." The recent plays are almost
unactable.

1102 Hudson, Lynton. THE TWENTIETH-CENTURY DRAMA
(Lond, Sydney, Toronto, Bombay & Stockholm: George G.
Harrap [The Harrap Library No 58], 1946), pp. 17-22,
23-24, 26, 29, 33, 47, 54, 57, 61, 62, 63, 64, 80,
espec 17-22.
Shaw's plays contain little action and much talk.
Reflecting his preaching, his wit, and his desire to shock,
they gave impetus to the new theater of ideas. Shaw's ideas
but not his dramatic form have been very influential on his
generation. [Passim references to Shaw's contributions to
modern drama.]

1103 Huxley, Aldous. "A Birthday Wish," G. B. S. 90,
p. 200.
The world would be a better place if it had listened to
Shaw's teaching as well as applauding his plays and
laughing at his prefaces.

1104 "I 90 anni di Shaw" (In Shaw's Ninetieth Year),
EMPORIUM (Bergamo), CIV (Oct 1946), 170-73.

Although Shaw has lived long enough to see himself become a
legend, the career of this living paradox does not seem to
have come to an end, and his work, containing elements of
expressive vitality, cannot be considered outdated. He may
seem a clown or a preacher, but he will be saved as an
artist. [In Italian.]

1105 "Idols of the Market-Place," CANADIAN FORUM,
XXVI (Sept 1946), 124-25.
Both Shaw and H. G. Wells "are now in the trough of
appreciation" given great artists who live to old age. They
both defied the label "artist" when it meant shirking
social responsibility. They popularized modern ideas and
preached a gospel of sane and balanced rationalism. Shaw is
not the Chesterton-labelled Puritan, but a pagan, the
"incarnation of Greek culture in the modern world."

1106 Inge, William Ralph. "Bernard Shaw: Socialist
or Rebel?" List, XXXVI (10 Oct 1946), 471; excerpted
in CRITICAL HERITAGE, pp. 372-73, Item 124.
Like other contemporary independent thinkers, Shaw rejects
nineteenth-century materialism and leans toward mysticism,
toward "essential Christianity," as represented by the Life
Force in Man and Superman.

1107 Inge, W[illiam] R[alph]. "Shaw as a
Theologian," G. B. S. 90, pp. 110-21.
Shaw is an "untypical theologian," quarrelling with the
church rather than with its founders. He and other critics
wrong Saint Paul, and Shaw's sketch of Jesus's life and
death in the Preface to Androcles and the Lion is
psychologically impossible. The Adventures of the Black
Girl in Her Search for God and Saint Joan are of little
importance to understanding Shaw's view of religion. The
Preface to Back to Methuselah, influenced by Samuel Butler
in its desire to shock clergy and tease scientists, attacks
"the theory of blind causation."

1108 Irvine, William. "G. B. Shaw's Musical
Criticism," MUSICAL QUARTERLY, XXXII (July 1946),
319-32; rptd as "The Music Critic," chap 16, in
Irvine, THE UNIVERSE OF G. B. S. (NY, Lond, &
Toronto: Whittlesey House [a division of McGraw-
Hill], 1949), pp. 125-36.

Shaw's music criticism for THE STAR (1888-90) and THE WORLD (1890-94) is varied in style and tone and of uniform high quality. Shaw was a propagandist for Wagner, for stage realism, and "for precise and intelligent execution." The criticism reflects his "passion for artistic perfection" and gives a picture of Shaw in the "very process of becoming himself"—the dramatist, the wit, the economist, the business man, and the "man of deep and even romantic feeling." The criticism is unbiased, though necessarily focussed more on the performance than on the composition. Shaw's test for the composer was feeling, thought, and inspiration.

1109 Irvine, William. "George Bernard Shaw and Karl Marx," JOURNAL OF ECONOMIC HISTORY, VI (May 1946), 53-72; incorporated into Irvine, THE UNIVERSE OF G. B. S. (NY, Lond, & Toronto: Whittlesey House [a division of McGraw-Hill], 1949).

Shaw learned from Marx that social phenomena are revolutionary, that facts and statistics contribute to sound thought and effective propaganda, and that the solution of practical problems requires abstract economic thinking. An Unsocial Socialist is an early and complete expression of Shaw's Marxist faith, which was later modified by Fabianism. Mrs. Warren's Profession and Major Barbara are based on the Marxist notion that the problem of poverty makes virtue impossible. But Saint Joan, The Apple Cart, and articles in the CLARION replace the conflict of economic forces with the conflict of ideas and personalities, especially the opposition of revolutionary creative genius and social convention. In Everybody's Political What's What Shaw puts his hope in "the revolutionary idealism of middle-class genius." [Much discussion of Marxian ideology and Shaw's response to W. S. Jevons and the Rev. Philip H. Wicksteed.]

1110 Isaacs, Hermine Rich. "The Films: Late Summer," TAM, XXX (Sept 1946), 517-20.

The film of Caesar and Cleopatra is "J. Arthur Rank's most expensive error." The scenic trappings obscure Shaw's wit, and the actors lack a sense of the historical Caesar and Cleopatra. [Photographs of Vivien Leigh as Cleopatra and of Shaw and Pascal. An earlier brief review by Isaacs of the film appeared in "Films: Good, Bad, and Rank," TAM, XXX (Feb 1946), 96-103.]

1111 Jennings, Richard. "Fair Comment," NINETEENTH CENTURY AND AFTER, CXL (July 1946), 38-40.
Shaw, soon to be 90, continues to talk hard and contradict everybody, including himself. His Shakespeare criticism is both truthful and diverting, pointing up Shaw's own achievements as moralist and philosopher. Shakespeare's characters, if they were Shavian, would be "good if capricious reformers"; they would not be dramatic, and most would be boring.

1112 Joad, C[yril] E[dwin] M[itchinson]. "Shaw's Philosophy," G. B. S. 90, pp. 57-76; rptd, with a Postscript, as chap vii in Joad, SHAW (Lond: Victor Gollancz, 1949), pp. 176-206; and in Louis Kronenberger (ed), GEORGE BERNARD SHAW: A CRITICAL SURVEY (Cleveland & NY: World, 1953), pp. 184-205.
Shaw's remarkably coherent philosophy of Creative Evolution, influenced by Samuel Butler and Lamarck and best expressed in Back to Methuselah, has as its center the need for life to subdue matter. According to this philosophy, man's raison d'etre is to fulfill Life's intentions; woman's purpose is more primitive and more fundamental (expressed in Lilith in Back to Methuselah). Like Plato, Shaw distrusts art, but he does not consider it a medium for the Form of Beauty; rather, he sees art as a substitute for reality for those unable to view reality directly. His thought demands "static and immutable perfection" in one element of the universe; yet Creative Evolution presupposes constant change. The contradiction is not resolved; nor does Shaw provide for any end or goal in life; account satisfactorily for the relationship between life and matter; or resolve the issue of individual freedom and the Life Force.

1113 Jones, Daniel. "G. B. S. and Phonetics," G. B. S. 90, pp. 158-60.
Shaw's work with phonetics includes a proposal for a new alphabet (the details to be supplied by others) and a series of booklets (Broadcast English) for the BBC. Pygmalion connects manner of speaking and success, and offers phonetics as "a key to social advancement."

246

1946: 1111-1117

1114 Karsh, Yousuf. FACES OF DESTINY, PORTRAITS BY KARSH (Chicago: Ziff-Davis, 1946), pp. 130-31.
[A black-and-white portrait of Shaw and an anecdote written by the author on his appointment with Shaw for the photographic session.]

1115 Kavanagh, Peter. THE IRISH THEATRE: BEING A HISTORY OF THE DRAMA IN IRELAND FROM THE EARLIEST PERIOD UP TO THE PRESENT DAY (Tralee, Ireland· Kerryman Limited, 1946), pp. 433-35.
[A list of Shaw's plays, without annotation or any analysis.]

1116 Keynes, Lord [John Maynard Keynes]. "G. B. S. and Isaac Newton," G. B. S. 90, pp. 106-9; rptd as "Bernard Shaw and Isaac Newton," in THE COLLECTED WRITINGS OF JOHN MAYNARD KEYNES, Vol. X: ESSAYS ON BIOGRAPHY (Lond: Macmillan; St. Martin's P, 1972), chap 36, pp. 375-81.
Shaw's portrait of Newton in In Good King Charles's Golden Days has historical and biographical inaccuracies.

1117 Krog, Helge. "Bernard Shaw," [trans from a Norwegian manuscript by O. F. Knudsen] NORSEMAN, IV (1946), 261-70.
Shaw combines youthful seriousness and fun and hides behind "the mask of ingenuousness." His plays reflect a struggle between poet and satirist, a conflict derived from his childhood in a "menage of romanticists and dreamers." His young life also accounts for his postponement of sexual experience and his hatred of poverty. His dramatic criticism is intelligent and witty, and The Quintessence of Ibsenism is "decidedly the best of all the books" about Ibsen. He was never an orthodox Marxist, though Marxism gave him his dramatic method—dialectical materialism. Plays Unpleasant blames the system and the victims' actions, not the victims themselves. In these and other plays (Candida is an exception), Shaw places social criticism above character development. Shaw is an evolutionist, not a revolutionist; above all, he opposes the status quo. His mysticism in Major Barbara, Heartbreak House, and Back to Methuselah is "pretty obscure."

1118 Krutch, Joseph Wood. "Drama," NATION, CLXII (9 Feb 1946), 176.

Pygmalion (Theater Incorporated, Barrymore Theater, NY) and Shakespeare's THE WINTER'S TALE both abandon probability, creating fabulous and fantastic characters in Hermione and Eliza, and Leontes and Higgins. And both have witty dialog and a satiric thrust (e.g., in the characters of Autolycus and Mr. Doolittle, blood brothers who articulate the case for the Undeserving Poor).

1119 Krutch, Joseph Wood. "Drama," NATION, CLXII (20 April 1946), 487.

Shaw is now a living classic, but outmoded. Candida (Cort Theater, NY), a comedy but not a problem play, is mentally vigorous. But Shaw fails to make Marchbanks convincing, for Shaw cannot express physical love.

1120 Laing, Allan M. "Bernard Shaw and the Business Man," LIVERPOOL ECHO (6 Dec 1946) [not seen in this form]; rptd in ISh, VII (1968-69), 23.

[Shaw on businessmen as civil servants, white collar men doing part time manual labor, a special moral code for the businessman, and other business-related questions.]

1121 "Libros: 'Guía política de nuestro tiempo' por George Bernard Shaw" (Books: Everybody's Political What's What, by George Bernard Shaw), QUE (Argentina), I, No 2 (15 Aug 1946), 33.

Everybody's Political What's What could very well be considered the ideological will of a very singular dramatist. Its style is not a literary one, but springs from meditation and a profound concept of esthetics. It contains two important elements: humor and independence with regard to all common literary, social, and political conventions. [In Spanish.]

1122 Limbert, Roy. "The Inspiration of Shaw," G. B. S. 90, pp. 181-89.

[An appreciative account by the Director of the Malvern Festival of Shaw's support. Shaw attended the Festivals, aided in rehearsals, wrote articles for the Festival Book, lent his voice to "Tea-Time Talks," participated in a Pageant of British Film, and wrote five plays especially for the Festival.]

1123 Loewenstein, F[ritz] E[rwin]. "Do You Remember, Mr. Shaw?" ADAM INTERNATIONAL REVIEW, XIV (Aug 1946), 9-17.
[An account of Shaw's early years in London, including his work for the Edison Telephone Company, based on Loewenstein's collection of Shaw letters, unreprinted pamphlets, leaflets, and contributions to periodicals, papers, and books.]

1124 Loewenstein, F[ritz] E[rwin]. THE HISTORY OF A FAMOUS NOVEL. Lond: Pvtly ptd, 1946; rptd Folcroft, Pa.: Folcroft Library Editions, 1973.
[A publishing history of An Unsocial Socialist from its beginning 9 July 1883 to March 1946.]

1125 Loewenstein, F[ritz] E[rwin]. "What Richard Mansfield Thought of 'Candida,'" DRAMA, ns II (Autumn 1946), 8-10.
Candida has the usual love triangle, with an unusual solution; it is a married woman's play, unheroic, with an evangelic message that remains topical. [Included is the text of Richard Mansfield's 1895 letter to Shaw rejecting the play as lacking in dramatic qualities.]

1126 Luzuriaga, Lorenzo. "Bernard Shaw y la educación" (Bernard Shaw and Education) LA NACIÓN (Buenos Aires), 21 July 1946; rptd in REPERTORIO AMERICANO (Costa Rica), XLII, No 22 (30 Nov 1946), 345-46.
Shaw is a true educator, arguing in Everybody's Political What's What that the way to eradicate social class discrimination in education is to abolish poverty. He sees education as a life-long process, and art as the greatest educator. Some of his theories are, however, unsound, e.g., his opposition to schooling past fourteen years of age, and his belief in state intervention in education. [In Spanish.]

1127 M., H. G. "'Man and Superman,'" THEATRE WORLD (Lond), XLII (May 1946), 8.
The King's Theater (Hammersmith) production of Man and Superman humanizes Shaw's "dialectal fireworks." Tanner is not merely the author's mouthpiece; Ramsden is "a very eminent Victorian indeed"; Octavius, "a gorgeous ninny."

1128 MacManus, M. J. "Shaw's Irish Boyhood,"
G. B. S. 90, pp. 31-45.
[Biographical sketch of the years before Shaw moved to
London.]

1129 Martin, Kingsley. "G. B. S. at Ninety," NATION,
CLXIII (27 July 1946), 97, 100.
Shaw's work contains "some consistent strains of thought"
concerning human history and religion; but it also contains
contradictions, e.g., Shaw's rebelliousness versus his
approval of Russian authoritarian education. He is
primarily a stimulator of thought, a moralist, a reformer,
and a satirist. [Summation of Shaw's life on his ninetieth
birthday: his personality and physique, his contributions
to the British stage, his likeness to Carlyle.]

1130 Masefield, John. "On the Ninetieth Birthday of
Bernard Shaw," G. B. S. 90, p. 17; also in SRL, XXIX
(27 July 1946), 10.
[Poem celebrating the "bright mind ever young."]

1131 Morley, Christopher. "G. B. S.—1856—?" SRL,
XXIX (27 July 1946), 25.
[A four-line poem in tribute to Shaw, on his ninetieth
birthday.]

1132 Morozov, Mikhail M. "Dramaturgiia Bernarda
Shou" (Dramaturgy of Bernard Shaw), PIGMALION
(Moscow: Malyi teatr, 1946); rptd in Morozov,
SHEKSPIR, BERNS, SHOU... (Shakespeare, Burns,
Shaw...) (Moscow: Iskusstvo, 1967), pp. 254-68.
Shaw had no immediate predecessors in English dramaturgy,
being a realist whose characters, their thoughts and
feelings, belong to the reality surrounding their author.
As a satirist, he hated the spirit of Victorian
respectability. His satire is often far-reaching,
especially in the early Three Plays for Puritans, which
outraged reactionary critics and the censorship. But Shaw
did not pursue that path: instead, he continued seeking—in
Fabian socialism, biological evolution, Puritan moralizing.
Shaw's plays must be acted seriously, not grotesquely or as
caricatures, even though his use of paradox in situations
and dialog is a kind of "grotesque," natural to the Irish.
Shaw was not the first English writer to admire Chekhov.

One factor in Shaw's plays which makes them classics is
that they can be read as well as seen in stage performance.
[In Russian.]

1133 Murray, Gilbert. "A Foreword," G. B. S. 90,
pp. 13-15.
Shaw can be characterized as a devotee of the life of the
mind, a reformer using ridicule and logic rather than
emotional appeal, a satirist free of malice, and a
courageous light-bringer and truth-teller.

1134 Nathan, George Jean. "Candida. April 3, 1946,"
THE THEATRE BOOK OF THE YEAR, 1945-1946 (NY: Knopf,
1946), pp. 353-57.
Candida is sentimental, as is Shaw (though he denies it).
The Cort Theater (NY) production has Katharine Cornell in
one of her better interpretations.

1135 National Book League (Lond). BERNARD SHAW:
CATALOGUE OF AN EXHIBITION AT 7 ALBEMARLE ST, LONDON
TO CELEBRATE HIS NINETIETH BIRTHDAY (Lond: Cambridge
UP, 1946); rptd Folcroft, Pa.: Folcroft Library
Editions, 1973.
[Exhibition, 26 July to 24 Aug 1946, included "first
editions of all the major works..., as well as copies of
all the first-night programmes." Catalog lists The Works;
The Novels; The Plays; Essays and Literary Criticism;
Pamphlets, Lectures and Articles in Periodicals; Political
Writings; Art; Shaviana; Books about G. B. S.; Recent and
Forthcoming Publications. Does not attempt completeness.]

1136 Neill, A. S. "Shaw and Education," G. B. S. 90,
pp. 140-51.
Shaw's 1910 theory of education as a dynamic, lifetime
process was heretical and shocking, filled with Freudian
psychological truths and very readable. But Shaw mistakenly
thinks of children as "little G. B. S.'s," and sees them in
relation to the adult rather than to the child's world.
Furthermore, he distrusts, dislikes and fears children: he
"loves the theoretical idea of a child better than he loves
the actual factual brat." In ignoring the unconscious and
refusing to see sex in anything, Shaw offers a theory of
education that is now or will be soon dated. His only

chance for immortality is in the few plays (e.g., How He Lied to Her Husband) which omit propaganda.

1137 Nichols, Lewis. "The Play," NYT, 4 April 1946, 33.
Katharine Cornell's Candida (Cort Theater, NY) continues to be fresh and alive, but Wesley Addy's Morell is colorless, and Marlon Brando's Marchbanks is a "monotonously intoning poet."

1138 Nichols, Lewis. "Three to Broadway: A Revival of Shaw's 'Pygmalion' Included Among the New Arrivals," NYT, 6 Jan 1946, II, p. 1.
Pygmalion (Theater Incorporated, Barrymore Theater, NY) is still humorous and touching; "it glows with good will."

1139 Nicoll, Allardyce. A HISTORY OF LATE NINETEENTH CENTURY DRAMA 1850-1900, Vol. I (Lond: Cambridge UP, 1946; rptd 1949; 2nd ed 1959; rptd 1962 as Vol. V of A HISTORY OF ENGLISH DRAMA, 1600-1900), pp. 1, 3, 12, 21, 22, 61, 70, 78, 90-91, 100, 105, 129, 169, 187, 189, 193-204, 211, Index, espec 193-204.
Like Shakespeare, Shaw emerged as a playwright during a dramatic renaissance, basing his technique on his predecessors but introducing a new epoch in drama. By 1900 his criticism and plays made him a dominant theatrical force, with his dramaturgic skill surpassing his prophetic powers. His plays combine Shakespearean humor, Jonsonian satire, and wit à la Congreve, with serious purpose and Shavian fun. He adds an element of imaginative fantasy to the drama of realism. In his best plays he has completely removed himself from his characters and omitted all emotion, as in Arms and the Man, The Devil's Disciple, and The Man of Destiny. Conversely, The Philanderer, Mrs. Warren's Profession, and Candida lack Shaw's characteristic comic detachment.

1140 "The Ninetieth Birthday Dinner for GBS," PUBLISHERS' WEEKLY, CL (3 Aug 1946), 474-75.
[Account of the Waldorf-Astoria (NY) dinner of 25 July honoring Shaw, sponsored by Dodd, Mead and the SRL. Friends and business acquaintances recalled Shavian witticisms and the president of Dodd, Mead spoke. Details of plans for the dinner appear in earlier copies of PUBLISHERS' WEEKLY:

"Dodd, Mead and the Saturday Review Plan for Shaw Anniversary," CXLIX (15 June 1946), 3121-22; "Speakers Announced for Shaw Birthday Dinner," CL (13 July 1946), 181; "'Information Please' at the Shaw Dinner," CL (20 July 1946), 287.]

1141 North, Sterling. "G. B. S. Denounces Imprisonment," CHICAGO SUN BOOK WEEK, 28 April 1946, p. 2.
The arguments in The Crime of Imprisonment are valid today. There is indeed a fine line between "business" and "crime," and between justice and vengeance.

1142 Orwell, George [pseud of Eric Blair]. "As I Please," TRIBUNE (Lond), 27 Dec 1946; rptd in THE COLLECTED ESSAYS, JOURNALISM AND LETTERS OF GEORGE ORWELL, ed by Sonia Orwell and Ian Angus. Vol. IV: In Front of Your Nose, 1945-1950 (NY: Harcourt, Brace & World, 1968), pp. 259-62.
Shaw correctly asserts that this is a credulous age, "more gullible and superstitious" than the Middle Ages.

1143 Orwell, George [pseud of Eric Blair]. "In Front of Your Nose," TRIBUNE (Lond), 22 March 1946; rptd in THE COLLECTED ESSAYS, JOURNALISM AND LETTERS OF GEORGE ORWELL, ed by Sonia Orwell and Ian Angus. Vol. IV: In Front of Your Nose, 1945-1950 (NY: Harcourt, Brace & World, 1968), pp. 122-25.
Shaw's Preface to Androcles and the Lion cites an example of schizophrenic thinking in the Gospel of Matthew.

1144 Pascal, Gabriel. "Shaw as a Scenario-Writer," G. B. S. 90, pp. 190-93.
Shaw is not only a great playwright and scenario-writer but a great actor and director as well. He has "unbelievable visual knowledge," a "genuine instinct for camera angles and...rhythmical sense of movie continuity." [Account of Shaw's creation of film scripts for Pygmalion, Major Barbara, and Caesar and Cleopatra.]

1145 Passfield, Lord [Sidney Webb]. "'Everywhere I Gained Something,'" G. B. S. 90, p. 46.
[Brief statement of the value of Webb's travels with Shaw.]

1146 Peacock, Ronald. "Shaw," THE POET IN THE THEATRE (NY: Harcourt, 1946; rptd NY: Hill and Wang, 1960), pp. 86-93; also rptd in Louis Kronenberger (ed), GEORGE BERNARD SHAW: A CRITICAL SURVEY (Cleveland & NY: World, 1953), pp. 178-83.
Shaw is the culmination in drama of the application of social thought to the theater and of art as parable. His originality is in his point of view and his use of naturalistic technique in comedy. Unlike Molière, who isolates the unreasonable character, Shaw isolates the reasonable one and imposes an unconventional character on a group of conventional ones. But Shaw lacks the imaginative power to create living comic characters. His realism made him abandon the traditional mechanical construction of plays, though he uses "the prerogatives and tricks of comedy, without...being chained to them."

1147 Pearson, Hesketh. "Bernard Shaw at Ninety," BRITISH BOOK NEWS, LXXII (July 1946), 255-57.
Shaw's novels contain the germ of his dramatic message and technique. The plays fall into four creative periods: the ten early plays; the "plays solely to please himself" (1903-1916); Heartbreak House (1919) through The Apple Cart (1930); and the late plays. Shaw exerted a tremendous influence on the social thought of the generation before World War I.

1148 Pearson, Hesketh. THE LIFE OF OSCAR WILDE (Lond: Methuen; Toronto: S.J.R. Saunders, 1946); also as OSCAR WILDE: HIS LIFE AND WIT (NY & Lond: Harper, 1946), pp. 1, 2, 46, 122, 127, 155-58, 171, 183, 191, 207, 235, 246, 249-50, 258, 260, 277, 286-87, Index; revised edition Lond: Macdonal and Jane's, 1975; rptd Westport, Conn.: Greenwood P, 1978.
Shaw and Wilde treated each other courteously, but were not friends; they each appreciated the other's genius. Shaw admired Wilde's witty attacks on conventional morality; Wilde admired Shaw's early works, including The Quintessence of Ibsenism and Widowers' Houses.

1149 Potter, Stephen. "Plays: Man and Superman, at The Arts Theatre," NS&Nation, XXXII (20 July 1946), 46.

To see Man and Superman is like "revisiting the university of one's youth," and the play (Arts Theater, Lond) seems "delightfully fresh." John Slater interprets the Devil along romantic lines, as Shaw would have it.

1150 Priebatsch, Heinz. "G. Bernard Shaw ein Künstler?" (G. Bernard Shaw an Artist?), SCHWEIZER ANNALEN (Aarau), III (1946-47), 401-7.
Shaw is an artist because he has proved that the realm of the intellect and the spirit has no fixed terms and rules. He is a brilliant comedian, a fierce fighter, and a Puritan full of exaggerations. [In German.]

1151 Priestley, J. B. "G. B. S.—Social Critic," G. B. S. 90, pp. 50-54; also as "Shaw as Social Critic," SRL, XXIX (27 July 1946), 5-7; excerpted in CRITICAL HERITAGE, pp. 368-69, Item 122.
Shaw is basically a religious man, insisting that theory and practice coincide and that all humanity is a living entity. His weaknesses are in overrating dictators and undervaluing democracy. In his plays, he manages to tell the truth provocatively without being offensive. His drawing room courtesy and good humor may seem out of place today, but they are nevertheless appealing.

1152 "'Pygmalion': Gertrude Lawrence adds new luster to an old favorite by G. B. Shaw," LIFE, XX (14 Jan 1946), 67-68, 70.
Pygmalion (Barrymore Theater, NY) is wise, witty, and funny. [Photographs of the production, with Gertrude Lawrence and Raymond Massey.]

1153 Rossi, Mario Manlio. "George Bernard Shaw," VERSO UNA TEOLOGIA (Towards a Theology) (Bari: Laterza, 1946), pp. 41-45.
One may criticize Shaw, but one cannot help enjoying his plays. Saint Joan, which marked Shaw's conversion, springs from the same source as Androcles and the Lion, which shocked believers. [In Italian.]

1154 Routh, H[arold] V. ENGLISH LITERATURE AND IDEAS IN THE TWENTIETH CENTURY (Lond: Methuen, 1946; 2nd ed 1948), pp. 16, 32-38, 45, 48, 69, 70, 81, 99, 101, 121, 184, Index, espec 32-38.

Shaw, like Wells, is "of the school of Rousseau," believing in human progress and perfectability—a faith reflected in his Fabian socialism and optimistic humanism. His drama combines the continental technique of Ibsen and of the pièces à thése with English emotional steadiness. He enlivened his satire with current issues, unexpected reversals, and elements of wild romance. But he failed to provide constructive thought and frequently let clowning obscure his message. He will be remembered as a pioneer in stagecraft for externalizing the interior monolog; for abolishing the "curtain," the "aside," and the "one-man play"; and for introducing "conversational argument" to the stage. [Scattered comparisons of Shaw to other turn-of-the-century writers.]

1155 S., H. [Harrison Smith]. "Hail," SRL, XXIX (27 July 1946), 24.
Shaw is a playboy and genius who has put his ideas to the test of two world wars, the threat of the atom bomb, and communist dictatorship. He has been announcing fundamental truths for sixty years.

1156 Saroyan, William. "My Visit with G.B.S.," NEW REPUBLIC, CXV (22 July 1946), 80.
[A rambling description of an afternoon Saroyan spent with Shaw.]

1157 Scholefield, R. S. "What Bernard Shaw Thinks at Ninety," COLLIER'S, CXVIII (3 Aug 1946), 23.
[Shaw answers Scholefield's questions about life, death, the future of the race, war, and Ireland.]

1158 "Shaw and the Ancients," TLS, XLV (27 July 1946), 349-50.
Back to Methuselah, though not Shaw's best play, is the culmination of his belief. Shaw is more a religionist than a moralist or artist. He says in Caesar and Cleopatra and in Back to Methuselah that people must will their own improvement; yet he also believes in an evolutionary force that holds them in its grip. He does not know if human beings are free or slave. Furthermore, his faith in longevity is problematic. In Back to Methuselah, longevity occurs by accident, not by will. And who would want to become an Ancient?

1159 Shipley, Joseph T. (ed). ENCYCLOPEDIA OF LITERATURE (NY: Philosophical Library, 1946), pp. 267-68, 1164.
Shaw is the most outstanding English dramatist since 1890, combining "brilliance of intellect with moral reform." Wit is his weapon; his major theme is the conflict of wills; his goal, a community of supermen. [Mentions Man and Superman, Back to Methuselah, Pygmalion, and Heartbreak House, perhaps his best work. Brief biographical sketch.]

1160 "Shorter Notices," SPECTATOR, CLXXVII (9 Aug 1946), 152.
In the ten-volume Penguin Shaw, one has the intellectual foundations of the twentieth century; if war-damaged, still the future will have to build on them or "on the gaps they leave."

1161 Stonier, G. W. "Deeds, not Words," NS&Nation, XXXII (20 July 1946), 51.
In Florence Farr, Bernard Shaw, W. B. Yeats: Letters, edited by Clifford Bax, Shaw is "rude, gallant, flying off at a tangent," talking about everything from Fabianism to bicycling.

1162 "Teatro: En la voz reside el magico secreto" (Theater: The Magic Secret Resides in the Voice), QUÉ (Argentina), I, No 6 (12 Sept 1946), 37.
The production of Saint Joan in German at the Lassalle Theater (Buenos Aires) was acclaimed by the critics and the German-speaking audience. [In Spanish.]

1163 "Temas y autores" (Themes and Authors), REVISTA DE AMÉRICA (Colombia), VI, No 18 (June 1946), vii.
At ninety, Shaw has won the fame of being the foremost humorist because of his innovative attitude toward life. [Reference to the Spanish productions of The Devil's Disciple, Major Barbara, and Candida, by Losada, Buenos Aires.] [In Spanish.]

1164 "The Theater," NEWSWEEK, XXVII (15 April 1946), 84-86, espec 84.
The Cort Theater (NY) production of Candida, with Katharine Cornell, is well acted, except for the role of Morell, who is "duller than Shaw intended."

1165 "Theater: Gertie's Pygmalion," NEWSWEEK, XXVII (7 Jan 1946), 82.
The Theater Incorporated (Barrymore Theater, NY) production of Pygmalion is good but not great. The play is not Shaw's best, but the wit remains "pointed and pungent."

1166 "Theater: Irishmen and Christians," NEWSWEEK, XXVIII (30 Dec 1946), 71.
Androcles and the Lion, produced by the American Repertory Theater (International Theater, NY), stands up well because of Shaw's acid wit.

1167 "The Theatre: Old Play in Manhattan," TIME, XLVII (7 Jan 1946), 89, 90.
Pygmalion, produced by Theater Incorporated (Barrymore Theater, NY), is an actable and entertaining fairy tale satirizing the middle class and aristocratic pretensions. The satire "has worn less well than the comedy."

1168 "The Theatre: Old Play in Manhattan," TIME, XLVII (15 April 1946), 90-91.
[Comments on the acting in the Katharine Cornell (Cort Theater, NY) production of Candida.]

1169 "The Theatre: Old Play in Manhattan," TIME, XLVIII (30 Dec 1946), 34.
Androcles and the Lion (American Repertory Theater production, International Theater, NY) reduces a serious subject to farce; it is mostly Shavian "high jinks."

1170 "Transition: Surprise," NEWSWEEK, XXVII (18 Feb 1946), 74.
Shaw turned up unexpectedly at the studio where Caesar and Cleopatra was being filmed and wrote a bedroom scene on the spot.

1171 Trebitsch, Siegfried. BERNARD SHAW DEM NEUNZIGJÄHRIGEN (Bernard Shaw the Nonagenarian) (Zürich: Artemis-Verlag, 1946).
[Detailed account of Trebitsch's 45-year working relationship with Shaw as translator and advocate of Shaw's plays. Especially interesting is the account of Trebitsch's intense labor during the one-year period granted him by

Shaw to translate and have one or more of Shaw's plays
produced and published in Germany.] [In German.]

1172 Trebitsch, Siegfried (trans) and Wiedner,
Laurenz (ed). BERNARD SHAW: DER GESUNDE MENSCHEN
VERSTAND. EINE AUSWAHL AUS DEN WERKEN (Bernard Shaw:
The Healthy Human Intelligence. A Selection from the
Works) (Zurich: Pegasus Verlag, 1946).
[Brief excerpts from Shaw's works arranged thematically
(poverty and wealth, the state, war, marriage and love,
etc.)] [In German.]

1173 Trewin, J. C. "Shaw as a Wit," G. B. S. 90, pp.
161-66.
Shaw is "the Chief Wit of his time," utilizing visual wit
(e.g., Androcles and the lion waltzing off stage), jokes
with "enviable staying power," and obvious, unsubtle comic
effects (as in Too True to Be Good). The Don Juan in Hell
scene reflects his wit, "a stream of persuasiveness," at
its height. His prose is unmatched in modern time, with
"strong and supple" dialog (e.g., in In Good King Charles's
Golden Days). His prefaces are a must to readers.

1174 Turner, W. J. "Lively Letters," SPECTATOR,
CLXXVI (21 June 1946), 642.
In Florence Farr, Bernard Shaw, W. B. Yeats: Letters, Shaw
and Yeats give themselves away in the letters "in
spontaneous fits of artful frankness."

1175 Turner, W. J. "Shaw's 'World Classic,'"
SPECTATOR, CLXXVII (30 Aug 1946), 224.
Back to Methuselah is "a comic masterpiece of the utmost
brilliance" that is assured of, but will have to await,
rediscovery after the present vogue for French existential
pessimism passes.

1176 Underhill, Frank H. "Fabians and Fabianism,"
CANADIAN FORUM, XXV (March 1946), 277-80, and XXVI
(April 1946), 8-12.
[A brief history of Fabian socialism and its place in the
current English government; discussion of Fabian political
ideas and criticism made of them.] Shaw has made the most
far-reaching criticism of Fabianism. His plays before World
War I reflect his Fabianism as well as his artistic insight

into society; but <u>Heartbreak House</u> and <u>Back to Methuselah</u> reflect his disillusion with the politics he once embraced. These latter plays are marred by "dreary...twaddle" about the Superman, but in <u>Saint Joan</u> Shaw's "pessimistic insight is unblurred."

1177 Usigli, Rodolpho. "Dos conversaciones con George Bernard Shaw y algunas cartas" (Two Conversations with George Bernard Shaw and Some Letters), CUADERNOS AMERICANOS, V (Nov 1946), 249-75; rptd in CORONA DE SOMBRA, PIEZA ANTIHISTORICA EN TRES ACTOS (Crown of Shadow, An Antihistorical Piece in Three Acts) (Mexico: Ediciones Cuadernos Americanas, 1947).
[Extensive narration of Usigli's visit to Shaw in 1945, with letters to Shaw, and from Shaw.] When Usigli was undergoing a writer's crisis, he turned to Shaw for advice. Shaw read his play CORONA DE SOMBRA (Crown of Shadow), and praised it. Molière and Shaw originally directed Usigli to the theater; after reading <u>Heartbreak House</u>, Usigli became influenced by Shaw the political thinker. [In Spanish.]

1178 [Wells, H(erbert) G(eorge)]. "A Letter from H. G. Wells," G. B. S. 90, p. 55; rptd in CRITICAL HERITAGE, pp. 366-67, Item 121.
[An affectionate letter to Shaw (dated 16 April 1941) commenting on the "delightful" film <u>Major Barbara</u> and alluding to their Fabian experience, to their education, and to growing old.]

1179 Winsten, S[tephen] (ed). G. B. S. 90: ASPECTS OF BERNARD SHAW'S LIFE AND WORK (NY: Dodd, Mead; Lond & NY: Hutchinson, 1946; rptd NY: Haskell House, 1975).
[A collection of essays, letters, and poetry dedicated to Shaw on his ninetieth birthday. Includes many photographs of Shaw, his friends, and contemporaries. Contents, abstracted separately under 1946: "Editorial Note," pp. 11-12 (not abstracted); Gilbert Murray, "A Foreword," pp. 13-15; John Masefield, "On the Ninetieth Birthday of Bernard Shaw," p. 17; S(tephen) Winsten, "Introduction," pp. 18-30; M. J. MacManus, "Shaw's Irish Boyhood," pp. 31-45; Lord Passfield (Sidney Webb), "'Everywhere I Gained Something,'" p. 46; Laurence Housman, "G. B. S. and the Victorians," pp.

47-49; J. B. Priestley, "G. B. S.—Social Critic," pp. 50-54; "A Letter from H. G. Wells," p. 55; "A Letter from Sir Max Beerbohm," p. 56; C. E. M. Joad, "Shaw's Philosophy," pp. 57-76; James Bridie, "Shaw as Dramatist (including a Surrealist Life of G. B. S.)," pp. 77-91; Lord Dunsany, "A Permanent Quality," p. 92; J. D. Bernal, "Shaw the Scientist," pp. 93-105; Lord Keynes (John Maynard Keynes), "G. B. S. and Isaac Newton," pp. 106-9; W. R. Inge, "Shaw as a Theologian," pp. 110-21; Edward J. Dent, "Corno di Bassetto," pp. 122-30; Maurice Dobb, "Bernard Shaw and Economics," pp. 131-39; A. S. Neill, "Shaw and Education," pp. 140-51; A. Emil Davies, "G. B. S. and Local Government," pp. 152-57; Daniel Jones, "G. B. S. and Phonetics," pp. 158-60; J. C. Trewin, "Shaw as a Wit," pp. 161-66; William Haley, "The Stripling and the Sage," pp. 167-70; Val Gielgud, "Bernard Shaw and the Radio," pp. 171-73; Kenneth Barnes, "G. B. S. and the R. A. D. A.," pp. 174-80; Roy Limbert, "The Inspiration of Shaw," pp. 181-89; Gabriel Pascal, "Shaw as a Scenario-Writer," pp. 190-93; S. I. Hsiung, "Through Eastern Eyes," pp. 194-99; Aldous Huxley, "A Birthday Wish," p. 200.]

1180 Winsten, S[tephen]. "Introduction," G. B. S. 90, pp. 18-30.
[Anecdotal sketch of Shaw at Ayot St. Lawrence.] Writing plays was an extension of Shaw's platform propaganda. Shaw tackles social problems in a prose as rich as poetry (e.g., in John Bull's Other Island). His characters, all "shades of himself," are alive and entertaining; his greatest creation is G.B.S. Personally, Shaw is a "compound of contradictions," interested in many things—economics as well as esthetics.

1181 Winsten, S[tephen]. "Shaw at 90—Still the Conventional Heretic," NYTMag, 21 July 1946, pp. 10-11.
Shaw is still the "downright thinker" and "upright figure," the most conventional heretic. He seems the only optimist left in the world. He knows the possibilities for humanity, and has helped it through laughter.

1182 Wyatt, Euphemia Van Rensselaer. "The Drama: Candida," CATHOLIC WORLD, CLXIII (May 1946), 167-71, espec 167-68.

Candida (Cort Theater, NY) is a brilliant play. Morell may have a "finer character" than Candida, who relentlessly exposes his weakness before Marchbanks.

1183 Wyatt, Euphemia Van Rensselaer. "The Drama: Pygmalion," CATHOLIC WORLD, CLXII (Feb 1946), 453-58, espec 455-56.
In the Theater Incorporated production (Ethel Barrymore Theater, NY) of Pygmalion, Eliza suggests in her closing lines that she will continue to fetch and carry for Higgins. Unlike the movie version, this production does not dramatize Eliza's triumph.

1184 Young, Stark. "Theater Incorporated," NEW REPUBLIC, CXIV (21 Jan 1946), 91-92.
Pygmalion can be played two ways—one ridicules class distinctions, and the other portrays the fight between a tyrannical yet charming man and a strong and eventually self-sufficient woman. In the Barrymore Theater production (NY), Raymond Massey plays Higgins a bit too heavily, and Gertrude Lawrence should be a bit more biting as Eliza.

1947

1185 Anderson, Maxwell. "Poetry in the Theater," OFF BROADWAY: ESSAYS ABOUT THE THEATER (NY: Sloane, 1947), pp. 47-54, 66.
As Shaw says, the theater is "essentially a cathedral of the spirit." However, such playwrights as Synge, O'Casey, O'Neill, and Shaw are limited in that they cannot produce the poetry that such a theater demands.

1186 Anderson, Maxwell. "Saint Bernard," OFF BROADWAY: ESSAYS ABOUT THE THEATER (NY: Sloane, 1947), pp. 12-17.
Shaw illuminates the modern intellectual landscape and is "at the head of all modern playwrights." After he saw that he could not save the world through reform, he turned to evolution and the Life Force. In turn, he grew to doubt these, and his doubts led him into the "Kingdom of despair" of Shakespeare and Sophocles. It is this kingdom that he

illumines in <u>Saint Joan</u> and <u>Heartbreak House</u>. He ended as a mystic who knew that "all faiths are delusions." [From a dinner address in 1946 celebrating Shaw's ninetieth birthday.]

>   **1187** "Arts Theatre: 'Back to Methuselah,'" TIMES (Lond), 19 Feb 1947, p. 6; Parts II and III, 20 Feb 1947, p. 6; Part IV, 26 Feb 1947, p. 7; Part V, 6 March 1947, p. 6.

The story in Part I of <u>Back to Methuselah</u> evolves naturally and delightfully; the straightforward production (Arts Theater, Lond) "leaves the subtleties to the actors," with Adam the least interesting of Eden's inhabitants. The middle of <u>Back to Methuselah</u> is tedious because of Shaw's use of topical satire in his political figures, which is now dated. However, the dialog and stage fun are still fresh and entertaining. <u>The Tragedy of an Elderly Gentleman</u> becomes dramatic only in the last minutes of the play. Before that are talk and jokes, some of which are stale; but others have been given new point by recent history. Shaw's idea in <u>As Far As Thought Can Reach</u> surpasses the dramatic expression of it. Though the production is good, the play reads better than it acts.

>   **1188** Atkinson, Brooks. "'Man and Superman': Maurice Evans Brings to Bernard Shaw's Comedy Talents That Illuminate It," NYT, 19 Oct 1947, II, p. 2.

<u>Man and Superman</u> "does run on interminably," but the Maurice Evans production (Alvin Theater, NY) keeps the dialog intelligible, the tempo and tone brisk and bright. In the play, Shaw lacks pity but not understanding or a sense of humor about humanity. A "radiant comedy" like <u>Man and Superman</u> cannot be written in today's anxious, insecure world.

>   **1189** Atkinson, Brooks. "The New Play in Review," NYT, 9 Oct 1947, p. 31; rptd in ON STAGE: SELECTED THEATER REVIEWS FROM THE NEW YORK TIMES 1920-1970, ed by Bernard Beckerman and Howard Siegman (NY: Arno P, 1973), pp. 281-82.

<u>Man and Superman</u> is "a witty play scrupulously staged" in the Maurice Evans production (Alvin Theater, NY).

1190 Atkinson, Brooks. "Theatre Arts Bookshelf," TAM, XXXI (Nov 1947), 74.
Geneva, Cymbeline Refinished, and In Good King Charles's Golden Days discuss interesting ideas, but they are too tedious to be good plays for the theater. The prefaces are Shaw at his best, writing with the humble and compassionate detachment of a prophet.

1191 Bentley, Eric [Russell]. BERNARD SHAW: A RECONSIDERATION (Norfolk, Conn.: New Directions [The Makers of Modern Literature], 1947; Lond: Hale, 1950; amended ed as BERNARD SHAW, 1856-1950, Norfolk: New Directions Paperbook, 1957; 2nd ed Lond: Methuen; NY: New Directions, 1967; rptd NY: Norton, 1976).
Shaw succeeds as an artist where he fails as a propagandist. He presents many sides of human nature and is passionately committed without being prejudiced. His socialism appeals to heroism, human will, and the Superman; it places faith in the gentleman, and is a part of "vital economy," a Life Force out of which a better world is evolving. The central paradox in Shaw is that what he takes as the essence of humanity—impulse, activity, and passion —evolves ultimately into thought and pure ideas; Shaw is thus at once rationalist and irrationalist. His method is polemic, using exaggeration and paradox, with Shaw playing the devil's advocate. His drama depicts the struggle between human vitality and conventional ethics (e.g., Widowers' Houses, Mrs. Warren's Profession, Three Plays for Puritans, Pygmalion), and goes beyond Ibsen in combining the personal with the disquisitory (Getting Married, Misalliance, Heartbreak House, and the late plays). The comic confrontation is often between Ironist and Imposter. The characters also fall into practical, effective people of action or contemplative types, all in search of a philosopher king. The tension in Shaw's plays comes from the portrayal of characters depraved by the system they live in or from the representation of human vanity generally. Unfortunately, Shaw's clown's mask, assumed because he was always an Outsider in society, obscures his message. But, unlike most modern artists, he is not dismayed by his estrangement from the world: he embraces neither the "tough" nor the "tender" schools of art but brings elements of both to his work. [An invaluable

commentary on Shaw's art, politics, and philosophy. Possibly the best single introduction to Shaw.]

1192 Bentley, Eric [Russell]. "Three Plays By Shaw," NYTBR, 23 Nov 1947, p. 16.
The ideas in three new prefaces and two new plays—Geneva, Cymbeline Refinished, In Good King Charles's Golden Days— may give the impression of newness, but it is all "old stuff, and at times distressingly so." His reworking of Shakespeare's play, however, is not "merely silly." Shaw parodies the Elizabethan and makes the play a naturalistic tragi-comedy.

1193 Beyer, William. "The State of the Theatre: Midseason Highlights," SCHOOL AND SOCIETY, LXV (5 April 1947), 250-52.
Androcles and the Lion is "a jolly lark," funny as well as contemplative. Initial reactions to Shaw as sacrilegious and blasphemous are being replaced by the better understanding of Shaw as "a true prophet and crusader for Christianity and democracy, and genuinely devout."

1194 Bissell, Claude T. "The Novels of Bernard Shaw," UNIVERSITY OF TORONTO QUARTERLY, XVII (Oct 1947), 38-51.
The early works are not merely juvenilia but indicators of Shaw's intellectual and artistic development. In his early novels Shaw has no consistent point of view toward society, but socialism released his "romantic imagination and his power of comic invention." Immaturity is a spiritual autobiography grounded in lower middle class life. The Irrational Knot tries to avoid the structural failures of Immaturity by limiting the cast of characters and focussing the conflict. Love Among the Artists is "solemnly didactic" about art, and the characters are sketchy. The tone of Cashel Byron's Profession and An Unsocial Socialist is comic; the prose, improved. Shaw's change from his early to late novels reflects his change from scientific rationalism to romantic individualism.

1195 "Briefly Noted," NYer, XXIII (22 Nov 1947), 135-40, espec 137-38.

In <u>Geneva</u>, <u>Cymbeline Refinished</u>, and <u>In Good King Charles's Golden Days</u>, Shaw has lost his grip. The plays trail off into nowhere.

> **1196** Brown, John Mason. "Seeing Things: O Eastern Star!" SRL, XXX (20 Dec 1947), 22-25; rptd in Brown, SEEING MORE THINGS (NY & Toronto: McGraw-Hill, 1948), pp. 238-48; and in Brown, DRAMATIS PERSONAE: A RETROSPECTIVE SHOW (NY: Viking, 1963), pp. 227-35.

Shaw is outraged by the raw sexuality of Shakespeare's ANTONY AND CLEOPATRA. <u>Caesar and Cleopatra</u> tries to "laugh off the whole business as a bad joke"; the work of a rationalist rather than of a romantic like Shakespeare, <u>Caesar and Cleopatra</u> does not deal with the eternal verities.

> **1197** Brown, John Mason. "Seeing Things: Progress and the Superman," SRL, XXX (1 Nov 1947), 28-32; rptd in Brown, SEEING MORE THINGS (NY & Toronto: McGraw-Hill, 1948), pp. 188-99; and in Brown, DRAMATIS PERSONAE: A RETROSPECTIVE SHOW (NY: Viking, 1963), pp. 121-29.

Shaw's theory of the improvement of the race through selective breeding, expressed in <u>Man and Superman</u>, has its problems: "Sex has proved harder to nationalize than the coal mines." But at least the critical reception of <u>Superman</u> has evolved since its first performance, when critics said that it was amusing, but not a play. The definition of theater has broadened since then, and Shaw is now accepted as a playwright. In the current production of <u>Superman</u> (Alvin Theater, NY) the comedy is delightful and the flow of words musical. Most of the ideas are not out of date.

> **1198** Brown, John Mason. "Seeing Things: Straight from the Lion's Mouth," SRL, XXX (11 Jan 1947), 24-27; rptd in Brown, SEEING MORE THINGS (NY & Toronto: McGraw-Hill, 1948), pp. 179-87.

<u>Androcles and the Lion</u> (American Repertory Theater, International Theater, NY) is meant not only to amuse children but also to force adults to think about faith—the kind of faith that makes Lavinia go to her death when she is not sure what she is dying for.

1199 Cerf, Bennett. "Trade Winds," SRL, XXX (8 Nov 1947), 5-6.
[Anecdotes concerning why Shaw chose Ayot St. Lawrence to live in, and a child's impression of God as Rodin's Shaw.]

1200 Ciarletta, Nicola. "Filosofia sociale e religione in George Bernard Shaw" (Social Philosophy and Religion in George Bernard Shaw), INDAGINE, I (1947), 169-80.
Shaw's anarchism is ambiguous: he is not a Christian because he does not believe in religion as a divine fact; he is not a communist because he believes in religion as a human fact. Religion and science have credulity in common; Shaw's ambiguity as a playwright stems from his mistrust of science because it is as fideistic as religion, which however is a social need. [In Italian.]

1201 Clark, Barrett H. and George Freedley. A HISTORY OF MODERN DRAMA (NY: Appleton, 1947), pp. 138-39, 162.
Shaw "is the one giant dramatic talent since the Elizabethan period." He is English, not Irish, and "modern English drama without Shaw would be as complete as the Elizabethan without Shakespeare." Candida is the best of his early plays. Caesar and Cleopatra is the best drama of his first decade as a playwright. Saint Joan is his best play. The Apple Cart, while it is not "top-flight" Shaw, contains "some of his best writing and most ingenious horseplay."

1202 Clarke, David Waldo. MODERN ENGLISH WRITERS (Lond, NY, & Toronto: Longmans, Green [Essential English Library], 1947), pp. 53-59.
Shaw's major achievement is in the creation of characters who are like real people. His dramatic genius is also reflected in vivid openings, witty dialog, inspired fantasy, and an ability to handle topical as well as historical themes. Though he offers no innovations in dramatic technique, he is nevertheless to be ranked with Shakespeare, Molière, and Ibsen.

1203 Coates, J[ohn] B[ourne]. "Bernard Shaw," LEADERS OF MODERN THOUGHT (Lond, NY, & Toronto:

Longmans, Green [Essential English Library], 1947;
rptd Lond: Longmans, 1960), pp. 23-39.
Unlike Shakespeare, Shaw is primarily a propagandist
dealing in ideas; yet his best plays compare favorably to
Shakespeare's in their eloquence and their mastery of comic
and ironic situations. [Biographical-historical summary of
Shaw's life and work.]

1204 d'Amato, Guy Albert. "The Successful Failure,"
PORTRAITS OF IDEAS (Boston: Christopher Publishing
House, 1947), pp. 43-44.
Shaw had the rare gift of clearly seeing the simple and the
obvious, but his ideas were ignored by a world that saw
only his clowning. By stimulating laughter and anger, he
defeated his own serious purposes.

1205 D'Ors, Eugenio. "Candida," NUEVO GLOSARIO
(Madrid: Aguilar, 1947), II, 371.
The character Candida resembles a flayed statue since both
she as well as the other characters in the play have the
appearance of statues in which one can perceive the bodily
fibers and muscles. The main fault of the performance was
the lack of injecting life into Candida and the others. [In
Spanish.]

1206 D'Ors, Eugenio. "¿Otro viaje de ida y vuelta?"
(Another Round Trip?) NUEVO GLOSARIO (Madrid:
Aguilar, 1947), I, 1041-42.
There is no novelty in Shaw's treatment of Joan in Saint
Joan. She conforms to Shaw's ideas, particularly to English
Protestantism, with little or no relevance to French
history. [In Spanish.]

1207 Eastman, Fred. "From Shakespear to Shaw,"
CHRIST IN THE DRAMA (NY: Macmillan, 1947), pp. 40-60.
Androcles and the Lion and Saint Joan dramatize the
conflict between saints and the social order. The
characters and ideas in Androcles reflect the Sermon on the
Mount; Joan resurrects the historical character of Joan.
Both plays show the influence of Christ on the central
characters and the author's vision of the life of the
spirit. [One of the Shaffer Lectures of Northwestern
University, 1946.]

268

1208 Eaton, Walter Prichard. "Plays Round Shaw's Record," NYHTBR, XXIV (26 Oct 1947), 5.
Geneva is in places very funny, though it is overlong, without a clear plot line, and about a dead issue. In Good King Charles's Golden Days starts and ends nowhere, but has some delightful dialog. Shaw's Cymbeline Refinished is forgiveable only in view of the failure of Shakespeare's own ending.

1209 "Embassy Theatre: 'John Bull's Other Island,'" TIMES (Lond), 3 Dec 1947, p. 7.
The Dublin Gate Theater Company production (Embassy Theater, Lond) substitutes farce for Shaw's comedy in John Bull's Other Island, omitting all the humanity and pathos in the play.

1210 Evans, Herbert M. and Dorothy A. A VISIT WITH G.B.S. (Berkeley: University of California P, 1947).
Shaw "has shown us that paradox may sometimes be very near the truth." Though he may be persona non grata to many scientists for his "unsound" views, he has nevertheless urged the entertainment of new ideas. [Account of a visit made by Herbert M. Evans, his wife, Dorothy, and O. Kyllman, chief of Constable and Company, to Shaw at Ayot St. Lawrence in January 1947. Shaw was interested in discussing hormones, his own education, medicine, scientific breeding.]

1211 Evans, Maurice. "See for Yourself: On the Boards," TAM, XXXI (Dec 1947), 2-4.
In Man and Superman (Alvin Theater, NY) the paradoxes and "twisted arguments" still take one by surprise.

1212 Fleming, Peter. "The Theatre," SPECTATOR, CLXXIX (10 Oct 1947), 460.
You Never Can Tell (Wyndham's Theater, Lond) conquers all the obstacles of age through its disciplined, harmonious, vital prose.

1213 Frahne, Karl Heinrich. VON CHAUCER BIS SHAW: EINE EINFÜHRUNG IN DIE LITERATUR ENGLANDS (From Chaucer to Shaw: An Introduction to English Literature) (Hamburg: J. P. Toth, 1947), pp. 108, 114, 130, 131-33, 136, 191, 297-303, 340.

[An introduction to Shaw's works (emphasis on his Puritanism, his idea of the Life Force, his indebtedness to Ibsen) and a biographical sketch (emphasis on Shaw's Fabian ideas).] Shaw tries to unmask the hypocritical late-Victorian society. His early phase of negative social criticism was soon followed by a positive goal, the creation of the Superman and the idea of the Life Force. [In German.]

1214 "G. B. S. on Love," NYTMag, 5 Oct 1947, p. 36. [A series of pictures from the Maurice Evans production of Man and Superman (Alvin Theater, NY) is captioned with a thematic synopsis of the play.]

1215 Gatch, Katherine Haynes. "'The Real Sorrow of Great Men': Mr. Bernard Shaw's Sense of Tragedy," COLLEGE ENGLISH, VIII (Feb 1947), 230-40.
Shaw's views on the nature and destiny of humanity are not the traditional ones; they are tied to his desire to reform human politics. So long as the critical intelligence evolves, a tragic view of life is not necessary. Shaw believes intolerance creates tragedy, "and that every defeat of the critical intelligence is a catastrophe." His sense of tragedy can be seen through his criticism of Ibsen and Shakespeare and in such plays as Back to Methuselah, Heartbreak House, and Saint Joan.

1216 Gibbs, Wolcott. "The Theatre: And Still They Come," NYer, XXIII (18 Oct 1947), 51-57, espec 54-55.
Man and Superman is not one of Shaw's best plays. The joke of woman-as-huntress is very old by now and the style of the speeches does not make up for it. In fact, Jack Tanner talks too much. The Maurice Evans production (Alvin Theater, NY) is handsome, but not superb.

1217 Gilder, Rosamond. "Broadway in Review: Actors All," TAM, XXXI (Dec 1947), 10-14.
In Man and Superman Shaw employs "Bardian periods" in Tanner's "witty diatribes against the female species." The Maurice Evans production (Alvin Theater, NY) is first-rate theater.

1218 Gilder, Rosamond. "Too Much of a Good Thing: Broadway in Review," TAM, XXXI (Feb 1947), 12-18, espec 17-18.

Androcles and the Lion is a discussion of the "poignant theme of what men die for." "Shaw's outward garment is of course motley, but the core of his argument is wonder." The American Repertory Theater production (International Theater, NY) emphasizes "Shaw the jester rather than Shaw the prophet."

1219 Green, E. Mawby. "Echoes from Broadway," THEATRE WORLD (Lond), XLIII (Dec 1947), 30, 32, 34, espec 32.
The Maurice Evans production (Alvin Theater, NY) of *Man and Superman* proves that the play "is basically a superb farce," "with hardly a speck of dust on it after 43 years."

1220 Grigor'ev, M. S. (ed). SOVETSKII TEATR (Soviet Theater) (Moscow: Vserossiiskoe teatral'noe obshchestvo, 1947), pp. 335-36.
Shaw holds the first place in Soviet theater as regards the number of productions in the foreign repertoire, especially *The Devil's Disciple* (1933) and *Pygmalion* (Malyi Theater, Moscow, 1943). The Malyi Company could not accept the ending of *Pygmalion* (after Eliza's metamorphosis, she remains the same limited bourgeois and Higgins the same egoist and celibate) and blamed Shaw because all his characters remained caricatures. D. V. Zerkalova as Eliza proved to be an unusual individual, who could struggle for her own life and happiness. In the end, she metamorphosed Higgins, though this did not concur with the author's intentions. Unfortunately, Soviet theater has forgotten Shaw's early plays, with their social satire. [In Russian.]

1221 Guardia, Alfredo de la. "La creación intelectual de Shaw" (The Intellectual Creation of Shaw), EL TEATRO CONTEMPORANEO (Buenos Aires: Editorial Kier, 1947), pp. 257-306.
[Sketch of Shaw's life and works, including his Life Force religion, his relationship to Christianity, his concept of love and art, his sociology, his intellectual humor. Defends Shaw's drama of ideas, which frequently transcends mere sociology, notably in *Caesar and Cleopatra* and *Saint Joan*.] [In Spanish.]

1222 Hobsbawm, E. J. "Bernard Shaw's Socialism," SCIENCE AND SOCIETY, XI (Fall 1947), 305-26.

Shaw was struck by two aspects of Marx: the literary power of the indictment against capitalism and the historical perspective which promises the final victory of socialism. For Shaw, capitalism was "fundamentally unjust and wrong." Unfortunately, however, his contribution to socialist theory is "scattered, contradictory and unsystematic." His defeatism fatally handicapped him in waging a more active fight for socialism. Still, he produced a remarkable critique of imperialist civilization.

> **1223** Irvine, William. "Bernard Shaw's Early Novels," TROLLOPIAN, II (June 1947), 27-42; rptd as "Five Novels in a Vacuum," chap 4, in Irvine, THE UNIVERSE OF G. B. S. (NY, Lond, & Toronto: Whittlesey House [McGraw-Hill], 1949), pp. 22-34.

Shaw's five novels represent an "embryonic development toward genius." In them Shaw shows creative power but lacks technique. Immaturity "hovers between a clinical record and a diary." The Irrational Knot, which is "compact, forceful, and witty," explores the dramatic possibilities in situations. Love Among the Artists, an "early attempt at Candida," is technically better but shows less spirit. Cashel Byron's Profession is "less witty, less distinguished, and less concentrated" than the preceding two novels, but An Unsocial Socialist anticipates Man and Superman. It is a "complete Shaw," with "all his literary vices and virtues" and "nearly all his ideas and poses."

> **1224** Irvine, William. "Man and Superman, A Step in Shavian Disillusionment," HUNTINGTON LIBRARY QUARTERLY, X (Feb 1947), 209-24; rptd as chap 27 in Irvine, THE UNIVERSE OF G. B. S. (NY, Lond, & Toronto: Whittlesey House [McGraw-Hill], 1949), pp. 235-48.

Man and Superman has multiple themes, combining Shaw's characteristic brilliance with his most characteristic ideas. It is a self-satire, "a Hamlet play" condemning "its most interesting character to passivity and inaction," and an intellectual drama. At times it "seems slow, abstract, unrealistic, undramatic, and even trivial"; the heavy load of theory staggers the slight plot. The conflict between Ann Whitefield and Jack Tanner "is carefully built up, elaborately motivated, and brilliantly comic." Yet the play lacks the satire, irony, realism, "deep feeling," "dramatic complication and varied character portrayal" of Shaw's other plays.

1225 Irvine, William. "Shaw and Chesterton," VIRGINIA QUARTERLY REVIEW, XXIII (Spring 1947), 273-81; rptd as chap 37 in Irvine, THE UNIVERSE OF G. B. S. (NY, Lond, & Toronto: Whittlesey House [McGraw-Hill], 1949), pp. 336-42.

Shaw and G. K. Chesterton agreed only about science, of which both were critical. Both owe much to "fin-de-siècle effrontery and witty insult." But their politics, religion, and temperaments were in opposition: Chesterton looked to a past ideal of freedom, self-reliance, and humane behavior, whereas Shaw looked forward to a better world and a "higher humanity." The two learned little from each other. Chesterton's book on Shaw is a sound, brilliant contribution to Shaw criticism.

1226 Irvine, William. "Shaw, the Fabians, and the Utilitarians," JOURNAL OF THE HISTORY OF IDEAS, VIII (April 1947), 218-31; rptd in Irvine, THE UNIVERSE OF G. B. S. (NY, Lond, & Toronto: Whittlesey House [McGraw-Hill], 1949), pp. 218-31.

Shaw's socialism owes more to John Stuart Mill than to Marx, in its middle-class, utilitarian, materialist, intellectual orientation. Shaw "exploits the comic possibilities of utilitarianism," applying frequently the test of utility, distrusting the masses, advocating female equality, and reflecting other Millite values. "It is wonderful that a movement apparently so modern and international as socialism could have been made into anything so English and conservative as Fabianism."

1227 Irvine, William. "Shaw, War and Peace, 1894-1919," FOREIGN AFFAIRS, XXV (Jan 1947), 314-27; incorporated into Irvine, THE UNIVERSE OF G. B. S. (NY, Lond, & Toronto: Whittlesey House [McGraw-Hill], 1949), pp. 314-27.

Shaw's political analyses tend to be "Benthamite or Marxist with aristocratic qualifications," with an emphasis on Fabian evolutionary thought. His Fabian pamphlet of 1899 on the Boer War attacked the principle of absolute sovereignty and militarism, and advocated a global federation of "Great Powers." But it is marred by romantic individualism.

Fabianism and the Empire argues that the welfare of the Empire and the world depends on Fabianizing the Empire. Arms and the Man, The Man of Destiny, Caesar and Cleopatra, and Major Barbara drain the heroism out of war and present a vision of war as a "logical and precise kind of madness." Heartbreak House predicts catastrophe; Common Sense about the War is "coolly judicial"; and the Case Against Germany warns against German monarchy and militarism without fully understanding the sinister implications of the latter. After the Treaty of Versailles, Shaw became increasingly impatient with compromise and political gradualism, and moved toward a more Marxist "philosophy of force." But with Everybody's Political What's What he once again advocated democratic socialism.

1228 Irvine, William. "Shaw's Quintessence of Ibsenism," SOUTH ATLANTIC QUARTERLY, XLVI (April 1947), 252-62; rptd in Irvine, THE UNIVERSE OF G. B. S. (NY, Lond, & Toronto: Whittlesey House [McGraw-Hill], 1949), pp. 137-46.

Shaw adds romantic individualism to his socialism and rationalism: influenced by Schopenhauer, Ibsen, and others, "by a very rational process he comes to deny reason as a guide to life." Shaw found in Ibsen the Life Force religion, an attitude toward idealism, realistic dramatic treatment, expository and analytical technique, and ready-made situations. He interpreted all of Ibsen as truth versus illusion, but Ibsen is more complicated than this. Shaw's account of the plays from Ibsen's middle period is best because he simply explains, and makes no critical estimate. His analysis of Ibsen's contributions to drama needs qualification: Ibsen is less "prosaically 'suburban'" than Shaw thinks; he did not originate discussion drama; he uses realistic plot as well as realistic characters.

1229 Johns, Eric. "Discussion Play," THEATRE WORLD (Lond), XLIII (April 1947), 19, 31.

Back to Methuselah "is not a play at all." It has no plot and no suspense, only an intellectual problem for discussion and solution. Noël Willman, who produced Back to Methuselah (Arts Theater, Lond) says that, in order to make a Shaw conversation-piece good theater, the producer must employ stage movement, prevent actors from declaiming their lines, and help actors see the feeling in back of their lines. Shaw's characters are not mere mouthpieces for the author; each has "thought-development" if not character development. Shaw's lines are difficult to learn, but beautiful when mastered. And Shaw offers scope to a stage designer.

1230 Koizumi, Shinzo. "Bernard Shaw (Dokusho Zakki sono 2)" (Bernard Shaw, Reading Notes 2), BUNGEI SHUNJU (Tokyo), XXV, No 6 (July 1947), 14-22; rptd in KOIZUMI SHINZO ZENSHU (Collected Works of Shinzo Koizumi) (Tokyo: Bungei Shunju, 1967), Vol. XIV, pp. 34-50.
Shaw's plays make delightful and amusing reading despite the fact that they are always full of serious discussions on serious matters. As a critic Shaw grasps the gist of matters securely and accurately, and his arguments are not merely eccentric, but based on academic authority. His free and sometimes acrobatic expressions make his style attractive. [In Japanese.]

1231 Krutch, Joseph Wood. "Drama," NATION, CLXIV (4 Jan 1947), 25-26.
Androcles and the Lion (American Repertory Company, International Theater, NY) is "a joyously irresponsible little farce," treating the battle of the sexes, Nietzscheism, and the Revolution in a "soft-hearted" way. The Preface, however, is burdensome.

1232 Krutch, Joseph Wood. "Drama," NATION, CLXIV (29 March 1947), 375, 377-78.
The Chocolate Soldier (Century Theater revival, NY) has every convention of romantic operetta, and just misses being tiresome. To some it is "delightfully quaint."

1233 Krutch, Joseph Wood. "Drama," NATION, CLXV (25 Oct 1947), 454-55.
Man and Superman (Maurice Evans production, Alvin Theater, NY) shows Shaw in the tradition of classical comedy. Jack Tanner and Ann are merely Shaw's Benedict and Beatrice, or Mirabell and Millamant.

1234 Krutch, Joseph Wood. "G.B.S.: Geneva, Cymbeline Refinished, and In Good King Charles's Golden Days," NATION, CLXV (11 Oct 1947), 388.

<u>Geneva</u>, <u>Cymbeline Refinished</u>, and <u>In Good King Charles's Golden Days</u> repeat familiar ideas and, at worst, read like a Max Beerbohm parody of Shaw. The characters all talk like Shaw, defining their intellectual positions "more sharply and clearly than their alleged prototypes could ever have done it."

1235 Lamm, Martin. "Ibsen och Shaw" (Ibsen and Shaw), EDDA (Oslo), XLVII (1947), 130-40.

Unlike his contemporaries, Shaw correctly saw that Ibsen's theme was that "there is no golden rule" and therefore every decision must be based on the facts of the individual situation involved. Shaw's first three plays show a much greater influence of Ibsen than his later plays, but even in the first three some of the ideas are not Ibsen's, e.g., the concept that all ownership is theft. <u>The Philanderer</u> satirizes both the advocates and the opponents of Ibsenism; <u>Mrs. Warren's Profession</u> owes a great deal to Ibsen's GHOSTS in situation, plot, technique, and manner of characterization. Though he abandoned plays in the "strict Ibsen-style," Shaw always held on to what he saw as Ibsen's basic theme, that people should be themselves and not allow themselves to be lured by a romantic view of life into playing a role which is foreign to them. A technique which Shaw frequently used was to have two major characters discover their unrealistic assessments of themselves and in effect exchange characters by the end of the play. Ibsen's A DOLL'S HOUSE tends to use this technique, but Shaw usually pushed the contrast between the characters to much greater extremes, as in <u>Candida</u> and <u>The Devil's Disciple</u>. With <u>Man and Superman</u>, Shaw began to introduce mystic and religious ideas into his hitherto prosaically realistic dramas. He never gave up writing the problem drama, however, as witness <u>The Doctor's Dilemma</u>. Though Shaw's plays are in some respects deeper in social and religious philosophy than Ibsen's, his ideas have never been taken seriously, as Ibsen's were, largely because his plays have a quality which Ibsen's lack—humor. [In Swedish.]

1236 Langner, Lawrence. "Mr. Shaw Discusses Mr. Shaw et al.," NYTMag, 16 Feb 1947, pp. 11, 60, 61; translated as "Visitando a Bernard Shaw" (Visiting Bernard Shaw) REVISTA DE REVISTAS (Mexico), 20 April 1947, pp. 30-32.

Shaw's conversation is as lively as ever. [Compares Shaw at ninety with Shaw at sixty five; reports a two-hour conversation with Shaw on sundry subjects, e.g., English socialism, the atomic bomb, the English and American theater.]

1237 Lawrence, Gertrude, with notes by Richard Aldrich. "Eliza Crossing the Land," TAM, XXXI (May 1947), 22-27.
[An account of Theater Incorporated's tour of Pygmalion (Wilmington, Washington, D.C., Pittsburgh, Toronto, Chicago, Mexico City) in Lawrence's diary and in comments by Aldrich, the managing director. Chit-chat about hotels, audience reception, celebrities met, etc.]

1238 Lennig, Walter. "Zweimal englische Komödie" (Two English Comedies), SONNTAG (Berlin), II (1947), No 4.
[Review of Maugham's THE CIRCLE and Arms and the Man.] Arms has proved more prophetic than Shaw could have imagined: it is as relevant today as when it was written. The performance (Renaissance Theater, Berlin) was not satisfying overall. [In German.]

1239 Lloyd, L. C. "On the Air," SPECTATOR, CLXXVIII (13 June 1947), 685.
[Review of the radio broadcast of Saint Joan.] Shaw evaded answering the question of what gave Joan the power to make men do her bidding; thus the play's early scenes are less convincing than the later ones.

1240 Loewenstein, F[ritz] E[rwin]. "The Autograph Manuscripts of George Bernard Shaw," BOOK HANDBOOK, I (1947), 85-92.
In spite of Shaw's denial that Shaw manuscripts and autographed editions exist for sale, there exist a longhand manuscript of John Bull's Other Island (in private hands); a shorthand version of Saint Joan (at the British Museum); a longhand manuscript of Widowers' Houses (Berg Collection, NY Public Library); the typescript of You Never Can Tell (Berg Collection); six pages of Love Among the Artists (Berg Collection); and the manuscript of Passion, Poison and Petrifaction (sold at a bazaar in 1905 for the Actors' Orphanage).

1241 "Lyric Theatre, Hammersmith: 'Pygmalion,'" TIMES (Lond), 19 June 1947, p. 6.

Higgins, "the irresistible bear," is modelled on Shaw. Pygmalion (Lyric Theater, Hammersmith) "mixes brutality with the fairy tale," especially in the third act when the men ignore Eliza after the bet is won.

1242 M., H. G. "'Back to Methuselah,'" THEATRE WORLD (Lond), XLIII (March 1947), 6; (April 1947), 6; (May 1947), 9.

Back to Methuselah (Arts Theater, Lond) is too long and lacks action. In Part 1 "the Serpent is the outstanding success." "Adam and Eve inevitably seem undressed, rather than in a state of Nature." The Gospel of the Brothers Barnabas contains Aristophanic satire on public men; and in The Thing Happens the long-livers are impressive. The play is stimulating, if not dramatic. The Elderly Gentleman (Part 4) is played "with a sort of sober comicality." As Far As Thought Can Reach depicts "a somewhat arid Arcadia," and the eternal wheel comes full circle with Lilith's "vague benediction" at the end. [Photographs of the production, May 1947, p. 9.]

1243 M., H. G. "'Pygmalion,'" THEATRE WORLD (Lond), XLIII (Aug 1947), 6-7.

The problem of what happens to Cinderella if there is no Prince Charming is raised but not solved in Pygmalion (Lyric Theater, Hammersmith); the last scene has "dry wordiness." Only Doolittle's appearance saves Act V "from being one of the worst last Acts on the English stage."

1244 Macqueen-Pope, W. CARRIAGES AT ELEVEN: A STORY OF THE EDWARDIAN THEATRE (Lond: Hutchinson, 1947; rptd Port Washington, NY, & Lond: Kennikat P, 1970), pp. 52, 71, 138, 144, 193, 195, 196.

"Shaw is a thing apart" from the Edwardian theater—"for no particular time, like Shakespeare." [Brief references to Shaw plays produced in the Edwardian theater; John E. Vedrenne and Harley Granville Barker at the Court Theater credited with introducing Shaw to England as a major dramatist.]

1245 "Man and Superman: Maurice Evans revives Shaw's witty tirade about the sexes," LIFE, XXIII (27 Oct 1947), 107-8, 110, 115.
Man and Superman is "the wordiest and most brilliant of all Shaw's comedies." [Photographs of Maurice Evans production, Alvin Theater, NY, with a feature on the difficulties of producing a Shaw play.]

1246 Marshall, Norman. THE OTHER THEATRE (Lond: J. Lehmann, 1947), pp. 14, 18, 20, 23, 28, 29, 58, 91, 115, 132, 162, 163, 166, 169-71, 173, 201, 202, 207, 215, 221, 229.
[Passim references to Shaw plays produced in English experimental theaters.]

1247 Middleton, George. THESE THINGS ARE MINE, THE AUTOBIOGRAPHY OF A JOURNEYMAN PLAYWRIGHT (NY: Macmillan, 1947), pp. 209-12, 334-36, 339-41, 346.
[An account of a conversation with Shaw concerning British censorship of plays; of Shaw's method of handling his own contracts and fees; and of his contract with the Dramatist's Guild of the Author's League of America.]

1248 Mortimer, Raymond. "Books in General," NS&Nation, XXXIII (3 May 1947), 317.
The prefaces to Geneva, Cymbeline Refinished, and In Good King Charles's Golden Days are interesting and provocative, as usual. Shaw's main aim seems to be an assault upon democracy. He proposes that all parliamentary candidates pass an examination and that capable women enter politics.

1249 Murray, Gilbert. "The Early G.B.S.," NS&Nation, XXXIV (16 Aug 1947), 128.
[Anecdotes from Murray's early friendship with Shaw.]

1250 Nathan, George Jean. "Androcles and the Lion. December 19, 1946," THE THEATRE BOOK OF THE YEAR, 1946-1947 (NY: Knopf, 1947), pp. 231-39, espec 231-32.
Androcles and the Lion is still lively, wise, and better than usual theater, though the American Repertory Theater (International Theater, NY) production is amateurish.

1251 Nathan, George Jean. "The Chocolate Soldier. March 12, 1947," THE THEATRE BOOK OF THE YEAR, 1946-1947 (NY: Knopf, 1947), pp. 338-39.

The ironic view of romance in Arms and the Man combined with Straus's romantic music in THE CHOCOLATE SOLDIER produces a comic paradox. Yet Shaw's play seems "as naturally suited to the operetta form as almost anything of Gilbert's."

1252 Nethercot, Arthur H. "The Quintessence of Idealism; or, The Slaves of Duty," PMLA, LXII (Sept 1947), 844-59.

Stage conflicts in end-of-the-century English drama reflect a revolution in the public attitude toward duty, self-sacrifice, idealism, nature, etc. Shaw began an attack on the Victorian concepts in The Quintessence of Ibsenism, and continued it in his Unpleasant plays. [Includes discussion of defenders and other attackers of duty.]

1253 "New Theatre: 'Saint Joan,'" TIMES (Lond), 4 Dec 1947, p. 6.

Celia Johnson's Joan has a "frank and trusting simplicity" in this excellent revival of Saint Joan (New Theater, Lond).

1254 Nicoll, Allardyce. BRITISH DRAMA, 4th ed (Lond: Harrap, 1947), pp. 343, 358, 360-61, 367, 369, 372, 373, 380, 386, 391, 425, 429, 432, 434, 435-45, 447, 456-58, 467, 472, 489, Index.

Shaw is "a peculiar admixture of Ibsen and Wycherley." "His aim is as serious, his analysis is as deep, as those of any of the more solemn dramatists, yet he cloaks that seriousness of purpose with a gaiety and a wit which has rarely been equalled in any time." He was and is the outstanding figure in the British theater, towering over modern thought. He is essentially a playwright, however, not a philosopher. To the theater he has contributed a "new incisiveness of utterance," a new kind of dramatic dialog, and fresh principles of characterization. His later turn from modified naturalism to frankly imaginative treatment of his themes indicates his sensitivity as a kind of dramatic barometer, catching the changing mood of his audience after 1920.

1255 Pearson, Hesketh. "Introduction: The Topolski Treatment," in Feliks Topolski, PORTRAIT OF G.B.S. (NY: Oxford University P, 1947), pp. 7-12.
Topolski captures the protean nature of Shaw: "the canny politician," "the industrious committee-man," the actor, the legalistic business man, the comedian, the Yoga singer, "the encyclopaedist," "the social mixer and the prophet." Over all is his incredible energy. [Book contains 33 plates of sketches of Shaw by Topolski.]

1256 "People: In the Pink," TIME, L (4 Aug 1947), 33-34.
Shaw has not mellowed with age, but still rails at reporters and makes biting political comments.

1257 Phelan, Kappo. "The Stage & Screen: <u>Androcles and the Lion</u>," COMMONWEAL, XLV (10 Jan 1947), 325.
<u>Androcles and the Lion</u> (American Repertory Theater, International Theater, NY) could be set to music. It is thoughtful, funny, and "neat." It deals with evolutionary Butlerian religious conclusions. The dancing, grateful lion is particularly charming.

1258 Phelan, Kappo and Phillip T. Hartung. "The Stage and Screen: Man and Superman," COMMONWEAL, XLVII (24 Oct 1947), 41-42.
Without its third act, <u>Man and Superman</u> (Maurice Evans production, Alvin Theater, NY) makes Tanner appear "a Superman merely because of his ability to talk a little longer, and jump a little further, than anyone else."

1259 "Piccadilly Theatre: 'Candida,'" TIMES (Lond), 28 March 1947, p. 6.
Morell is Shaw's best character, a combination of human strength and weakness. Except for a third act, when the poet's thought is too "fustian" and Candida's love too maternal, <u>Candida</u> (Piccadilly Theater, Lond) might be Shaw's best play.

1260 Ransan, André. "Bernard Shaw," in EN DÉJEUNANT AVEC... (Breakfasting with...) (Paris: Les Deux Sirènes; Bruxelles: L'Ecran du Monde, 1947), pp. 59-72.

[An account of overhearing, while hiding under Shaw's window, a conversation in 1932 between the theater manager of l'Oeuvre, Shaw, and Augustin Hamon. The reported conversation is interspersed with gossip and comments on Shaw's career.] Speaking of the Paris production of Too True to be Good, Shaw was alert, youthful, facetious, caustic, insolent. [In French.]

1261 Robinson, Lennox (ed). LADY GREGORY'S JOURNALS: 1916-1930 (NY: MacMillan, 1947), pp. 66-67, 199-216, 295-96.
[References to Shaw's comments on his mother's spiritualism, on William Morris, on the rejection of his novels, on the reception of Heartbreak House in America, on Mark Twain, and on plays that make a lasting impression on the audience.]

1262 Root, E. Merrill. FRANK HARRIS (NY: Odyssey P, 1947), pp. 4, 12, 22-23, 52, 59, 66, 72-75, 84, 91-93, 103, 111, 120-23, 126, 127, 129, 131, 136, 137, 141, 142, 152, 164, 169, 174-75, 190, 196, 198, 200, 206-9, 212, 214, 228, 231, 237, 239, 253, 284-85, 291-97, 310-13.
Shaw, the "unsocial socialist," gave a "sense of perfect unconstraint." Though he had disciples, he was largely alone. He was cool in the face of criticism, and he "seemed to have all the luck."

1263 S., F. "'You Never Can Tell,'" THEATRE WORLD (Lond), XLIII (Nov 1947), 7-8; XLIV (Jan 1948), 25-28.
You Never Can Tell is the "most uncomplicated of Shaw's plays." The Wyndham Theater (Lond) production is lighthearted and skillful. [Photographs of the production in XLIV, Jan 1948.]

1264 Shaw, Irwin. "Theater: In Praise of Impudence," NEW REPUBLIC, CXVII (20 Oct 1947), 38.
Man and Superman (Maurice Evans production, Alvin Theater, NY) bears no relation to life. It avoids emotion, and uses characters to convey early twentieth-century ideas. The acting is good.

1265 "Shaw Plus Evans," NEWSWEEK, XXX (20 Oct 1947),
88, 91.
Shaw undeniably "wrote some clever plays." The Maurice
Evans production (Alvin Theater, NY) of Man and Superman is
delightful.

1266 Skawroński, Zdzisław. "Arcyheretyk
współczesności--G.B.S." (Arch-heretic of the
Contemporary—G.B.S.), TEATR (Warsaw) (1947), 1/2,
33-39. [Not seen but listed in POLSKA BIBLIOGRAFIA
LITERACKA ZA 1947 (Warsaw, 1958), No 4732.] [In
Polish.]

1267 "St. Peter and 'St. Bernard': An apostle
resembling atheist Shaw pops up in Royal Academy,"
LIFE, XXII (19 May 1947), 40.
In Frederick Elwell's painting "I Dreamt St. Peter Sat for
His Portrait," in the Royal Academy of Arts, St. Peter
looks very much like Shaw. Elwell insists that it is not
Shaw; Shaw admits that he "might become a second St.
Bernard."

1268 Stokes, Sewell. "Methuselah, Hattie and Some
Shamrock," TAM, XXXI (May 1947), 35-37.
Back to Methuselah (Arts Theater, Lond) always has to be
"an interesting event, if only because it is the play its
author considers to be his most important." He often
reaches poetic heights in the plays, though The Gospel of
the Brothers Barnabas is dull.

1269 Stuckenschmidt, H. H. "Shaw und Wagner," (Shaw
and Wagner), STIMMEN; MONATSBLÄTTER FÜR MUSIK
(Berlin) I, No 4 (1947-48), 107-11.
While in his early music criticism Shaw defended Wagner
enthusiastically, he presented a conception of Wagner which
England's conservative friends of music less readily
accepted than that of the Bayreuth Prince and pious invoker
of the Good Friday Spell. Corno di Bassetto made no attempt
to conceal his sympathy for Wagner the political
revolutionary and democrat of the Dresden years. The
Perfect Wagnerite is simply a defense of the young Wagner
against the old Wagner, of the revolutionary of 1848
against the Schopenhauerian of the second half of his life.

[With extended quotations from The Perfect Wagnerite.] [In German.]

1270 Talmay, Allene. "Vogue's spot-light," VOGUE, CX (15 Nov 1947), 112, 190-91, espec 112.
Man and Superman (Alvin Theater, NY) is "beautiful romantic nonsense," with much "crude vitality." Shaw creates magnificent women characters. Usually he contrasts the strong woman with a strong and a weak man, as in this play.

1271 "The Theater: Old Operetta in Manhattan," TIME, XLIX (24 March 1947), 66.
THE CHOCOLATE SOLDIER is a "mighty steep" descent from Arms and the Man and is a bore in its present revival, in spite of the "Old World dash and melodiousness" of the songs.

1272 "The Theater: Old Play in Manhattan," TIME, L (20 Oct 1947), 66-68, 71-73.
Man and Superman (Maurice Evans production, Alvin Theater, NY) is longwinded and no longer shocking in its woman in pursuit of man thesis. But it is nevertheless "wickedly witty comedy."

1273 Thomas, Sir William Beach. "G. B. S. as Fellow Countryman," ATLANTIC MONTHLY, CLXXIX (June 1947), 115-19.
Shaw is known to most as an urban individual. But his country home at Ayot St. Lawrence allows him to cultivate his extraordinary senses of sight and hearing and to exercise in natural scenery. [Anecdotes about Shaw's vegetarianism, interchanges with neighbors, talk with animals, lack of appreciation for sport.]

1274 Thompson, Alan Reynolds. "Shaw: Ironist or Paradoctor?" PACIFIC SPECTATOR, I (Winter 1947), 113-29; revised and rptd in THE DRY MOCK; A STUDY OF IRONY IN DRAMA (Berkeley & Los Angeles: U of California P, 1948), pp. 103-27.
Shaw's plays take one to an articulate, passionless, amusing "never-never land"; they "are the escape literature of the intellectual." Shaw's central technique is paradox dramatized. [Examples from the plays and from biographical and philosophical data.] His work does not have the bitterness and pain that irony implies, except in Saint

Joan, his only play with "genuinely tragic emotion." The Doctor's Dilemma is not tragic: Dubedat's death has pathos combined with wit, and the ending of the play is happy. There are poetic moments in some of his plays.

1275 Tindall, William York. FORCES IN MODERN BRITISH LITERATURE, 1885-1946 (NY: Knopf, 1947), pp. 6n, 33-45, 46, 47, 48, 49, 50, 52, 54, 55n, 69, 101-2, 132, 178, 190-95, 196, 217, 218, 324-25, 332-33, 338, 362, Index, espec 33-45, 101-2, 190-95, 324-25; rptd NY: Random House (Vintage), 1956.
[Discusses Shaw's place in the Left, the New Drama, the Right, the search for a Superman, and exploration of the unconscious.] Shaw began in the New Drama and outlasted it. He replaced the religion of socialism with the search for a Superman, rejecting materialism and accepting Butler's Lamarckian evolution. He also moved in some plays toward Freud's province, "discussing sex like a sociologist" and describing the mother complex. His plays brought intellect and gaiety to the theater, though his work is characterized by a "cruel brilliance," a physiological or psychological inhumanity and lack of passion.

1276 Trewin, J. C. "The World of the Theatre: Book of the Play," ILN, CCXI (27 Oct 1947), 474.
You Never Can Tell (Wyndham's Theater, Lond) is a charming pot boiler, though one misses Shaw's stage directions, which are a treasure in this and other plays.

1277 Trewin, J. C. "The World of the Theatre: The Spoken Word," ILN, CCXI (27 Dec 1947), 730.
Shaw is a master of long, majestic speeches, as in Saint Joan (New Theater, Lond) with its radiantly inspired Joan, or in John Bull's Other Island (Dublin Gate Theater production, Embassy Theater, Lond) with its "exuberantly comic" Broadbent.

1278 von Stein, Irmgard. "Die Logik im Taschentuch. Eine Begegnung mit Shaw" (The Logic in the Handkerchief. A Meeting with Shaw), ATHENA (Berlin), I, No 10 (Sept 1947), 39-41.
[An account of a luncheon with Shaw, who had a cold and gave a lecture on colds (logic in the handkerchief).] [In German.]

1279 Warren, Virginia Lee. "'Pygmalion' Given in Mexican Capital: Gertrude Lawrence Scores a Success in Shaw Play—Use of English Cuts Attendance," NYT, 6 Feb 1947, p. 29.

Gertrude Lawrence's Theater Incorporated production of Pygmalion opened in Mexico City to a small but appreciative audience, which was apparently predisposed to judge the play by the movie version (an immense success in Mexico).

1280 Wavell. "The Theatre," SPECTATOR, CLXXIX (12 Dec 1947), 741.

Saint Joan (Old Vic production, New Theater, Lond) may be Shaw's finest achievement and contribution to the English stage and literature.

1281 Worsley, T. C. "The Theatre: Saint Joan, at the New Theatre," NS&Nation, XXIV (13 Dec 1947), 468.

Shaw makes an "astounding story credible" for a skeptical and misinformed modern age in Saint Joan. But the production at the Old Vic is deplorable, for it abrogates Shaw's miracle with a miscast Joan (Celia Johnson) and unworthy acting.

1282 Wyatt, Euphemia Van Rensselaer. "The Drama: Androcles and the Lion," CATHOLIC WORLD, CLXIV (Feb 1947), 453-58, espec 456-57.

Shaw's version of Christianity in Androcles and the Lion (American Repertory Theater, International Theater, NY) is unreal, and its Preface is "balderdash." Shaw captures the spirit of joy in Christianity but misses the point of Christian sacrifice. Saint Joan, on the other hand, shows an acceptance of God as the foundation of faith.

1283 Wyatt, Euphemia Van Rensselaer. "The Drama: Man and Superman," CATHOLIC WORLD, CLXVI (Nov 1947), 167-72.

Act III of Man and Superman (Alvin Theater, NY) can be omitted without damaging the story. The text of the play is "flashing," "like vintage wine."

1284 "Wyndham's Theatre: 'You Never Can Tell,'" TIMES (Lond), 4 Oct 1947, p. 6.

You Never Can Tell (Wyndham's Theater, Lond) is "the liveliest show in town," though thematically it is one of

Shaw's most diffuse plays. The characters, dialog, and production are "light hearted" and delightful.

1285 Zanco, Aurelio. "George Bernard Shaw," STORIA DELLA LETTERATURA INGLESE (History of English Literature), (Turin: Chiantore, 1947), II, 777-84; rptd Turin: Loescher, 1964.
[Long bio-bibliographical sketch with detailed plot summaries.] [In Italian.]

1948

1286 Aronin, Isobel Joy. "I Saw Shaw: A brash young lady gets her man," LIFE, XXV (15 Nov 1948), 75-76.
[Account of how Aronin, a Vassar junior, managed to get an interview with and movie of Shaw. Description of Ayot St. Lawrence and what she discussed with Shaw.]

1287 "Arts Theatre: 'Major Barbara,'" TIMES (Lond), 31 March 1948, p. 2.
The Western Theater Company (Arts Theater, Lond) has a vivacious production of Major Barbara, neglecting neither the fun nor the earnestness of the play.

1288 "Arts Theatre: 'Too True to be Good,'" TIMES (Lond), 14 July 1948, p. 7.
The jokes in Too True To Be Good are cheap, but the theme has a "stark dignity" and the prose is superb. The production (Arts Theater, Lond) is brilliant.

1289 Atkinson, Brooks. "At the Theatre," NYT, 11 Feb 1948, p. 33.
John Bull's Other Island is too verbose and too grounded in outdated politics; and the Dublin Gate Theater production (Mansfield Theater, NY) did not enliven it much.

1290 Atkinson, Brooks. "At the Theatre," NYT, 11 March 1948, p. 31.
You Never Can Tell has a lot "of old-fashioned stock material" and a lot of not very good talk. The Theater Guild production (Martin Beck Theater, NY) is not

particularly praiseworthy; the direction aims too much at ingeniousness and gems of wit, thus overplaying Shaw's already overplayed hand in this comedy.

1291 "Bernard Shaw," OBSERVER PROFILES, with an Introduction by Ivor Brown (Lond: Allan Wingate, 1948; rptd Freeport, NY: Books for Libraries P, 1970), pp. 147-50.

Shaw, who preached that Creative Evolution is a matter of resolve, not destiny, in Back to Methuselah, not only has survived the crises of his early years and endured into an atomic age but has also lived his own sermon and become the model "Methuselist."

1292 Beyer, William. "The State of the Theater: British Stars Over Broadway," SCHOOL AND SOCIETY, LXVII (24 April 1948), 314-16.

Even though "authentically 1900" in its treatment of subject matter, Man and Superman does not become dated. There is some technical fumbling, especially in the over-long first act, but when Shaw's "penchant for pausing to interpolate pointed aphorisms" grows out of his development of the plot and the extraordinary characters, the combination is dramatically integrated and illuminating. "Shaw's moral persuasiveness, fortunately, outweighs his capacity for social satire and political lampooning," so that he avoids topicality and touches universality with his perceptions.

1293 Brown, John Mason. "Seeing Things: The Old Look," SRL, XXXI (24 April 1948), 32-34.

In You Never Can Tell (Theater Guild, Martin Beck Theater, NY) Shaw wrote to appeal to West End theater managers, succumbing to the technical fads of 1896. Thus the well-made play is out of date; the characters of Dolly and Phil are obnoxious; and the class-conscious waiter absurd. Gloria and Valentine are pale forerunners of Ann Whitefield and Jack Tanner.

1294 Chew, Samuel C. A LITERARY HISTORY OF ENGLAND, ed by Albert C. Baugh (NY: Appleton-Century-Crofts, 1948), pp. 1483, 1488, 1518-19, 1520-25; espec 1520-25.

Shaw is too voluble and repetitious, and confuses art and ethics; furthermore, he is not an original thinker, but gives "vigorous enunciation and brilliant illustration" to others' ideas. He examines the faults of society, which is the only villain of his plays, and treats ideas, not emotions. [A brief survey of Shaw's works, asserting that Man and Superman is more philosophical than dramatic; that Saint Joan is too rational to encompass the character of a saint; and that Shaw's powers generally declined after he wrote Major Barbara, his masterpiece.]

1295 Clarke, Winifred. GEORGE BERNARD SHAW: AN APPRECIATION AND INTERPRETATION. Altrincham: John Sherratt and Son, 1948.
Shaw, both idealist and realist, is "the greatest educationist of his time." His theme is humanity, its self-development through life-long "inner revolutionary activity"; and the theme is traceable throughout his works. Saint Joan is Shaw's "most beautiful poem," symbolizing the power of spiritual freedom.

1296 Clurman, Harold. "The Play Isn't Everything," NEW REPUBLIC, CXVIII (29 March 1948), 30.
In You Never Can Tell (Martin Beck Theater, NY) Shaw's wit sparkles. The play is not out of date. It is really about the Waiter, who "is willing—against reason—to give life a chance."

1297 "Copywriter," NYer, XXIV (31 July 1948), 11-12.
Shaw wrote for Pan American World Airways an advertisement (currently in print) encouraging American tourism in Ireland. Not only did he write the copy, but he edited the proof—even the captions for the pictures. [For accounts of the same event, see also "Ireland: Approved by G.B.S.," NEWSWEEK, XXXI (21 June 1948), 32, and "Ireland," TIME, LII (19 July 1948), 42.]

1298 D., F. J. "'Major Barbara,'" THEATRE WORLD (Lond), XLIV (May 1948), 7-8.
The Arts Theater (Lond) production of Major Barbara was competently acted and entertaining. Shaw's thought in the play is virile.

1299 da Costa, R. "Pilgerfahrt zu Bernard Shaw" (Pilgrimage to Bernard Shaw), DIE WELTWOCHE (Zürich), XVI, No 748 (12 March 1948), 19.
[Account of a visit of da Costa and a female friend with Shaw. Describes their reception at Ayot St. Lawrence; Shaw's workplace; Shaw himself; and their brief, tense, trivial conversation.] [In German.]

1300 Darlington, W. A. "London Letter: Old Vic's Offering of 'Saint Joan' and the Question of Shaw's Durability," NYT, 11 Jan 1948, II, p. 3.
Shaw's chance of becoming a theater classic rests on Saint Joan and You Never Can Tell, for neither play is limited by topical subjects. But Saint Joan (New Theater, Lond) has too much of the lecture and too little of the drama in it. Will it offer character and emotion to future generations?

1301 Dougherty, Joseph Charles. "The Political Thought of G. B. Shaw as Expressed in His Drama." Unpublished dissertation, University of Washington, 1948. [Listed in Paul F. Breed and Florence M. Sniderman, DRAMATIC CRITICISM INDEX (Detroit: Gale, 1972), p. 609.]

1302 Evans, Ifor. "G. B. Shaw," A SHORT HISTORY OF ENGLISH DRAMA (Harmondsworth: Penguin, 1948; 2nd ed rev & enlarged, Boston: Houghton Mifflin, 1965), pp. 123, 150-58, 162, 163, 167, 168, 196, espec 150-58, Index.
Shaw is the only English dramatist with a world reputation. He did not touch tragedy; his dialog contains some dramatic improprieties; some of the late plays have obvious dramatic devices; and he neglects theatrical visual arts. Yet his drama is a rare combination of his interest in music and in ideas. He delighted the theatrical world. [A chronological survey of his major works.]

1303 F., M. "Das neue Babylon" (The New Babylon), DIE GEGENWART, III, No 17 (1 Sept 1948), 23.
Shaw favors a new political dictionary. In a letter to the London TIMES he advocates a Royal Commission which should determine all political terms. Shaw, however, in his own writings is not even able to distinguish between

"capitalism" and "communism." Instead of destroying the old Babylon he creates a new one. [In German.]

1304 "G. B. S. und die Todesstrafe" (G. B. S. and Capital Punishment), JUNIOR (Bremen), II (1948), 14.
[A translation of The Crime of Imprisonment with a brief introduction.] Shaw is independent of any theory or dogma. [In German.]

1305 Gassner, John. "The Theatre Arts," FORUM (Phila), CIX (April 1948), 212-14.
John Bull's Other Island (Dublin Gate Theater production, Mansfield Theater, NY) lacks dramaturgy but has "wit and perspicacity." The beginning is slow, and the play lacks plot. Shaw's satire gives way to an affirmation in the speeches of Father Keegan.

1306 Gibbs, Wolcott. "The Theatre: The Great Man Again," NYer, XXIII (21 Feb 1948), 53-54.
John Bull's Other Island (Mansfield Theater, NY) is "languid and antique."

1307 Gibbs, Wolcott. "The Theatre: Hollywood, Shaw and Sartre," NYer, XXIV (27 March 1948), 45-46, 48.
You Never Can Tell (Martin Beck Theater, NY) is not funny. The woman question is out of date; the characters are not effective; and the dialog is only interesting when no one is discussing sex, which is not very often.

1308 Glicksberg, Charles. "Shaw vs. Science," DALHOUSIE REVIEW, XXVIII (Oct 1948), 271-83.
Shaw did not oppose the advance of scientific knowledge, but regarded science as a religion whose credentials needed constant examination. He objected to scientists who transgress the moral laws of humanity to further knowledge, regarding them as no less immune to human weaknesses than the members of any other profession. He challenged scientific problems, particularly Darwinism, which he addressed in Man and Superman and Back to Methuselah and which he considered disastrous if applied to social and political problems. He approached scientific matters as an enlightened but violently prejudiced layman who aired opinions outside his sphere of competence with deplorable results. In the final analysis, Shaw rejected science

because it did not give him the very thing which, by its nature, it cannot give: a faith to live by.

1309 Henderson, Archibald. "George Bernard Shaw and Communism," CAROLINA QUARTERLY, I (Fall 1948), 11-14. Shaw encourages the critical confusion around his inconsistency of thought, though of late he has become more cautious, after having praised Hitler's and Mussolini's executive efficiency. His socialism, after 1911, was not Fabian but his own (known as Distributism). He maintains that everybody should be given "from birth, an equal share in the national income." After his 1931 visit to Russia, he "really 'went dotty' for Russia." He "has been an avowed Communist" since then, though he "is not opposed to private enterprise operating under Socialism."

1310 Horzyca, Wilam. "Lepsze niż Shakespeare" (Better Than Shakespeare), PROGRAM TEATRU ZIEMI POMORSKIEJ (Toruń), No 6 (1947/1948); rptd in Horzyca, O DRAMACIE (About Drama) (Warsaw: Wydawnictwa artystyczne i filmowe, 1969), pp. 214-18. In Caesar and Cleopatra, Shaw seeks to answer the question "What is history?." In declaring humorously that his play is "better than Shakespeare," Shaw is not suffering from megalomania, but proposing that his Caesar is a livelier character than Shakespeare's. The key to Shaw's concept of history is in humor. [In Polish.]

1311 House, Humphrey. "G. B. S. on Great Expectations," DICKENSIAN, XLIV (March 1948), 63-70; (Sept 1948), 183-86. Shaw's Introduction to GREAT EXPECTATIONS, first published by the Limited Editions Club in 1937 in the United States, is not well known. But its sixteen pages are more valuable than sixteen volumes of some Dickens criticism: it lacks "the drivelling and trivial verbosity that passes so often for criticism of Dickens." Shaw correctly identifies Dickens's lack of "culture," the greatness of the art of GREAT EXPECTATIONS, the freeing up of Dickens' "more open, social autobiographical self" in the novel, and the increasingly dark view Dickens had of the bourgeois world. Shaw is less correct about Pip's final despair of the bourgeois world, about Estella's being "a born tormentor," and about Pip's unreclaimed snobbery. At times Shaw seems to see the novel as an essay in ethics—which it is not. Shaw sees Dickens as a radical social reformer, but in fact Dickens was opposed to philosophic radicalism. He was individualistic, humanistic, authoritarian to an extent. Even LITTLE DORRIT is not as subversive as Shaw thinks.

1312 Iizuka, Tomoichiro. "Bernard Shaw no Engekikan" (Bernard Shaw's View of the Theater), ENGEKIGAKU JOSETSU (An Introduction to Theater Studies), Vol. I (Tokyo: Yuzankaku, 1948), pp. 230-34.
Shaw chose the theater as the most effective means of propagating his ideas. He maintained that the theater should serve for the betterment of society. [In Japanese.]

1313 Johnson, Falk. "An Additional Judgement," QUARTERLY JOURNAL OF SPEECH, XXXIV (Dec 1948), 503-4.
Shaw's alphabet is theoretically desirable, but is too radical for public acceptance.

1314 Krutch, Joseph Wood. "Drama," NATION, CLXVI (21 Feb 1948), 219-21.
John Bull's Other Island (Mansfield Theater, NY) will never be a classic because it depends too much upon a special time and place. On the subject of Ireland, Shaw is a bit provincial.

1315 Krutch, Joseph Wood. "Drama," NATION, CLXVI (27 March 1948), 361.
Reviewers find You Never Can Tell (Theater Guild, Martin Beck Theater, NY) "tedious, stuffy, outmoded, and tiresome." But it is in fact "gay, lively, high-spirited, shrewd, wise, exuberant, and overflowing with intelligent fun."

1316 Lamm, Martin. DET MODERNA DRAMAT (Stockholm: A Bonnier, 1948); translated as MODERN DRAMA by Karin Elliott (Oxford: Basil Blackwell, 1952; rptd NY: Philosophical Library, 1953), pp. xii, xv, xvii, 136, 142-43, 147, 150, 190, 215, 251-84, 285-86, 292, 293, 317, 325, 334, Index, espec 251-84.
Shaw most resembles Ibsen, writing problem plays with multiple points of view and using debate and discussion. Yet Shaw utilizes a variety of dramatic forms, including French comedy, French vaudeville-farce, and melodrama. His

plays reflect the characteristics of a public speaker in their careless structure and their wordiness. His characterization depends in part on the stage directions, and his dialog lacks the impression of real life. His greatness lies in his psychological clarity, his ability to capture situations and moods, and his combination of pathos and foolery. The early plays attack romantic conventions and morals and support a realistic view of life. But with Man and Superman Shaw abandons rationalism for a mystical faith in the Life Force. [Also discussed are Arms and the Man, The Devil's Disciple, Captain Brassbound's Conversion, The Man of Destiny, Caesar and Cleopatra, Candida, Major Barbara, The Doctor's Dilemma, The Shewing-Up of Blanco Posnet, Androcles and the Lion, Back to Methuselah (Shaw at his worst) and Saint Joan (Shaw at his best).] [In Swedish.]

1317 Lavalette, Robert. LITERATURGESCHICHTE DER WELT (Literary History of the World) (Zürich: Orell Füssli, 1948), pp. 25, 383, 395-96, 397, 415.
[A brief portrait of Shaw, with emphasis on his theory of the Life Force.] Shaw is a typical author of the age of transition. [In German.]

1318 Lennig, Walter. "Durchbruch des Wahren Menschen" (The Emergence of the True Self), SONNTAG (Berlin), III, No 19 (1948), 7.
The Devil's Disciple contains a central human truth: that the innermost nature of a person shows itself in a decisive hour. The acting (Hebbel Theater, Berlin) was on the whole good, and the audience enthusiastic. [In German.]

1319 Lennig, Walter. "Verworrenheit, Ironie, Satire" (Intricacy, Irony, Satire), SONNTAG (Berlin), III, No 1 (1948).
[Generally favorable review of current production of Androcles and the Lion.] Shaw's brilliant paradoxes and sparkling dialog are partially lost in this production. Androcles is slightly dated. [In German.]

1320 Loewenstein, F[ritz] E[rwin]. "Introduction," BERNARD SHAW THROUGH THE CAMERA (Lond: B & H White, 1948), pp. 9-10; ptd as THE PICTORIAL RECORD OF THE

LIFE OF BERNARD SHAW (Lond: H. A. & W. L. Pitkin, 1951?).
Shaw, one of the world's most photographed people, consented to and aided with the collection of photographs which makes up this book [which includes "Introduction"; a chronology, "Bernard Shaw: Chief Events and Principal Works," pp. 11-15; "Photographs," pp. 17-123; and "List of Pictures and Credits," pp. 124-28. The photographs are divided into sections: "Ancestors, Relations, early Portraits and Dublin Pictures," "Early Days," "Ayot St. Lawrence and London," "Hands, Handlines and Horoscope," "Travels," "Caricatures, Sculptures, Portraits and Book Illustrations," "Friends, Contemporaries, famous Actors and notable occasions."]

1321 "Lyric Theatre, Hammersmith: 'Captain Brassbound's Conversion,'" TIMES (Lond), 14 Oct 1948, p. 6.
Captain Brassbound's Conversion does not have startling ideas about justice and vengeance or woman's power, but the characters and situations have wit and eloquence. Flora Robson's Lady Cecily enchanted and conquered the audience (Lyric Theater, Hammersmith).

1322 M., H. G. "'John Bull's Other Island'—'The Old Lady Says "No"'—'Where Stars Walk,'" THEATRE WORLD (Lond), XLIV (Jan 1948), 39-40.
John Bull's Other Island (Dublin Gate Theater Co., Mansfield Theater, NY) is old fashioned, "refreshing," but too long. Broadbent is a "caricature of the self-deluding Englishman"; Doyle seems real enough.

1323 McIntosh, Ronald. "Shaw's Boswell," CHRISTIAN SCIENCE MONITOR MAGAZINE, 10 July 1948, p. 5.
F. E. Loewenstein, Founder of the Shaw Society, is "Shaw's Boswell." He is joint editor of the SHAVIAN, has been working on an authoritative bibliography of Shaw's work for ten years, and works at "Shaw's Corner." [Two photographs of Shaw.]

1324 Macqueen-Pope, W[alter]. HAYMARKET: THEATRE OF PERFECTION (Lond: W. H. Allen, 1948), p. 352, Index.
[Account of an abortive attempt to produce You Never Can Tell at the Haymarket Theater in 1897.]

1325 Madero, Ernesto. "A los 90 años Bernard Shaw dice a <u>Hoy</u> ya soy viejo" (At 90 Years Bernard Shaw Says to <u>Hoy</u> That He is Too Old), HOY (Mexico), No 609 (23 Oct 1948), 24-25.
[Shaw's witty response in 1945 to members of the World Youth Council, who invited Shaw to lecture or join the Club.] [In Spanish.]

1326 Madero, Ernesto. "Bernard Shaw, de charlacon <u>Hoy</u>" (Bernard Shaw, from a Conversation with <u>Hoy</u>), HOY (Mexico), No 608 (16 Oct 1948), 12-13.
[Madero recalls his 1948 visit to Shaw, who is for Madero a "cute child, roguish, ill-bred, saucy, and an eater of candies."] [In Spanish.]

1327 Madero, Ernesto. "Con el brujo de Ayot St. Lawrence" (With the Wizard of Ayot St. Lawrence) HOY (Mexico), No 607 (9 Oct 1948).
[Description of Shaw at his ninetieth birthday; the first of three interviews.] [In Spanish.]

1328 Martin, Kingsley. "Marx and the Fabian," NS&Nation, XXXVI (24 July 1948), 78.
Shaw justifies his approach to socialism in the postscript to <u>Fabian Essays</u>, Jubilee Edition. He contends that Fabians must remain a "minority of cultured snobs and genuinely scientific Socialist tacticians," for they have no time to converse with "illiterates or political novices." Moreover, he believes that the Soviet Union "completely converted to Fabianism." In reality, the Fabians have been influenced by the Soviet Union. The political democracy that Shaw and the Webbs once espoused cannot be discovered in their recent writings. Today, Shaw is a Marxist.

1329 Mencken, H. L. "An American Reaction to Bernard Shaw's Forty Letter Alfabet," QUARTERLY JOURNAL OF SPEECH, XXXIV (Dec 1948), 503.
Shaw overestimates the disadvantages of English spelling. Like all reformers, Shaw is "too eager for quick results," and, like all spelling reformers, he is imprudent and foolish.

1330 Nathan, George Jean. "John Bull's Other Island. February 10, 1948," THE THEATRE BOOK OF THE YEAR, 1947-1948 (NY: Knopf, 1948), pp. 262-66.
John Bull's Other Island (Dublin Gate Theater Players, Mansfield Theater, NY) is far from Shaw's best, but is nevertheless superior to contemporary drama. Its ideas are the most important aspect of the play.

1331 Nathan, George Jean. "Man and Superman. October 8, 1947," THE THEATRE BOOK OF THE YEAR, 1947-1948 (NY: Knopf, 1948), pp. 84-94; rptd as "Shaw and the Dramatic Style," THE WORLD OF GEORGE JEAN NATHAN, ed by Charles Angoff (NY: Knopf, 1952), pp. 417-29.
Man and Superman (Alvin Theater, NY) now seems "respectably tame and conservative." Its style is what lends it interest.

1332 Nathan, George Jean. "You Never Can Tell. March 16, 1948," THE THEATRE BOOK OF THE YEAR, 1947-1948 (NY: Knopf, 1948), pp. 322-26.
You Never Can Tell (Martin Beck Theater, NY, Theater Guild revival) remains amusing in spite of its age because of Shaw's "lively wit, character observation and literary velvet." Shaw is able to make the audience feel the play was casually written; his mastery is in knowing how far to go and when to stop.

1333 Nowakowski, A. "Die heilige Johanna" (Saint Joan), DIE ZEIT (Hamburg), 16 Sept 1948, p. 6.
Shaw's Saint Joan (Theater der Jugend, Hamburg) displays his skill of dramatic composition and psychological insight. But sometimes his irony seems to fail. [In German.]

1334 "The Old Vic Theatre Company in 'Saint Joan,'" THEATRE WORLD (Lond), XLIV (Feb 1948), 13-20.
The Old Vic's is a "faultless" production of Saint Joan (New Theater, Lond), a play with "The stamp of greatness ...upon it." [Pictorial primarily.]

1335 Papini, Giovanni. "G. B. Shaw ovvero il piu matti dei savi" (G. B. Shaw or the Maddest of the Sages), IL CORRIERE DELLA SERA (Milan), 24 Dec 1948;

rptd in SCRITTORI E ARTISTI (Writers and Artists) (Milan: Mondadori, 1959), pp. 1136-40.
Shaw's intellectual development was not humanistic or philosophical, but biblical and biological. His diffidence toward pure art derives from his Puritanism. Shaw sought to be an occultist out of social blindness. Polemic and dramatic radicalism are the fundamentals which inspired Shaw's works. [In Italian.]

1336 Peiper, Tadeusz. "Spostrzeżenia: Żolnierz i bohater" (Observations on Arms and the Man), TEATR (Warsaw), 3/5 (1948), 59-62. [Not seen but listed in POLSKA BIBLIOGRAFIA LITERACKA ZA 1948 (Warsaw), 1956.] [In Polish.]

1337 Perry, Henry Ten Eyck. "Master and Disciple," YALE REVIEW, XXXVII (March 1948), 544-47.
Geneva "is almost as dated as the League of Nations and the Hague Tribunal," and, after World War II, the dictators are not amusing. However, its thesis, that humankind has failed politically and needs to mature into competent statesmanship, remains true. Cymbeline Refinished has creditable verse and makes an appreciative comment on CYMBELINE. In Good King Charles's Golden Days has a "thoroughly Shavian cast of characters"; their contrasting views and occasional farcical action keep the essentially plotless play lively. Eric Bentley's BERNARD SHAW interprets Shaw well, but having "become a classic in his own lifetime," Shaw needs no interpreter.

1338 Phelan, Kappo and Phillip T. Hartung. "The Stage and Screen: John Bull's Other Island," COMMONWEAL, XLVII (27 Feb 1948), 494-96.
The parliamentary arguments of John Bull's Other Island (Dublin Gate Theater, Mansfield Theater, NY) are "mainly historically interesting." But the chief premise of the comedy—the sentimental Englishman versus the realistic Irishman—is still timely, original and witty.

1339 Phelan, Kappo. "The Stage and Screen: You Never Can Tell," COMMONWEAL, XLVII (16 April 1948), 635-36.
You Never Can Tell (Theater Guild, Martin Beck Theater, NY) needs cutting, for the first two acts drag. Curiously, the play has no moral.

1340 Rebora, Piero. BERNARD SHAW COMICO E TRAGICO (Bernard Shaw the Comic and the Tragic) (Florence: Vallecchi, 1948).
Shaw's creative activity falls into four phases, the comic and the tragic occurring in all four: 1876-1892, 1892-1903, 1903-1923, and 1924 to date. The mechanisms of his ideological utterances may irritate or amuse, according to one's response to the comic or tragic aspects. [Bibliography, pp. 277-78.] [In Italian.]

1341 S., F. "'St. Joan,'" THEATRE WORLD (Lond), XLIV (Jan 1948), 10.
Celia Johnson plays Saint Joan (New Theater, Lond) with "other-worldly sincerity." The trial scene is "unbearably poignant"; the epilog, anticlimactic.

1342 Schucking, Levin L. "Bernard Shaws Liebesbriefe" (Bernard Shaw's Love Letters), ESSAYS ÜBER SHAKESPEARE, PEPYS, ROSSETTI, SHAW UND ANDERES (Essays on Shakespeare, Pepys, Rossetti, Shaw and Others) (Wiesbaden: Dieterich, 1948), pp. 142-72.
Ellen Terry and Bernard Shaw: A Correspondence introduces Ellen Terry to the German reading public. Shaw's so-called love letters are really commercial letters. They are void of any feeling. [In German.]

1343 Shand, James. "Author and Printer: G. B. S. and R. & R. C.: 1898-1948," ALPHABET AND IMAGE (Lond), No 8 (Dec 1948), 3-38.
Shaw dealt directly with his printer and binder. Influenced by William Morris, he had definite preferences in the format of his books. His method of composition was a first draft in shorthand; then double-spaced typescript, emended and revised; and meticulous proof-reading. He made particularly careful revisions in final proof.

1344 "The Shape of Things: George Bernard Shaw, Never Bashful," NATION, CLXVII (4 Sept 1948), 245-47.
Words are "a major weapon in modern war" because they can be used any way a speaker wants. Shaw proposes a new political dictionary to make negotiations clearer and to head off war. As a contribution to the peace, Shaw's proposal should "proceed informally."

1345 Shaw, Irwin. "Theater: The Irish on the Irish," NEW REPUBLIC, CXVIII (1 March 1948), 24.
John Bull's Other Island (Mansfield Theater, NY), one of Shaw's worst plays, has lectures rather than a plot.

1346 Shawe-Taylor, Desmond. COVENT GARDEN (NY: Chanticleer P [World of Music Series], 1948), pp. 40, 47-48, 50.
Shaw was a thorough musician, and an operatic expert. He wittily, but pointedly, criticized in THE STAR and THE WORLD Covent Garden opera under Augustus Harris as impresario. He urged Harris to perform TRISTAN and THE RING, and he ridiculed the artistic laziness of the singers Jean and Edouard De Reszke, who subsequently triumphed in Wagnerian opera.

1347 Sheen, Fulton J. PHILOSOPHY OF RELIGION (NY: Appleton-Century-Crofts, 1948), p. 346, Index.
Shaw and Wells are the best known interpreters of "the Liberal Man," i.e., a social being who "needs neither faith for his intellect nor grace for his will." Shaw's values are materialistic, utilitarian, and cynical, though Christian assumptions appear occasionally in his work.

1348 [Sheerin, John B.] "Bernard Shaw Has Fun," CATHOLIC WORLD, CLXVIII (Dec 1948), 180-81.
[Response to an article by Shaw in the DAILY WORKER (Lond) on the definition of communism.] Shaw uses the word communism etymologically and not "in its 1948 meaning." He has added to the world's humor but lacks seriousness, using his extraordinary talent to proliferate chitchat, quips and puns.

1349 Stokes, Sewell. "Charades by Old Favorites," TAM, XXXII (Jan 1948), 47-49, espec 47.
You Never Can Tell is the least attractive in revival of Shaw's early plays. Such a "fashionable" comedy is unlike Shaw, and less amusing than one by Oscar Wilde. The Wyndham Theater (Lond) production is "full of tedious fooling and obvious humor."

1350 Tetauer, Frank. BERNARD SHAW. SPULUTVŮRCE SOCIALISTICKÉHO DNEŠKA (Bernard Shaw. Co-creator of Present-Day Socialism) (Prague: Prace, 1948).

[Biography with 21 chapters on Shaw as Fabian socialist, novelist, critic, dramatist, with a synthesis of Shaw's philosophy and ideology (to 1938). Bibliography, pp. 137-38.] [In Czech.]

1351 "The Theatre Guild: Season 1923," TAM, XXXII (Fall 1948), 43.
The Theater Guild (NY) "cornered the market" in Shaw plays and had a great 1923 season (which included The Devil's Disciple and Saint Joan). [Photographs of these productions.]

1352 "The Theater: Old Play in Manhattan," TIME, LI (23 Feb 1948), 56.
John Bull's Other Island (Dublin Gate Theater Players, Mansfield Theater, NY) makes a friendly but mercilessly accurate comment on the English and Irish. But at times the play is talky and tedious.

1353 "The Theater: Old Play in Manhattan," TIME, LI (29 March 1948), 56.
You Never Can Tell (Theater Guild, Martin Beck Theater, NY) is a diverting "scrambly farce" that anticipates Shaw's mature comedy in places. It is old-fashioned, garrulous, and attempts to satirize too many things. Like Wilde and no one since, Shaw can be "sharp without being snide, mischievous without being nasty."

1354 "Theater: Shaw, Circa 1896," NEWSWEEK, XXXI (29 March 1948), 82.
You Never Can Tell (Theater Guild, Martin Beck Theater, NY) is amusing and engaging, though dated.

1355 "Theater: Shaw's Other Island," NEWSWEEK, XXXI (23 Feb 1948), 80.
John Bull's Other Island (Dublin Gate Theater, Mansfield Theater, NY) is witty, and the satire on Shaw's "ironic realist" Celt and "impulsively romantic Briton" remains topical.

1356 Trewin, J. C. THE ENGLISH THEATRE (Lond: Paul Elek [Life and Leisure 1], 1948), pp. 16-19, 20-23, 69, 91-92, 100, espec 20-23.

Shaw became an "Old Master," a legend in his own time. His contribution to the English theater in both plays and prefaces is to incite thought through provocative argument --presented with "utmost levity." He requires "room in which to detonate"; thus his longer plays are better than his one-act plays. Heartbreak House is a long debate, too diffuse, though with some poetic passages. Back to Methuselah unites intellect and imagination, but the central plays are too flippant for his lofty theme. Saint Joan is a modern classic. His later plays vacillate between slapstick and majesty.

1357 Trewin, J. C. "The World of the Theatre: The Plot Thickens," ILN, CCXIII (6 Nov 1948), 528.
Buoyant Billions, just produced at Zurich, "is apparently plotless." On the other hand, Captain Brassbound's Conversion (Lyric Theater, Hammersmith) has an implausible but lively plot, dominated by the wit and attractiveness of Lady Cicely. "Unlike most of the Shavian comedies it acts better than it reads."

1358 W., E. "G. B. Shaw muss herhalten" (G. B. Shaw Must Bear the Responsibility for That), RUF (Munich), III (Nov 1948), 13.
[An article primarily about the Surrealist painter Robert Schuppner, who quotes Shaw to the effect that a picture should never please more than ten percent of the people who go to an exhibition.] [In German.]

1359 Webb, Beatrice. OUR PARTNERSHIP, ed by Barbara Drake and Margaret I. Cole (NY: Longmans, Green, 1948), pp. 9, 14, 28, 34, 36, 37-38, 53, 109-14, 121, 134, 175, 188, 189, 193-94, 204, 224, 249, 256-57, 271, 282-84, 290, 294, 303, 309, 310-11, 312, 313-15, 352, 373, 380, 385, 447-49, 470-71.
Shaw the playwright is a masterful artist and craftsman. But Shaw the man is difficult to understand. He is a "devoted propagandist," an excellent friend to many, and an instrumental figure in politics. Fabianism and the Empire explains the Fabian position on the Boer War and presents fairly the opinions of partisans of the Boers as well as patriots. Man and Superman is a play combining essay, treatise, interlude, and lyric, all illustrating the same

idea. Major Barbara is a "dance of devils," which ends in an "intellectual and moral morass."

1360 [Welti, Jakob]. [Review of Buoyant Billions].
ZÜRCHER ZEITUNG, 22 Oct 1948, p. 5; rptd in CRITICAL
HERITAGE, pp. 374-76, Item 125.
Buoyant Billions (Trebitsch translation, Schauspielhaus, Zürich production) repeats, in a rather mild tone, well-known Shavian themes. Shaw preaches reason in love and marriage and takes a rationalist look at the propertied class. The play is witty, but drawn out and heavy handed.

1361 West, E. J. "G. B. S. on Shakespearean Production," STUDIES IN PHILOLOGY, XLV (1948), 216-35.
Shaw attacked butcheries and rewritings of Shakespeare, demanding that Shakespeare's scripts be played as Shakespeare had left them. He regarded Shakespeare as a professional craftsman and dramatic technician, and offered mature criticism of Shakespearean production. Given Shaw's tremendous knowledge of Shakespeare's plays, it is not surprising that some of his prose is Shakespeare-influenced.

1362 Winsten, Stephen. DAYS WITH BERNARD SHAW (Lond
& NY: Hutchinson, 1948; NY: Vanguard, 1949; Lond:
Reader's Union, 1951; rptd Lond & NY: Hutchinson,
n.d. [c. 1973-77]).
[An anecdotal biography by Shaw's neighbor at Ayot St. Lawrence. Quotes Shaw at length on many subjects, including his reminiscences of famous contemporaries. A valuable portrait of the aging Shaw, but it must be taken with caution. Contains inaccuracies and quotations apparently elaborated by Winsten. Shaw said of the book, "In hardly any passage in the book as far as I have had time to examine it...has Mr. Winsten's art not improved on bare fact and occurrence by adding the charm of his own style to the haphazard crudity of nature" (quoted in Robert E. Sherwood, "Self-Illumination by G.B.S.—and a Reverent Chronicle," NYTBR, 27 March 1949, p. 17).]

1363 Wyatt, Euphemia Van Rensselaer. "The Drama:
Dublin Gate Theater," CATHOLIC WORLD, CLXVII (April
1948), 70-73 espec 71-72.

John Bulls' Other Island (Dublin Gate Theater players, Mansfield Theater, NY) is "long-winded"; the politics are "now merely historical."

1364 Wyatt, Euphemia Van Rensselaer. "The Drama: You Never Can Tell," CATHOLIC WORLD, CLXVII (May 1948), 168-70.
In You Never Can Tell (Theater Guild production, Martin Beck Theater, NY) the Waiter is the pivotal character. The comedy deft and light-hearted; the acting is good, though the twins are too cute.

1949

1365 Aldridge, John W. "Books in Review: Artful Dodger," NEW REPUBLIC, CXX (23 May 1949), 20-24, espec 21.
Stephen Winsten's DAYS WITH BERNARD SHAW (1949) does not show Shaw the man—Shaw when he is not acting. Sixteen Self Sketches does not portray the whole of Shaw either, but it contains intimate and moving passages.

1366 "Arts Theatre: Widowers' Houses," TIMES (Lond), 3 Feb 1949, p. 6.
Widowers' Houses contains elements of later Shaw: nonsense, wit, experimental characters, logical argument. The portrait of Blanche is "brutally realistic." The last act is the most substantial.

1367 Atkinson, Brooks. "At the Theatre," NYT, 17 May 1949, p. 28.
The Maurice Evans production of Man and Superman (City Center, NY) is not as expert as that of last season, though Evans continues to perform Tanner with common sense and wit. The play is, however, Broadway's only first-rate comedy of the season.

1368 Atkinson, Brooks. "First Night at the Theatre: Shaw's 'Caesar and Cleopatra' With Cedric Hardwicke and Lilli Palmer," NYT, 22 Dec 1949, p. 28.

Caesar and Cleopatra treats great historical figures as mortals in a witty and wise play. The opening night performances (National Theater, NY) were at times too "heavy going," perhaps because Cedric Hardwicke (Caesar) was ill.

1369 Basso, Hamilton. "Books: Foxy Like a Grandpa," NYer, XXV (7 May 1949), 105-6, 109.
Sixteen Self Sketches and Stephen Winsten's DAYS WITH BERNARD SHAW recall two important facts about Shaw: he is always fun to read, and he consistently adopts the esthetic point of view, so that sanitation, economics, politics, and religion are all ultimately intertwined with art.

1370 "Bedford Theatre, Camden Town: 'Major Barbara,'" TIMES (Lond), 14 June 1949, p. 7.
Major Barbara (Bedford Theater, Camden Town) is profound and moving, containing "a mixture of poetry and wit, and wicked argument and real feeling."

1371 "Bedford Theatre, Camden Town: 'Mrs. Warren's Profession,'" TIMES (Lond), 28 June 1949, p. 7.
Mrs. Warren's Profession is a disappointing play in that it lacks the human dimension. Yet the duel between Vivie and Mrs. Warren "is exhilarating."

1372 "Bedford Theatre, Camden Town: 'The Inca of Perusalem,'" TIMES (Lond), 31 May 1949, p. 7.
The Inca of Perusalem (Bedford Theater, Camden Town) is now a collector's piece. The Inca resembles Shaw in his vanity, self-assurance, and humor.

1373 "Books: A Man of Wealth & Very Old," TIME, LIII (4 April 1949), 106, 109-10.
[Review of Sixteen Self Sketches, Fabian Essays, and DAYS WITH BERNARD SHAW, by Stephen Winsten; mostly direct and indirect quotation of Shaw.]

1374 Bookwright. "Reprints, New Editions," NYHTBR, XXVI (6 Nov 1949), 31.
Shaw's Selected Plays (Dodd, Mead) vary in excellence; e.g., The Dark Lady of the Sonnets and In Good King Charles's Golden Days are "farcical trifles." Some Shaw characters lack flesh and blood. But Shaw excels in

intellect, wit, and truth-telling. THE QUINTESSENCE OF G. B. S., by Stephen Winsten, is an uneven work, and many quotations suffer from being out of context.

1375 Brailsford, H. N. "Shaw on Himself," List, XLI (21 April 1949), 663-64; rptd as "Shaw über sich selbst," DIE BRÜCKE (Essen), No 132 (13 May 1949), pp. 11-14; also rptd in CRITICAL HERITAGE, pp. 379-80, Item 127.

Sixteen Self Sketches reveals many of the influences that helped form Shaw's character. His father's drinking destroyed Shaw's belief in "the perfect and omniscient father-image" and also affected his "ascetic Puritanism." Shaw has always been shy of expressing or admitting emotion, and he still conceals his emotions in this book. Three decisive events in Shaw's life occurred in the mid-eighties: reading DAS KAPITAL, being introduced to Ibsen's plays, and meeting Sidney Webb and the Fabians.

1376 Castelli, Alberto. "Introduzione a George Bernard Shaw" (Introduction to George Bernard Shaw), HUMANITAS, IV (May 1949), 512-22.

Shaw cultivated and displayed his sense of beauty in his long career as critic and playwright. He wants to show that he knows everything and that he likes nothing, and that anything may be reformed if his teachings are followed. His artistry appears especially in his essays and prefaces. [In Italian.]

1377 Castro Oyanguren, Enrique. "La temporada de la Compañía de Comedias" (The Season of the Compañía de Comedias), MERCURIO PERUANO, Año XXIV, No 271 (Oct 1949), 436-38.

It was feared that the Peruvian public would not understand the grace and subtlety of Candida, but the public of Lima widely attended the performance and reacted favorably to it. [In Spanish.]

1378 "The Check List: Biography," AMERICAN MERCURY, LXVIII (June 1949), 759.

The Sixteen Self Sketches are no substitute for Shaw's autobiography. They offer few new facts, but are magnificently written.

1379 Christ, Ernst. "G. B. Shaw. Die Quintessenz seiner Einsichten" (G. B. Shaw. The Quintessence of His Points of View), WELTSTIMMEN (Stuttgart), XVIII, No 10 (July 1949), 1-7.

Everybody's Political What's What might be considered the quintessence of Shaw. It contains extensive commentary on education, war, economics, and the future of humankind. According to Shaw, the playwright should be a biologist, a philosopher, and a prophet as well. [In German.]

1380 Cole, Margaret (ed). THE WEBBS AND THEIR WORK (Lond: Frederick Muller, 1949), pp. 3-14, 17, 19, 21, 22, 25, 30, 33, 42, 59, 61, 64-65, 76, 119, 127, 128, 133, 134, 136, 140, 156, 167, 168, 197, 237, 239, 242, 245, 267, 289, 291, 292, Index.

[Passing references in essays by various authors to Shaw's relationship to the Fabians, to the NEW STATESMAN, and to the Webbs; pp. 3-14 contain Shaw's answers to a questionnaire about the Webbs.]

1381 Cole, Toby and H. K. Chinoy (eds). ACTORS ON ACTING (NY: Crown, 1949), pp. 346-52; rev ed 1970, pp. 370-76.

[Brief summary of Shaw's career as drama critic and his relationship to acting and actors; introduction to Shaw's essay "The Point of View of the Playwright," rptd from HERBERT BEERBOHM TREE: SOME MEMORIES OF HIM AND OF HIS ART, ed by Max Beerbohm (Lond: Hutchinson, n.d.).]

1382 Collins, John Stewart. "Bernard Shaw und die Frauen" (Bernard Shaw and Women), BERLINER HEFTE FUR GEISTIGES LEBEN (Berlin), IV (1949), 143-55.

[Discusses Shaw's relations with Ellen Terry, his wife, and Mrs. Patrick Campbell.] Shaw's relations with women have never been painful. In his plays two types of women predominate: the self-reliant and proud woman, such as Candida or Lady Cicely Waynefleet, and the forward, passionate, and quick-tempered woman, such as Blanche in Widowers' Houses and Flavia in On the Rocks. [In German.]

1383 Constable & Co. Ltd. "Unsolicited Reviews," TLS, 19 March 1949, p. 185.

A.L.H. sent a hostile review of Sixteen Self Sketches in advance of its publication to "a leading Yorkshire newspaper." This review is not a literary note such as publishers sometimes send concerning new publications but a "mysterious," "unsolicited," and "jauntily impudent" review.

1384 Darlington, W. A. "Shaw's New Play Seen at Festival: 'Buoyant Billions' Entertains Malvern Audience—Ranked Among His Trivial Works," NYT, 14 Aug 1949, p. 58.
Buoyant Billions contains familiar Shaw ideas and the play ranks as one of Shaw's more trivial works. But the audience (Malvern Festival production) was not bored.

1385 DeWitt, William A. "George Bernard Shaw: Most Independent Man on Earth," ILLUSTRATED MINUTE BIOGRAPHIES (NY: Grosset, 1949; rev ed 1953), p. 138.
Shaw's genius alone does not explain his "Olympian position in the English speaking world." His position is explained by the fascination of his personality and by his "caustic, extravagant, utterly outspoken opinions." His three best plays are Saint Joan, Heartbreak House, and Back to Methuselah.

1386 "Dressing the Part," TLS, XLVIII (12 March 1949), 166.
Sixteen Self Sketches shows that Shaw is less sentimental than he is thought to be; he refuses to soften loss, yet is not defeatist. He is charming, chivalrous, and sane.

1387 Dunkel, Wilbur Dwight. "Bernard Shaw's Religious Faith," THEOLOGY TODAY, VI (Oct 1949), 369-76.
Shaw is more Christian than he admits. He clearly admires the precepts and example of Jesus. He portrays clergymen sympathetically (e.g., Morell), and shows concern for the development of human spirit (e.g., in Caesar, in Eliza Doolittle). His Superman reflects Christian ethics, and his heaven is union with God through contemplation. Ferrovius in Androcles and the Lion exemplifies Christian strength through conviction; Lavinia exemplifies faith that transcends knowledge; and the play contrasts followers of Jesus and nominal Christians. Saint Joan shows that Christianity has not yet been tried by society.

1388 Dunkel, Wilbur D[wight]. "The Essence of Shaw's Dramaturgy," COLLEGE ENGLISH, X (March 1949), 307-12. Shaw shows technical skill in handling plot and situation; e.g., the triangle plot in Man and Superman has characters group and regroup as new ideas are introduced. In contrast, Oscar Wilde's drama is filled with forced entrances and exits, and the wit is not integrated into the theme. The Philanderer, Candida, The Devil's Disciple, and The Doctor's Dilemma also rely on triangle plots; in each the woman makes an unexpected choice, thus giving the turn to the plot. Shaw creates Jonsonian humours comedy, with characters based on the four humours. He also turns the well-made play to his own use. [Understands Jonson and Wilde less than Shaw.]

1389 Fergusson, Francis. "The Theatricality of Shaw and Pirandello," PARTISAN REVIEW, XVI (June 1949), 589-603, espec 589-96; rptd in Fergusson, THE IDEA OF A THEATER (Princeton: Princeton UP, 1949, pp. 178-93; rptd Garden City, NY: Doubleday, 1953; NY: Doubleday Anchor, 1955), pp. 190-98. The idea of the theater as something primitive, subtle and direct was realized by Shakespeare and Sophocles and by the DIVINE COMEDY of Dante. It was not realized by Shaw, who was too conscious of his audience and, in the plays written prior to World War I, too willing to use the "machine-made" conventions of the well-made play that he professed to scorn. In the beginning, Shaw based his plays upon the drawing-room conventions used by Oscar Wilde. Major Barbara, for example, may be "read as a typical sentimental parlor comedy for the carriage-trade." It contains no attacks on the values of its audience. Except for Barbara, all characters are unresolved paradoxes, and the play thus is a "parlor-game," acceptable "as a string of jokes which touch nothing." After World War I, however, Shaw came closer to "the integrity and objectivity of art." Influenced by Chekhov, in Heartbreak House Shaw established a reality outside the play against which the characters in the play can be measured. In this play, Shaw came closest to realizing the "Shavian farcical inspiration" by creating the unreal characters appropriate to farce, although this play, too, is flawed, both by the character of Ellie and by the tendency of the playwright to lecture. Audrey, the burglar-preacher, ends Too True To Be Good by dismissing

309

the other characters of the play as fantastic, unreal, and perverse. He might be describing all of Shaw's characters.

1390 Fleming, Peter. "The Theatre," SPECTATOR, CLXXXIII (14 Oct 1949), 498.
Buoyant Billions is a piece of "dramatic doodling," plotless, purposeless, dull.

1391 "G. B. S.," TAM, XXXIII (Aug 1949), 11.
Shaw will probably celebrate his ninety-third birthday at Ayot St. Lawrence, chatting with neighbors, walking down the country lanes, reading and listening to music. [Brief item follows "Shaw's Rules for Directors," pp. 6-11; Margaret Webster comments that in it Shaw is "his usual self--...sound, healthy, common sensible and...humane... also dogmatic, egotistical and arbitrary."]

1392 Gassner, John. "The Bookshelf," TAM, XXXIII (June 1949), 9, 99-100.
The best of Sixteen Self Sketches are Shaw's comments on himself—"his penchant for anticlimax," the importance of music in his life, his rejection of "the notion that he was frivolous," "his insistence on antipathy to aestheticism." He "made the cake of modern comedy rise by mixing the yeast of economics into the batter." He is a Creative Evolutionist rather than a rationalist or materialist; and he thanks the Fabian Society for knocking "much nonsense, ignorance, and vulgar provinciality out of his system."

1393 Hood, Samuel Stevens (ed). ARCHIBALD HENDERSON: THE NEW CRICHTON (NY: Beechhurst P, 1949).
[A collection of essays in tribute to Henderson, Shaw's authorized biographer. Section on "Literature" contains praise by various writers of Henderson's GEORGE BERNARD SHAW: HIS LIFE AND WORKS (1911) and BERNARD SHAW: PLAYBOY AND PROPHET (1932). Bibliography of Henderson's works on Shaw, pp. 221-29.]

1394 "In Passing: Shaw at 93," NEWSWEEK, XXXIV (8 Aug 1949), 34.
Shaw spent his ninety-third birthday at Ayot St. Lawrence entertaining his friend, Sir Robert Hotung. The next day Shaw lashed out at the Labor government.

1395 Irvine, William. THE UNIVERSE OF G. B. S. (NY, Lond, & Toronto: Whittlesey House [a division of McGraw-Hill], 1949; rptd NY: Russel & Russel, 1968).
Like G. K. Chesterton, Shaw reacted against the "decadent aestheticism" of the 1890's, but was influenced by its idiom (the wit and rhetoric) and its "many-sided romanticism." Shaw combined common sense and virtue with his esthetics; his truth is "forensic and dramatic." The central conflict in his plays is between "realistic vitalism and dead, unreal convention." All the plays are variations on two basic themes: "an individual convicts himself of robbing society," or "society is convicted of martyring an individual." During the years, Shaw's political opinions have vacillated; they are "a long satirical dialectic between political events and a somewhat refractory yet deeply serious critical intelligence." [A political and historical approach to Shaw's life and works. Includes discussion of Shaw's early years; the rise and decline of Fabian socialism; World War I and its aftermath; Shaw's love affairs and his marriage; his old age as a "British institution." Comments on all the plays in a biographical-historical context. Primary and secondary bibliography, pp. 417-25. Incorporates the following (q.v.): "Bernard Shaw's Early Novels," TROLLOPIAN, II (June 1947), 27-42; "Shaw, the Fabians, and the Utilitarians," JOURNAL OF THE HISTORY OF IDEAS, VIII (April 1947), 218-31; "George Bernard Shaw and Karl Marx," JOURNAL OF ECONOMIC HISTORY, VI (May 1946), 53-72; "G. B. Shaw's Musical Criticism," MUSICAL QUARTERLY, XXXII (July 1946), 319-32; "Shaw's The Quintessence of Ibsenism," SOUTH ATLANTIC QUARTERLY, XLVI (April 1947), 252-62; "Man and Superman, a Step in Shavian Disillusionment," HUNTINGTON LIBRARY QUARTERLY, X (Feb 1947), 209-24; "Shaw, War and Peace, 1894 to 1919," FOREIGN AFFAIRS, XXV (Jan 1947), 314-27; "Shaw and Chesterton," VIRGINIA QUARTERLY REVIEW, XXIII (April 1947), 273-81.]

1396 Joad, C[yril] E[dwin] M[itchinson]. SHAW (Victor Gollancz, 1949; rptd Norwood, Pa.: Norwood Editions, 1976).
Shaw had a liberating effect on early twentieth-century youth, releasing them from romantic notions about women, war, Empire, wealth, labor, poverty, funerals, families, and revenge. Essentially a rationalist, Shaw believes that

truth is "something clear, close, definite, and stateable"; therefore, he cannot relay mystical insight or write poetry. His style has an effect of "imperturbability and drive"; his wit relies on "ready repartee" and "quick and surprising argument." Both derive from logic and thought. Though Shaw is more interested in ideas than in plays, his characters are recognizable human beings, in plays that have plenty of action; in fact, the dramatic presentation sometimes obscures Shaw's message. But Shaw's late plays reflect an indifference to dramatic form. [Includes personal encounters with Shaw, an analysis of Shaw's politics, and a character analysis. Chap VII, "Shaw's Philosophy," appeared originally in G. B. S. 90, pp. 57-76. The analysis of Shaw's style is taken, without acknowledgment, and at times verbatim, from Dixon Scott, "The Innocence of Bernard Shaw," MEN OF LETTERS (Lond & NY: Hodder & Stoughton, 1916; first pub BOOKMAN [Lond], 1913). "An Imaginary Dialogue," with Shaw's reply, pp. 135-44, originally appeared in NS&Nation, XXVI (3 July 1943), 6-7.]

1397 Jones, Margo, Joshua Logan, Lee Strasberg, George Abbott, Alfred De Liagre, Jr., Margaret Webster, Herman Shumlin. "In Reply to Mr. Shaw...," TAM, XXXIII (Sept 1949), 8-9.
[Seven noted American directors reply to "Shaw's Rules for Directors," TAM, XXXIII (Aug 1949), 6-11. Each finds areas of agreement/disagreement. Consensus on the need for more flexibility in directing methods.]

1398 Jones, W. S. Handley. "One of Our Conquerors," LONDON QUARTERLY AND HOLBORN REVIEW, Jan 1949, pp. 10-19, and April 1949, pp. 136-45; rptd in THE PRIEST AND THE SIREN AND OTHER LITERARY STUDIES (Lond: Epworth P, 1953), pp. 44-60.
Shaw was the spokesperson for the change from romance to fact, from sensibility to sense, attributing cool judgment and "unflinching realism" to the Irish mind. Arms and the Man was prompted by Shaw's reaction to Gladstone's sentimental defense in the late 1870's of Bulgaria against the Turks. Shaw became a showman in order to call attention to his message. [Account of his years as music critic, as drama critic and Ibsen prophet, as Fabian, as married man.] He combines caution with verbal violence, and "is the most didactic artist that ever lived," with a "passion for

explaining himself." His "well-meaning" characters have an authoritarian temper. He combines politics and religion, rejecting Christian ethics, democracy, and l'art pour l'art. Because his accepts "the responsibilities of genius," he demands of himself both style and craft. He is "a double-minded man," combining intuition and reason, mysticism and theology. He is an evangelist for (not the creator of) his Life Force religion, influenced by Butler and Shelley. Above all, he has faith in life.

1399 Kosh, E. "Novi komad B. Shoa Bojantovi Bilioni" (Shaw's New Comedy Buoyant Billions), KNJIZEVNOST (Belgrade), IX (1949), 517-18.
Buoyant Billions is an unpretentious farce which cannot of course be compared to Saint Joan, nor can we expect it to be comparable. [In Serbian.]

1400 Krutch, Joseph Wood. "G. B. Shaw: At 92, a Puzzle Still Unsolved," NYHTBR, XXV (27 March 1949), 1-2.
Both Sixteen Self Sketches and DAYS WITH BERNARD SHAW, by Stephen Winsten, show Shaw the man of "dazzling gifts," writing "in language the most perspicuous since Jonathan Swift." But neither really explains Shaw, who remains an enigma. Taking ideas from many nineteenth-century writers, he is self-contradictory. He is primarily a dramatist, asking—not answering—questions and making people aware of the interaction of ideas.

1401 Laing, Allan M. (ed). IN PRAISE OF BERNARD SHAW: AN ANTHOLOGY FOR OLD AND YOUNG (Lond: Frederick Muller, 1949; rptd Folcroft, Pa.: Folcroft Library Editions, 1974).
[Brief tributes by various authors, excerpts from various works on Shaw, Shaw on himself, photographs—all reflecting Shaw's life and personality. Includes Max Beerbohm, "A Testimonial," from the firm where Shaw had his first job, William Rothenstein, Henry Arthur Jones, Ivor Brown, Robert Louis Stevenson, Doris Arthur Jones, J. B. Priestley, Frank Swinnerton, Arnold Bennett, item from THE RADIO TIMES, J. L. Garvin, Sybil Thorndike, Winston S. Churchill, item from "Profile" in THE OBSERVER (1946), Mrs. Patrick Campbell, Gordon Craig, William Archer, Cecil Chesterton, C. E. M. Joad, James Agate, A. E., a Welsh miner, R. B. (in

THE OBSERVER), Hesketh Pearson, Gilbert Murray, Kingsley Martin, A. M. L. (in THE OBSERVER), John Drinkwater, Rutland Boughton, Charles Graves, Albert Einstein, B. Ifor Evans, Martin Armstrong, Compton Mackenzie, St. John Ervine, Maurice Dobb, H. J. Tomlinson, Denis Saurat, W. R. Anderson, G. K. Chesterton, Anatole France, John Masefield, item from TLS (1946), Stanley J. Sharpless, Karel Capek, Denis Johnston, Lord Baldwin, Hilaire Belloc, Christopher St. John.]

> **1402** Limentani, Uberto. "Mazzini's and G. B. Shaw's Ideas on the Function of Art," ITALIAN STUDIES, IV (1949), 57-65.

Shaw's theory of the educational mission of art and of the artist as prophet echoes Mazzini's literary theory. Both conceive of art as having a religious, missionary purpose; both consider the artist the conscience of humanity, interpreting events and making them coherent. Mazzini considers historic drama the ideal literary form for this purpose. Saint Joan puts into practice Mazzini's demand that literature should present religious principles found in religious events. But Shaw lacks Mazzini's fanatic insistence on the subordination of art to a sense of mission: his Joan is a living, breathing character. Shaw never loses sight of the esthetic factor. And he sees art as rising from a new religion, whereas Mazzini sees a revitalized religion brought about by the artist.

> **1403** Loewenstein, F[ritz] E[rwin]. "Bernard Shaw, Music Critic," HINRICHSEN'S MUSICAL YEARBOOK, VI (1949), 147-52.

[An account of Shaw's career as a music critic, followed by a resume of Shaw's opinion of major composers. Stresses the influence of Vandaleur Lee.]

> **1404** Lyons, Hilary H. "Books: The Irish are at their most winning best when writing short stories; far surpassing English and Americans," HOLIDAY, VI (Aug 1949), 22, 24-25, espec 22.

Unlike other important early-century Irish writers, Shaw did not find his inspiration in nationalism, though he is proud of being Irish. No one in Ireland today is as influential as "the Four Masters"—Joyce, Yeats, O'Casey, and Shaw. The latter two, however, are past their prime.

1405 M., A. P. "Mr. Shaw," MANCHESTER GUARDIAN, 15 March 1949, p. 3.

Sixteen Self Sketches, in Shaw's "nervous and impatient prose," lets one glimpse a person who is "more of a phenomenon than a man"—almost all intellect.

1406 M., H. G. "'The Apple Cart': 'Mrs. Warren's Profession,'" THEATRE WORLD (Lond), XLV (Aug 1949), 6-8.

The Apple Cart "is not drama, but it is great fun." Its prophecies have mostly been fulfilled. Mrs. Warren's Profession is one of Shaw's best plays, but Vivie Warren never comes to life. She speaks common sense, while Mrs. Warren "stands for romance"; the two manage "to stir the heart" at the end of Act II in the Bedford Theater (Lond) performance.

1407 M., H. G. "'Pygmalion': 'Candida': 'The Inca of Perusalem': 'Arms & the Man': 'Major Barbara,'" THEATRE WORLD (Lond), XLV (July 1949), 8-10.

The Bedford Theater (Lond) has replaced Shakespeare with Shaw. The performance of Pygmalion made even the fifth act, "which often seems long, tedious and unnecessary," interesting. The Inca of Perusalem, a "shapeless playlet," is no longer topical—and was never well-received. Candida was "breath-taking," though "it is next to impossible to make Marchbanks human." Only Raina's make-believe turned "to matter of fact reality" and Bluntschli's realism saved Arms and the Man. Major Barbara is old-fashioned, but its discussion of human goodness never ages. To call poverty a crime "still seems an over-statement." Barbara's loss of innocence is touching, though the reason for her final conversion in the armaments factory is "a mystery."

1408 M., H. G. "'Widowers' Houses,'" THEATRE WORLD (Lond), XLV (March 1949), 10.

In spite of its documentary nature, Widowers' Houses has more human characters than in other Shaw. Lickcheese and Cokane are two of his best creations. The Arts Theater (Lond) revival "was straightforward, tending to over-simplification."

1409 "Malvern Festival: 'Buoyant Billions,'" TIMES (Lond), 15 Aug 1949, p. 7; rptd in CRITICAL HERITAGE, pp. 377-78, Item 126.

Buoyant Billions (Malvern Festival production) is only a postscript to Shavian drama, yet it has "intellectual gaiety" and vibrant dialog. Particularly rewarding are the discussion of eternal values by a jungle native, the passionate defense of world bettering, and the hint of a woman in love in "the odd Shavian female."

1410 Marshall, Margaret. "Drama," NATION, CLXIX (31 Dec 1949), 650-51.

Caesar and Cleopatra (National Theater, NY) is exuberant comedy deriving its depth from the portrait of Caesar and, to a lesser degree, Apollodorus.

1411 Martin, Kingsley. "Self-Illuminations by G.B.S.—and a Reverent Chronicle," NYTBR, 27 March 1949, p. 3.

Sixteen Self Sketches tells little that is not already known about Shaw. The book is worthwhile to newcomers to Shaw, because it gathers together facts about his life. Interestingly enough, he modestly asserts that he never claimed to be a greater dramatist than Shakespeare.

1412 Martin, Kingsley. "Shaw's Persona," NS&Nation, ns XXXVII (26 March 1949), 304.

Sixteen Self Sketches does not reveal much new about Shaw, nor does it show much of the inner Shaw, who always pays "conscious and artistic attention to the persona." Winsten's DAYS WITH BERNARD SHAW gives a glimpse of private Shaw, and has superb photographs.

1413 Matthews, Harold. "Malvern in 1949," THEATRE WORLD (Lond), XLV (Sept 1949), 11-12, 29, 34, 38-39, espec 11-12, 29.

Buoyant Billions is in Shaw's "Malvern period" style: it is a conversation piece. It has no story and no theme, but the characters and talk are good. Shakes versus Shav (Lanchester Marionette Theater, Malvern) has "dolls of striking personality." It opens a wonderful vista for puppetry, with public figures in a marionette play.

1414 Muller, H. J. "It Still Isn't a Science: A Reply to George Bernard Shaw," SRL, XXXII (16 April 1949), 11-12, 61.

Shaw's defense of the genetics of Lysenko is "outside the range of science." Whereas Darwinian natural selection undermined mysticism, Shaw and the Lysenkoists are turning back the clock, attacking the irrevocable laws of nature as "fatalism." Humanists should learn to embrace scientific thought.

1415 Nathan, George Jean. "Caesar and Cleopatra. December 20, 1949," THE THEATRE BOOK OF THE YEAR, 1949-1950 (NY: Knopf, 1950), pp. 130-42.

Caesar and Cleopatra (National Theater, NY) electrifies the stage with its style, wit, intellect, and satirical spirit. But Caesar's "rococo and defeatist attitude" toward aging dates the play. Unlike current drama, its emotion derives from its intellect. Shaw's plays succeed because of the element of the novel and unexpected.

1416 Nethercot, Arthur H. "The Truth About Candida," PMLA, LXIV (Sept 1949), 639-47.

In Candida Marchbanks represents the realist; Morell, the idealist; and Candida, the Philistine—as defined in The Quintessence of Ibsenism. Candida is mother-woman as well. Only Prossy sees her clearly, while the men do not.

1417 Nicoll, Allardyce. "Purposeful Laughter: George Bernard Shaw," chap v in WORLD DRAMA, FROM AESCHYLUS TO ANOUILH (Lond: George G. Harrap, 1949), pp. 741-53.

Of all living authors, Shaw is the greatest social thinker. His characters embody intellectual concepts; his scenes are often debates, varied by the "clowneries" introduced in them; and his plays are "dances of thoughts." The atmosphere of his plays is distinct from past theater: in them "the mask is the character." He uses melodrama, opera, and extravaganza as models, but they are not recognizable once Shaw adds his characteristic verbal brilliance. Saint Joan, his best play, is more subtle and deep than his earlier work. His later plays have inconclusive themes, structural weaknesses, and characters lacking human warmth.

1418 Pacheco Vélez, César. "Notas de teatro: Cándida" (Theater Notes: <u>Candida</u>), MERCURIO PERUANO (Peru), XXIV, No 269 (Aug 1949), 351.
Shaw satirizes English conventions and attacks Pharisaism. Though he makes use of the theater for social propaganda, his characters never become ridiculous nor grotesque caricatures. They are always elaborated, intellectual, complex, and keen. The performance by the Compañía Nacional de Comedias failed to understand <u>Candida</u>, producing a play irregular in its development, and absurd in some situations. [In Spanish.]

1419 Pearson, Hesketh. "GBS by Propagandist and Dreamer," SRL, XXXII (2 April 1949), 19-20.
<u>Sixteen Self Sketches</u> is the work of a propagandist. It is repetitive, providing material for a psychoanalyst but not for a biographer. Shaw omits the anecdotes, gossip, and details that make a good biography; he insists that his philosophic life did not lend itself to the biographical art. Winsten's DAYS WITH BERNARD SHAW does not present the true Shaw, either.

1420 Pearson, Hesketh. "Memories of 'G. B. S.' and Granville Barker," List, XLI (24 Feb 1949), 324-25.
[Anecdotal account of the first production of <u>Androcles and the Lion</u> (1913, Granville Barker).] <u>Androcles</u> is Shaw's best comedy.

1421 "People: Young in Heart," TIME, LIV (22 Aug 1949), 28.
<u>Buoyant Billions</u>, according to critics at the Malvern Festival, has no plot and no point. It repeats ideas from earlier Shaw; yet it is never dull.

1422 Perry, Henry Ten Eyck. "Shaw: Pure and Adulterated," YALE REVIEW, XXXVIII (June 1949), 749-51.
The effect of Winsten's DAYS WITH BERNARD SHAW is desultory—not so <u>Sixteen Self Sketches</u>. Shaw is both an intellectual of "studied eccentricity" and a warm-hearted, perceptive man. Therefore some of his characters are rigid, whereas others are imaginative triumphs.

1423 "Plays and Pictures: Widowers' Houses, at the Arts," NS&Nation, XXXVII (12 Feb 1949), 153.
Widowers' Houses (Arts Theater, Lond) has dialog that "crackles," but Shaw is unable to focus on "one brand of irritant." Instead, he pricks the audience in a hundred places.

1424 "Princes Theatre: 'Buoyant Billions,'" TIMES (Lond), 11 Oct 1949, p. 8.
Buoyant Billions rearranges old Shavian ideas in a brief, entertaining, intellectual, discursive play. [Continuation of the Malvern Festival production.]

1425 Ray, Cyril. "Shaw on Himself," SPECTATOR, CLXXXII (18 March 1949), 368.
Sixteen Self Sketches and Shaw's prefaces constitute an autobiography. Neither his life nor his prose is dull. The witty fragments in Sixteen Self Sketches omit reference to Shaw's philandering and his marriage—indeed, "they omit emotions."

1426 Reynolds, Ernest. MODERN ENGLISH DRAMA: A SURVEY OF THE THEATRE FROM 1900 (Lond: Harrap, 1949; rptd Norman: U of Oklahoma P, 1951), pp. 16, 19-21, 27, 32, 33, 37, 44, 48, 49, 51, 52, 57, 58, 71, 73, 81n, 116, 123-33, 136-38, 143-47, 150, 152, 157, 161, 162, 164, 165, 170, 178, 182, espec 123-33; Index.
Shaw dominates English drama of the twentieth century. He brought questions of social reform into a literature historically resistant to them; he was "the Prince" who awakened "the Sleeping Princess" of English theater. His style is operatic, not poetic. Back to Methuselah, perhaps his major work, has a cosmic philosophic sweep—but is dull as drama. Saint Joan is Shaw's greatest character. His other works stress "the gospel of Socialism." His greatest qualities are "an ability to make people think by making them laugh," a view of life that encompasses all areas of knowledge, strong social satire, a keen sense of theatrical effect, and an "indifference to conventional dramatic construction."

1427 Robinson, Kenneth J. "The Theatre," SPECTATOR, CLXXXIII (26 Aug 1949), 264.

In <u>Buoyant Billions</u> (Malvern Festival), Junius gives one more of Shaw than any other character in the play, though each utters at least one Shavian maxim. Shaw seems less dogmatic about the Life Force; he may feel it futile to try to teach a religion without rites and legend.

1428 Rolo, Charles J. "On being a genius," ATLANTIC MONTHLY, CLXXXIII (May 1949), 87-89.
<u>Sixteen Self Sketches</u> reveals the influences that made Shaw "seem paradox personified." The "driving impulse . . . has been profoundly conventional." Winsten's DAYS WITH BERNARD SHAW shows Shaw as garrulous, vain, egotistical, and at times silly. Both works reinforce Edmund Wilson's view that Shaw is a considerable artist but his ideas are confused and uncertain.

1429 Ross, Julian L. PHILOSOPHY IN LITERATURE (Syracuse: Syracuse UP, 1949), pp. 124-26, 207-9, Index.
In the Preface to <u>Androcles and the Lion</u>, Shaw wisely contends that civilization cannot endure without Christian ethics, i.e., equal regard for every human soul, and a repudiation of vicarious redemption. Shaw is a "strenuous" optimist, rejecting indolence and purposelessness (e.g., in <u>Heartbreak House</u>) and advocating conscious evolution toward an eternal (also evolving) goal (e.g., in <u>Man and Superman</u> and <u>Back to Methuselah</u>).

1430 S., J. P. "The Theatre: Shavian Prank Presented," NYT, 7 April 1949, p. 38.
<u>The Millionairess</u> is only "a shallow Shavian prank" producing "uneasy ennui" and not deserving revival (Dramatic Workshop of the New School, President Theater, NY).

1431 "Shakes vs. Shav—The Bout of the Centuries," NYTMag, 4 Sept 1949, pp. 14-15, 33.
The Malvern Festival presented a puppet show, <u>Shakes vs. Shav</u>. In the play Shaw, of course, has the best lines as well as the last word.

1432 Spender, Stephen. "Books and the Arts: The Riddle of Shaw," NATION, CLXVIII (30 April 1949), 503-10, espec 503-5; rptd in Louis Kronenberger (ed),

GEORGE BERNARD SHAW: A CRITICAL SURVEY (Cleveland & NY: World, 1953), pp. 236-39.
Sixteen Self Sketches and Winsten's DAYS WITH BERNARD SHAW seem to be "frozen left-overs." Both Shaw and his plays are two-dimensional. "His art is the direction of dialogue from the outside, not the creating of character from within." At the center of his work is good sense, not feeling or joy; his best is "serious laughter."

1433 "Totschläger Petrus" (The Murderer Saint Peter), EVANGELISCHE WELT. INFORMATIONSBLATT FÜR DIE EVANGELISCHE KIRCHE IN DEUTSCHLAND (Bethel), III (1949), 16.
[Comments on an interview which Shaw gave to the DAILY WORKER.] Shaw could not draw a parallel between Christ and Marx, for there is an essential difference between communist and Christian views of the world. [In German.]

1434 Trewin, J. C. "The World of the Theatre: Good King Bernard," ILN, CCXV (27 Aug 1949), 320.
Buoyant Billions is formless, but it has "verbal knockabout" and "buoyancy." It has no new ideas, yet some of Shaw's wisdom, and it is the best thing at the Malvern Festival.

1435 Trewin, J. C. "The World of the Theatre: Period Pieces," ILN, CCXIV (26 Feb 1949), 280.
The Arts Theater (Lond) production of Widowers' Houses gets "a salute." "The young Mr. Shaw of 1892 was quite a dramatist," showing Lickcheese transformed "from a crushed worm to tiger burning bright."

1436 West, E. J. "Barry Sullivan: Shavian and Actual," ETJ, I (Dec 1949), 140-58.
Shaw's estimate of Barry Sullivan in "Sullivan, Shakespeare, and Shaw" (1948) is impressionistic, garrulous, and rambling. [A history of Shaw's criticism of the actor and of Sullivan's acting career.]

1437 West, E. J. "Days with Bernard Shaw. By S. Winsten." and "Sixteen Self Sketches. By Bernard Shaw," QUARTERLY JOURNAL OF SPEECH, XXXV (Oct 1949), 372-75.

Winsten's DAYS WITH BERNARD SHAW makes Shaw appear anecdotal and garrulous in his old age, and suffers from its author's ego and lack of structure. On the other hand, Sixteen Self Sketches is "invaluable." Shaw brings knowledge and a fine analytical sense to his criticism, platform speaking, and drama. His revision of "The Art of Rehearsal" (rptd as "Shaw's Rules for Directors") should be required reading for directors.

> **1438** Williams, Harcourt. OLD VIC SAGA (Lond: Winchester Publications, 1949), pp. 20, 25, 51, 54, 56, 66-67, 76, 88-89, 100-101, 120-21, 124, 136-37, 147-48, 162, 165, 169, 172, 186, 194, 214, Index.

[References to productions of Shaw plays at the Old Vic (Lond). Appendices list "Old Vic Plays and Their Producers," 1914-1949, and Old Vic players.]

> **1439** Winsten, S[tephen]. "A Conversation Piece," WORLD REVIEW, ns V (July 1949), 21-22.

[Account of Shaw's meeting Danny Kaye at Winsten's place. The actor and Shaw chatted about modern music halls, holding an audience, etc.]

> **1440** Winsten, S[tephen]. "George Bernard Shaw in the Village," THE SATURDAY BOOK, ed by Leonard Russell (Lond: Hutchinson, 1949), pp. 257-63.

[A description of Ayot St. Lawrence and Shaw's working habits, with an imaginary visit of Shakespeare to Shaw.] Shaw has created a persona of depth and imagination for the public.

> **1441** Winsten, Stephen. "Introduction," THE QUINTESSENCE OF G.B.S.: THE WIT AND WISDOM OF BERNARD SHAW, ed by Stephen Winsten (NY: Creative Age P, 1949; rptd NY: Collier Books, 1962), pp. vii-xiii.

Shaw's early convictions have not changed through the years. He "was a centipede with a foot in every cause" who "proved that truth is funnier than comedy." Essentially an optimist, his laughter is based in thought and expressed in art.

> **1442** Winsten, Stephen and Esmé Percy. "A Play of the Month: Comments on George Bernard Shaw's new play

'Buoyant Billions,'" WORLD REVIEW, ns No 7 (Sept 1949), 17-22.
[Includes "The Author Explains," pp. 17-18; Winsten, "How 'Buoyant Billions' Was Written," pp. 19-21; and Percy, "How 'Buoyant Billions' Was Produced," p. 22. "The Author Explains" is a series of questions about the play, answered by Shaw in his own handwriting.] Winsten: No one has replaced Shaw as dramatist. "His creative power has not waned." Buoyant Billions adds something new to the Shaw canon: a sense of peace. But Shaw should not focus his "worldbettering" on mathematical perfection, Eastern mysticism, or animal magnetism. Percy: In Buoyant Billions the ideas "are the real dramatis personae"; therefore the director has to concentrate on the delivery of the speeches rather than on stage business. The effect is music.

1443 Winstone, Reece. "GBS 'At Home,'" CHRISTIAN SCIENCE MONITOR MAGAZINE, 8 Oct 1949, pp. 8-9.
[A brief description of Ayot St. Lawrence and a pictorial essay of the village and Shaw.]

1444 Worsley, T[homas] C[uthbert]. "The Arts and Entertainment: G. B. S. and Cymbeline," NS&Nation, XXXVIII (2 July 1949), 11.
In Our Theatres in the Nineties Shaw takes the theater seriously, and has absolute sureness about the direction it should take. His comments on Shakespeare's CYMBELINE attack Bardolatry and display his gift for penetrating analysis. The current production of CYMBELINE (in the Stratford repertoire) bears out Shaw's objections to the play.

1445 Worsley, T[homas] C[uthbert]. "The Arts and Entertainment: The New Show," NS&Nation, XXXVIII (20 Aug 1949), 193.
Shaw's latest play is "very far from senile." Buoyant Billions provides a "fresh, light, even rather gay-hearted, evening in the Shaw late manner." It seems to "ramble around the contemporary scene"; yet it is not so "utterly erratic" as it may appear.

1446 Wyart, E. V. R. "16 Self Sketches. Bernard Shaw. Dodd Mead. $3.50," COMMONWEAL, L (13 May 1949), 130-32.

<u>Sixteen Self Sketches</u> has "a pleasing 18th century directness." Shaw seems mostly interested in himself as a speaker; this may explain the long speeches weighing down his drama.

1447 Z., B. "Djavolov učenik" (<u>The Devil's Disciple</u>)," IZVOR (Zagreb), II (1949), 832-35.
After reading Marx's KAPITAL, Shaw became a fervent student of Marxism and political economy, and greeted the Oct 1917 Revolution with sympathy. The recent (1949) production of <u>The Devil's Disciple</u> in Zagreb was well received. [In Croatian.]

1950

1448 "A Comedy of No Manners," TLS, 16 June 1950, p. 370.
<u>Buoyant Billions</u> is lively, argumentative, and assertive. The debates in Acts III and IV repeat former ideas of Shaw; however, the play holds the theater. Shaw can still write better plays than many contemporary West End dramatists.

1449 "Adiós a G. B. S." (Good-bye to G. B. S.), DESTINO (Spain), No 692 (11 Nov 1950), 9.
Shaw's humor and witticisms were endless. [Includes some of Shaw's observations on America, autobiographies, love, posterity, success, politics, war and peace, the English, and his wife.] [In Spanish.]

1450 a'Green, George. "A Roadfarer's Log-Book," CTC [Cyclists' Touring Club) GAZETTE (Dec 1950).
Shaw was a member of the CTC from 1895 to his death. [Résumé of his comments to the Club in 1898 on the tone the GAZETTE should adopt, and reference to a 1947 letter for publication.]

1451 Alford, Walter. "G. B. S. Corner on Broadway," CHRISTIAN SCIENCE MONITOR MAGAZINE, 4 March 1950, pp. 5, 17.
<u>Caesar and Cleopatra</u> (National Theater, NY) and <u>The Devil's Disciple</u> (Royal Theater, NY) have parallel stage histories:

written only two years apart for popular players, both
premiered in the United States, then were not revived for a
quarter of a century. [Brief stage history shows Shaw's
keen interest in staging and in money.]

1452 Anderson Imbert, Enrique. "Un autógrafo de
Bernard Shaw" (Bernard Shaw's Autograph), SUR, No 193
(Oct Dec 1950), 282-84.
[Recollections of Anderson Imbert, an Argentine socialist
who tried to establish a Shavian society in Argentina and
attempted through reviews of Shaw's plays to arouse the
interest of the public in Shaw's message.] [In Spanish.]

1453 "Arts Theatre: 'Heartbreak House,'" TIMES
(Lond), 6 July 1950, p. 8.
In Heartbreak House Shaw's inner artistic self appears to
give the play a "strong, haunting appeal" in spite of the
dull and somewhat incoherent parade of ideas.

1454 "Arts Theatre: 'Mrs. Warren's Profession,'"
TIMES (Lond), 26 Jan 1950, p. 7.
Mrs. Warren's Profession is excellent comedy, though Vivie
is somewhat unbelievable. The Arts Theater (Lond) revival
is handsome.

1455 Atkinson, Brooks. "About the Play," TAM, XXXIV
(Sept 1950), 52.
Caesar and Cleopatra [rptd pp. 53-88] is a human portrait
rather than an analysis of a ruler. Shaw's hero-worship of
Caesar is narcissistic, since there is much of Shaw in the
portrait. [Includes with text of play photos of the
National Theater (NY) production, 1949.]

1456 Atkinson, Brooks. "At the Theatre," NYT, 26 Oct
1950, p. 39.
Mrs. Warren's Profession, influenced by both Ibsen and
Pinero, combines melodrama and Marxism. The Bleeker Street
Playhouse (Theater Venture, NY) production is uneven, but
Mrs. Warren and Vivie are played with force and character.

1457 Atkinson, Brooks. "At the Theatre: Shaw's 'Arms
and the Man' Acted With Francis Lederer and Sam
Wanamaker," NYT, 20 Oct 1950, p. 34.

It is too bad that the entire performance does not come up to the animated acting of Petkoff (Lederer) and Sergius (Wanamaker) in the Arena Theater (NY) production of Arms and the Man.

1458 Atkinson, Brooks. "First Night at the Theatre," NYT, 26 Jan 1950, p. 23.
The Devil's Disciple uses "flamboyant theatricals"; the trappings of romance lead to the hilarious trial scene, "a comic masterpiece." [Praise for the NYC Theater Company revival, City Center, NY. Another review of the same production by Atkinson, "He's Here Again: Shaw Is Represented at the City Center By 'The Devil's Disciple,'" NYT, 5 Feb 1950, II, p. 1.]

1459 Atkinson, Brooks. "First Night at the Theatre: City Center Opens Its Winter Theatre Series With One of Shaw's Early Plays," NYT, 28 Dec 1950, p. 21; rptd in ON STAGE: SELECTED THEATER REVIEWS FROM THE NEW YORK TIMES 1920-1970, ed by Bernard Beckerman and Howard Siegman (NY: Arno P, 1973), pp. 324-26.
Like The Devil's Disciple, Captain Brassbound's Conversion begins with tedious exposition, "gathers lightness, satire and drollery," and ends hilariously. Though a minor Shaw play, it has intelligence, a dry style, and gentle satire. [Appreciative of the NYC Theater Company production, City Center, NY.]

1460 Atkinson, Brooks. "Shaw in Fine Fettle: 'Caesar and Cleopatra' Is the Keenest Drama of the Season," NYT, 8 Jan 1950, II, p. 1.
Shaw treats Caesar and Cleopatra as people. "Caesar is Shaw's masterpiece"jaunty and quick-witted but also analytical and kind. [High praise for Lilli Palmer's Cleopatra, less for Cedric Hardwicke's Caesar (National Theater, NY).]

1461 Bacon, Josephine Daskam. "G. B. S. 1856-1950," NYHT, 10 Nov 1950; rptd in ShawB, I (May 1952), 16.
[Bad poem; tribute to Shaw.]

1462 Baker, A. E. "Christianity and Bernard Shaw," CHURCH TIMES (Lond), CXXXIII (10 Nov 1950), 826.

Shaw "had a philosophy of life rather than a religion." His concept of God, derived principally from Samuel Butler, is of an immanent force (like the Third Person in the Trinity); he was not Christian, but admired Jesus's teaching. Shaw knew little about the Bible or the Book of Common Prayer, and, like H. G. Wells, had a crude notion of Atonement.

1463 "Bernard Shaw," HOY (Mexico), No 716 (11 Nov 1950), 54.
A great dramatist, novelist, poet and humorist, Shaw left a tremendous legend and thousands of anecdotes. [Photo of Shaw.] [In Spanish.]

1464 "Bernard Shaw," SEMANARIO PERUANO, IV, No 45 (6 Nov 1950), 14-15.
Shaw's humor has not ceased even with his death, since he chose to die on the day Truman was attacked, and on the same day the King of Sweden died, thus upstaging in the news both Truman and the King. [In Spanish.]

1465 "Bernard Shaw," TIMES (Lond), 3 Nov 1950, p. 5; rptd in CRITICAL HERITAGE, pp. 383-85, Item 129.
Shaw will be remembered more as artist than as preacher. Intensely histrionic, he invented the outrageous "G.B.S." and a drama of ideas that was vigorous, lucid, and witty. But he did not understand the impulsive side of humanity, so that his characters are not people, but ideas. His genius was for dramatizing the clash of ideas. [Obit—leading article.]

1466 "Bernard Shaw," TLS, 10 Nov 1950, p. 709.
Shaw was an institution, having dominated the literary and public scene for years. He castigated both enemies and friends, and both regarded him with affection. His plays have power and craft; his prefaces and pamphlets make "sociology as fascinating as romance." His prose is precise, unaffected, profound (yet fun); the Preface to Man and Superman is perhaps his best piece of prose. Shaw was self-contradictory, an "insatiable adopter and adapter" of others' ideas. Many of his arguments are outdated; he himself was a brave, brilliant, and incongruous gift from "an era already receding into the legendary and strange."

1467 "Bernard Shaw en Hoy," HOY (Mexico), No 710 (30 Sept 1950), 33.
[A note on some of Shaw's witty remarks concerning government, nutrition, smoking, and cycling.] [In Spanish.]

1468 "Bernard Shaw la figura más original de la moderna literatura inglesa" (Bernard Shaw The Most Original Figure of Modern English Literature), LA NACIÓN (Argentina), 3 Nov 1950; rptd in REVISTA EXCELSIOR (Peru), XVI, No 208 (Nov-Dec 1950), 21-22.
Shaw's originality was in his contributions to drama, criticism, politics, humanism, and humor. [In Spanish.]

1469 "Bernard Shaw's World—And Ours," NEW REPUBLIC, CXXIII (13 Nov 1950), 5.
Before World War I Shaw's challenge to old ideas based on argument and fact appealed to readers; after World War I Shaw ceased to appeal because disillusioned readers doubted that ideas led to progress. However, Shaw deservedly became a "pillar of English culture."

1470 Betancur, Cayatano. "George Bernard Shaw," EL SIGLO (Colombia), 12 Nov 1950, p. 1. [Obit.] [In Spanish.]

1471 Beyer, William. "The State of the Theatre: Actors Take the Honors," SCHOOL AND SOCIETY, LXXI (8 April 1950), 213-17.
Caesar and Cleopatra is a better play than The Devil's Disciple because Shaw uses more of his characteristic "wry wisdom and ascerbic wit." In The Devil's Disciple, Shaw concentrates on mechanical plotting in order to produce a money-making melodramatic potboiler, sacrificing the "lusty character delineation" that shows Caesar as "a man of modern complexities, an urbane humanist." Both plays are best and most lively in the final acts.

1472 Boor, Jan. "Umrel G. B. Shaw" (Death of G. B. Shaw), SLOVENSKÉ POHL'ADY (Martin), LXVI (1950), 783-85.
Shaw is said to have been a socialist, but he was individualistic, disorganized, unorthodox—a Utopian. He visited the Soviet Union in 1931, and his visit caused great indignation among the English bourgeoisie. Shaw was

328

never a consistent Marxist because of his Protestant upbringing and his belief in the Life Force. His prefaces suggest that Shaw was a thinker, rather than a dramatist, though he was master of English speech. [In Slovak.]

1473 Brailsford, H. N. "G. B. S.," NS&Nation, ns XL (11 Nov 1950), 421-22; also in NATION (NY), CLXXI (25 Nov 1950), 476-77.

Shaw perfectly "incarnated his time." His success derived from his sincerity, craftsmanship, and "poetical surprises." Rejecting art for art's sake, he wrote to persuade or to amuse, finding expression for intense emotion in irony and argument. The plays with a social message may date, but his comedies and philosophy (indebted largely to Shelley) will not.

1474 Brenner, Theodor. "When I Met Shaw," WESTERN HUMANITIES REVIEW, IV (Spring 1950), 137-40.

[Reminiscence of an afternoon visit with Shaw in June 1945 at Ayot St. Lawrence.]

1475 Bridie, James. "The Play of Ideas," NS&Nation, ns XXXIX (11 March 1950), 270-71.

Shaw's plays are not tracts, his characters not automata. His plays are well constructed; his characters, if not better than Shakespeare's, are better than Shaw's contemporaries'. Shaw has liberated drama for future experimentation. [Response to Terence Rattigan, "Concerning the Play of Ideas" (1950), q.v.]

1476 Bridie, James. "Shaw as Playwright," NS&Nation, ns XL (11 Nov 1950), 422; rptd in CRITICAL HERITAGE, pp. 389-91, Item 131.

Shaw was not a theatrical innovator: his plays resemble his contemporaries' in style and construction. His contributions to theater were his unconventional ideas. He rediscovered the didactic impulse in drama, understood human nature, had "unflagging eloquence." He avoids stock characters and makes non-erotic subjects exciting. His tragedies leave hope, and his pessimistic plays dissolve in laughter.

1477 Brown, Ivor. "The Future of G. B. S.,"
OBSERVER, 5 Nov 1950, p. 4; also in SATURDAY NIGHT,
21 Nov 1950, p. 42.
Shaw's plays with "narrative value will outlast the
discussion-pieces." Saint Joan, Heartbreak House, and Back
to Methuselah contain enduring poetry. While Shaw's
politics will fade, his prose will remain a model of
lucidity and strength.

1478 Brown, John Mason. "GBS: Headmaster to the
Universe," SRL, XXXIII (18 Nov 1950), 11-13, 31; rptd
as "Professional Man of Genius," in Brown, AS THEY
APPEAR (NY, Toronto & Lond: McGraw-Hill, 1952), pp.
59-70, and Brown, DRAMATIS PERSONAE: A RETROSPECTIVE
SHOW (NY: Viking, 1963), pp. 148-56.
Shaw had an extraordinary, paradoxical, incisive mind. An
egoist, he could be "downright silly"—yet he had grandeur.
"An artist in spite of himself" (though not as good as
Shakespeare), Shaw was a skillful writer with an important
message. His musical training was reflected in his writing.

1479 Brown, John Mason. "Seeing Things: Hail,
Caesar—and Cleopatra," SRL, XXXIII (14 Jan 1950),
26-28; rptd in Brown, STILL SEEING THINGS (NY, Lond,
& Toronto: McGraw-Hill, 1950), pp. 160-66; and in
Brown, DRAMATIS PERSONAE: A RETROSPECTIVE SHOW (NY:
Viking, 1963), pp. 136-40; also as "Caesar and
Cleopatra," in Louis Kronenberger (ed), GEORGE
BERNARD SHAW: A CRITICAL SURVEY (Cleveland & NY:
World, 1953), pp. 247-49.
Shaw deals with grand topics in a serious way. In Caesar
and Cleopatra (National Theater, NY) he portrays Caesar as
a great man and avoids a tawdry, passionate Cleopatra.
Shaw's history plays, viewing the past in contemporary
terms, are witty, impudent, and human.

1480 Brück, Max von. "G. B. S.," GEGENWART (Freiburg
im Breisgau), V, No 22 (1950), 13-15.
[Obituary sketch, including Shaw's impact on the
development of the drama and his philosophy.] Shaw is "an
eclectic who occupies an isolated standpoint but seeks to
build bridges to his fellow men in parody and wit." [In[
German.]

1481 Bryant, Arthur. "Our Notebook," ILN, CCXVII (18 Nov 1950), 806.
Counter to prevailing eulogistic praise, Shaw was not the greatest literary artist of his time. He was a masterful dramatic technician and pamphleteer, but he had no historical sense, and his characters did not live. However, even if he lacked creative capacity, he did have poetic insight, as in the closing scene of Saint Joan.

1482 Bullrich, Silvina. "Comedias desagradables, por Bernard Shaw" (Plays Unpleasant, by Bernard Shaw), ATLÁNTIDA (Argentina), XXXII, No 996 (Feb 1950), 75.
The three Plays Unpleasant are bitter but very realistic studies of social injustice. In content and dramatic technique, Shaw has not been surpassed. [In Spanish.]

1483 Bullrich, Silvina. "Hombre y Superhombre, por Bernard Shaw" (Man and Superman, by Bernard Shaw), ATLÁNTIDA (Argentina), XXXIII, No 1004 (Oct 1950), 92.
Man and Superman is a masterpiece that belongs to all time. Shaw is the only writer who has shocked the world using truth as his only weapon. His analysis of the relationship between men and women is excellent, but he should have also been more specific on the means by which a woman could attract men. [In Spanish.]

1484 "CAESAR AND CLEOPATRA," TAM, XXXIV (March 1950), 8.
Shaw's Caesar is "witty and humane"; the action of Caesar and Cleopatra is a "garnish to a feast of Shavian views," which are "at least heard" in the National Theater (NY) production. [Photograph of production included.]

1485 Cano, José Luis. "Bernard Shaw," INSULA (Spain), No 59 (15 Nov 1950), 8.
Numerous anecdotes about Shaw reveal his genius and humor. Yet the anecdotes, as well as Shaw's phrases and paradoxes, have created a myth and obscured the individual genius of Shaw. [In Spanish.]

1486 Cardus, Neville. "Shaw and Music," HALLE: A MAGAZINE FOR MUSIC LOVERS (Manchester), Dec 1950, pp. 9-12.

Shaw made music criticism comprehensible and entertaining to the ordinary reader. But his musical taste was middle-class, which led him to misunderstand Schubert and to overrate Goetz and Elgar. He also forgot that music is "related to beauty and sensibility."

1487 Carrington, Norman T[homas]. G. BERNARD SHAW: SAINT JOAN (Lond: James Brodie [Notes on Chosen English Texts], n.d. [1950?]).
[A study guide for students, containing a general introduction; a "life of Joan of Arc"; sketches of the plot, theme, and characters; explanatory notes; and study questions. Introduction, "The Author," pp. 5-14, is a cursory review of Shaw's life and work, tending not to take seriously Shaw's opposition to schooling, his politics, his vegetarianism.] Shaw likes to advertise himself as a crank; he is not so versatile as John Galsworthy or John Drinkwater [other authors in this series]. Because his plays are problem plays, they will not endure as long as plays of human character. Shaw appeals to the head, not the heart, and lacks "genial human tolerance."

1488 Catlin, George. "Contra GBS," SRL, XXXIII (30 Dec 1950), 19-20.
John Mason Brown is wrong about Shaw in "GBS: Headmaster to the Universe" (1950). Shaw approved of both Stalin and Mussolini, and in the interest of efficiency and economics became an anti-democratic fascist. [Letter to the editor.]

1489 Cerf, Bennett. "Trade Winds," SRL, XXXIII (30 Sept 1950), 4, 6.
Shaw has been hospitalized after a fall while trimming a tree. His Farfetched Fables, which have opened in private performance (Watergate Theater, Lond) are terrible.

1490 Chassé, Charles. "G. Bernard Shaw, auteur social et satiriste puritain" (G. Bernard Shaw, Social Critic and Puritan Satirist), FRANCE ILLUSTRATION, No 265 (11 Nov 1950), p. 520.
[Obit. Admires the spellbinder and the mountebank in Shaw, and the themes of a few plays.] Shaw refused to sum up his ideas in a few principles. He preached for too many causes and was termed once "a Puritan in cap and bells." [In French.]

1491   Chauviré, Roger. "Bernard Shaw," REVUE DES CEUX
      MONDES, No 23 (1 Dec 1950), 476-84.
Shaw's tone is practical, because he thinks that art has
the purpose of edification and teaching, of pedagogy (like
Voltaire) rather than pleasure (like Molière). The
importance that money has in his thought and work is due to
his humble origins and experience of hardship. He affects
Irish humor and Irish loyalty in order to magnify his non-
conformist image, so that he will be more pleasing to an
English audience. The Irish forgive Shaw for his aberrance,
and the English like him because they do not take him
seriously. Shaw is in fact serious, and his ideas and works
will effect social change. [In French.]

1492   Ciardi, John. "Elegy for G. B. Shaw," NYer,
      XXVI (16 Dec 1950), 110. [Poem.]

1493   Clark, Barrett H. "Broadway Plays Pass in
      Review," DRAMA MAGAZINE (NY), XXI (May 1931), 9-11.
"Shaw is a real playwright only occasionally and, as it
were, by accident." His plays date quickly; some are
"exceedingly dull." The Theater Guild (NY) production of
Getting Married proves this. [Photo on p. 9.]

1494   Clurman, Harold. "Theatre: C. Channing and
      Others," NEW REPUBLIC, CXXII (2 Jan 1950), 21-22.
The Lilli Palmer-Cedric Hardwicke Caesar and Cleopatra
(National Theater, NY) is bad; and the play is "boyish and
very nearly silly."

1495   Clurman, Harold. "Theatre: Change of Mood," NEW
      REPUBLIC, CXXII (27 Feb 1950), 20-21.
The Devil's Disciple is "a trifle dull in its exposition,"
but the courtmartial scene is delightful. Shaw's characters
are theatrical foils, and many of his plays are
"ideological autobiographies."

1496   Clurman, Harold. "Theatre: A Little on Shaw,"
      NEW REPUBLIC, CXXIII (13 Nov 1950), 20-21.
Arms and the Man (Arena Theater, NY) holds the best of
Shavian style, and Mrs. Warren's Profession (Bleecker
Street Playhouse, NY), the best of the Shavian message. An
assessment of the two plays depends on whether one prefers

art or philosophy, and whether or not one agrees with Shaw's philosophy.

1497 Colby, Reginald. "Begegnung mit Miss Patch" (Meeting with Miss Patch), WELTWOCHE (Zürich), XVIII (22 Sept 1950), 11.
[Anecdotal account of details of Shaw's personal routine provided by Shaw's secretary, Blanche Patch.] [In German.]

1498 Coll, Julio. "Ha muerto el último bufón: George Bernard Shaw" (The Last Buffoon Has Died: George Bernard Shaw), DESTINO (Spain), No 692 (11 Nov 1950), 19-20.
Shaw was the first to undermine Victorian traditions; his theoretic and impracticable socialism has to be analyzed from this point of view. The prophet of a new religion, he exaggerated in order to be heard. His works are cerebral—all thought and little feeling; Saint Joan, Great Catherine, The Devil's Disciple, and Man and Superman are long, ingenious explications executed with keen intelligence. [In Spanish.]

1499 Confalonieri, Giulio. "Ricordo di George Bernard Shaw" (In Memory of George Bernard Shaw), IL RADIOCORRIERE, 12 Nov 1950, pp. 4, 11.
[Obit by Italian musicologist with personal remembrances of Shaw.] [In Italian.]

1500 Crisler, B. R. "Miss Gish as a Wealthy Eccentric," CHRISTIAN SCIENCE MONITOR MAGAZINE, 28 Oct 1950, p. 8.
Arms and the Man "is probably the pleasantest of Shaw's Plays Pleasant and Unpleasant," and the Arena Theater production (NY) is "fun" and well-acted.

1501 Crisler, B. R. "A New Play by Lonsdale, an Old One by Shaw," CHRISTIAN SCIENCE MONITOR MAGAZINE, 4 Nov 1950, p. 6.
Shaw wrote Mrs. Warren's Profession under "the superstitious belief that economics is all." He therefore confuses "immorality with capitalism" in the play and sympathizes at the end with Vivie, the representative of morality.

1502 Critic. "Dublin Diary," NS&Nation, XL (11 Nov 1950), 417-18.
Dublin received the news of Shaw's death with numerous obituaries, in which nobody wanted to discuss his controversial attitude toward politics or religion.

1503 D., F. G. "'Mrs. Warren's Profession,'" THEATRE WORLD (Lond), XLVI (March 1950), 9.
It is hard to believe that Mrs. Warren's Profession (Arts Theater, Lond) was banned. "Shaw's mind...has a force and clarity which makes our contemporary theater seem a little pale and lifeless."

1504 Dempsy, David. "G. B. S. on Joyce," NYTBR, 23 July 1950, p. 8.
In a recent letter, Shaw called ULYSSES "a revolting record of a disgusting phase of civilization." For some it may be appealing as art, but for Shaw it is "hideously real." Shaw admires the impulse "to force people to face it," but he feels that 150 francs is a bit much for such a book. When Joyce saw the letter, he remarked that Shaw probably subscribed anonymously.

1505 Dempsy, David. "Shaw Again," NYTBR, 26 Nov 1950, p. 8.
Archibald Henderson has conceived the idea of a Shaw Society of America, which will be loosely affiliated with the parent society in London headed by F. E. Loewenstein. Shaw, before dying, uncharacteristically stated his deep appreciation in a letter to Henderson.

1506 Desnica, V. "G. B. Shaw: Đavolov učenik" (G. B. Shaw: The Devil's Disciple), HRVATSKO KOLO (Zagreb), III, No 1 (1950), 121-24.
Shaw's plays have been known in Zagreb since 1922, when they were enthusiastically received. Shaw's work is characterized by original twists in plot, unexpected psychological reactions, absurd logical situations, and paradox. In The Devil's Disciple, Shaw mingles pathos and comedy with cynicism and sarcasm, which disorients audiences. Nor is it easy for the producer to harmonize these elements. [In Croatian.]

1507 "The Devil's Disciple," TAM, XXXIV (April 1950), 13.
The Devil's Disciple (NYC Theater Company, City Center, NY) is well acted and well directed. [Photograph of Burgoyne at Dudgeon's hanging.]

1508 Dickmann, Enrique. EL MENSAJE DE SHAW AL CUMPLIR 94 AÑOS (The Message of Shaw on Completing 94 Years) (Buenos Aires: La Vanguardia, 1950).
Shaw's main interest, the social problem, shaped his works. His message was synthesized in five branches of his philosophy: religion, ethics, politics, esthetics and pedagogy. [In Spanish.]

1509 Dodderidge, Morris. "G. B. Shaw—The Man, the Legend, and the Achievement," LETTERATURE MODERNE (Milan), I (1950), 476-82.
The view that Shaw's characters are mouthpieces for his ideas and have no imaginative reality of their own is a fallacy, as witness Saint Joan, which time will probably acclaim as Shaw's masterpiece. However, it is the least Shavian of his plays. His philosophy of Creative Evolution is best expressed in the third act of Man and Superman and in Back to Methuselah. The message of Shaw's work is one of positive encouragement.

1510 Duffin, H[enry] C[harles]. CREATIVE EVOLUTION. DEFINITIONS BY HENRY CHARLES DUFFIN. Revised by Shaw. (Lond: Shaw Society [Shavian Tract No 1], 1950).
Darwinian natural selection and other "godless scientific descriptions" of evolution are unacceptable philosophically because they ignore design and purpose. True evolution was preached by Erasmus Darwin and revived by Butler, Shaw, and Bergson. All the Creative Evolutionist knows is that the Life Force works by trial and error; the Life Force is "Paley's watchmaker with his watches mostly going wrong." This force seems to aim at greater mental capacity and more control of circumstances. Evolution cannot be brought about by any individual conscious act of will.

1511 Dutli, Alfred. "Die Religiöse Bedeutung des Evolutionsgedankens bei Bernard Shaw" (The Religious Significance of Evolutionary Thought in Bernard Shaw's Works). Published dissertation, University of

336

Zurich, 1950; pub under same title Bern: Benteli, 1950.
According to Shaw the concept of Creative Evolution is the religion of the twentieth century. Shaw is a vitalist who attacks mechanistic Darwinism and its principle of circumstantial selection. Shaw's idea of the Life Force is based upon Lamarck's philosophy and is influenced by Samuel Butler's evolutionism. Shaw does not believe in an individual God; he sees the creative impulse in all nature. His whole work is an "everlasting Yea." Shaw accepts the irrational forces of this world as well as the scientific facts. His philosophy is more consistent than most critics think. His plays are sermons at the service of Creative Evolution. [In German.]

1512 D[utt], R[ajani] P[alme]. "George Bernard Shaw," LABOUR MONTHLY, XXXII (Dec 1950), 529-40; rptd PENSEE (Paris), XXXIV (Jan 1951), 62-68.
Shaw always "kept the red flag flying." He was an artist, not a thinker. There were too many contradictory strands in his thought; therefore he was best in his plays (which will outlive his prefaces). His artistic integrity rests on his "broad humanity." His strength was that he tried to awaken the British public to challenge capitalism. His weakness: "The truths...always come forth in a twisted shape." He felt "individualist helplessness," knowing no real Marx and settling for "the tenth rate platitudinous commonplaces of a Jevons or a Marshall." Yet his heart, though not his head, supported socialist revolution. He and the Webbs were finally convinced by the Russian Revolution of the failure of Fabianism and Labour Party Reformism. [In French.]

1513 Dz., P. "B. So na srpskam u posebnim izdanjima" (B. Shaw in Serbian and Additional Editions), KNJIŽEVNOST (Belgrade), V, No 12 (1950), 640-41.
The following plays by Bernard Shaw have been produced in Belgrade: Mrs. Warren's Profession (1921), Pygmalion (1922), The Doctor's Dilemma (1923), The Devil's Disciple (1924), Saint Joan (1926), Caesar and Cleopatra (1933). A company calling themselves "The English Players" presented Candida in 1931. Shaw visited Yugoslavia in 1929 and 1931. Translations have included Saint Joan (1926), Pygmalion (1947), The Devil's Disciple (1948), The Doctor's Dilemma (1949), Mrs. Warren's Profession (1950). [In Serbian.]

1514 The Editor. "Our Private Shaws," NS&Nation, ns
XL (11 Nov 1950), 415.
Shaw was so encompassing a figure that everyone has a
different Shaw. His witticisms during the dark months of
1942 often upset people. Yet he "always held that life is
unbearable if one thinks of it in terms of individual
success or suffering, but fascinating if one analyzes
biological and economical changes." He never let "humane
sympathies enter into his public judgments," although in
private life he was generous and benevolent.

1515 "Education of a Queen," LIFE, XXVIII (30 Jan
1950), 46-48.
[A pictorial essay of Caesar and Cleopatra, as produced on
Broadway with Cedric Hardwicke and Lilli Palmer. Short
synopsis of plot.]

1516 "El viejo rebelde" (The Old Rebel), SEMANA
(Colombia), IX (8 July 1950), 24-27.
Shaw is for many a charlatan, but for the intellectuals of
his generation he is a liberator. He is an old rebel who
fought against everything, including senility. [Some
biographical information based on Frank Harris's
biography.] [In Spanish.]

1517 Ervine, St. John. "Bernard Shaw," SPECTATOR,
CLXXXV (10 Nov 1950), 454-55.
Shaw was an engaging and infuriating man, though he was
infuriating only as a public figure. At times he seemed to
be cruel, mainly to pretentious people whose vanity he
disturbed with his frankness. His mind was orderly, and he
was fastidious in appearance. Basically he was a shy,
solitary person, and often ungainly at first meetings. Most
importantly, Shaw "would do more for his friends than they
would do for themselves." He was a socialist because he
wished to free all from mean labor. His contempt for
democracy was tremendous, and his "respect for dictators
was unbounded."

1518 Ervine, St. John and Hesketh Pearson. "Tributes
to Bernard Shaw," List, XLIV (9 Nov 1950), 487-88.
"I—By ST. JOHN ERVINE": At the end of the nineteenth
century, Shaw provided wit and courage for despairing
youth. He "was a great laugher," and always stimulated

thought. He was impressive looking, surprisingly shy, with little need for others yet with no rancor toward humanity. He faced disappointment in his early career and loneliness in old age with courage. "II—by HESKETH PEARSON": Shaw was "the most tolerant of men" and "essentially humble." His "explanatory nature" dominates his novels, criticism, and plays. "He revolutionized the British drama, lifted criticism to a level of intelligent entertainment it had never reached before and has not attained since, profoundly influenced the philosophy of his age, and was largely instrumental in creating a new political power in England." [Very overstated.]

1519 Evans, N. Dean. "I Called on George Bernard Shaw," SCHOLASTIC TEACHER, LVI (5 April 1950), 8-T; rptd as "Man and Superman," SCHOOL REVIEW, LVIII (April 1950), 187-88; as "Visit with George Bernard Shaw," EDUCATION, LXXI (Sept 1950), 45-46; as "George Bernard Shaw on Education," SCHOOL AND SOCIETY, LXXII (14 Oct 1950), 245-46.
[Evans called on Shaw at Ayot St. Lawrence, and—to his surprise—was met by Shaw. They discussed English and American education, Shaw's interest in audio-visual technology, student enjoyment of classes and question asking, and early sex education. Shaw explained his maxim, "he who cannot, teaches" thusly: "a man who is 'doing' all the time does not really have time to teach."]

1520 Faggin, Giuseppe. "G. B. Shaw," PAIDEIA (Genoa), V (1950), 289-96.
Shaw disconcerts anyone who wishes to evaluate his work. Although primarily known as dramatist, his temperament was probably the least dramatic of his age, and he was incapable of understanding the dramatic aspects of the human condition. He was not a dramatist of genius, being too cerebral and detached. The dramatic aspect of his plays is always secretly mocked and denied. The stage was his pulpit, and he was always present. His plays bear witness to his interest in vital problems of his time, but his ideas lack coherence. The unsystematic nature of his thoughts and work is clearly symptomatic of his moral inadequacy. Faith in any idea must have seemed to him enslavement. His freedom from good and evil, from prejudice, from tradition was empty, abstract, and

destructive. The only theory Shaw adopted with a certain satisfaction was the Life Force, but this was not a novelty in Europe. In Shaw, it is represented by woman in the battle of the sexes. Saint Joan provided him with an opportunity to exalt the original, irrational power of the spirit. In a bourgeois materialistic age with its cult of science, Shaw dared to celebrate mystical inspiration and faith. But Saint Joan is a rare moment of grace in Shaw's work. Future generations will learn from his comedies to be vigilant in the face of ideological tyranny, but will search in vain for human examples wherein to find their own torments, secret aspirations, and passions of the flesh and the spirit. [In Italian.]

>1521 "Farewell to a Giant: G. B. Shaw's career as dramatist, scoffer and wit ends at age of 94," LIFE, XXIX (20 Nov 1950), 51-52.

[A pictorial essay of Shaw on his deathbed, funeral scenes, and some of the mourners. Brief facts of his life, his "variable ideals" and "constant foes."]

>1522 Finci, E. "Smrt Bernarda Soa" (Death of Bernard Shaw), KNJIŽEVNOST (Belgrade), V (1950), 636-38.

In Serbia, readers and theater-goers only know Shaw's Mrs. Warren's Profession, Pygmalion, Saint Joan, and The Devil's Disciple. His works should be better known, as they would enrich Serbian culture. [In Serbian.]

>1523 Flake, Otto. "Der journalistische Mensch: Ausblick auf G. B. Shaw" (Journalistic Man: A View of G. B. Shaw), LITERARISCHE DEUTSCHLAND (Heidelberg), I, No 2 (1950), 3-4.

With Shaw "journalistic man breaks into the realm of values and raises a demand which will knock at the gates so long as this new eon, the journalistic, lasts." Although one easily sees the young Shaw as a journalist and self-made man, without respect for experts and trusting in something he might have called critical human understanding, "his critical stance grew from deeper layers, where the philosophical impulse resides." [In German.]

>1524 Fraser, George S. "Shawou o itamu" (Lament over Shaw), THE MAINICHI (Tokyo), 3 Nov 1950, p. 4; rptd in Fraser, NIPPON INSHO (Impressions of Japan and

Other Essays), ed by Mikio Hiramatsu (Tokyo: Asahi
Shimbunsha, 1952), pp. 103-6; also as "Bernard Shaw:
1950," ShawB, I, No 5 (May 1954), 13-14. The original
English version appears in the English Section of
NIPPON INSHO, pp. 81-84.
[Tribute to Shaw's political and literary importance on the
occasion of his fatal accident.] [In Japanese.]

1525 Fukuhara, Rintaro. "Bernard Shaw—Ningen to
Shakai no kibishii Hihyoka—" (Bernard Shaw—Severe
Critic of Man and Society), ASAHI HYORON (Tokyo), V,
No 11 (Nov 1950), 93-101; rptd in EIGAKU ZATSUDAN
(Idle Talks on English Studies) (Tokyo: Kenkyusha,
1955), pp. 130-44.
The problem that Shaw pursued throughout his long life was
how intellectuals should live. The quality of the Shavian
expression lay in his mastery of the art of conveying
commonsensical matters as if they were not so at all. That
is the secret of his popularity. [In Japanese.]

1526 Fuller, Edmund. GEORGE BERNARD SHAW: CRITIC OF
WESTERN MORALE (NY & Lond: Scribner [Twentieth
Century Library, ed by Hiram Haydn], 1950).
Shaw is not an original thinker; he is eclectic—a
synthesizer adopting "Both/And" rather than "Either/Or" as
his mode of inquiry and using irritation and overstatement
to attract attention. His prose works are only lengthy
footnotes to his plays. His drama falls into three periods:
(1) the attack on hypocrisy and social pretensions (from
Widowers' Houses through Captain Brassbound's Conversion);
(2) the immensely creative stage, Shaw's development of a
systematic moral and social philosophy (Man and Superman
through Saint Joan); (3) a steady diminution of power in
poor plays which have only a few splendid effects (The
Apple Cart and later). Shaw is both debunker and prophet,
and his work can be divided into "The Indictment and The
Program." He failed to formulate a modern creed, partly
because he is too discursive and partly because he confuses
faith and politics.

1527 Furst, Henry. "L'inesauribile Bernard Shaw"
(The Inexhaustible Bernard Shaw), IL BORGHESE, 15 Nov
1950, pp. 520-21; rptd in IL MEGLIO DI FURST (The
Best of Furst) (Milan: Longanesi, 1970), pp. 112-17.

Shaw was not a great artist like Molière; he did not defend
the oppressed like Voltaire; nor was he a prose writer like
Wilde (even though he was often compared to the three of
them). But he had a keen mind and clarified any problem he
turned to. However, his talent should not be exaggerated
(his defence of vegetarianism was ridiculous), though his
brilliant paradoxes will always amuse. When the Labour
Party scorned Mussolini, Shaw, who regularly visited Italy,
praised the valid elements of fascism, affirming his right
to judge everything without passion or prejudice. [Right
wing opinions of an Italianate American in a right wing
journal.] [In Italian.]

1528 "G. B. S.," LA PRENSA (Argentina), 3 Nov 1950,
p. 5.
[Brief biographical note on the occasion of Shaw's death;
some details about where, how, and why he died.]

1529 "G. B. S.," MANCHESTER GUARDIAN, LXIII, No 19
(3 Nov 1950), p. 9; rptd in CRITICAL HERITAGE, pp.
386-88, Item 130.
[Obit.] The diversity of Shaw's activities complicates an
assessment of him. As a dramatist, he will endure. In the
drama of life, he played countless roles. He wrote little
about death, for it was the "brightness of life that he
valued." Future generations will not let him perish.
[Another obit. on p. 5, under title "George Bernard Shaw:
Moral Philosopher."]

1530 [Gassner, John?]. "George Bernard Shaw," List,
XLIV (2 Nov 1950), 448.
Shaw is best known for his unfailingly entertaining plays,
but he exerted little power over the English theater. "Only
stupid people ever treated Shaw as a clown." He needed a
platform, and preached Creative Evolution in Man and
Superman and in Back to Methuselah, "his most significant
play." His practical goal was State socialism. Many of his
ideas have become a part of the fabric of society.

1531 "George Bernard Shaw," DER AUFSTIEG
(Wiesbaden), II, No 18 (30 Sept 1950), 79 o25-26.
[A survey of Shaw's life.] Shaw is an Irishman, a Puritan,
a critic and progressive politician, a playwright and a

philosopher. His main aim is to destroy illusions and so-
called ideals. [In German.]

1532 "George Bernard Shaw," ILN, CCXVII (11 Nov
1950), 761-63.
[Brief account of Shaw's death; brief sketch of his life.
Photographic essay of his life.]

1533 "George Bernard Shaw, Dubliner Who Mocked Man's
Works, Rose from Poverty," NYT (2 Nov 1950), p. 28.
[Full-page obit.] Shaw lived a life of contradictions; he
was a dogmatic and controversial master of paradoxes.

1534 Gibbs, Wolcott. "The Theatre: Morality Play,"
NYer, XXVI (4 March 1950), 58, 60.
The first half of The Devil's Disciple (Royal Theater, NY)
is boring. The characters are not interesting nor witty;
the plot is confined to family bickering. But the second
act is Shaw at his best.

1535 Gielgud, Val. "G. B. S.: His Contribution to
Broadcasting," RADIO TIMES, 17 Nov 1950, p. 7.
[An account of Shaw's relations with the BBC, regretting
that broadcasting came too late for Shaw to write drama for
the radio. Adds nothing new to the earlier "Bernard Shaw
and the Radio," in Winsten, G. B. S. 90 (1946).]

1536 Gilkes, A. N. "G. B. S., G. K. C. and Paradox,"
FORTNIGHTLY REVIEW, CLXXIV (Oct 1950), 266-70.
Shaw's paradoxes "dwindle into mere exaggerations," while
Chesterton's are "perfection." The paradoxes of Shaw can be
comprehended by remembering that he is a Puritan, an
Irishman, and "one of the ablest, and most conceited, and
in some ways the most modest, man living."

1537 Goddard, Scott. "Shaw on Music," TRIBUNE
(Lond), No 720 (1 Dec 1950), 12-13.
Shaw used music criticism as a way of getting a hearing, of
finding a pulpit. The criticism is brilliant, but
superficial. Shaw shared with Elgar "a common flamboyance."

1538 Guyard, Marius-François. "Bernard Shaw,"
ETUDES, CCLXVII (Oct 1950), 397-99.

[Obit.] France was reluctant for a long time to accept Shaw the playwright. His plays met with unequal success; many of them are outdated, but they are redeemed by Shaw's satirical and destructive humor. Yet in Saint Joan, the old atheistic Irish Puritan has approached Joan's mystery with more respect than would a French philosopher. [In French.]

> **1539** Haloche, M. "G. B. Shaw," LE THRYSE (Dec 1950), pp. 447-51.

[Obit, with a review of some plays and the criticism with which they were received.] When Candida was produced in Paris in 1907, the Parisian audience adopted Shaw. Mrs. Warren's Profession is a mixture of sentimental comedy and melodrama, but it is not ill-constructed. The Apple Cart is a politico-ideological entertainment but impossible to listen to. Shaw has none of Molière's qualities; he is excessively caustic and insolent. But Saint Joan is deeply moving. [In French.]

> **1540** Hare, Peter. "George Bernard Shaw und die Nachwelt" (George Bernard Shaw and Posterity), BRITISH BULLETIN (Cologne), III, No 45 (9 Nov 1950), 7-12.

[Obit, with emphasis on Shaw's Puritan philosophy, his Fabian ideas, and his concept of the Life Force.] In spite of various critics' opinions, Shaw is a real poet, whose work will survive. [In German.]

> **1541** Herbst, Carl Ludwig. "George Bernard Shaw: der Spötter von der Grünen Insel nimmt das Fahrrad ernst" (George Bernard Shaw: The Mocker from the Emerald Isle Takes the Bicycle Seriously), RADMARKT (Bielefeld), LXI, No 3 (1950), 26-27.

Although Shaw had not gone cycling in ten years, he renewed his membership card (#156) in his 93rd year—an act of deep importance. "The old gentleman who has won so many mental races naturally can no longer think of remaining active as a cyclist as he did earlier with such enthusiasm." In his physical limitations he may also recognize that nature, which so perfectly displays itself to the cyclist, has revealed to him "that he too is a part of nature." [In German.]

1542 Hobson, Harold. "'Second Mrs. Tanqueray'
--'Farfetched Fables,'" CHRISTIAN SCIENCE MONITOR
MAGAZINE, 16 Sept 1950, p. 7.
Shaw's contribution to the theater was to find dramatic
conflict in advanced ideas. This is missing in Farfetched
Fables (Watergate Theater, Lond). Shaw has abandoned the
dramatic for "the regions of pure thought." The play does
not "hang together," has little humor, and no original
thought.

1543 Hodess, J. "George Bernard Shaw and the Jews,"
ZION MAGAZINE (Jerusalem), II (Dec 1950), 1-14: rptd
in CShav, V (Nov-Dec 1964), 13-17.
Shaw had deep sympathy and respect for Jews, as exemplified
by Jewish characters in his plays (e.g., the Jewish doctor
in The Doctor's Dilemma and Mendoza in Man and Superman).
Though he attacked Max Nordau in The Sanity of Art, he
found himself on the same moral ground as Nordau. He
consistently defended himself from the charge of anti-
Semitism, though his reaction to Nazi treatment of Jews was
inadequate, and he doubted the success of Zionism. He was a
religious man; his politics were basically ethical and
esthetic, influenced more by William Morris than by Karl
Marx.

1544 Höffinghoff, Gerda. "George Bernard Shaw als
Publizist" (George Bernard Shaw as Journalist).
Unpublished dissertation, University of Münster,
1950. [Listed in McNamee, and in Altick and Matthews,
Item 1727.] [In German.]

1545 "Hondo pesar causó en todo el mundo la muerte
de George Bernard Shaw" (The Death of George Bernard
Shaw Caused Deep World-wide Sorrow), LA PRENSA
(Argentina), 3 Nov 1950, p. 4.
The world will miss the witty remarks of one of the most
humane and intelligent beings of the twentieth century.

1546 Hone, Joseph. "A Note on Bernard Shaw's
Ancestry," TLS, 10 Nov 1950, p. 709.
Shaw's family originally was Scottish, of the Clan Chattan.
[Genealogy from William Shaw, who "came to Ireland in the
army of William III," to Bernard Shaw.] Shaw's mother was a
Gurley, of County Carlow; Shaw inherited some property in

Carlow through the Gurleys. [Eric Gillett, "Bernard Shaw's Ancestry," TLS, 24 Nov 1950, p. 747, corrects a small misprint in Hone's letter.]

1547 Husserl, Edmund. "Shaw und die Lebenskraft des Abendlandes" (Shaw and the Life-Force of the West), HAMBURGER AKADEMISCHE RUNDSCHAU, III (1948-1950), 743-44.
Why should one fear the concept of "the decline of the West" at a time when Shaw's comedies, which "conquer all hearts," express a faith which so effectively disperses such skepticism? "Shaw the artist is the most effective preacher of present-day Europe, and its most radical drill sergeant—inexhaustible in the laying bare of all lying and well-meant falseness, of all intellectual and practical prejudices in all conceivable dress. But no one surpasses him with respect to pure love of mankind . . . and to genuine truthfulness which does not even spare itself." [Convincingly traces parallels between Shaw's thinking and that of the founder of phenomenology.] [In German.]

1548 "Inglaterra: La Muerte de un mensajero" (England: The Death of a Messenger), SEMANA (Colombia), IX, No 212 (11 Nov 1950), 18-20.
Shaw is the messenger of the new, modern era. [An account of Shaw's last days and some biographical notes.]

1549 Isaacs, J. "Bernard Shaw and the Jews," JEWISH CHRONICLE (Lond), 10 Nov 1950, pp. 13, 23.
Jews play a part, though a small one, in Shaw's art and life. [Brief account of Shaw's pronouncement on Jews in Geneva, Saint Joan, and The Devil's Disciple, and of his dealings with Max Nordau, Jacob Epstein, Siegfried Trebitsch, and Israel Zangwill.]

1550 Ishida, Kenji. "Emerson to Akuma no Deshi" (Emerson and The Devil's Disciple), AMERIKA-BUNGAKU NO KENKYU (Studies in American Literature) (Tokyo: Kenkyusha, 1950), pp. 210-21.
Abandon heteronomous morality and return to your nature, and you can really practice the higher morality: this is one of Shaw's basic ideas, and it is the theme which is developed in many of his works, notably in Immaturity, The Shewing-Up of Blanco Posnet, and The Devil's Disciple. Shaw

has a great deal in common with Ralph Waldo Emerson. Possibly the title and the structure of The Devil's Disciple originate in some passages in Emerson's SELF-RELIANCE. That the scene of the play is laid in a Puritan home in New England should also be noted. [In Japanese.]

1551 Jaffé, Gerhard. "Shaws Oppfatning Av Dramatisk Diktkunst Sammenlignet Med Shakespeares" (Shaw's concept ot Dramatic Art Compared with Shakespeare's), EDDA, L (1950), 56-92.

In his essays and prefaces, Shaw recognizes two kinds of plays: salon drama and the drama of ideas. Shaw prefers the latter, and recognizes Ibsen as its leader and himself as the only playwright capable of following Ibsen. Shaw's Puritanism makes him loathe romantic sexuality and focusses him on social problems. Unfortunately, his drama is neither original nor serious, nor does it show any understanding of the artistic problems of playwrighting. Shaw also identifies two kinds of artists: pure artists, such as Shakespeare and Dickens, and philosopher-artists, such as Bunyan, Blake, and himself. Shaw's boast of being "greater than Shakespeare" shows a critical blindness which is also responsible for his artistic shortcomings and failures. A comparison of Antony and Cleopatra with Caesar and Cleopatra demonstrates that Shakespeare was a true artist with a serious poetic theme, and that Shaw lacked dramatic art, and that his vaunted ideas are trite and hackneyed. [In Norwegian.]

1552 Jannattoni, Livio. "Omaggio a George Bernard Shaw" (Homage to George Bernard Shaw), L'ITALIA CHE SCRIVE, XXXIII (Nov-Dec 1950), 201.

Shaw was a great lover of Italy; he supported for a while the fascist cause and contributed an essay full of admiration for Mussolini and Hitler to a leading Italian journal ["La guerra non ci sarà" (There Won't Be Any War), NUOVA ANTOLOGIA, CCCLXXXVII (Sept-Oct 1936), 260-64]. [In Italian.]

1553 Jhering, Herbert. "Shaw und die deutschen Schauspieler," (Shaw and German Actors) AUFBAU (Berlin) VI, No 12 (1950), 1201-3.

[Reminiscences about Jhering's exposure and response to early Shaw performances in Germany.] [In German.]

1554 Joad, C[yril] E[dwin] M[itchinson]. "Tribute to Shaw," NS&Nation, ns XL (18 Nov 1950), 454, 456.
[Obit.] Shaw liberated the pre-World War I generation from Victorianism and turned it to socialism. He also provided an optimistic philosophy.

1555 Kerr, Walter. "The Stage: Arms and the Man," COMMONWEAL, LIII (10 Nov 1950), 120-22.
Arms and the Man is old but playable, but the Edison Arena Theater (NY) production is "at about half-voltage."

1556 Kindermann, Heinz and Margarete Dietrich (eds). LEXIKON DER WELTLITERATUR (Encyclopedia of World Literature) (Wien & Stuttgart: 1950), pp. 751-52.
[A bio-bibliographical survey. Emphasis on Shaw's idea of the Superman and on his attacks against capitalism.] [In German.]

1557 Knapp, Friedrich. "Der säkularisierte Puritaner. Zum Tode von George Bernard Shaw" (The Secularized Puritan. On the Death of George Bernard Shaw), RHEINISCHER MERKUR (Koblenz), V, No 46 (11 Nov 1950), 7.
[Obit.] A nomadic intellect is characteristic of Shaw, the most troublesome of all modern writers. He is successful as a poet and preacher, but unsuccessful as a theologian. [In German.]

1558 "Kommunalpolitiker Shaw" (The Municipal Politician Shaw), DER STÄDTETAG (Stuttgart), III, No 12 (Dec 1950), 355.
Shaw was a fierce fighter for municipal socialism. [A brief survey of Shaw's activities in municipal policy.] [In German.]

1559 Kupferberg, Herbert. "Death of a Music Critic," SRL, XXXIII (25 Nov 1950), 60-61.
As a music critic, Shaw had emulators but no successors. No critic has "ever applied words to music more artfully or more artistically."

1560 L., C. E. "Der 94 jährige G. B. S." (The 94-year-old G. B. S.), ZEIT (Hamburg), 20 July 1950, p. 2.

Shaw was a rediscoverer of a lost art form: comedy. "The new Socrates appeared to his generation in the form of a new Aristophanes and transformed it." [In German.]

1561 LaFarge, John. "Methuselah in search of a God," AMERICA (NY), LXXXIV (18 Nov 1950), 190.
[Obit.] Though he believed in Creative Evolution, Shaw never transcended himself. His comedies were mere "tracts and theses," a result of Shaw's religious spiritual rebellion. His "heretical heroes...lapsed into grimacing antics once they had strutted their impressive little part." Shaw had a "vivid and original exterior," but he could not escape from his self-imposed spiritual prison.

1562 Laing, Allan M. "G. B. S. in Heaven," NS&Nation, XL (18 Nov 1950), 456.
[Poem on how Shaw will "stir up" Heaven (or Hell) with Shavian argument.]

1563 Laing, Allan M. "My Shaw Postcards," NS&Nation, XL (16 Dec 1950), 621-22.
[An account of Laing's correspondence with Shaw from 17 July 1921 to 10 March 1949 concerning grammatical and other errors in Shaw's published works. Laing read all his books as they were published and mailed a list of corrections to Shaw, who sometimes rewrote and sometimes disagreed. On a card of 4 March 1949 Shaw appointed Laing "Honorary Proof Reader."]

1564 "Las occurrencias de Bernard Shaw" (The Witticisms of Bernard Shaw), SEMANARIO PERUANA (Costa Rica), IV, No 45 (6 Nov 1950), 17.
[Anecdotes about some of Shaw's jokes and bright sayings.]

1565 Levy, Benn W. "Bernard Shaw," TRIBUNE (Lond), No 719 (17 Nov 1950), 9-10.
Shaw cannot be pigeon-holed. Though a thoroughgoing socialist, he was not a propagandist but an artist, capable of characterizing weak socialists and capable capitalists. His comic view precluded despair but not poetic valuation of human life, as in passages of <u>Saint Joan</u>, <u>Heartbreak House</u>, and <u>Caesar and Cleopatra</u>. [Brief sketch of his opinions and character.]

1566 Levy, Benn W. "The Play of Ideas," NS&Nation, ns XXXIX (25 March 1950), 338.
Shaw refused to subjugate character to propaganda and rebelled against ideological playwrighting. It is foolish to speak of "schools" of drama, for "There are only good plays and bad plays." [Part of the controversy over Terence Rattigan's "Concerning the Play of Ideas" (1950), q.v.]

1567 Loewenstein, F[ritz] E[rwin]. THE REHEARSAL COPIES OF BERNARD SHAW'S PLAYS: A BIBLIOGRAPHICAL STUDY (NY: Theatre Arts; Lond: Reinhardt & Evans, 1950; rptd Folcroft, Pa.: Folcroft P, 1969).
[A descriptive bibliography of Shaw's play-rehearsal copies; "no attempt has, however, been made to give a complete descriptive and critical list." Arranged chronologically, beginning with The Shewing-Up of Blanco Posnet (1909). In two sections: I, the green-cloth Constable edition; II, the Standard Edition (from 1931). "Introduction," pp. 7-10, discusses characteristics and uses of rehearsal copies.]

1568 Lupis-Vukić, Ivan. "Povodom smrti G. B. Shawa: tri dana s velikim piscem u Splitu god. 1929 i jedna njegova pisana izjava koja se sada prvi put objavljuje" (On the Occasion of the Death of G. B. Shaw: Three Days in Split in 1929 and a Written Statement of Shaw's Here Published for the First Time), REPUBLIKA (Zagreb), VI, Nos 11/12 (1920), 819-23.
Despite surveillance by the dictatorial regime of King Alexander, the present writer interviewed Shaw in Split (May 1929) and Dubrovnik, and acted as his guide and interpreter. The censorship in Jugoslavia did not allow Shaw's interview to be published. [Shaw's statement on ethnographical and strategic frontiers is printed on p. 832.] [In Croatian.]

1569 MacCarthy, Desmond. "George Bernard Shaw," SUNDAY TIMES (Lond), 5 Nov 1950, p. 3.
[Obit.] Shaw the penetrating writer and thinker actually died a number of years ago. Like Voltaire, Shaw was witty, iconoclastic, "benevolent without love." His philosophy was "a chaos of clear ideas," and it culminated in a pernicious approval of liquidating opponents of the ruling authority.

1570 MacLiammóir, Micheál. THEATRE IN IRELAND (Dublin: Publ. for the Cultural Relations Committee of Ireland [Irish Life and Culture Series], 1950; rptd 1964), pp. 13-15, 28, 41, 42.

John Bull's Other Island is not, as Shaw said, an "uncompromising picture" of old Ireland; it is instead a picture of Ireland in the 1880's. But Shaw's example influenced younger Irish writers to turn from fantastic to realistic themes.

1571 Marquerie, Alfredo. "En la muerte de George Bernard Shaw" (On the Death of George Bernard Shaw), CORREO LITERARIO (Spain), I, No 13 (1 Dec 1950), 1.

All Shaw's theater was "nothing more than dialectic" which amused those who enjoyed protest. His work could never be reduced to a coherent philosophical system. Shaw is corrupt, dissipated, a disturber, never a builder like Chesterton or Belloc. His prefaces and essays are "intellectual perturbations and confusions." He fought monogamy, and lived as a bourgeois in marriage; preached socialism, and died rich and was even avaricious. His selfish and tranquil life was the mirror of his restlessness and subversive propaganda. As a dramatist he was good. [In Spanish.]

1572 Marshall, Margaret. "Drama," NATION, CLXX (4 Feb 1950), 110-15.

The Devil's Disciple (City Center, NY) is witty and well acted in Margaret Webster's production.

1573 Marshall, Margaret. "Drama," NATION, CLXXI (4 Nov 1950), 418.

Mrs. Warren's Profession contains "infantile leftism." Shaw could not resolve his attack on capitalism, and left his only "good" character, Vivie, living "grimly ever after." There are, however, good scenes; witty and intelligent dialog filled with conviction; and skillful characterization.

1574 Marx, Henry. "Corno di Bassetto," MUSIC NEWS, XLII (Dec 1950), 5, 10.

[Brief obit and appreciation.]

1575 Maurois, André. "Bernard Shaw par Bernard Shaw" (Bernard Shaw by Bernard Shaw), REVUE DE PARIS, LVII (Dec 1950), 5-11.
Maurois' lecture on Shaw published in MAGICIENS ET LOGICIENS (Magicians and Logicians) (Paris: Grasset, 1935) was sent to Shaw by the English publisher translating the book. Shaw returned the proofs to Maurois with the margins filled with notes. Shaw was vigilant as to the exactitude of his portrait and of the ideas attributed to him. [Maurois also recalls Shaw's devastatingly sarcastic speech at H. G. Wells's seventieth birthday celebration.] Man and Superman is "the finest Don Juan ever written—and the most profound." [In French.]

1576 Meister, Charles W. "Comparative Drama: Chekhov, Shaw, Odets," POET LORE, LV (Autumn 1950), 249-57.
Heartbreak House satirizes and condemns the aristocracy in "glittering, humorous dialogue." Unlike Chekhov, Shaw is all surface and intellect, with no emotional depth. Heartbreak House is more a "philosophical pamphlet," with two-dimensional characters, than a Chekhovian dramatic portraiture.

1577 Meyer, Alfred Richard. "Shaws prismatisches Genie" (Shaw's Prismatic Genius), AUSBLICK: MITTEILUNGSBLATT DER DEUTSCHEN AUSLANDSGESELLSCHAFT (Lübeck), I (Dec 1950), 73-74.
[Rambling thoughts on Shaw; obit. Briefly compares Shaw and Jonathan Swift.] [In German.]

1578 "A Mind That Never Grew Old," CHRISTIAN CENTURY, LXVII (15 Nov 1950), 1349.
Shaw remained contemporary with people and events because of his "undiminished mental energy." His writings are not outdated. He was a socialist and atheist, but his atheism seemed to stem from a disbelief in "orthodox definitions of God" rather than a disbelief in God. He had faith in humanity's ability to rise above the commonplace.

1579 Mizener, Arthur. "Poetic Drama and the Well-made Play," ENGLISH INSTITUTE ESSAYS, 1949, ed by Alan S. Downer (NY: Columbia UP, 1950; rptd NY: AMS P, 1965), pp. 33-54, espec 45-54; also in LITERARY

CRITICISM: IDEA AND ART, ed by W. K. Wimsatt (Berkeley, Los Angeles, & Lond: University of California P, 1974).
Shaw uses the familiar conventions of drama in superb poetic drama. For example, at the end of Scene IV of Saint Joan, he uses a piece of frozen action to sum up character as it relates to the larger play—as Pinero does at the curtain of Act III of THE NOTORIOUS MRS. EBBSMITH. Yet Shaw's imagination infuses the language and action with a variety and depth of meaning that Pinero lacks. So too Heartbreak House uses the conventional techniques of character revelation and the tableau curtain in a profound, imaginative exploration of theme and character.

1580 Nathan, George Jean. "The Devil's Disciple. January 25, 1950," THE THEATRE BOOK OF THE YEAR, 1949-1950 (NY: Knopf, 1950), pp. 210-12.
Shaw transforms "faded hokum" into original work by "philosophical paradox." In The Devil's Disciple, gaudy melodrama is a means of turning upside down the audience's view of the conventional. Perhaps the stage machinery is too obvious; but the play (Old Vic production, NY) is fun.

1581 Nathan, George Jean. "The Theatre: More on G. B. S.," AMERICAN MERCURY, LXX (March 1950), 308-12; also ptd as part of "Caesar and Cleopatra. December 20, 1949," in THE THEATRE BOOK OF THE YEAR, 1949-1950 (NY: Knopf, 1950), pp. 130-42, espec 138-42.
Much current criticism of Shaw is hypocritical. His themes and jokes, though sometimes dated, are witty and wise. Shaw himself is honest, modest, unpretentious, capable of self-parody, fair, playful, and a great showman. His original style varies from "smoothly active" to "disjointedly supine."

1582 Nicolson, Harold. "Marginal Comment," SPECTATOR, CLXXXV (10 Nov 1950), 460.
[Editorial comment on Shaw obits, registering shock at H. G. Wells's posthumously published attack and remembering a conversation with Shaw, Wells, and others on fame.]

1583 Nucete-Sarde, José. "Shaw, la mejor creación de George Bernard Shaw" (Shaw, the Best Creation of

George Bernard Shaw) "Homenaje a Bernard Shaw" (Homage to Bernard Shaw) CULTURA UNIVERSITARIA (Venezuela), XLI (Nov-Dec 1950), 85-100.
GBS aimed only at being GBS. He was proud of being his own personality, and in this respect he shared with Graham, Kipling, and Chesterton the sign of originality. [In Spanish.]

1584 "Obituaries: George Bernard Shaw," MUSICAL AMERICA, LXX (15 Nov 1950), 38.
[Brief obit, emphasizing Shaw's early and "unusually brilliant" music criticism for the STAR and the WORLD, and mentioning The Perfect Wagnerite and THE CHOCOLATE SOLDIER.]

1585 "Obituary Notes," PUBLISHERS' WEEKLY, CLVIII (11 Nov 1950), 2143-45.
[Obit, with emphasis on Shaw's association with Dodd, Mead.] Shaw never gave an unlimited publishing contract and disliked textbook editions of his plays. Contrary to the general impression, he was kind and generous.

1586 O'Casey, Sean. "Bernard Shaw: An Appreciation of a Fighting Idealist," NYTBR, 12 Nov 1950, pp. 41, 44; rptd in HIGHLIGHTS OF MODERN LITERATURE, ed by Francis Brown (NY: Mentor Books, 1954).
Shaw was a born fighter who struggled courageously to abolish poverty. He was not only a first-rate dramatist, but an "original theologian" who deftly analyzed Christianity, particularly in his Preface to Androcles and the Lion. As time passes, Shaw will endure as "a sage standing in God's holy fire."

1587 O'Casey, Sean. "The Play of Ideas," NS&Nation, ns XXXIX (8 April 1950), 397-98.
Shaw combines reform with "the fanciful guile of a dramatist," e.g., in The Devil's Disciple, a melodrama filled with "intelligent emotion." He and Ibsen brought a "dead drama" to life. Most great plays "are strongly tinted with social significance." [Part of the controversy over Terence Rattigan's "Concerning the Play of Ideas" (1950) q.v.]

1588 Onnen, Frank. "GBS als Musiekcriticus" (GBS as Music Critic), MENS EN MELODIE, V (Dec 1950), 392-95. Although not what one would call a "musical" personality, Shaw spent a considerable portion of his early career as a music critic; he originally began to write on music and other non-political subjects simply because the editors of his newspaper, the STAR, refused to print his political essays. His reviews tended to be personal rather than expert since he had no extensive musical background. He preferred the music of Wagner, as amply documented in The Perfect Wagnerite, although the attraction was more intellectual than musical. In spite of his amateur status as musician, however, Shaw's pronouncements were original and stimulating. [In Dutch.]

1589 P., I. "George Bernard Shaw," FUNK UND SCHULE (Leipzig), IV (1950), 51-53.
[A survey of Shaw's life and works from a Marxist point of view. Emphasis on Shaw's remarks on Lenin and Stalin.] According to Shaw the models of humanity are the hard-working people. [In German.]

1590 Panter-Downes, Mollie. "Letter from London," NYer, XXVI (30 Sept 1950), 56, 58-59.
Farfetched Fables (Watergate Theater, Esmé Percy production) is "only a string of very tenuously connected charades, or fables, that...sounded something like a culling from all the words Shaw ever wrote." Perhaps the know-it-all but intellectually searching being of the last fable "symbolizes Shaw himself."

1591 Payan Archer, Guillermo. "El homenaje a Shaw" (Homage to Shaw), EL TIEMPO (Colombia), 12 Nov 1950, p. 4.
[Brief obit.] [In Spanish.]

1592 Pearson, Hesketh. G. B. S.: A POSTSCRIPT (NY: Harper; Lond: Collins, 1950; rptd with G. B. S., A FULL LENGTH PORTRAIT [NY & Lond: Harper, 1942] as G. B. S., A FULL LENGTH PORTRAIT, AND A POSTSCRIPT [NY: Harper, 1952]; rptd as BERNARD SHAW: A BIOGRAPHY, Introd by Richard Ingrams [Lond: Macdonald & Jane's, 1975]).

[First ten chaps deal with difficulties that Pearson
experienced in gathering materials (1939-1940) for
G. B. S., A FULL LENGTH PORTRAIT. Chaps 11-23 concern
Shaw's life from the end of 1939 to 1950—a "postscript" to
the earlier biography based on reminiscences, personal
encounters, and written exchanges. Included are Shaw's
reaction to the earlier biography and to Pearson's life of
Shakespeare; sundry comments on Oscar Wilde, Henry Irving,
and others; the death of Charlotte Shaw; additional details
on the women in Shaw's life; an obit Shaw wrote for
himself. Final chaps (24-29) include a characterization of
"Shaw the man, the playwright, and the reformer"; an
introduction to Shaw's first printed writing; and an obit
by Pearson.] Shaw was an essentially serious, sincere, sane
man who played many roles, including that of clown. He was
a cautious man of simple tastes, whose "only form of self-
indulgence was overwork." He renovated the English stage
with plays that seemed original but which in fact draw on
the tradition of Euripides, Molière, and Shakespeare. His
influence as a reformer, thanks to his prefaces and
speeches as well as his plays, is felt on every field of
modern thought.

1593 Pearson, Hesketh. THE LAST ACTOR-MANAGERS.
(Lond: Methuen; NY: Harper, 1950), pp. 3, 4-6, 10,
13-14, 17, 18, 20, 25-26, 29, 30-31, 41, 43, 51, 53,
56-57, 62, 71, 72-73, 74, 75-76, 77, 79, Index.
[References to Shaw as he related to actor-managers of his
plays, e.g., Johnston Forbes-Robertson, Herbert Tree,
George Alexander, John Martin-Harvey, and Harley Granville-
Barker.]

1594 Perruchot, Henri. "Bernard Shaw, ou un cynisme
de l'authenticité" (Bernard Shaw or the Cynicism of
Authenticity) SYNTHÈSES, Dec 1950, pp. 50-61; rptd in
LA HAINE DES MASQUES: MONTHERLANT, CAMUS, SHAW (The
Hatred of Masks) (Paris: La Table Ronde, 1955), pp.
157-206.
Shaw's plays are not well-made plays but plays of ideas
with a didactic purpose. Each play deals with a particular
subject or idea dear to Shaw. His work is an attack on
traditional morals and on respectability, but he aims at
establishing a superior kind of morals. He is an anti-
romantic, a realist, and a humorist. His paradoxes are

meant to reveal the truth by a dialectical argument. Respectable Philistines or Pharisees are contrasted with true, lucid heroes, who face facts and tear off masks. They are urged by a life power, which is Nietzschean in spirit, and they have a mission. Artists, men of action, who are apparently selfish people, mark in fact a step toward the Superman. Shaw's socialism is hardly Marxist, because his ideas are not materialistic. He criticizes democracy, but the well-organized society he dreams of would preserve individual freedom. [In French.]

1595 Pettis, Ashley. "G. B. S.: In Tune With the Infinitesimal," CATHOLIC WORLD, CLXXI (July 1950), 266-71.
Shaw's music criticism is shallow, unjust, and inept, using verbal wit to cover a lack of morality and judgment. Shaw probably liked Wagner because of Shaw's own revolutionary tendencies. Though he is presently revered, he is overrated, and his plays and ideas are on the wane.

1596 Phelan, Kappo. "The Stage: Caesar and Cleopatra," COMMONWEAL, LI (13 Jan 1950), 390.
Caesar and Cleopatra (National Theater, NY) is still entertaining.

1597 Phelan, Kappo. "The Stage: The Devil's Disciple," COMMONWEAL, LI (24 Feb 1950), 535-36.
The Devil's Disciple (Maurice Evans production, Royale Theater, NY) satirizes melodrama: the first act follows the usual pattern; the second and final acts reverse it. It is not an experiment in form but in understanding.

1598 Philipp, Günter B. "Bernard Shaws Stellung zu Demokratie und Faschismus" (Bernard Shaw's Position on Democracy and Fascism). Unpublished dissertation, University of Münster, 1950. [Listed in McNamee, and in Altick and Matthews, Item 1745.] [In German.]

1599 Pineda, Rafael. "Prefacios y apéndices de George Bernard Shaw" (Prefaces and Appendices of George Bernard Shaw), "Homenaje a Bernard Shaw" (Homage to Bernard Shaw), CULTURA UNIVERSITARIA (Venezuela), XLI (Nov-Dec 1950), 97-100.

Shaw's prefaces and appendices are the key to understanding his thought. They are forms by which he kills romantic illusions. [In Spanish.]

1600 Pritchett, V. S. "G. B. S.: 1856-1950," TIME, LVI (13 Nov 1950), 30-31; rptd in Louis Kronenberger (ed), GEORGE BERNARD SHAW: A CRITICAL SURVEY (Cleveland & NY: World, 1953), pp. 240-46.
An eighteenth-century man, Shaw was early in danger of becoming a dilettante. But he became an artist who could transform "disruptive debate into a kind of classical Mozartian music." However, his plays lead one to "the boredom of the over-stimulated."

1601 Rattigan, Terence. "Concerning the Play of Ideas," NS&Nation, ns XXXIX (4 March 1950), 241-42; rptd in TAM, XXXIV (Aug 1950), 14-16, with reply by Shaw, pp. 16-17; also rptd in CRITICAL HERITAGE, pp. 381-82, Item 128.
Shaw led modern drama nowhere, because he did not tolerate any form of drama but the play of ideas. He found Shakespeare lacking because Shakespeare wrote "about people and not about things." Playwrights are now expected to write topical, controversial drama, and this cripples them. Character and narrative count in drama; ideas at best take third place. [A controversy ensued, with responses (q.v.) on "The Play of Ideas" by James Bridie, 11 March 1950; Benn W. Levy, 25 March 1950; Peter Ustinov, 1 April 1950; Sean O'Casey, 8 April 1950; Ted Willis, 15 April 1950 (nothing on Shaw); Shaw, 6 May 1950, pp. 510-11; and sundry letter writers. Rattigan closed the controversy, 13 May 1950, pp. 545-46, reiterating his preference for plays of character.]

1602 Rattray, R. F. "Bernard Shaw's Origins," QUARTERLY REVIEW, CCLXXXVIII (Jan 1950), 46-61.
[Sketch of Shaw's ancestry, his education, his youth up to his move to London, based on Shaw's own autobiographical writings, espec Sixteen Self Sketches.] Shaw's and Samuel Butler's lives were parallel: "both had loveless homes and childhoods and were lonely and diffident," and both "found compensation in art."

1603 Rey Tosar, Manuel. GEORGE BERNARD SHAW CONTRA
M. REY TOSAR (George Bernard Shaw Against M. Rey
Tosar) (Buenos Aires: Americana, 1950).
[Subtitled "A coarse maneuver in which the famous writer
appears at the service of foreign capitalism, and against
Argentinean cultural interests." A partially fictitious
treatise in which Shaw appears as a character to expose the
current malpractices of the publishing companies of
Argentina as well as the conflict between native and
foreign publishing companies. Describes a confrontation
between Shaw and Tosar, an editor who has published
translations of Shaw, violating Shaw's copyright.] [In
Spanish.]

1604 Riding, George A. "The Candida Secret,"
SPECTATOR, CLXXXV (17 Nov 1950), 506; rptd in A
CASEBOOK ON CANDIDA, ed by Stephen S. Stanton (NY:
Crowell, 1962), pp. 166-69.
[Correspondence between members of a play-reading society
at Rugby and Shaw on "the secret in the poet's heart" in
Candida.]

1605 Rivas-Lázaro, Manuel. "Por el dédalo de la
paradoja hacia Bernard Shaw" in "Homenaje a Bernard
Shaw" (Homage to Bernard Shaw), CULTURA UNIVERSITARIA
(Venezuela), XLI (Nov-Dec 1950), 87-90.
Paradox is the key to understanding Shaw as an apostle of
virtue and the leader of a new religion without dogmas.
Ibsen, Pirandello, and Shaw are three apparently
contradictory spiritual forces, who, when they wrote, were
able to encompass everything, even being revolutionaries.
[In Spanish.]

1606 Robinson, Lennox. "Bernard Shaw: A Playwright's
Tribute," TIMES (Lond), 7 Nov 1950, p. 8.
[A tribute to "the finest (prose stylist) since Swift" from
his erstwhile "secretary" (i.e., apprentice playwright).]

1607 Roch, Herbert. "Hofnarr der Bourgeoisie. Zum
Tode von G.B. Shaw" (Court Jester of the Bourgeoisie.
On the Death of G.B. Shaw), WELTBÜHNE, V (1950),
1427-29.
Throughout his life Shaw fought against superstition,
dogmatism and hypocrisy. His weapons were wit, irony and

satire. He followed the revolutionary development of the Soviet Union with keen interest. [In German.]

1608 Romero, Héctor M. "En memoria de un autor que nunca leí" (In Memory of an Author Whom I Never Read), MAÑANA, XXXVII, No 377 (10 Nov 1950), 26-27.
[A tribute to Shaw by an author who states that he does not feel remorse at not having read Shaw, except for <u>Pygmalion</u> and <u>The Adventures of the Black Girl in Her Search for God</u>. He is more interested in Shaw as a man who defended Wagner's music and Ibsen's plays than as a dramatist.] [In Spanish.]

1609 Rosati, Salvatore. "George Bernard Shaw," NUOVA ANTOLOGIA, CDXLX (Sept-Dec 1950), 362-65.
Shaw's last comedy, <u>Buoyant Billions</u>, was acknowledged to have brilliant craftsmanship but ideas that were not new; more significantly, there was an unconsciously cruel expectation that the one-time champion was about to fall in his last battle. The dominance of Shaw's political and social consciousness obscured not only his artistic capabilities but his purely personal capacities as well. When his ideas on society and economics are outdated, the artistic nucleus of his rich production will go on living for many generations. [In Italian.]

1610 Rushmore, Robert. "Taps for the Basset Horn," OPERA NEWS, XV (27 Nov 1950), 31-32.
Shaw's music criticism, especially that of Corno di Bassetto, is still valid, and promises to remain so. Shaw "cut through the popular second rate and championed the neglected first rate." Except for his opinion of Brahms, he was invariably right in his comments on music and musicians.

1611 S., F. "'Macbeth' and 'Heartbreak House,'" THEATRE WORLD, XLVI (Aug 1950), 6.
The Arts Theater (Lond) revival of <u>Heartbreak House</u> was brilliant. "Even the wordiest passages commanded undivided attention." The play's philosophy is "apt for today."

1612 Sainz de Robles, Federico C. "En torno a un tipo paradigmático y eterno" (Concerning a

Paradigmatic and Eternal Type), ESCORIAL (Spain), XX, No 60 (Aug 1949), 1205-1223.
Shaw shows less understanding of Don Juan than do others who have written on the subject. Shaw wants to teach Don Juan to be a reasonable and socialist being. This attitude is dangerous since it gives the myth a tendency toward social exemplarization. Shaw's Don Juan is more rationalist, more hypocritical, and less Don Juan than the one by Molière. [In Spanish.]

1613 Sandwell, B. K. "Shaw and His Stage People," SATURDAY NIGHT, 21 Nov 1950, p. 7.
Shaw had a passion for paradox and achieved popularity with the young because of his denunciation of authority. Though they are attractive to intellectual actors and actresses, his characters are dry and flat, reflecting Shaw's own lack of human passion. Over time, his ideas will lose importance.

1614 Santos Gaynor, Juan. "El credo de Bernard Shaw" (The Creed of Bernard Shaw), REVISTA DE LA UNIVERSIDAD DE BUENOS AIRES, XLVI, No 340 (Oct-Dec 1950), 567-79.
Shaw was not a materialist nor a rationalist but a spiritualist, a moralist whose main preoccupation was philosophy. [In Spanish.]

1615 Schonberg, Harold C. "Facing the Music," MUSICAL COURIER, CXLII (15 Nov 1950), 4.
[Brief obit and appreciation of Shaw as a music critic.] "Was there a greater music critic who wrote in the English language? If so, who?"

1616 Schonberg, Harold C. "Musical Metaphysics . . . Its Cause and Cure," ETUDE, LXVIII (March 1950), 13, 62, 64.
Like a few other major authors (James Joyce, Romain Rolland, Thackeray), Shaw had a thorough understanding of music. He had "impeccable taste and intuition," and no one has equaled him in criticism for a "combination of wit and essential solidity."

1617 "Sección de teatro y cinematografía" (Theater and Film Section), LA PRENSA, 22 Jan 1950, p. 8.

[Reference to the permit Mexican comic Mario Moreno Cantinflas obtained from Shaw and Gabriel Pascal to film a version of Androcles and the Lion.] [In Spanish.]

1618 Sempronio. "El teatro en el mundo" (The Theater in the World), DESTINO (Spain), No 692 (11 Nov 1950), 12.
Among the descendents of Ibsen's revolutionary theatrical thought, Shaw belongs to the group of poets and reasoners. His masterpiece is Saint Joan, where, alongside the religious and nationalistic intentions of the author, there is poetry and liveliness. [In Spanish.]

1619 Sempronio. "Medio siglo de teatro: ¿Cuál ha sido desde su punto de vista el mayor acontecimiento teatral español de estos últimos 50 años?" (A Half-Century of Theater: What Has Been from Your Point of View the Best Spanish Theatrical Event of the Last 50 Years?), DESTINO (Spain), No 652 (4 Feb 1950), 18-19.
[A poll conducted in 1950 by DESTINO (Barcelona) on the most important theatrical events during the first half of the twentieth century revealed that Saint Joan as performed by Margarita Xirgu in 1925 was an important milestone.] [In Spanish.]

1620 Shah, Hiralel Amritlal. "Bernard Shaw in Bombay," ShawB, I (Nov 1956), 8-10; rptd from PRABUDDHA JAIN (Bombay), 15 Nov 1950.
Shah took Shaw on a tour of two Jain temples when Shaw visited Bombay in 1933, and accompanied Shaw to a boring reception by the "Three Arts Circle." The temples delighted Shaw; the reception did not. The next day Shah showed Shaw (on shipboard) photographs of Indian art, architecture, and costume. [Anecdotal.]

1621 Shanks, Edward. "John Bull's Other Dramatist (In Memoriam G. B. S., 1856-1950)," SUNDAY TIMES (Lond), 5 Nov 1950, p. 6. [Poem.]

1622 "The Shape of Things," NATION, CLXXI (11 Nov 1950), 421-23.
[Obit.] Shaw "outshone every other dramatist of the English-speaking world." The issues in his plays may be dated, but his sense of humor and admirable prose keep them

alive. He was seduced by the twentieth-century myth of the efficacy of dictatorship and salvation through an elite— or perhaps only "half-seduced," since the late plays on this theme do not carry real conviction.

1623 "Shaw's Shenanigans: 'Devil's Disciple' has fun with American Revolution," LIFE, XXVIII (6 March 1950), 53-54, 56.
[A pictorial essay on The Devil's Disciple.] Burgoyne is "a perfect mouthpiece" for Shavian jibes.

1624 "Shaw's Triumph: At 94 he survives a broken thigh and gets to be a picture censor," LIFE, XXIX (23 Oct 1950), 44.
[Pictorial essay on Shaw's homecoming after recuperating in hospital from a broken thigh.]

1625 "'Shaw's Village' Hears an Occasional Snort of Protest," CHRISTIAN SCIENCE MONITOR MAGAZINE, 12 Aug 1950, p. 16.
The villagers of Ayot St. Lawrence celebrated Shaw's birthday while he was in London. Shaw writes from ten o'clock to one; he walks around the village as one of the citizens. He writes lots of letters, is delighted with press clippings, lives quietly, is a camera enthusiast. His wit "seems to be spontaneous but is really carefully contrived." Shaw's house has become a pilgrimage. His friend F. E. Loewenstein protects him from reporters. [Photograph of Loewenstein and Shaw.]

1626 Spenker, Lenyth. "The Dramatic Criteria of George Bernard Shaw," SPEECH MONOGRAPHS, XVII (1950), 24-36.
In his drama criticism, Shaw consistently argued that theater was to be taken seriously and that esthetic experience was impossible without ethical substance. In his analysis of drama, he looked for attacks on conventional morality and affirmations of the value of human life. For example, plays that treat women as inferior were assumed by Shaw to be hopelessly dated, and Shaw disliked the pessimism he perceived in HAMLET and the lack of conviction he perceived in plays by Beaumont and Fletcher and by Pinero. When he turned from ethics to character, dialog, and technique, then Shaw attacked "staginess," the

detachment of stage life from real life that he found in such disparate works as Shakespeare's OTHELLO and Pinero's THE NOTORIOUS MRS. EBBSMITH.

1627 [Staples, Leslie]. "Bernard Shaw," DICKENSIAN, XLVII (Dec 1950), 9.
Shaw acknowledged his indebtedness to Dickens. [Résumé of Shaw's contributions to Dickensian scholarship.]

1628 Starr, Mark. "'Headmaster to the Universe,'" SRL, XXXIII (9 Dec 1950), 24.
Unlike most intellectuals, Shaw did not avoid political drudge work. His opinions of the totalitarians of both the right and left, however, prove that "even the sharpest intellect may go astray." [A Letter to the Editor.]

1629 Stoppel, Hans. "Das Bild Manschlicher Grösse bei Bernard Shaw" (The Picture of Human Greatness in Bernard Shaw). Unpublished dissertation, University of Kiel, 1950. [Listed in McNamee, and in Altick and Matthews, Item 1758.] [In German.]

1630 Strauss, E[rich]. GEORGE BERNARD SHAW (Lond, NY, & Toronto: Longmans, Green [Essential English Library, ed by C. E. Eckersley], 1950).
Shaw's style "is less moving than interesting," though perfect for his expository purposes. The novels have a stiff and formal style, but they have interesting dialog and characters and imaginative, original stories. The essays are characterized by a strong personal note and criticism of accepted conditions and ideas. The political writings helped to make socialism known and respected in England. Shaw's distinguishing characteristic as a dramatist is the moral passion he brings to bear on world problems. His best characters (Joan, Lavinia, Barbara Undershaft) share this passion to improve the world. Though influenced by Ibsen and sharing the wit and comic brilliance of W. A. Gilbert and Oscar Wilde, Shaw occupies a unique place in modern literature: his art and thought have taught people to question and challenge formerly accepted ideas and systems. [A balanced survey of Shaw's life and work in a series "intended mainly for foreign students."]

1631 "Thanks for Your Shilling," TIME, LVI (25 Dec 1950), 20, 23.
[Announces publication (and sale, in Ayot St. Lawrence, at Mrs. Lyth's post-office shop) of Bernard Shaw's Rhyming Picture Guide to Ayot St. Lawrence. Quotes some of the verse, with description of accompanying photographs.] "Not yet Stratford-on-Avon, Ayot St. Lawrence was on the way to becoming a shrine."

1632 "Theater: Education of a Queen," LIFE, XXVIII (30 Jan 1950), 46-48.
The excellent revival (National Theater, NY) of Caesar and Cleopatra owes much to Cedric Hardwicke's portrayal of Caesar and Lilli Palmer's infusion of worldly glamour in Cleopatra.

1633 "Theater: New Plays: Arms and the Man," NEWSWEEK, XXXVI (30 Oct 1950), 78.
Arms and the Man is perennially charming, though the Arena Theater (NY) production is below its previous standard.

1634 "The Theater: Old Play in Manhattan," TIME, LV (2 Jan 1950), 52.
Caesar and Cleopatra (National Theater, NY) has vigor and makes an astute comment on the ancient world. The tone is wry and ironic. Caesar is a non-vindictive conqueror "with a lonely rather than a loving heart." Shaw hand-picked Sir Cedric Hardwicke as Caesar, and watched the Broadway revival closely. He earlier refused a production by the non-profit Theater, Incorporated. "He has no interest in non-profit enterprises."

1635 "The Theater: Old Play in Manhattan," TIME, LVI (6 Nov 1950), 57-58.
The greater part of Mrs. Warren's Profession produced by Theater Venture (Bleeker Street Playhouse, NY) is "deadwood —obsolete in method, lean on wit, smacking of 19th-century melodrama." But the two big scenes between Vivie and Mrs. Warren are "profoundly Shavian" and powerful.

1636 "The Theater: Old Plays in Manhattan," TIME, LV (6 Feb 1950), 66.
The NY City Theater Company's production (City Center, NY) of The Devil's Disciple "left the critics cheering." The

second half is the better. The trial scene is the gayest in modern drama.

1637 "Theater: Openings: Mrs. Warren's Profession," NEWSWEEK, XXXVI (6 Nov 1950), 88-89.
The Bleeker Street Playhouse (NY) production of Mrs. Warren's Profession shows that the play is indestructible, though "Time may have cushioned the impact."

1638 "Theater: Revival: 'Caesar and Cleopatra,'" NEWSWEEK, XXXV (2 Jan 1950), 48.
Caesar and Cleopatra has aged very little. The Hardwicke/Palmer Broadway revival (National Theater, NY) is excellent.

1639 "Theater: Revival: 'The Devil's Disciple,'" NEWSWEEK, XXXV (6 March 1950), 82.
The Devil's Disciple is not Shaw "at his acidulous best," but Dick Dudgeon "is a fine romantic rebel," and Burgoyne is delightful.

1640 "Tribuna del conferenciante: Una evocación de Bernard Shaw" (The Lecturer's Platform: An Evocation of Bernard Shaw), DESTINO (Spain), No 692 (2 Dec 1950), 14.
[Praise of Shaw and information about his death.] [In Spanish.]

1641 Ustinov, Peter. "The Play of Ideas," NS&Nation, ns XXXIX (1 April 1950), 367.
Both Terence Rattigan and James Bridie isolate one element of Shaw: Rattigan identifies Shaw's ideas with a dreary social message; Bridie claims too much for Shaw's influence. Shaw is like Jonson and Aristophanes—"a great independent tributary," but too didactic. [Part of the controversy over Terence Rattigan's "Concerning the Play of Ideas" (1950), q.v.]

1642 Vergani, Orio. "Ricordo minimo de George Bernard Shaw" (A Brief Memory of George Bernard Shaw), L'ILLUSTRAZIONE ITALIANA, 12 Nov 1950, pp. 13, 32.
[Obit, with description of meeting with Shaw; of no critical interest.] [In Italian.]

1643 Vilanova, Antonio. "El pensamiento de Bernard Shaw" (The Thought of Bernard Shaw), DESTINO (Spain), No 692 (2 Dec 1950), 14.
Shaw is a genius at sarcasm, with the corrosive irony of Voltaire and the satiric humor of Swift. He is considered the incarnation of the Protestant spirit and of the anti-dogmatic liberal man of the nineteenth century. He has been a fanatic for truth and a destroyer of supernatural myths, romantic conventions, rhetorical heroism, and moral hypocrisy. His thought was inspired by a strange mixture of Utopian doctrines bordering on pure mediocrity. [In Spanish.]

1644 Villari, Luigi. "Ricordi di G. B. S.," (Recollections of G. B. S.), L'ITALIA CHE SCRIVE (Rome), XXXIII (1950), 199-200.
Shaw visited Italy several times. In a conversation many years ago in Venice, he declared that the best theatrical impresario he ever knew was Adelaide Ristori. He also referred to knowing Mrs. Pat Campbell. [In Italian.]

1645 Ward, A[lfred] C[harles]. BERNARD SHAW (Lond & NY: Published for the British Council by Longman Group Ltd.; Lond: F. Mildner & Sons, 1950; rvd Lond & NY: Longmans, Green, 1951, 1957, 1960, 1963, 1966; rptd with minor amendments and additions to bibliography Harlow: Longman, 1970).
Shaw's place in literature will be determined by his quality as an imaginative artist, not by his stature as a political thinker and social reformer. [Survey, generally favorable, of all Shaw's work. A good introduction for the non-specialist.]

1646 "Watergate Theatre: 'Farfetched Fables,'" TIMES (Lond), 6 Sept 1950, p. 6.
Farfetched Fables (Shaw Society production) is a not very witty parody of Back to Methuselah. It is playful but not entertaining fare.

1647 West, Alick. "Debate and Comedy (A note on the unresolved dissonance in Bernard Shaw's early plays)," ARENA, I (1949-50), 37-41.
Shaw typically has saints and realists battle, and allows the realists to win. The "revolutionary creative energy" of

Louka, Gloria, Brassbound, Anderson, and Keegan is
repressed; Shaw uses stock comic themes and undercuts the
philosophy and the class issue, as in Man and Superman. The
laughter and dreams are unresolved, thus making "Shaw
almost a clown against his will."

> **1648** West, Alick. GEORGE BERNARD SHAW, "A GOOD MAN
> FALLEN AMONG FABIANS" (NY: International Publishers,
> 1950; Lond: Lawrence & Wishart, 1950; rptd Freeport,
> NY: Books for Libraries P, 1970; Folcroft, Pa.:
> Folcroft Library Editions; Lond: Lawrence & Wishart,
> 1974; pp. 158-66 rptd as "Saint Joan: A Marxist
> View," in Stanley Weintraub [ed], SAINT JOAN: FIFTY
> YEARS AFTER [Baton Rouge: Louisiana State UP, 1973],
> pp. 106-13).

Shaw's artistry is flawed by his Fabianism, which reduces
revolution to legislative reformism. His novels grow out of
his early sense of isolation within the family, his
separation from respectable society in Dublin, and his
loneliness in London. In them he wrote for society,
expressing "not only personal resentments, but also a human
vitality"; his novelistic heroes reveal Shaw's art to be on
the side of the people, of the workers, and against
bourgeois hypocrisy. Shaw's political plays, Widowers'
Houses and Mrs. Warren's Profession, expose capitalist
society but reject class struggle and collective unity in
favor of bourgeois individualism and rationalism. So too
his critical works of the 1890's are marred by bourgeois
idealism which causes him to look for values outside
socialism. In fact, his work from An Unsocial Socialist to
Major Barbara moves "from the direct attack on capitalism
as an inhuman system of exploitation to praise of the
capitalists for following their healthy instincts." His
standards are confused—his realism is merely an acceptance
of the existing order of things. His dramatic vision is
always in conflict with his Fabianism; finally he retreats
into mysticism, so that, in Saint Joan and Back to
Methuselah, "religious consciousness has become an end in
itself." [An interesting though thesis-heavy analysis of
Shaw's major works.]

> **1649** West, E. J. "Shaw, Shakespeare, and Cymbeline,"
> THEATRE ANNUAL, VIII (1950), 7-24.

[An analysis of Shaw's various comments on CYMBELINE, in the letters to Ellen Terry concerning her role as Imogene, in Shaw's 1896 SATURDAY REVIEW review of the play, and in Cymbeline Refinished.] In Cymbeline Refinished Shaw tried to keep the characters, especially "the wooden king," alive and consistent.

1650 "When A Great Man Dies," List, XLIV (9 Nov 1950), 484.
The B.B.C. owes much to Shaw, for both he and his plays broadcast well. At his death, some of the press published hostile remarks on his vanity, his attitude in wartime, his lack of humanity. "It can be said that a prophet is never honoured in his own country." But his teaching has profoundly influenced modern life.

1651 Wyatt, Euphemia Van Rensselaer. "Theater: Caesar and Cleopatra," CATHOLIC WORLD, CLXX (Feb 1950), 384-87, espec 384.
In Caesar and Cleopatra (National Theater, NY), both Shaw and the audience seem amused. Caesar is a just, "urbane, amusing man of the world." Cleopatra is a minx.

1652 Wyatt, Euphemia Van Rensselaer. "Theater: Heartbreak House," CATHOLIC WORLD, CLXXI (May 1950), 148-49.
Heartbreak House is too long. But at the Bleeker Street Theater (NY), the On Stage group makes the dialog seem purposeful, the wit sharp, and the characters human.

1653 Wyatt, Euphemia Van Rensselaer. "Theater: Mrs. Warren's Profession; Arms and the Man," CATHOLIC WORLD, CLXXII (Dec 1950), 226-28.
In Mrs. Warren's Profession (Theater Venture production, Bleeker Street Theater, NY) Vivie is a precursor of Saint Joan in her lonely stand for "her ideal of decency" and honest work. Arms and the Man (Arena Theater, NY) is played as a farce. It requires a good production since it is not Shaw at his best.

1654 Yamamoto, Shuji. "Bernard Shaw o Itamu" (Mourning the Death of Bernard Shaw), ASAHI SHINBUN (Osaka), 4 Nov 1950; rptd in ENGEKISUNSHI (A Sketch

of the Theater) (Kobe: Chugai Shobo, 1958), pp. 181-83.
The modern English drama began and ended with Shaw. He was
both a brilliant dramatist and dramatic critic. While
creating the Life Force theory out of Schopenhauer,
Nietzsche, and Marx, and taking up various kinds of
subjects including marriage, prostitution, social classes,
and war, he enlarged markedly the intellectual horizon of
drama. [In Japanese.]

1655 Yano, Hojin. "Shaw to Nippon" (Shaw and Japan),
OTANI DAIGAKU SHINBUN (Kyoto), 6 Dec 1950; rptd in
HIKAKU BUNGAKU--KOSATSU TO SHIRYO--(Comparative
Literature--Observations and Materials) (Tokyo:
Nanundo, 1956), pp. 87-90; rvd and enlgd ed (1978),
pp. 94-97.
Though it is now difficult to ascertain when Shaw was
introduced to Japan, his name seems to have attracted
attention in the early 1900's as the author of The
Quintessence of Ibsenism. His fame as dramatist was short-
lived in Japan, and his influence over the Japanese was
generally negligible. However, there is a writer who
attained to greatness under the influence of Shaw: Kan
Kikuchi. A comparative study of them is a good subject as
yet untouched. [In Japanese.]

1656 Żuławski, Juliusz. "G.B.S.," TWÓRCZOŚĆ
(Warsaw), VI, No 12 (1950), 158-59.
Shaw was a great denunciatory critic of the bourgeois
world, but could never draw the proper conclusions from his
critical attitude and collaborate with the anti-bourgeois
social revolution. Fabianism was not entirely to blame: he
outgrew it, though never renounced allegiance to it. He
criticized his own social class, but did not want to
renounce his own comfortable position in it. He often
stressed his admiration for the Soviet Union, but did not
take the decisive step which progressive writers did. [In
Polish.]

1951

1657 Andrassy, Caterina. "G.B.S. in Moscow,"
NS&Nation, XLI (3 March 1951), 240-41.
[Reminiscence of seeing Shaw in Moscow. F. L. Whelan,
"G.B.S. in Moscow," NS&Nation, XLI (17 March 1951), 305,
replies, noting that he found paintings of Shaw and Lady
Astor at a penal settlement for delinquent children,
Bolshevo, near Moscow; Whelan includes text of Shaw letter
describing his visit to Bolshevo.]

1658 Atkinson, Brooks. "At the Theatre," NYT, 5 Oct
1951, p. 23.
Saint Joan is an inspired play, and Uta Hagen (Cort
Theater, NY) does not let it down.

1659 Atkinson, Brooks. "At the Theatre," NYT, 23 Oct
1951, p. 34.
Since Don Juan in Hell was written separately, it is
logical to play it as an independent enterprise. The
performance by the First Drama Quartet (Carnegie Hall, NY)
will never be forgotten by anyone who witnessed it.

1660 Atkinson, Brooks. "First Night at the Theatre,"
NYT, 20 Dec 1951, p. 13.
Laurence Olivier and Vivien Leigh in Caesar and Cleopatra
are a triumph. Olivier plays Caesar less for wit than
character; Vivien Leigh's contribution is not large.

1661 Atkinson, Brooks. "Maid of Orleans," NYT, 14
Oct 1951, p. 1.
Saint Joan crowned Shaw's career. It is an untraditional
drama, possibly because Shaw used the original sources and
not the nineteenth-century interpretations. It is an
impartial examination of human institutions reacting to a
revolutionary girl who recognizes only the authority of
God. Shaw's thesis is confirmed by the persecutions of
heresy in our own society. Today there is no doubt that the
Epilog is essential.

1662 Baeza, Ricardo. "Recuerdos de Bernard Shaw" (Memories of Bernard Shaw), SUR (Argentina), CC (June 1951), 7-21.

More than anything else Shaw is a social reformer whose goal is the improvement of society. [Baeza met Shaw several times; in 1922 he spoke to Shaw about the poor Spanish translations and pointed out to him common mistakes.] [In Spanish.]

1663 Baiwir, Albert. "The Legacy of George Bernard Shaw," REVUE DES LANGUES VIVANTES (Brussels), XVII (1951), 2-10.

The test of Shaw's influence should be based on what one remembers of him without consulting books. The lasting impression of Shaw's dramatic works "is that of a curiously inverted world, with little claim to objectivity or even reality, and of a nerve-racking atmosphere somehow evocative of that of a madhouse." His characters are remembered as mental attitudes rather than as living personalities. There are two groups of Shavian characters: one, a mass of rather stupid, conventional characters, and two, a minority of typically Shavian heroes. The latter group are surprisingly less individualized and more easily forgotten than their opponents. Some of Shaw's characters are real and human: Mrs. Warren of the first group, Joan and Candida of the exceptional type. Caesar and Cleopatra and The Man of Destiny do not produce realistic and human characters. Shaw's plays exhibit perpetual motion but lack harmonious development and a central dramatic purpose. However, Shaw, as an exceptional craftsman, preserved the illusion of drama by employing paradoxical situations reversed by a single, aptly chosen word as seen in Caesar in the anticlimactic episode of Caesar at the foot of the Sphinx. Shaw's wit and clowning belong to histrionics. Shaw's message is not as impressive as his artistry. Thus, Shaw the dramatist will outlive Shaw the thinker, not because he created a new kind of comedy, the comedy of purpose, but because of the unique quality of his histrionics, his expression, his style.

1664 Baldi, Sergio. "Per l'Arte de Shaw" (Through Shaw's Art), RIVISTA DI LETTERATURA MODERNE E COMPARATE, II (June 1951), 282-86.

Shaw died at such an advanced age that immediately afterwards the young generation considered him technically and socially a has-been. His work did not contribute anything to deepening the ideas that he held; he was only a propagator of those ideas. His merit lies in reaching people who would not read Marx and Darwin directly. In his theater of oratory, the plot is only a pretext for the thesis. Yet there are exceptions to this: Mrs. Warren's Profession, Pygmalion, and his masterpiece, Saint Joan, where art dominates the thesis. The limitation in Shaw's art is the lack of inner battle or affect. In Candida only the scene where she must choose between husband and poet touches the edge of true drama, of poetry. Shaw's poetry lies in the individual's effort to affirm his morality against an inimical society. [In Italian.]

1665 Barzun, Jacques. "Introduction," PLEASURES OF MUSIC: A READER'S CHOICE OF GREAT WRITING ABOUT MUSIC AND MUSICIANS FROM CELLINI TO BERNARD SHAW, ed by Jacques Barzun (NY: Viking P, 1951; Lond: Michael Joseph, 1952), pp. 1-18.
Shaw wrote "higher criticism" which can be understood by the laity.

1666 Bax, Clifford. "Shaw As Dramatist: A Criticism," DRAMA, ns XX (Spring 1951), 19-21.
[A photograph of Shaw with Lord Howard de Walden, William Archer, G. K. Chesterton, and J. M. Barrie.] Candida is essentially unsound because the managing type woman has no sensibility and appetite for the arts. Getting Married is "mere back-chat." Back to Methuselah must be impressive to materialists but dull to students of metaphysical philosophies. Heartbreak House may come to be considered Shaw's best play. Saint Joan, about a visionary, was written by a rationalist. Androcles and the Lion is "sheer vulgarity."

1667 Bentley, Eric [Russell]. "Bernard Shaw Dead," TAM, XXXV (Jan 1951), 22-24; rptd in IN SEARCH OF THEATRE, by Eric Bentley (1953), q.v.
[Tribute to Shaw at his death, calling him the first civilized man and the happiest great writer who ever lived, his worthy predecessor being Don Quixote. Photograph.]

1668 Bentley, Eric [Russell]. "Hinter der Maske des Narren" (Behind the Mask of the Fool), DER MONAT, III (Jan 1951), 355-65.
The real meaning of Shaw was that he was a tool of something greater than himself. It was his aim to give our civilization new directions, but most people never saw beyond G.B.S. the buffoon. Shaw's plays reveal more about his real character than about his teachings. Shaw failed as propagandist but he survived as an artist. [In German.]

1669 Bentley, Eric [Russell]. "Shaw Dead," ENVOY: A REVIEW OF LITERATURE AND ART, 1951, pp. 8-12.
[Obit.] Shaw was the great taskmaster of our age and the first civilized man.

1670 "Bernhard [sic] Shaw o učenju modernih jezikov" (Bernard Shaw on the Study of Modern Languages), GLEDALŠKI LIST DRAMA (Ljubljana), VII (1950/51), 237-41. [Not seen.] [In Croatian.]

1671 Besenbuch, Max L. "Shaw Als Historiker" (Shaw as Historian). Unpublished dissertation, Erlangen University, 1951. [Listed in DAID.]

1672 Beyer, William H. "Shaw in the Spotlight," SCHOOL AND SOCIETY, LXXIV (22 Dec 1951), 405-9.
Saint Joan is Shaw's finest play. The Epilog is weak because Shaw cannot resist editorializing in it, and it is best to eliminate it in production. Uta Hagen in the Theater Guild revival (Cort Theater, NY) fails to reveal the "light and heat" in the role perhaps because it escapes Margaret Webster in her directorial approach.

1673 Boas, Frederick S. "Joan of Arc in Shakespeare, Schiller, and Shaw," SHAKESPEARE QUARTERLY, II (Jan 1951), 35-45.
Shakespeare's Joan La Pucelle in I HENRY VI and Schiller's Joan in JUNGFRAU VON ORLEANS are false representatives of history. Shaw's Saint Joan is not. Dissatisfied with those dramatists' interpretations of Joan, Shaw represented her truly by understanding her environment. Thus, Shaw's play exhibits the conflict not so much between Joan and her antagonists (as the other plays do) but rather between the

Church, as well as the feudal system, and Private
Judgement, as well as the spirit of nationality.

1674 Borges, Jorge Luis. "Nota sobre (hacia) Bernard
Shaw" (Note on Bernard Shaw), SUR (Argentina), No 200
(June 1951), p. 3; rptd as "For Bernard Shaw," in
Borges, OTHER INQUISITIONS, 1937-1952, trans by
Ruth L. C. Simms (Austin: University of Texas P,
1964; NY: Washington Square P, 1966); also in Shaw R,
IX (May 1966), 52-55.
Shaw's eminence in literature rests on the great characters
he creates, the most ephemeral of which is G. B. S. His
"basic subjects are philosophy and ethics," and his work
"leaves an aftertaste of liberation." [In Spanish.]

1675 Brown, John Mason. "The Prophet and the Maid,"
SRL, XXXIV (27 Oct 1951), 27-29; rptd in AS THEY
APPEAR (NY: McGraw-Hill, 1952), pp. 71-76.
Saint Joan, Shaw's greatest play and one of the greatest
plays of the modern theater, is magnificent not because
Shaw retells the story of the Maid but because the "story
comes to life in a new and memorable way." Though a
Catholic, Shaw's Joan is one of the first Protestant
martyrs. Shaw's Epilog is essential to understanding his
meaning and Joan's canonization. Although the production of
Joan at the Cort Theater (NY) is commendable, Joan eludes
the actress Uta Hagen. Her performance at best is
competent, at worst "plainly inadequate." The "Joan of all
Joans" was Shaw himself when he read the part to Sybil
Thorndike's company.

1676 Brown, John Mason. "What—Shaw Again?" SRL,
XXXIV (10 Nov 1951), 22-26; rptd in AS THEY APPEAR
(NY: McGraw-Hill, 1952), pp. 77-85, and in DRAMATIS
PERSONAE: A RETROSPECTIVE SHOW (NY: Viking Press,
1963), pp. 129-35.
[A laudatory review of the Carnegie Hall (NY) reading of
Don Juan in Hell from Man and Superman directed by Charles
Laughton and read by Laughton, Charles Boyer, Cedric
Hardwicke, and Agnes Moorhead. Illustrations in article
include photographs of the Drama Quartet and a drawing of
Shaw.]

1677 Bullrich, Silvina. "Dieciséis esbozos de mí mismo, G.B.S." (Sixteen Self Sketches, G.B.S.), ATLÁNTIDA (Argentina), XXXIV (April 1951), 70.
[Review of the Spanish translation of Sixteen Self-Sketches.] This autobiography truly reveals Shaw the man and the artist. [In Spanish.]

1678 Byington, Steven T. "Colons in Shavian Prose," SRL, XXXIV (18 Aug 1951), 23.
Shaw's liberal use of colons does not result from his reading of the Bible, but instead the colon is rhetorical. His notion of the effectiveness of speech does not derive from the theater, but from his experience as a platform speaker.

1679 Caballero y Lastres, Daniel. "Prefacio a la dramática de Shaw" (Preface to the Drama of Shaw), MERCURIO PERUANO, XXXI (1951), 41-46.
Shaw is an intellectual writer who deserves respect despite all the apparent complexities and contradictions in his personality. He was a humorist but also a man deserving affection. He was both attractive and repulsive because of his lack of humanity and because of the excess of rich ideology. [In Spanish.]

1680 Camerino, Aldo. "L'ultimo Shaw" (The Last Shaw), SCRITTORI DI LINGUA INGLESE (English Authors) [first published in 1951, place unknown] (Milan: Ricciardi, 1968), 201-3.
Bernard Shaw's Rhyming Picture Guide to Ayot St. Lawrence is saddening, though a pleasure for a lover of Shaw to glance through. After many years, Shaw admirers have finally lost patience with him. Over the past twenty years, readers have come to ask whether Shaw's reputation was really what remains in the mind, or was his work clever witchcraft by a clown of genius? Yet the fascination of Shaw at his best remains. Scenes, if now without the freshness and surprise of first reading, can still touch and amuse us. [In Italian.]

1681 Cardona, Rafael. "Memorias de una entrevista fracasada" (Memories of an Interview that Failed), REPORTORIO AMERICANO (Costa Rica), XLVII (15 April 1951), 65-66.

Shaw is a man sick with terror of life. While in Mexico, he ridiculed and frustrated reporters. [In Spanish.]

1682 Casson, Lewis. "G.B.S. and the Court Theatre," List, XLVI (12 July 1951), 53-54.
Shaw's plays as well as his artistic partnership with Granville Barker assured the success of the Court Theater and brought the British theater more into line with the more advanced theater of the Continent. John Bull's Other Island is important in that its success made the continuance of the Court Theater's season possible. After the successes of You Never Can Tell and Man and Superman, being assured of an audience at the Court Theater, Shaw began to write plays to please himself. The next play, Major Barbara, overemphasized the polemical. [From a talk on the BBC Third Programme. Photograph of scene from John Bull.]

1683 Casson, Lewis. "G.B.S. at Rehearsal," DRAMA, ns XX (Spring 1951), 9-13.
[Includes two photographs: one of Saint Joan, a second probably the last photograph of Shaw before his death.] Candida set the foundations of the famous Vedrenne-Barker management at the Court Theater. From Major Barbara on, with the exceptions of The Doctor's Dilemma and Saint Joan, Shaw tended to use the theater rather than serve it. Exceedingly careful about directing his own plays in England, Shaw was distinctly careless about foreign presentations. Shaw was a great director, but he sometimes overdid the comic side.

1684 Castelli, Alberto. "Bernard Shaw e la Religione" (Bernard Shaw and Religion), SCUOLA CATTOLICA, LXXIX (1951), 163-70.
The Adventures of the Black Girl in Her Search for God signals the beginning of Shaw's thoughts on the origin and development of the concept of God. Shaw demonstrates that God changes with the times and that the old concepts of the God of the scriptures are passé. Unfortunately Shaw never considered Dante's explanation in Canto IV of the PARADISO. Shaw's Saint Joan is a "Galtonian visionary" who produces the visions she desires. In Back to Methuselah he reveals his confusion about the dogmas of the Immaculate Conception and the Virginity of Mary, and he denies original sin. Shaw

is capable of humanism and is a better soul than the ideas he expresses. [In Italian.]

1685 Chappelow, Allan. "An Ideal Model," PHOTOGRAPHIC JOURNAL, XCI (Jan 1951), Sec A, 36-39. [Account of photographing Shaw. Six photographs.]

1686 Clemens, Cyril. "Notes on Bernard Shaw," HOBBIES, LV (Feb 1951), 137-38. [Very brief notes on plays by Shaw: Candida, John Bull's Other Island, Captain Brassbound's Conversion, Man and Superman, Androcles and the Lion, Back to Methuselah, Saint Joan. Includes letters from Shaw to Clemens.]

1687 Coburn, Alvin Langdon. "George Bernard Shaw: 26 July 1856 to 2 November 1950," PHOTOGRAPHIC JOURNAL, XCI (Jan 1951), Sec A, 29-30. [Anecdotes of Shaw and photography. Photograph.]

1688 Cole, Margaret. "G.B.S. and Fabian Socialism," FABIAN JOURNAL, III (Feb 1951), 11-14. Shaw's most important contribution to Fabian socialism is his style. Secondly, he helped establish the tradition of hard work. Thirdly, he helped create the spirit of tolerance. [Photograph of Shaw with a group from an early Fabian Summer School.]

1689 Collins, A. S. ENGLISH LITERATURE OF THE TWENTIETH CENTURY (Lond: University Tutorial P, 1951), pp. 2, 5, 281, 282-84, 288, 296, 314-27, 402-3. The most important development in the English theater in the nineties was Shaw, who dwarfs all other dramatists in the twentieth century before World War I. In the history of English drama he is second only to Shakespeare.

1690 Corrigan, Andrew J. "No Peace for Printers," BRITISH PRINTER, July-Aug 1951, pp. 58-61. Shaw's provision in his will to change the English alphabet will not work. "English may have become what it is by accident . . . but it has not remained as it is by accident."

1691 Crane, Milton. "Pygmalion: Bernard Shaw's Dramatic Theory and Practice," PMLA, LXVI (Dec 1951), 879-85.
Shaw's own plays do not support his theories of the discussion play. Pygmalion, Man and Superman, and The Doctor's Dilemma show that Shaw's dramatic technique is old fashioned, because Shaw recognized the soundness of traditional drama.

1692 Dahlhaus, Carl. "Bernard Shaws Heilige Johanna" (Bernard Shaw's Saint Joan) BDDTG, No 1 (1950-51).
Saint Joan is both a dramatic chronicle and a parable. The play is marked by serene reserve rather than by angry bitterness. [In German.]

1693 "Der Tod Methusalems" (Methuselah's Death), DER MONAT, III, (Jan 1951), 365-68.
[Quotations of international reactions to Shaw's death and some information about his last years, his death and his testament.[[In German.]

1694 Deutsch, Otto Erich. "The Reception of Schubert's Works in England," MONTHLY MUSICAL RECORD, LXXXI (Nov 1951), 236-39.
Shaw was not alone in wronging Schubert in England.

1695 Eaton, Walter Prichard. "Bernard Shaw as a Playwright," BULLETIN OF THE SHAW SOCIETY OF AMERICA, I (Autumn 1951), 6-7.
[Brief history of early Shaw productions in NY.] Shaw's plays are God's gift to the players; his characters, often Shaw in disguise, are a joy to the players. The Great Catherine, Cleopatra, Joan, Dubedat, Eliza Doolittle, and General Burgoyne are all choice roles for actors.

1696 Editor. "The Last Prophet," BRITAIN TODAY, CLXXVI (Jan 1951), 1-3.
Shaw set the pace in emancipating humankind from the obsolete ideas of a crumbling society.

1697 Eells, George. "The Third Saint Joan," TAM, XXXV (Nov 1951), 32-33, 88-89.
[Review of Uta Hagen's performance (Cort Theater, NY) as Saint Joan.]

1698 Ervine, St. John. "The Mind of Bernard Shaw,"
List, XLVI (15 Nov 1951), 840-41.
The major theme which runs through the whole of Shaw's work
is his belief that humankind has been given a brain to
comprehend the purpose of the Life Force. Thus, the
conflict in his plays is between the exceptional
individual, the person who uses his or her mind
constructively, and the obstinate and immovable mob, as in
You Never Can Tell, Major Barbara, and Caesar and
Cleopatra. The plays of affirmation or great belief are
Heartbreak House, Back to Methuselah, and Saint Joan. The
plays of decline are The Apple Cart, Too True To Be Good,
and On the Rocks, which show Shaw's fear that humans will
go the same way as the dinosaurs. Proper appreciation of
Shaw depends upon knowing four facts about his life: he was
a proud Irish Protestant; he belonged to an upper class
family, declining in place; he was a Victorian; and he was
a genial Puritan. [From a talk on the BBC Third Programme.]

1699 Fatur, Bogomil. "Komediograf G. B. Shaw
(Kritična študija)" (G. B. Shaw the Writer of
Comedies: A Critical Study), NOVI SVET [Ljubljana],
No 1 (1951), 30-42.
[Obit that places Shaw in the world events of his lifetime
and among the major world writers.] [In Slovene.]

1700 Filipovíc, Rudolf. "G. B. Shaw i lingvistika"
(G. B. Shaw and Linguistics), REPUBLIKA, VII (Feb
1951), 203-6.
Two elements of the English language interested Shaw while
he was still in his twenties: pronunciation and spelling.
He worked unsuccessfully to secure a chair at Oxford for
the English phonetician, Henry Sweet, so that he could use
him to influence reform. Pygmalion was more effective; he
had already dealt with the issue in the Preface to Captain
Brassbound's Conversion. Shaw always tried to be up-to-
date, and in the 1946 Preface to Pygmalion he eliminated
some old rules and introduced new ones. Two of his findings
are very important: 1) In America Sweet's phonetic
stenography is successful; and 2) An exact and complete
phonetic alphabet is neither practical nor necessary for
everyday use. [In Croatian.]

1701 Fiske, Irving. BERNARD SHAW'S DEBT TO WILLIAM BLAKE. WITH FOREWORD AND NOTES BY G.B.S. (Lond: Shaw Society [Shavian Tract No 2], 1951; rptd Folcroft, Pa.: Folcroft P, 1970); rptd in G. B. SHAW: A COLLECTION OF CRITICAL ESSAYS, ed by R. J. Kaufmann (Englewood Cliffs, NJ: Prentice-Hall, 1965).
Both Shaw and Blake deal with humankind and the world from a religious point of view. Both write directly and with no adornment; both have little use for the romantic emotions; both reject the notion of progress in art and human affairs; for both religion and politics are the same; both are incensed by the corruption of the substance of religion into its forms; both insist on the unity of all human drives; both measure human conduct, not in terms of good and evil, but in terms of profit and loss; both preach the need for sound intellectual judgment; and both regard the only sin to be subjection to the concept of sin.

1702 Fukase, Motohiro. "Bernard Shaw, Bunun no Shocho" (Bernard Shaw, the Vicissitudes of Literary Fate), TENBO (Tokyo), No 61 (Jan 1951), 66-69.
Shaw seems to have lost his power to effect change, in the sense that all his ideas and ideals have virtually been realized under the Labour government administrations. The decisive factor that makes Shaw dated is his lack of poetry, such as that identified with D. H. Lawrence. Poetic drama is the major trend of modern English literature and is now flourishing. [In Japanese.]

1703 Gassner, John. "Shaw as Drama Critic," TAM, XXXVI (May 1951), 26-29, 91-95; rptd in THE THEATRE IN OUR TIMES (NY: Crown Publishers, 1954), pp. 123-33.
Shaw's considerable dramatic criticism, though perhaps most memorable for its polemics and Olympian judgments, was most importantly a constructive and creative force in the development of English theater, emphasizing as it did the intellectual element in drama. His reviews in the 1890's took modernists like Pinero to task for conveying conventional sentiments while pretending to the realism of Ibsen. Realism for Shaw was not characterized by verisimilitude achieved technically but rather by an interest in ideas that capture and hold the audience's attention. Similarly, a character was real who demonstrated

intelligence in discussion. Discussion is not an anti-dramatic device, but rather a reflection of intelligence permeating the work as it does in the plays of Ibsen in a non-formulaic way. Just as he tried to encourage genuine admiration for Ibsen, Shaw tried to free Shakespeare from his idolaters and to bring his plays to a dramatic audience rather than solely to a reading one. Always concerned with the play in production, Shaw's criticism suggested that even Shakespeare's sense of character owes much to mood or temperament conveyed in the sound of the line, not in its mundane content. He opposed revivals of Shakespeare that obscured his genius with costuming and elaborate scenery. He often depreciated Shakespeare for his sometime conventional and moral point of view and his "potboiling proclivities." Yet, he constantly championed Shakespeare as the supreme poet-playwright. He objected only to uncritical admiration of the Bard and the unchallenged substitution of his plays for modern dramas of ideas on the British stage.

1704 "G. B. S.: 1856-1950," ENGLISH, VIII (Spring 1951), 169.
Shaw's title to greatness lies in the totality of his activities and gifts. Comparison of Shaw and Shakespeare is impossible. Shaw compares with Ibsen and Strindberg and in some ways with Aristophanes.

1705 "George Bernard Shaw, der große kritische Realist. Zum 95. Geburtstag des Freundes der Sowjetunion und des Friedens" (George Bernard Shaw, Critical Realist. Commemorating the 95th Birthday of the Friend of the Soviet Union and the Friend of Peace), BÖRSENBLATT FÜR DEN DEUTSCHEN BUCHHANDEL (Leipzig), CXVIII (28 July 1951), 376-78.
Shaw is the most important critical realist of bourgeois society. Throughout his life he never tired of uncovering the rotten state of capitalist society. Although some elements in his plays seem dated, in The Apple Cart he correctly anticipated American imperialism. Shaw also thought highly of Stalin. [In German.]

1706 Gernsheim, Helmut. "G.B.S. and Photography," PHOTOGRAPHIC JOURNAL, XCI (Jan 1951), Sec A, 31-36.
"The purpose of this paper is . . . to illuminate [Shaw's] opinions on photography and to quote from the

correspondence that passed between us, in which he disclosed for the first time some information about his photographic activity." [Some of Shaw's correspondence reproduced.]

1707 Glicksberg, Charles I. "The Criticism of Bernard Shaw," SOUTH ATLANTIC QUARTERLY, L (1951), 96-108.
Shaw the critic, like Shaw the dramatist, is, despite disguises, primarily the artist; he is only completely at home in the world of the arts, as he says in the introduction to Immaturity. Shaw is an impressionistic critic. Criticism for him was a passion for the ideal of artistic perfection. His criticism is always written in the first person; he is always looking at the work of art for the creative power it communicates. As a critic of painting, of music, of the drama, what he was fighting for so violently was to vindicate the freedom and integrity of the artist against the indifference and inertia of the Philistines. In Love Among the Artists he insists that earnestness of intention is not enough to compensate for lack of inherent ability, that genius carries everything before it. Shaw considers the test of great literature to be the artist in full revolt against ready-made morality, as can be seen in The Irrational Knot.

1708 Glicksberg, Charles I. "Shaw the Novelist," PRAIRIE SCHOONER, XXV (1951), 1-9.
In spite of their technical flaws, Shaw's novels have a forward-looking morality and anticipate the ideas in the dramas. The novels were rejected not because they lacked competence, but because they advanced ideas that ran counter to Victorian morality. Immaturity is pedantic. But The Irrational Knot is a remarkable performance anticipating a revolt from conventional values. Shaw uses joking as a way of telling the truth. In Love Among the Artists some vital characters appear. Conflict between wealthy and poor classes appears again as well as the conflict of the true artist and the conscientious second-rater. Shaw, however, does not romanticize the life of the artist; the artist is a hard worker, contemptuous of flattery and wealth, of worldly prizes and social distinctions. However, Shaw has not yet begun to formulate his militant conception of art as essentially didactic.

Cashel Byron's Profession attacks the brutality of prizefighting. The cure will come not from moral indignation but from a total reform of society. An Unsocial Socialist is an exposition of the tenets of socialism. Shaw's harshness toward artists who demand special privileges differs greatly from his attitude toward artists in Love. Shaw's novels are based on a false aesthetic; they are exercises aimed at earning a living and gaining a reputation. He hated the art of novel-writing as a form of make-believe.

1709 Goddard, Scott. "George Bernard Shaw," CHESTERIAN, XXV (Jan 1951), 58-59.
[Obit for a famous subscriber.]

1710 Guernsey, Otis L., Jr. "ANTA's Finale," NYHT, 14 May 1951.
The company presenting Getting Married is barely adequate, and the play becomes a tedious succession of witticisms.

1711 Hackett, Francis. "Shaw — and Wells," ATLANTIC MONTHLY, CLXXXVIII (May 1951), 73-76.
[A eulogistic letter about Shaw to U.S. Supreme Court Justice Felix Frankfurter reflecting on Shaw's personal biography and his career.] Although Shaw had obvious limitations of temperament, as Wells knew so well, his brain was first-rate and used for effectiveness, and his gift was histrionic and forensic. As a dramatic critic he used his reviews as a vehicle for propaganda. In his own dramas he invented a community of ideas. He had an aversion to the physical, with sex excluded or made comic, or denied. He could see his heroine as a figure walking out of William Morris's sagas into Candida and Major Barbara and Saint Joan. Comedy was his weapon. Pygmalion is festive. His surefootedness in the dialectic of the theater is a craftsman's joy, though Broadway was too brutally numb to know it. Joan is simple enough for a child to understand. In his dramas he was a social critic, and his characters came from the most unconventional sources until The Doctor's Dilemma. His greatness as a playwright was that he had "fertility of invention, alacrity in devising contrast, power of impact, and novelty of thinking."

1712 Hain, D. E. "Correspondence," RECORD NEWS (Brighton, England), II (Jan 1951), 253-55.
[Comment on Shaw's views on singing methods.]

1713 Harvey, C. J. D. "George Bernard Shaw," ONS EIE BOEK (Capetown), XVII (March 1951), 6-8.
There can be no serious doubt that Shaw is among the five or six most important English dramatists.

1714 Heard, Gerald. "Memories of Shaw and Wells," TOMORROW, X (Feb 1951), 25-30.
Shaw was the epitome of his age. In his first plays the watchword is efficiency. Undershaft, Julius Caesar, Bluntschli and Bohun, perhaps even Mrs. Warren, are types that face the facts of life. The Doctor's Dilemma and Pygmalion represent Shaw's middle phase showing a "Pavlovian conditioning of man through reflexes." Saint Joan, Heartbreak House, Candida, Caesar and Cleopatra, You Never Can Tell, and Back to Methuselah represent Shaw's final phase and the demise of drama as the voice of the seer arrests the actors. Shaw "closed the romantic movement which in its largest span stretches from Sophocles to Shaw--the idea of man meeting woman and together defying the Gods. He has, therefore, also closed that revolutionary period which we call the modern age and which began with the religious revolution." And Shaw has "closed that vast instrument for the molding of individualized man—the theatre."

1715 Henderson, Archibald. "Bernard Shaw and France: Gaelic Triumph or Gallic Repulse?" CAROLINA QUARTERLY, III (March 1951), 42-56.
[A consideration of the impact of Shaw as a dramatist upon the cultivated and enlightened French public, which appears in a slightly different form in Henderson's GEORGE BERNARD SHAW: MAN OF THE CENTURY (1956).]

1716 Henderson, Archibald. "Creative Evolution," BULLETIN OF THE SHAW SOCIETY OF AMERICA, I (Feb 1951), 4-5.
[A letter which was sent to the NYT on 27 Nov 1950, but which was never published in the TIMES.] Shaw first set forth the tenets of his religious faith in the Preface to Man and Superman and in the Don Juan in Hell dream, and

later in <u>Back to Methuselah</u>. Shaw believed that the purpose of life is the Life Force which will continue to try to realize itself. Humankind is only a stage in Shaw's doctrine of Creative Evolution.

1717 Henderson, Archibald. "Shaw's Stature," QQ, LVIII (Spring 1951), 14-22; rptd as "Where Shaw Stands Today," ShawB, I (Autumn 1951), 1-6, and in SUPPLEMENT TO SHAW SOCIETY BULLETIN, XXXIX (June 1951).

As drama critic for the SATURDAY REVIEW, Shaw chose deliberately to create a public alter ego. He is not a critic at all; he is either an advocate or a prosecutor, and he is the most successful artist in self-exploitation in literary history. He was both man and myth. Shaw has the best prose style among writers of the first half of the twentieth century. However, his novels fail as a result of bad timing. <u>Man and Superman</u> is the most brilliant comedy ever penned. Shaw first wrote in the Aristotelian manner. <u>Major Barbara</u> introduces the disquisitory play, the two most conspicuous examples of which are <u>The Doctor's Dilemma</u> and <u>Heartbreak House</u>. Shaw moved to the discursive drama of which <u>Getting Married</u> is the type-form. He dispensed with plot and said that it could hardly be called a play. The greatest British drama since the time of Shakespeare is <u>Saint Joan</u>. Shaw's best plays in addition to <u>Saint Joan</u> are <u>Candida</u>, <u>Superman</u>, <u>Androcles and the Lion</u>, <u>Heartbreak</u>, and <u>Back to Methuselah</u>. Other plays which will surely hold the boards for a long time are <u>Arms and the Man</u>, <u>The Doctor's Dilemma</u>, <u>John Bull's Other Island</u>, <u>You Never Can Tell</u>, <u>Caesar and Cleopatra</u>, <u>Barbara</u>, and <u>Dilemma</u>. Certain of his plays wear the badge of opera: <u>Disciple</u>, <u>Arms</u>, <u>The Man of Destiny</u>, <u>Captain Brassbound's Conversion</u>, <u>Caesar</u>, <u>The Apple Cart</u>, and <u>Methuselah</u>. Shaw transferred the Socratic dialog from the Acropolis to the modern stage and by expanding the group of interlocutors evolved the Shavian drama. [Eulogy before the Shaw Society of America at Shavian Vespers meeting, the Grolier Club, Feb 1951.]

1718 Hudson, Lynton. THE ENGLISH STAGE, 1850-1950 (Lond: George G. Harrap & Co., Ltd. 1951), pp. 100, 105, 115, 119, 120, 121, 124, 128-34, 140, 149-50, 155, 161, 163, 166, 169-70, 171, 175-76, 200, 211, 216.

[Decade by decade survey of play production on the English stage.]

1719 Iijima, Kohei. "Shaw to Chekhov—Shoshin no Ie to Sakura no Sono tono Kankei nitsuite—" (Shaw and Chekhov; the Relationship between Heartbreak House and THE CHERRY ORCHARD) EIBUNGAKU, KENKYU TO KANSHO (Waseda U, Tokyo) No 2 (June 1951), 27-38; rptd in SHAKESPEARE OBOEGAKI (Papers on Shakespeare) (Tokyo: Waseda Daigaku Shuppanbu, 1956), pp. 121-38.
The influence of THE CHERRY ORCHARD on Heartbreak House has often been pointed out, and there are, in fact, many similarities between them. They show, however, more marked differences, particularly in the quality of laughter. [In Japanese.]

1720 Insúa, Alberto. "Cleopatra y Bernard Shaw" (Cleopatra and Bernard Shaw), LA VANGUARDIA (Argentina), 20 Feb 1951, p. 7.
Shaw follows the tradition of Plutarch and Shakespeare in depicting Cleopatra's love affairs in human and real terms. [In Spanish.]

1721 Irving, Laurence. HENRY IRVING: THE ACTOR AND HIS WORLD (Lond: Faber & Faber, 1951), passim.
Shaw was an implacable enemy of Irving. Art was a sounding-board for Shaw's polemics. The critical method which he applied to music worked for the theater: to startle his readers to attention by comic destruction of their contemporary idols. "He had championed Wagner by disparaging Brahms and mocking at Paderewski; now he would force the public to listen to Ibsen and himself by decrying Shakespeare and ridiculing Irving." Though Shaw and Irving wrought lasting changes in the English theater, they turned their backs on each other. Irving was orthodox and established; Shaw was the dissenter. The rift was complete when Irving rejected The Man of Destiny. Shaw battled Irving to get Ellen Terry in Shavian parts and away from Irving. Irving dismissed Shaw the critic as an eccentric. Shaw was obsessed by Irving as the symbol of an outworn romanticism.

1722 Ishida, Kenji. "Bernard Shaw to Eigo no Hatsuon" (Bernard Shaw and Pronunciation of English), KAICHOON (Kyoto), No 1 (June 1951), pp. 2-9.
[A brief survey of Shaw's interest in the English language.] [In Japanese.]

1723 Ishida, Kenji. "Shaw," in GENDAI BUNGAKU (Modern Literature), ed by the editorial office of Chikuma Shobo (Tokyo: Chikuma Shobo [Bungaku Kozo, V], 1951), pp. 197-201.
[A brief survey of Shaw's life and works up to Saint Joan, which Ishida regards as Shaw's last great play.] [In Japanese.]

1724 Isobe, Yuichiro. "GBS to Igirisu no Shinbun" (GBS and the British Press), EIGO SEINEN (Tokyo), XCVII (March 1951), 105-7.
[Summary of news report by the British press when Shaw died. Isobe lists over 30 obit notices.] [In Japanese.]

1725 Jackson, Barry. "Shaw At Malvern," DRAMA, ns XX (Spring 1951), 29-31.
[A history of Shaw plays at the Malvern Festival; a photograph of Shaw and Elsie Fogerty.]

1726 Johnson, A. E. "Encounters with G.B.S.," DALHOUSIE REVIEW, XXXI (April 1951), 19-22.
Shaw was not a great dramatist; he was a great craftsman. Shaw could never have written such plays as MACBETH, OTHELLO, and LEAR, and even Saint Joan is overestimated and cannot approximate them. Shaw used up his immortality while living. He may have understood ideas, but he was not a philosopher, and he lacked the gift of poetry. Instead of being a seer, Shaw was a typical Victorian reactionary. He had the worst of modern diseases—self insistence. His own dazzle hurt his perception. Of blood, sweat, and tears, he was deficient in the first and last.

1727 Jovanović, S. A. "Bernar So, Odlomak iz Rada" (Fragment from a Major Work), LETOPIS MATICE SRPSKE (Chronicle of the Serbian Mother) (Novi Sad), III (1951), 240-66.
Shaw created a new form, the discussion drama, which was and is difficult for the audience. It is a question of

whether the prefaces or the plays are more interesting. Shaw is the English Ibsen, even though Shaw is a poet and Ibsen is not. He also resembles Brieux, though Shaw avoided having a thesis. He is a true writer of the ideological theater, though he draws no conclusions. [Survey of the variety of objects of Shaw's witty attacks in his plays.] [In Serbian.]

1728 Kawatake, Shigetoshi. "Nippon ni okeru Bernard Shaw" (Bernard Shaw in Japan), EIGO SEINEN (Tokyo), XCVII (March 1951), 103-5.

Ibsen, Hauptmann and Shaw were driving forces of the early modern drama movement in Japan. However, Shaw's influence on Japanese writers has been slight, mainly because his comedy has not been understood properly. [Chronicles major Shaw productions in Japan from 1910 through the 1930's.] [In Japanese.]

1729 Kerr, Walter F. "The Theaters," NYHT, 20 Dec 1951.

Olivier has become almost too world-weary in Caesar and Cleopatra. Vivien Leigh dominates most of the way.

1730 Krokover, Rosalyn. "Shaw as a Dance Critic," MUSICAL COURIER, CXLIII (15 Jan 1951), 15.

Shaw exposed the pre-Diaghilev ballet in England and visualized the psychological ballet of the future. He castigated those dance critics who concealed their lack of sensibility with technical jargon.

1731 Kropotkin, Princess Alexandra. "Pleasant Memories of Bernard Shaw," AMERICAN MERCURY, LXXII (Jan 1951), 23-29.

[Reminiscences in an article filled with Shavian comments and quips of the times when the author was together with Shaw.]

1732 Krutch, Joseph Wood. "Shaw's Last Play," NATION, CLXXII (16 June 1951), 565.

[Review of THIRTY YEARS WITH G.B.S. by Blanche Patch and of Buoyant Billions.] Shaw's last play, Buoyant Billions, lacks coherence, but his passion and wit are still quite evident.

1733 Langner, Lawrence. THE MAGIC CURTAIN: THE STORY OF A LIFE IN TWO FIELDS, THEATRE AND INVENTION (NY: E. P. Dutton & Co., Inc., 1951), passim.
[Autobiography of Lawrence Langner, founder of the Theater Guild, containing anecdotes and lengthy discussions of Shaw and Shaw's relationship to the Theater Guild, as well as photographs of some Shaw productions.]

1734 Langner, Lawrence. "Saint Joan—a Play for Today," NYT, 30 Sept 1951, II, pp. 1, 3.
Shaw's Joan is a saint of freedom of conscience. No other saint has so important a message for today in light of the Kremlin's oppression. Joan is also a saint of the kind of patriotism we honor. [Recollections of original Theater Guild production of Saint Joan.]

1735 Langner, Lawrence. "Shaw and Back to Methuselah," TAM, XXXV (Nov 1951), 22-23, 78-80.
[Langner's recollections of the first production of Back to Methuselah, given in New York in 1922.] Because Methuselah was so long, there was a need to cut it. Thus, The Tragedy of an Elderly Gentleman, which was part of the second bill, was cut drastically by Shaw, who had in the past refused to cut plays. [Photograph of a painting of Shaw.]

1736 Luis, Rafael de. "Un deseo lingüístico de Shaw" (A Linguistic Wish of Shaw), LA VANGUARDIA (Argentina), 25 March 1951, 11.
[Describes Shaw's will, especially the provisions for reforming the English language.] [In Spanish.]

1737 Lynch, Vernon E. "George Bernard Shaw and the Comic." Unpublished dissertation, University of Texas, 1951. [Listed in Frederic M. Litto, AMERICAN DISSERTATIONS ON THE DRAMA AND THE THEATRE.]

1738 McCord, Bert. "The Theaters," NYHT, 5 Oct 1951.
Saint Joan is great theater. Uta Hagen's performance (Cort Theater, NY) does not attain magic.

1739 MacKaye, Percy. "A Note Concerning Arnold Daly and Bernard Shaw," ShawB, I (Autumn 1951), 7-8.
At a time when Shaw's plays were being scoffed at by leading New York critics in 1901, actor Arnold Daly

launched a "Shavian crusade," producing Shaw plays off-Broadway. Daly's persistent efforts advanced Shaw's influence in America.

1740 M[ackerness], E. D. "Obituary: George Bernard Shaw (1856-1950)," MUSIC SURVEY, III (1951), 84-85.
As a music critic, Shaw avoided technical jargon. His prose style is honest with an economy of statement. He was skilled in separating great performances from shallow exhibitionism.

1741 Mann, Thomas. "He Was Mankind's Friend," List, XLV (18 Jan 1951), 98-99, 102; rptd and trans in whole or in part in "George Bernard Shaw," BULLETIN OF THE SHAW SOCIETY OF AMERICA, I (Feb 1951), 2; "G.B.S.—Mankind's Friend," YALE REVIEW, XL (1951), 412-20; "Die Götter gehen dahin: Eine Rede über Bernard Shaw" (The Gods are Leaving: A Speech about Bernard Shaw), NEUE LITERARISCHE WELT (Heidelberg), IV (10 Feb 1953), 3-4; "Bernard Shaw (1950)," ALTES UND NEUES (Frankfurt/Main: S. Fischer, 1953), pp. 237-47; trans Louise Servicen, "L'Impertinence Libératrice," CAHIERS DES SAISONS, XXXVII (Spring 1964), 167-72; and CRITICAL HERITAGE, pp. 395-402.
Germany recognized Shaw's importance before the English did, and it was because of the performance of his plays in Germany that the London Independent Theater began to produce them. Shaw claimed to have a great indebtedness to German culture, but in fact he seems to have been little influenced by the literature; it was German music that influenced him strongly. He developed his own distinctive style, a style as unrealistic as that of opera but very effective, both in his prefaces, where he used it in his own voice, and in the plays, where he used it in the speeches of his characters. This style is well illustrated in the Preface to Saint Joan, a Preface so good that it almost makes the play superfluous. The two sides of Shaw were Shaw the radical socialist, who worked to advance socialist causes through speeches, through books such as The Intelligent Woman's Guide to Socialism and Capitalism, and through his plays; and Shaw the theater critic and dramatist, who paid homage to the two greatest influences on his plays in The Perfect Wagnerite and The Quintessence of Ibsenism. Saint Joan, Shaw's "closest approach to

tragedy," deserves its world reputation, and <u>Heartbreak</u> <u>House</u> is in the "highest rank of comedy." Among his other enduring plays are <u>Caesar and Cleopatra</u>, <u>Man and Superman</u>, <u>Pygmalion</u>, <u>Androcles and the Lion</u>, and <u>The Apple Cart</u>.

In the plays not only the physical, but also the spiritual, qualities are depicted with a touch of meagerness and frigidity which does not seem consistent with the idea of greatness. Perhaps Shaw was a "laughing prophet" of future times when the goal of all art will be to rise above the difficulties and agonies of life to a level where they can be treated lightly, or perhaps the lightness of touch was so easy for him that he was really not the right person to deal with these difficulties and agonies. In any case, he loved humankind and throughout his life used his wit and art to fight against stupidity, which he felt is the greatest obstacle to rising to ever-higher levels of maturity. There is something frigid and haggard about his work and his person, but he was undoubtedly "mankind's friend." [Speech for Third Programme of the BBC.]

> **1742** Maurois, André. "Bernard Shaw über Bernard Shaw" (Bernard Shaw on Bernard Shaw), UNIVERSITAS, VI (1951), 1305-10.

[Maurois on Shaw's comments scribbled on the margins of Maurois' critical essay on Shaw, and his personal encounters with Shaw and H. G. Wells.] [In German.]

> **1743** Monterroso, Augusto. "G. B. S., Mala noticia," (G. B. S., Bad News), REVISTA DE GUATEMALA, I (1 April 1951), 188-90.

Shaw is the first contemporary humorist, not only because of his engaging manner or the formal hilarity of his style, but also because of the originality of his stand on life. There were in his life, thought and work, a fund of ideas and clear and sincere feeling that has contributed to rejection of aberration and prejudice. [In Spanish.]

> **1744** Morgan, L. N. "Bernard Shaw the Playwright," BOOKS ABROAD, XXV (Spring 1951), 101-4.

Whatever doubts may exist about Shaw's influence, there can be no debate on the stimulus which he gave to other writers. In 1933 the publication of <u>The Adventures of the</u> <u>Black Girl in Her Search for God</u> stimulated several

publications: THE ADVENTURES OF THE BLACK MAN, THE
ADVENTURES OF THE BROWN GIRL, THE ADVENTURES OF THE WHITE
GIRL, all searching for God, and THE ADVENTURES OF GOD IN
HIS SEARCH FOR MR. SHAW. Numerous publications have been
written about Shaw. In 1913 Androcles and the Lion was
criticized not as a play but as an enormously clever insult
thrown in the face of the British people. However, by 1950
no critic would interpret his essays as anything but drama.
His plays were often considered essays because of the
prefaces accompanying them and because they were often
published for readers before they were performed. His plays
are characterized by elements of farce; sermonizing; fat
parts for performers; friends as models for his characters;
and comic names to reveal character types. He followed
other traditions of the English playhouse. The Devil's
Disciple depends on mistaken identity, reversals of
situation, and a last minute rescue with musical
accompaniment. Getting Married and Misalliance were
experiments in classical unities; Saint Joan concludes with
a comic epilog just like the tragedies of the late
seventeenth and early eighteenth centuries. As an artist in
his profession he fiddled variations on whatever themes
came his indefatigable way. [Photograph.]

1745 "Mr. Shaw's Final Irony," NYT, 23 March 1951,
p. 20.
The last irony of Shaw's life is his will. Shaw, who once
may have hoped to reform humanity, has left a will which is
merely a futile attempt to reform the alphabet.

1746 Mumford, Lewis. "Patrick Geddes and His CITIES
IN EVOLUTION," MAGAZINE OF ART, XLIV (Jan 1951), 25-
31.
In almost every particular Shaw was the opposite of Patrick
Geddes, his contemporary, but they were equals in their
brilliance, the breadth of their scope, and their contempt
for sham.

1747 Murray, Gilbert. "A Few Memories," DRAMA, ns XX
(Spring 1951), 7-9.
Cusins in Major Barbara does in fact resemble Murray, as
Shaw suggested. The satirist Shaw was a "world-changer" and
"free from personal malice." While people spoke of Shaw's
conceit, he did not overrate his powers.

1748 Nakano, Yoshio. "G. B. Shaw nokoto" (On G. B. Shaw), NINGEN (Tokyo), VI (Jan 1951), 224-26.

From the turn of the century until World War I Shaw exerted a wide-spread influence as an iconoclast and a born writer of comedy, a laughing philosopher. [In Japanese.]

1749 Nathan, George Jean. "Mr. Nathan Goes to the Play," TAM, XXXV (Dec 1951), 20-21, 80; rptd in Nathan, THE THEATRE IN THE FIFTIES (NY: Knopf, 1953), pp. 192-94.

Saint Joan is such a notable work that nothing can damage its inner life and vitiate its effect. It might be acted successfully by marionettes. Uta Hagen (Cort Theater, NY) is the picture of an actress operating by a clocked mechanism.

1750 Nishiwaki, Junzaburo. "Bernard Shaw no Issho" (Bernard Shaw's Life), GAKUTO (Tokyo), XLVIII (Jan 1951), 22-25.

Shaw is a modern Aristophanes, and his achievement shows a brilliant fusion of journalism and theater. He is essentially a man of the nineteenth century. Although he is a literary celebrity throughout the early twentieth century, his contribution to modern English literature since World War I is not great. [In Japanese.]

1751 Ocampo, Victoria. "The Mighty Dead," SUR (Argentina), CC (June 1951), 57; rptd in TESTIMONIOS, 5th series (1950-1957), Buenos Aires, 1957, 33-39.

Lady Nancy Astor invited Victoria Ocampo to meet Shaw at his home early in the 1940's. [In Spanish.]

1752 O'Hegarty, P. S. "Shaw," DUBLIN MAGAZINE, ns XXVI (July-Sept 1951), 47-51.

Shaw was original; he borrowed from no one. An iconoclast, to whom nothing was sacred, he was a prime destroyer of illusions. For fifty years Shaw was the "greatest all-round intelligence writing in England." Man and Superman is his masterpiece. After Saint Joan Shaw wrote nothing significant.

1753 Pacheco, Eleonora. "Las cenizas de George Bernard Shaw" (The Ashes of George Bernard Shaw), HISTORIUM (Argentina), XII (March 1951), 44-45.

Shaw's writings and religion are vital causes of crime
because he and the evolutionists in general have glorified
the eradication of ideas on morality. He is responsible for
the decision of a drug addict, Joan Lee, to kill her blind
and sick child. [In Spanish.]

1754 Panter-Downes, Mollie. "A Reporter at Large:
The Shrine," NYer, XXVII (14 April 1951), 82-96.
[A brief historical perspective on Ayot St. Lawrence, and a
fuller description of Shaw's Corner, including anecdotal
reminiscences of Mrs. Alice Laden's years as Shaw's
housekeeper, who became tour guide of Shaw's Corner when it
was opened to the public.]

1755 Patch, Blanche. THIRTY YEARS WITH G.B.S. (Lond:
Victor Gollancz; NY: Dodd, Mead, 1951).
Shaw and Sidney Webb were alike in having efficient and
strong-willed wives coming from upper-middle class homes.
Both men had encyclopedic minds, accepted men and women as
they found them, and handled their own publishing. Shaw's
Common Sense about the War caused a hubbub, and his
comments bout the sinking of the Lusitania got him expelled
from the Dramatists' Club. All of Shaw's characters are
creatures of a dramatic situation already determined
despite Shaw's belief that, when he began a play, the fate
of the characters was not predestined. For example,
Heartbreak House grew from a story of Lena Ashwell's about
the character who became Captain Shotover. Before he had a
secretary Shaw wrote all his plays in longhand. Afterwards
he used Pitman shorthand. Shaw never wrote the prefaces
until he had completed the plays. Shaw's mind lay fallow
four years between the writing of Jitta's Atonement, which
ran one week after its opening, and The Apple Cart. Shaw
regarded Hollywood with scorn and his own plays sacrosanct,
but he allowed Gabriel Pascal to film Pygmalion. What Shaw
consistently declined to acknowledge was the right of
people to govern themselves. Shaw declared himself an
atheist, but he seemed a mystic, with his faith in the Life
Force. He was not worldly, was unimpressed by rank, was not
greedy. He said, without Sidney Webb, he might have been a
mere literary wisecracker, like Carlyle or Ruskin. Shaw
thought William Morris was four great men rolled into one.
[Many details--e.g., sources of names of characters,

originals of characters, etc.—from Shaw's secretary of thirty years.]

1756 Pearson, Hesketh. "Bernard Shaw," SIXTEEN PORTRAITS OF PEOPLE WHOSE HOUSES HAVE BEEN PRESERVED BY THE NATIONAL TRUST, ed by L. A. G. Strong (Lond: Naldrett P, 1951), pp. 170-82.
Shaw's main characteristics are traceable to his father and mother and his childhood conditions. [A brief character sketch of Shaw. Illustration of Shaw's Corner by Joan Hassall.]

1757 Pease, Edward. "Early Days," FABIAN JOURNAL, III (Feb 1951), 9-11.
[Personal recollections of Shaw and the Fabian Society. Photograph.]

1758 Percy, Esmé. "Esmé Percy's Last Visit with Shaw," ShawB, I (Feb 1951), 2-3.
[Records a portion of Percy's last visit with Shaw.]

1759 Pettet, Edwin Burr. "Shavian Socialism and the Shavian Life Force; An Analysis of the Relationship between the Philosophic and Economic Systems of George Bernard Shaw." Unpublished dissertation, New York University, 1951. [Listed in DAID.]

1760 Pettet, Edwin Burr. "Shaw's Socialist Life Force," ETJ, III (May 1951), 109-14.
The Life Force philosophy appears to be a paradox. For man the Life Force is a drive toward genius; for woman it is a drive toward security. However, Shavian socialism provides the condition of security, both economic and social, which makes the Life Force philosophy consistent. The early Shaw treated women as static creatures; then, in his Creative Evolution theories, he gallantly defended women against man's bestiality. His preoccupation with Creative Evolution crystallized into the Life Force philosophy of Man and Superman and Back to Methuselah, in which the chattel-woman of the Victorian world metamorphosed into a biologically precocious force in whose power the supposedly dominant male became merely slave labor. In Methuselah femaleness is represented as being more primitive than maleness in that it is more fundamental to the reproductive process. In

<u>Superman</u> the primary work of woman is a biological drive. Woman needs to dominate and control man for purposes of subsistence. However, if society were more effectively organized according to Shaw's socialism, then the special business of the Life Force could be realized. Equality of income would mean the equalizing of intellectual opportunity. Both men and women in Shavian socialism would then be free to develop in themselves the Life Force that is genius, work toward godhead and the triumph of mind.

1761 Phillpotts, Eden. FROM THE ANGLE OF 88 (Lond, NY, Melbourne, Sydney, Capetown: Hutchinson, 1951), pp. 53-59.
"There was never any 'Colossus-complex' about Shaw; he just happened to be a colossus."

1762 Picón Salas, Mariano. "Bernard Shaw en tiempo pasado" (Bernard Shaw in the Past Tense), REVISTA DE AMERICA, XXII (1951), 126-29; rptd in OBRAS SELECTAS (Madrid: Edime, 1953), pp. 1122-26.
"Shavian" or "choviano" or "chaivano" indicates that which is characteristic of a historical personage who has lived long, a literary method of treating ideas by annoying or laughing at all people, and giving plasticity and figurative clothing to the most abstract concepts, all of which Shaw has done so well. [In Spanish.]

1763 Predan, Jože. "G. B. Shaw," MLADINSKA REVIJA, VI (Feb 1951), 262-68.
Shaw was a socialist from the beginning, though behind his socialism lurks a trace of the aristocrat, sympathy for individualism and the will. His socialism is a battle of the individual against the exploitation of the masses. The strength of his satire against the bourgeoisie lies in his intellectual emancipation; he never loses his balance. His greatness results from his fight against human stupidity and exploitation. We can recognize Swift in Shaw, though where Swift was inarticulate [!], wild, natural, and rude, Shaw was always artistic, never bloody, possessing calm as he cuts the painful abscess of society. Like Anatole France he loved unhappy, lost humanity, but his love of justice was never sentimental. His heritage is the combination of intellect and laughter. [In Slovene.]

1764 Pritzker, Lee. "What Shaw Did," BULLETIN OF THE SHAW SOCIETY OF AMERICA, I (Autumn 1951), 9.
[Eulogy.]

1765 Purdom, C. B. "Shaw as Dramatist: An Appreciation," DRAMA, ns XX (Spring 1951), 16-19.
At the same time that Shaw wrote from inspiration, he was the most practical dramatist. While Shaw wrote in the classical manner, his climax came early in the plays, for which he was criticized. In Man and Superman Shaw depended on talk; talk was excessive in the last act of Major Barbara. His later plays were almost wholly talk. Shaw's plays appear easy to act; they are not. Shaw did not lack heart even though he was a playwright of the head (a weakness). The merit of Shaw's rhetoric is in feeling, but he is not a romantic. Shaw was a comic genius, not a satirist or skeptic. His plays are not a joke but a vision. He is a prophet of the future. [Photograph of Heartbreak House, 1943.]

1766 Robertson, Archibald. "What Shaw Has Taught Us," MONTHLY RECORD [South Place Ethical Society, Lond], March 1951, pp. 10-12.
The changes in the mental climate in the past sixty years are not the work of one man, but Shaw played a notable part. The first article of Shaw's faith is human collective responsibility for the world. He also challenged the concept of good conduct. Morell in Candida is a good man on the right side of the battle against human exploitation, but he cannot see that his wife belongs to herself and not to him. The urge to understand the world and work to change it is humanity's greatest passion. [Summary of an address delivered on 28 Jan.]

1767 Robson, William A. "Bernard Shaw and the Political Quarterly," POLITICAL QUARTERLY, XXII (July 1951), 221-39.
Shaw's financial assistance and encouragement made it possible for the POLITICAL QUARTERLY first to be published. [A history of Shaw's relationship to the POLITICAL QUARTERLY, including Shaw's and the founder's, Robson's, correspondence.]

1768 Rubinstein, H. F. "Shaw as Dramatist: The Shavian Technique," DRAMA, ns XX (Spring 1951), 14-15.

Shaw's drama does not echo back the public voice; he is a good schoolmaster. Heartbreak House is Shaw's HAMLET. Shaw's tour de force non-stop debate, Don Juan in Hell, overtaxes the ordinary human mind. But Shaw's style is flexible, and what grace and charm of personality he can impart.

1769 Russell, Bertrand. "George Bernard Shaw," VIRGINIA QUARTERLY REVIEW, XXVII (1951), 1-7.

Shaw was an almost perfect example of the shy man with an inferiority complex. His wit was developed entirely as a sensitive man's armor against an intrusive world. The greatest service Shaw did was in dispelling humbug by laughter; however, plays about humbug are timely, not eternal. Shaw the playwright was clever but not wise. His wit does sometimes light up absurdities in a manner which is quite astonishing, for example in Arms and the Man. His plays are not as enjoyable when they are wholly serious, like Saint Joan. His disagreements with Darwin led him to admire and popularize Bergson's élan vital in Back to Methuselah. His plays are a reversion to a much earlier type, for his characters do not aim at being complete, rounded human beings, but are each an embodied point of view in an argument. The final judgment upon Shaw will be that he was enormously useful as a reformer, but that his effectiveness as an artist was, to a large extent, temporary. Shaw was both kind and cruel, and both were essential parts of an incredibly vigorous personality.

1770 S., J. P. "Getting Married Revived by ANTA," NYT, 14 May 1951, p. 28.

Even as a Shavian novelty Getting Married is not impressive.

1771 S., N. "Bernard Shaw's Last Play," MANCHESTER GUARDIAN WEEKLY, LXIV (18 Jan 1951), 7.

[Review of the first public performance of Farfetched Fables.]

1772 Salenius, Elmer W. "Harley Granville Barker and the Modern English Theater." Unpublished dissertation, Boston University, 1951. [Listed in McNamee.]

1773 Salter, William. "Radio Notes," NS&Nation, XLI (27 Jan 1951), 97.
The English treated Shaw's death perfunctorily, except for the B.B.C. broadcast of Thomas Mann's talk on Shaw.

1774 Scharff, Erich. "Shaws Androklus und der Löwe" (Shaw's Androcles and the Lion), DIE VOLKSBÜHNE, I, No 7 (1951), 15.
[Mainly describes content of the play.] [In German.]

1775 Scott-James, R. A. FIFTY YEARS OF ENGLISH LITERATURE, 1900-1950 (Lond: Longmans, Green, 1951).
Shaw and Wells produced talkative literature. Shaw's characters are puppets for ideas rather than individualized persons in his plays, with a few exceptions: Candida perhaps, Saint Joan, and Captain Shotover in Heartbreak House. Shaw said in Mrs. Warren's Profession that society rather than the procuress was to blame for the evils of prostitution; in Widowers' Houses society rather than the individual landlord created abuses of the right to property; in Getting Married modern home life is unnatural; in The Doctor's Dilemma the superstition of medical infallibility is exposed. Caesar and Cleopatra does not aim at proving any general proposition; thus, it comes nearer to being a play. In Saint Joan Shaw reaches a higher level because grander emotions are involved. Shaw was a propagandist; his criticism is destructive.

1776 Scott-James, R. A. "George Bernard Shaw," BRITAIN TODAY, CLXXVII (Jan 1951), 4-10.
Shaw's distinctive ideas do not derive from his Fabianism or socialism, but from his reading at the British Museum: Samuel Butler, Henrik Ibsen, and Friederich Nietzsche. His qualifications for reforming society's morals in the guise of a playwright: he was a writer of forceful English; he got to know the stage thoroughly; he was a skillful debator; he was witty. No man who was so fierce in his attack made so very few enemies. [Reproductions of Augustus John portrait and photograph.]

1777 Seresia, Cécile. "G.B. Shaw," LA REVUE
NOUVELLE, IV (15 April 1951), 356-65.
Shaw's legend and personage are his own creation. His only
passion was intellectual, and he had no vices. As a
dramatist he cannot portray passion; he is a dramatic
lecturer. Shaw's ideas in the Preface to Androcles and the
Lion are too optimistic. His conception of art is
puritanical and didactic, and he cannot understand
sentiment and sexual passion. Man and Superman is only an
amusing farce. Saint Joan, like Androcles, is not truly
religious because Shaw is impervious to mysticism. He is
too detached and can never take anyone or anything
seriously. This serves his didacticism well. He is himself
a paradox, a committed writer with an uncommitted spirit.
[In French.]

1778 "Seven Ideas of Joan," NYTMag, 14 Oct 1951, p.
17.
[Photographs of Uta Hagen, Winifred Lenihan, Sybil
Thorndike, and Katharine Cornell, as Shaw's Saint Joan.]

1779 Sheenan, Vincent. "My Last Visit with Shaw,"
ATLANTIC MONTHLY, CLXXXVII (Jan 1951), 19-24.
[Recollections of visits and conversations with Shaw.] Shaw
agreed with Gandhi that all his plays had a religious
center.

1780 Slonimsky, Nicolas. "Musical Oddities," ETUDE,
LXIX (June 1951), 4-5.
[Reports Shaw's unusual method for playing the C major
scale on the piano.]

1781 Stokes, E. E., Jr. "William Morris and Bernard
Shaw: A Socialist Artistic Relationship." Unpublished
dissertation, University of Texas, 1951. [Listed in
McNamee.]

1782 Stresau, Hermann. "George Bernard Shaw (1856-
1950)," MERKUR, V (Jan 1951), 1-12.
Shaw's dilemma is that his attacks on conventions and
institutions are virtually buried by the artistic form in
which he carries them out. The conflict between the artist
and the preacher in his work points to the conflict between
art and life which underlies the whole nineteenth century.

Shaw attempts to solve the conflict with the principle of the Life Force; his heroes believe in the superiority of the mind. Shaw's artistic solution to the dilemma is to transpose the conflict between mind and matter to the higher plane of comedy in which the great game of his figures demonstrates the eternal cadence of being. [In German.]

1783 Suga, Yasuo. "Shaw to Wilde" (Shaw and Wilde), KAICHOON (Kyoto), No 1 (June 1951), 20-21.
Though they appeared to stand in direct opposition, Shaw and Wilde shared in common a spirit of rebellion against Victorian conventionality. [In Japanese.]

1784 Swinnerton, Frank. THE BOOKMAN'S LONDON (Lond: Allan Wingate, 1951; NY: Doubleday, 1952; rev Lond: John Baker, 1969), pp. 9, 53, 57, 138, 141.
[References to Shaw in London.]

1785 Taketomo, Sofu. "Shisoka, Geijutsuka—G.B.S. Kanken—" (Ideas or Art? A Personal View of G.B.S.), KAICHOON (Kyoto), No 1 (June 1951), 9-12.
Shaw is primarily a writer of comedy. His philosophy and dramatic techniques are all employed to make the audience laugh. [In Japanese.]

1786 Terlecki, Tymon. "Kronika Kultwralna: Shaw w Polsce" (Cultural Chronicle: Shaw in Poland), KULTURA (Paris), X (Oct 1951), 127-36.
A thorough study of Shaw in Poland under present circumstances is impossible. Books, magazines, theatrical archives (if they have survived), and the correspondence between Shaw and Florian Sobieniowsky, his translator, would be necessary. Productions of Shaw in Poland were among the first on the continent. Buckle, Spencer, Marx, and Ibsen certainly paved the way for Shaw's acceptance. He was undoubtedly an important influence on the "bio-chemistry" of independent Warsaw. There existed a rivalry between Berlin and Warsaw for Shaw premieres. All of Shaw's plays but Back to Methuselah were performed. He was more successful in Poland than in France because he spoke to Polish feelings about independence. But as the present shows, his influence was not lasting. His plays, though enormously popular on stage, were not published. His

prefaces could not be read. Probably the cause of this failure is the Polish notion that plays are not literature. Nothing remains of Shaw as nothing remains of witty, mocking pre-war Warsaw. There was not even a just critical estimate. [Includes survey of performances of Shaw, with emphasis on the actors. Exceptionally interesting.] [In Polish.]

1787 "To Be a Memorial and Shrine for Shavians: 'Shaw's Corner' Now Open to the Public," ILN, CXXVIII (17 March 1951), 407.
Shaw's home, at Ayot St. Lawrence, Hertsford, was opened to the public by the National Trust today. [Photographs of the house and its interior.]

1788 Torbarina, Josip. "Pogovir" (Afterword), ČETIRI DRAME (Four Plays) (Zagreb: Matica Hrvatska, 1951), 309-56.
Shaw attacks bourgeois society in Widowers' Houses; the economic system in Mrs. Warren's Profession; puritanism in The Devil's Disciple; whereas Candida is warmer and less typical. [Brief discussion of Shaw on the Jugoslav stage, Shaw's Marxism, critical views of Shaw, especially of Miroslav Krleža, and Jugoslav translations of Shaw. Bibliography (especially Jugoslav works). Photograph of Shaw.] [In Croatian.]

1789 Trewin, J[ohn] C[ourtenay]. DRAMA, 1945-1950 (Lond, NY, & Toronto: Longmans, Green [The Arts in Britain], 1951), pp. 14-15, 35, 42, 47.
Shaw is still first among living playwrights. Buoyant Billions has shown that Shaw, well past ninety, can still hold an audience. It is in the tradition of The Simpleton of the Unexpected Isles and Too True To Be Good. [Bibliography. Illustrated.]

1790 Trewin, J[ohn] C[ourtenay]. "G.B.S. as Dramatic Critic," DRAMA, ns XX (Spring 1951), 32-33.
[A speech delivered in St. Pancras Town Hall on the occasion of the Evening of Tribute offered by the Borough and the British Drama League in memory of Shaw.]

1791 Trewin, J[ohn] C[ourtenay]. THE THEATRE SINCE 1900 (Lond: Andrew Dakers, 1951).

Shaw wrote the wittiest sermons a dramatic critic has ever delivered. He admired Henry Arthur Jones, trampled on Augustin Daly, rebuked Irving, cheered Ibsen. [Survey of Shaw's major plays.] In Shaw's golden age, the 1920's, there appeared the often eloquent but rather too lengthy Heartbreak House; the Creative Evolution parable, Back to Methuselah; and the cogent, warm, and witty, but not romantic Saint Joan. In the thirties, despite his age, Shaw was still in command of the theater, writing good drama, although the plays were often lengthy with sometimes too much talk and too little action.

1792 Tunney, Gene. "G. B. Shaw's Letters to Gene Tunney," COLLIER'S, CXXVII (23 June 1951), 16-17, 51-53.
[Brief history of the friendship and correspondence of Shaw and Tunney. Photograph.]

1793 "Una comedia de Bernard Shaw" (A Comedy of Bernard Shaw), BIBLOS (Argentina), X (1951), 11.
[Short parody of Shaw's comedies. In each act a man asks the woman if she loves him. Shaw explains that the argument resides in the woman's being always the same but in each case with a different man.] [In Spanish.]

1794 Usigli, Rodolfo. "El destructor de ídolos (Sentido y forma de George Bernard Shaw) (The Destroyer of Ideals [Meaning and Form of George Bernard Shaw]), CUADERNOS AMERICANOS (Mexico), X (Jan-Feb 1951), 180-210, and (July-Aug 1951), 251-76.
Shaw is a destroyer of idols because he began the battle of intelligence and common sense against sentimentality, sex and Victorian conventions. He understood his own time and worked to improve it, condemning its stupidities, injustices, and social inequities. He deserves to be studied because he is an excellent example of the writer who rejected the idea of art for art's sake as trivial, selfish, and hedonistic. He intellectualized the theater, taking current social, political, religious, and philosophical problems for analysis and using humor to satirize the oddities of society. [In Spanish.]

1795 Ussher, Arland. "Bernard Shaw's 'Feast of Reason,'" List, XLVI (9 Aug 1951), 228-29.

Shaw's mind lacked color and mystery, but there was nothing common or mean in him. It is ironical to remember that, after he wrote Candida, Shaw was hailed as Defender of the Hearth, and that after Saint Joan he almost received popular canonization as a Defender of the Faith. He was the most consistent of socialists in making perfect equality of income the touchstone of true socialism. His greatness was that he put both philosophy and life upon the boards. However, Shaw had a lack of historical sense—evident in his Caesar, who has nothing of the pagan sense of fate, his Joan of Arc, who has none of the intimate, and his Adam and Eve. His portrait of Joan is sensitive, with the danger that it may replace the historic one. Shaw was not a dramatist in the traditional sense; he created a genre of his own, the dialectical extravaganza which one can imagine as the drama of the future. His heroines are often wily and feline, such as Ann Whitefield in Man and Superman and Candida, who is a bit of a fraud. Captain Brassbound's Conversion is a play devised simply to glorify a charming and clever woman. Like The Doctor's Dilemma it has no clear-cut problem. Arms and the Man is Shaw's nearest approach to a popular drawing-room comedy. His works are conversations, the best the world has to offer. [From the Third Programme of the BBC. Photograph of Shaw with Hilaire Belloc and G. K. Chesterton.]

1796 Vandewalle, G. G. B. SHAW EN HET BRITSE SOCIALISME (G. B. Shaw and British Socialism) (Ghent: De Vlam, 1951). [Not seen.] [In Dutch.]

1797 Vidan, Ivo. "Uz Izdanje Četiriju Drama Bernarda Shawa" (Comment on Four Dramas by Bernard Shaw), HRVATSKO KOLO (Zagreb), III-IV (April 1951), 361-65. Four poorly chosen plays, Mrs. Warren's Profession, The Devil's Disciple, Candida, and Widowers' Houses, are insufficient for the first Croatian edition of Shaw. His early plays failed because of his attacks on capitalism. To gain an audience he became amusing. His later plays are each unique, and after World War I, except for Saint Joan, his work demonstrates a decline. The prefaces are a sign of weakness, because they indicate that Shaw lacked the artistic means to express himself completely in his plays, but it is a shame that they are eliminated here. [In Croatian.]

1798 Wade, Allan. "Shaw and the Stage Society," DRAMA, ns XX (Spring 1951), 23-27.
[Two photographs: one taken in 1893, the other taken sometime in his last years. A history of Shaw's participation in the Stage Society.]

1799 Walker, Kenneth. "The Philosophy of Bernard Shaw," WORLD REVIEW, July 1951, pp. 18-21.
Shaw was everything by turns and never anything very long. His knowledge was remarkable for its breadth, not its depth. Shaw was never taken seriously. But one thing Shaw took seriously was Creative Evolution, which is the central theme of the third act of Man and Superman. It is more closely knit throughout Back to Methuselah. The Doctor's Dilemma is only a semi-philosophical, semi-scientific jaunt. Only once does Dilemma become serious, when Shaw touches on the vexed question of vivisection. The greatest service Shaw did was to startle others and make them think. He was extremely clever but not very wise.

1800 Ward, A[lfred] C[harles]. "Shaw, George Bernard," THE OXFORD COMPANION TO THE THEATRE, ed by Phyllis Hartnoll (Lond, NY, Toronto: Oxford UP, 1951, 1957, 1967), pp. 878-79.
[Brief biography of Shaw and brief analysis of Shaw's theory and practice as a writer.] Shaw used the stage to propagandize for reform of society, but he did so in a witty and entertaining manner. The criticism that he could not draw real characters on the stage has been refuted by the fact that his characters continue to live. [There is no indication that there has been any addition to or revision of this essay since the first edition.]

1801 Weber, Carl J. "A Talk with George Bernard Shaw," COLBY LIBRARY QUARTERLY, III (May 1951), 26-33.
[Recollections of Shaw's comments on co-education, Shakespeare, phonetics, especially some of the differences between English and American pronunciation.]

1802 West, E. J. "An Epitaph for Bernard Shaw," WESTERN HUMANITIES REVIEW, V (1951), 323-32.
What Shaw gave to the twentieth century may be summed up in the line "smiling comedy with some hope in it" from Buoyant

Billions. Yet the world wanted more. His The Sanity of Art
(1895) and his essay "On Going to Church" (1896) show how
Shaw equated art and religion, making a religion of
purposeful art and an art of purposeful religion. His
purpose was to be a dramatic artist. However, his plays
were continually criticized as not being plays because he
was not a dramatist. Shaw is unlucky in his authorized
biographers, Pearson and Henderson, for both misunderstood
the plays. The discussions in Getting Married, in The Apple
Cart, and in Heartbreak House on the potentialities of life
and of love, and his dialogs in Hell in Man and Superman
and in the tent scene in Saint Joan create a compelling
emotional crescendo in drama far greater than, for
instance, the sheer dramatic thrill of the air raid in the
last act of Heartbreak. Despite comments Shaw made in the
Envoy to his Everybody's Political What's What, he was
often mystical. He could give a perspective of history and
the intimations of ultimate significance. His comedy is
serious. His irrepressible gaiety of genius he achieved in
the trance-scene of Married, in the tremendous ending of
the fifth of the Methuselah plays, at the end of Too True
to Be Good, often in Caesar and Cleopatra, in John Bull's
Other Island, in Major Barbara and Androcles and the Lion,
frequently in Joan, and almost throughout Heartbreak, his
masterpiece.

1803 Whitworth, Geoffrey. THE MAKING OF A NATIONAL
THEATRE (Lond: Faber & Faber, 1951).
[Includes photograph of Shaw and letter from Shaw to
Gollancz, 31 Nov 1925, and a speech by Shaw to a Drama
League meeting, 31 Jan 1930.] During the historic three
year period of 1904 to 1907 at the Royal Court Theater,
Shaw's plays topped the list with performances of eleven
plays. Shaw was for once in agreement with many when a
National Theater as a memorial to Shakespeare was proposed.
He wrote The Dark Lady of the Sonnets as a plea for the
National Theater.

1804 Whitworth, Geoffrey. "Shaw and the Drama
League," DRAMA, ns XX (Spring 1951), 27-29.
[A history of Shaw's relationship to the British Drama
League.]

1805 Williams, Raymond. "Criticism into Drama, 1888-
1950," ESSAYS IN CRITICISM, I (Jan 1951), 120-38.

For Shaw the reform of drama was a matter of subjects of social importance and of a framework for moral teaching. His career is an obvious example of the making of criticism into drama.

1806 Williams, Stephen. "Bernard Shaw as Music Critic," MUSICAL TIMES, No 1295 (Jan 1951), 9-13.
Shaw turned the world of music inside out within two years as a critic of music by writing about it as a music lover and a hater of shoddy productions or bad performances. Shaw embraced music in terms of human enjoyment and wrote about it in exciting human terms, not in technical musical terms as other critics did. Shaw could play the buffoon as critic only because he had such a thorough knowledge of music.

1807 Williamson, Audrey. THEATRE OF TWO DECADES (Lond: Rockliff; NY: Macmillan, 1951), pp. 19, 21, 30, 37, 38, 107-26, 127, 129, 173, 256, 262, 263, 291, 318, 321.
For the first time in theatrical history, the greatest stage honor belongs to a writer "whose primary challenge is the intellect." Shaw's plays are full of good parts and have made many actors' reputations. His characters have lives outside their personal relationships. But Candida is a "fireside" woman, and Candida is popular for this reason. [Survey of British productions of Candida, Geneva, In Good King Charles's Golden Days, The Doctor's Dilemma, Heartbreak House, Man and Superman, and Back to Methuselah, with passing reference to other plays.]

1808 Wilshire, Lewis. "Shaw's Last Play," ENGLISH, VIII (Spring 1951), 193-95.
The puppet play Shakes Versus Shav is "a little pathetic." Shakespeare accepted his world as he found it; Shaw never could. Shaw's characters were types and opinions; Shakespeare's were individuals. Shaw made considerable noise in the theater and will remain a force even though his New Drama has faded somewhat.

1809 Wilson, A[lbert] E. EDWARDIAN THEATRE (Lond: Arthur Baker, 1951).
Edwardian theater was interesting, momentous and important in the history of British theater, with Shaw as one of its pioneers. A renaissance of dramatic criticism had occurred

408

in the 1890's when Shaw headed that profession with his brilliant and unsurpassed essays in the SATURDAY REVIEW. Shaw wrote the prolog to TODDLES, produced by Cyril Maude; and in 1907 he joined with others to write a letter protesting the banning of several playwrights' plays, among them his own Mrs. Warren's Profession.

1810 Winsten, Stephen. SALT AND HIS CIRCLE (Lond: Hutchinson, 1951), passim.
[Contains many excerpts from conversations between Shaw and Henry S. Salt and others and many anecdotes about Shaw. Appendix One is an essay by "Salt on Shaw."]

1811 Winstone, Reese. "Shaw's Corner," COMING EVENTS IN BRITAIN, June 1951, pp. 36-37.
On a visit to Ayot St. Lawrence Shaw read a tombstone inscription, "Her time was short." The lady died aged 90; Shaw decided this was the place for him. [Photographs.]

1812 Worsley, T. C. "Shaw's Edwardian Comedies," BRITAIN TODAY, CLXXVII (Jan 1951), 11-14.
Audiences will know Edwardian England from Shaw's plays; such knowledge is only a by-product of comedy, but only of the highest comedy. Shaw's plays do not survive on their ideas, but on their fun. Shaw was interested in human beings, primarily as social animals.

1813 Yamanouchi, Kuniomi. "Shaw Nenpyo" (Chronological Table of Shaw's Life and Works), KAICHOON (Kyoto), No 1 (June 1951) 13-19.
[Includes brief biographical comments, major works and other important data in Shaw's lifetime.] [In Japanese.]

1952

1814 Atkinson, Brooks. "At the Theatre," NYT, 23 April 1952, p. 23.
Olivia de Havilland's Candida is not a perceptive one.

1815 Atkinson, Brooks. "At the Theatre," NYT, 18 Oct 1952, p. 17.

The Millionairess is a senile play. Katharine Hepburn (Shubert Theater, NY) does little to relieve the tiresomeness of the title character.

1816 Atkinson, Brooks. "Quite a Dame," NYT, 6 Jan 1952, II, p. 1.
Shaw's account of the relations between Caesar and Cleopatra is not reliable, for it omits sex.

1817 A[tkinson], B[rooks]. "Shaw's Pygmalion in the Bronx," NYT, 9 Feb 1952, p. 11.
Pygmalion (Equity Community Theater) seemed more like Arthur Wing Pinero than Shaw.

1818 Bab, Julius. "Shaw's 'Life-Force,'" BDDTG, No 15 (1951-52).
[A brief note on the Life Force and the energy of Shaw's personality.] [In German.]

1819 Bab, Julius. "Shaws strahlende Unbescheidenheit" (Shaw's Shining Immodesty), BDDTG, No 25 (1951-52).
Shaw liked to shock by his "shining immodesty." [In German.]

1820 Bałutowa, Bronisława. "Komizm postaci dramatu Bernarda Shaw w służbie ideologii" (The Comic in Characters of Bernard Shaw's Plays in the Service of Ideology), PRACE POLONISTYCZNE (Łódz), X (1952), 345-62.
For many years, Shaw was reproached by critics because of the unclear, ambiguous, and contradictory statements of his views and because it was difficult to determine whose side he was on in the dramatic conflicts of his plays. The main element in Shaw's plays is the comic element, which is the proper weapon in an ideological battle, because comic characters represent an inappropriate attitude toward reality. Examples can be drawn from Widowers' Houses, Candida, Caesar and Cleopatra, Man and Superman, Major Barbara, and The Doctor's Dilemma. The apparent contradictions in the expressions of opinions are usually motivated by artistic aims. Shaw's influence passed relatively quickly, and he created no lasting foundations for the social changes he intended. [In Polish.]

1821 Barzun, Jacques. "In Hell Again," Notes to the Columbia Recording of <u>Don Juan in Hell</u> (1952); rptd ShawSB, XLVIII (March 1953), 11-13.
Shaw composes a quartet with words and ideas in <u>Don Juan in Hell</u>. In listening to Shaw's sonata, you do not mind the returns and repeats as you do in reading. It is the greatest moral document of our century to date. And it is true drama.

1822 Barzun, Jacques. "Love and the Playwright," NEW REPUBLIC, CXXVII (3 Nov 1952), 17-18.
[Barzun praises <u>Bernard Shaw and Mrs. Patrick Campbell: Their Correspondence (1952)</u>, and discusses Shaw's feelings about love and sex.] This is not a novel in letter form, but a complete drama. Shaw's love was unmistakably physical for Stella Campbell, who was not equal to him. Contrary to the argument that Shaw's intelligence and vegetarianism preclude his lack of strong sexual desire, Shaw's plays testify to a lively and direct awareness of sexual magnetism, as in the <u>Liebeskampf</u> in the third act of <u>Widowers' Houses</u>, the bold dialog between Boxer and Lesbia in <u>Getting Married</u>, the emotional climaxes in <u>Man and Superman</u> and <u>You Never Can Tell</u>, and the actualization of the old triangle problem in <u>Candida</u>. Shaw's unrequited love for Stella Campbell is the tragedy of an elderly genius.

1823 Bellyei, László. "G. B. Shaw," VILÁGIRODALMI TÁJÉKOZTATÓ, No 9-10 (1953). [Not seen.] [In Hungarian.]

1824 Beltroy, Manuel. "<u>Don Juan en el Infierno</u> de Bernard Shaw y el Teatro Universitario de San Marcos" (<u>Don Juan in Hell</u> and the Teatro Universitario of San Marcos), EL COMERCIO (Peru), 6 July 1952, p. 13.
The performance of <u>Don Juan in Hell</u> (Teatro Universitario, San Marcos) was an appropriate tribute to the Irish genius because of its philosophical depth, its sociology, its humor, and its style. [In Spanish.]

1825 "Bernard Shaw Commemorated," ShawSB, XLVIII (March 1953), 13-14 [from CULTURAL NEWS FROM HUNGARY, December 1952, published by the Hungarian News and Information Service, London, W.2.]

Professor György Lukács, in an address on the second anniversary of Shaw's death, discussed attempts by the Horthy administration in Hungary to censor Shaw and lauded Shaw's opposition to the exploitation of workers and other oppressed groups.

1826 Brown, John Mason. "Joey and Stella: The Letters of GBS and Mrs. Pat," SRL, XXXV (6 Dec 1952), 20-22, 39-40.
[Review of Bernard Shaw and Mrs. Patrick Campbell: Their Correspondence; photograph of Mrs. Patrick Campbell.] A prolific letter writer, Shaw's writing was an indispensable spiritual and intellectual release, as well as a physical need.

1827 Brown, John Mason. "Katherine Without Petruchio," SRL, XXXV (1 Nov 1952), 24-25.
The Preface to The Millionairess is far superior to the play, which is tedious and tired. However, Katharine Hepburn's performance (Shubert Theater, NY) is energetic and brilliant. Shaw's wittiest and most satisfying autumnal drama is In Good King Charles's Golden Days. But his writing career reached its peak with Saint Joan. In spite of the vitality of The Apple Cart six years later, there was an unmistakable decline. Although his last plays betrayed signs of age, Shaw's prefaces, letters, postcards, and such expository tracts as The Intelligent Woman's Guide to Socialism and Capitalism and Everybody's Political What's What continued through his final days to be as eruptive as ever.

1828 Clark, Eleanor. "Shaw, Fry, and Others," PARTISAN REVIEW, XIX (1952), 217-24.
Three plays by Shaw dominate the 1952 theater season; a fourth, Pygmalion, is effective. Man and Superman stands above all. Shaw's two most nearly titanic characters, Joan and Caesar, speak morality. Superman's dream act is one of the world's great moral dialogs. The part of Joan is an impossible role for an actress and will trouble actresses for at least a few centuries. Joan is made to be as much like a boy as possible, reflecting Shaw's problems in creating a heroine.

1829 Clark, William Ross. "The Literary Aspects of Fabian Socialism," DA, XII (1952), 615-16. Unpublished dissertation, Columbia University, 1952.

1830 Clinton-Baddeley, V. C. THE BURLESQUE TRADITION IN THE ENGLISH THEATRE AFTER 1660 (Lond: Methuen, 1952), pp. 71, 120-22, 135.
Shaw borrowed from Henry Carey's CHRONONHOTONTHOLOGOS for The Admirable Bashville, a burlesque of his own Cashel Byron's Profession. The result is a blank verse joke.

1831 Cole, Margaret. "G.B.S. & Fabian Socialism," FABIAN JOURNAL, III (1952), 11-14.
Shaw's contributions to socialism were his incomparable style, his hard and constant work, and his magnanimous and co-operative spirit. He helped establish the spirit of tolerance in the Fabian Society and the Labour Party which it helped form.

1832 Craig, Gordon. "Reflections on the Irving-Shaw Controversy," List, XLVIII (17 July 1952), 107-8.
Henry Irving and Shaw quarreled because the two men were too alike in being ambitious. There could be no partnership between them because Shaw's plays were not equal to those being presented at Irving's Lyceum Theater; furthermore, his plays did not appeal to the great British public—the pit and the gallery public, who were not interested in paradox, Shaw's special fancy.

1833 Critic. "London Diary," NS&Nation, XLIV (6 Sept 1952), 257.
Shaw's eccentric bequest of 400,000 pounds to the alphabet fad is regretful. His failure to provide for the upkeep of Shaw's Corner is a second error of his will. [Discussion follows in Marjorie Deans, "Shaw's Corner," NS&Nation, XLIV (20 Sept 1952), 320; and Allan M. Laing and Augustus Baker, "Shaw's Corner," NS&Nation, XLIV (27 Sept 1952), 351.]

1834 d'Agostino, Nemi. "Ritratti Critici di Contemporanei: Bernard Shaw" (Critical Portraits of Contemporaries: Bernard Shaw), BELFAGOR, RASSEGNA DI VARIA UMANITA, VII (March 1952), 188-204.
Shaw was a typically bourgeois phenomenon. Among the intelligentsia, admiration lasted a short time only. [Many

quotations from Daudet, Pound, H. James, Yeats among others to support the above judgment.] Only the Americans and Germans considered the theatrical works and not the ideology. Shaw's philosophy is one of the will. Some have thought that from John Bull's Other Island through Heartbreak House to Saint Joan Shaw lost faith in this ideology and turned to a deeper reality; in effect the opposite is true. To reach the truth of Shaw's achievement, one must consider his ideology as a necessary convention to organize and develop his sensibility toward artistic synthesis. [Surveys the plays up to Man and Superman to show that the real conflict in Shaw's drama is between Shaw and his audience to whom he offers the problem of its own behavior.] Heartbreak, among Shaw's best works, is "on the surface" in the sense T. S. Eliot meant describing Ben Jonson's comedies. Back to Methuselah is a failure because of its lack of faith in reality. Joan is limited and uneven, but because Joan is born from lyric intuition and is not merely an expression of ideology, the play is successful. The plays after Joan reveal Shaw's inability to create true poetic intuition out of his theories. He never captured the totality of experience because he could never conceive of a truly guilty character; he expresses one of the essential motifs of the art of our time: a relativity that deepens the mystery of life. Shaw is the link between the Restoration and popular theaters. He is different from Yeats, Synge, Eliot, Auden and Isherwood, Duncan, Nicholson, MacNiece and Fry in that he does not fight on the side of experimental drama against the commercial theater. [Short bibliography. Interesting in spite of the florid style.] [In Italian.]

1835 Dent, Alan. "Editor's Preface," BERNARD SHAW AND MRS. PATRICK CAMPBELL: THEIR CORRESPONDENCE (Lond: Victor Gollancz, 1952; NY: Alfred A. Knopf, 1952; Toronto: Longmans, 1952), pp. ix-xii.
Almost nothing has been deleted except some gibberish from the correspondence, which begins in 1899, when Shaw was a trenchant critic and Mrs. Campbell was at the height of her fame, and ends in 1939.

1836 Dodd, Edward H., Jr. "Dear World," ShawB, I (May 1952), 1-2.

Shaw was a prodigious, overwhelming letter writer. The Shaw-Campbell letters will be published under the rights of Mrs. Campbell's daughter, according to provision in Shaw's will.

1837 Elliott, Robert C. "Shaw's Captain Bluntschli: A Latter-Day Falstaff," MODERN LANGUAGE NOTES, LXVII (1952), 461-64.
Bluntschli, anti-hero but exemplar of the modern soldier in Arms and the Man, parallels, albeit as a pale imitation, Falstaff in HENRY IV, PART I. Sergius exemplifies the kind of manhood Hotspur represents as foil to Falstaff. Sergius's Byronic self-doubt measures the inadequacy of the Hotspurian values in the world of the late nineteenth century. In Arms there is no choice possible between the conflicting worlds. Louka, the real man in the play, is the only character who in any sense transcends these worlds as Hal transcends his.

1838 Emmel, Felix. "Major Barbaras Weg" (Major Barbara's Way), BDDTG, No 15 (1951-52).
[Plot summary of Major Barbara.] Major Barbara is Shaw's most aggressive attack against poverty. [In German.]

1839 Emmel, Felix. "Shaws Arzt am Scheideweg" (Shaw's The Doctor's Dilemma), BDDTG, No 25 (1951-52).
[Plot summary of The Doctor's Dilemma.] Dubedat is the first non-romantic artist of the modern European theater. [In German.]

1840 Ervine, St. John. "Is Shaw Dead?" SPECTATOR, No 6491 (21 Nov 1952), 657-58.
The memorial Fund Appeal failed partly because the English show little inclination to honor men of genius. Shaw's opinions are dead, but his plays are alive. [Angus Watson, "Is Shaw Dead?" SPECTATOR, No 6492 (28 Nov 1952), 734, 736, disagrees: Shaw will not survive because he was not sincere.]

1841 F., R. SHAW'S CORNER, AYOT ST. LAWRENCE, HERTFORDSHIRE, A PROPERTY OF THE NATIONAL TRUST (Lond: Curwen P, 1952).

[Description of Shaw's house and its furnishings. Photograph.]

1842 Gassner, John. "The Puritan in Hell," TAM, XXXVI (April 1952), 67-70; rptd in ShawSB, XLVII (Dec 1952), 7-14; THE THEATRE IN OUR TIMES (NY: Crown Publishers, 1954), pp. 156-62.

Don Juan in Hell, incorporating an anti-amorist view of the Spanish lover, is probably the most puritanical play in English since Milton's SAMSON AGONISTES. When A. B. Walkley commented on Shaw's ignorance of the non-rational life and suggested he try to write a play about Don Juan as a remedy, Shaw answered with Man and Superman, the only real treatment of sex ever written, according to Shaw; and he did it unromantically and unsentimentally. Don Juan in the interlude does not pursue women or seek sex. Shaw saw Don Juan as a man with a purpose, as a believer and a moralist; he used him to expound his ideal of the Superman and his religion of Creative Evolution. Don Juan, though essentially plotless, is engrossing theater because the discussion has variety, pacing, and purpose. The discussions depend on skillful delivery.

1843 Gilkes, A. N. "Candour about Candida," FORTNIGHTLY, ns CLXXI (Feb 1952), 122-27.

Candida has conceit and a kind of bright stupidity. She does not understand her husband, nor does she understand loyalty in marriage; neither did Shaw. Morell, following the Christian standards of behavior, reaches a higher level than Candida or Shaw ever reached. The play is a tragedy on the well-worn theme of a good-natured, capable idealist smothered by the dominating maternal instinct of a wife who has never known the meaning of love and has never understood the contents of the marriage vow.

1844 Grendon, Felix. "Buoyant Billions," ShawB, I (May 1952), 9-10.

Buoyant Billions, Shaw's last full-fledged play, has been unjustly depreciated--like all Shaw plays with the exception of Saint Joan. Billions is a play of ideas in which the characters are made real through their ideas and desires.

1845 Haro Tecglen, Eduardo. "<u>Cesar y Cleopatra</u> por George Bernard Shaw" (<u>Caesar and Cleopatra</u> by George Bernard Shaw), TEATRO (Argentina), I (Nov 1952), 46-48.
In <u>Caesar and Cleopatra</u> Shaw discredits the romantic concept of the hero and at the same time fights Shakespeare. It is an excellent play, which was erroneously considered an "historical comedy" by Jacinto Benavente. [In Spanish.]

1846 Háy, Gyula. "Megjegyzések G.B. Shaw drámai müveszetéröl" (About G.B. Shaw as a Playwright) (Budapest: Szepirodalmi, 1952), pp. 7-22. [An introduction? Not seen.] [In Hungarian.]

1847 Henderson, Archibald. "Collectors and Collections of Shaviana in the U.S.A.," ShawB, I (May 1952), 7-9.
[Names of persons who collect Shaviana.]

1848 Hettner, Willy. "Posthume Komödie um G.B.S." (Posthumous Comedy about G.B.S.), BÜHNENGENOSSENSCHAFT (Hamburg), IV (1952), 12.
[On Shaw's testament: the wish for a phonetic alphabet.] [In German.]

1849 Hirai, Hiroshi. "Bernard Shaw to Oscar Wilde—Frank Harris no Wilde Den omeguru Ronso—" (Bernard Shaw and Oscar Wilde—a Controversy on a Life of Wilde by Frank Harris), EIBUNGAKU KENKYU (Tokyo), XXVIII (March 1952), 42-58; rptd in OSCAR WILDE NO SHOGAI (A Life of Oscar Wilde) (Tokyo: Shohakusha, 1960), pp. 263-67.
[Traces in detail the process of the controversy between Shaw and Robert Harborough Sherard on the life of Wilde by Frank Harris, beginning in 1933 and continuing until Sherard's death in 1943. Sherard was preparing a book to refute OSCAR WILDE: BY FRANK HARRIS WITH A PREFACE BY BERNARD SHAW (1938) under the title PERNICIOUS AMNESIA. His project, however, was not completed owing to World War II and his death.] [In Japanese.]

1850 Jacobson, Sol. "Androcles in Hollywood," TAM, XXXVI (Dec 1952), 66-69.

GEORGE BERNARD SHAW

[Account of the filming of <u>Androcles and the Lion</u> with brief history of the play.]

1851 Kerr, Walter F. "The Theaters," NYHT, 23 April 1952, p. 22.
Olivia de Havilland's production of <u>Candida</u> is without any wit, charm or serenity.

1852 Kerr, Walter F. "The Theaters," NYHT, 18 Oct 1952).
<u>The Millionairess</u> (Shubert Theater, NY) is not much of a play, and Katharine Hepburn is not very good in it.

1853 Kindermann, Heinz. MEISTER DER KOMÖDIE. VON ARISTOPHANES BIS G.B. SHAW (Masters of Comedy. From Aristophanes to G.B. Shaw) (Wien, München: Donau-Verlag, 1952), pp. 274-89.
In Shaw logic triumphs over ethics. He was undoubtedly the greatest satirist among recent European dramatists. His irony hides serious truths; his rational distance often serves as self protection. [In German.]

1854 Kirchner, Gustav. "Shaw's <u>Pygmalion</u> und Smollett's PEREGRINE PICKLE," DIE NEUEREN SPRACHEN, Neue Folge, No 10 (1952), 409-17.
Since the plots of Shaw's <u>Pygmalion</u> and Smollett's PEREGRINE PICKLE agree in all major aspects, it can be concluded that Shaw was heavily indebted to Smollett's novel. [In German.]

1855 Kronenberger, Louis. "Shaw," THE THREAD OF LAUGHTER (NY: Alfred A. Knopf, 1952), pp. 227-78.
Even though not one of Shaw's plays can be confidently pronounced great, his plays stand unchallenged by any other body of dramatic work since Ibsen's. Love has little passion or sexuality about it for Shaw; for example, Candida's job is to make Morell and Marchbanks understand themselves. <u>The Devil's Disciple</u> is a comparative failure, attempting to be satiric but lacking any specific compulsion. Burgoyne brings the play to life in the trial scene because he does not fit the formula of the melodrama. Caesar of <u>Caesar and Cleopatra</u> is a Shavian hero, full of contradictions, resembling Shaw. The Hell scene makes <u>Man and Superman</u>, otherwise a traditional Shaw comedy, one of

his most brilliant. In the other acts Shaw's Life Force seems little more than what other poets have termed Nature. Don Juan, Tanner's ancestor, is most purely Shavian, believing that the brain is far superior to the flesh, abandoning women not from boredom but from fear. The Hell scene is a triumph of Shaw over sense. Concerning the English in Ireland, John Bull's Other Island is not a good play, but it is one Shaw had to write. Major Barbara has Shaw exploding Barbara's attitude to exalt Undershaft's. God is totally dependent on Mammon; that is the tragic irony. Shaw is a better wit, artist, playwright than he is a propagandist, philosopher, political moralizer. Getting Married, full of dramatic ingredients, is not a play in the ordinary sense but a dialog, since all is resolved by argument. Androcles and the Lion, in which there is no real religious issue, is about Christianity and martyrdom. Heartbreak House, a major play but not a major success, is a kind of Noah's Ark in which all of the species, if not saved, can be observed. Heartbreak as symbolism seems impaired by its conclusion. Though Saint Joan is not a comedy, it is widely regarded as the outstanding work of the outstanding comedy writer of today. Shaw fails to make Joan real by making her realistic. The epilog, announcing the canonization of Joan, makes its point in comic terms although the point is tragic. Shaw saw both sides of an argument. In having a real compulsion to criticize the one by the other, he seems a little unprincipled. He is a socialist who admires industrialists and capitalists, a Puritan who will turn intellectual playboy, whose Life Force becomes meaningless as soon as fulfilled. But Shaw, with comic genius, is one of the great masters of dialog in English literature.

1856 Krutch, Joseph Wood. "GBS Enters Heaven (?),"
SRL, XXXV (24 May 1952), 19-21.
[A fictional barbed conversation between Thoreau and Shaw in which Thoreau's point of view is that Shaw died without knowing he had lived. Shaw's point of view is that Thoreau blasphemes the Life Force. It appears that the conversation takes place in Hell.]

1857 Krutch, Joseph Wood. "Shaw the Shavian,"
NATION, CLXXV (6 Dec 1952), 524-25.

[Review of Bernard Shaw and Mrs. Patrick Campbell: Their Correspondence (1952).] The climax of Shaw's correspondence with his Stella occurs in 1912 at the time of the production of Pygmalion. The love letters are ambiguous. The mystery, if there is one, is as mysterious as ever, although sexual shyness could explain both his behavior toward Mrs. Campbell and the whole protective doctrine of the thinker and doer with no time for child's play.

1858 Laing, Allan M. and R. K. Mosley. "Letters from England," ShawB, I (May 1952), 13-15.
[Letters discuss current British Shaviana and performances of Shaw; blunders in Stephen Winsten's SALT AND HIS CIRCLE (1951); and new photographs in R. F. Rattray's BERNARD SHAW: A CHRONICLE AND AN INTRODUCTION (1934).]

1859 Loewenstein, F[ritz] E[rwin]. "The Copyrighting of Shaw's Early Dramatic Work, Containing Also a Word on the Vicissitudes of Mrs. Warren's Profession," ShawSB, Supplement No 2 (Feb 1952).
[List of plays having copyright-performances, with places and dates: Candida, The Devil's Disciple, You Never Can Tell, Mrs. Warren's Profession, The Philanderer, Caesar and Cleopatra, Captain Brassbound's Conversion, The Admirable Bashville, Man and Superman, and How He Lied to Her Husband.]

1860 Lutter, Tibor. G. B. SHAW (Budapest: Müvelt Nép, 1952).
Shaw was a great progressive in spite of such early errors like Fabianism. His moment of glory was meeting the greatest of all men, Stalin. The bourgeois public and critics wish to see him as a jester—but the Hungarians know better. [Critical biography.] [In Hungarian.]

1861 Maurois, André. "Bernard Shaw—My Editor," SRL, XXXV (6 Dec 1952), 22-23, 39.
[A detailed account comparing Maurois' biographical commentary about Shaw with Shaw's changes to Maurois' essay on Shaw in PROPHETS AND POETS (1935).]

1862 Molnar, Joseph. "Shaw's Four Kinds of Women," TAM, XXXVI (Dec 1952), 18-21, 92; rptd "Shaw's Living Women," ShawSB, XLIX (June 1953), 7-11.

Since Shaw's first play, critics have been writing Shaw's obituary as a dramatist, insisting that he cannot create living characters. An examination of Shaw's women belies this charge. Shavian types who are particularized as individuals are the womanly woman in The Devil's Disciple, the self-sacrificing mother in Too True to Be Good, Raina in Arms and the Man, and Julia Craven in The Philanderer; the Emancipated Woman, free from romantic illusions, Eliza in Pygmalion, Lady Cicely in Captain Brassbound's Conversion, and Fanny in Fanny's First Play; the Life Force Woman, Ann in Man and Superman, Sweetie in Too True, Gloria in You Never Can Tell, and Lilith in Back to Methuselah; and the New Woman, representing both freedom and responsibility, Major Barbara, Saint Joan, and Lavinia in Androcles and the Lion. Rummy Mitchens in Major Barbara is a typical victim of lower class poverty but is individualized by her sharpness and sense of humor. Because Shaw was socialist before artist, he understood human characters moving in a world of complex reality, which is seen in Vivie's clash with her mother in Mrs. Warren's Profession, in Raina's romantic illusions, in Barbara's problem of faith, and in Joan's historical destiny. Shaw was most the artist when he was most the philosopher.

1863 Nathan, George Jean. "Don Juan in Hell," TAM, XXXVI (Jan 1952), 80; rptd THE THEATRE IN THE FIFTIES (NY: Knopf, 1953), pp. 200-201.
[Review lauding the production of Don Juan in Hell, performed at Carnegie Hall by Charles Laughton, Cedric Hardwicke, Charles Boyer, and Agnes Moorehead.]

1864 Nathan, George Jean. "Kid Hepburn vs. Rocky Shaw," TAM, XXXVI (Nov 1952), 18-20; rptd in THE THEATRE IN THE FIFTIES (NY: Knopf, 1953), pp. 185-92.
The Millionairess (Shubert Theater, NY), like Buoyant Billions, is one of Shaw's weaker plays. Plays of his later life, such as Geneva and The Simpleton of the Unexpected Isles, were often repetitions of earlier plays and were no more verbose and just as sprightly as Getting Married and Misalliance.

1865 Nathan, George Jean. "Two Cleopatras," TAM, XXXVI (March 1952), 18-19, 70; rptd in THE THEATRE IN THE FIFTIES (NY: Knopf, 1953), pp. 197-200.
[Critical review of Laurence Olivier and Vivien Leigh in the successive bills of Shaw's Caesar and Cleopatra and Shakespeare's ANTONY AND CLEOPATRA.]

1866 Nethercot, Arthur H. "The Schizophrenia of Bernard Shaw," AMERICAN SCHOLAR, XXI (1952), 455-67.
It is ironic that Shaw is being lauded; he was one of the most complete "againsters" that the world has ever known. His prefaces are clearer statements of his opinions than are his plays. He made his works palatable to the public by putting details of character and interpretation in stage directions, not in the dialog. The public considers Candida sweet, though she is a Shavian Philistine and Mother Woman with a strong streak of shrewdness, unscrupulousness, materialism, and even cruelty in her nature. In Pygmalion the audience gets a feeling that Higgins cannot possibly be as cold-blooded as he really is, and that he and Eliza will marry. Secondly, Shaw made his plays palatable by writing an epilog, as in The Doctor's Dilemma, Saint Joan, and Caesar and Cleopatra, which nullifies the story-line or characterization in the play itself. Thirdly, Shaw suppressed his own diagnoses of some of the plays, as for example the omission of Act III of Man and Superman in acted versions. He consistently softened his ideas, so that their impact on his audiences would not be too obnoxious, as in the agreeable portraits of diabolonians such as Dick Dudgeon and Undershaft. Violence is made to appear merely symbolic or relatively painless and even comical, as in Heartbreak House, The Inca of Perusalem, The Simpleton of the Unexpected Isles, Back to Methuselah, Geneva, and in the prefaces to Androcles and the Lion and Getting Married.

1867 Norman, Frank. WHITEHALL TO WEST INDIES (Lond: Bodley Head, 1952), p. 60; summarized as "Cover Man," ShawSB, XLVIII (March 1953), 10.
During a week's Fabian Society Summer School at Haslemere [where Norman met Shaw], Shaw identified Miss Hankinson, who led the physical exercise group, as "the prototype for his Saint Joan."

1868 Parmenter, Ross. "Shaw and Mozart," ShawB, I (May 1952), 3-5.
Shaw and his favorite composer, Mozart, parallel as comic and revolutionary playwrights, both juxtaposing the comic with the serious. [Considers You Never Can Tell, Saint Joan, Back to Methuselah, The Devil's Disciple, The Apple Cart, On the Rocks, and In Good King Charles's Golden Days.]

1869 Pearson, Hesketh. "The Origin of Androcles and the Lion," List, XLVIII (13 Nov 1952), 803-4.
[History of the first production of Androcles and the Lion and comments on reviews of the play.] Androcles was inspired by Shaw's dislike of James Barrie's PETER PAN.

1870 Pease, Edward R. "G. B. S. 1856-1950: Early Days," FABIAN JOURNAL, XII (1952), 9-11.
[Photograph of Shaw and history of Shaw's relationship to the Fabian Society.]

1871 Pettet, Edwin Burr. "Shavian Socialism and the Shavian Life Force: An Analysis of the Relationship between the Philosophic and Economic Systems of George Bernard Shaw," DA, XII (1952), 622-23. Unpublished dissertation, New York University, 1952.

1872 Pogson, Rex. MISS HORNIMAN AND THE GAIETY THEATRE, MANCHESTER. With a Foreword by St. John Ervine (Lond: Rockliff Publishing Corporation, 1952), pp. vii, ix, 8-10, 13, 15, 19, 24-25, 32-35, 47-48, 59, 62, 69-70, 76-80, 84-85, 93, 101, 103, 116, 135, 138, 148, 152-53, 164, 169, 177, 182, 185.
Miss Horniman financed the first public production of a Shaw play in London, Arms and the Man, and thus launched the modern theater movement in England. Shaw acknowledged his indebtedness to Miss Horniman in the Preface to John Bull's Other Island. Plays Miss Horniman produced at the Gaiety were The Man of Destiny, How He Lied to Her Husband, The Devil's Disciple, Candida, Major Barbara, and The Doctor's Dilemma.

1873 Russell, Diarmuid. "Introduction," THE SELECTED PROSE OF BERNARD SHAW (NY: Dodd, Mead, 1952), pp. 5-18.

In Shaw's writing, the intellect is a passion, giving his prose a cold feeling. The Novels seem odd but not out of date. Shaw is not a pioneer in economic thought, but he is readable and lucid. His dramatic criticism is better than his music criticism. The major difference between his prose and his plays is that in his prose he did not choose to be an entertainer.

1874 Schwartz, Jacob. "The Extraordinary Shaw Collection of Dr. T. E. Hanley," ShawB, I (May 1952), 12-13.
[Description of Hanley's collection.]

1875 Smith, J. Percy. "Superman Versus Man: Bernard Shaw on Shakespeare," YALE REVIEW, XLII (1952), 67-82; rptd in abbreviated form in ShawSB, L (Sept 1953), 11-17.
Beneath the paradox, invective, and hyperbole in which it is often clad, Shaw's Shakespearean criticism is a body of integrated and self-consistent ideas. Shaw's review of CYMBELINE, played at the Lyceum in 1896, reveals him opposing Bardolatry while acknowledging Shakespeare's genius. Shaw's abridgments of CYMBELINE proposed to the actress Ellen Terry suggest his desire to awaken the audience with the maximum intellectual stimulation. Shakespeare failed to represent the Shavian view of comedy as social corrective, and his treatment of women was outmoded for Shaw. While Shaw viewed Shakespeare's politics as detestable, as in his treatment of Julius Caesar, in the Preface to The Dark Lady of the Sonnets Shaw comes just short of making Shakespeare an honorary member of the Fabian Society. The change of mind suggests an error in Shaw's criticism of identifying the dramatist with his characters. Shaw's criticism of HAMLET, played at the Lyceum in 1897, suggests that Shakespeare failed to understand in his characterization of Hamlet what Schopenhauer calls Immanent Will, which is not a long step from Shaw's Life Force. Shaw's ultimate reason for wanting to leave Shakespeare behind is that the business of modern drama is with the future.

1876 Smoker, Barbara. "The Shavian Subconscious," ShawSB, XLVI (Sept 1952), 9-10.

[Abstract of a talk by R. F. Rattray, dealing with "the subconscious of creative artists in general, then of Shaw." The talk was published as "The Subconscious and Shaw," QUARTERLY REVIEW, CCXCI (April 1953), 210-22, q.v.]

1877 Steinhardt, Maxwell. "Shaw's Plays in Performance," ShawB, I (May 1952), 10-12.
Saint Joan (Cort Theater, NY) is impressive. Vivien Leigh is excellent in Caesar and Cleopatra; Laurence Olivier is not so good. AFFAIR OF LETTERS is the title of a reading by Sarah Churchill and Edward Thommen of selections from the Shaw-Terry correspondence.

1878 Suckling, Norman. "Shaw and Schubert," MONTHLY MUSICAL RECORD, LXXXII (Jan 1952), 22.
Shaw is correct that Schubert's music is brainless. [Answer to Otto Erich Deutsch, "The Reception of Schubert's Works in England," MONTHLY MUSICAL RECORD, LXXXI (Nov 1951), 236-39.]

1879 Treugutt, Stefan. "Na scenach warszawskich" (On the Warsaw Stages), TWÓRCZOŚĆ (Warsaw), VIII (1952), 162-68.
In Mrs. Warren's Profession ("Współczesny" Theater, Warsaw), Shaw's criticism of the social position of women is not restricted to the problem of work, prostitution, emancipation, etc.; from criticism of manners and customs, Shaw moved to social problems and the unmasking of the constitutional foundations of England and the capitalist exploitation of one person by another. The play is a critical, relentless look at the fate of individuals caught in the meshes of a capitalist machine. Fifty years have passed, but the picture of contrasts within the disintegrating social life of England has not changed; only the colors and contrasts have become clearer. [In Polish.]

1880 Ussher, Arland. "Bernard Shaw: Emperor and Clown," THREE GREAT IRISHMEN: SHAW, YEATS, JOYCE (Lond: Victor Gollancz, 1952; NY: Devin-Adair, 1953), pp. 13-61; partly rptd in SAINT JOAN: FIFTY YEARS AFTER, 1923/24, ed by Stanley Weintraub (Baton Rouge: Louisiana State UP, 1973), pp. 119-24.
While Shaw's mind lacked color and mystery, there was nothing common or mean in him. However, The Philanderer

suggests that he was not angelic. Nor was he a Puritan. Yet he was an epicure in thoughts more than in sensations. His humanitarianism is that of an ascetic dictator, being a demagog more than a leader. Yet Shaw was the most consistent and logical of all socialists in making perfect equality of income the touchstone of true socialism. Shaw hated poverty, and often created unpleasant characters belonging to the class that Marxists call Workers. As philosopher he had an explanation of existence, derived mainly from Nietzsche, Schopenhauer and (perhaps) Bergson; as artist he admired strong, vital, unmoral personages of all sorts of both sexes. His greatness was that he put both philosophy and life on the boards and succeeded in fascinating his audience; but it was his weakness that he over-rationalized and over-moralized them both. Mrs. Warren is convincing; Undershaft is too Shavian to be real. Keegan and Saint Joan are Shaw's finest characters. Candida, Pygmalion, and Saint Joan are his finest works. [Comments on John Bull's Other Island, Androcles and the Lion, Back to Methuselah, Man and Superman, Misalliance, Captain Brassbound's Conversion, Arms and the Man.] After the failure of Widowers' Houses and the suppression of Mrs. Warren's Profession, Shaw ceased writing dramatic social criticism. He was always a moralist but, unlike Ibsen, ceased writing about personal problems and the individual soul in later life. Shaw's religious plays, Superman and Methuselah, are tedious except for their wit, which is often silly like that in The Tragedy of an Elderly Gentleman. His works are not quite art or philosophy, but they are conversation--and the best the world has to give.

1881 Ward, A[lfred] C[ourtenay]. "Introduction," PLAYS & PLAYERS: ESSAYS ON THE THEATRE, by Bernard Shaw (Lond: Oxford UP, 1952), pp. vi-xv.
There is much of Shaw in John Tanner, who speaks of moral passion, aesthetic passion, and intellectual passion. Those passions are the root of Shaw's uniqueness as a critic. To him art was a function of life. No one else has written dramatic criticism like Shaw's. He was the only first-rate critic who took Marie Corelli seriously. Shaw objected to Henry Irving's distortion of Shakespeare and others, but he was constantly aware of Irving's greatness. He was passionately convinced in an age that exploited and distorted Shakespeare that Shakespeare's genius lay in his

mastery of poetry. Shaw refused to accept Shakespeare as a man of ideas for modern times when he saw Ibsen, the one contemporary man of ideas, being ignored. Shaw was right in wanting to link the greatest living playwright, Ibsen, with the greatest actor, Irving, but wrong in singling Irving out as an instrument to conform to Shaw's literary and sociological ideals. A selection of Shaw's weekly articles from the SATURDAY REVIEW offers a cross-section of English theater history in the eighteen-nineties and demonstrates his gift of writing intelligently and illuminatingly.

1882 Webb, Beatrice. BEATRICE WEBB'S DIARIES, 1912-1924, ed by Margaret I. Cole with an introduction by the Rt. Hon. Lord Beveridge (Lond, NY, Toronto: Longmans, Green, 1952), pp. v, ix, x, 4, 6, 11, 12, 17, 21, 27, 31, 37, 47-48, 68, 69, 70-71, 75-79, 82, 84, 95, 129, 137, 162, 200, 201, 216, 217, 225, 227-28, 238.
[References to Shaw and Beatrice and Sidney Webb, especially relating to the Fabian Society.]

1883 Welsh, Henry. "How Bernard Shaw Smelt the Rat," ShawSB, XLIV (April 1952), 4-6.

[Extended anecdote explaining how the author obtained an autographed photograph of Shaw, Shaw's comment on his own music criticism, and a comment on a speech by Napoleon from The Man of Destiny.]

1884 West, E. J. "The Critic as Analyst: Bernard Shaw as Example," ETJ, IV (Oct 1952), 200-205.
Shaw's success as a drama critic is owed to his power of analysis.

1885 Williams, Raymond. DRAMA FROM IBSEN TO ELIOT (Lond: Chatto & Windus, 1952; NY: Oxford UP, 1953), pp. 11, 22, 41, 42, 49, 51, 138-53, 176, 192, 231, 262-63, 270, 271-72.
Shaw misrepresented Ibsen in The Quintessence of Ibsenism, but his book was one of the forces that produced the New Drama. The social context of Shaw's reputation is responsible for his greatness, since his work actually lacks the complexity of great art. [Survey of the major

plays.] The emotional inadequacy of Shaw's plays denies him major status as a playwright.

1886 Winsten, Stephen. SHAW'S CORNER (Lond: Hutchinson, 1952; NY: Roy Publishers, 1953).
[A record of Winsten's walks and talks with Shaw from 1945 to October 1950. Photographs.]

1887 Zuñiga, Angel. "En la muerte de Shaw" (On the Death of Shaw) and "En Shaw todo es representación" (In Shaw Everything is Theater), PALABRAS DEL TIEMPO (Barcelona: Barna, 1952), pp. 304-10.
Shaw sums up a brilliant period of English literature because of his talent, intellectual capacity, original view of the world, and rich human and social ideology. He fails only in believing that everything would be perfect once socialism is achieved. [Includes a review of G.B.S., A FULL-LENGTH PORTRAIT AND A POSTSCRIPT (1952), by Hesketh Pearson.] [In Spanish.]

1953

1888 Altman, George, Ralph Freud, Kenneth Macgowan and William Melnitz. THEATER PICTORIAL: A HISTORY OF WORLD THEATER AS RECORDED IN DRAWINGS, PAINTINGS, ENGRAVINGS, AND PHOTOGRAPHS (Berkeley and Los Angeles: U of California P, 1953), picture numbers 284, 329, 331, 335, 354, 369, 395, 427, 436, 448, 449.
[Primarily a book of pictures, with minimal text. Shaw plays represented in the pictures are The Apple Cart, Back to Methuselah, Caesar and Cleopatra, Saint Joan, and Too True to Be Good.]

1889 Atkinson, Brooks. "Barry Jones Heads a Capital Cast in a New Staging of Shaw's Misalliance," NYT, 19 Feb 1953, p. 20.
Misalliance (City Center, NY) apparently has no central theme but expressed Shaw's views on many topics in the best Shavian style. The actors contribute much to the success of the play, particularly Barry Jones, who is the perfect

Shavian because of the "comic insincerity" with which he
plays his part, and Roddy McDowell, who plays his role like
a cynical Marchbanks. [This production is also reviewed
favorably by Atkinson in NYT, 22 March 1953, II, p. 1.]

1890 Atkinson, Brooks. "News Notes on G.B.S.: He Is
Still a Controversial Figure in the World He Left
Three Years Ago," NYT, 18 Jan 1953, II, p. 1.
There is no reason why the public should support
financially the upkeep of Shaw's house at Ayot St. Lawrence
as a memorial to him. The true memorial to him is his plays
and other writings, which continue to interest the public,
as is evident from the highly favorable reception accorded
The Millionairess in its just-completed run, in the fact
that the New York City Center is planning a new production
of Misalliance, and in the success of two recent
collections of Shaw's prose. The "true lesson" of Shaw is
skepticism.

1891 Baake, Friedrich. "George Bernard Shaw als
Musikkritiker" (George Bernard Shaw as Music Critic),
ARCHIV FÜR MUSIKWISSENSCHAFT, X (1953), 233-52.
In the history of music criticism, Shaw holds a unique
position as an extremely subjective critic. His criticism
highlights the relationship between art and life but it
does not provide a model for other critics to follow.
Shaw's relationship to music is determined by two factors:
his musicality and his socialism. The former enabled him to
understand music on its own terms; the latter made him
intolerant of all art for art's sake. Thus we find very
good judgments, based on musical insight, next to very
distorted views, based on ideological convictions. [In
German.]

1892 Baake, Friedrich. "George Bernard Shaw als
Musikschriftsteller" (George Bernard Shaw as a Writer
on Music). Unpublished dissertation, University of
Kiel, 1953. [Listed in McNamee, p. 534.] [In German.]

1893 Baird, A. Dunmore. "Welcome to New York, Mr.
Shaw," ShawB, I (Summer 1953), 1920.
[Report of Shaw's arrival in New York 11 April 1933 on the
Empress of Britain; his reception by a crowd of laborers at
the dock.]

1894 Baker, Julius. "Theatre News," ShawSB, XLIX (June 1953), 25-26.
[Comments on the successful current NY production of Misalliance; the current Lond production of The Apple Cart (Theater Royal, Haymarket); and an item by "A Correspondent" on "Happy Accidents" in Shaw productions (TIMES, Lond, 1 April 1953), q.v.]

1895 Barber, George Stanley. "The Musical Criticisms of Bernard Shaw," PENNSYLVANIA STATE UNIVERSITY ABSTRACTS OF DOCTORAL DISSERTATIONS, XV (1953), 427-31. Unpublished dissertation, Pennsylvania State College, 1952.

1896 Barker, Felix. THE OLIVIERS: A BIOGRAPHY (Philadelphia & NY: J. B. Lippincott, 1953), pp. 19, 47, 48, 50, 113, 166, 230-32, 259, 260, 263-68, 277-78, 347, 353-58.
Very early in Laurence Olivier's career Shaw saw and approved his subtle interpretation of Parolles in ALL'S WELL THAT ENDS WELL. Though the production of ANTONY AND CLEOPATRA and Caesar and Cleopatra together was very successful on both the London and the New York stages, "it was really a marriage of incompatibles" in which Caesar and Cleopatra was the weaker partner. Laurence Olivier became very impatient with Shaw's play, particularly with its insistence that there was no romance between Caesar and Cleopatra. When playing Sergius, of Arms and the Man, Olivier, in an effort to avoid making him a caricature, tried to play him honestly, but thus lost the comedy of the role without gaining sympathy for the character.

1897 Barzun, Jacques. "The Inexhaustible Bernard Shaw," GRIFFIN, II (1953), 1-3, 8; rptd, abridged, as "The Prose of Bernard Shaw," ShawSB, XLIX (June 1953), 14-17.
Now that many of the ideas for which Shaw fought in his writings have been widely accepted, readers can begin to appreciate his prose for its artistic, rather than its didactic, qualities. The "Rejected Statement" on censorship from the Preface to The Shewing-Up of Blanco Posnet is one of the three great masterpieces on censorship in English. [Review of The Selected Prose of Bernard Shaw, ed by Diarmuid Russell (1952).]

1898 Barzun, Jacques. "Introduction: Byron and the Byronic in History," THE SELECTED LETTERS OF LORD BYRON, ed by Jacques Barzun (NY: Grosset & Dunlap, 1953), vii-xli.

Mendoza in Man and Superman satirizes the Byronic hero of the melancholy, world-weary noble outlaw type. This hero epitomizes courageous, lonely individuality and therefore became outmoded when democratic structures made group action, such as that of the Fabian Society, more effective than individual action. Shaw's Cashel Byron has more than just his name in common with Lord Byron. In their correspondence with their publishers William James, Byron, and Shaw revealed similar attitudes toward those publishers.

1899 Bentley, Eric [Russell]. "Acting and Reciting," NEW REPUBLIC, CXXVIII (26 Jan 1953), 22-23.

The Drama Quartet should not be praised for reciting rather than acting. Shaw believed that in Shakespeare's time speeches in the plays were declaimed with a minimum of stage business, rather than acted. In insisting on such presentation of Shakespeare Shaw had a valuable influence on Shakespearean productions in his time, but he carried his ideas too far.

1900 Bentley, Eric [Russell]. IN SEARCH OF THEATER (NY: Alfred A. Knopf; Toronto: McClelland & Stewart, 1953), pp. 118-20, 251-55 ["Bernard Shaw Dead" (1951)], passim.

Margaret Webster's production of Saint Joan suffers from the same failing as her productions of Shakespeare, the attempt to popularize the play by over-stressing the obvious and failing to bring out the underlying meaning of events of dialog. In spite of this misdirection, Uta Hagen's performance as Joan is good precisely because she does not attempt to soar.

1901 Bentley, Eric [Russell]. "On Acting," NEW REPUBLIC, CXXVIII (19 Jan 1953), 22-23.

Shaw's preference for Duse's acting over Bernhardt's is often thought to be based on his preference for "natural" acting over "artificial" acting, but this conclusion seems to be inconsistent with Shaw's criticism of the natural actor John Hart.

1902 Beyer, William H. "The State of the Theatre: The Devil at Large," SCHOOL AND SOCIETY, LXXVII (21 March 1953), 183-87.

Misalliance is the most stimulating and consistently amusing play on Broadway this season. The narrative is "obviously intentional hokum," but the theme, criticism of Victorian institutions and traditions of marriage and family life, still has point today.

1903 Blum, Daniel. THEATRE WORLD: SEASON 1952-1953 (NY: Greenberg, 1953), pp. 6, 27, 28, 29, 128, 129, 142, 179.

Two successes of the 1952-53 New York season were Shaw's The Millionairess and Misalliance. [Photographs of Don Juan in Hell, Heartbreak House, The Millionairess and Misalliance.]

1904 "Books in Brief," NATION, CLXXVI (3 Jan 1953), 17-18.

Shaw's nondramatic prose gives the reader more insight into the paradoxes of Shaw's nature than do his plays. [Review of The Selected Prose of Bernard Shaw, ed by Diarmuid Russell (1952).]

1905 Brown, Ivor. "At the Theatre: Royal and Ancient," OBSERVER (Lond), 10 May 1953, p. 13.

The current revival of The Apple Cart (Haymarket, Lond) is well staged and well performed. Noel Coward's style of delivery makes the most of the high comedy of his part.

1906 "Budapest, Pygmalion," ShawSB, L (Sept 1953), 9.

A review in MAGYAR NEMZET of the current production in Budapest of the Dezsö Mésröly translation of Shaw's Pygmalion praises the play and Shaw for fighting against established institutions and bourgeois beliefs and practices.

1907 Carroll, Joseph. "Shaw's Journal to Stella," TAM, XXXVII (Jan 1953), 10-12.

The recently published Bernard Shaw and Mrs. Patrick Campbell: Their Correspondence (1952) is not as satisfactory as the Shaw-Terry letters, probably because Terry was closer to being an intellectual equal of Shaw's than Mrs. Campbell was and because Terry felt no need to pose in her letters, whereas Mrs. Campbell is constantly playing the part of a coquette.

1908 Cerf, Bennett. "Trade Winds," SRL, XXXVI (9 May 1953), 6, 8.
Currently there is a successful revival of Shaw's Misalliance (Barrymore Theater, NY) with a notable cast performing it well.

1909 Chapman, John. "Shaw's Misalliance in Genial Performance at the City Center," DAILY NEWS (NY), 18 Feb 1953.
Misalliance, now being presented at the City Center, is a "spoof" with an insubstantial plot designed to bring together characters of different classes, ages, and interests to give Shaw ample opportunity for witty social criticism.

1910 Chapman, John (ed). THEATRE '53 (NY: Random House, 1953), pp. 6, 7, 12-13, 33, 466, 477-78, 507-8, 540, 545, 547, 548.
Though the recent production of The Millionairess was a popular success, many critics attributed its success to the fame of Shaw and of Katharine Hepburn rather than to the qualities of the play or its production. Misalliance, which many critics had considered a minor Shaw play, elicited their praise and ran far longer than had been expected.

1911 Chase, Harrison V. "A Note on Spiritual Meagreness," ShawB, I (Summer 1953), 15-16.
In refutation of the charge that Shaw's philosophy of the Life Force is an intellectual and materialistic concept lacking in spirituality, it might be pointed out that the concept is in many respects similar to the Elan Vital of Henri Bergson, the Reverence for Life of Schweitzer, and the Satyagraha, or Truth Force, of Mahatma Gandhi—none of which has ever been accused of such a lack of spirituality.

1912 Cloten, Claud. "Theatre News," ShawSB, XLVIII (March 1953), 26-29.
[An account of current and forthcoming performances of Shaw and of radio broadcasts relating to Shaw.]

1913 Clurman, Harold. "Theater," NATION, CLXXVI (7 Mar 1953), 212-13.

The theme of Shaw's Misalliance is the same as that of Heartbreak House—the disastrous irresponsibility and blindness of the English upper classes—but the play was written at a time when this decay of the ruling classes could still be viewed with good humor and optimism. The present production of the play at the Barrymore is a highly enjoyable visit to a world which is no more.

1914 Coleman, Robert. "Misalliance Is Real Fun and Splendidly Acted," DAILY MIRROR (NY), 18 Feb 1953.

Misalliance is minor Shaw but better than most contemporary plays. Much of the credit for the success of the current production by the New York City Drama Company must go to Cyril Ritchard's direction.

1915 A Correspondent. "Happy Accidents," TIMES (Lond), 1 April 1953.

On one occasion when Esmé Percy was playing in The Doctor's Dilemma an unintended but theatrically effective illusion of a ghostly presence was created by a defect in the scenery. When Sybil Thorndike was rehearsing Saint Joan she added a line of dialog that Shaw liked so well he incorporated it into the text.

1916 Coward, Noel. "Coward Upsets His Apple Cart," TAM, XXXVII (Sept 1953), 30-32.

The Apple Cart, dealing with the relationship between a constitutional monarch and his cabinet, is a more appropriate play to present in this coronation year than any new play could be. Though King Magnus is a spokesman for Shaw's ideas, he is also humanized, especially through his relationship with his wife and his daughter.

1917 Croome, Honor. "The Show Goes On," SPECTATOR, CXC (5 June 1953), 724.

Though many theaters held no performances on coronation night because they anticipated a meager audience, the Noel Coward production of The Apple Cart (Haymarket Theater, Lond) presented its nightly performance as usual. King Magnus's defense of the monarchy seemed more pertinent than usual, but it was actually a "shower of Shavian rhetoric, dated Fabianism, beautifully turned and beautifully irrelevant'."

1918 Cuthbertson, Joseph. "Piscatorial Androcles and Other Theatricals," SHAVIAN, I (Dec 1953), 15-17.
[A report on Shaw productions around the world, including Androcles and the Lion and You Never Can Tell in The Hague; Arms and the Man, by Eric Elliot's touring company, in Ahmedabad, India; and Don Juan in Hell, on tour in Germany. In the latter, the German actor's interpretation of the devil lacks the "suave slipperiness and self-indulgence" which the lines call for.]

1919 Dalton, Hugh. "Shaw as Economist and Politician," SHAW AND SOCIETY: AN ANTHOLOGY AND A SYMPOSIUM, ed by C[yril] E[dwin] M[itchinson] Joad (Lond: Odhams P, 1953; rptd Norwood, Pa.: Norwood Editions, 1976), pp. 250-62 [first presented as a Fabian Memorial Lecture on 27 Feb 1951].
Shaw derived his economic theories first from Henry George, then from Marx's DAS KAPITAL, and finally from Jevons. Shaw's attitude toward poverty is made clear in Major Barbara and in the Preface to that play. His economic theories are set forth in such works as Fabian Essays, a 1930 Preface to Fabian Essays, The Intelligent Woman's Guide to Socialism and Capitalism, Everybody's Political What's What, and Common Sense of Municipal Trading. In the Intelligent Woman's Guide Shaw advocated equality of income for all, feeling that it was a basic tenet of socialism, but sixteen years later, in Everybody's Political What's What, he indicated that he no longer held this opinion.

Though Shaw was very influential as a political theorist, he was a very poor political candidate, largely because a too rigorous honesty led him at times to speak well of his opponents and ill of his supporters.

1920 d'Amico, Silvio. "Cesare e Cleopatra di G. Bernard Shaw" (Caesar and Cleopatra by G. Bernard Shaw), PALOSCENICO DEL DOPOGUERRA, II: 1949-1952 (Turin: Radio Italiana, 1953), pp. 256-59.
The audience at the Eliseo last night expected a comedy, but despite its brilliance, Caesar and Cleopatra is basically serious, even bitter. Shaw admits that Caesar

contains something of himself. The play is one of misunderstandings, depicted in dialogs, scenes, and episodes that are often caustic and satirical. It was published in 1901, an age of fin-de-siècle hedonism, and can be described as prophetic. [Script of broadcast talk, Turin, Radio Italiana (13 Oct 1952).] [In Italian.]

> **1921** Darlington, W. A. "First Nights: Shaw Revived at Haymarket," DAILY TELEGRAPH & MORNING POST (Lond), (8 May 1953), p. 10.

The current revival of The Apple Cart (Haymarket Theater, Lond) supports the contention that in this play Shaw's preaching, though obviously present, is properly kept secondary to the dramatic action.

> **1922** Dolar, Jaro. "Ob Shawovi zgodovinski komediji" (Shaw's Birthday Comedy), GLEDALIŠKI LIST, VII (1952/53), 1678.

[On Caesar and Cleopatra. Not seen.] [In Croatian.]

> **1923** Dunsany, Lord [Edward John Moreton Drax Plunkett]. "Irish Writers I Have Known," ATLANTIC MONTHLY, CXCII (Sept 1953), 66-68.

Shaw had a "magnificent" short story published first in the Irish periodical SHANACHIE. Shaw's reputed "gruffness" must have been a protective pose since he always seemed kind in person. The original viewpoint expressed in Shaw's plays came as a shock to the English people.

> **1924** Eyrignoux, L. "Études Critiques: Bernard Shaw et Mrs. Patrick Campbell" (Critical Essays: Bernard Shaw and Mrs. Patrick Campbell), ÉTUDES ANGLAISES, VI (Nov 1953), 350-53.

Bernard Shaw and Mrs. Patrick Campbell: Their Correspondence amply supports Hesketh Pearson's view of Shaw's relations with Mrs. Campbell, making it clear that they never involved an actual sexual consummation. During the first period of letters, of "l'amour explosif," from 1912 to 1914, Shaw's letters are characterized by the baby-talk and adolescent romantic fire which needlessly dismay so many of his English admirers. In most of these letters discussions having to do with money or with the performances of some of his plays are intermingled with the declaration of passion. Even during this period Shaw's letters are full of phrases which indicate an attitude toward romantic love later reflected in Man and Superman and Back to Methuselah, the attitude that such love is a diversion from the important tasks of life. During the next period, 1914 to 1920, the passion is dead; friendship flourishes, but there is little of interest about Shaw personally. The letters of the last period, from 1920 to the year before the death of Mrs. Campbell, should have been withheld from publication out of respect for the memory of both Shaw and Mrs. Campbell, since they present both in an unfavorable light.

1925 F., L. "At the Theatre: Equity Community Theatre Revives Shaw's Man and Superman at High School in Bronx," NYT, 21 Feb 1953, p. 11.
Man and Superman espouses one of Shaw's favorite themes, the idea that it is the woman, not the man, who does the pursuing in a romance.

1926 Fell, James B. BERNARD SHAW ARRIVES: A FANTASY IN ONE ACT (Lond: Samuel French Ltd., 1953).
[This one-act play, which consists entirely of a debate between Shaw, Shakespeare, and Mephistopheles in hell, owes much to Shaw's own Shakes versus Shav and Act III of Man and Superman. It contains brief critical remarks on Saint Joan and Back to Methuselah.]

1927 Franklyn, Julian. THE COCKNEY: A SURVEY OF LONDON LIFE AND LANGUAGE (Lond: Deutsch, Feb 1953; rev ed May 1953; NY: Macmillan, 1953), pp. 10, 226-29, 233-38, 248, 251, 253, 278.
Shaw was right to object to the inaccurate rendering of Cockney dialect in the stereotype established by Dickens, but his own rendering of Cockney was also inaccurate—in Drinkwater, of Captain Brassbound's Conversion, and in Eliza, of Pygmalion. In Shaw's attempt to convey the dialect sounds through phonetic spelling he was often unsuccessful, partly because of his Irish background and partly because of the unobjective, superior attitude he took toward the speakers of Cockney. Shaw was unaware of the pride which the Cockney takes in his speech. [Franklyn delivered a speech containing this material to the Shaw Society on 29 June 1953. It was summarized by Barbara Smoker in SHAVIAN, I (Dec 1953), 9-11.]

1928 Fraser, G[eorge] S[utherland]. THE MODERN
WRITER AND HIS WORLD (Lond: Derek Verschoyle, 1953),
pp. 16, 17, 45-46, 48, 49, 62, 63, 139, 144, 146,
148-52, 162, 166-68, 296.

Shaw and Oscar Wilde supplied the impetus to modern English
drama, Shaw reviving the "comedy of ideas." Shaw did not
add anything new to the dramatic forms inherited from Ibsen
and Chekhov, and his plays lack the poetry with which they
invested their plays through their use of symbols. The hell
scene from <u>Man and Superman</u>, in spite of its brilliance,
does nothing to advance the action, and <u>Back to Methuselah</u>,
though it may have some merits, is lacking in dramatic
pleasure. <u>The Quintessence of Ibsenism</u> misses the painful
poetry in Ibsen and the insecurity about moral judgments.
Shaw's plays fall into two principal categories—those
dealing with contemporary social problems presented in very
prosaic, realistic terms (<u>Mrs. Warren's Profession</u>,
<u>Widowers' Houses</u>, and <u>The Philanderer</u>) and those dealing
with his philosophic beliefs and hence allowing the
incorporation of fantasy into the basically realistic
format of his plays (<u>Superman</u> and <u>Methuselah</u>). The lack of
a sense of poetic tragedy evident in his plays—even <u>Saint
Joan</u> is not really a tragedy, but rather an inspiring and
ennobling pageant—is also evident in his irreverent
criticisms of Shakespeare, the grand coherence of whose
mind Shaw is unable to grasp. <u>John Bull's Other Island</u> has
more of the atmosphere of real life than do his other
plays. In the plays of his later years Shaw introduced no
new ideas and showed himself to be out of touch with the
realities of his age. His continued defense of the powerful
dictators of the time did not come from any love of
brutality but stemmed from two deficiencies in him: his
failure to question the inevitability of progress; and his
lack of the kind of poetic imagination which could foresee
the inevitable decay of old traditions which had respected
and protected the individual, but could not see that in
decaying they would unleash cruelty and barbarism. About
half a dozen of Shaw's plays, including <u>Heartbreak House</u>
and <u>John Bull</u>, have the quality of timelessness, but the
others are already beginning to seem dated, though the
brilliance of Shaw's wit and his skill at dramatic dialog
will keep them alive.

1929 Gassner, John. "When Shaw Boils the Pot...,"
TAM, XXXVII (July 1953), 63-64, 92; rptd in THE
THEATRE IN OUR TIMES (NY: Crown, 1954), pp. 163-69.
If he were alive, Shaw might well have been amused at the
remarkably favorable reception of the revival of his
Misalliance (New York's City Center Theater), for when the
play opened originally in London in 1910, it was an
unqualified failure. The New York critics, however, are not
unwarranted in calling it the most stimulating play of the
1952-53 season, for Misalliance is still one of the
greatest farces in the English language. "Misalliance"
refers to the mismatching of parents and children in the
play, not to the upper middle class's relationship to the
aristocracy. Furthermore, there are characters and
situations in the discursive play that presage Heartbreak
House, Back to Methuselah, Man and Superman, and The
Millionairess. In Misalliance, as in his other plays, Shaw
delighted in playing with ideas and making them into
theater. Perhaps if Shaw had not considered the play a
potboiler, the critics would have been able to relax and
enjoy the farce.

1930 Gibbs, Wolcott. "The Theatre: Miss Russell and
Mr. Shaw," NYer, XXIX (7 March 1953), 59-61.
Though Shaw himself had a low opinion of Misalliance, it is
very entertaining.

1931 Gjesdahl, Paul. "Kaptein Brassbounds
forvandling på Nasjonalteatret" (Captain Brassbound's
Conversion at the National Theater), ARBEIDERBLADET
(Oslo), 30 March 1953, p. 4.
When Shaw's plays were first produced, his paradoxes were
considered outrageous and were forgiven only for the
brilliance of the wit with which they were expressed.
However, time has shown that they are true paradoxes and
that Shaw was simply ahead of his time in recognizing them.
For example, the paradoxes about the treatment of one
nation by another uttered by Lady Cicely in Captain
Brassbound's Conversion have by now become widely accepted
as truths about international relations. [In Norwegian.]

1932 Glicksberg, Charles I. "Shaw on Education,"
EDUCATIONAL FORUM, XVIII (Nov 1953), 38-48.

Shaw saw his task in all of his writings as educational. The Preface to <u>Immaturity</u> describes his own upbringing with very little formal education. <u>An Unsocial Socialist</u> shows the hero finding it necessary to educate the working classes about the effects of capitalism on their lives. His essay on "Schools and Schoolmasters" in the 1918 EDUCATION YEAR BOOK describes the educational system as a prison system in which the children have no rights and are taught to conform; he asserts that this keeps them from learning. Later, when he wrote <u>The Intelligent Woman's Guide to Socialism and Capitalism</u>, he had changed his mind to the extent of advocating the necessity of teaching a child certain fundamental rules of good behavior and one's obligation to one's own soul. <u>Everybody's Political What's What</u> points out that in the socialist future it will be necessary for everyone to be educated in order to choose the proper leaders for society. Shaw recognized that there are differences of individual ability and that the educational system must be flexible enough to adapt to these. "A Treatise on Parents and Children" (1910) is based on his belief that every person is an attempt by the Life Force to advance itself through the evolutionary process and that the educational system will only serve to interfere with this process. A major theme of <u>Misalliance</u> is the difficulties of childrearing. <u>Pygmalion</u> points to the importance of environment in education. The Preface to <u>Back to Methuselah</u> asserts that political science, as it is taught, upholds "the morality of feudalism corrupted by unsocialism" and sets up "the military conqueror, the robber baron, and the profiteer" as heroes to be emulated. Shaw's support for the freedom for each child to develop in its own direction is tempered by his socialist beliefs.

1933 Goffin, Peter. THE ART AND SCIENCE OF STAGE MANAGEMENT (NY: Philosophical Library, 1953; Lond: J. Garnet Miller, Quality P, 1953), pp. 23, 26, 27-28, 30-33, 88, 90.

Through his support of Ibsen's plays, through his own writing of plays, and through the publishing of his plays with his own prefaces and detailed stage directions to prevent their misinterpretation and alteration by producers, Shaw had a great part in the movement toward introducing realistic social drama in place of the melodrama which was popular in his early years.

1934 Gould, Jack. "Television in Review: 'Omnibus' Closes Series with Arms and the Man, but Shavian Pleasantry Is Not Quite Captured," NYT, 4 May 1953, p. 31.
The tone of the Omnibus production of Arms and the Man would have been more appropriate to the musical comedy THE CHOCOLATE SOLDIER.

1935 Gould, Symon. "George Bernard Shaw and His Latter-day Vegetarian Abuses," AMERICAN VEGETARIAN, 1 Feb 1953, pp. 1, 4; 1 March 1953, pp. 1, 5; 1 April 1953; 1 May 1953.
[In this four-part article Gould includes and criticizes two Shaw letters, excerpts from a third letter which originally appeared in the spring 1947 VEGETARIAN QUARTERLY, and a printed postcard, all on the subject of vegetarianism.] Shaw was not a true vegetarian in the last decade or so of his life. Not only did he admit to taking liver extract to treat pernicious anemia, but he advocated taking other gland extracts to cure other physical disorders and he tried to separate vegetarian practice from its true ethical motivation, the desire to avoid the slaughter of animals. Thus, in his last years he abandoned vegetarian beliefs, indicating that "the titan's mind was tottering."

1936 Grau, Jacinto. "Bernard Shaw," DON JUAN EN EL TIEMPO Y EN EL ESPACIO (Don Juan in Time and Space) (Buenos Aires: Raigal, 1953), pp. 205-8.
Shaw's Don Juan is a character who, rather than being the conqueror, is conquered by a woman. Being seduced is not peculiar to Jack Tanner; it is the condition of all men, although male vanity and the common foolishness of most professional rakes have ignored it. However, to create a philosophical Don Juan is to deny the essence of the true Don Juan, who does not care to meditate on either pleasant or unpleasant things. [In Spanish.]

1937 Green, Paul. "Mystical Bernard Shaw," DRAMATIC HERITAGE (Lond, NY: Samuel French, 1953), pp. 112-31.
Shaw expressed the belief that there are "only two great principles in man—his mystic nature and his common sense" and that anything which denies either or both of these principles or stifles their operation leads humanity into

confusion and darkness, as the predominance of the views of Darwin and his followers has done. Einstein, on the other hand, had a true understanding of both the common sense appearance of things and the miracle in the reality behind that appearance. Shaw felt that critics misinterpreted his plays because they considered him to be stressing fact and proceeding by reasoned argument, whereas really he is a mystic and his plays are mystical "interludes . . . between two greater realities." His favorite among his own plays was <u>Heartbreak House</u> because "it has more of the miracle, more of the mystic belief." Of contemporary dramatists Shaw had highest praise for O'Casey. He felt that Strindberg, though a great genius, had failed to achieve a proper balance between the mystical sense and common sense in his plays.

1938 Grendon, Felix. "Felix Grendon Replies to George Jean Nathan," ShawB, I (Summer 1953), 13-15.
Despite the popular success of the current production of <u>The Millionairess</u>, George Jean Nathan, in TAM (1952), viciously criticized not only this production, but also the play itself, Shaw as a playwright, the Shaw Society for its interest in Shaw, and the author [Grendon] for his favorable review of <u>Buoyant Billions</u>. Nathan gave no particulars in his criticisms, but merely reviled everything in generalities.

1939 Grendon, Felix. "Hedgerow Theater," NATION, CLXXVII (22 Aug 1953), 157.
The Hedgerow Theater players, in Moylan-Rose Valley near Philadelphia, who have a Shaw festival each July, included in this year's performances <u>Too True to Be Good</u>, <u>Heartbreak House</u>, and <u>Man and Superman</u>.

1940 Grendon, Felix. "The Quartette in John Tanner's Dream," ShawB, I (Summer 1953), 21-22.
In the most enthralling debate in the world's literature, the Devil, the Statue, and Doña Ana defend the life-style which Shaw consigns to Hell, whereas Don Juan opts for the hard, creative life of Heaven. Despite the fact that the "Dream Scene" of <u>Man and Superman</u> was originally criticized as unplayable, the First Drama Quartet have held audiences spellbound.

1941 G[rendon], F[elix]. "Village Wooing," ShawB, I
(Summer 1953), 24-25.
At the 25 Nov 1952 meeting of the New York Chapter of the
Shaw Society a dramatic reading of Village Wooing was
presented. In this little masterpiece Shaw develops on a
modest scale the same theme which he develops in heroic
proportions in Man and Superman—the duel between the
sexes, with the Life Force aiding the woman because through
her success will eventually come the superior human beings
of the future.

1942 Gruber, E. L. "Letter to the Editor," ShawSB,
XLIX (June 1953), 27.
"Current Stages" has been performing You Never Can Tell
with great success on a very small stage in a converted
loft in Manhattan.

1943 Guezuraga, Margot. "Bernard Shaw, El Vínculo
Irracional" (Bernard Shaw, The Irrational Knot),
HISTORIUM (Argentina), XV (Oct 1953), 54-55.
In The Irrational Knot, Shaw was ahead of his time in
viewing the great commotions of the twentieth century.
Moreover, in it can be found the beginnings of his later
dialog and themes. [In Spanish.]

1944 Guinness, Alec. "Prologue," AN EXPERIENCE OF
CRITICS by Christopher Fry and THE APPROACH TO
DRAMATIC CRITICISM by Ivor Brown, W. A. Darlington,
Alan Dent, Harold Hobson, Philip Hope-Wallace, Eric
Keown, J. C. Trewin, T. C. Worsley; ed by Kaye Webb
(NY: Oxford UP, 1953), p. 7.
[Guinness lists Shaw among critics he feels compelled to
read when preparing for a classical role.]

1945 Gurko, Leo. HEROES, HIGHBROWS AND THE POPULAR
MIND (NY & Indianapolis: Bobbs-Merrill Company,
1953), pp. 95, 260, 261.
[Contains brief references to Shaw's theory of the
development of supermen.]

1946 Gussow, Mel. "And Now, Diana at the Stake,"
NYT, 31 Dec 1953, II, pp. 1, 4.
Diana Sands finds the part of Saint Joan "huge," because
Joan plays so many roles in her short life (and even

reappears as a ghost). She sees some similarities between the role of Joan and her role in A RAISIN IN THE SUN. Sands does not believe that her race presents any difficulties in her playing Joan.

1947 Haas, Willy. "Ein Menschenleben mit G. B. Shaw: Siegfried Trebitschs Selbstbiographie" (A Lifetime with G. B. Shaw: Siegfried Trebitsch's Autobiography), ENGLISCHE RUNDSCHAU (Köln), III (1953), pp. 540-41.
Though Trebitsch showed early promise of ranking as an original writer with such other Viennese writers of his time as Hofmannsthal, Arthur Schnitzler, Richard Beer-Hoffmann, and Hermann Bahr, when he became Shaw's official German translator he knowingly sacrificed his own career as a writer to Shaw's genius and became known simply as "Shaw's translator." He was more than just Shaw's translator, however, since it was through Trebitsch's efforts that Shaw's plays were first produced in Germany, and it was their success in Germany that opened the way for their successful public production in England. Trebitsch's autobiography is full of interesting anecdotes involving Shaw. [In German.]

1948 Haas, Willy. "Eitle Künstlerliebe: G. B. Shaws Briefwechsel mit Stella Patrick Campbell" (Mere Artists' Love: G. B. Shaw's Exchange of Letters with Stella Patrick Campbell), ENGLISCHE RUNDSCHAU (Köln), III (1953), pp. 662-64.
Shaw's love affairs give evidence of the same careful planning which went into his every other activity. Having wisely married a rich woman, he cleverly chose to court by mail successful actresses whom he wanted to play the starring roles in his new plays. The love letters of Shaw and Mrs. Campbell were obviously written by both with an eye on posterity. In this correspondence Shaw has written, quite unintentionally, his most brilliant satire, on the theme of the tragedy and comedy of the love of artists, who even in the midst of their love can never really forget themselves and their art. The tragicomic aspects of the letters are heightened in those written after the love affair was over, when the letters are filled with recriminations and with pleadings and arguments about the possible publication of the letters. In spite of the

obvious self-consciousness of the love expressed in the letters, however, there is also an undercurrent of genuine feeling for one another that occasionally comes through. [In German.]

1949 Handley-Taylor, Geoffrey (comp). LITERARY, DEBATING AND DIALECT SOCIETIES OF GREAT BRITAIN, IRELAND AND FRANCE, Sections III and IV (Lond, NY, Frankfurt: Hinrichsen, 1953), pp. 9, 14, 15, 19, 21, 31, 34.
[Lists, with a few anecdotes, societies which have had permanent or occasional interest in Shaw.]

1950 Hare, Peter. "Rückblick auf G. B. Shaw: Aus Anlass einer deutschen Gesamtausgabe seiner Dramen" (A Retrospective View of G. B. Shaw: On the Occasion of a German Collected Edition of His Dramas), ENGLISCHE RUNDSCHAU (Köln), III (1953), p. 355.
The Siegfried Trebitsch translation of the complete dramatic works of Shaw reads well though it is at times marred by minor faults and unevenness. Many of Shaw's plays create living characters, as do Candida, Pygmalion, The Doctor's Dilemma, Saint Joan, and In Good King Charles's Golden Days. These, along with Caesar and Cleopatra, Androcles and the Lion, and many others will surely achieve immortality on the stage. [In German.]

1951 Hatcher, Harlan [Henthorne]. "George Bernard Shaw," A MODERN REPERTORY, ed by Harlan [Henthorne] Hatcher (NY: Harcourt, Brace & World, 1953), pp. ix, x, 1-7.
Shaw had an uneventful life but early learned how to dramatize himself to catch public attention. When he could not get his plays performed, he published them with prefaces and thus made them an enduring part of the English tradition of wit and comedy. In spite of the topical nature of their themes, at least six of his plays—Candida, Caesar and Cleopatra, Man and Superman, Androcles and the Lion, Saint Joan, parts of Back to Methuselah, and possibly Pygmalion and The Devil's Disciple—seem likely to survive as classics.

1952 Hawkins, William. "Shaw's <u>Misalliance</u> Played to Hilt of Wit," NEW YORK WORLD-TELEGRAM & THE SUN, 19 Feb 1953.
The New York City Drama Company's current production of <u>Misalliance</u> is the most delightful production of its varied history. <u>Misalliance</u> reverses the traditional relationships between the various classes, sexes, and generations.

1953 Hayes, Richard. "The Stage: <u>Misalliance</u>," COMMONWEAL, LVII (3 April 1953), 648-49.
Though <u>Misalliance</u>, about people who have lost the motive force for action and can only talk incessantly, is "sunny and humane," it nevertheless reminds us of how much discipline it took for Shaw to achieve this light-hearted outlook on the failings of human relationships.

1954 Haynes, Renée. HILAIRE BELLOC (Lond, NY, Toronto: Longmans, Green [Writers and Their Work, No 35], 1953; rptd 1958), pp. 5, 28.
Belloc, Shaw, Chesterton, and Wells rebelled against the complacency and rigidity of the Victorian middle and upper classes and tried to shock them into an awareness of the realities of human life which the Victorian illusions and conventions denied. The ideas which Shaw and Wells set forth have now become widely accepted, unlike those of Belloc.

1955 Heilbroner, Robert L. THE WORLDLY PHILOSOPHERS: THE LIVES, TIMES, AND IDEAS OF THE GREAT ECONOMIC THINKERS (NY: Simon and Schuster, 1953), pp. 145, 241, 258-59.
The mild and well-meaning Marxist Second International included Shaw and similar socialists.

1956 Heiseler, Bernt von. "Über Bernard Shaw" (About Bernard Shaw), ZEITWENDE (München), XXII (1953), 566-68.
Shaw can be compared with Erasmus and Voltaire in his deserved reputation for cleverness, but like them he was not so deep a thinker as some of his contemporaries. Though he was no poet, on some occasions his work came close to poetry. His works were distinguished by his wit, his powers of observation, and his knowledge of human nature, and yet they displayed a weakness when looking into the human

heart. In <u>Candida</u>, for example, Shaw's understanding of the characters is so comprehensive that they almost, but only almost, come to seem like real people; when Shaw overstepped his own limitations to write a mocking work on the subject of Joan of Arc, he somehow broke out of the usually narrow scope of his understanding and lighted up the holiness of Joan's life. Often a problem is not really grappled with but is merely shunted aside by an ingenious verbal parry, and yet this parry throws a bright light on the problem. His mockery did much to expose the cant by which the English social system was often defended, and yet when England was attacked in World War II, he advocated support of his country's war effort. [In German.]

1957 Henderson, Archibald. "The Decline and Fall-Off of the Shavian Empire?" ShawB, I (Summer 1953), 8-13. The failure of the Shaw Memorial Committee to raise the projected 250,000 pounds should not be taken as an indication that the interest in or value of Shaw's works died with him, but it should be attributed instead to failings of the committee itself.

1958 Hennecke, Hans. "Bernard Shaws Vermächtnis" (Bernard Shaw's Legacy), DEUTSCHE RUNDSCHAU, LXXIX (1953), 1168-73; rptd in Hennecke, KRITIK: GESAMMELTE ESSAYS ZUR MODERNEN LITERATUR (Criticism: Collected Essays in Modern Literature) (Gütersloh: Bertelsmann, 1958), pp. 235-42.
Shaw's prefaces still provide many valuable insights and plenty of food for thought. Although Shaw never talked much about his art, his best plays constitute great literature. He considered it his most important task to uncover and castigate the follies of his contemporaries. Whether his own philosophy is a consistent whole is open to question. Certain basic principles, however, occur throughout his work, the two most prominent of them being the evolutionary Life Force and the decisive importance of money. Behind the mask of a "superman" Shaw was actually shy and sensitive. He mastered the art of debunking and of unmasking others, but he himself remained elusive. [In German.]

1959 Hewes, Henry. "Broadway Postscript: London Bridge," SRL, XXXVI (1 Aug 1953), 24-25.

The Apple Cart (Haymarket Theater) is probably the most popular of a number of revivals in London this season. ESCAPADE, by Roger MacDougall, has been strongly influenced by Shaw's Misalliance.

1960 Hewes, Henry. "Broadway Postscript: PICNIC & More Fun," SRL, XXXVI (7 March 1953), 33-35.
Though Misalliance is one of the too talky plays which Shaw wrote in the period between the greater plays of 1906 and 1912, it is nevertheless very entertaining, and the current revival on Broadway makes the best of its good qualities.

1961 Hobson, Harold. THE FRENCH THEATRE OF TO-DAY: AN ENGLISH VIEW (London, Toronto, Wellington, Sydney: George G. Harrap, 1953), pp. 39-40, 202, 203.
During the German occupation of France, plays about Joan of Arc, particularly Shaw's Saint Joan, had a strong influence in strengthening the spirit of those who were resisting the invaders. John Tanner, of Man and Superman, was a pioneer in the establishment of a fundamental attitude of twentieth-century literature, the attitude that women have a right to have sexual experiences without marriage.

1962 Hobson, Harold. THEATRE (Lond: Burke Publishing Co. [Pleasures of Life], 1953), pp. 126, 152, 233.
As a critic Shaw was perceptive and witty but often unfair. Man and Superman and Saint Joan are fine plays, but not great plays.

1963 Hobson, Harold. THE THEATRE NOW (Lond, NY, Toronto: Longmans, Green and Co., 1953), pp. 56, 128, 149, 150-52.
Ann Whitefield of Man and Superman is a "cold-blooded liar and hypocrite" and "a singularly repulsive creature," but in the New Theater production in 1951 Kay Hammond brought to the part the charm which Shaw had failed to give it. The 1951 Olivier productions of Caesar and Cleopatra and Shakespeare's ANTONY AND CLEOPATRA on alternate nights revealed surprising affinities between the genius of the two authors.

1964 Hoffman, Theodore. "Thrown to the Lions," NEW REPUBLIC, CXXVIII (15 June 1953), 22-23.

Gabriel Pascal's film version of <u>Androcles and the Lion</u> is just the sort of religious spectacle that Shaw always vigorously opposed. Though much of the Shavian wording is retained, it is presented in such a way as to sentimentalize both character and theme.

1965 Holberg, Stanley Marquis. "The Economic Rogue in the Plays of Bernard Shaw," UNIVERSITY OF BUFFALO STUDIES, XXI (Oct 1953), 33-119; rptd Folcroft, Pa.: Folcroft P, 1971.
In order to attack capitalism and advance the cause of socialism, Shaw created in five of his plays an economic rogue--a character who disregards both the accepted morality of his day and the welfare of his fellow human beings in his selfish pursuit of financial success. The first two of these, Sartorius of <u>Widowers' Houses</u> and Mrs. Warren of <u>Mrs. Warren's Profession</u>, are victims as well as exploiters, and although they are ruthless and immoral in their business lives, they are affectionate and well-intentioned in their personal lives. Thus, their economic roguery is primarily attributable not to their own faults but to the evils of the capitalistic system. The depictions of Undershaft in <u>Major Barbara</u> and Epifania in <u>The Millionairess</u> add to the concept of the economic rogue the notion that the Life Force works through such a character in its striving toward an improved world. Boss Mangan of <u>Heartbreak House</u> illustrates the shallowness and weakness of the economic rogue when he is allowed, through the apathy of the educated and cultured classes, to become the sole power in government.

1966 Holmes, Oliver Wendell, and Harold J. Laski. HOLMES-LASKI LETTERS: THE CORRESPONDENCE OF MR. JUSTICE HOLMES AND HAROLD J. LASKI: 1916-1935, ed by Mark DeWolfe Howe (Cambridge, Mass.: Harvard UP, 1953), pp. 8, 18, 81, 196, 212, 344, 352, 368, 399, 407-8, 429, 448, 454, 480, 566, 570, 603, 613, 629, 631, 635, 636, 642, 656, 683, 740-41, 749, 853, 864-65, 902, 989, 991, 1014, 1016, 1018-19, 1024, 1056, 1057, 1059, 1072, 1157, 1181-82, 1187, 1191, 1194, 1200, 1206, 1211, 1286-87, 1296, 1403, 1419, 1438, 1458, 1466.
[The Holmes letters are all critical of Shaw, finding him and his plays witty but shallow. The 24 Laski references to

Shaw up to 1928 are full of high praise for his conversation, for his social, political and economic thinking, and for his plays, especially <u>Saint Joan</u>. The remainder of the Laski references are highly critical of Shaw's taste and manners in conversation and of the superficiality of the thought in his writings. Laski found <u>The Apple Cart</u> "mediocre and vulgar."]

1967 Hood, Sam[uel Stevens]. "George Bernard Shaw's Pittsburgh Cousins," PITTSBURGH PRESS FAMILY MAGAZINE (Sunday Supplement), 31 May 1953, pp. 3-5.
[An account of Shaw's correspondence with a first cousin in Pittsburgh, Constance Ann Gurly, married to an American, William Hamilton. During World War I Shaw helped her locate her son, William, Jr., who had been reported missing in action in France. In the years 1927-28 Shaw wrote three letters to her other son, Douglas, advising him in a disagreement which Douglas was having with his father about whether Douglas should go to college.]

1968 Hummert, Paul A. "Marxist Elements in the Works of George Bernard Shaw," DA, XIII (1953), 1183. Unpublished dissertation, Northwestern University, 1953; pub with revisions as BERNARD SHAW'S MARXIAN ROMANCE (Lincoln: U of Nebraska P, 1973).

1969 Jacobsohn, Siegfried. "<u>Candida</u>," BDDTG (1952-53), No 34.
The superficially simple but actually quite complex structure of <u>Candida</u> is appropriate to the content of the play: through the seemingly simple events of the play, some of which even appear to lack relevance to its advancement, the depths and complexities of the characters, as well as their growth and development, are gradually revealed. [In German.]

1970 Joad, C[yril] E[dwin] M[itchinson]. "Editor's Introduction," SHAW AND SOCIETY: AN ANTHOLOGY AND A SYMPOSIUM, ed by Joad (Lond: Odhams P, 1953; rptd Norwood, Pa.: Norwood Editions, 1976), pp. 7-19.
The hero worship of Shaw by the generation that grew up between the turn of the century and World War I resulted from Shaw's having freed them from the false ideals of the Victorian era; from his contributions to socialist thought;

from the intellectual stimulation of his plays; from the inspirational effect of his philosophy, which looked forward to the improvement of humankind through its own efforts; and from the versatility which made Shaw both a creative thinker and an able practitioner in many fields.

1971 Joad, C[yril] E[dwin] M[itchinson]. "Editor's Introduction to Section II," SHAW AND SOCIETY: AN ANTHOLOGY AND A SYMPOSIUM, ed by Joad (Lond: Odhams P, 1953; rptd Norwood, Pa.: Norwood Editions, 1976), pp. 69-71.

The extracts from Shaw's Fabian tracts, Fabian speeches, and letters to the Fabian Society printed in this section have been chosen with two principal purposes in mind: first, to show Shaw as the chief writer and editor, the literary expert, of the Fabian Society, constantly revising and correcting the essays written by others and by himself, considering calmly and fairly the views and criticisms expressed by other members, no matter how foolish those criticisms might sometimes be; and second, to show Shaw as a business-like administrator of the affairs of the Fabian Society.

1972 Joad, C[yril] E[dwin] M[itchinson] (ed). SHAW AND SOCIETY: AN ANTHOLOGY AND A SYMPOSIUM, (Lond: Odhams P, 1953; rptd Norwood, Pa.: Norwood Editions, 1976).

[Sections include "Shaw—The Man, the Socialist" (original essays, I); "Tracts, Speeches and Letters" (excerpts from Shaw, II); "Extracts from Prefaces, Plays, Essays and Articles" (III); "Three Fabian Memorial Lectures" (originally delivered Feb and March 1951). Essays on Shaw abstracted separately under 1953: Joad, C. E. M., "Editor's Introduction," "Editor's Introduction to Section II," and "Shaw the Philosopher"; Martin, Kingsley, "G.B.S."; Woolf, Leonard, "The Early Fabians and British Socialism"; Ratcliffe, S. K., "Some Reminiscences of Shaw as a Young Socialist"; Dalton, Hugh, "Shaw as Economist and Politician"; Levy, Benn W., "Shaw the Dramatist."

1973 Joad, C[yril] E[dwin] M[itchinson]. "Shaw the Philosopher," SHAW AND SOCIETY: AN ANTHOLOGY AND A SYMPOSIUM, ed by Joad (Lond: Odhams P, 1953; rptd Norwood, Pa.: Norwood Editions, 1976), pp. 233-49.

[First presented as a Fabian Memorial Lecture on 20 Feb 1951]. Shaw's concept of a Life Force directing an evolutionary process by which the two opposing forces in the universe, Life and Matter, interact, becoming pure thought, is set forth in the Don Juan in Hell scene in Man and Superman, throughout all five parts of Back to Methuselah, and in the Preface to Methuselah. Shaw never indicated what this pure thought would be thinking about, once it had eliminated matter. Shaw did manage to use this evolutionary theory as the basis for a very practical philosophy of human behavior, according to which man should not strive to live his life in the service of his own desires and happiness, but instead in the service of some cause which will advance the purposes of the Life Force. In addition, this philosophy views woman as mainly intent upon making man into a provider for her children because her role is to advance the Life Force through biological reproduction. Man may even, as Dubedat does with Jennifer in The Doctor's Dilemma, use and exploit woman in the furtherance of his creative work. If his genius is in the realm of art, he must eschew romantic art and produce didactic art since only such art advances the purposes of the Life Force. Though Shaw's philosophy has been largely ignored, partly because he stated it so clearly and plainly that it does not seem deep enough to be impressive, he was nevertheless a great philosopher, remarkable for power and originality of thought.

1974 Johnson, A. E. "Drama Mailbag: Shaw, like Socrates, Found to Corrupt the Youth—Assorted Attitudes," NYT, 1 Feb 1953, II, p. 3.
The deleterious effect that the works of Shaw, even Saint Joan, have had is evidence of our literary decadence. Shaw had very little of value to say. [Letter to the Editor, answered in "Drama Mailbag," NYT, 8 Feb 1953, II, p. 3, by George Marquisee, "Another Retort,": Johnson's opposition to what he considers the immorality of Shaw's works puts him in the company of those throughout the ages who have opposed the exposing of cant; by Victor Conrad Norman, "Easy Targets": Shaw always exercised his wit on easy targets like Johnson in order to open the minds of the young; and by Walter R. Storey, "Letter Criticizing Shaw Draws Replies from His Admirers—Comments": Shaw still

offers wisdom and entertainment in <u>Man and Superman</u>, <u>Pygmalion</u>, <u>Saint Joan</u>, and at least nine other plays.]

1975 Johnson, Edgar. "Dickens and Shaw," ShawB, I (Summer 1953), 1-7.
Shaw had a very high regard for Dickens and his work, and Shaw's own works were clearly influenced by Dickens. The two were similar in their love of farce and slapstick, in which respect <u>Great Catherine</u>, <u>Major Barbara</u>, and <u>Saint Joan</u> show passages similar to some in Dickens. <u>The Doctor's Dilemma</u>, <u>Man and Superman</u>, <u>Pygmalion</u>, <u>You Never Can Tell</u>, <u>Captain Brassbound's Conversion</u>, and <u>Barbara</u> use comic characters similar to some of Dickens's comic characters, even the names of such characters often showing the Dickensian influence. In the expression of deep feeling Shaw is also like Dickens, as witness certain passages in <u>Candida</u>, <u>Barbara</u>, <u>Caesar and Cleopatra</u>, and <u>Joan</u>. The most important parallel between the two, however, is no doubt in the purpose underlying most of their work: "a developing criticism of society was the lifework of both and the very soul of their art."

1976 Karr, Harold Solomon. "Samuel Butler: His Influence on Shaw, Forster, and Lawrence," DA, XIII, No 4 (1953), 551-52. Unpublished dissertation, University of Minnesota, 1953.

1977 Keen, Alan. "Shaw and Shakespeare," ShawSB, XLVIII (March 1953), 18-19.
There is a parallel between Shakespeare and Shaw, but whereas Shaw's message was social, Shakespeare's was universal. [Summary of an address given to the Shaw Society.]

1978 Kemp, T. C., and J[ohn] C[ourtenay] Trewin. THE STRATFORD FESTIVAL: A HISTORY OF THE SHAKESPEARE MEMORIAL THEATRE (Birmingham, England: Cornish Brothers, 1953), pp. 7, 10, 42-43, 45, 83, 118, 127, 131, 133, 138-39, 143, 149.
Shaw praised highly Barry Sullivan's acting, particularly in HAMLET. He criticized severely almost all aspects of Augustin Daly's production of AS YOU LIKE IT (1897), except for the acting of Ada Rehan. His criticism of the last act of CYMBELINE is not justified. The Spring Festival of 1919

opened with Candida. Getting Married is a "verbose debate,"
but Heartbreak House presents a clear picture of pre-World
War I Europe and an eloquent exposition of Shaw's ideas.
Shaw criticized the original Shakespeare Memorial Theatre
building, appealing for funds to build a replacement, and
after the fire in 1926 he strongly endorsed Elisabeth
Scott's design for a new theater. Shaw felt that
Shakespeare would have enjoyed Charlie Chaplin's acting.

1979 Kerr, Walter F. "The Theaters," NYHT, 19 Feb
1953.
Misalliance may be the funniest subjectless play.

1980 Krim, Seymour. "Shaw: The Man Behind the Mask,"
COMMONWEAL, LIX (6 Nov 1953), 120-23.
Despite Shaw's ardent support of such realistic playwrights
as Ibsen and his insistence that drama should deal with
reality, his own plays are not realistic, do not have truth
to life, and are sentimentalized. Shaw's plays sink to the
level of the audience in order to be entertaining instead
of maintaining a high standard of truth and raising the
audience to that standard. Shaw identified himself with the
heroic figures he created in his plays and became his own
greatest work of art.

1981 Kronenberger, Louis (ed). THE BEST PLAYS OF
1952-1953: THE BURNS MANTLE YEARBOOK (NY, Toronto:
Dodd, Mead, 1953), pp. 7, 14, 17, 25, 29, 40, 262,
292.
[Contains passing references to performances of The Apple
Cart, Don Juan in Hell, Major Barbara, The Millionairess,
Misalliance, and The Shewing-Up of Blanco Posnet and
factual data concerning productions of Millionairess and
Misalliance.]

1982 Kronenberger, Louis (ed). CAVALCADE OF COMEDY:
21 BRILLIANT COMEDIES FROM JONSON AND WYCHERLEY TO
THURBER AND COWARD (NY: Simon and Schuster, 1953),
pp. xiv, xv, 343-44, 400.
The greatness of Shaw's work consists not in one or a few
single outstanding plays but in the large body of his work,
with its immense variety of characters, settings, ideas,
and points of view. In Androcles and the Lion, in spite of
the wildly comic form, Shaw awakes in the audience an

emotional and thoughtful response to the characters and their actions. The most significant element in Pygmalion, both dramatically and intellectually, is its reversal of the Pygmalion legend.

1983 Kronenberger, Louis (ed). GEORGE BERNARD SHAW: A CRITICAL SURVEY (Cleveland & NY: World Publishing Co., 1953).
[Critical articles are arranged chronologically by date of their first publication. Contents, abstracted under year of first publication: "A Short Chronology" [not abstracted]; Louis Kronenberger, "Introduction," pp. ix-xvii (1953); Max Beerbohm, "A Cursory Conspectus of G.B.S.," AROUND THEATERS (1930); James Huneker, "The Quintessence of Shaw," ICONOCLASTS (1905, 1933); G. K. Chesterton, "The Critic," GEORGE BERNARD SHAW (1909); John Palmer, GEORGE BERNARD SHAW: HARLEQUIN OR PATRIOT? (1915); P. P. Howe, "Shaw's Economics," BERNARD SHAW: A CRITICAL STUDY (1915); Dixon Scott, "The Innocence of Bernard Shaw," MEN OF LETTERS (1916); Philip Littell, "The Bondage of Shaw," NEW REPUBLIC (1917); Ludwig Lewisohn, "Shaw among the Mystics," THE DRAMA AND THE STAGE (1922); George Jean Nathan, "Mr. Shaw and the Ogre," TESTAMENT OF A CRITIC (1931); Joseph Wood Krutch, "The Shavian Dilemma," NATION (1935); Edmund Wilson, "Bernard Shaw at Eighty," THE TRIPLE THINKERS (1938, 1948); W. H. Auden, "The Fabian Figaro," COMMONWEAL (1942); Jacques Barzun, "Bernard Shaw in Twilight," KENYON REVIEW (1943); Ronald Peacock, "Shaw," THE POET IN THE THEATRE (1946); C. E. M. Joad, "Shaw's Philosophy," G.B.S. 90 (1946); Eric Bentley, "Shaw's Political Economy," BERNARD SHAW (1947); Stark Young, "Heartbreak Houses," IMMORTAL SHADOWS (1948); Stephen Spender, "The Riddle of Shaw," NATION (1949); V. S. Pritchett, "G.B.S.: 1856-1950," TIME (1950); John Mason Brown, "Caesar and Cleopatra," STILL SEEING THINGS (1950); Thomas Mann, "He Was Mankind's Friend," LISTENER (1951).

1984 Kronenberger, Louis. "Introduction," FOUR PLAYS BY BERNARD SHAW: CANDIDA; CAESAR AND CLEOPATRA; PYGMALION; HEARTBREAK HOUSE (NY: Modern Library-Random House, 1953), pp. vii-xii.
Shaw's works have a continental variety and extensiveness and a torrential wit and rhetoric which more than compensate for their faults and deficiencies. Perhaps most

455

prominent among those faults is his treatment of sex, but his plays gain more from his unconventional treatment of characters and situations than they lose through the sexlessness of the characters. Though Candida is like a curiously sexless Portia, though Caesar and Cleopatra is not about a sexual encounter between its two protagonists but is instead a philosophic and political play, though Higgins has no sexual interest in Eliza, and though in Heartbreak House the animals do virtually everything except pair off, the very sexlessness where sex was expected becomes a positive virtue in each of the plays.

1985 Kronenberger, Louis. "Introduction," GEORGE BERNARD SHAW: A CRITICAL SURVEY, ed by Kronenberger (Cleveland & NY: World Publishing Co., 1953), pp. ix-xvii; rptd "Shaw," REPUBLIC OF LETTERS (NY: Alfred A. Knopf, 1955), pp. 167-77.

Despite his wide-ranging interests and fine intelligence, Shaw is more a showman of ideas than a philosopher. He never achieved any synthesis of his many contradictory views, nor was there any one core or essence to his thought. He lacked a tragic view of life, an awareness of the evil side of humanity, to give depth to his mind. Of the criticisms written of his work and thought, the best, those of Chesterton, Dixon Scott, and Beerbohm, were among the earlier ones. Recent critics have tended to ignore Shaw, partly because the unpoetic and didactic nature of his art violates the most cherished current concepts of what constitutes true art and partly because his plays are studies of society, not of character. Whatever he may lack in philosophy and poetry, however, none can deny the brilliance of his "free, volatile, unvindictive, dazzlingly gymnastic play of mind."

1986 Krutch, Joseph Wood. "Bernard Shaw and the Inadequate Man," "MODERNISM" IN MODERN DRAMA: A DEFINITION AND AN ESTIMATE (Ithaca, NY: Cornell UP, 1953), pp. 43-64.

[Printed without substantial change from the series of Messenger Lectures delivered by Krutch at Cornell University in October 1952. The thesis of the book is that "modernism" in modern drama represents a complete break with the values of the past, and that, in contradiction of the great hopes of the originators and exponents of this "modernism," it is leading civilization "not to a bright future, but to something like intellectual and moral paralysis."] With Shaw, who in his defense of Ibsen's plays and in his own plays opposed a new morality to Victorian morality, true "modernism" came to the English stage. The Revolutionist's Handbook of Man and Superman concludes by supporting the established voting procedures as the means to improvement of English society. In these years the strongest influence on Shaw's thought was that of Marx. In time Shaw's optimism was eroded by the course of world events; three representative plays show the development of his thought away from his early optimism. In Major Barbara, as a consequence of living in the security of prosperity, the munitions workers will, through improved education and the development of the spiritual side of their nature, learn to make the choices which will lead society in the direction of a socialist Utopia. With the advent of World War I, however, Shaw's increasing pessimism is evident in Heartbreak House, where the capitalist, Boss Mangan, is not a producer, like Andrew Undershaft, but is a pure parasite whose operations consist solely of the manipulation of money with no profit to anyone but himself. Later, in Back to Methuselah, Shaw is even more pessimistic, for he no longer believes that one lifetime is long enough for a person to learn to steer properly. Despite his determined optimism, Shaw's "modernism" eventually leads him to a view of the future which seems decidedly pessimistic.

1987 Krutch, Joseph Wood. "The Not So Good Old Days," TAM, XXXVII (Oct 1953), pp. 78-80, 93.
[Among Krutch's reminiscences are his defense of the religious views expressed by Androcles and the Lion and his rating of The Simpleton of the Unexpected Isles as "good fun but not really meaning anything at all."]

1988 Laing, Allan M. (ed). LAUGHTER AND APPLAUSE: ANECDOTES FOR SPEAKERS (Lond: Allen & Unwin, 1953), pp. 9 [unnumbered], 12, 13-14, 15, 22-23, 39, 57, 60-61, 68, 73, 85, 86, 87, 89, 95, 97, 98, 111, 116, 122, 123-24, 151, 152, 153, 160, 168, 175, 182, 184.
[Many brief anecdotes by and about Shaw.]

1989 Landstone, Charles. OFF-STAGE: A PERSONAL RECORD OF THE FIRST TWELVE YEARS OF STATE SPONSORED

DRAMA IN GREAT BRITAIN (Lond: Elek, 1953), pp. 30, 53, 109, 114, 117, 126, 127, 151, 161, 185.
[Shaw plays mentioned as having been performed are Candida, Village Wooing, The Man of Destiny, Pygmalion, You Never Can Tell, The Apple Cart, Saint Joan, Arms and the Man, Caesar and Cleopatra, and Man and Superman.]

1990 Laurence, Dan. "Shaw's Life Force: The Superpersonal Need," ShawSB, XLVIII (March 1953), 14-17.
Shaw was a deeply religious man. [Description of Shaw's religion and its functions. Summary of an address given to the Shaw Society.]

1991 Le Gallienne, Eva. WITH A QUIET HEART: AN AUTOBIOGRAPHY (NY: Viking, 1953), pp. 42, 43, 110, 186, 254, 258, 275, 276.
[Passing mention of Shaw or one of his plays.] Madame Ludmilla Pitoëff's performance in Saint Joan was extremely well received but created an impression of Joan quite different from what Shaw probably had in mind. In the days before he achieved fame, Marlon Brando gave an extremely good performance as Marchbanks in Candida.

1992 "Lebensdaten Bernard Shaws" (The Dates of Bernard Shaw's Life), BDDTG, No 34 (1952-53).
[A very brief chronology of Shaw's life and of the major events in it.] [In German.]

1993 LeRoy, Gaylord C. PERPLEXED PROPHETS: SIX NINETEENTH-CENTURY BRITISH AUTHORS (Phila: U of Pennsylvania P; Lond, Bombay, Karachi: Oxford UP, 1953), pp. 33, 115, 126, 131, 148, 149, 153, 154, 156, 157, 159, 161, 178.
[This book, discussing Carlyle, Arnold, Ruskin, James Thompson, Rossetti, and Wilde, is liberally sprinkled with quotations from Shaw about capitalism, socialism, and social reform.]

1994 Levy, Benn W. "Shaw the Dramatist," SHAW AND SOCIETY: AN ANTHOLOGY AND A SYMPOSIUM, ed by C[yril] E[dwin] M[itchinson] Joad (Lond: Odhams P, 1953; rptd Norwood, Pa.: Norwood Editions, 1976), pp. 263-79.

Shaw criticized not only the well-made play but also the problem play which did not treat realistically the problem, the characters, or the society from which the problem arose. Yet he did not maintain a strictly naturalistic kind of realism in his plays. He wrote comedy because he was an optimist, believing that humanity can by its own efforts change the future; however, the speeches of both Saint Joan and Caesar are evidence that Shaw had an awareness of the tragic aspects of life. Shaw's habit of giving his characters a chance to set forth their own defense to their own best advantage resulted in the confusion of actors, audiences, and critics as to who were the good and who were the bad characters. The plays contain both the clash of personality and the clash of ideas, and his best plays—Major Barbara, Saint Joan, and Heartbreak House—have both to the greatest extent.

1995 Lewis, Theophilus. "Theatre," AMERICA, LXXXVIII (7 March 1953), 632-33.
Though Misalliance is not Shaw at his best and though the ideas it discusses, which shocked its original audiences, are now routinely accepted, nevertheless it is a solid and enduring comedy of manners presenting characters of real interest.

1996 "London Sees Apple Cart: Critics Praise Revival of Shaw Play with Noel Coward," NYT, 8 May 1953, p. 29.
London critics of the TIMES and the DAILY TELEGRAPH were somewhat dissatisfied with Noel Coward's performance in The Apple Cart, but for the most part the reviews of the production were favorable and found the play fresh and witty.

1997 McClain, John. "Everybody Had a Wonderful Time," JOURNAL AMERICAN (NY), 19 Feb 1953.
Misalliance (City Center, NY) has little motivation or plot but does have very witty, apt dialog and very clear and penetrating depiction of character types.

1998 McCleary, G. F. "Some Early Recollections of G.B.S.," FORTNIGHTLY, CLXXIX (Feb 1953), 119-23.
Shaw exhibited from the beginning the style and wit which later made him famous. He was a great reader of Artemus

Ward. He felt that at the school of economics proposed by Sidney Webb all the teachers, regardless of their subjects, should be socialists who would advance the cause of socialism. Shaw cared little for the music of such composers as Brahms, Chopin, Schubert, Schumann, and Mendelssohn. Although he cared little for the work of Elgar on first exposure to it, he later became a good friend of Elgar and a great admirer of his music. The verses about Shaw beginning "Shaw golden crowned and ivory faced," which have been attributed to Lord Olivier and to Charles Burton, were actually written by a woman. Though in his writing Shaw could often be perverse and irritating, in person he was always kind, courteous, and encouraging.

1999 McDowell, Frederick P. W. "Technique, Symbol, and Theme in Heartbreak House," PMLA, LXVIII (June 1953), 335-56.

An important key to the technique of Heartbreak House may be found in its subtitle, A Fantasia in The Russian Manner on English Themes. The Chekhovian influence is evident in that, to a greater extent than in Shaw's early plays, the characters are symbolic abstractions. To the discussion of ideas which had been a prominent feature of such earlier plays as Captain Brassbound's Conversion, Major Barbara, the Hell scene in Man and Superman, and Getting Married, Shaw in this play adds the Chekhovian effect of the "perpetually dissolving scene" created by the continual and unmotivated entrances and exits of the characters. Instead of resulting in a dreamlike quality, as this technique does in Chekhov's plays, in Heartbreak this technique produces a nightmare quality. The plays which follow Heartbreak show the influence of this play in their technique, often having characters which are to an even greater extent abstractions.

Among the themes which emerge through the interaction of characters are the concepts that truth is relative and shifting, a dynamic mosaic of conflicting forces in which it is difficult to distinguish between madness and sanity, reality and absurdity; that the aristocracy of Europe has been corrupted by its search for pleasure, by its self-centered neuroticism, and by its lack of real concern for the well-being of society; that the chief sins of modern society are hypocrisy and an adherence to, or at least a toleration of, capitalist values; that the apathy and blindness of the aristocracy are so great that it will take a terrible catastrophe to awaken them to the need for a spiritual renewal; and that self-recognition and spiritual understanding are not enough without the presence of a directing will and the energy to act upon that recognition and understanding.

2000 Macqueen-Pope, W[alter James]. SHIRTFRONTS AND SABLES: A STORY OF THE DAYS WHEN MONEY COULD BE SPENT (Lond: Hale, 1953), pp. 259, 267, 273.
The role of Candida was the greatest part Kate Rorke ever played. One of the first persons to be photographed with the use of the Banfield-Foulsham flashlight process was Shaw, who professed to be "dazzled" by this art.

2001 Martin, [Basil] Kingsley. "G.B.S.," SHAW AND SOCIETY: AN ANTHOLOGY AND A SYMPOSIUM, ed by C[yril] E[dwin] M[itchinson] Joad (Lond: Odhams P, 1953; rptd Norwood, Pa.: Norwood Editions, 1976), pp. 23-38.
Most of the time Shaw was able to keep his public personality, the "irresponsible jester," separated from his private person, the serious thinker and writer. In the few times when he did not, he was led to the statements of opposition to democracy and praise of dictatorships which did his reputation much harm. In spite of his reputation, he was one of the easiest of authors for an editor to work with, and he was not upset by criticism. He loved debate, but he avoided hurting the feelings of his opponents in argument. Jung once suggested that Shaw's coolness might have resulted from his never having been deeply in love and thus having managed to evade real experience. Such an explanation might also account for the lack of passion which characterizes Shaw's plays despite their intellectual brilliance, as for example in the Hell scene in Man and Superman and the last act of Major Barbara. Shaw's mind and energy remained great to the end of his life; in his last year his contribution to a series of articles on the drama was the most vital article of the series. His greatness will be recognized permanently because "his mind and personality dominated an epoch."

2002 Martin, [Basil] Kingsley. HAROLD LASKI (1893-1950): A BIOGRAPHICAL MEMOIR (Lond: Victor Gollancz, 1953), pp. 83, 88-89, 94.

In 1931 Laski, Shaw, and others, contributed to a symposium on the economic "crisis in democracy" published in the POLITICAL QUARTERLY. In 1932, as the crisis continued, Shaw wrote to Laski, asserting that Fabian socialism was incapable of dealing with the crisis and had become the "extreme Right" in its opposition to Soviet-style communism, which he now espoused. In 1934, when Laski was severely criticized in the Western press for a speech he made in Moscow which was being interpreted as pro-communist, Shaw publicly praised him for his sensible remarks.

2003 Mehta, Lehar Singh. "Shaw—The Successor to Shakespeare," MODERN REVIEW (Calcutta), XCIV (Aug 1953), 149-50.

Shaw enjoyed saying unpleasant things that hurt and startled people because he knew it would be good for them. He exaggerated in order to shock people into seeing the truth beneath the exaggeration. "Bernard Shaw was the mind looking out with quick and thrilling interest upon the play of life."

2004 Meister, Charles W. "Chekhov's Reception in England and America," AMERICAN SLAVIC AND EAST EUROPEAN REVIEW, XII (1953), 109-21.

During the first World War Shaw became an admirer of Chekhov's work, asserted that "after reading a play of Chekhov's he felt like tearing up his own plays," and was much influenced by Chekhov in his own Heartbreak House. However, he did not long continue to reflect the spirit of disillusionment which made Chekhov's plays gain critical appreciation after World War I.

2005 "Membership and Other Notes," ShawSB, L (Sept 1953), 4-8.

St. John Ervine suggested that the Interlude in The Apple Cart is derived from an incident in The Irrational Knot, and Sir Lewis Casson pointed out a possible relationship between the play and Laurence Housman's novel JOHN OF JINGALO.

2006 Mendip, Thomas. "Around and About," ShawSB, XLIX (June 1953), 27-28.
"Cassandra" in the DAILY MIRROR has complained about the bequests in Shaw's will, particularly those relating to language reform, and the CHICAGO DAILY NEWS deplores current work on a new alphabet inspired by the provisions of Shaw's will.

2007 Mendip, Thomas. "Lions and Shadows," SHAVIAN, I (Dec 1953), 14-15.
The Gabriel Pascal film of Androcles and the Lion is very poor. Even where it follows Shaw's lines closely, it loses entirely the spirit of those lines. It will probably be very popular, however.

2008 Nathan, George Jean. "George Jean Nathan's Monthly Critical Review," TAM, XXXVII (May 1953), 14-16, 88; rptd in THE THEATRE IN THE FIFTIES (NY: Knopf, 1953), pp. 24-25.
Though Misalliance (City Center, NY) has been thought an unplayable play, this year's revival proves otherwise.

2009 Nathan, George Jean. "Sample British Imports: Bernard Shaw," THE THEATRE IN THE FIFTIES, by George Jean Nathan (NY: Knopf, 1953), pp. 157-60.
Shaw's wit has continued to be popular because he has mingled with it other forms of humor less biting and more palatable to the general public; furthermore, his wit, intellectual though it be, views life from the standpoint of the average person, as opposed to the inherently class-conscious standpoint of such social wits as Wilde, Sheridan, and Coward.

2010 Nethercot, A[rthur] H. "Shaw's Women and the Truth about Candida," SHAVIAN, I (Dec 1953), 12-13.
[A summary by Barbara Smoker of Nethercot's speech to the Shaw Society on 11 Sept 1953.] MEN AND SUPERMEN: THE SHAVIAN PORTRAIT GALLERY (1954) divides the characters of all of Shaw's plays, using the three basic categories Shaw set up in The Quintessence of Ibsenism and then subdividing those categories. In Candida Marchbanks is a "developing Realist," Morell is a "wavering Idealist," and Candida is a "static Philistine." The categories cannot be considered as entirely rigid and distinct, however.

2011 Ostergaard, Geoffrey. "G.B.S.--Anarchist,"
NS&Nation, XLVI (21 Nov 1953), 628.
A little-known fact about the development of Shaw's
political and economic thought is that, before he became a
socialist, he was for a short time an anarchist.

2012 Pearson, Hesketh. "The Origins of The Apple
Cart," List, 4 June 1953, pp. 936-37.
Shaw once suggested that he himself was the original of
King Magnus of The Apple Cart. Orinthia was modeled on Mrs.
Patrick Campbell, and the wrestling match between Orinthia
and Magnus was suggested by a similar incident between Mrs.
Campbell and Shaw. Labor leader John Burns inspired
Boanerges, and Proteus has qualities taken from three
prominent public men—Asquith, Lloyd George, and Ramsay
MacDonald. The queen is somewhat reminiscent of Shaw's
wife.

2013 Perdeck, Albert. "G. B. Shaw en J. W. Stalin,"
DE GROENE AMSTERDAMMER, 28 March 1953, p. 4.
[After surveying some of the more sensational aspects of
Shaw's 1931 trip to Russia with Lady Astor and Lord
Lothian, Perdeck attempts to place Shaw's Russian
experience, and especially the interview with Stalin,
within the context of his strong intellectual commitment to
socialism.] In Too True to Be Good and On the Rocks, Shaw
displays the changes in political ideology which he was
forced to undergo after meeting Stalin. Even in old age, he
continued to have a strong, positive recollection of
Stalin. [In Dutch.]

2014 "The Plain View," TLS, 22 May 1953, pp. 325-
26.
In Bernard Shaw: Selected Prose (1952), Diarmuid Russell
included some works which might lead the reader to question
the value of Shaw's writings. In these works, such as Crude
Criminology (1931), Shaw fails to take into account the
achievements of the past. In other works Shaw displays a
behaviorist attitude toward human beings, as in his
accounts of his parents in the prefaces to Immaturity and
to his collected music criticism, in The Perfect Wagnerite,
and in three separate erroneous criticisms of Ibsen's
LITTLE EYOLF. In his plays, however, Shaw explores the
inner lives of his characters. A comparison of THE MASTER

BUILDER and Heartbreak House—in which Ibsen and Shaw treat the same theme, the special relationship which sometimes develops between a young woman and an old man—reveals Shaw's superiority in exploring this archetypal relationship. Shaw's Preface to Heartbreak House, however, might cause the unwary reader to miss this theme entirely and to believe the "great nonsense" that the play is about the disastrous irresponsibility of England's ruling classes. Shaw belonged to an age in which those who had left traditional religion behind felt compelled to demonstrate the earnestness of their lives by giving serious political interpretations to their works. Without understanding what he had done, Shaw created the great archetypal figures Ann and Tanner, Ellie and Captain Shotover, and Saint Joan.

2015 Popkin, Henry. "Romance of an Intellectual," KENYON REVIEW, XV (1953), 331-35.
Many parallels can be drawn between Shaw's plays and his correspondence with Mrs. Patrick Campbell—parallels between the types of women he was drawn to and those he drew, parallels in the evidence of sexual inhibition, and to some extent parallels in the disillusionment concerning love, although the extent of the disillusionment and loss of love between Shaw and Mrs. Campbell was far greater than that in any of the plays. [Review of Bernard Shaw and Mrs. Patrick Campbell: Their Correspondence.]

2016 Prideaux, Tom. WORLD THEATRE IN PICTURES: FROM ANCIENT TIMES TO MODERN BROADWAY (NY: Greenberg; Toronto: Ambassador Books, 1953), pp. 136-44, 146-51. [Photographs, mostly from the files of LIFE, covering 18 years of Broadway productions, with very brief comments on the plays. Shaw plays represented in the photographs are You Never Can Tell, Androcles and the Lion, The Doctor's Dilemma, Candida, The Millionairess, The Devil's Disciple, Misalliance, Caesar and Cleopatra, Man and Superman, and Pygmalion.]

2017 Ratcliffe, S. K. "Shaw As a Young Socialist," SHAW AND SOCIETY: AN ANTHOLOGY AND A SYMPOSIUM, ed by C[yril] E[dwin] M[itchinson] Joad (Lond: Odhams P, 1953; rptd Norwood, Pa.: Norwood Editions, 1976), pp. 54-65.

465

In the only known instance of his being directly influenced by an orator, Shaw became interested in economics and in socialist thought as a result of hearing an address by Henry George. After a thorough reading of DAS KAPITAL, he had what many British socialist thinkers lacked, an understanding of the Marxian theoretical basis of the socialist theories he was advocating. Graham Wallas believed that the Fabian hostility to Marx resulted from debates about Marxist theory between Shaw and Philip H. Wicksteed published in TODAY. Although Shaw had to work with people who could go at his pace and therefore did not join groups of working-class socialists, his interest in them is indicated by his being attracted to Fabianism by the tract "Why Are the Many Poor?" The earliest of Shaw's Fabian essays show that all his fundamental views were present from the first. He felt that his styles in speaking and in writing were the same, but his written works contain some passages of elaborate structure, whereas he was always direct in his speeches. He felt that his pose as jester was necessary to attract the attention of audiences and readers, but probably a person of his genius would have been heard and read without it.

2018 Ratcliffe, S. K. "Shaw as I Knew Him," ShawSB, L (Sept 1953), 17-18.
[Summary of a speech made by Ratcliffe at the 27 April 1953 meeting of the Shavian Society.] In the many debates in which Shaw engaged before World War I he revealed a mastery of oratorical techniques; his manner in those debates never indicated the contempt for the masses which he revealed later in his career. His speaking style showed a limitation of vocabulary and certain tricks of verbal economy which did not characterize his written language.

2019 Rattray, R. F. "The Subconscious and Shaw," QUARTERLY REVIEW, CCXCI (April 1953), 210-22.
Through "the subconscious inheritance of sex," Shaw felt that he was able to see the world as a woman does; through "the subconscious inheritance of race" he acquired the traits of both Mediterranean and Nordic races, but with a predominance of the imaginative traits of the Mediterranean. Both Keegan and Doyle, of John Bull's Other Island, are reflections of the author, Keegan reflecting his Mediterranean traits and Doyle his Nordic ones. Shaw

also inherited traits from various members of his family. Captain Brassbound's Conversion, Pygmalion, Heartbreak House, and Back to Methuselah all illustrate the way Shaw's plays use characters, incidents, or ideas subconsciously derived from his personal life, from conversations with others, and from his reading.

    2020 Rebora, Piero. "Ricordi Culturali Italiani di Bernard Shaw" (Italian Cultural Memories of Bernard Shaw), ENGLISH MISCELLANY, IV (1953), 179-86.
Classical and Italian culture have had a limited effect on Shaw's work, especially when compared with the German influence. When asked to explain precisely his interest in Italian culture, Shaw replied that he was influenced from his earliest years by Italian music from Rossini to Verdi and later Palestrina and Monteverdi. Italian literature meant Dante and Boccaccio; he knew the name Papini, and he enjoyed Pirandello. He attended in London a reading of F. T. Marinetti in 1914 and expressed his admiration for Futurism because of its "audacity, energy, and vital force." The libretto of IL TROVATORE was his textbook for Italian. [Includes quotations in Italian from Shaw letters to the author.] [In Italian.]

    2021 "Rediscovering a Shavian Gem," TAM, XXXVII (Sept 1953), 33-35.
[An introduction to the reprinting of the text of Misalliance on pp. 35-63. Brief stage history, with a sampling of critical comments by reviewers of the current NY revival.]

    2022 Reyes, Alfonso. "Sobre un decir de Bernard Shaw" (On a Remark by Bernard Shaw), OBRAS COMPLETAS, II (Mexico: Fonde Cultura Económica, 1953), 144-48.
Shaw's remark that the best way to understand verses is to put them to music did not refer to elegance of form but to the "music of ideas." [In Spanish.]

    2023 Riewald, J. G. SIR MAX BEERBOHM, MAN AND WRITER: A CRITICAL ANALYSIS WITH A BRIEF LIFE AND A BIBLIOGRAPHY (The Hague: Martinus Nijhoff, 1953), pp. 15, 16, 17, 26, 43, 53, 63, 87, 143, 146, 148, 150, 151, 155, 156, 157, 158-61, 162, 165, 169, 171, 172, 173, 176, 181, 196, 205, 206, 223, 225, 226, 227,

228, 229, 230, 231, 246, 256, 258, 260, 263, 267, 269, 274, 278, 281, 282, 284, 293, 300, 317, 328. Shaw's critical honesty and his analytic approach to criticism influenced Beerbohm's style, yet Beerbohm's dramatic criticism was principally aesthetic and subjective, whereas Shaw's was more concerned with the intellectual and ethical content of the plays. Shaw brought to the movement for realistic drama an extremely funny but didactic comedy of the intellect. Beerbohm rated Shaw's style of fantasy below that of Wilde or Barrie. He found Shaw's satire rather inhuman. Beerbohm wrote more critical articles about the plays of Shaw than about those of any other dramatist then living, yet he complained of his inability to make a final, unwavering evaluation of Shaw as a dramatist. Beerbohm found many of the plays—Mrs. Warren's Profession, Captain Brassbound's Conversion, You Never Can Tell, The Philanderer, Getting Married—marred by their mingling of comic and serious elements, a failing he also found in many of Shakespeare's plays. Beerbohm praised the wit, high spirits, and brilliance of such plays as The Doctor's Dilemma, The Devil's Disciple, Arms and the Man, Man and Superman, John Bull's Other Island, and the spiritual beauty of Major Barbara, but found that he enjoyed them for their philosophic content, not as drama, and he criticized Misalliance as unstructured even as a debate. Beerbohm looked upon Shaw as an innovator and as almost machinelike in his efficiency and integrity.

2024 Rowell, George. "Introduction," NINETEENTH CENTURY PLAYS, ed by George Rowell (Lond: Oxford UP [World's Classics], 1953, 1956, 1960, 1965, 1968), p. xii.
Shaw's genius enabled him to write well-made plays that shocked his own age but have delighted audiences since that time.

2025 Rubinstein, Annette T[eta]. THE GREAT TRADITION IN ENGLISH LITERATURE FROM SHAKESPEARE TO SHAW, 2 vols. (NY: Citadel, 1953; NY: Arco, 1955; NY, Lond: Modern Reader Paperbacks, 1969), pp. 191, 192, 308, 516-18, 675, 686, 734, 747, 850, 852, 854, 857, 863, 864, 867, 868, 874, 875-926.
Shaw's fatal flaw was his inability to see the masses as partners in the struggle for socialism. Though Love Among

the Artists expresses the potential power of the lower classes in the struggle to improve their conditions, already in The Irrational Knot the hero, who has risen from the lower classes, eventually rejects his earlier idealism, and An Unsocial Socialist establishes a pattern that appears often in the plays—i.e., it exposes the injustices of capitalism but sees the lower classes as unable to correct this system and reposes its faith instead in the effectiveness of a single superior leader. Only Widowers' Houses and Mrs. Warren's Profession are really socialistic, and even they do not suggest a solution to the evils of capitalism. Arms and the Man, Candida, You Never Can Tell, Misalliance, and John Bull's Other Island satirize Shaw's former idealism and socialist beliefs and activities. The concept of a great individual whose most important quality is a passionless nonhumanity appears in The Perfect Wagnerite, Caesar and Cleopatra, Captain Brassbound's Conversion, and in all the later plays except Saint Joan. Man and Superman rejects both imperialism and revolution, and in Major Barbara Shaw deserts to the capitalists and fascists. Joan, except in its self-contradictory epilog, gives a true picture of the revolutionary hero whose source of strength is the common people; Heartbreak House is a powerful expression of the evils of capitalism. Common Sense about the War shows that the powers ruling England were as guilty of causing World War I as were the powers ruling Germany, but it fails to suggest a way to alter the system which produced this situation. Shaw's comments on Bunyan, Shelley, Dickens, and Morris show that he saw their greatness not simply in the artistic qualities of their works but in their criticisms of society.

2026 Russell, Bertrand. "Bernard Shaw, the Admirable Iconoclast," List, L (3 Sept 1953), 380-81; rptd in PORTRAITS FROM MEMORY (NY: Simon and Schuster, 1956), pp. 75-80.
Shaw's life could be divided into three periods: the early period, in which he was a music critic, novelist, and Fabian activist; the middle period, in which he was primarily a writer of comedies; and the last, in which he acted as "a prophet demanding equal admiration for St. Joan of Orleans and St. Joseph of Moscow." In the first two phases he was admirable; in the third, less so. His vanity was great, as was indicated in his meetings with Bergson

and with Masaryk, on both of which occasions he spoke at length and dogmatically on subjects on which they were experts, giving them no opportunity to contribute or reply. He had a foolishly exaggerated admiration for Samuel Butler. His vegetarianism and his opposition to vivisection were not inspired by humanitarian feelings, but simply suited his ascetic nature and his indefensible attitude toward science. He was an excellent iconoclast but was not very effective in setting forth any constructive systems of belief.

2027 S., B. "The Annual Dinner," ShawSB, XLVIII (March 1953), 19-20.
[An account of the comments of Hubert Humphreys, Alan Keen, Dan Laurence, Ellen Pollock, Benn Levy, and Esmé Percy at the Shaw Society annual dinner, 5 Dec 1952.]

2028 Saint-Aulaire, Le comte de. "De Viviani à la Jeanne d'Arc de Bernard Shaw" (From Viviani to the Saint Joan of Bernard Shaw), LES OEUVRES LIBRES (Paris), April 1953, pp. 107-38.
[A series of recollections of literary and political figures with whom Saint-Aulaire had contact during his tenure as ambassador from France to England in the early 1920's. The fifth section, "La Saint Jeanne de Bernard Shaw" (The Saint Joan of Bernard Shaw), is devoted entirely to Shaw and his play.] Shaw's impudence extended even to his reactions to royalty and to the most celebrated women of his day. Shaw allayed Saint-Aulaire's fears that Joan might treat "France's national heroine" with disrespect by inviting him to attend the premiere and sending him a copy of the play so that he might see that there was nothing in it that might cause embarrassment to a representative of France. For political reasons attempts to have it included in the repertoire of the Comédie-Française failed; it was finally presented instead at the small Théâtre des Arts by Georges and Ludmilla Pitoëff. [In French.]

2029 Salas, Francisco Chica. "Teatros independientes: Androcles y el León" (Independent Theaters: Androcles and the Lion), SABER VIVIR (Argentina), IX (Dec 1953), 55-56.
The performance of Androcles and the Lion was excellent; Shaw's humor could easily be perceived. [In Spanish.]

2030   "Shaw and Stella," ShawSB, XLVIII (March 1953), 21-22.
Although containing possibly "some of the most exquisite love-letters penned by mortal man," <u>Bernard Shaw and Mrs. Patrick Campbell: Their Correspondence</u> has "a strangely un-Shavian flavour of dust and ashes," partly because the correspondence continued long after the love between the two was dead and partly because Mrs. Campbell's letters cannot match the verbal genius of Shaw.

2031   "Shaw in Tasmania," ShawSB, L (Sept 1953), 8-9.
Clive Sansom reports that in the last few years there have been in Tasmania professional performances of <u>Saint Joan</u> and <u>Pygmalion</u>, and since 1927 local amateur theatrical groups have presented <u>Pygmalion</u>, <u>Major Barbara</u>, <u>Heartbreak House</u>, <u>The Devil's Disciple</u>, <u>The Doctor's Dilemma</u>, <u>The Man of Destiny</u>, <u>The Dark Lady of the Sonnets</u>, and <u>Man and Superman</u>.

2032   "Shaw Slapstick Cheers Broadway," LIFE, XXXIV (13 April 1953), 155-56.
Though <u>Misalliance</u> is a very talky play, the talk on a wide range of subjects is brilliant and is relieved by occasional slapstick; the result is very amusing.

2033   "Shaw's Last Play: <u>Why She Would Not</u> Not to Be Performed," TIMES (Lond), 5 Dec 1953, p. 9.
After consulting drama critics and other literary advisers, the Public Trustee, as Shaw's executor, has decided that Shaw's last play, the incomplete "comediettina" <u>Why She Would Not</u>, will neither be published nor performed. The play has been put into the hands of the British Museum.

2034   "Shaw Society Meets," NYT, 16 March 1953, p. 22.
In an address to the Shaw Society, Archibald Henderson attributed Shaw's failure as a novelist to the appetite of the British reading public of the time for sensational thrillers instead of social criticism.

2035   Shiras, Mary. "G.B.S.: A Profile," CHICAGO REVIEW, VII (Fall-Winter, 1953), 26-34.

The public probably will remember Shaw primarily as an artist, a dramatist, not a thinker. Nevertheless, he insisted that drama must be didactic and cited Pygmalion in refutation of those who claimed that didactic drama could not be successful. In his plays the laughter often coincides with a sudden insight, as it frequently does in Major Barbara, or responds to sarcastic wit, as in Saint Joan and Man and Superman. There is also sometimes physical humor for comic relief, as in Androcles and the Lion and Pygmalion. The most commonly used technique in his plays is probably anti-climax.

2036 Smith, Robert McCaughan. "Modern Dramatic Censorship: George Bernard Shaw," DA, XIV, No 1 (1954), 133-34. Unpublished dissertation, Indiana University, 1953.

2037 Sprague, Arthur Colby. SHAKESPEARIAN PLAYERS AND PERFORMANCES (Cambridge, Mass.: Harvard UP, 1953; Lond: A. & C. Black, 1954), pp. 104, 107, 111, 118, 140, 143-44, 146-47, 148, 159, 202, 205, 210, 211, 212.
Shaw was highly critical of Henry Irving's Shakespearian performances, his stage voice, and his mutilation of the texts of Shakespeare. He gave strong support to the principles of Shakespearian production set forth and carried out by William Poel and the Elizabethan Stage Society, especially their return to the unaltered Shakespearian texts and to the bare platform stage. Shaw's The Art of Rehearsal advises how the playwright can influence the performances of the actors.

2038 Stamp, Henry E. "Letters to the Editor: Bernard Shaw," PUBLISHERS' CIRCULAR AND BOOKSELLERS' RECORD, 26 Sept 1953.
A visit to Shaw's house at Ayot St. Lawrence is well worth anyone's time. [Letter to J. G. Wilson.]

2039 Steinhardt, Maxwell. "Shaw's Plays in Performance," ShawB, I (Summer 1953), 22-23.
Though some critics have been harsh in their reviews of the current NY production of The Millionairess, audiences have been extremely enthusiastic. It is certainly not Shaw's best play, but it is a hilarious farce-comedy with many

examples of his keen wit and many valid critical comments on economic and social institutions. Katharine Hepburn successfully recreates the complex character of Epifania.

2040 Stephens, Frances. THEATRE WORLD ANNUAL (LONDON): A PICTORIAL REVIEW OF WEST END PRODUCTIONS WITH A RECORD OF PLAYS AND PLAYERS, No 4: 1st June 1952-31st May, 1953 (Lond: Rockliff, 1953), pp. 11-12, 19, 23, 24, 37-40, 128-32.
[Photographs, brief plot summaries, cast lists, and other production data from the 1953 productions of The Millionairess and The Apple Cart.] The Millionairess, though not one of Shaw's best, is nevertheless included among the most distinguished revivals in the West End, as is Cart.]

2041 Stokes, E. E., Jr. "Shaw and William Morris," ShawB, I (Summer 1953), 16-19.
Though Shaw and Morris were in two different camps of socialism, they often worked together at socialist meetings and collaborated on works promoting socialism, as in their articles on "The Socialist Ideal" in the NEW REVIEW (Jan 1891) and in their contributions to the Joint Manifesto of British Socialists (1893). In private their conversations centered on art and literature, particularly on their shared interest in Dickens, Ruskin, and the Pre-Raphaelite artists. Morris's influence on Shaw is evident in The Sanity of Art, in "On Going to Church," and in some of Shaw's drama criticism in the SATURDAY REVIEW.

2042 Stokes, James Paul. "The Reception of THE SECOND MRS. TANQUERAY," FLORIDA STATE UNIVERSITY STUDIES, II (1953), 89-94.
Shaw had a higher opinion of THE SECOND MRS. TANQUERAY when he saw it performed with Mrs. Patrick Campbell in the title role than when he read the play after it had been published.

2043 Storey, Walter R. "Drama Mailbag: Letter Criticizing Shaw Draws Replies from His Admirers—Comments," NYT, 8 Feb 1953, II, p. 3.
Though many of the Shavian ideas which were shocking in his time are now no longer so, Shaw still has both wisdom and entertainment to offer in such plays as Man and Superman, Pygmalion, Saint Joan, and at least nine others.

2044 Stresau, Hermann. "Bernard Shaw und die Frauen" (Bernard Shaw and Women), BDDTG, No 34 (1952-53).
Candida is perhaps the most personal of Shaw's plays. Both Marchbanks and Morell are parodies of Shaw himself— Marchbanks of his suppressed poetic qualities and Morell of his public personality as preacher and advocate of social causes. However, both of these characters are parodies only in the context of their relationship with Candida, who is not a parody but who, as the archetypal wife, mother, and unattainable beloved, embodies for Shaw the mysterious secret of life. [In German.]

2045 Stresau, Hermann. "Mit dem süssesten Anstand . . . G. B. Shaws dramatische Werke und das Problem des Übersetzens" (With the Sweetest Propriety . . .: G. B. Shaw's Dramas and the Problem of Translating), DEUTSCHE UNIVERSITÄTSZEITUNG, VIII (1953), 14-16.
Siegfried Trebitsch's translation of Shaw's works (1946), revised by Trebitsch in cooperation with the publisher (Zurich: Artemis), is still full of mistakes. Trebitsch mastered neither German nor English. [In German.]

2046 "The Theater: Old Play in Manhattan," TIME, LXI (2 March 1953), 74-75.
In spite of its reputation as an unplayable play and in spite of the fact that it has not been seen on Broadway since 1917, Misalliance proved very successful in last week's performance there. It is full of uninhibited and violent action, but it lacks focus on any one theme.

2047 "Theater: Reviews," NEWSWEEK, XLI (2 March 1953), 84.
Misalliance (City Center, NY) is a little long-winded, but on the whole the dialog is witty and full of penetrating insights on a wide range of subjects.

2048 Trebitsch, Siegfried. CHRONICLE OF A LIFE, trans Eithne Wilkins and Ernst Kaiser (Lond: William Heinemann, 1953), pp. 12, 96-99, 122-31, 145-48, 151, 158, 163-64, 167, 169-75, 177-85, 187-90, 196-99, 204, 207-9, 211-12, 218, 229-31, 254-58, 261, 263-77, 283-84, 286-98, 303-7, 310-11, 319, 324-29, 346-51, 368-75, 378, 381-83, 390-91, 393-97, 400-401, 404-5.

[This autobiography of Shaw's German translator contains much factual information about dates, places, casts, and other circumstances of the performances and publication of Shaw's plays in Germany and many anecdotes drawn from the author's personal visits and meetings with Shaw.]

2049 Trewin, J[ohn] C[ourtenay]. DRAMATISTS OF TODAY (Lond: Staples P, 1953), pp. 11, 12, 14, 17, 21, 24-25, 27-36, 49, 61, 91, 116, 134, 137, 142, 153, 172, 192, 197, 202-3.

Shaw might be compared to Marlowe in that each of them ushered in a new age in the English theater. Shaw felt that the function of the drama was to discuss problems bearing on real life in the real world, especially problems of ethics and morality, and he had the verbal gift to do this with style. With the passage of time he began to be more expository than dramatic, as in Getting Married and Misalliance. At the same time he was also writing "brisk stage pieces," such as Pygmalion, which was popular for its theatricality, not for its ideas. Even a much greater play, Heartbreak House, is twice as long as it should be, as is true of most of the later Shavian plays. Yet these plays, even Buoyant Billions, still show great vitality, the sole exception being Farfetched Fables. Even Shaw's worst plays are better than the work of most of his contemporaries in the theater. His best work includes the Don Juan in Hell scene of Man and Superman, In the Beginning and As Far As Thought Can Reach from Back to Methuselah, Saint Joan, Heartbreak, Candida, and In Good King Charles's Golden Days, with John Bull's Other Island and Androcles and the Lion almost making the list.

2050 Tynan, Kenneth. ALEC GUINNESS. (NY: Macmillan [Theatre World Monograph, No 1], 1953), pp. 11, 28, 33, 52, 62, 63, 80, 106, 107.

[Brief references to Shaw and his plays, the most significant of which have to do with Guinness's interpretations of the roles of Louis Dubedat in The Doctor's Dilemma and the Dauphin in Saint Joan.]

2051 Tynan, Kenneth. PERSONA GRATA (Lond: Wingate, 1953; NY: Putnam, 1954), pp. 31, 45, 57, 74, 94.

[Shaw is not included among the persona grata discussed, but there are brief, mostly laudatory, references to him on

the pages cited.] The title role in The Millionairess is
"just close enough to being unplayable" to provide the
right challenge to Katharine Hepburn's talents.

2052 U. "Bernard Shaws Liebesbriefe: Zur posthumen
Veröffentlichung des Briefwechsels mit Mrs. Patrick
Campbell" (Bernard Shaw's Love Letters: On the
Posthumous Publication of His Exchange of Letters
with Mrs. Patrick Campbell), DER STANDPUNKT (Bozen),
VII (16 Jan 1953), p. 8.
Bernard Shaw and Mrs. Patrick Campbell: Their
Correspondence reveals clearly why Shaw fought to prevent
the publication of these letters during his lifetime.
Shaw's letters constitute a unique mixture of two extremes
of tone: on the one hand the dry language of a text of
economics and on the other the baby talk of childish terms
of endearment and outpourings of passion which suggest the
real feelings that in other areas of his life Shaw
suppressed. Campbell clearly understood that, although Shaw
might sometimes write as though nothing existed except his
love for her, nevertheless his work, his political
lectures, and his life with his wife were at the same time
proceeding undisturbed. Occasionally in the letters Shaw
appears also as the jester who tries to teach through shock
and mockery. [In German.]

2053 van Druten, John. PLAYWRIGHT AT WORK (NY:
Harper, 1953), pp. 3, 36, 48-49, 64, 84, 117, 127,
130, 194-95, 199.
[In brief references van Druten cites, usually with
approval, plays and dramatic criticism of Shaw to
illustrate or support some of the concepts he sets forth,
referring specifically to Shaw's Dramatic Opinions, Mrs.
Warren's Profession, Candida, and Saint Joan.]

2054 Walker, Roy. "Theatre Royal," TWENTIETH
CENTURY, CLIII (June 1953), 466-70.
The theme of The Apple Cart (Theatre Royal production), the
deficiencies of democracy, seems very relevant today, not
simply because references to the United Nations have been
substituted for references to the League of Nations in the
original, but also because of the royal mistress who wants
to be made queen and the king who talks of abdication,
circumstances which have prevented the play's production in

London since 1935. Noel Coward, who plays Magnus, was influenced by Shaw in the writing of his own plays. Coward's THE YOUNG IDEA was so strongly influenced by You Never Can Tell that Coward feared he was plagiarizing. Furthermore, a scene in PRIVATE LIVES parallels almost exactly the scene in The Apple Cart in which Sempronius discovers Magnus and Orinthia wrestling on the floor. The moving performances of Noel Coward as Magnus and Margaret Rawlings as Lysistrata should disprove forever the contention that Shaw cannot create real people and that his drama is of the head and not the heart. In the course of the play Shaw uses the repetition of identical images to link the romantic and the political plots, a technique he learned from Shakespeare.

2055 Warnock, Robert (ed). REPRESENTATIVE MODERN PLAYS: BRITISH (Chicago: Scott, Foresman, 1953), pp. 1, 4, 6-7, 8, 9, 105-14.
Shaw always incorporated a strong idea content into his plays, but the best of them also exhibit convincing characterization and highly dramatic and poetic qualities. The Doctor's Dilemma is a characteristic Shaw play in its satire of the pompous and arrogant members of a professional class, in its conception of the artist, in its examination of the relationship of the sexes, in its posing of a moral dilemma, and in its wit.

2056 Watts, Richard, Jr. "Shaw's Misalliance a Joy at City Center," NEW YORK POST, 19 Feb 1953 [not seen in this form]; rptd in NEW YORK THEATRE CRITICS' REVIEWS, XIV (23 Feb 1953), 357.
Misalliance (City Center, NY) is so entertaining as to raise the question of why the play has been so little appreciated and so infrequently performed. Perhaps the explanation lies in its slightness of plot and emotion and its lack of concentration on one central theme. These qualities, however, are offset by its comic confrontations, its wit, style, and high spirits. Even its wordiness is an expression of its vitality and exuberance and thus is an asset rather than a drawback.

2057 Weales, Gerald. "Old Letters, Same Shaw, New Impetus," NEW MEXICO QUARTERLY, XXIII (1953), 343-48.

Shaw's manner of speaking about his characters in <u>Bernard Shaw and Mrs. Patrick Campbell: Their Correspondence</u> contradicts the common critical assumption that Shaw's characters are mere mouthpieces for his ideas.

2058 "'Wee Frees' Again Attack Shaw," ShawSB, XLVIII (March 1953), 14.
THE MONTHLY RECORD OF THE FREE CHURCH OF SCOTLAND asserted after his death that Shaw had a brilliant but unclean mind and that there is something healthy in the collapse of the Shaw Memorial Fund.

2059 Welland, D. S. R. THE PRE-RAPHAELITES IN LITERATURE AND ART (Lond, Toronto, Wellington, Sydney: George G. Harrap, 1953), pp. 31, 43, 195.
In <u>Man and Superman</u> Tanner rejects the respectable domesticity represented by Coventry Patmore's ANGEL IN THE HOUSE. Shaw was influenced by the Pre-Raphaelites, as is evidenced by his statement that <u>Candida</u> was intended to be "a modern Pre-Raphaelite play."

2060 West, E. J. "'<u>Arma virumque</u>' Shaw Did Not Sing," COLORADO QUARTERLY, I (Winter, 1953), 267-80; rptd in <u>ARMS AND THE MAN</u>, ed Henry Popkin (NY: Avon Books, 1967), pp. 161-75.
Disappointed that few playgoers or critics saw the serious purpose of his foolery in <u>Arms and the Man</u>, Shaw reacted by writing "A Dramatic Realist to His Critics," in which he demonstrated that, because he was not pessimistic or cynical about human nature and human ideals, he could write about them realistically. To interpret Sergius as a caricature is to miss the serious purpose that Shaw had in mind in the play; Sergius should be seen as truly disturbed over his inability to live up to ideals which, though false, he believes in. The play should be seen as a serious attack on both the romantic view of war and the romantic view of love.

2061 West, E. J. "Hollywood and Mr. Shaw: Some Reflections on Shavian Drama-Into-Cinema," ETJ, V (Oct 1953), 220-32.
The very quality which Shaw criticized most in Hollywood films—spectacle—has been made the major element of the film version of <u>Androcles and the Lion</u>. In 1931 and 1932

Shaw did permit the filming, in England under his direct supervision, of How He Lied to Her Husband and Arms and the Man, but he was not pleased with the results. In the 1938 film version of Pygmalion, produced in Hollywood by Gabriel Pascal, the directors worked closely with Shaw and retained his dialog; the resulting film was both a popular and critical success. Shaw was so pleased that he allowed Pascal to produce Major Barbara as a film, with gratifying results. Caesar and Cleopatra, filmed by Pascal at intervals during the war years, was characterized by Shaw as a very bad film. The film of Androcles and the Lion does not even use Shaw's dialog as written.

2062 West, E. J. "Shaw's Criticism of Ibsen: A Reconsideration," UNIVERSITY OF COLORADO STUDIES, SERIES IN LANGUAGE AND LITERATURE, IV (July 1953), 101-27.
Shaw was not a blind worshipper of Ibsen, nor did he value Ibsen's plays solely for the themes which he found in them, without regard to their artistic and dramatic qualities. His Ibsen criticism contains negative as well as positive judgments about the plays, and his criticism of individual performances shows him to be concerned about the art and stagecraft of the performances, not the ideas developed in the plays. The 1891 and 1913 prefaces to The Quintessence of Ibsenism assert that the purpose of the volume is merely to stimulate intelligent discussion and thought about Ibsen's plays. Shaw again and again repudiated the idea that his own plays or views were influenced by Ibsen, often pointing out that works in which critics found heavy Ibsen influence had been written before he had read any Ibsen.

2063 Whitman, Willson. "New Plays from GBS," ShawSB, XLVIII (March 1953), 6-10.
Shaw's plays were always incomprehensible at the time of first production. Too True to Be Good is a faithful reflection of the postwar years. The pirates of The Simpleton of the Unexpected Isles now fly the black flag above the American in Korea. Heartbreak House continues to show that it is nice people who, through their inaction, bring on wars.

479

2064 Williams, Raymond. DRAMA FROM IBSEN TO ELIOT (NY: Oxford UP, 1953), pp. 138-53, et passim; rvd 1964, 1968.

The Quintessence of Ibsenism, though its analyses of Ibsen's plays are not valid, was important for its support of the new drama and its insistence on making drama again a serious form of literature. Through his insistence on writing long prefaces and interpretive stage directions, Shaw made his plays into hybrid creations with some of the qualities of novels and some of the qualities of plays but inferior to both. Not only did he insist that his plays were didactic, but he was able to describe the subject of each in a simple phrase, thereby revealing the shallowness of his works. Widowers' Houses is very thin stuff. The Philanderer fails to distinguish, without reference to the stage directions, between the dialog intended to mock conventional stage romance and that intended to express serious and sincere emotions of the characters. Arms and the Man succeeds largely because it is negative, like most are derived from fantasy and unrelated to real human experience. The plays of Shaw are to be admired for their ability to satirize pretension and foolishness and for their wit, but the emotional inadequacy of his plays denies him major status.

2065 Woolf, Leonard. "The Early Fabians and British Socialism," SHAW AND SOCIETY: AN ANTHOLOGY AND A SYMPOSIUM, ed by C[yril] E[dwin] M[itchinson] Joad (Lond: Odhams P, 1953; rptd Norwood, Pa.: Norwood Editions, 1976), pp. 39-53.

That socialism in England never became attached to a blind worship of the writings of early socialist thinkers such as Marx, Engels, and Lenin, as it did in Germany and Russia, is largely the result of the work of the Fabians, especially Shaw and the Webbs. Though Shaw and the Webbs were the principal developers of British-style socialist theory, its adoption through the British political system must be credited to Sidney Webb alone, not to Shaw, for Shaw was good only at destruction.

2066 Woolf, Leonard. "Shaw and Fabians," NS&Nation, XLVI (14 Nov 1953), 601.

[Woolf protests against a misinterpretation of some of his remarks in a chapter which he contributed to SHAW AND SOCIETY, by C. E. M. Joad (1953).]

2067 Worthington, Mabel Parker. "Don Juan: Theme and Development in the Nineteenth Century," DA, XIII, No 3 (1953), 399. Unpublished dissertation, Columbia University, 1953.

2068 Wyatt, Euphemia Van Rensselaer. "Theater," CATHOLIC WORLD, CLXXVII (April 1953), 67-70.
Though intended as a study of family relationships, Shaw's Misalliance deals entertainingly with many subjects.

1954

2069 Bannal, Flawner, Jr. (pseud). "Theatre Notes. Strawhat Shaw," ShawB, I (Sept 1954), 22-23.
On the summer barn theater circuit in America, 31 productions of 15 different plays by Shaw were performed. The most important one of the season was Too True to Be Good with Zachary Scott and Ruth Ford. Although it was unevenly cast, it was very funny.

2070 Bentley, Eric [Russell]. "Theatre," NEW REPUBLIC, XXXVII (26 June 1954), 20-21; rptd as "Shaw and the Actors," SHAVIAN, ns No 3 (Autumn 1954), 12-15.
Shaw's interest in actors to some extent reflects the completeness of his interest in the theatrical medium. The difficulty in acting Shaw's plays is to render the speeches fully, for they cannot be easily cut. Shaw's instructions to actors suggest that the success of the performance relies on the training of the actor not on any gimmickry.

2071 Bentley, Eric [Russell]. "What Is Acting?" DRAMATIC EVENT, AN AMERICAN CHRONICLE (NY: Horizon P, 1954), pp. 50-53.
The London production of The Millionairess perverts Shaw's meaning in the play. Katharine Hepburn imposes her interpretation on the role rather than allowing her

portrayal to arise from the character. Consequently, her Epifania has ferocity and energy, but not vitality.

2072 Brower, Reuben A. "George Bernard Shaw," MAJOR BRITISH WRITERS, II, ed by C. B. Harrison (NY: Harcourt, Brace, 1954), pp. 521-34; rptd NY: Harcourt, Brace & World, pp. 681-97.
Though no one of Shaw's "fifteen reputations" is satisfactory, some are partially appropriate. He was an inventor of the twentieth-century temper. [Brief survey of Shaw's career; an examination of the relationship between comedy and ideas, with an analysis of Man and Superman.]

2073 Brück, Max von. "In der Hölle Shaws" (In Shaw's Hell), DIE GEGENWART, IX (2 Jan 1954), 15-16.
Shaw's interlude Don Juan in Hell from Man and Superman, in German and with German star actors, is a tremendous success in West Germany. The play itself is a fascinating fossil. [In German.]

2074 "A Continuing Check-List of Shaviana," ShawB, I (May 1954), 24.
[This bibliography is a continuing feature; it has been prepared by various hands, some anonymous, including E. E. Stokes, Jr., Charles A. Carpenter, Jr., Stephen S. Stanton, John Rodenbeck, and John R. Pfeiffer.]

2075 Emerson, Flora Elizabeth. "English Dramatic Critics of the Nineties and the Acting of the 'New Theatre,'" DA, XIV, No 2 (1954), 356. Unpublished dissertation, Bryn Mawr College, 1953.

2076 Ervine, St. John. "Introduction," BERNARD SHAW IN HEAVEN, by H. F. Rubenstein (Lond: William Heinemann [The Drama Library], 1954), pp. 1-4.
Shaw would have coped better with the discovery of himself in the next world than Rubinstein allows, but BERNARD SHAW IN HEAVEN is good entertainment. Shaw had many friends, and he was a generous man.

2077 Fechter, Paul. "George Bernard Shaw," DENKER UND DEUTER IM HEUTIGEN EUROPA (Thinkers and Guides in Contemporary Europe), ed by Hans Schwerte and Wilhelm

Spengler (Oldenburg, Hamburg: Gerhard Stalling, 1954;
Vol 2 of GESTALTER UNSERER ZEIT), pp. 24-35.
Shaw was basically a romantic who covered his romanticism
with a cloak of rationality. [Article includes excerpts
from Shaw's work.] [In German.]

2078 Fisher, Desmond M. "Shaw's Other Dustman,"
AMERICAN MERCURY, LXXVIII (March 1954), 119-21.
Pygmalion's Alfred Doolittle is the dustman Shaw's readers
remember, but there is another dustman, Patrick O'Reilly of
Dublin, who has worked hard to have Shaw remembered in his
home city. A friend to Shaw in his last years, Dustman
O'Reilly collected money from the people to erect a
memorial plaque on Number 33 Synge Street, where Shaw was
born; and he is now trying to get the city to give Shaw a
more impressive and suitable memorial, such as a statue at
Trinity College.

2079 Foster, Milton Painter. "The Reception of Max
Nordau's Degeneration in England and America," DA,
XIV (1954), 1078-79. Unpublished dissertation,
University of Michigan, 1954.

2080 Gassner, John. THE THEATRE IN OUR TIMES. A
SURVEY OF THE MEN, MATERIALS AND MOVEMENTS IN THE
MODERN THEATRE (NY: Crown Publishers, 1954), pp. 6,
8, 10, 17, 25, 26, 28, 29, 30, 32, 59, 70, 73, 79,
90, 97, 105, 111, 120, 122, 123-69, 171, 174, 208-11,
212, 230, 240, 247, 270-76, 284, 291, 324, 388, 389,
412, 413, 421-24, 431-33, 436, 445, 447, 461, 470,
471, 472, 484, 486, 491, 519, 522, 534, 543-48.
["Shaw as Drama Critic" (1951), "The Puritan in Hell"
(1952), "When Shaw Boils the Pot..." (1953),
abstracted under date of original publication.
Reprints essays, sometimes with major revision,
published earlier.]
"Saint George and the Dragons," pp. 135-55. Shaw, a latter-
day Saint George, combined austerity with a zeal for a full
life on earth, hunting down Victorian morality,
sentimentality, competitiveness, war, and vivisection.
Interestingly, his own ideals of Marxism, Fabianism, and
feminine emancipation turned into twentieth century
dragons. The value of Shaw's plays is always most evident
in the theaters where the plays become epiphanies when they

come to life, as in the Theater Guild production of <u>Saint Joan</u> (1951); the First Drama Quartet opening of <u>Don Juan in Hell</u> (1951); and the Lawrence Olivier production of <u>Caesar and Cleopatra</u> (opened 1951). Shaw's Fabianism, his lack of realism, and his lack of a sense of evil are bound to be attacked in ensuing decades. His poetry is communicative rather than formalistic; and his characters are open to attack as types. However, the world Shaw creates on the stage is a token of reality, and it is still quite commodious.

From "T. S. Eliot: The Poet as Anti-Modernist," pp. 270-76. Eliot's and Shaw's plays differ in tone. Whereas Eliot works in darkness, even in a comedy of manners, Shaw radiates confidence, optimism, and a certain carefree attitude. Eliot was aware of sin, but Shaw never really created an evil character. His plays are informal in style and directly communicative; Eliot's are formalistic with allusive meanings.

"The Gloss of English Stage Production," pp. 421-24. The Olivier company productions of <u>Caesar and Cleopatra</u> and ANTONY AND CLEOPATRA were the best of the New York season in 1952.

"Fabianism and the British Playwright," pp. 431-32. Shaw was the most exciting Fabian playwright. He upset all apple carts in the service of effecting reform.

"The Gertrude Lawrence <u>Pygmalion</u>," pp. 543-45. Theater Incorporated revived <u>Pygmalion</u> successfully in 1945-46, portraying the "spine" of the comedy for the audience-- that the difference between a flower girl and a lady is in how she is treated, not how she behaves.

"The Risks Remain for Even Shakespeare and Shaw," pp. 545-48. The fact that a play is good does not assure its success on the stage. If even <u>Saint Joan</u> or <u>Candida</u> could fail in production as in Spring 1952, then how much more likely was a lesser play, <u>You Never Can Tell</u>, to fail, as in the London production of 1948?

2081 Gillilan, Strickland. "The Will Rogers of the Solar System," MARK TWAIN JOURNAL, IX (Summer 1954), 8.
[Personal reminiscence.] Shaw thought serious things but said them frivolously.

2082 Gorelik, Mordecai. "Metaphorically Speaking," TAM, XXXVIII (Nov 1954), 78-80, 91.
The setting of a play like Saint Joan is not just background. It is documentation of the geography and history of a time; it is an environment for human beings; it is a machine for theater, relating to and working within the physical limitations of a stage. But it can also be a metaphor; and as such, it is most nearly related to the script. In Joan, some scenes have an underlying metaphor, such as the bright sky overhead in Scene 1 or the meager elegance of Scene 3. The governing metaphor of the play, however, is descent. The Saint journeys from naive visions of heaven to the hell of her martyrdom and finally to a puckish reluctance to return to plodding earthly life.

2083 Grendon, Felix. "Meeting Notes," ShawB, I (Sept 1954), 20-21.
[Summary of Maxwell Steinhardt's speech about Shaw's letters to Mrs. Patrick Campbell and Ellen Terry.] The correspondence between Ellen Terry and Shaw dispels the myth that he was sexually frigid. The letters indicate that the affair between the famous actress and the equally famous dramatist existed in the flesh as well as on paper.

2084 Grendon, Felix. "Shaw's Annajanska," SHAVIAN, ns No 3 (Autumn 1954), 26-28.
Though a sparkling comedy, Annajanska the Bolshevik Empress has a distinct intellectual purpose—to encourage the British in 1917 to think seriously about the Russian Revolution of 1917. In this and in other plays, Shaw shows himself to be an advocate of democracy that is an outgrowth of a socialist economy. Neither the form of democracy linked to America's free enterprise system nor the autocracy of the Kremlin qualified as Shavian democracy.

2085 Griffin, Alice. "Sketches by Shaw," TAM, XXXVIII (Jan 1954), 70-71.

Shaw's sketches reveal the dramatist's touch. He confessed that "his ambition at one time [was] to be Michelangelo, not Shakespeare." [Reviews Shaw's sketches and John Farleigh's illustrations for The Adventures of the Black Girl in Her Search for God.]

    2086 Guttmann, Bernhard. "Der Gott der Evolution" (The God of Evolution), DIE GEGENWART, IX (11 Sept 1954), 594-95.
Back to Methuselah is Shaw's testament. But after two world wars, Shaw's belief in rational and intellectual human evolution seems questionable. [In German.]

    2087 Haussler, Franz. "Androcles: Shaw's Fable Play," trans by Felix F. Strauss, ShawB, I (May 1954), 8-9.
There is real comedy in Androcles and the Lion, his Fable Play as Shaw called it; but as usual the humor conveys some truths, though not bitter ones. In one of his most humane plays, Shaw examines the question of religious conviction, using Androcles and the Christians as examples of those who affirm their faith unconditionally and the Romans as skeptics who do not believe in anything at all. Shaw examines both sides in all their complexities. He does not present a case history of Christianity's opposition to Rome. Rather, both the Christians and the Romans serve to help Shaw illustrate that pure motives and, consequently, pure actions result from faith, not from lip service to any particular code.

    2088 Henderson, Archibald. "Shaw and Shakespeare," ShawB, I (Sept 1954), 1-6.
[In substance the same as the address given by Henderson at the Annual General Meeting of the Shaw Society of America on 28 March 1954.] Shaw's crusade against Shakespeare lasted about 50 years and was for the most part greatly misunderstood. His good-humored caricature of the Bard in The Dark Lady of the Sonnets was denounced as a character created in Shaw's own image. The campaign against Bardolatry began in 1900; until then he often jocularly associated himself with Shakespeare. He always attacked productions of Shakespeare's plays that violated their integrity. In a sense, his denigration of Shakespeare began with The Quintessence of Ibsenism, in which Shaw measured

Ibsen's mind--his psychological position--against Shakespeare's. No one who cannot remember Ibsen's impact in England after 1889 can really know how devastatingly Ibsen dwarfed Shakespeare in that respect.

2089 Hickin, R. A. "The Christian Debt to George Bernard Shaw," LONDON QUARTERLY AND HOLBORN REVIEW, Jan 1954, pp. 46-50.

For a sincere Christian, Shavian discipline is priceless. His attitude toward Jesus is the real kernel of his thought, especially in Androcles and the Lion. Shaw's Jesus was without sin, personally strong, and possessed of intellectual stature; he would have repudiated the church. But Shaw failed to account for the change in the church from the materialism of the time of his own early days, as Bill Walker in Major Barbara reveals.

2090 Hull, William. "Shaw on the Joyce He Scarcely Read," ShawB, I (Sept 1954), 16-20.

Shaw and Joyce have in common their exile from Dublin and a moral imperative--Joyce to incite conscience in the audience of his moral history; Shaw to make his audience examine its morality. Shaw persisted in not purchasing ULYSSES; however, he read snatches of it when it was serialized in THE LITTLE REVIEW. He probably had not read DUBLINERS or PORTRAIT OF THE ARTIST AS A YOUNG MAN. Still, Shaw felt that Joyce had accurately reflected what Dublin had to offer its young men; and he admired the fact that Joyce had documented it. In Zurich in 1918, Joyce was probably responsible for the choice of Shaw's The Dark Lady of the Sonnets and Mrs. Warren's Profession in the repertory of the English Players.

2091 Krutch, Joseph Wood. "Why Not 'Methuselah'?" TAM, XXXVIII (June 1954), 24-25, 96.

Although Back to Methuselah is one of Shaw's talkiest and most philosophical plays, it could be cut down to a manageable size and be relevant to audiences. The most recent and successful Shaw productions have been those which present Shaw as a philosopher. The most salient characteristic of his work is his determination to reconcile doctrines like Butler's common sense, Bunyan's Puritanism, Marx's dialectical materialism, and Bergson's creative evolution with each other. However, the ideas in

Methuselah are dramatized well and are punctuated with sparkling dialog and humor. One of the best stories of the world lends itself extraordinarily well to Shaw's reinterpretation, one which optimistically sets up human cooperation with the Life Force in evolution against determinism. And it ought to be produced.

  2092 Küsel, Herbert. "Shaw übt sein Stück ein. Aus der Bühnengeschichte des Pygmalion" (Shaw Rehearses His Play. From the Stage History of Pygmalion), DIE GEGENWART, IX (27 March 1954), 209-12.
[Küsel quotes mainly from Shaw's letters to Mrs. Patrick Campbell, which appeared in a German translation in 1953. These quotations are intermingled with references to a Pygmalion performance in 1954 in Frankfurt/Main.] [In German.]

  2093 Küsel, Herbert. "Weihe am kleinen Kornmarkt. Shaws Pygmalion, beinahe im neuen Haus gespielt" (Sacred Action in the Theater at the Kleiner Kornmarkt. Shaw's Pygmalion, Almost Played in the New House), DIE GEGENWART, IX (27 Feb 1954), 141-44.
Siegfried Trebitsch's translation of Pygmalion, virtually unchanged since the Fischer edition of 1913, despite claims to the contrary in the "new and revised editions" by Artemis (1948) and Suhrkamp, is woefully out of date. [In German.]

  2094 Laurence, Dan H. "Bernard Shaw and the PALL MALL GAZETTE: An Identification of His Unsigned Contributions," ShawB, I (May 1954), 1-7.
In 1855, W. H. Stead, editor of the PALL MALL GAZETTE, retained Shaw's services as a reviewer; from May 1885 to December 1888, Shaw wrote essays on subjects as wide-ranging as art, music, drama, theology, and science in which he analyzed the works of Ouida, George Moore, Marie Corelli, and Henry James, and commented on Marx, Madame Blavatsky, and Jevons. Defying contemporary rules of criticism, his reviews were colloquial and informal with a humorous tone. They were always to the point. Shaw began to tire of book reviewing though, and in 1888 he accepted the post of music critic for THE STAR. [Two reviews reprinted in this article are representative of his early (1885) and late (1888) book reviews in the PALL MALL GAZETTE.]

2095 Laurence, Dan. "Bernard Shaw and the PALL MALL GAZETTE: II," ShawB, I (Sept 1954), 7-12.
George Moore thought Shaw was totally lacking in aestheticism and able to carry a train of thought only long enough to make a joke. Shaw thought Moore a romancer, writing for a coterie, until he read A MUMMER'S WIFE at the urging of William Archer. Still, Shaw's commentary on Moore's work, though sparse, does not completely contradict his original opinion of Moore. In Shaw's review of Moore's A MERE ACCIDENT in the PALL MALL GAZETTE [rptd in this article] on 19 July 1897, Shaw does not object to Moore's introduction of the subject of rape, but he does object to its being described for its own sake. "Christian Names," the first literary piece for which Shaw was paid, appeared in ONE AND ALL for the week ending 11 Oct 1879. Under the pseudonym (and in the persona) of an "English Mistress," Shaw humorously reviewed George R. Sim's purported true confession of a backstairs domestic, MARY JANE'S MISTRESS [review rptd in this article].

2096 Mai, Werner. "Das Drama George Bernard Shaws auf der deutschen Buehne und in der deutschen Kritik" (George Bernard Shaw's Drama in the German Theater and in German Criticism). Unpublished dissertation, Tübingen University, 1954. [Listed in DAID.]

2097 MARK TWAIN JOURNAL, IX (Summer 1954).
[An issue devoted to personal reminiscence and appreciation of Shaw by many hands.] Table of contents, not abstracted: Archibald Henderson, "Mark Twain and Bernard Shaw"; Adolphe de Castro, "An American Author Meets Shaw"; W. R. Inge, "My Acquaintance with George Bernard Shaw"; Carl Milles, "Shaw Seen by a Sculptor"; Cyril Scott, "Impressions of Bernard Shaw"; Francis Brett Young, "Shaw the Most Entertaining of Companions"; Robinson Jeffers, "A Great Man in Our Time"; C. S. Lewis, "Comedian of the Highest Order"; Hesketh Pearson, "First Impressions of Shaw"; Faith Baldwin, "Brought Up on Shaw"; A. E. Coppard, "Idolater of Shaw"; James Hilton, "Took the Trouble to Write"; Chard Powers Smith, "A Dramatist Too Close in the Wings"; Harrison Smith, "Shaw the Educator"; Mazo de la Roche, "Bernard Shaw at Malvern"; Viscountess Astor, "His Mind as Clear as Crystal"; Phyllis Bottome, "A Successful Guy Fawkes"; DeLancey Ferguson, Untitled; William H. Kilpatrick,

"Contributor to the Hearst Papers"; August Derleth, "Sui Generis"; Lawrence Housman, "A Halo of Popularity and Applause"; Susan Ertz, "Shaw's Flashing, Bloodless Rapier"; Norman Rockwell, "Personal Tribute"; Bertrand Russell, "Personal Reminiscence"; Sigmund Spaeth, "Shaw as a Music Critic"; James Montgomery Flegg, "The Emperor of Effrontery"; Padraic Colum, "My Short and Simple Recollections of George Bernard Shaw"; Christopher Fry, "Nearer to a Spiritual Positive."

> **2098** Montes, Jorge. "Androcles y el leon de Bernard Shaw, hecho por Nuevo Teatro" (Androcles and the Lion by Bernard Shaw, Performed by the New Theater), TEATRO (Argentina), X (Jan-March 1954), 25.

Pedro Asquini's production of Androcles and the Lion was described by him as a "scenic insanity" because of the costumes, decoration, and background music. It also included parts of Shaw's prolog. [In Spanish.]

> **2099** Morilia, Roberto. "G. B. Shaw, o dell'Amor Platonico" (G. B. Shaw, or Concerning Platonic Love), LETTERATURE MODERNE, V (Aug 1954), 466-70.

Even though in his letters to Mrs. Patrick Campbell Shaw claimed that nothing but his affection for her mattered, she wrote that actually his work, his political meetings, his home, and his wife took precedence. Candida is probably the best example of his marital relations, with Shaw as Morell. The Intelligent Woman's Guide to Socialism and Capitalism contains Shaw's ideas about socialism and marriage. Order and self-control regulated Shaw's life, and he remained faithful to these virtues in his relationship with Mrs. Campbell. When she wished to publish the letters, his objections revealed his respect for convention. Permission for publication was given in his will when death freed him from convention. [In Italian.]

> **2100** Nethercot, Arthur H. "Bernard Shaw, Philosopher," PMLA, LXIX (March 1954), 57-75.

Shaw would never have been a good teacher of philosophy (nor would he have wanted to be), for his knowledge of philosophy, evidenced in his writings, is too fragmentary. Yet he did develop a system of philosophy over the years which he insisted informed his intellectual and artistic life. He was interested in Schopenhauer, Nietzsche, Ibsen,

Hegel and Marx. He refers to Leibniz, Lao Tse, Socrates, Aristotle, and Plato. He had something to do with Nietzsche's popularity in England. Comte and Voltaire appealed to him. He only rarely and then briefly referred to Bacon, Locke, and Hobbes. He referred most often to Herbert Spencer of the English philosophers. Of his contemporaries, Bertrand Russell, Dean Inge, and Benedetto Croce interested him. However, Shaw does not engage in any discussion or critique of any of these philosophers. Rather, he refers sporadically to individuals and their work, using them as examples of some generalization. Of course, he is most interested in Samuel Butler and Henri Bergson, who, other than Shaw himself, are exponents of the creed he was most comfortable with——Creative Evolution.

2101 Nethercot, Arthur H. MEN AND SUPERMEN: THE SHAVIAN PORTRAIT GALLERY (Cambridge: Harvard UP, 1954; NY: Arno, 1966).
A number of clearly recognizable and repeated types, classifications and categories of characters appear in Shaw's novels and plays. In The Quintessence of Ibsenism, Shaw set out his basic categories: the Philistines, the Idealists, and the Realists. In the third chapter of Quintessence, Shaw contrasts the New Woman with three former categories into which women have fallen in order to demonstrate the obstacles to women's independence from and equality with men: the womanly woman, the pursuing woman, and the mother-woman. The last type of woman is the manly woman. Although there are more distinctive female types in the plays and novels, there is some variety among the males: the new man, the philanderer, and the artist-man. Techniques of characterization often take the form of fastening on blemishes in a national character. Underlying Shaw's cynicism about the professions is his disappointment in social and political systems for not using the best people as leaders. Dictators and Strong Men presage the Supermen, but no Superman really appears in any of the plays. The names of Shaw's characters give clues to their nature. The classification of the variety of humankind into types that interact with each other in dramatic situations characterizes the comedy of humors as well as the medieval morality play. Shaw uses types of human beings, often more articulate and self-analytical than ordinary people, to speak for him with complexity and richness. [The various

categories of character types are explained and illustrated from the novels and plays.]

2102 O'Casey, Sean. "Shaw's Corner," SUNSET AND EVENING STAR (NY: Macmillan, 1954); rptd in MIRROR IN MY HOUSE, II (NY: Macmillan, 1956; rptd Lond: Pan Books, 1973), pp. 226-70 et passim; trans and rptd "O Bernarde Shou—iz t͡sykla Zakhod slont͡sa i vercheniai͡a zvezda" (On Bernard Shaw—From Sunset and Evening Star) INNOSTRANAĬA LITERATURA, No 7 (1956), 87-89 [In Russian].

[O'Casey's creative autobiography has many references to Shaw in its six books, but of particular interest is "Shaw's Corner." O'Casey recounts the relationship with the Shaws, especially the luncheon dates in which O'Casey was frequently scolded by Mrs. Shaw for his independent nature, Shaw keeping silent until he needed to intervene, ending one such episode with the explanation that O'Casey was like himself in needing to express the holy ghost within him as he saw fit, whatever the consequences. In general, Shaw in this chapter serves as a weapon in O'Casey's attack on Chesterton and modern Catholicism. O'Casey takes particular delight in imagining what great bishops Shaw, Joyce, and Yeats would make. Includes a moving account (some of which has been published elsewhere) of the deaths of the Shaws and a tribute to Shaw's dramatic art.]

2103 "Premiéry Slovenských Divadiel 1945-1953" (First Nights at Slovak Theaters 1945-1953), SLOVENSKE DIVADLO (Bratislava), II (1954), 299-334.
The Devil's Disciple was produced at the Slovak National Theater, Bratislava, in the 1946/47 season. Candida was produced at the Martin Theater in the 1945/46 season, and Great Catherine at the National Theater, Košice in the 1946/47 season. Mrs. Warren's Profession was produced at the Worker's Theater, Žilin, in the 1949/50 and 1950/51 seasons, at Zvolen in 1950/51 and at the New Theater of the National Theater, Bratislava, in 1949/50. The Devil's Disciple was also produced at Zvolen in 1951/52. [In Czechoslovak.]

2104 Purdom, C. B. "Shaw and Granville-Barker," SHAVIAN, ns No 3 (Autumn 1954), 16-18.

[Summary by Barbara Smoker of the talk given by Purdom on 28 June 1954.] Shaw and Granville-Barker met in 1899 when Shaw was 43 and Barker 22, and they remained close friends until 1916 when Barker's first marriage to Lillah McCarthy broke up and he married Helen Huntington. His second marriage ended Barker's close association with Shaw and with the theater. The conjecture is that the second Mrs. Barker was hostile to Shaw and also did not want Barker to remain in the theater. He became a professor and a lecturer.

2105 Rattray, R. F. "The Butler-Shaw Philosophy," SHAVIAN, ns No 3 (Autumn 1954), 8-10.
[Summary by Barbara Smoker of Rattray's talk.] Both Shaw and Samuel Butler felt that the nineteenth-century conception of evolution, emphasizing primarily the physical aspect of life, did not fit observable facts. The Life Force does not have to be documented in a laboratory, for it can be verified by anyone, according to Shaw. The body's cells cooperate with the mind. Both Butler and Shaw are mystics.

2106 Rubinstein, H[arold] F[rederick]. BERNARD SHAW IN HEAVEN (Lond: William Heinemann, Ltd [The Drama Library], 1954).
[A one-act play first produced at the Royal Court Theater on 26 July 1952, about Shaw's death and entry into heaven with Candida, Frank Harris, Shakespeare, and Rosalind as the other major characters.]

2107 S., J. P. "At the Theatre," NYT, 12 Jan 1954, p. 19.
The Simpleton of the Unexpected Isles is one of Shaw's least distinguished works; it drags on unmercifully.

2108 Schindler, Gerhard. "Shaws Kritik am English Way of Life" (Shaw's Criticism of the English Way of Life). Published dissertation, Leipzig University, 1954. Published as GEORGE BERNARD SHAW, SEINE KRITIK AN DER ENGLISCHEN LEBENSFORM IN SEINEN SOZIALKRITISCHEN DRAMEN (1956) (George Bernard Shaw: His Criticism of the English Way of Life in His Drama of Social Criticism). [Listed in DAID.]

2109 Sharp, William L. "The Relation of Dramatic Structure to Comedy in the Plays of George Bernard Shaw," DA, XIV (1954), 1007-8. Unpublished dissertation, Stanford University, 1954.

2110 Sinka, Grzegorz, and Tadeusz Grzebieniowski. "George Bernard Shaw," TEATR KRAJÓW ZACHODNIEJ EUROPY XIX I POCZĄTKU XX WIERKU (The Theater of the Countries of Western Europe from the XIXth to the Beginning of the XXth Century), I (Warszaw and Łodź; Państwowe Wydawnictwo Naukowe, 1954), pp. 90-110. [Short biography. Description of almost all major plays from the socialist point of view.] Plays Pleasant make fun of the revolutionary position; they are opposed to scientific thinking. Candida is a capitulation to capitalism. Caesar in Caesar and Cleopatra is a funny old gentleman, and Cleopatra is not very clever. Captain Brassbound's Conversion dramatizes the capitulation of the revolutionary. Shaw could not continue rejecting his revolutionary ideas. He needed to fight injustice and evil. Rejecting historical materialism, he interpreted human behavior in terms of evolution and, taking his cue from Schopenhauer and Nietzsche, called it "will" in Man and Superman. Human progress is the result of the Life Force and not the class struggle. Capitalism triumphs in Major Barbara. Shaw has no solution to the problem of poverty. The accusation in the media that Shaw was a traitor and a German agent during World War I provoked his greatest work: Heartbreak House, Back to Methuselah and Saint Joan. Here he dramatized the breakdown and decline of bourgeois society. In Joan he made his peace with the Catholic Church. The Apple Cart is a play very important for Poland. It was presented in 1929 and is linked to Polish internal conditions. It dramatizes the idea that bourgeois democracy is a fiction that depends upon capitalism. After 100 years of sentimentality, Shaw's laughter in the theater was liberating; he told the truth. He turned to the reading public with his prefaces, some of which are excellent political pamphlets, not always in harmony with the plays. Shaw is luckily superior to his Fabian ideas, and his fidelity to reality often contradicts those ideas. He was an excellent critic of the theater and actors, but he was less successful with plays because he was always most concerned with his own ideas. [In Polish.]

2111 Smith, Robert McC. "Modern Dramatic Censorship:
George Bernard Shaw," DA, XIV (1954), 133-34.
Unpublished dissertation, Indiana University, 1953.
[Listed in McNamee.]

2112 Spiel, Hilde. "Shaw und die Frauen. Methusalem
zwischen Gefühl und Sinnlichkeit" (Shaw and Women.
Methuselah between Feeling and Sensuality), DER
MONAT, VII (Nov 1954), 113-28.
For Shaw sex was indecent and a waste of time. He was no
ascetic but full of inhibitions which, however, never
gained control over him. The reasons for his sexual
inhibitions must be traced back to his childhood and youth.
Shaw, the disappointed romantic, differentiated between
sensual and Platonic love. Although he had some encounters
with sensual love, he preferred the Platonic kind as
evidenced by his relationship with Ellen Terry, Mrs.
Patrick Campbell and his wife Charlotte. [In German.]

2113 Stokes, Sewell. "Shaw, Frank Harris and St.
Joan," JOHN O'LONDON'S WEEKLY, 28 May 1954, 534.
[Anecdote of Shaw's attitude about the necessity of a
knowledge of French to write about Saint Joan. Text of Shaw
letter.]

2114 Strauss, Felix F. "Shaw's Appeal to Mid-Century
Austrian Intellectuals," ShawB, I (May 1954), 15-17.
In the 20 or so issues of NEUE WEGE (New Ways) from 1950-
53, nine brief essays and two notes concern Shaw. During
those years Pygmalion, The Doctor's Dilemma, Caesar and
Cleopatra, and Saint Joan were staged in Vienna, and Arms
and the Man, The Apple Cart, and Androcles and the Lion
probably were staged there. One of the notes, "Theater
Without Props" (VII, 71/72, 544) suggests that Shaw
demonstrates in Don Juan in Hell that the theater's
possibilities are not yet depleted. The other note,
"Ancient Dramas on the Modern Stage" (VI, 58, 62) by Georg
Schreiber refers in passing to Shaw's successful adaptation
of an ancient fable to the modern stage in Androcles. Four
of the nine articles were written by Wilhelm Halbwidl:
"Shaw, the Teacher and the Wag," (VI, 59, 99); "About
Bernard Shaw's Arms and the Man," (VII, 71/72, 54); "The
Pygmalion Myth and Shaw," (VI, 57, 32); and "About
Androcles and the Lion," (IX, 91, 10). The other five

articles are Wilhelm Gross, "Shaw's Saint Joan as a Human and as a Hero," (VI, 59, 98); Robert Prantner, "Caesar and Cleopatra," (VI, 65, 12); August Hochst, "Deheroized History by Bernard Shaw," (VI, 65, 11); Herwig Kellner, "Bernard Shaw's Apple Cart," (IX, 91, 10); and Richard Kogl, "Preachers from the Stage: Shaw and Nestroy [sic]," (IX, 91, 10). In general, Austrian writers appreciate Shaw's constructive social criticism and his optimistic belief in the primacy of creative humanity. None of the essays considers the prefaces to his plays or his economic discourses.

> **2115** Stresau, Hermann. "Bernard Shaw's [sic] Helden" (Bernard Shaw's Arms and the Man), BDDTG, No 54 (1953-54).

Arms and the Man is a comedy and not a satire. The comic moments of the play refer to both the sober realist and the romantic sentimentalist. [In German.]

> **2116** "Theatre Notes. No Better Than Shakespeare—On Broadway or TV," ShawB, I (May 1954), 22-23.

In the New York theater season of 1953-54, there were no productions of Shaw's plays on Broadway. The Vaughn-James production of The Simpleton of the Unexpected Isles at the Davenport Theater made the play seem a closet drama. The production of Heartbreak House at Hofstra College on Long Island was well-acted and imaginatively staged. The Omnibus television production of The Man of Destiny bore little resemblance to Shaw's play.

> **2117** Trewin, J[ohn] C[ourtenay]. "Shaw as Dramatic Critic," SHAVIAN, ns No 3 (Autumn 1954), 11-12.

[Summary by Barbara Smoker of the talk given by Trewin on 28 May 1954.] Any drama critic who has a feeling for his job will think often and respectfully of Shaw, who did not leave his brains in the cloakroom when he attended the theater and who paid no attention to the rules of dramatic criticism.

> **2118** Weber, Carl J. "A Talk with George Bernard Shaw," ShawB, I (May 1954), 18-22.

[Personal reminiscence of a conversation with Shaw on 9 July 1929, at a garden party at Taplow-on-Thames. Subjects covered were co-education in American schools, attempts to edit Shaw's plays, differences in pronunciation within the British Isles and between Great Britain and America.]

2119 West, E. J. "Saint Joan: A Modern Classic Reconsidered," QUARTERLY JOURNAL OF SPEECH, XL (Oct 1954), 249-59; rptd in SAINT JOAN FIFTY YEARS AFTER, 1923/24-1973/74, ed by Stanley Weintraub (Baton Rouge: Louisiana State UP, 1973), pp. 125-40.
Though commentary on Shaw's Saint Joan ranges from uncritical praise to outright attack, most critics agree that this play is Shaw's greatest. The play has undeniable power in moving audiences and not merely with theatrical devices. Shaw recognized in Joan's story the potential for a tragedy as great as that of Prometheus; and he succeeded, in his own estimate, where Shakespeare, Voltaire, and modern writers failed. Joan is a great play because the characters are credible and embody the complexity of human nature.

2120 Worsley, T. C. "An Irish Joan," NS&Nation, XLVIII (9 Oct 1954), 434-36; rptd in SAINT JOAN FIFTY YEARS AFTER, 1923/24-1973/74, ed by Stanley Weintraub (Baton Rouge: Louisiana State UP, 1973), pp. 141-43.
Siobbhan McKenna's Joan is the best in memory. In her portrayal of a naive farm girl who learns in the course of her trial to walk with royalty of church and state, McKenna's Irish accent works to mark Joan off from the others and to make the Irish rhetoric in Shaw's dramatic language come to life.

2121 Zerke, Carl F. "George Bernard Shaw's Ideas on Acting," DA, XIV (1954), 1850-51. Unpublished dissertation, Florida State University, 1954.

1955

2122 Atkinson, Brooks. "Theatre: The Doctor's Dilemma," NYT, 12 Jan 1955, p. 22.
The sardonic crackle of Shaw is missing from the Phoenix production of The Doctor's Dilemma. [Also reviewed in Atkinson, "Forever Shaw," NYT, 23 Jan 1955, II, p. 1.]

2123 Barzun, Jacques. "Shaw and Rousseau: No Paradox," ShawB, I (May 1955), 1-6.
Although Shaw can be predictably compared with Voltaire since they were both dramatists and satirists, he and Rousseau also can be paralleled. First of all, both Shaw and Rousseau used their writing skills throughout their lifetimes to present their readers with systems of social reform imbued with a religiosity. Both hoped current society could be replaced with a better one, although neither favored a bloody revolution. Voltaire used his biting wit to criticize society. Neither Shaw nor Rousseau approved of the status quo. They believed in equality for all individuals and were convinced that the government that could achieve this end was not possible without a non-theological or non-metaphysical religion to insure morality in its actions and goals. Both shared a regard for simplicity, evident in their works and in their lives, which antagonized some people. Neither man could tolerate enslavement to desires for luxuries or entertainment; yet, each defended the passions. Both also realized the power of the stage and worried about drama that was not moral and educational. Rousseau and Shaw were each faddists, wearing unconventional clothing for their day, promoting new musical notation (Rousseau), or a reformed alphabet (Shaw).

2124 Batson, Eric J. "Hyperion and the Yahoos," ShawB, I (Jan 1955), 16-18.
Shaw's Britain seems to be conspiring against giving Shaw his due. There was only one revival (Saint Joan) in England last year. The National Trust has not publicized the opening of Shaw's Corner at Ayot St. Lawrence nor made directions very accessible to tourists. The press tries to make Shaw seem unpopular, although his plays in the English Penguin edition continue to be best sellers. And critics, like Norman Carrington, imply that Shaw's battle with censorship was a publicity stunt.

2125 Benedek, Marcell. "Öt Éve Halt Meg G. B. Shaw" (G. B. Shaw Died Five Years Ago), IRODALMI UJSÁG (Literary Gazette), 5 Nov 1955, p. 5.
Shaw is remembered as the socialist deplorer of dangerous prejudices and social lies. [In Hungarian.]

2126 "The Blanco Posnet Controversy," ShawB, I (Jan 1955), 1-9.
[Commentary connects the documents in the case: "Blanco Posnet Banned by the Censor," by Bernard Shaw; "Shaw's Battle with the Censor," by James Joyce; and "The Religion of Blanco," by William Butler Yeats. Shaw's The Shewing-Up of Blanco Posnet was censored by the Lord Chamberlain (1909) because it was irreligious. Shaw responded in a statement distributed to Sir Herbert Beerbohm Tree's audiences at His Majesty's Theatre, "Blanco Posnet Banned by the Censor," in which he disagreed with the decision and indicated plans to publish the play and allow it to be performed in Europe and America. He then offered the play to W. B. Yeats and Lady Gregory for possible production at Dublin's Abbey Theatre. [History of subsequent events.] James Joyce was at the play's premiere in Dublin, reviewing it for IL PICCOLO DELLA SERA (Trieste). He summarized the events in the censorship battle and then found the play unconvincing as drama.

2127 Campbell, Douglas. "Canadian Players on the Snowplow Circuit," TAM, XXXIX (April 1955), 71-73, 88; "Afterword" by Ann Casson rptd as "Saint Joan of the Snows," SHAVIAN, ns No 5 (Sept 1955), 19-21.
The success of the Canadian Players in taking Saint Joan to communities in northern Ontario made it evident that a great play can be produced with a minimum of scenic properties and without period costumes or other glamorous accoutrements of the theater. In fact, it seems that the less the audience-actor contact is interfered with, the more exciting the experience of the theater is.

2128 Casson, Sir Lewis. "GBS at Rehearsal," THEATRICAL COMPANION TO SHAW. A PICTORIAL RECORD OF THE PLAYS OF GEORGE BERNARD SHAW, by Raymond Mander and Joe Mitchenson (Lond: Rockliff Publishing Corporation; NY: Pitman Publishing Corporation, 1955), pp. 16-18.
Shaw's interest in the production of a play was primarily in acting and casting. Good actors took detailed direction from him very well because he was a good actor himself. While he directed the first English production and subsequent London revivals of his plays from 1900-1920, he was not very solicitous about foreign productions. Shaw

felt that an audience's interest can only be held if the number of ideas conveyed in any production was high. He did not waste any of his ideas; each was carefully planned to hit a mark. He was prone to overdo the slapstick and comic effects.

2129 Casson, Sir Lewis. "Granville-Barker, Shaw and the Court Theatre," THEATRICAL COMPANION TO SHAW. A PICTORIAL RECORD OF THE PLAYS OF GEORGE BERNARD SHAW, by Raymond Mander and Joe Mitchenson (Lond: Rockliff Publishing Corporation; NY: Pitman Publishing Corporation, 1955), pp. 288-92.

The Stage Society, first of the Sunday Club Theaters, was immune from the Censor's ban and thus had remarkable artistic license, giving dramatists like Shaw some exposure and security. With the performance and success of John Bull's Other Island, Shaw's first unpublished play to be produced, Shaw saw that he did not have to doubt his market. The remarkable partnership of Shaw and Barker provided successful theater because the actors in their employ had been trained in the art of stage speech. Even the worst of them was audible, and the best could make effective stage speech seem natural.

2130 Cecchi, Emilio. "L'Eclisse di Shaw" (Shaw's Eclipse), NUOVA ANTOLOGIA, REVISTA DI LETTERE, SCIENZE, ED ARTI, XC (June 1955), 217-22; rptd in SCRITORI INGLESI E AMERICANI (English and American Writers) (Milan: Il Saggiatore, 1962), pp. 186-94.

Public lack of interest followed immediately after Shaw's death; people were tired of his courting fame through publicity, letters, and causes. Though Thomas Mann's essay is full of praise, it raises doubts whether Shaw ever took serious things seriously. Only Aristophones and Molière are equal to Shaw's dramatic dialog. There is no point in criticizing Shaw for not producing a theater of passions and moral contrasts; his is one of cultural polemic and in some cases of simple conversation. [Cites Chesterton, Nietzsche, Barbellion, Mansfield, Blunt, and a caricature of Beerbohm.] Saint Joan is something different, and it reveals an untypical Shaw, an artist with pathos, color, and plasticity. [In Italian.]

2131 Clunes, Alec. "The Arts Theatre," THEATRICAL COMPANION TO SHAW. A PICTORIAL RECORD OF THE PLAYS OF GEORGE BERNARD SHAW, by Raymond Mander and Joe Mitchenson (Lond: Rockliff Publishing Corporation; NY: Pitman Publishing Corporation, 1955), pp. 300-301.
One seventh of the Arts Theater's program in 11½ years was comprised of Shaw material because audiences wanted to see his plays.

2132 Code, Grant. "Shaw at Hedgrow," ShawB, I (Jan 1955), 22-24.
Shaw supported repertory theater as it existed in the Malvern Theater in Britain and the Hedgrow Theater in the U.S. In fact, Shaw indicated that royalty checks to him from Hedgrow could be paid in any manner convenient to the theater, a way of cooperating with a theater trying to remain solvent. Founded in April 1923, by Jasper Deeter, the theater was the most active Shaw Theater in the U.S., producing over 200 plays, 18 of them plays by Shaw.

2133 Connolly, Thomas E. "Shaw's Saint Joan," EXPLICATOR, XIV (Dec 1955), Item 19; rptd in Roy Bentley (comp), STUDENT'S SOURCES FOR SHAKESPEARE'S HAMLET, SHAW'S SAINT JOAN, CONRAD'S HEART OF DARKNESS (Agincourt, Ontario: Book Society of Canada, 1966), pp. 47-48.
Joan's use of a mixture of archaic and modern English in the play is not haphazard. She consistently uses archaic speech each time she refers to the child-like Charles familiarly as "Charlie." She does not use the archaic second-person singular (equivalent to the French tu) in the coronation scene. She uses the archaic form in only one other scene—her trial. There, she scornfully employs the familiar in addressing the priest who shows himself to be beneath her intellectually.

2134 Coxe, Louis O. "You Never Can Tell: G. B. Shaw Reviewed," WESTERN HUMANITIES REVIEW, IX (Autumn 1955), 313-25; rptd in ENABLING ACTS, SELECTED ESSAYS IN CRITICISM (Columbia and Lond: U of Missouri P, 1976), pp. 125-42.
Shaw is writing in the tradition of dramatists like Shakespeare, Ben Jonson, Wycherly and Congreve, whose art

seeks to make the audience more fully conscious of reality and points to discrepancies between seeming and reality. Shaw dramatizes the pressure of reality upon illusion. In You Never Can Tell, talk gives rise to action as the audience's attention moves from a single character to a group of them. And the movement starts outside the play, for Shaw sets the play in motion with the ideas in his Preface, and he drives the meaning toward the circumference of the play as characters move from types to human beings, from illusion to reality, under the stress of a social question or a moral problem. The moral center in Shaw's plays is often a concrete image, such as the dentist's office in You Never Can Tell, that can be modulated a number of times in the play and allows for some humor. If caricatures like Alfred Doolittle or Androcles will facilitate Revelation for the audience, Shaw will employ them as well as lofty types such as Caesar and Saint Joan. Shaw always urges his audience to be fully conscious by having his finest characters strive to know themselves so that they may cooperate with the Life Force in evolution. Never Can is a classic comedy that does not really entertain. Its exposure of inhumanities makes us laugh, not for our amusement but to make us fully and painfully human.

2135 "Critics' Dilemma?" SHAVIAN, ns No 5 (Sept 1955), 27-29.
The study of a great playwright's limitations is as significant and interesting as a study of his successes. The Doctor's Dilemma, while it expresses the inability to judge others objectively, is not a masterpiece like Pygmalion or Man and Superman. Still, in the play there is a tragic vision, underscored by Shaw's faith in evolution.

2136 Cubeta, Paul M. (ed). MODERN DRAMA FOR ANALYSIS (NY: Dryden, 1955; rptd NY: Holt, Rinehart & Winston, 1962), pp. 1-81.
[The Devil's Disciple with Biography, Selected Bibliography, Shaw's Notes, Commentary, and Questions.]

2137 Dolgonos, Berta. "Del Don Juan de Molière al Hombre y Superhombre de Bernard Shaw" (From the DON JUAN of Molière to the Man and Superman of Bernard Shaw), DAVAR (Argentina), LVIII (May-June 1955), 82-87.

Shaw's interpretation of Don Juan is completely new. Shaw's Don Juan incarnates the superman, prototype of the human race who adds the intellectual and spiritual perfection of the philosopher to the physical perfection of the athlete. Don Juan's essence does not lie in his adventurous and loving spirit but in the revolt of his natural instincts against laws and religious institutions. [In Spanish.]

2138 Douglas, James. "'Shakes versus Shav' Battle of the Centuries," UNESCO COURIER, VIII (June 1955), 8-9.

According to Shaw's Preface to his puppet play, Shakes versus Shav, the unchangeable facial expressions of puppets keeps the audience's imagination constantly engaged.

2139 Drew, Arnold P. "'Pygmalion' and 'Pickwick,'" N&Q, ns II (May 1955), 221-22.

Dickens's influence on Shaw is evidenced in the opening scene of Pygmalion, which closely parallels the first scene of chapter 2 in PICKWICK PAPERS. Higgins, in attempting to record the Cockney dialect, and Pickwick, in attempting to record the age of the cab-driver's horse, become involved in a street quarrel as a result of their arousing suspicions. Both scenes introduce the main character and present a comic weakness in him. Both Pickwick and Higgins are unable to make their good intentions understood.

2140 "Einstein and Shaw," SHAVIAN, ns No 5 (Sept 1955), 6.

Einstein and Shaw admired each other. Einstein considered Shaw the supreme artist because of his ability to delight and to educate his generation. Shaw said Einstein's portrait suggests a musician more than a mathematician, to which Einstein eventually replied that nothing precludes scientists being artists as well.

2141 Ervine, St. John. "Portrait of Bernard Shaw," List, LIV (18 Aug 1955), 249-50.

Shaw was an uncommonly generous man whose friends were numerous and affectionate and so varied that some of them, if they had met, would never have endured each other. Both G. K. Chesterton and Auguste Rodin remarked at separate times that Shaw was Christ-like. Chesterton's view of life was antithetical to Shaw's, but he nonetheless admired and respected him. As a sculptor, Rodin noted that Shaw's head had the proportions of the traditional figure of Jesus. [Photograph. Commentary in Letters to the Editor by Oliver Cope and Harold Binns, List, LIV (25 Aug 1955), 298.]

2142 f[alkenberg], h[ans] g[eert]. "Zur Entstehungs —und Bühngeschichte von Shaws 'Brassbound'" (On the Genesis and Stage History of Shaw's Captain Brassbound's Conversion), BDDTG, No 94 (1955-56). Captain Brassbound's Conversion was written for Ellen Terry and is based on Cunninghame Graham's MOGREB-EL-ACKSA. [On Ellen Terry performing Lady Cicely.] [In German.]

2143 Ford, George H. DICKENS AND HIS READERS. ASPECTS OF NOVEL CRITICISM SINCE 1836 (Princeton UP for the University of Cincinnati, 1955; NY: W. W. Norton, 1955, 1965), pp. 160, 172, 233-36, 242, 251, 258. Shaw's admission of his debt to Dickens may puzzle those who see Dickens as a bourgeois writer and Shaw as an iconoclast and socialist. However, Shaw's Dickens (of LITTLE DORRIT, OUR MUTUAL FRIEND, and GREAT EXPECTATIONS, more than of PICKWICK PAPERS) was an indignant muckraker. Shaw's tone more than his criticism of society is Dickensian. And Shaw says he owes his characters to Dickens, who demonstrated the possibility of joining verisimilitude in characterization to humorous expression and grotesque situation.

2144 Forter, Elizabeth T. "A Study of the Dramatic Technique of Bernard Shaw." Unpublished dissertation, University of Wisconsin (Madison), 1955. [Listed in McNamee.]

2145 Gassner, John. "The Practicality of Impractical Criticism," TAM, XXXIX (Feb 1955), 22-23, 95-96. Shaw's destructive criticism was essentially constructive. [Photograph of Shaw.]

2146 Gatch, Katharine Haynes. "The Last Plays of Bernard Shaw: Dialectic and Despair," ENGLISH STAGE COMEDY, ed and with intro by W. K. Wimsatt, Jr. (NY: Columbia, 1955), pp. 126-47.

Shaw's later plays may never compare in quality with those of his prime. Still, plays such as <u>Heartbreak House</u>, <u>The Apple Cart</u>, <u>Fanny's First Play</u>, <u>Major Barbara</u>, <u>Too True to Be Good</u>, <u>On the Rocks</u>, <u>The Simpleton of the Unexpected Isles</u>, and <u>The Millionairess</u> are samples of Shaw's attempts to create a genre of English stage comedy. The plays' themes are often political, and so, too, is their dialectical structure. Shaw was impressed with Meredith's essay on "Comedy and the Uses of the Comic Spirit" and Meredith's contention that comedy civilizes. Shaw's indebtedness to the comic tradition often takes the edge off the excesses of doctrine. When structured, the last plays, like <u>Barbara</u>, <u>Too True</u>, and <u>Heartbreak</u>, demonstrate the dialectic clearly; and when without structure, the plays, like <u>Simpleton</u>, exhibit no dialectic at all. For instance, in <u>Barbara</u>, the protagonist is Cusins, professor of Greek, and the antagonist is Undershaft, who feels he is beyond good and evil. Barbara Undershaft is both comic and heroic when she accepts Cusins's vision that one cannot have power for good without risking power for evil. All the late plays are tragicomedies that attempt in their comic treatment of important themes to find new modes for that peculiar time of history between the World Wars.

2147 Gibbs, Wolcott. "Shaw at the Phoenix," NYer, XXX (22 Jan 1955), 74-76.
The first half-hour of <u>The Doctor's Dilemma</u>, with its jokes about medical practices at the beginning of the century, detracts from the performance (Phoenix Theater). The problem dramatized receives impressive arguments, but the solution is ambiguous and ironic. This particular production is not distinguished. Geraldine Fitzgerald is too animated as Mrs. Dubedat and Roddy McDowell, as the youthful Dubedat, is more suggestive of an educated juvenile delinquent than an evil man of genius.

2148 Grendon, Felix. "Theatre Notes. The Phoenix's Dilemma," ShawB, I (May 1955), 22-24.
The Phoenix Theater production of <u>The Doctor's Dilemma</u> overlooks the presence of the personified community at whom the play's barbs are aimed. Not once did Sidney Lumet's production make the audience feel its complicity in a social crime. Shaw's most meaningful speeches were reduced to wisecracks. This production proves that, despite fine

performances by actors, the play will be wooden unless the director understands Shaw's intentions.

2149 Griffin, Alice. "The New York Critics and Saint Joan," ShawB, I (Jan 1955), 10-15.
Saint Joan premiered in New York in 1923 with Winifred Lenihan in the lead and was revived there in 1936 with Katharine Cornell and again in 1951 with Uta Hagen. Though it garnered mixed reviews in these 28 years and though the quality of its production varied, the play had become a world masterpiece by 1951. The play was not included in the Burns Mantle "ten best" plays of the 1923-24 season; and New York critics thought there was some greatness in it, but that it needed better editing. Others, like Percy Hammond, thought the Epilog tiresome. Nonetheless, it was a popular success. By the 1936 revival, Hammond thought the Epilog moving and had, as other critics did, high praise for Cornell's portrayal of Joan. Critics of the 1951 revival with Uta Hagen acknowledged the play as a masterpiece and directed any unfavorable comments toward the production. The gist of such criticism is that a great play needs a great and distinguished production to fulfill its potential.

2150 Henderson, Archibald. "Shaw's Novels: And Why They Failed," DALHOUSIE REVIEW, XXXIV (Winter 1955), 373-82; rptd in ShawB, I (May 1955), 11-18.
Brought up on Dickens, Shelley, Shakespeare, the Bible, SWISS FAMILY ROBINSON, ROBINSON CRUSOE, and the novels of Sir Walter Scott, Shaw began his literary career by writing novels because everyone then was writing them. Though undoubtedly financial failures, Shaw's novels were not complete artistic failures. His style was stilted and devoid of the idiomatic style that characterizes his plays, but Shaw felt sure the antagonism toward his novels was due not to literary incompetence on his part, but to his social and political ideas. Still, there are some flaws in the novels: they are very episodic, with two-dimensional characters.

2151 Herrin, Virginia T. "Bernard Shaw and Richard Wagner: A Study of Their Intellectual Kinship as Artist Philosophers." Unpublished dissertation,

University of North Carolina (Chapel Hill), 1955. [Listed in McNamee.]

2152 Homeyer, Fritz. "Große Zeitgenossen im Buchladen" (Great Contemporaries in the Bookstore), BÖRSENBLATT FÜR DEN DEUTSCHEN BUCHHANDEL (Frankfurt, Federal Republic of Germany), XI (8 March 1955), 153-54.
[Homeyer's personal encounter with Shaw at an exhibition of musical scores, which he arranged as head of the Foreign Department of Bumpus, Oxford Street, London, Booksellers to H.M. the King.] When he was 26, Shaw heard his first German mass. It was Bach's mass, and during its performance, he also heard a "corno di bassetto" for the first time. [In German.]

2153 Honan, William. "A Presentational 'Saint Joan,'" ShawB, I (Jan 1955), 19-21.
The production of <u>Saint Joan</u> (Group 20 Players, Theater on the Green, Wellesley, Mass., 1954) met with unreserved praise. The actors became orators, willing vehicles for the points of view and ideas in the play. Stage movement was minimal to accentuate the interplay of ideas. The setting, too, aimed to gain and focus the audience's attention, not to distract it. The play was produced as a presentation of ideas and human voices.

2154 Jackson, Sir Barry. "Introduction," THEATRICAL COMPANION TO SHAW. A PICTORIAL RECORD OF THE PLAYS OF GEORGE BERNARD SHAW, by Raymond Mander and Joe Mitchenson (Lond: Rockliff Publishing Corporation; NY: Pitman Publishing Corporation, 1955), pp. 1-2.
Shaw was fundamentally courteous and helpful. He kept abreast of developments in the theater and world affairs. His mind was always clear and incisive.

2155 Kaye, Julian B. "Bernard Shaw and the Nineteenth Century Tradition," DA, XV (1955), 269. Dissertation, Columbia University (New York), 1954. [Listed in McNamee. Published Norman, Okla.: U of Oklahoma P, 1958.]

2156 Kerr, Walter F. "Theater," NYHT, 12 Jan 1955.
It is Shaw who most needs saving in the Phoenix production
of The Doctor's Dilemma.

2157 Kisfaludy Stróbl, Zsigmond. "Emlékezések G. B.
Shaw-ra" (Memories of G. B. Shaw), CSILLAG (Star), IX
(1955), 620-29.
[Kisfaludy Stróbl, a well-known sculptor, reminisces about
Shaw's sitting for a bust and about their subsequent
friendship.] [In Hungarian.]

2158 Krabbe, Henning. "Bernard Shaw on Shakespeare
and English Shakespearian Acting," ACTA JUTLANDICA,
Aarsskrift for Aarhus Universitet, XXVII,
Supplementum B, Humanistisk Serie 41 (1955).
Shaw was an opponent of uncritical admiration of
Shakespeare's plays, for he felt that idolatry of
Shakespeare created a barrier against new progressive
drama. Shaw wished Shakespeare performed uncut and under
stage conditions as close to the original as possible, with
respect for the meaning as well as the music of the verse.
The Dark Lady of the Sonnets discusses Shakespeare's social
position, his character, his relations with women, his
outlook on life and his relations with the British public.
Shaw had an intense dislike for Shakespeare's
contemporaries. [Detailed survey of Shaw's criticism of
Shakespeare and productions of his plays with extensive
quotation.]

2159 Laing, Allan M. "The Centenary Message. A
Tragical Topical Episode," SHAVIAN, ns No 5 (Sept
1955), 3-5.
[A very short play about Shaw being interviewed in heaven
about the centenary planned for him; also about the play
Shaw is collaborating on in heaven with Ibsen.]

2160 Lansdale, Nelson. "Joans of London," TAM, XXXIX
(Sept 1955), 70-71, 93.
Siobbhan McKenna's interpretation of Saint Joan is
superlative. It is based on an appreciation of the
playwright's intentions and on her investigation of the
transcripts of the trial and current biographies of Joan in
English.

2161 Laurence, Dan H. "Shaw's Final Curtain," ShawB, I (Sept 1955), 19-21.
After Shaw's death, his last play, <u>Why She Would Not</u>, was deposited by his executor at the British Museum and declared unfinished. The play is not innovative and indeed seems to have inverted the plot of <u>The Millionairess</u>, with a man in the money-making position instead of a woman. Some old Shavian themes are repeated. Bossborn, like Dick Dudgeon, is under the power of an evolutionary force. The name Serafina suggests decaying England in its translation as "evening's end." Furthermore, Shaw's handwritten note at the bottom of a holograph copy of the play suggests that <u>Would Not</u> is complete.

2162 Leavis, F. R. "Shaw against Lawrence," SPECTATOR, CXCIV (1 April 1955), 397-99.
In an introductory essay to SEX, LITERATURE, AND CENSORSHIP, by Harry T. Moore, H. F. Rubinstein calls D. H. Lawrence a "determined Shaw-hater," but no one who understands Lawrence would use those words. Lawrence's opposition to Shaw was because Shaw represented, as well as any other modern writer, what was wrong with modern life. Shaw's work was devoid of emotion.

2163 Lennartz, Franz. "George Bernard Shaw," AUSLÄNDISCHE DICHTER UND SCHRIFTSTELLER UNSERER ZEIT (Foreign Poets and Writers of Our Time) (Stuttgart: Kröner, 1955), pp. 611-23.
With his penchant for paradox and wit Shaw is partially responsible when critics called him Europe's greatest buffoon. But with his plays he propagated a socialism of freedom and human rights. [Mostly a brief survey of Shaw's life and work.] [In German.]

2164 Lewis, C. S. SURPRISED BY JOY (NY: Harcourt Brace, 1955), p. 102.
Shaw was a favorite of Lewis's, not so much because Shaw was fashionable reading but because he had been accessible in Lewis's father's library and had written on Wagner, another favorite of Lewis's.

2165 Lüdeke, H. "Some Remarks on Shaw's History Plays," ENGLISH STUDIES, XXXVI (1955), 239-46.

What endures in Shaw's plays is not his message or wit so much as his philosophy. His optimism becomes in the history plays a mystic belief in the final victory of humanity. In creating heroes for his history plays, Shaw sacrifices historical accuracy for portraits that interested him. His Napoleon in The Man of Destiny is intentionally an unromantic figure, a shrewd professional soldier with huge ambition and a jealous nature. His General Burgoyne in The Devil's Disciple is first a gentleman and then a soldier. His Caesar in Caesar and Cleopatra is not so much a lover as an astute political tutor for the young queen and a model of the moral ruler in his purposefulness. Shaw's portrait reiterates his optimism about human nature. Saint Joan is not historically accurate, but again Shaw bent history to his dramatic purposes. The revolutionary aspect of Joan's position captured his imagination; and in her, he embodied the will, the Life Force, that endures even in a hostile context. Joan is conquered by human limitations, not by evil forces.

2166 McCarthy, Mary. "Shaw at the Phoenix," PARTISAN REVIEW, XXII (Spring 1955), 252-59; rptd in SIGHTS AND SPECTACLES (NY: Farrar, Straus and Cudahy, 1956), pp. 151-62.
The Phoenix Theater production of The Doctor's Dilemma does not succeed. Its veteran cast substitutes staginess for acting. Throughout the play, the audience has to figure out the characters' motivations and the moral questions asked. Shaw's characters often step out of themselves to make a speech or a joke. Shaw spoke reason to a deaf world, stating problems as dilemmas and paradox with an amazing clear-mindedness that eventually isolated him. He became a crank peddling panaceas like equal distribution of money, anti-vivisectionism, anti-vaccinationism, and phonetic spelling. He was the most original playwright of his day; still, he missed greatness.

2167 Mander, Raymond, and Joe Mitchenson. THEATRICAL COMPANION TO SHAW. A PICTORIAL RECORD OF THE PLAYS OF GEORGE BERNARD SHAW, with an introduction by Sir Barry Jackson (Lond: Rockliff Publishing Corporation; NY: Pitman Publishing Corporation, 1955).
[The prefatory and appended material include remembrances and introductions by people close to Shaw--actors,

producers, directors. This material includes lists of
Shaw's plays done in repertory with the casts, comments on
Shaw as a producer and director, and valuable information
about the private theater clubs helpful to innovative
dramatists, like Shaw, in finding their audience. It
includes also information about the production of Shaw's
plays in London, in the provinces, in foreign countries, on
radio, television, and film. The body of the book concerns
Shaw's plays in the order in which they were written. It
includes for each play the history of its production, lists
first performances, copyright performances, and revivals;
it lists casts of various productions, includes synopses of
the plots, and contains informative notes about each play's
production. A generous number of photographs is included to
record scenes from the various performances.] Contents,
abstracted separately under author's name: Sir Barry
Jackson, "Introduction"; Dame Sybil Thorndike, "Thanks to
Bernard Shaw"; Sir Lewis Casson, "G.B.S. at Rehearsal";
Allan Wade, "Shaw and the Stage Society"; Sir Lewis Casson,
"Granville Barker, Shaw and the Court Theatre"; Esmé Percy,
"Charles Macdona and the Macdona Players. An Appreciation";
Alec Clunes, "The Arts Theatre." Not abstracted: Mander and
Mitchenson, "Preface," "Bernard Shaw, the Producer," "The
Plays," "Copyright Performances," "The Incorporated Stage
Society," "The Royal Court Theatre (Vedrenne and Barker),"
"The Everyman Theatre, Hampstead," "The Macdona Players,"
"The Old Vic," "The Arts Theatre Club," "'Q' Theatre," "The
Lyric Theatre, Hammersmith," "The Bedford Theatre, Camden
Town," "The Malvern Festival," "The Malvern Company,"
"First Foreign Translations and Productions," "American
Productions," "Bernard Shaw and the Films," "Broadcasts,
Television and Recordings," "First Publication of the
Plays," "Record Runs in London," and "Casts of London
Revivals."

2168 Martz, Louis. "The Saint as Tragic Hero. Saint
Joan and Murder in the Cathedral," TRAGIC THEMES IN
WESTERN LITERATURE, ed by Cleanth Brooks (New Haven:
Yale UP, 1955), pp. 150-78; rptd in G. B. SHAW: A
COLLECTION OF CRITICAL ESSAYS, ed by R. J. Kaufmann
(Englewood Cliffs, NJ: Prentice-Hall, 1965); rptd in
SAINT JOAN: FIFTY YEARS AFTER, 1923/24—1973/74, ed
by Stanley Weintraub (Baton Rouge: Louisiana State
UP, 1973), pp. 144-65.

The question of whether or not a play about a saint can be tragic leads inevitably to a discussion of the nature of tragedy. Both Saint Joan and MURDER IN THE CATHEDRAL draw their power from the schism of faith in the audience; they depend on the audience's uncertainty in accepting their saintly heroes as being divinely inspired. The tragic sense in these plays emerges from the interaction of the hero, who represents some secret cause, and the other characters, who are the human sufferers. Joan is not a tragic hero, but Shaw creates tragic tension in the play by opposing her to the whole range of responses to her voices. She resembles an Aristotelian hero in her abject confidence in her voices; her only lapse in the play is her moment of recantation. Joan can certainly be called tragic if we do not demand an Aristotelian hero and if we see the subject for tragedy as the relative tension between doubt and affirmation, between secret cause and human suffering.

2169 Mendip, Thomas. "The Play of the Moment," SHAVIAN, ns No 4 (May 1955), 22-24.
Saint Joan is enjoying revivals in Holland and England, as well as America.

2170 Nethercot, Arthur H. "G.B.S. and Annie Besant," ShawB, I (Sept 1955), 1-14.
Though the actual nature of the relationship between Annie Besant and Shaw may never be known, the daily and Sunday newspapers, house organs of the socialist and secularist societies of the eighties and nineties, and the personal letters and records of the pair can help flesh out their eight year acquaintance.

2171 O'Casey, Sean. "Shaw's Corner," SHAVIAN, ns No 4 (May 1955), 2-5.
Though many have criticized Shaw's plays for his socialism and his philosophy, the charge that there is no poetry in them is the least supportable. There is powerful poetry and emotion in the description of the Syrian sky in Caesar and Cleopatra, in Joan's sorrow when she realizes the world is not ready to accept her, and in every scene of Heartbreak House.

2172 O'Donnell, Norbert F. "On the 'Unpleasantness' of 'Pygmalion,'" ShawB, I (May 1955), 7-10.

512

Studies of <u>Pygmalion</u> which treat it as a wholly pleasant play ignore the social significance of Eliza Doolittle's transformation from guttersnipe to lady to human being. They ignore, too, Alfred Doolittle's denunciation of conventional morality as the morality of intimidation. It is a key to understanding the play's meaning, explaining as it does Doolittle's plight as well as Eliza's. The ending reflects Shaw's optimism in that Eliza's human vitality triumphs over conventional morality. Her anger at Higgins's arrogance completes her transformation and gives her direction. The unpleasant implications of the play are immanent in the hostility between Eliza and Higgins at the conclusion; yet, actors and directors persist in sentimentalizing the ending with a suggestion of love and marriage for Pygmalion and his Galatea.

2173 Percy, Esmé. "Bernard Shaw: A Personal Memory," List, LII (26 May 1955), 929-31.
At rehearsals Shaw's method was to act out the character as he conceived it, a method maddening to producers but helpful to actors. He never demanded anything from an actor that was beyond the actor's capabilities, but he did believe an actor should never let an audience's attention wander. He did not like actors to throw his lines away, and he envied D. H. Lawrence's dialog in THE WIDOWING OF MRS. HOLROYD. Until his fatal accident, Shaw was dynamically and intensely alive. A deeply religious man with a sense of fun, he will be remembered as a great dramatist, even if he is forgotten as a philosopher.

2174 Percy, Esmé. "Charles Macdona and the Macdona Players: An Appreciation," THEATRICAL COMPANION TO SHAW. A PICTORIAL RECORD OF THE PLAYS OF GEORGE BERNARD SHAW, by Raymond Mander and Joe Mitchenson (Lond: Rockliff Publishing Corporation; NY: Pitman Publishing Corporation, 1955), pp. 296-97.
The Macdona Players "did more than anyone to bring the Shavian Theatre to the consciousness of the general public."

2175 Popović, Dušan. "Dve Jednočinke Bernarda Šoa," LETOPIS MATIČA SRPSKE (Novi Sad), CCCLXXVI (1955), 501-5.

[Essay-review of the first Serbian productions of The Man of Destiny and Great Catherine.] [In Serbian.]

2176 Purcell, Victor. "Shaw, Russell, Toynbee, and the Far East," SHAVIAN, ns No 4 (May 1955), 15-19.
[A talk at the National Book League on 25 Feb 1955, summarized by the speaker.] Though Shaw and Bertrand Russell were often associated in the public mind, they were quite dissimilar. Shaw hated Darwinism because its followers used it to justify laissez faire and because it did not account for "mind" in the universe. Russell was concerned with the historical importance of Darwinism, not its contemporary relevance. Furthermore, Russell was not impressed with Marx as a thinker, whereas Shaw was always sympathetic to the Russian experiment. Still, the two men are associated because they placed greater store on feeling, guided by experience, than on authority or revelation. Toynbee represented a transcendental approach to world affairs.

2177 Rattray, R. F. "The Shavian Religion I Believe In," SHAVIAN, ns No 5 (Sept 1955), 7-9. [Reported by Barbara Smoker.]
With a mind not structured by a university education, Shaw was able to see more easily the way the creative faculty operates. He was always striving for betterment and thus found it difficult to understand where evil and suffering fit into creation and evolution. He concludes that the Life Force experiments—that God is all-good but not perfect. Shaw was a mystic and an idealist who over-estimated human goodness. He felt religion must be adapted to the people and that it must be based on beauty as well as on intellect.

2178 Reyes, Alfonso. "La danza de las esfinges" (The Dance of the Sphinxes), OBRAS COMPLETAS, III (Mexico: Fonde Cultura Económica, 1955), 96-98.
[A creative-poetic essay in which the relationships between men and women are analyzed in terms of Candida, the Pastor, the Poet, and the Secretary.] [In Spanish.]

2179 Rosselli, John. "The Right Joan and the Wrong One," TWENTIETH CENTURY, CLVII (April 1955), 374-83.

In John Fernald's <u>Saint Joan</u> (St. Martin's Theater), Siobbhan McKenna gives a fine performance; however, Jessie Evans in Peter Lambert's production of the play (at a small theater in the basement of Manchester Central Library) gave a most moving performance of the role, one which seems to be an example of the right way to do a play by Shaw. He wrote classical comedy, and the methods of it are operatic. Anyone who produces <u>Joan</u> should pay attention to Mozart's methods in DON GIOVANNI, where the women characters are universal types brought to life through the music. In Shaw's play, voice is important, too. Dunois's speech in the cathedral scene is like an aria. Shaw states a theme, varies it in repetition, summarizes it, introduces another, and combines the two. Joan has an aria, too. If the actors playing the characters try to be more than instruments, the effect is diminished.

2180 Salazar Chapela, E. "Los Amores de Bernard Shaw" (The Loves of Bernard Shaw), INSULA (Spain), X (15 Nov 1955), 12, 16.
[A discussion of Shaw's relations with women: Jenny Patterson, Alice Lockett, May Morris, Annie Besant, Janet Achurch, Mrs. Shaw, Mrs. Patrick Campbell, Ellen Terry, and Blanche Patch.] [In Spanish.]

2181 Sanín Cano, Baldomero. "Un genio de la observación y la burla (G.B.S.)" (An Observant and Humorous Genius [G.B.S.]) and "Un plácido censor de su época" (A Benevolent Censor of His Time), EL HUMANISMO Y EL PROCESO DEL HOMBRE (Humanism and the Progress of Man) (Buenos Aires: 1955), pp. 105, 116-25. Shaw was a genius of common sense who made use of irony and humor to criticize human nature in order to improve it. [In Spanish.]

2182 Schermel, Ronald. "Theatre in Holland," SHAVIAN, ns No 4 (May 1955), 21-22.
Two important productions of Shavian drama in the Netherlands were <u>Saint Joan</u> (Amsterdam Theater Group: Douglas Seale, director of the Birmingham Repertory Theater, producer) and <u>Caesar and Cleopatra</u> (Hague Theater Group; Erwin Piscator, director). The <u>Joan</u> performance was able, with undue emphasis on the quarrels between members of the ecclesiastical court.

515

2183 Scott, Russell. "Shaw's Place in the History of Alphabet Reform," SHAVIAN, ns No 5 (Sept 1955), 15-17.

[A talk at Hope House on 24 June 1955 reported by Barbara Smoker.] Shaw was not original in his desire for alphabet reform. The movement goes back as far as the fifteenth century. Shaw and phonetics experts thought that the alphabet should contain 40 letters to represent all the sounds in the language.

2184 Seduro, Vladimir. THE BYELORUSSIAN THEATER AND DRAMA (NY: Research Project on the U.S.S.R., 1955) pp. 54, 71.

The Devil's Disciple, produced at the Byelorussian State Theater (Minsk) during the 1922/23 season, was selected for the repertoire solely because of its revolutionary scenes and motifs. [Bibliography, pp. 428-80.]

2185 Shattuck, Charles H. "Bernard Shaw's 'Bad Quarto,'" JOURNAL OF ENGLISH AND GERMANIC PHILOLOGY, LIV (1955), 651-63; rptd in CShav, V (Jan-Feb 1964), 11-17.

Widowers' Houses, Shaw's first play, is the only one he was thoroughly ashamed of. Yet a study of his revisions of the 1893 version for Plays Pleasant and Unpleasant (1898) demonstrate Shaw's growing mastery of the drama and the development of his distinctive style. In the 1898 revisions he expands stage directions greatly so that they indicate purpose, mood, and manner. He expunges superfluous dialog, needless puns, and silly quibbles. His characters consequently are more precisely drawn. A complete collation of Shaw's early plays with the text of the Standard Edition is necessary to assess his growth between 1898 and 1930. But even this study shows that he had found his stride by 1898.

2186 "Shaw Has Been Here Before," ShawB, I (Jan 1955), 15.

Shaw is not alive to comment on the positions of America, Britain, and France on the re-arming of Western Germany, but in a letter turning down an invitation to lecture at a Fabian Summer School Session in America in 1918, he worried about the dominance of America in any peace dictated by the Allies.

2187 Silverman, Albert H. "Bernard Shaw's Political Extravaganzas." Unpublished dissertation, Tulane University, 1955.

2188 Smith, J. Percy. "A Shavian Tragedy: <u>The Doctor's Dilemma</u>," THE IMAGE OF THE WORK, ESSAYS IN CRITICISM, by B. H. Lehman and others (Berkeley & Los Angeles: U of California P, 1955), pp. 189-207.
Shaw looked for theater that was informed by high seriousness and purpose. He saw drama as the presentation of the problem of human will in conflict with the environment and he presented the individual circumstance. The term <u>problem</u> refers to the generalization of the idea which is worked out in a specific set of circumstances, the <u>plot</u>. According to Shaw, it is the playwright's ability to deal with the problem, not with the plot, that makes drama come to life. In <u>The Doctor's Dilemma</u>, the plot deals with a problem the universal nature or relevance of which is not explored. The problem in <u>Dilemma</u>, which could as effectively be the Teacher's or the Soldier's or the Clergyman's Dilemma, is simply the inability to judge other men's lives without being affected by irrelevant information. The specific situation in which the problem is examined gives rise to the social criticism, in this case, criticism of the medical profession.

2189 Stanton, Stephen S. "English Drama and the French Well-Made Play," DA, XIV (1955), 2194-95. Unpublished dissertation, Columbia University, 1955. [Listed in McNamee.]

2190 Stoppel, Hans. "Shaw and Sainthood," ENGLISH STUDIES, XXXVI (April 1955), 49-63; rptd in STUDENTS' SOURCES FOR SHAKESPEARE'S HAMLET, SHAW'S SAINT JOAN, CONRAD'S HEART OF DARKNESS, comp by Roy Bentley (Agincourt, Ontario: Book Society of Canada, 1966); rptd in SAINT JOAN: FIFTY YEARS AFTER, 1923/24-1973/74, ed by Stanley Weintraub (Baton Rouge: Louisiana State UP), pp. 166-84.
Joan is the expression of Shaw's ideal human figure for the years 1910-30 and is linked to his earlier as well as to his later figures. In his early novels there are figures that revolt against old forms. They were soon followed by characters who also are assertive and individualistic but

who have an irrational or intuitive strain. Shaw presents Joan as a synthesis of all his requirements for the ideal human figure. She is a genius who strives to help others see things as they really are, but she also has a creative imagination which raises her rational faculties to the higher plane of prophecy. Shaw's saints diverge from any Christian conception of sainthood in a number of ways. Revelations stem not from God but from the imagination. Furthermore, Shaw's heroes aim to establish progress in this world, and their failures are not due to sin and temptation but to mental or physical frailty. And their mystical experiences return the saint to the world; and that world, in turn, returns the saint to a new mystical experience.

2191 Suenaga, Kuniaki. "Cymbeline to G. B. Shaw" (CYMBELINE and G. B. Shaw), KINDAI NO EIBUNGAKU, ed by Fukuhara Rintaro Sensei Kanrekikinenronbunshu Kankokai (Tokyo: Kenkyusha, 1955), pp. 215-25.
[Surveys briefly Shaw's long-term concern for Shakespeare's CYMBELINE, which extended over 50 years from his famous attack on Henry Irving's presentation in 1896 to his Forward to Cymbeline Refinished.] [In Japanese.]

2192 Thorndike, Dame Sybil. "Thanks to Bernard Shaw," THEATRICAL COMPANION TO SHAW. A PICTORIAL RECORD OF THE PLAYS OF GEORGE BERNARD SHAW, by Raymond Mander and Joe Mitchenson (Lond: Rockliff Publishing Corporation; NY: Pitman Publishing Corporation, 1955), pp. 11-15.
[Personal remembrance of Shaw's ability to shock humanity into awareness of responsibilities.] Shaw felt that actors could not be good unless they wanted to express something they had humanly felt. He was not a cold character, but there was a breathtaking quality about him, like cold air at the heights, that sometimes carried people who knew him to new vision. He was dynamic and stimulating, something of an actor himself, who was intensely interested in human beings and who could inspire confidence in actors.

2193 Untermeyer, Louis. MAKERS OF THE MODERN WORLD (Chicago: Spencer P, 1955), pp. 24, 33, 113, 115, 118, 119, 175, 182, 247-61, 283, 451, 469, 498, 666, 668, 676, 773.

[Brief biography, stressing Shaw's role as critic and teacher. Also passing references to Shaw in the biographies of others.]

2194 Wade, Allan. "Shaw and the Stage Society," THEATRICAL COMPANION TO SHAW. A PICTORIAL RECORD OF THE PLAYS OF GEORGE BERNARD SHAW, by Raymond Mander and Joe Mitchenson (Lond: Rockliff Publishing Corporation; NY: Pitman Publishing Corporation, 1955), pp. 285-87.

The forty who attended the first meeting of the Stage Society decided to establish a private society to produce plays unlikely to be sponsored by established theater managements. You Never Can Tell was the first play performed, and the Society produced a number of Shaw's plays when London theaters were not interested in him. By 1904, when the Society was incorporated, Shaw's plays were being produced in London. Shaw and Mrs. Shaw became life members of the society, and Shaw served many years on the production committee in support of the Society.

2195 West, E. J. "Introduction," ADVICE TO A YOUNG CRITIC AND OTHER LETTERS, by Bernard Shaw (NY: Crown Publishers, 1955), ix-xvi.

[The collection of Shaw's letters to R. Golding Bright, with annotations, is edited by a good Shavian—someone who is favorably disposed to Shaw and avidly reads his works and the works of the Shavian essayists. The volume contains a one-sided correspondence, for although Bright saved Shaw's letters, he did not apparently keep copies of his own letters to Shaw.]

2196 Williamson, Audrey. "Wagner and Shaw," SHAVIAN, ns No 4 (May 1955), 9-12.

[Summary by Barbara Smoker of Williamson's address to the National Book League.] Though Shaw admired Wagner, definite differences exist between the work of Shaw and of Wagner. For example, Shaw seems to have little knowledge of women as human beings, whereas Wagner's understanding of them seemed based on wide personal experience and the feminine in his own nature. Wagner brought nature into his writings, whereas Shaw preferred to deal with people and ideas. Wagner's drama requires elaborate staging and effects, whereas Shaw's plays are carried by dialog and action.

2197 Yeats, W[illiam] B[utler]. THE LETTERS OF W.B. YEATS, ed by Allan Wade. (NY: Macmillan, 1955), pp. 59, 67, 231, 233, 335, 383, 385, 387, 392, 395, 407, 420, 442, 453, 473, 474, 490, 500, 507, 513, 535, 541, 543, 549, 564, 565, 566, 623, 671, 717, 724, 767, 771, 794, 800, 801, 802, 803, 876, 884.
[References to Shaw in Yeats's correspondence.]

1956

2198 Adler, Henry. "The Artist Philosopher," ADAM INTERNATIONAL REVIEW, Nos 255-256 (1956), 17-23.
Upon his centenary, Shaw is being attached with "buckshot from blunderbusses of low calibre." All such criticism suffers from superficial understanding and partial viewing. The failure to grasp the interrelationship of all Shaw's work, its essential religious nature, has misled many critics. Shaw "approaches God through the back door." He becomes the Devil's Disciple because, in a world of inverted morality that uses individuals for base purposes, one must seek virtue through a double inversion of morality. This paradox of the Devil in search of God governs Shaw's electric dialog and thought.

2199 Adler, Henry. "Bertholt Brecht's Contribution to Epic Drama," List, LV (12 Jan 1956), 51-52; rptd in John Gassner, DIRECTIONS IN MODERN THEATRE AND DRAMA (NY: Holt, Rinehart, Winston, 1966), pp. 309-17.
Brecht's presentation of Galileo's story seems intellectually naive when compared with the independent intellectualism of Shaw in his Preface to Saint Joan.

2200 Albert, Sidney P. "Bernard Shaw: The Artist as Philosopher," JOURNAL OF AESTHETICS AND ART CRITICISM, XIV (June 1956), 419-38.
Shaw as artist-philosopher used drama not only to expound philosophy but also to show how it could work in human situations. Shaw's concept of the philosopher's role is three-fold: to discover the inner will of the world, inventively to discover means of fulfilling that will, and

in action to do that will. Shaw was influenced by many different philosophers, but perhaps Hegel's dialectical theory is the most crucial to an understanding of Shaw's plays. Shaw was unique, however, in his application of a sense of humor to the realm of philosophy, accounting for his escaping martyrdom.

2201 Alt, Eduard Otto "Shaw und der Fabianismus. Umrisse einer Neuwertung des Denkers und Politikers" (Shaw and Fabianism. Outlines of a Revaluation of Shaw, the Thinker and Politician). Unpublished dissertation, University of Freiburg, 1956. [Listed in McNamee.]

2202 "Andrew Undershaft: Economic Rogue," SHAVIAN, VII (1956), 57-59.
[A discussion at the National Book League on 23 March 1956, reported by Barbara Smoker.] Shaw, as usual, gave the devil some good arguments, but in the case of Undershaft, failed to knock them down. Major Barbara is pre-atomic age and thus not literally applicable to the present. The point may be that, unless we arrange the social structure on a more equitable basis, we are laying ourselves open to Undershaftism as the lesser of two evils.

2203 Anikst, A. "Bernard Shou (k 100-letiiu tso dnia rozhdeniia)" (Bernard Shaw on His Centenary), ZNANIIA (Moscow) (1956). [Not seen.] [In Russian.]

2204 Anikst, A. "Kak stat' Bernardom Shaw—vmesto iubileinoi stat'i" (How to Become Bernard Shaw—In Place of a Jubilee Essay), TEATR (Moscow), No 7 (1956), 127-32.
Shaw's secret of dramatic art is simple: choose an ordinary situation and turn it upside down, as in Candida or The Devil's Disciple. The function of Shaw's paradoxical situations, characters and action is to make the audience think. In Pygmalion, Eliza speaks in a vulgar way but her soul is not vulgar. The denouements in Shaw's plays are not only unexpected but in many cases are not denouements at all—nothing has ended, everything is beginning, including thought. One of Shaw's most important qualities, of course, is humor. [In Russian.]

2205 Anikst, A. "Uchenik d'iavola" (<u>The Devil's Disciple</u>), TEATR (Moscow), No 9 (1956), 145-46.
[Comment on a production at the Bolshoi Gorky Theater, Leningrad, 1956.] Many producers think irony does not reach an audience, so they often take refuge in unnecessary buffoonery and the grotesque. More attention should be paid to the intellectual character of Shaw's heroes. Unfortunately, in the Soviet Union "scenic variants" or adaptations of Shaw's plays are still used when the texts do not require any assistance. [In Russian.]

2206 Anisimov, I. I. "Bernard Shou k stoletiiu so dnia rozhdeniia" (Bernard Shaw on the Centenary of His Birth), PRAVDA (Moscow), 26 July 1956; rptd in SOVREMENNYE PROBLEMY REALIZMA, by Anisimov (Moscow: "Nauka," 1977), 270-74.
All progressive humankind marks Shaw's centenary. His long life was a struggle against social injustice. The Great October Revolution of 1917 caused marked changes in Shaw's work, and he greeted it with high hopes. [In Russian.]

2207 Anisimov, I. I. "Vtoraia epokha v tvorchestve B. Shou" (The Second Period of Shaw's Work), INOSTRANNAIA LITERATURA (Moscow), No 11 (1956), 192-202.
Marked changes occur in Shaw's work after World War I and the October Revolution (1917). The Preface to <u>Heartbreak House</u> complements the strong political overtones in the play, and the dominant ship symbolism in the last scenes allows Shaw to reveal his conclusions. <u>Back to Methuselah</u> has Faustian characteristics and develops the idea of Creative Evolution. <u>Saint Joan</u> is Shaw's most serious play: its Preface shows the close connections between what occurred in the Middle Ages and in the twentieth century, though the former was more humane than the latter period. The great cycle of the thirties began with <u>The Apple Cart</u>, a political masquerade with political paradoxes, and includes farces with historical settings, all permeated by contemporary crises. The political comedies of the thirties result from everything Shaw had already written: the external dissimilarity of <u>Widowers' Houses</u> and <u>The Apple Cart</u> should not prevent us from seeing the inner logic of their relationship. [In Russian.]

2208 Anosova, N. A. "Vydaiushchiĭsia pisatel'-gumanist" (Leading Writer and Humanist), NAUKA I ZHIZN (Moscow), No 7 (1956), 58-59. [Not seen.] [In Russian.]

2209 Archer, William. "Extracts from a lecture by William Archer on Galsworthy, Barrie and Shaw, Delivered to the College Club, New York, in 1921," DRAMA, XLII (Fall 1956), 29-36.
[A partial publication of Archer's famous 1921 speech, noteworthy for its account of Archer's friendship with Shaw.] Shaw is an idealist of exactly the sort Shaw criticized in The Quintessence of Ibsenism. He does not live in the real world but in an a priori world of his own construction. He sees things not as they are, but as it suits him to think they are.

2210 Arnot, R. Page. "Shaw and the Soviet Union," LABOUR MONTHLY, XXXVIII (1956), 421-28.
Shaw rejoiced in the Soviet Union, which had translated ideas into action. [A brief history of Shaw's appreciation of the Soviet Union.]

2211 Atkinson, Brooks. "Saint Joan," NYT, 16 Sept 1956, II, p. 1.
As a rude peasant girl, Siobbhan McKenna's performance of Saint Joan is effective. But McKenna's acting does not blossom into the saint. The trial scene is a brilliant statement of the instinct public institutions have for self-preservation in the presence of individuals who adhere to private conscience. [Reviewed by Atkinson also in "First Night at the Theatre," NYT, 12 Sept 1956, p. 42.]

2212 Atkinson, Brooks. "Shaw's The Apple Cart," NYT, 28 Oct 1956, II, p. 1.
The Apple Cart is still timely. In 1929 Shaw was not horrified by the European dictatorships, but after World War II broke out, he was shocked by their inhumanity. We do not have to accept Shaw's political ideas to recognize the liveliness and the conscience of Cart. [Photograph. Also reviewed by Atkinson, "Theatre: Apple Cart," NYT, 19 Oct 1956, p. 23.]

2213 Atkinson, Brooks. "Theatre: <u>Major Barbara</u>," NYT, 31 Oct 1956, p. 27.
In the current production of <u>Major Barbara</u> Charles Laughton and Shaw reach a draw.

2214 Atkinson, Brooks. "Theatre: <u>My Fair Lady</u>," NYT, 16 March 1956, p. 20.
Shaw's mind is the genius of MY FAIR LADY.

2215 Avenarius, G. "Bernard Shou i kinematograf" (Bernard Shaw and the Cinematograph), ISKUSSTVO KINA (Moscow), IX (1956), 99-109.
Shaw declared that the invention of the cinematograph was more important than the invention of printing, because it was accessible to the illiterate. He was negative toward American cinema and its representatives, for profiteering. One of the first to appreciate the opportunities of the cinema as art, Shaw did less for its development than he might have done. [In Russian.]

2216 Balashov, N. "Velikii master dramy" (Great Master of the Drama), OGONEK (Moscow), XXXIV (1956), 13.
Shaw depicted social life realistically by means of paradox. After 1917, Shaw paid most attention to the general crisis of the capitalist world and was one of the first Western writers to take the side of the Soviet Union. [In Russian.]

2217 "Banning of <u>Pygmalion</u>," STAGE (6 Dec 1956), p. 1.
[A news item covering the controversy over the banning of <u>Pygmalion</u> performances during the run of MY FAIR LADY.]

2218 Barnet, Sylvan. "Bernard Shaw on Tragedy," PMLA, LXXI (Dec 1956), 888-99.
Shaw's criticism of Shakespearean tragedy necessarily has ethical as well as esthetic implications. Shaw's objection to tragedy was that of a romantic, who believes the universe is an evolving organism rather than the static machine of classical thinking. His attitude is teleological. He could see no alternative to Creative Evolution except pessimism, which he equates with a tragic view of life. Thus he converted to a comic pattern the

material of tragedy, for the traditional protagonist is a
heroic variation from the norm, who is (at least in some
sense) destroyed. But for Shaw commendable variations
(especially women imbued with the Life Force) survive, get
married, and live happily ever after. Because he sees the
significant variant as a person allied with the Life Force,
he is impatient with tragic heroes. For Shaw, existence, a
continual state of becoming, lacks the finality against
which the tragic hero struggles, reveals his capabilities,
and is spent. [The Doctor's Dilemma, Heartbreak House, and
Saint Joan are used to illustrate.]

2219 Barzun, Jacques. "From Shaw to Rousseau," THE
ENERGIES OF ART: STUDIES OF AUTHORS CLASSIC AND
MODERN (NY: Harper, 1956), pp. 245-80; rptd NY:
Vintage Books, 1962, pp. 248-83.
Shaw is particularly important as an example of the modern
because, first, he was so encyclopedic, and, secondly, like
many other modern artists, Shaw kept abusing romanticism
while exemplifying it in his thought or praising its
representative figures. The romanticism he attacked
consisted of the clichés of secondhand romance; but high
Romanticism remains the groundwork of his philosophy,
reflected in his many-sidedness, love of dramatic
opposition, and conversion of esthetic into social
standards. His fusion of scientific skepticism with
religious faith, of individualism with collective
discipline, of the primacy of the will with the use of
reason, of a taste for heresy with a taste for legalism—
these dialectical opposites are the mainspring of his
intellectual energy. Shaw has the vision, though not the
temperament, of Rousseau. Both men used their literary
talents to set forth explicit programs of social reform
rooted in a religious view of life. They wanted society and
humanity made new by a system embodying a new faith. Both
believed that God pervades our being and cannot work out
His purpose except through us. [Excellent criticism.]

2220 Bellu, Pavel. "George Bernard Shaw (1856-
1956)," STEAUA, VII (1956), 56-60.
Shaw introduced the theater of ideas in England. The
prefaces to the plays are meant to develop one's wit,
whereas the plays themselves are merely amusing. Shaw's
novels are facile. His poverty-stricken childhood helps to

explain his admiration for the Soviet Union, his acts of
charity, and his refusal of a title. [In Romanian.]

2221 Bellyei, László. "George Bernard Shaw (1856-
1950)," NÉPMÜVELÉS, VI (1956), 16-17.
[Socialist party-line praise of Shaw on his hundredth
birthday, with emphasis on the plays and on his social
conscience.] [In Hungarian.]

2222 Berry, Wallace. "Opera. The Admirable
Bashville," ABSTRACT OF DISSERTATIONS (1956 [1957]),
53-54. Unpublished dissertation, University of
Southern California, 1956.

2223 Bhakri, A. S. "Shaw's Dramas in Relation to His
Social and Philosophical Ideas." Unpublished
dissertation, University of Leeds, 1956. [Listed in
McNamee.]

2224 Bibesco, Princess Marthe. "Memories of Bernard
Shaw," List, LV (26 April 1956), 503-4.
[The cousin of Antoine Bibesco reports his wedding to
Elizabeth Asquith, which Shaw stealthily attended and later
satirically described in a letter he sent to the bride as a
wedding present. Accounts also of Mrs. Shaw's role in
getting Shaw to write Saint Joan, and of how Anthony
Asquith got him to add a scene to Pygmalion for the film
version.]

2225 Boor, Jan. "G. B. Shaw: k stému výročiu
narodenia" (G. B. Shaw: On His Centenary), SLOVENSKÉ
DIVADLO (Bratislava), IV (1956), 375-80.
Shaw came to the theater when capitalism was at its height
and experienced two wars caused by imperialists. He refused
to accept any philosophy or doctrine without question and
in this was English, despite his Irish origins. Though
careless about form, he cared for language and sense—a
classical, almost French, tendency. Dialog is the vital
nerve of his plays. Many of his characters are only
variations on one type: mothers, emancipated women,
constructive realists—all depicted with humor. But his
other characters are often schematic. [In Czechoslovak.]

2226 Borinski, Ludwig. "Shaw und die Stilexperimente des frühen 20. Jahrhunderts" (Shaw and the Stylistic Experiments of the Early Twentieth Century), DIE NEUEREN SPRACHEN, Neue Folge, No 8 (1956), 361-71.
The beginning of the twentieth century is characterized by radical stylistic experiments in literature and the arts. Shaw shocked his contemporaries more with his ideas, but beginnings of formal experiments are also evident in his work. These experiments consisted mostly in the dissolution of formal structures. Technical innovations, many of them derived from the film (flashbacks, montage), take the place of intuitive art. Barriers between art and literature on the one side and journalism and advertising on the other side begin to disappear. Shaw is most of all a journalist with a keen eye for details. He achieves his greatest effects through the use of paradox and surprise; these, however, wear thin with repetition and constitute the most questionable aspect of his art. In combining the most heterogeneous elements in his work Shaw comes close to the experiments of T. S. Eliot and James Joyce. But he is separated from them by his optimistic belief in progress and by his wittiness. [In German.]

2227 Casson, Sir Lewis. "Thoughts on Shaw's Centenary," SHAVIAN, VII (1956), 10-12.
Shaw had much in common with Sheridan, Shakespeare, and Molière; his plays are already going through the usual course of classical plays. They are played in period costume (leading to "overdressing and guying"); the next step is over-elaboration of the settings, to distract attention from the words and their meaning. Then will arise another William Poel who will insist on going back to what Shaw himself liked. "simplicity of setting, concentration on significant extrovert acting, and stylised rhetorical stage speech, produced as word-music."

2228 "Centenary Year News Notes," ShawB, I (Nov 1956), 3.
Edward Chodorov has just finished his dramatization of The Irrational Knot; the Berlin Cultural Festival presented Village Wooing and Fanny's First Play; RCA Victor will soon release its recording of Saint Joan; a Shaw Collection has been established at Cornell University; Graham Greene will

write the screenplay for the film to be made of <u>Saint Joan</u> by Otto Preminger.

2229 Charrington, Norman T. G. BERNARD SHAW, PYGMALION (Lond: James Brodie [Notes on English Texts], 1956).
[A student guide to Shaw's life, career, and especially <u>Pygmalion</u>, including maps, notes, and questions. Contains standard biographical summary and familiar critical formulas.] Shaw was all head and no heart, a cynic who sneered at his fellow creatures, who wrote problem plays that lack art and emotional depth. [All of this is then contradicted by a helpful account of <u>Pygmalion</u>.]

2230 Chiaromonte, Nicola. "Shaw, le Parole e la Minestra" (Shaw, the Words and the Soup), MONDO, 16 Oct 1956; rptd in LA SITUAZIONE DRAMMATICA (Milano: Bompiani [Portico: Critica e Saggi], 1960), pp. 54-57.
Possibly Shaw and not Brecht is the true creator of "alienated theater." He understood that didactic theater teaches nothing; it upsets existing opinions. The variety of Shaw's characters who cannot be reduced to a simple doctrine places him in the company of Aristophanes, Molière, and Voltaire. <u>Major Barbara</u>, never shown in Italy, is the most socialist-Marxist of Shaw's works. As in <u>Saint Joan</u>, the action shows the passage from weak to clear conscience. Shaw's characters stop talking when the argument is exhausted; <u>Barbara</u> should end with Act II when Barbara learns to trust only the truth of her vital impulses. The theme of <u>Barbara</u> is belief in the modern world; the key is that Barbara has learned something in her loss of faith. [In Italian.]

2231 Clurman, Robert. "G.B.S. 100," NYTBR, LXI (22 July 1956), 8.
Americans adore Shaw because he was never civil to them: witness the gala celebration of his centenary in Chicago. The British are content with dignified runs of his plays and documentaries.

2232 Collis, John Stewart. "The Two Bernard Shaws," DUBLIN MAGAZINE, XXXI (1956), 36-40.

Shaw functioned on two levels: Fabian and playwright. Essentially he did not know how humanity was to be saved, for he was "incapable of consecutive thought" and only an emotional writer. [Illustrates with Major Barbara, John Bull's Other Island, and Heartbreak House.]

2233 Comarnescu, Peter. "G.B. Shaw," SCRISUL BĂNĂTEAN (Timisoara), No 6 (1956), 94-102. [Not seen.] [In Romanian.]

2234 Couchman, Gordon W. "Shaw, Caesar, and the Critics," SPEECH MONOGRAPHS, XXIII (1956), 262-71. Originally Caesar and Cleopatra was called an "opera-bouffe" by critics and its historical trappings derided as fantastical inventions. Shaw attacked such views in 1908 and 1913, indicting all reviewers as not "worth a cent." Although many critics appreciated the validity of his historical details and the characterization of Caesar, Shaw felt the play had not received its due from the press.

2235 Crisan, Ion. "Testamentul lui Shaw" (Shaw's Testament), CONTEMPORANUL, 28 Oct 1956. Shaw's last prank was his Will, for British scholars are still confused about the 40 letter English alphabet. [In Romanian.]

2236 Daiches, David. "G.B.S., Spokesman for Vitality," SRL, XXXIX (21 July 1956), 8-10. Shaw's plays are still lively and entertaining; his prose is still provocative. Shaw was at his best when discussing topical rather than universal questions. Victorian themes and contemporary situations are his forte. He stood for vitality against convention, for creative will against the lethargy of custom and the hypocrisy of social pretensions. Such ideas are not original, but Shaw's contribution was in his particular dramatization of the human complexity of this conflict.

2237 Diakonova, N. Ia. "Istoricheskaia drama Shou Sviataia Ioanna" (Shaw's Historical Drama Saint Joan), VESTNIK LENINGRADSKOGO UNIVERSITETA (Leningrad), No 29 (1956), pp. 112-28. In Saint Joan, Shaw developed old tendencies, dealing with the problems of historical and contemporary processes, the relation of the individual to the crowd, as in <u>Three Plays for Puritans</u>. <u>Joan</u> is the most straight-forward of all Shaw's work. The tragedy of Joan was that of Shaw himself. Her portrait expresses many of his old, favorite ideas (Life Force, etc.). His pessimistic concept of the passivity of the masses leads Shaw to the ironic negation of social progress. He introduces obvious parallels between past and present, e.g., the authority of the Church, political convenience, nationalism, and the social structure. But <u>Joan</u> cannot be taken too seriously, as witness the comic impression made by Shaw's use of contemporary idiom in the dialog. [In Russian.]

2238 Dobrev, Chavdar. "Za Shou i za negoviĭa 'Pigmalion' na teatŭr 'Trudov Front'" (On Shaw and his <u>Pygmalion</u> at the "Labor Front" Theater), TEATŬR (Sofia) VII (1956), 45-54.
Shaw's works are permeated with hatred of and protest against the inhuman structure and moral norms of society. He depicted the stagnation of contemporary capitalist society in his own, original way. The general impression of the production of <u>Pygmalion</u> at the "Labor Front" Theater (Sofia) is amusing, light, effective, though the producer has tried to reveal the basic ideas of the play. The use of Bulgarian dialect amused the audience. [In Bulgarian.]

2239 "Eastern Eyes on Bernard Shaw," ShawB, I (Nov 1956), 8.
[A summary of the Shaws' world cruise on the Empress of Britain in 1932-33.]

2240 Erdely, I. "Marginalii: Faţâ de Textul lui Shaw" (Marginalia: As Compared With Shaw's Text), CONTEMPORANUL, 14 Sept 1956, p. 2.
Deviations from Shaw's text in certain Romanian translations used on the stage or for radio broadcast have distorted Shaw's plays. The introduction of non-existent burlesque characters is especially misleading. [In Romanian.]

2241 Erikson, Erik H. "The Problem of Ego Identity," JOURNAL OF THE AMERICAN PSYCHOANALYTIC ASSOCIATION, IV (1956), 56-121; rptd PSYCHOLOGICAL

ISSUES, I (1959), 101-64; rptd IDENTITY AND THE LIFE CYCLE (NY & Lond: W. W. Norton, 1979), pp. 108-75.
[The section "Biographic: G.B.S. (70) on George Bernard Shaw (20)" and section 5 deal with Shaw.] The public identity of G.B.S. was one of Shaw's masterpieces. He describes a crisis at the age of 20, an identity crisis caused by too much success and too defined a role. Shaw then granted himself a prolongation of the interval between youth and adulthood. The occupational part of this "psychosocial moratorium" was reinforced by an intellectual part. Shaw had three parents, the third being Vandeleur Lee. Three elements of identity formation from Shaw's alcoholic father, his impersonal, but disillusioned mother, and his musical third parent are The Snob, The Noisemaker, and The Diabolical One. The Fabian socialists provided Shaw "a coherent . . . over-all orientation in space and time, in means and ends."

2242 Ervine, St. John. BERNARD SHAW: HIS LIFE, WORK AND FRIENDS (NY: William Morrow; Lond: Constable, 1956).
The role of Ireland in Shaw's life has been insufficiently developed. [Traces influences on Shaw's life.] The Fabian Society gave Shaw a family and a cause and contributed a "reasoned opposition to the economic dogmas of Marx." Shaw blossomed as a persuasive wooer of intelligent young ladies, but he enjoyed the female mind perhaps more than the body. The greatest of Shaw's plays is Man and Superman. It reveals the philosophical dilemma that plagued Shaw all his life, frequently resulting in contradictory attitudes, as Shaw vacillates between a deterministic Life Force and a Life Force utterly dependent upon human free creativity. As he became more celebrated and less heeded, Shaw became more extreme in his doctrines. Nevertheless, the mistakes of his last years, and the life-long mistake of his collectivist politics, do not cancel out Shaw's great gift to the world of the wit and wisdom of a generous and courageous man. He was "a beacon in a time of intellectual darkness. And that flame still brightly burns."

2243 Ervine, St. John. "G.B.S. in the Theatre," List, LVI (12 July 1956), 50-51.
Shaw, at first told that he had no talent for writing plays, was a master of drama, largely attributable to an

exceptionally acute sense of theater. [Illustrations from Saint Joan and Widowers' Houses.]

2244 Fennel, Desmond. "George Bernard Shaw," NUESTRO TIEMPO (Spain), XXVI (Aug 1956), 42-62.
Attention should be paid to Shaw's work, because of his socialism. He was a good music critic and a revolutionary in the theater. Saint Joan is perhaps his finest play; in the years after it his public personality obscured the real Shaw. He changed from socialism to admiring Mussolini and satirized Labour Party policies in The Apple Cart. [In Spanish.]

2245 Frank, Joseph. "Major Barbara—Shaw's Divine Comedy," PMLA, LXXI (March 1956), 61-74; rptd in TWENTIETH CENTURY INTERPRETATIONS OF MAJOR BARBARA, ed by Rose Zimbardo (Englewood Cliffs, NJ: Prentice-Hall [Spectrum Books], 1970).
Both Major Barbara's message and method represent Shaw at the height of his career. Dante's and Shaw's works progress from sin to repentance to salvation. Dante's art provides a penetrating insight into the medieval period, comprehending the politics, economics, psychology and ethics of his era. Major Barbara is equally inclusive—its subject matter covers the same fields; its time span is the present and future; and the characters represent all men. Whereas Dante emphasizes individual salvation through personal righteousness, Shaw believes the individual is personally responsible for the reform of institutions.

2246 Frankel, Charles. "Efficient Power and Inefficient Virtue (Bernard Shaw: Major Barbara)," GREAT MORAL DILEMMAS IN LITERATURE, PAST AND PRESENT, ed by Robert M. MacIver (NY: Harper, 1956), pp. 5-23.
Shaw pleasantly upsets the audience with Major Barbara by offering unusual insights into the human conflict of Might versus Right. The choice is not between efficient power and inefficient virtue, but between using power blindly or for deliberate ends. There is a difference between idle talk about virtue and employing power to its limit. Political reform does not follow from moral regeneration, but moral regeneration follows from social reform. Finally, power is not inherently immoral, but becomes a curse when it is cheapened for some and made impossibly important to others.

2247 Gallo, Raúl Blas. EL IMPORTANTE G.B.S. (The Important G.B.S.) (Buenos Aires: Quetzal, 1956).
Shaw is a cynic, a clown with convictions. After Ibsen, no author is more dramatic than Shaw. Only in this way can the fact that he created a drama with themes and motifs forbidden to the theater be explained. [In Spanish.]

2248 Gassner, John. "Shaw and Realism," FORM AND IDEA IN MODERN THEATRE (NY: Dryden, 1956), pp. 64-66; rptd in an expanded edition as DIRECTIONS IN MODERN THEATRE AND DRAMA (NY: Holt, Rinehart and Winston, 1966).
As a playwright as well as critic Shaw belongs to realism because he exemplifies the belief that the theater is the place for the examination of facts and issues rather than a place for the service of beauty and the worship of universals. His use of discursive prose and his fundamental adherence to the fourth-wall convention also classify him as a realist.

2249 Gelb, Arthur. "Evans Takes on G.B.S.," NYT, 7 Oct 1956, II, pp. 1, 5.
Maurice Evans is taking the responsibility of "sporting" The Apple Cart by embellishing Shaw's directions with further business. He has made two small changes in dialog also.

2250 Girosi, Pablo. "Pirandello y Shaw" (Pirandello and Shaw), REVISTA DE LITERATURAS MODERNAS (Argentina), I (1956), 47-72.
Whereas Pirandello is an innovator who created a literary tradition, Shaw is a rejuvenator who failed to establish a literary school. Both deal with the conflict between appearances and reality, but in Shaw's plays the outward appearance of the individual represents the social reality. The reality of being in Pirandello is unknown. Shaw's optimism is reflected in his preaching. His humor springs from his vision of the external social world; Pirandello's comes from the inner psychological world. Shaw's problems are contingent upon time; Pirandello's are universal and everlasting. [In Spanish.]

2251 Goldberg, Albert. "Shaw's Musical Criticism," LOS ANGELES TIMES, 5 Aug 1956; rptd in CShav, I (March-April 1960) [2 pp].
Shaw is perhaps the greatest and easily the most readable of all music critics. Though it was popularly believed that he was "a clown playing at being a music critic," he knew his subject thoroughly. In addition to his reviews, The Perfect Wagnerite remains a Wagnerian classic, and at Verdi's death he wrote "the best critical summation of Verdi's work that we have."

2252 Golovenchenko, A. "Dzhordzh Bernard Shou (1856-1950): k stoletiîu so dnîa rozhdeniîa" (George Bernard Shaw [1856-1950]: On the Centenary of His Birth), LITERATURA V SHKOLE (Moscow), CCVII (1956), 72-75.
Like some of his great contemporaries, Shaw understood the role and significance of the people, and he depicted in his works progressive ideas. He fought bravely on the side of opponents of reaction. He often admitted he became a socialist under the influence of Marx's KAPITAL, though he did not follow Marx's teachings consistently. In all his works, Shaw unmasked imperialism, which seemed to him a terrible threat to civilized humanity, and he often pointed to the Soviet Union as a model. [In Russian.]

2253 Gomez Valderrama, Pedro. "Los cien años de un Irlandés vegetariano" (The Hundred Years of an Irish Vegetarian), MITO (Venezuela), II (Aug-Sept 1956), 186-94.
[Brief biography and survey of Shaw's ideas and plays.] Shaw has a definite and specific meaning for Latin America. His works were the beginning of a new world, an introduction to the twentieth century. [In Spanish.]

2254 Goodykoontz, William Francis. "John Bunyan's Influence on George Bernard Shaw." Unpublished dissertation, University of North Carolina, 1956. [Listed in INDEX TO AMERICAN DOCTORAL DISSERTATIONS 1955/56—1966/67, and in Frederic M. Litto, AMERICAN DISSERTATIONS ON THE DRAMA AND THE THEATRE—A BIBLIOGRAPHY (Kent, Ohio: Kent State UP, 1969) pp. 38, 141.]

2255 Gorbunov, Arnold M. BERNARD SHOU 1856-1950: PAMIATKA CHITATELIIU (Bernard Shaw 1856-1950: Readers' Handbook) (Moscow: Lenin State Library, 1956), pp. 42-49.

Shaw's work has not lost its importance. Even now it aids the progressive forces of the world in their struggle against imperialist reaction and advocates humanistic ideals and friendship between nations. [Includes bibliography and editions in Russian.] [In Russian.]

2256 Grendon, Felix, Dan H. Laurence, and Richard Watts, Jr. "Centenary Year Theatre Notes," ShawB, I (Nov 1956), 15-19.

[Review by Grendon of Village Wooing, produced at the Greenwich Mews theater and the Davenport Theater.] The production is excellent in all respects. [Review by Laurence of The Admirable Bashville, produced at the Lenox Hill Playhouse by the Equity Library Theater.] Bashville shows how even minor Shaw proves dramatically practicable in the theater. [Review by Watts of Saint Joan at the Phoenix Theater.] An excellent production overall is highlighted by the acting of Siobbhan McKenna, who portrays Joan with deep instinctive feeling.

2257 Grindea, Miron. "G.B.S. and France," ADAM INTERNATIONAL REVIEW, Nos 255-256 (1956), 1-14.

Shaw was such a complex, unpredictable man that he was frequently misunderstood; this is particularly the case in his relations with France and the French theater. Shaw's partial failure in France was due to his perverse determination in choosing Augustin Hamon, who was totally unconnected either with literature or with the theater, as the exclusive translator of his works. Hamon's translations overemphasize political and sociological content at the expense of comic art. Shaw compounded matters by scorning the two actors, the Pitoëffs, who conquered Paris for him with their production of Saint Joan. Finally, Shaw insisted upon ridiculing France's intellectual and artistic pretensions to such a degree that literal-minded Frenchmen, not seeing the jest in Shaw's tone, found it difficult to forgive him. [Followed by three Shaw letters to the Pitoëffs.]

2258 Grunfeld, Fred. "Discography: GBS on Records,"
      SRL, XXXIX (21 July 1956), 11.
[A brief account of Shaw's voice and Shaw's plays on
records.]

2259 Halasi, Andor. "Találkozásom Bernard Shaw—val"
      (My Meeting with Bernard Shaw), SZINHÁZ--ES
      FILMMÜSVÉZET (Theater and Film Art), 1956, pp. 479-
      80.
[Anecdote about and quotation from Shaw's address to the
audience on the occasion of the Budapest premiere of
Candida in Jan 1916.] [In Hungarian.]

2260 Hamon, Henriette. "Bernard Shaw, A Teacher for
      the Younger Generation," SHAVIAN, VII (1956), 48-49,
      51.
Shaw was essentially a teacher and continues to live as
one. His method was to make people think for themselves,
not to impose his own views. His dramatic work is a school
for practical psychology. His life is a model of
perseverance, altruism, and the highest sense of justice.

2261 "Handsome Soapbox for Shaw," LIFE, XLI (10 Dec
      1956), 125-28.
[A pictorial review of the Laughton production of Major
Barbara, with emphasis upon the sets designed by Donald
Oenslager.]

2262 Henderson, Archibald. "Biographer's Breviary,"
      ShawB, I (Nov 1956), 1-3.
[Announces the publication of his biography, GEORGE BERNARD
SHAW: MAN OF THE CENTURY, and summarizes his opinions of
Shaw's chief qualities and major accomplishments.]

2263 Henderson, Archibald. GEORGE BERNARD SHAW: MAN
      OF THE CENTURY (NY: Appleton-Century-Crofts, 1956).
      [An expanded version of Henderson's GEORGE BERNARD
      SHAW: HIS LIFE AND WORKS (Lond: Hurst & Blackett;
      Cincinnati: Stewart & Kidd, 1911; rptd NY: Boni &
      Liveright, 1918), and of his BERNARD SHAW, PLAYBOY
      AND PROPHET (NY & Lond: Appleton, 1932)].
[The standard biography of Shaw by his authorized
biographer. Begins with a Preface explaining how Henderson
came to write biographies of Shaw and how Shaw reacted and

contributed to his efforts.] Shaw was a "true genius: inexplicable, untraceable, unmanageable, unpredictable, incalculable." One can find in him "few traceable hereditary influences." Environmental influences are more to the point. Exalting will above rationality, genius above gentility, independence above dutifulness, Shaw's novels reveal the growth of Shaw's conception of the modern hero, who ruthlessly pursues human betterment at the expense of happiness, finding it necessary to stand alone, the intelligent outsider, against a mob of fools and the knaves who exploit them. The signal lack of success Shaw had in getting his novels published at first made such fierce self-sufficiency necessary. Shaw developed into a master debator and became notorious as a devil's advocate. Though he later abandoned the "class war" theory, he found in the economic jeremiads of Marx a sweeping indictment of capitalism that was essentially religious in its transcendent purposefulness and its hatred of base living. [History of Shaw's writing for the theater.] Whatever Shaw's foibles or limitations as a human being, one must agree with Dean Inge that he was close to the Kingdom of God. He will surely live on. [Biography is anecdotal, and badly organized, but filled with a wealth of information about Shaw. Concludes with appendices on productions of Shaw's plays around the world, Shaw's ghost-writing of Vandeleur Lee's pamphlets on "voice," Arms and the Man in London and the provinces, 1894-1895, and a brief memoir of Charlotte Frances Payne-Townshend by her nearest kinswoman.]

2264 Henn, T. R. "The Shavian Machine," THE HARVEST OF TRAGEDY (Lond: Methuen, 1956), 188-96; rptd in G. B. SHAW: A COLLECTION OF CRITICAL ESSAYS, ed by R. J. Kaufmann (Englewood Cliffs, NJ: Prentice-Hall, 1965), 162-69.
Shaw failed as a tragedian because the social and intellectual climate of England from 1880 to 1920 was perhaps less fitted to provide favorable conditions for a tragic Anschauung than either the Norway of Ibsen or the Ireland of Yeats or O'Casey. England offered magnificent material for the social satirist but little or nothing toward a constructive vision based upon conflicting antinomies. Nevertheless, The Doctor's Dilemma, Mrs.

Warren's Profession, and Saint Joan are tragedies; but all
of them are wanting.

2265 Heslin, J. J. "Shaw and the American
Reformers," SHAVIAN, VI (1956), 30.
[A talk given to the New York Regional Group on 5 Nov 1955,
reported by Barbara Smoker.] Unlike the American reformer,
Shaw was not driven by sentimentality and feelings of guilt
inherited from an early Puritanical background.

2266 Horzyca, Wilam. "Rodowód Małgorzaty Knox"
(Origin of Margaret Knox), PROGRAM PANSTWOWEGO TEATRU
IM. J. SLOWACKIEGO (Program of the State Slowacki
Theater) (Cracow) 1956/57 season; rptd in Horzyca, O
DRAMACIE (About Drama) (Warsaw; Wydawnictwa
artystyczne i filmowe, 1969), pp. 226-32.
Anyone familiar with Shaw's work might think that Fanny's
First Play is a repetition of Mrs. Warren's Profession. Had
the latter been set anywhere but in Protestant England,
Vivie, crushed by reality, would have had no recourse but
to enter a convent. Instead, she goes into a business
office. Margaret Knox (Shaw's favorite and his mouthpiece)
is prepared for a crusade against the evils of the world
and even achieves a childish, symbolic rebellion. When
Vivie goes out into the world, she changes her name to
Barbara, who is a reincarnation of Vivie and forerunner of
Margaret. First Play is a hymn to human creative strength,
in which Shaw appears to see religious values. But it is
Dionysian religion, and Margaret is a Maenad in the hands
of the unfortunate policemen. This is how First Play
differs from Shaw's other plays. Neither Vivie nor Barbara
would have knocked out a policeman's teeth. Saint Joan is
another matter. [In Polish.]

2267 Hughes, Glenn. "Shaw Not Met," TRIVIA: POETIC
FOOTNOTES FOR AN UNWRITTEN AUTOBIOGRAPHY (Seattle: U
of Washington Book Store, 1956), 61-62.
[A free-verse poem-anecdote about the author's attempt to
visit Shaw to seek permission to quote from a book and his
being rebuffed by a secretary while Shaw was week-ending in
the country.]

2268 Iosifescu, Silvian. "Shaw, iconoclastul" (Shaw: Iconoclast), SHAW, TEATRU (Bucresti: ESPLA, 1956), pp. 5-50. [Not seen.] [In Romanian.]

2269 Irvine, William. "Major Barbara," SHAVIAN, VII (1956), 43-47.
Undershaft's munitions point to the limitations of laissez-faire morality—"to the neglect of ultimate ends, to pride —in property, to emphasis on 'good business' and cash payment as the sole nexus between individuals. Undershaft does not care what his bombs do to civilization." Ultimately, Undershaft's policy is self-destructive. But Undershaft has another side: as a mystic he sees that poverty means weakness and slavery and that power means freedom and action. To this creed Barbara and Cusins are converted, but not without the understanding that they will qualify it by their philosophy and their religion.

2270 Kárpáti, Aurél. "Bernard Shaw: A modern Arisztofanész" (Bernard Shaw: The Modern Aristophanes), orig pub 1956, rptd in TEGNAPTÓL MÁIG, VALOGATT IRODALMI TANULMÁNYOK (From Yesterday to Today, Selected Literary Essays) (Budapest: Szépirodalmi Könyvkiadó, 1961), pp. 400-404.
Shaw's strength derived from his use of humor to expose human, especially capitalistic, failings. Unfortunately, he was only a Fabian and not a Marxist, but he redeemed himself by his support of the USSR in the 1930's. [In Hungarian.]

2271 Katona, Jenö. "G. Bernard Shaw (1856-1950)," KÖNYVTÁROS, No 7 (1956), 521-23.
[A laudatory article on Shaw, "the greatest theatrical writer of the first half of the twentieth century."] [In Hungarian.]

2272 [Kelling, Lucille.] EXHIBITION CHECK-LIST: AN EXHIBITION OF SELECTIONS FROM THE ARCHIBALD HENDERSON COLLECTION OF BERNARD SHAW (Chapel Hill: Louis Round Wilson Library, U of North Carolina, 15 Nov—31 Dec 1956).
[Notes for the 219 items in the Henderson Collection, prepared by the curator.]

2273 Kerans, James. "A Study of the Hero in the Novels of George Bernard Shaw." Unpublished dissertation, Harvard U, 1956. [Listed in McNamee.]

2274 Kerr, Walter F. "Theater," NYHT, 12 Sept 1956. Siobbhan McKenna forces the audience to share Saint Joan's vision.

2275 Kerr, Walter F. "Theater," NYHT, 19 Oct 1956. It is splendid that Maurice Evans decided to bring The Apple Cart out for inspection, but, finally, the play does not capture one's interest.

2276 Kerr, Walter F. "Theater," NYHT, 31 Oct 1956. In spite of all the virtues of Charles Laughton's production of Major Barbara, it is disappointing.

2277 Khristova, M. "Bernard Shou" (Bernard Shaw), RABONTNICHESK DELO (Sofia), No 191 (9 July 1956), 2. [Not seen.] [In Bulgarian.]

2278 King, Carlyle. "GBS and Music, with a Moral for Canadians," QQ, LXIII (1956), 165-78. As a music critic Shaw insisted that it was not his business to be polite or judicious, or to praise, but to find fault "until the limit of attainable perfection is reached." Art for Shaw is ethically serious. Shaw especially berated the performer or composer who demonstrated technical proficiency without understanding. Though Shaw gradually came to value the "absolute music" of a Brahms, his preference was for the composer who had something to say. Music being one of the chief means of grace, and the arts being the only effective instrument of education, Shaw argued that the spiritual health of society requires their support.

2279 Komatsu, Motoya. "Shaw no Hiteiteki Taido ni tsuite" (On Shaw's Negative Attitude), AKITA DAIGAKU GAKUGEIGAKUBU KENKYUKIYO (Akita) (Jinbun, Shakai, Kyoiku), VI (Feb 1956), 173-88. The basis of Shaw's negation of Christianity is his optimistic view that human beings will do good when they are left free. Shaw's optimism is closely related to his theory of the Life Force. It is, however, not his religion at all, but a means of exposition of his ideals. [In Japanese.]

2280 Korsunskaîa, S. "Bernard Shou k ˆstoletiiˆu" (Bernard Shaw's Centenary), SOVETSKAIˆA UKRAINA (Lvov), VII (1956), 165-67.
Shaw welcomed the 1917 October Revolution and from the beginning regarded the Soviet Union with sympathy and love. His attitude to the Soviet people was one of steadfast friendship to which they responded warmly and sincerely. Shaw was dear to all progressive humankind. [In Russian.]

2281 Korzeniewski, Bohdan. "Shaw dzisiaj us nas" (Shaw Today in Poland), PAMIĘTNÍK TEATRALNY (Warsaw), V (1956), 247-59.
Shaw is known as an "apostle of good sense," but in Poland history has taught us not to respect "good sense"—Poles prefer romanticism. The Teatr Polski (Warsaw) has produced more Shaw plays than almost any other theater in Europe, but badly and carelessly. Shaw's translator, Sobieniewski, has exercised a relentless and jealous dictatorship in clear contradiction to Shaw. His translations are eccentric, full of obscure barbarisms and provincialisms without rhyme or reason. [In Polish.]

2282 Krog, Helge. "Bernard Shaw," in SANT Å SI: ARTIKLER (To Tell the Truth: Articles) by Helge Krog (Oslo: H. Aschehoug, 1956), pp. 11-23.
[A collection of articles by Krog published earlier elsewhere. "Bernard Shaw" was originally a radio speech occasioned by Shaw's death and then enlarged for journal publication by the inclusion of material from other articles which Krog had written about Shaw.] Important qualities of Shaw which influenced his work throughout his life were the youthful spirit he retained all his life; his fear of romanticism; his hatred of poverty; his wide range of solidly grounded knowledge in many fields; and his "oppositional" nature. The Quintessence of Ibsenism is the best of all books on Ibsen, and though Shaw's plays are quite different from those of Ibsen, they have their starting point in Ibsen. Though Shaw never really became a Marxist, the Marxist analysis of society not only gave him his understanding of how all aspects of society are intertwined, a theory underlying much of his drama, but

also gave him his basic dramatic method. His characters are usually types rather than individuals—only a means to social criticism. They are ultimately absolved of responsibility because the social system is the villain. Using the weapons of logic and laughter, Shaw fought all his life for human betterment, for truth, for freedom and the spirit. [In Norwegian.]

2283 Krohn, Paul Günter. "George Bernard Shaw," DEUTSCHUNTERRICHT, IX (1956), 373-86.
Shaw was a committed and rational humanist who believed in the future of socialism. His criticism of Marx was misguided, though he always acknowledged Marx's importance. His best plays are Candida, Caesar and Cleopatra and Saint Joan. Shaw's later plays are interesting, but they lack poetic power. [Mainly a brief survey of Shaw's life and work.] [In German.]

2284 Krutch, Joseph Wood. "An Open Letter to George Bernard Shaw," SRL, XXXIX (21 July 1956), 12-13.
Shaw is the most likely of all modern writers to achieve immortality, even though his utilitarian style is devoid of poetry and he was unable to reconcile a materialistic determinism with the mystical creed he preached at profounder moments.

2285 Laing, Allan M. "Why He Would Not: A Heavenly Exclamation Mark in One Scene," SHAVIAN, VI (1956), 4-7.
[A brief dramatic sketch in which Shaw, now in heaven, informs an official from the Office of the Public Trustee that he does indeed wish his last play, Why She Would Not, to be published.]

2286 Lambert, J. W. "J. W. Lambert on Shaw: Time to Think Again," DRAMA, ns XLII (Fall 1956), 65-66.
Although Shaw paid lip service to the idea that the theater was to be used by a serious propagandist only as an alternative to a soap-box in Hyde Park, the fact is that his plays survive on the basis of their supreme theatricality and their regard for dramatic characterization.

2287 Lambert, J. W. "Plays in Performance," DRAMA, ns XLI (Summer 1956), 20-21.
Miriam Karlin, Roger Livesey, and Donald Pleasance were successful in <u>Misalliance</u> at the Lyric, Hammersmith.

2288 Lambert, J. W. "Plays in Performance," DRAMA, ns XLIII (Winter 1956), 21.
London's feeble celebration of the Shaw Centenary amounted only to <u>Major Barbara</u>, <u>Caesar and Cleopatra</u>, and <u>The Doctor's Dilemma</u>. <u>Dilemma</u> stands or falls, without an exceptional Jennifer Dubedat, on the interplay between the doctors. Michael Hordern as Bloomfield-Bonnington stole the play.

2289 Lansdale, Nelson. "Literary Landmark," SRL, XXXIX (21 July 1956), 34.
[A photo and account of "Shaw's Corner" in Ayot St. Lawrence.]

2290 Laughton, Charles. "The Passionate Major," NYT, 28 Oct 1956, II, pp. 1, 3.
The word "passion" can be applied to <u>Major Barbara</u> because it is a devastating and uninhibited attack upon the hypocritical philosophy of the sacrosanct blessedness of the poor. It is ironic that a practical humanist like Shaw should be accused of being an intellectual writer rather than a writer of the heart. Shaw is sometimes mistaken but never malicious. Seldom is a play so angry and so witty, too. Shaw attacks honestly but he does not despair. One can disagree with Shaw and still enjoy the play, and perhaps think a little better afterwards, too.

2291 Laurence, Dan H. "The Facts about <u>Why She Would Not</u>," TAM, XL (Aug 1956), 20-21, 89-90.
<u>Why She Would Not</u> is a complete and meaningful play, a variation on the Pygmalion archetype, a synthesis and summation of familiar Shavian themes, and obviously Shaw intended it to be published.

2292 LeCorre, Pierrette. "Les cent ans de George Bernard Shaw" (George Bernard Shaw's 100 Years), LA PENSÉE, ns No 70 (1956), 32-42. [Not seen.] [In French.]

2293 Lederer, Moritz. "In Memoriam George Bernard Shaw," DEUTSCHE RUNDSCHAU, LXXXII (July 1956), 762-65.

Unlike Gerhart Hauptmann, Shaw detested being a celebrated poet. Shaw continued Ibsen's line of social criticism although audiences often saw only the intellectual clown in him. Like Ibsen or Karl Kraus, Shaw presented his criticism with poetic power as did after him such writers as Jean Giraudoux, Thornton Wilder and Bertolt Brecht. Shaw was, after Shakespeare, the most popular author at Max Reinhardt's theater in Berlin. [In German.]

2294 Lerner, Alan Jay. "Pygmalion and My Fair Lady," ShawB, I (Nov 1956), 4-7.

Lerner and Loewe tried to musicalize Pygmalion in 1952, but gave it up as hopeless. In 1954 they discovered the secret: "to dramatize all the things that happened off-stage, and also, as much as possible, to illustrate with music and lyrics, the background of Eliza's life: the life she had as a Cockney and the life she would have as a grande-dame." Over 60 percent of the musical is directly from the play; the rest tries to be faithful to Shaw's intentions.

2295 Loebe, Horst. "Lady Cicely oder die Macht des Ungewohnten" (Lady Cicely or the Power of the Unusual), BDDTG, No 94 (1955-56).

The power of the unusual is the subject of Captain Brassbound's Conversion. [In German.]

2296 Logorio, Arturo. "Con Bernard Shaw, turista-express en Pompeya" (With Bernard Shaw, Tourist-Express in Pompeii), ATLANTIDA (Argentina), XXXIX (Oct 1956), 42-43, 92.

Meeting with Shaw in 1931 in Pompeii was the beginning of the author's dislike of Shaw's childish and selfish personality. His works, with the exception of Candida and Saint Joan, will not survive. [In Spanish.]

2297 Lokhorst, Emmy van. "Toneelkroniek: Honderd jaar geleden werd Shaw geboren" (Theater Chronicle: Shaw was Born One Hundred Years Ago), GIDS, CXIX (1956), 325-28.

Shaw created strong female characters in Candida, Major Barbara, Pygmalion, and Saint Joan. His personality as described by Blanche Patch in THIRTY YEARS WITH SHAW (1951) is especially attractive: polite, uncompromising and good-humored. [Review of recent Shaw productions in the Netherlands: The Apple Cart, Caesar and Cleopatra, Saint Joan, You Never Can Tell, Fanny's First Play, and Village Wooing. [In Dutch.]

2298 Lukeš, Milan. "Poslední shawova hra" (Shaw's Last Play), DIVADLO (Prague), VII (1956), 988-89.
Why She Would Not illustrates a very Shavian paradox and is a political allegory of Old England. It is connected with both The Millionairess and, less obviously, with Pygmalion. [In Czechoslovak.]

2299 Lupan, Radu. GEORGE BERNARD SHAW (Bucuresti: ESPLA, 1956 [?]).
[Lupan examines Shaw's esthetics and philosophy from the Marxist point of view. Commentary on Shaw's novels, his music and Ibsen criticism, his "unpleasant" theater, John Bull's Other Island. Includes a section on holy prophets and imposters, and calls Shaw a twentieth-century Molière.] [In Romanian.]

2300 Lupan, Radu. "Shaw, Critic de Artă" (Shaw As an Art Critic), VIATA ROMÎNEASCĂ, IX (Aug 1956), pp. 119-212; rptd in GEORGE BERNARD SHAW (Bucureşti: ESPLA, 1956 [?]), Chap IV.
[Considers Shaw's esthetics.] [In Romanian.]

2301 McDowell, Frederic P. W. "Everybody's Political What's What: A Twelfth Anniversary," SHAVIAN, VII (1956), 39-42.
Everybody's Political What's What is insistently concerned with the relationship of modern politics to modern spiritual life. Its principal concerns—the way to select qualified leaders, the class war between "barbarians and civilized citizens," the necessity of equal incomes—are familiar. Shaw mistakenly identified ideal democracy with Soviet communism, though he partly redeemed himself by also insisting upon freedom of speech.

2302 McKee, Irving. "Editing the Early Plays," SHAVIAN, VII (1956), 21-23.

[A talk at the National Book League, 25 Nov 1955, reported by Barbara Smoker. To forestall possible mutilations of Shaw's plays now out of copyright in America, McKee is working on definitive editions which will contain critical histories and Shaw's revisions. Details on Arms and the Man, Candida, and The Devil's Disciple.]

2303 [Magos, Mrs. G.?] BERNARD SHAW SZÜLETÉSÉNEK SZÁZÉVES ÉVFORDULÓJÁRA. AJÁNLÓ BIBLIOGRÁFIA, KÖNYVTÁROSOK SZÁMÁRA, KIÁLLÍTÁSOK RENDEZÉSÉBEZ, NEPNEVELÖK MUNKÁJÁBOZ (On the Occasion of Bernard Shaw's One Hundredth Birthday. An Annotated Bibliography for Librarians to Organize Exhibits to Aid the Work of Educators) (Budapest: A Fövárosi Szabó Ervin Könyvtár Röplap Bibliográfiája, 1956). [Not seen.] [In Hungarian.]

2304 Marín, Jorge. "Centenario de Bernard Shaw" (The Centenary of Bernard Shaw), DESTINO (Spain), CMXC (28 July 1956), 5-8.
Shaw was not an original thinker; he spread the ideas of others. He revolutionized English drama. He demonstrated the values of wit, irony, and provocation in criticism. His thought was more influential on his generation than that of any other writer. He was a force in English political reform. He showed that it was possible to disagree with opponents without being intransigent and to sustain a controversy while maintaining a sense of humor. [In Spanish.]

2305 Masefield, John. "Lines for a One Hundredth Birthday," SRL, XXXIX (21 July 1956), 7.
[Shaw centenary poem by England's laureate.]

2306 Möllmann, Horst. "G. B. Shaw," RUND UM DIE WELT, No 7 (1956), 65-68.
[A brief survey of Shaw's life and works.] Shaw's major theme is the debunking of heroes and saints. He is a fierce socialist with a proletarian consciousness. [In German.]

2307 Mosley, Sir Oswald. WAGNER AND SHAW: A SYNTHESIS (Lond: Sanctuary P, 1956; noted on the cover: "Reprinted from The European.").

[Commentary on Shaw's use of Wagner and his reading of the RING OF THE NIBELUNG.]

2308 Nakahashi, Kazuo. "Gekibungaku to Bernard Shaw" (Dramatic Literature and Bernard Shaw), GENDAI IGIRISUBUNGAKU NYUMON (Introduction to Modern English Literature) (Tokyo: Kenkyusha, 1956), pp. 26-36.
Shaw was not only the leading playwright of twentieth-century English drama but also the representative writer and thinker before World War I. He believed in progress firmly and optimistically. This faith stood out in sharp contrast to the general tendency after World War I. [In Japanese.]

2309 Nuñez y Domínguez, Roberto. DESCORRIENDO EL TELÓN: 40 AÑOS DE TEATRO EN MÉXICO (Opening the Curtain: 40 Years of Theater in Mexico) (Madrid: 1956).
Candida performed by Gloria Iturbe was sponsored by the Secretariat of Education. [In Spanish.]

2310 O'Brien, Terence and Ruth Spalding. "An Evening of Shavian Reminiscences and Extracts at the National Book League on September 23rd, 1955," SHAVIAN, VI (1956), 18-19.
[Reported by A. D. Pope: a program of eight extracts from Shaw's plays, many personal reminiscences, and an acted interview between Ruth Spalding and Shaw.]

2311 O'Casey, Sean. "G. B. Shaw: The Lord of a Century," NYT, 22 July 1956, II, p. 1.
Shaw was always annoyed to be called an English writer. He had many literary enemies, but they have done nothing in drama to compare with his achievement.

2312 O'Casey, Sean. THE GREEN CROW (NY: George Braziller, 1956), pp. 197-211; rptd in Sylvan Barnet (ed), THE GENIUS OF THE IRISH THEATRE (NY: New American Library, 1960), pp. 359-64.
Shaw is "seer, saint, and sage," one who fought "with laughing violence" for "the golden heresy of truth" and for "the glorious ascent of man." Yeat's notion that Shaw was a mere logician is contradicted by the evidence of his musical, poetic imagination.

2313 O'Hare, John. "How the Play Reached Publication," TAM, XL (Aug 1956), 22-23.
[Account of how a trip to the Society of Authors to gain statistical information of Shaw's increasing international popularity ended in O'Hare's being given the manuscript of Why She Would Not for publication.]

2314 Oppel, Horst. "George Bernard Shaw—Versuch einer Charakterskizze. Zur 100. Wiederkehr seines Geburtstages am 26. Juli 1956" (George Bernard Shaw —Attempt at a Character Sketch. Occasioned by his Hundredth Birthday on July 26, 1956), DIE NEUEREN SPRACHEN, No 7 (1956), 313-17.
In order to understand Shaw's works, it is absolutely necessary to understand the author. Somehow Shaw remains curiously elusive. He had no respect for authorities of any kind, but he himself demanded respect. Whether he was capable of true friendship is questionable: he put criticism, polemics and his fondness of contradictions above everything else. He was extremely egocentric and did not know loyalty or gratitude. His relation to Ibsen shows that he could not readily admit to influence by others. His work shows signs of hastiness; he always wrote before his talents had matured. One of his most admirable qualities is his inability to lie. Yet there is also a tragic shadow; the seeker of freedom never found it himself. [In German.]

2315 Papajewski, Helmut. "Bernard Shaws Chronicle Play Saint Joan," GERMANISCH-ROMANISCHE MONATSSCHRIFT, Neue Folge VI (1956), 262-77.
Saint Joan is one of Shaw's most lasting plays. The central question in it is how such faith can be resurrected. Faith is to be interpreted in an evolutionist, not a religious sense. For Shaw Saint Joan was a representative of the Life Force whose effect was blunted by her canonization. [In German.]

2316 Parandowski, Jan. "G.B.S.," originally published in 1956, place unknown; rptd in SZKICE: SERIA DRUGA (Warsaw: Pánstwowy Instytut Wydawn., 1968), pp. 139-43. [Not seen.] [In Polish.]

2317 Patch, Blanche. "Trying to Understand Shaw," ADAM INTERNATIONAL REVIEW, Nos 255-256 (1956), 23-24.

[Shaw's former secretary quotes from three letters that illustrate the many questions about Shaw that she has been asked. One letter is the one Tolstoy wrote criticizing Shaw for not realizing the importance of being earnest; another is from H. G. Wells reviewing a performance of John Bull's Other Island in which he sees a disgusting caricature of himself; and a third is from Shaw to a group of sportswomen turning down an invitation to speak to them on the grounds of being extremely unathletic and out of shape.]

2318 Payne, B. Iden. "No Blackleg," SHAVIAN, VII (1956), 52.
Shaw insisted on high pay for the staging of his plays in order to maintain a high standard for his fellow playwrights. But on special occasions he would reduce the usual fee so as not to undermine his fellow playwrights.

2319 Pearson, Hesketh. BEERBOHM TREE, HIS LIFE AND LAUGHTER (Lond: Methuen, 1956), passim.
Tree never resented Shaw's criticisms of his acting because he admired Shaw's wit and dramatic genius. In 1909 Shaw wrote The Shewing-Up of Blanco Posnet for Tree—but Tree rejected the play and waited another four years for their most notable joint venture, Pygmalion. During rehearsals (His Majesty's Theater) Shaw tried vainly to bring about some order to Tree's and Mrs. Campbell's unorthodox and often erratic displays of personality. Once the play was launched on a successful and profitable season, Shaw remained aloof, until at Tree's insistence he attended the one hundredth performance, only to be revolted by Tree's travesty of the ending. Shaw tried to make Tree see that he was violating the author's anti-romantic purposes, and Tree tried to make Shaw see that Higgins throwing flowers to Eliza was better box-office.

2320 Pearson, Hesketh. "Bernard Shaw as Producer," List, LVI (16 Aug 1956), 229-30.
Shaw from his earliest years was impregnated by the classical style of writing and acting, his own plays reminding Granville-Barker of Italian opera, and thus the naturalistic actors of the nineties did not know what to make of a Shaw play. But gradually Shaw as a director ["producer," in English terms] converted the actors to his

rhetorical, musical style. He was a very effective director, able to get the very best out of each actor.

2321 Pecháček, Jaroslav. "Ještě dvě shawovské inscenace" (Two More Shaw Productions), DIVADLO (Prague), VII (1956), 968-71.

Major Barbara (Ceske Budejovice Theater) is more interesting in its boldness than in its paradoxical arguments. The producer cut the undramatic discussions to an acceptable length. This production is the boldest step so far toward reviving Shaw's plays in Czechoslovakia. Arms and the Man was produced at the Comedy Theater (Prague). [In Czechoslovak.]

2322 Percy, Esmé. "Memories and Evocations of Bernard Shaw," SHAVIAN, VII (1956), 5-7, 9.

[A special meeting held in conjunction with the City Literary Institute Theater Club on 5 Nov 1955, reported by Barbara Smoker, and described as "the official opening of our celebrations for Shaw's centenary year." Esmé Percy talked of his first meeting with Shaw, his experience with Shaw as a director, and two encounters with Shaw when he was uncharacteristically emotional.]

2323 Pettet, Edwin B. "The Life Force: Shaw's Comedic Norm," SHAVIAN, VI (1956), 14-16.

[A lecture at the National Book League, 9 Sept 1955, reported by Barbara Smoker.] Shaw reverses the usual comedic pattern. Shavian wit is the cutting edge of a deviate turned back upon the audience and used in the service of what Shaw calls the Life Force.

2324 Phelps, Gilbert. THE RUSSIAN NOVEL IN ENGLISH FICTION (Lond: Hutchinson's University Library, 1956), pp. 139-41, 143, 150-54, 188.

Tolstoy influenced Shaw's philosophical thinking and his belief that art must have a social function. Shaw used Tolstoy's "shock-tactics" to wake people up from sterile lives. He also used Tolstoy's tragicomic method. Shaw saw the political and social implications of the melancholy in Chekhov's CHERRY ORCHARD.

2325 Possonyi, László. "A Százéves G. B. Shaw" (The Hundred Year Old G. B. Shaw), VIGILIA, XXI (Jan 1956), 16-19.
Shaw's best play is <u>Saint Joan</u>. The great Marxist used humor to tell the English audience how horrid they are. Enlightened, progressive Hungarians love him. [In Hungarian.]

2326 Priestley, J. B. "Thoughts on Shaw," NS&Nation, LII (28 July 1956), 96.
Shaw wrote his best plays in early middle age. He never appeared emotionally committed to his beliefs, advancing or defending them without anger. H. G. Wells was more emotional, therefore more frank and honest. Shaw never entered the post-1914 world, failing to comprehend the significance of dictators and other anti-social types. His women are either Strindbergian managers or vacuous kittens. His comedy of "light without heat" was a <u>tour de force</u> of his unique style and Irish temperament. He came at the right moment, as a great destroyer, to sweep out the Victorian era.

2327 Pritt, D. N. "A Socialist Tribute," SHAVIAN, VII (1956), 19-20.
Shaw rescued the author from his Tory upbringing by demonstrating that the individual is responsible for the whole of society.

2328 Przewoska, H. "Obchodzone w tym roku (Przegląd wystawién sztuk [Bernarda Shaw] w Teatrze Polskim i Teatrze Malym w Warszawie od 1914)" (Celebrated This Year: Survey of Productions of Shaw's Plays at the Teatr Polski and the Teatr "Maly" in Warsaw since 1914), STOLICA (Warsaw), V (1956), 10. [Not seen.] [In Polish.]

2329 Puff, Wilhelm. "Bernard Shaw und die Ironie" (Bernard Shaw and Irony), DER GESICHTSKREIS, ed by Ernst Niekisch (München: Beck'sche Verlagsbuchhandlung, 1956), pp. 164-85.
Everything resisting the process of evolution is exposed to ridicule in Shaw's form of irony. A better understanding of Shaw's irony is achieved by examining the concepts of irony shaped and sharpened through Hegel, Kierkegaard, Bertolt

Brecht and Hölderlin's concept of tragedy. Characteristic of Shaw's irony: contradictions are not solved; they are part of the evolutionary process. [In German.]

2330 Purdom, C. B. GRANVILLE BARKER: MAN OF THE THEATRE, DRAMATIST AND SCHOLAR (Lond: Rockliff, 1956; Cambridge, Mass: Harvard UP, 1956), passim.
[A biography of Granville Barker with many biographical references to Shaw and a full account of Shaw's relationship with the Vedrenne-Barker management of the Court Theater. Illustrated.]

2331 Purdom, C. B. "Shaw and Garden Cities," SHAVIAN, VI (1956), 20-22.
[A talk at the National Book League, 28 Oct 1955, reported by Barbara Smoker.] In the 1870's Shaw took a lively interest in the idea of "Garden Cities," as imagined by Ebenezer Howard and supported by Henry George, and later spoke for Letchworth Garden City (founded 1904) and Welwyn Garden City (founded 1919). It was all part of Shaw's belief that industrialized populations should be decentralized.

2332 Quirk, Randolph. "Pygmalion's Frenzy," List, LVI (30 Aug 1956), 311-12.
Language functions as a social activity, especially class dialects and jargon which can be used as barriers or forms of social assessment. Pygmalion illustrates the folly of being obsessed with outward linguistic forms.

2333 R. Ânea, G. "Homenaje a Bernard Shaw" (Homage to Bernard Shaw), CULTURA PERUANA, XVI (July 1956).
Overruled was performed by El Carro de Tespis in Lima to commemorate Shaw's centenary. [In Spanish.]

2334 Rattray, R. F. "The Greatness of Shaw," SHAVIAN, VII (1956), 31-33.
"Shaw was a distinguished philosopher, artist, statesman, publicist, critic of drama, music, literature and art of the highest integrity and probity, a prophet, a mystic, a saint."

2335 Richardson, Henry B. "The Pygmalion Reaction," PSYCHOANALYTIC REVIEW, XLIII (Oct 1956), 458-60.

In the myth of Pygmalion is the attempt "to convert love into a less powerful emotion by giving it a rarefied and overesthetic quality." The "Pygmalion reaction" is best illustrated in modern literature by Shaw's Pygmalion. The play is complicated by the fact that it concerns two statues, or counterfeit human beings: Pygmalion Higgins makes a counterfeit of himself to reinforce his aversion to women and marriage. After making himself into an automaton, he tries to force Eliza into the same role, with explosive results. In psychiatric terms, he himself adopts a pattern of behavior and then tries to project this on another person.

2336 Ring, Martin R. (trans). "Lusin Looks at Bernard Shaw," ShawB, I (Nov 1956), 11-13.
Lusin, a satirist of the pre-Communist government in China and now enshrined as "China's Gorki," gives a flippant and irreverent account of Shaw's visit to Shanghai in 1933. Lusin anticipated that he would like Shaw because he was disliked by the same people Lusin disliked, but he found Shaw more ordinary and less satirical than he had hoped.

2337 Rochester, Howard. "El conflicto tripartito en el teatro de Shaw" (The Tripartite Conflict in the Plays of Shaw), MITO (Venezuela), II (Aug-Sept 1956), 186-91.
Although it is possible to disagree with Shaw's political ideas and his philosophy and to reject his collective solutions and his faith, the man himself cannot be forgotten. He fought against injustice, hypocrisy, sentimentality and prejudice. His ideas are aggressive and attractive, but his plays are often repetitive, containing speeches that are too long. Shaw's writing reflect the confusion and conflict within his own mind between the poet, the practical man, and the prophet. [In Spanish.]

2338 Romm, A. S. "K voprosu o dramaticheskom metode Bernarda Shou" (On the Question of Shaw's Dramatic Method), IZVESTIIA AKADEMII NAUK SSSR (OTDELENIE LITERATURY I IAZYKA) (Moscow), XV (1956), pp. 315-29.
Shaw's philosophical and social views underwent complex evolution, as did his artistic method. This evolution occurred during two basic periods, with a break between 1914-1917. Although the plays of each period differ in

ideas and method, some features appear in both. Shaw's early works and themes deal with crises of the bourgeois world and the breakdown of its economic, social, and ideological stability. Shaw regarded art as a powerful factor in social change and sought to work on the feelings and intellects of his audiences—hence the apparatus of prefaces. Basic to all Fabian writers is the breakdown of bourgeois thought; but both Shaw and H. G. Wells went far beyond the shallow rationalism of the Fabians. The dramatic conflicts in Plays Unpleasant are not based on the encounter of real characters with the real facts of social life, but their ideological comprehension of the facts. Thus the brothels owned by Mrs. Warren are ideas, discussion of which forms the perepetia. Despite Shaw's close links with Ibsen, Shaw began where Ibsen left off. The dramatic method which Shaw invented suited his basic task. He provides no scrupulous analysis of the inner experience of his characters, but makes them think, judge, and discuss important questions of life. The Plays Pleasant are much more complex philosophically and psychologically and in dramatic form, e.g. the last scene of Candida, which realizes the potentialities inherent in Three Plays for Puritans. [In Russian.]

2339 Romm, A. S. TVORCHESTVO BERNARDA SHOU (Works of Bernard Shaw) (Leningrad: Obshchestvo po rasprostraneniiu politicheskikh i nauchnykh znanii, 1956).
Throughout his life, Shaw ruthlessly exposed the falsity of bourgeois society though he could not always solve complex problems under the rule of liberal and reformist illusions. Despite his mistakes, he consistently hated bourgeois imperialistic aggression and believed in the victory of intelligence and justice. He mistakenly believed that rational bourgeois practicality could overcome the faults of contemporary society. This was the weak side of Shaw's outlook, evident in Plays Pleasant and elsewhere. Later he shifted the center of his plays to ideological questions. Arms and the Man began his anti-war plays. The grandiose successes of socialism in the USSR and the increasing crises of capitalism brought about a turning point in his work. He was a faithful friend of the Soviet Union, and this is why the World Council of Peace celebrates his centenary. [In Russian.]

2340 Roppen, Georg. EVOLUTION AND POETIC BELIEF: A STUDY OF SOME VICTORIAN AND MODERN WRITERS (Oslo: Oslo UP, 1956), pp. 153, 352-402, 405, 406, 418, 428, 433, 446, 447-57, 461, 462.
Shaw is an original thinker in that he transforms the ideas he borrows in the heat of moral passion, but he is not consistent or comprehensive. [The Life Force creed, Man and Superman and Back to Methuselah are examined in detail.] Shaw set out from a point different from H. G. Wells, but both pursued parallel courses, and both arrive at the same evolutionary Utopia.

2341 Rosa-Nieves, Cesáreo. "Don Juan: Hombre y símbolo" (Don Juan: Man and Symbol), EL MUNDO (Puerto Rico), 17 Nov 1956, p. 21.
[Review of Man and Superman on the occasion of its premiere in Puerto Rico by the University of Puerto Rico.] [In Spanish.]

2342 Rowell, George. "Intellectual Drama: Shaw," THE VICTORIAN THEATRE: A SURVEY (Lond & NY: Oxford UP, 1956), 128-35.
Shaw responded to the demand of a small but influential section of the public for plays outside the established repertory of society drama, first by championing Ibsen, then by producing plays of his own that possessed a literary and artistic character of high intellectual caliber.

2343 Rubinova, E. "Bernard Shou: k 100-letiiu so dnia rozhdeniia" (Bernard Shaw: Centenary), SOVETSKII KAZAKHSTAN (Alma-Ata), No 7 (1956), 110-14.
Shaw's stage directions are a special kind of literature, a prose complement to his dramas, even though producers often cannot comply with them. Characters also are more detailed in stage directions than in action. The more active characters are often Shaw himself. Some of his plays are pamphlets satirizing political problems, e.g. Major Barbara. [In Russian.]

2344 "Saint Joan in Poland," NYT, 15 Dec 1956, p. 20.
The Polski Theater in Warsaw, where The Apple Cart was given its world premiere, was the scene of the Polish

premiere of <u>Saint Joan</u>. The celebrations included lectures on Shaw by Alan Dent.

2345 Schindler, Bernhard. "Bernard Shaw: Seine Kritik am 'English Way of Life'" (Bernard Shaw: His Criticism of the English Way of Life), WISSENSCHAFTLICHE ZEITSCHRIFT DER KARL-MARX-UNIVERSITÄT LEIPZIG, Gelellschafts-und Sprachwissenschaftliche Reihe, V (1955/56), 118.
Particularly after World War II, attention focused on Shaw's theory of evolution rather than his social criticism. He was a social critic but never trusted the history-shaping forces of the proletariat. [Summary of Schindler's book (1956) on Shaw.] [In German.]

2346 Schindler, Bernhard. "Die Erneuerung des englischen Dramas durch George Bernard Shaw. Zu seinem 100. Geburtstag am 26. Juli 1956" (Bernard Shaw's Revival of English Drama. Comment on his 100th Birthday on 26 July 1956), BÖRSENBLATT FÜR DEN DEUTSCHEN BUCHHANDEL (Leipzig), CXXIII (21 July 1956), 463-64.
After the censorship of the theater was introduced in 1737, English writers turned to the novel if they wanted to depict reality. It was left to Shaw to reintroduce reality to the stage with plays like <u>Widowers' Houses</u> or <u>Mrs. Warren's Profession</u>. To reach the widest possible audience, he had his plays printed in high quality book editions. [In German.]

2347 Schindler, Bernhard. GEORGE BERNARD SHAW. SEINE KRITIK AN DER ENGLISCHEN LEBENSFORM IN SEINEN SOZIALKRITISCHEN DRAMEN (George Bernard Shaw: His Criticism of the English Way of Life in His Plays Dealing with Social Criticism) (Halle, Saale: Niemeyer, 1956).
Shaw criticized the economic basis and the superstructure of British society. Throughout his life, Shaw was an inexorable critic of the English way of life; his strength lies in tearing the mask from a rotten society. His weakness, however, is that rather than trusting the history-shaping forces of one class, the proletariat, he relied on the mystical rule of the Life Force. [In German.]

2348 Schirmer-Imhoff, Ruth. "Saint Joan: Die Quelle und ihre Bearbeitung" (Saint Joan: The Source and Its Adaptation), ANGLIA, LXXIV (1956), 102-32.

Interpretations of Saint Joan as a representative of the Life Force of the emerging bourgeois class, convincing as they are, do not completely explain the greatness of the play. The figure of Joan transcends the usual Shaw characters as embodiments of Shavian principles and ideas; Joan "captivates and uplifts." Shaw's play reveals the overpowering influence of the source material: Jules Quicherat's five volume edition of Latin documents about Joan's trial and rehabilitation (1841-49), translated into French by Pierre Champion (1920). Shaw's artistic achievement is evident in his skillful selection and treatment of the sources. Shaw added some details of his own, rearranged some materials, limited the number of people involved, compressed the time. But as a close comparison shows, he never strayed far from his sources. Some passages, such as portions of the trial, are almost literally lifted from source. Altogether, Shaw's Saint Joan is remarkably close to the historic Saint Joan as portrayed in the historic documents. [In German.]

2349 Schlösser, Anselm. "Mitstreiter für eine bessere Welt. Zum 100. Geburtstag Bernard Shaws" (Co-Fighter for a Better World. To Shaw's 100th Birthday), NEUE DEUTSCHE LITERATUR, IV (July 1956), 100-109.

Shaw was, as Lenin said, a good man fallen among Fabians. His pills were too tasty; he could be integrated into bourgeois society as the fool at the court of capitalism. But with his sharp and analytic thought he did contribute his share to change the world. [In German.]

2350 Schonauer, Franz. "G.B. Shaws Puritanismus: Zum 100. Geburtstag von George Bernard Shaw" (G.B. Shaw's Puritanism: To George Bernard Shaw's One Hundredth Birthday), ECKART, XXV (1956), 312-20.

Shaw is a typical product of nineteenth-century rationalism. His Puritanism is not religious; it is characterized by strict discipline and severity. His theories of Life Force and evolution are merely functional, mechanistic, deterministic. What is lacking is human warmth and individual freedom. His plays serve merely as platforms for his ideas; there is no dramatic tension nor character development. Today they are only of historical interest. [In German.]

2351 Schonfield, Hugh J. "The Answer of Androcles," SHAVIAN, VII (1956), 35-37.
[A talk at the National Book League, 16 Dec 1955, reported by Barbara Smoker.] Natural religion, the religion of Androcles, rather than revealed religion, is the religion for modern times. Religion is the union of spirits, as exemplified by the gentleness of Androcles.

2352 Scott, Robert Lee. "Bernard Shaw's Rhetorical Drama: A Study of Rhetoric and Poetic in Selected Plays," DA, XVI (1956), 402-3. Unpublished dissertation, University of Illinois at Urbana-Champaign, 1955.

2353 Shah, Hiralal Amritlal. "Bernard Shaw in Bombay," ShawB, I (Nov 1956), 8-10.
[An account by one of Shaw's hosts of his stay in Bombay during the Shaw's 1932-33 world cruise.] Shaw was intensely interested in the Jain temples and intensely bored by the dramatic and musical entertainment provided.

2354 "Shall America Go It Alone?" SHAVIAN, VI (1956), 7.
[Reports several productions of Shaw's plays scheduled for American stages, in contrast to finding Shavian activity only on television and radio in Britain.]

2355 Sharenkov, Viktor. "Zabelezhitelen chovek i velik dramaturg: po sluchai 100 godini ot rozhdenieto na Shou" (Notable Man and Great Playwright: On the Centenary of Shaw's Birth), SEPTEVRI (Sofia), IX (1956), 175-81.
Shaw, undoubtedly the greatest English playwright since Shakespeare, lived and worked through the period of capitalist ascendancy and imperialism in England. Reading Marx revealed to Shaw everything that was happening around him: hence his frequent inconsistencies and contradictions. Disillusioned by bourgeois democracy, Shaw greeted the October Revolution with joy and became a devoted friend of

the Soviet Union. He remained to the end a fighter, humanist and artist. [In Bulgarian.]

2356 Sharp, William L. "<u>Misalliance</u>: An Evaluation," ETJ, VIII (March 1956), 9-16.
<u>Misalliance</u> examines the question of a satisfactory alliance of male and female, and secondarily the parent-child relationship. Its unusual structure gives the impression of lack of seriousness because it lacks a single focus. The parent-child problem is that of youth seeking experience but stifled by parental insistence on respectability and mental detachment. Tarleton exists in such an intellectual realm that he neither perceives objective reality nor particularly understands himself. This dichotomy is simultaneously comic and psychologically revealing.

2357 Shattuck, Charles H. "Sour Note," SRL, XXXIX (1 Sept 1956), 23.
[Takes SRL to task for reprinting a butchered version of Wells's "obituary" of Shaw, and corrects the false impression of Shaw created by Well's irrational statements.]

2358 "Shaving: Shaw Copyrights Valued," SHAVIAN, VII (1956), 56.
The high valuation of Shaw's copyrights by the Estate Duty Office will result in there being nothing left for alphabet reform after the death duty has been paid.

2359 "Shaw in Chicago," SRL, XXXIX (21 July 1956), 9.
[An account of the centenary salute to Shaw in Chicago.]

2360 Simon, Louis. "The Educational Theories of George Bernard Shaw," DA, XVI (1956), 2069-70. Unpublished dissertation, New York University, 1956.

2361 Sinko, Grzegorz. "G.B.S. po sto latach" (G.B.S. A Hundred Years After), PAMIETNIK TEATRALNY (Warsaw), V (1956), 239-46.
As a young man, Shaw quickly saw the scandals of his time and set about clearing them away in a cold, scientific and rational manner. But the treatment of social, philosophical

and scientific problems on the stage was never a novelty, though they had been treated emotionally. Shaw replaced this approach by wit aimed at making people think. His drama of ideas was a new form: his linking the text of stage plays with material for reading (e.g., the prefaces) was innovative and gave him a wider audience. Later Shaw could not understand that his "reality" had ceased to exist. This was not simply a matter of old age: history itself did not conform to his views. [In Polish.]

2362 Sion, Georges. "Bernard Shaw, le baladin du monde occidental" (Bernard Shaw, The Playboy of the Western World), REVUE GÉNÉRALE BELGE, Aug 1956, 1698-1711.

[A centenary reassessment of Shaw's life, his career, and his politics.] Shaw developed the theater of ideas, but in a comic version. The first encounter between Shaw and England was of opposites clashing, but they developed into a dazzling entente. Because he outlived the Victorian society to which he belonged, he became identified with a defunct world. As a revolutionary, he became outdated. His major failings are his inexhaustible flow of words, allowing his dialectical rage to get the better of his dramatic sense, and his wit at the expense of heart. He is a forceful and subtle writer—clear both morally and in literary terms. The Hamons, his translators into French, do not do justice to his theatricality; their translations are faithful but awkward. Shaw's life was strange and grandiose; his career brilliant. He was the Playboy of the Western World. [In French.]

2363 Smith, Warren S[ylvester]. "Bernard Shaw and the Quakers," BULLETIN OF THE FRIENDS HISTORICAL ASSOCIATION, XLV (1956), 105-18.

Shaw had a great deal in common with the Quakers, but more so with their historical position, as represented by the perhaps atypical George Fox, than with their contemporary practices. Though never attending a meeting of Quakers, Shaw thought of himself as a Quaker by temperament. Peace-loving (although not quite a pacifist), Shaw nevertheless, like George Fox, combatted traditional Protestantism and ecclesiasticism in order "to restore the voice of God to the individual, to revive prophecy, [and] to set up his life and behavior as a testimony to the Inner Light." As a playwright Shaw made the greatest use of Quaker thought in Saint Joan and in In Good King Charles's Golden Days.

2364 Smith, Warren S[ylvester]. "Shaw's Bout with Christianity," NATION, CLXXXIII (28 July 1956), 82-84.
[A summary of Shaw's opinions on Christianity.] Shaw opposed both official Christianity and Darwinian science in order to establish their meeting ground. He restated and reinterpreted the evolutionary theories of Lamarck in order to restore the idea of the Holy Spirit in human progress.

2365 Smoker, Barbara. "The British Museum Typescript," SHAVIAN, VII (1956), 30, 34.
[Report of an examination of the typescripts of Shaw's last play, Why She Would Not, at the British Museum. Concludes that Shaw did indeed want it published.]

2366 Smoker, Barbara. "On Marriage," SHAVIAN, VII (1956), 38.
[A review of recent productions of two of Shaw's plays dealing with marriage—Misalliance and Getting Married.]

2367 Smoker, Barbara. "On the Stage," SHAVIAN, VII (1956), 53-54.
[A report on the many Shaw productions scheduled for the centenary year in England, America, and elsewhere.]

2368 Smoker, Barbara. "The Simplified Spelling Society," SHAVIAN, VI (1956), 24.
[Report of a meeting of the Simplified Spelling Society, in which Professor Daniel Jones spoke on their successful efforts to achieve "one system of Nue Speling on both sides of the Atlantic."]

2369 Somló, István. "G. B. Shaw Ellen Terryről" (G. B. Shaw about Ellen Terry), SZINHÁZ-ES FILMMÜVÉSZET (Theater and Film Art) (1956), 423-29.
[Introduction to and translation of Shaw's Introduction to Ellen Terry and Bernard Shaw: A Correspondence (1931).] [In Hungarian.]

2370 Stanford, Derek. "British and American Criticism: A Contrast," SHAVIAN, VII (1956), 55-56.

American criticism is sometimes too creative and scientific and goes too far beyond the work in its search for meaning. British criticism is mostly academic and either historical or formal in its approach. The sort of criticism Shaw wrote, a general analysis of public ideas, is singularly lacking in both British and American criticism.

2371 Stokes, Sewell. "Conversation with Bernard Shaw," List, LVI (6 Sept 1956), 339-40.
[Stokes remembers meetings with Shaw, in which they discussed Isadora Duncan, Saint Joan, talking films, recording the voice, longevity, hell, regret, and style.]

2372 "Swimming with a Swell," TIMES (Lond), 5 Dec 1956, p. 12.
[The anonymous correspondent met Shaw in 1914 at a seaside resort where they talked and swam together. Anecdotes about Shaw on Chesterton, Freud and Jung, The Doctor's Dilemma, oratory, and palmistry are retold.]

2373 Szczawiej, Jan. "George Bernard Shaw," LAUR I CIERŃ (Laurel and Thorn) (Warsaw: Ludowa spoldzielnia wydawnicze, 1977), pp. 341-63. [First printed 1956, place unknown.]
In 1956, the World Council of Peace displayed a portrait of Shaw, among others, in Warsaw. Hundreds of thousands of persons have attended performances of Shaw's plays in Poland during the past decade. His plays exposed the most vital problems of the age. He was a reformer whose influence will endure long after his time. [In Polish.]

2374 Thomas, Geoffrey. "Shaw in Australia," SHAVIAN, VII (1956), 50-51.
Australia is not inclined to bother with Shaw's "intolerable burden of thought." Nevertheless the work of Creative Evolution goes on in Australia.

2375 Thorndike, Dame Sybil. "Tribute to GBS," SHAVIAN, VII (1956), 13-14.
Shaw, possessed of an adventurous spirit, impressed on one how worthwhile life can be. As a director he insisted on music in the delivery of lines, and on the "inward truth" he was seeking. Much of what Shaw taught has become commonplace today.

2376 Tienken, Arturo L. "Bernard Shaw, reformador" (Bernard Shaw, Reformer), ATENEA (Chile), CXXVI (1956), 80-96.
Shaw is mainly a social reformer. Through thesis plays he tried to destroy commonly accepted ideas. His ideas, expressed through characters, are of prime importance. [In Spanish.]

2377 Tippett, Michael. "An Irish Basset-Horn," List, LVI (26 July 1956), 119-20.
[A tribute to Shaw as a music critic.] Believing that he could make musical criticism readable even by the deaf, Shaw launched a formidable attack on academic music and formalist criticism. Shaw's first principle was that an esthetic judgment in music can only be based on what the sensibility perceives of what the ear hears, not on academically pre-conceived formulas.

2378 Trewin, J[ohn] C[ourtenay]. "G.B.S. 100," ILN, CCXXIX (28 July 1956), 156.
Though Shaw is still very much a force in the theater, he should not be taken for granted or for simply the librettist for MY FAIR LADY. Fortunately, there are still good productions of Shaw plays. [Concludes with a review of a London production of Major Barbara by the Bristol Old Vic Company.]

2379 Trewin, J[ohn] C[ourtenay]. "Rare Company," ILN, CCXXIX (28 Jan 1956), 136.
[Celebrates the double centenary of Shaw and Mozart.]

2380 Valency, Maurice. "Shaw the Durable Dramatist," TAM, XL (July 1956), 66-68, 86-87.
Shaw was the most "brilliant" of playwrights. His theater is monumental. It survives because of its utility—Shaw's subjects are still timely, and his manner of presenting them is still very playable. Further, it is not the spurious air of novelty but the fundamental nature of his material which assures his life upon the stage. His originality was in his use of traditional subjects to which he brought a well-developed philosophical system, an enveloping idea. In his plays the powers of brightness battle with the powers of darkness, the conclusion always a

draw or a synthesis. In watching a Shaw play the audience witnesses evolution.

2381 Vancura, Zdeněk. GEORGE BERNARD SHAW (Praha: Orbis [Knihovna Cekoslovenské Spolecnosti Pro Siřeni Polytickych Á Vědeských Znalosti, Svazek 144 (Library of the Czechoslovak Society for Dissemination of Political and Scientific Knowledge, V. 144), Jázyk, Literáturá Á Uměni, Svazek 33 (Language, Literature, and Art, V. 33)], 1956).
[Conventional but very solid survey of Shaw's career and introduction to his work for the Czechoslovak reader, with a table of Shaw's plays in Czechoslovak.] Table of Contents: 1. Shaw always alive. 2. Shaw's youth and the beginning of his literary career. 3. Shaw the critic and the fighter. 4. The Unsocial Socialist. 5. The beginning of Shaw's theatrical activity. 6. Dramatic mastery in Mrs. Warren's Profession. 7. Four pleasant plays. 8. Three Plays for Puritans. 9. From the real-politik to the unreal philosophy. 10. Dramas of life's pain and comedies of life's humor. 11. Utopia and legend. 12. Return to political comedy. 13. Shaw's own epilog. 14. List of Shaw's plays. [In Czechoslovak.]

2382 Verbitsky, Bernardo. "El carro de las manzanas, y Santa Juana, por George Bernard Shaw" (The Apple Cart and Saint Joan, by George Bernard Shaw), DAVAR (Argentina), LXV (July-Aug 1956), 117-18.
The Apple Cart and Saint Joan are excellent Shaw plays faithfully translated into Spanish by Floreal Mazia, much superior to previous translations by Julio Broutá. [In Spanish.]

2383 Vientós Gastón, Nilita. "El centenario de Bernard Shaw" (The Centenary of Bernard Shaw), INDICE CULTURAL, I (San Juan: Editorial Universidad de Puerto Rico, 1956), 249-51.
All the world is a stage, and Shaw was its greatest player. He is an original and enduring writer, whose works possess permanent value, ideas, and poetic qualities. [In Spanish.]

2384 Weinstein, Marybeth. "Out of G.B.S. on His Centenary," NYTMag, 22 July 1956, pp. 10-11.

"On these pages is a sampling . . . of the messenger boy of a new age!" [Quotations and photographs.]

2385 West, Alick. "The Enemy of Humbug," DAILY WORKER (Lond), 26 July 1956, 2.
Shaw's style will immediately make his reader feel alive.

2386 Wiemken, Helmut. "George Bernard Shaw," DIE VOLKSBÜHNE, VII (1956), 2-4.
In the history of European literature, there is no parallel to the phenomenon Shaw. He put his art to the service of social criticism, and he found comedy the most appropriate form of expression. [In German.]

2387 Williams, Harcourt. "Enter George Bernard Shaw," VIC-WELLS ASSOCIATION, CXI (July 1956), 1-3; rptd REGIONAL, II (March 1959), 1, 4.
[Anecdotes about the first Shaw production and several subsequent ones at the Old Vic during the seasons 1929-1933.]

2388 Wilson, Angus. "The Living Dead: Bernard Shaw," LONDON MAGAZINE, III (Dec 1956), 53-58.
[Begins as a review of Ervine's biography (1956).] Shaw's reputation as a playwright has recently suffered a great decline, but centenary tributes still praise the man. But "when we salute Shaw as a human being, we salute the virtues of inhumanity." Most of his lovable qualities "are surely the deliberate, controlled actions of a detached man." Shaw's drama of ideas, his greatest contribution to the theater, was in the service of the welfare state, and both Shaw's drama and the welfare state ignore the problem of evil. Shaw is also sexually naive in his plays; his battle of the sexes is "arch, artificial—a kind of male virgin's sex-teasing dream." His women strike an unpleasant note in their man-chasing. Although Shaw is seldom moving, he is a great comedian. The dramatists of the day can learn most from him in his power of putting real people on the stage instead of worn out stereotypes.

2389 Wilson, Colin. THE OUTSIDER (Lond: Gollancz, 1956), pp. 279-81; rptd with a new postscript NY: Dell, 1967.

[Wilson's first attempt at stating his "new existentialism," which incidentally sought to rescue Shaw from present neglect and undervaluation by declaring him "a major religious teacher."] Shaw's evolutionary faith explains the sense of alienation on the part of the dominant intellectual minority. Such alienation is necessary to motivate human evolution into a higher form.

2390 Winsten, Stephen. "Editorial Note," MY DEAR DOROTHEA: A PRACTICAL SYSTEM OF MORAL EDUCATION FOR FEMALES EMBODIED IN A LETTER WRITTEN TO A YOUNG PERSON OF THAT SEX, ed by Stephen Winsten (Lond: Phoenix House; NY: Vanguard P, 1956), 53-55.
Convinced that the fine arts were dead, the young Shaw of 1878 pursued the neglected art of living. His first principle was to think everything out for himself, facing all facts, however unpleasant. This was the basis for his advice in My Dear Dorothea, a piece which is the quintessence of Shaw's work and the germinating ground of his genius. It reveals, too, an uncanny understanding of the mind of a child.

2391 Winsten, Stephen. JESTING APOSTLE: THE PRIVATE LIFE OF BERNARD SHAW (Lond: Hutchinson, 1956; NY: E. P. Dutton, 1957).
[A biography based on both research and personal reminiscence.] It is difficult with Shaw to separate truth from fiction, to find the person behind the public mask, but it is time to begin the effort if the real Shaw is ever to be known. Much of what Shaw became can now be traced to his childhood experience. With so little support from the home, it is small wonder that Shaw came to think of discouragement as the greatest sin. He lived on the assumption that life was a jest, although to his credit he tried to make it the best possible jest. The unfortunate part is that, in different circumstances, in another age, he might have been more of a holy man and less of a fool, but the "Nineteenth Century had turned the mystic that he was by nature into a harsh realist." Paradoxically, he insisted on creating a religion out of the scientific negations of Creative Evolution and insisted further as its chief saint and prophet upon always being in a minority of one. However, Shaw was inordinately fond of wealth and power, for a saint. The basic Shaw is expressed in the

article of faith that Creative Evolution's struggle for survival inevitably produces Supermen who are deemed most fit to survive. Amusingly, it was his wife's money that allowed him to act up to his convictions. As time passed, Shaw more and more thought of himself as a unique superman who had risen far above average humankind; he lost all sense of sympathy and charity for the human race, all sense of justice even. Those who could not live up to his harsh ideal were to be exterminated. It is fitting that his will bequeathed to the world with whom he found communication so difficult a radical language reform, for in doing so he kept in the vanguard, posthumously and for some time to come, always a benefactor of humanity but never merely human.

2392 Worsley, T. C. "Shavian Comedy," NS&Nation, LII (28 July 1956), 102-3.
A large residue of Shavian drama will survive and will be even more effective after the perspective of another generation. Shaw's plays present the clash of both ideas and temperaments; the latter are rooted in the plays themselves and have a life out of time.

2393 Young, Percy. "Shaw, Shakespeare and Elgar," SHAVIAN, VI (1956), 10-12.
[A talk at the National Book League, 16 July 1955, reported by Barbara Smoker.] Elgar was a regular reader of Corno di Bassetto and agreed with many of Shaw's conclusions about music. After meeting in 1913, Shaw and Elgar struck up a friendship based on mutual esteem. They occasionally corresponded and generally attended each other's openings. SEVERN SUITE (1930) was dedicated to Shaw.

2394 Zemskov, V. and Iu. Khodzhaev. "Bernard Shou v Leningrade" (Bernard Shaw in Leningrad), NEVA (Moscow), VII (1956), 174-76.
Shaw saw as much as possible during his nine-day visit to the USSR. He met Stanislavskii in Moscow and Lunacharskii in Leningrad. The full text of his filmed speech on Lenin was published in the leading newspapers. He then visited Gorki in Gorki. [In Russian.]

Index

AUTHORS

Included here are authors, editors, and translators of articles and books on Shaw. Numbers after each name refer to the item(s) in the bibliography written, edited, or translated by the name.

Boza, Masvidal Aurelio:
327
Brailsford, H. N.: 1375,
1473
Branch, Lesley: 804
Brande, Dorothea: 230
Breîtburg, S.: 693
Brenner, Theodor: 1474
Brentano, Lowell: 400, 401
Bridges-Adams, W[illiam]:
929
Bridie, James [pseud of
Henry Mavor Osborne]:
402, 1053, 1475, 1476
Brinser, Ayers: 10
Brisson, Pierre: 11, 120
Brooks, Benjamin Gilbert:
694
Brooks, Donald: 985
Brophy, Liam: 1055
Broughton, Philip S.: 1056
Brower, Reuben A.: 2072
Brown, Ivor: 12, 13, 121,
122, 123, 231, 403, 404,
405, 472, 473, 474, 552,
619, 695, 696, 756, 1477,
1905
Brown, John Mason: 14,
406, 475, 805, 852, 853,
930, 986, 1057, 1058,
1059, 1196, 1197, 1198,
1293, 1478, 1479, 1675,
1676, 1826, 1827
Brück, Max von: 1480, 2073
Brüser, Ernst: 757
Bruton, J. G.: 1060
Bruton, Percy: 553
Bryant, Arthur: 1481
Bullock, J. M.: 15
Bullrich, Silvina: 1482,
1483, 1677
Burdett, Osbert: 232
Burnham, David: 854
Byington, Steven T.: 1678

Caballero y Lastres,
Daniel: 1679
Cabell, Branch: 233
Calverton, V. F.: 697
Camerino, Aldo: 1680
Campbell, Douglas: 2127
Canby, Henry Seidel: 476,
931
Cano, José Luis: 1485
Canton, Wilberto L.: 1062
Carb, David: 16, 124
Carbon, Emile: 17
Cardona, Rafael: 1681
Cardus, Neville: 1486
Carnegie, Dale: 932
Caro, J.: 18
Carrington, Norman
T[homas]: 1487
Carroll, Joseph: 1907
Carter, John: 758
Casson, Sir Lewis: 1682,
1683, 2128, 2129, 2227
Castelli, Alberto: 698,
989, 1376, 1684
Castro, Cristobal de: 125
Castro Oyanguren, Enrique:
1377
Catlin, George: 1488
Caudwell, Christopher
[pseud of Christopher St.
John Sprigg]: 621
Cecchi, Emilio: 477, 2130
Cehan, B.: 328
Cerf, Bennett: 933, 1063,
1199, 1489, 1908
Chaning-Pearce, M[elville]:
806
Chapman, John: 990, 1909;
(ed) 1910
Chappelow, Allan: 1685
Charrington, Norman T.:
2229
Chase, Harrison V.: 1911
Chassé, Charles: 1490

Index

TITLES OF SECONDARY WORKS

Titles of articles in periodicals and chapters in books are in quotation marks; book titles are in upper case. Numbers after each title refer to the item in the bibliography where the title appears.

587

601

INDEX OF TITLES OF SECONDARY WORKS

Index

PERIODICALS AND NEWSPAPERS

Included here are periodicals and newspapers for which entries occur in the bibliography. Numbers after each title refer to the number(s) of the item in the bibliography where the title appears.

INDEX OF PERIODICALS AND NEWSPAPERS

Index

FOREIGN LANGUAGES

Included here are the languages in which articles and books listed in the bibliography originally appeared. Numbers under each language refer to the items in the bibliography where the foreign language title is given. English language items are not listed.

2108, 2112, 2115, 2142,
2152, 2163, 2201, 2226,
2283, 2293, 2295, 2306,
2314, 2315, 2329, 2345,
2346, 2347, 2348, 2349,
2350, 2386
Hungarian: 78, 79, 298,
493, 494, 517, 596, 634,
636, 668, 672, 916, 1823,
1846, 1860, 2125, 2157,
2223, 2259, 2270, 2271,
2303, 2325, 2369
Italian: 86, 94, 137, 310,
364, 477, 591, 698, 718,
760, 847, 989, 1104,
1153, 1200, 1285, 1335,
1340, 1376, 1499, 1520,
1527, 1552, 1609, 1642,
1644, 1664, 1680, 1684,
1834, 1920, 2020, 2099,
2130, 2230
Japanese: 157, 202, 219,
221, 224, 244, 257, 261,
262, 267, 282, 288, 289,
296, 312, 313, 321, 361,
439, 570, 587, 709, 793,
1230, 1312, 1524, 1525,
1550, 1654, 1655, 1702,
1719, 1722, 1723, 1724,
1728, 1748, 1750, 1783,
1785, 1813, 1849, 2191,
2279, 2308
Norwegian: 679, 1551,
1931, 2282
Polish: 51, 419, 497, 498,
571, 645, 1098, 1099,
1266, 1310 1336, 1656,
1786, 1820, 1879, 2110,
2266, 2281, 2316, 2328,
2361, 2373, 1098
Romanian: 328, 365, 786,
883, 2220, 2233, 2235,
2240, 2268, 2299, 2300
Russian: 27, 56, 57, 58,

82, 268, 269, 305, 350,
693, 962, 1034, 1132,
1220, 2102, 2204, 2205,
2206, 2207, 2208, 2215,
2216, 2237, 2252, 2255,
2280, 2338, 2339, 2343,
2394
Serbian: 158, 526, 638,
661, 1399, 1513, 1522,
1727, 2175
Slovak: 1472, 1699
Slovene: 263, 745, 1699,
1763
Spanish: 1, 2, 110, 125,
184, 256, 323, 324, 327,
395, 469, 471, 496, 503,
546, 547, 584, 611, 688,
794, 829, 830, 871, 888,
919, 936, 963, 982, 995,
1012, 1018, 1033, 1060,
1062, 1067, 1091, 1096,
1121, 1126, 1162, 1163,
1177, 1205, 1206, 1221,
1325, 1326, 1327, 1377,
1418, 1449, 1452, 1463,
1464, 1467, 1468, 1470,
1482, 1483, 1485, 1498,
1508, 1516, 1545, 1548,
1564, 1571, 1583, 1591,
1599, 1603, 1605, 1608,
1612, 1614, 1617, 1618,
1619, 1640, 1643, 1662,
1674, 1677, 1679, 1681,
1720, 1736, 1743, 1751,
1753, 1762, 1793, 1794,
1824, 1845, 1887, 1936,
1943, 2022, 2029, 2098,
2137, 2178, 2180, 2181,
2244, 2247, 2250, 2253,
2296, 2304, 2309, 2333,
2337, 2341, 2376, 2382,
2383
Swedish: 1235, 1316
Ukrainian: 594

Index

PRIMARY TITLES

Included here are titles by Shaw occurring in titles of articles or books or in the abstracts. Numbers after each title refer to the number(s) of the item in the bibliography where the title appears.

2146, 2207, 2212, 2244,
2249, 2275, 2297, 2382
Arms and the Man 2, 69,
84, 194, 276, 323, 383,
409, 414, 417, 454, 456,
511, 565, 602, 645, 670,
833, 871, 888, 937, 961,
964, 967, 998, 1139,
1227, 1238, 1251, 1271,
1316, 1336, 1398, 1407,
1457, 1496, 1500, 1555,
1633, 1653, 1717, 1769,
1795, 1837, 1862, 1869,
1880, 1896, 1918, 1934,
1989, 2023, 2025, 2060,
2061, 2064, 2114, 2115,
2263, 2302, 2321, 2339
As Far As Thought Can Reach
1187, 1242
Back to Methuselah 213,
222, 228, 359, 383, 432,
587, 621, 786, 882, 903,
976, 1000, 1006, 1048,
1065, 1094, 1107, 1112,
1117, 1158, 1159, 1175,
1176, 1187, 1215, 1229,
1242, 1268, 1291, 1308,
1316, 1356, 1385, 1426,
1429, 1477, 1509, 1530,
1646, 1648, 1666, 1684,
1686, 1698, 1714, 1716,
1717, 1735, 1760, 1769,
1786, 1791, 1799, 1802,
1807, 1834, 1866, 1868,
1880, 1888, 1924, 1926,
1928, 1929, 1932, 1951,
1973, 1986, 2019, 2049,
2064, 2086, 2091, 2110,
2207, 2340
Bernard Shaw and Mrs.
Patrick Campbell: Their
Correspondence 1822,
1826, 1857, 1907, 1924,
2015, 2030, 2052, 2057

Bernard Shaw's Rhyming
Picture Guide to Ayot
Saint Lawrence 1631,
1680
Buoyant Billions 1357,
1360, 1384, 1390, 1399,
1409, 1413, 1421, 1424,
1427, 1434, 1442, 1445,
1448, 1609, 1732, 1789,
1802, 1844, 1864, 1938,
2049
Caesar and Cleopatra 94,
174, 182, 228, 349, 396,
409, 443, 456, 471, 768,
860, 874, 919, 983, 987,
992, 993, 1017, 1029,
1035, 1061, 1066, 1071,
1097, 1110, 1144, 1158,
1170, 1196, 1201, 1221,
1227, 1310, 1316, 1368,
1410, 1415, 1455, 1451,
1460, 1471, 1479, 1484,
1494, 1513, 1515, 1551,
1565, 1596, 1632, 1634,
1638, 1651, 1660, 1663,
1698, 1714, 1717, 1729,
1741, 1775, 1802, 1820,
1845, 1855, 1859, 1865,
1866, 1877, 1888, 1896,
1920, 1922, 1950, 1951,
1963, 1975, 1983, 1984,
1989, 2016, 2025, 2061,
2080, 2110, 2114, 2165,
2171, 2182, 2234, 2283,
2288, 2297
Candida 64, 94, 358, 383,
417, 421, 433, 444, 453,
454, 487, 520, 548, 549,
552, 557, 558, 563, 564,
572, 573, 574, 577, 585,
593, 597, 600, 606, 607,
608, 614, 672, 701, 704,
729, 730, 748, 768, 824,
848, 849, 850, 853, 854,